MANAGEMENT SCIENCE
AN INTRODUCTION TO
THE USE OF DECISION MODELS

MANAGEMENT SCIENCE

AN INTRODUCTION TO THE USE OF DECISION MODELS

KENNETH R. BAKER

DEAN H. KROPP

The Amos Tuck School of Business Administration
Dartmouth College

JOHN WILEY & SONS

New York / Chichester / Brisbane / Toronto / Singapore

Library of Congress Cataloging in Publication Data:

Baker, Kenneth R., 1943–
    Management science.

    Bibliography: p.
    Includes index.
    1. Industrial management—Mathematical models.
2. Management science.   3. Decision-making—Mathematical
models.   I. Kropp, Dean H.   II. Title.
HD30.25.B35   1985   658.4′033   84-21959
ISBN 0-471-87766-2

Printed in the United States of America

10 9 8 7 6 5 4 3 2 1

Preface

This book is designed for an introductory course dealing with quantitative models used in decision making. It is intended primarily for management curricula in which there is a one-term elementary course in management science. However, it contains enough material to support a two-term sequence if the text, exercises, and cases are used extensively. The four chapters on linear and integer programming require no previous college mathematics, while the chapters on other modeling techniques assume that the student has already studied probability and statistics.

Our exposition avoids using calculus, and we prefer intuitive justifications to rigorous arguments when that choice seems pedagogically effective. Nevertheless, we are not aiming our material at weak students or at a superficial level of knowledge. On the contrary, we expect students to have a good facility with algebraic notation and an ambition to learn more than technique.

The text material alone represents more than one term's coverage, even if the cases are neglected and the exercises are assigned very selectively. If fewer text chapters are covered, there is more time in class for discussion of the issues raised in the exercises and cases, or for reinforcing key concepts by repeated application. Nevertheless, it is important to view our material as providing only one component of a student's introductory course. The instructor has the discretion to resequence topics and to design lectures, discussions, computer assignments, and projects as other components in the course. The instructor selects which themes are emphasized and integrates the student's experiences. This book provides some of the resources to assist such an effort.

Our exposition is concise, consisting of a thorough (but not wordy) treatment of the main concepts. A more lengthy text could give details on special cases or variations of the models, or it could discuss specific applications. However, we feel that such topics, and the materials that support them, are best left to the individual instructor. Some instructors might well decide to supplement this book with material reflecting their own preferences. Those who want to emphasize recent applications could include readings and discussions of articles from such journals as *Interfaces* or the *Journal of the Operational Research Society*. On the other hand, someone who preferred to emphasize the detail and rigor of the techniques could compose specific handouts or assign reading from specialized texts on simulation, decision theory, integer programming, and the like. An instructor whose preference for cases extends beyond the material we have

v

included could supplement our text with one of the paperback case collections now available.

Although some instructors might find our coverage narrow, we do not believe in an introductory course aimed at a broad, cursory survey of all available techniques. In an introductory course, we much prefer a balanced treatment of building, analyzing, and applying models. Our mix of text material, examples, exercises, and cases is intended to help achieve this balance.

Each component in this mix is important. The text material provides a concise, systematic treatment of some fundamental analytic models and modeling concepts. The emphasis is on basic structure and logical reasoning, not on mathematical details and proofs. The examples make the models and concepts concrete, helping the student to understand specific details and generalize introductory topics. The exercises give the student feedback on his/her understanding of the concepts; and since they mostly involve word problems, they represent opportunities to practice building, analyzing, and applying models. The cases confront the student with realistic decision-making situations where models are useful, and they provide an opportunity to adapt, integrate, and extend the material in the text. The cases have been chosen largely for their pedagogical value, and they can be used in different ways, from serving as a basis for class discussion to providing more complicated problems for student projects. We provide details on the use of the cases in the Instructor's Manual.

In preparing computer-based materials to accompany our book, we have anticipated the trend toward greater use of personal computers for decision support. Our material on computer solutions for linear and integer programming relies on the LINDO package, which is widely available in a version that runs on the IBM PC (as well as on mainframe computers). We have also created personal computer programs written in BASIC to accompany some of the text material and to support some of the cases. Instructors who are interested in obtaining a copy of our course diskette should contact us directly.

For the most part the chapters are self-sufficient, but there are also topics that potentially integrate the material in two or more chapters. We have organized the material to support several teaching preferences, and we elaborate on the possibilities in the instructor's manual.

Our most important acknowledgment goes to Tammy Stebbins, whose administrative assistance has been vital to the progress of our manuscript. Her sense of organization and dedication to quality work have made us feel very well supported. In addition, we wish to thank Eugene Simonoff, whose efforts first brought us together to work seriously on this project. We also want to acknowledge the students at the Amos Tuck School, whose encouragement and criticism over several years helped us refine our material. We are indebted to James R. Freeland, University of Virginia; Jill A. Kammermeyer, Boston University Overseas Program; and Steven Nahmias, University of Santa Clara, whose comments reminded us to think about our book from different perspectives. Their constructive suggestions certainly improved our exposition. Finally, we want to acknowledge the help of Nina R. Lewis, our editor at John Wiley & Sons. Her guidance, support, and professionalism have been instrumental in bringing this book to publication.

Hanover, New Hampshire
September 1984

Kenneth R. Baker
Dean H. Kropp

Contents

Chapter 1

INTRODUCTION: MODELS AND MODELING

The material in this book is intended to help you develop a familiarity with certain models and a facility for the type of reasoning that accompanies their use. Our first objective is to acquaint you with the important principles and methods of management science. By doing so, this book will help you become an **intelligent consumer** of model-based analyses. Although you may not always perform the detailed analysis yourself, we expect that you will at least be able to evaluate someone else's analysis. By "intelligent consumption" we mean that you will recognize the capabilities and limitations of a particular modeling approach, that you will understand the analysis accompanying a given model, and that you will explore the effects of altering the model's assumptions.

Our second objective is to help you organize your decision making. In other words, this book will help you become a more **disciplined thinker.** Whether or not you use the specific models we treat in this text, we expect that after reading the book you will be better able to formalize the way you deal with the tangible aspects of a decision problem. By "disciplined thinking" we mean that you will identify choices and criteria in decision problems, that you will measure existing conditions and quantify decision outcomes, and that you will use logical reasoning to explain the consequences of particular choices.

To accomplish these objectives we have assembled a collection of text material, exercises, and cases. The text provides a concise treatment of the important models and techniques of management science. The exercises represent opportunities to practice formal analysis and to work with models. The cases describe specific settings in which modeling and analysis can be effective. We believe that all three elements are important to your learning process.

In this book we shall study a collection of models that can provide assistance to managers, consultants, engineers, analysts, and other people involved in the decision making process. In broader terms, we shall also study a systematic approach to solving decision problems. This **modeling approach** formalizes the description and analysis of decision problems that you face, and it provides you with an improved understanding of your situation. This improved understanding, in turn, helps you to organize your thinking effectively and to reach purposeful, rational decisions.

A **model** is a simplified representation of a real-world problem or phenomenon. The particular types of models we shall study are **mathematical** models, which means that they involve mathematical representations of real problems and phenomena. Of course, mathematical concepts are abstract, but this is no accident—the modeling approach relies on abstract reasoning to precede concrete action. Also, mathematical concepts are logical and precise, and their use in decision models helps to make the decision-making process more logical and precise.

Our coverage emphasizes **decision models,** that is, models used in support of decision making. In most applications, decision models contain certain common elements. The most important of these elements are decisions, data, outcomes, and structures. In order to convey a better sense of what we mean by decision models, we begin by describing each of these elements briefly.

Models must have a way to represent a **decision,** which is the choice of an action from a list of alternatives. Sometimes we represent the list explicitly. More frequently, however, we represent a decision in terms of a **variable,** and the specific numerical value for this variable implies a specific choice. Because the choice is under the control of the decision maker, we speak of a **controllable** variable in the model as representing a decision.

One of the key tasks in modeling is delineating a boundary for the decision problem and thereby distinguishing between "choices" and "givens." For example, we may be interested in building a model to help us minimize overtime hours at a factory in which compact cars are manufactured, given a fixed work-force size. Such a model would represent the number of overtime hours as a controllable variable (within limits) and the work-force size as a given or uncontrollable one. From a different perspective we might wish to represent both overtime hours and work-force size as controllable variables, with other conditions being fixed. Thus, the designation of controllable variables not only represents the measurable facet of a decision, but it also implies something about the problem's scope.

A second type of element in most models is information, or data. Here we refer to numerical descriptions either of conditions in the external environment or of technological factors within a system. These kinds of quantitative descriptors take the role of **uncontrollable** variables. For example, the rate at which cars are produced on a particular assembly line in the factory might be a technological parameter, which could be estimated by analyzing historical records. Similarly, the potential sales for the cars during the coming month might be an environmental parameter, which could be estimated by a forecasting technique. A decision about the length of a production run on the assembly line would not change either of these parameters, but decision makers would have to take them into account when alternative run lengths are considered. Thus, we want to represent parameters in a model so that we can capture the specific conditions surrounding the decision.

The third type of element involves quantifiable outcomes. We try to find an appropriate "yardstick" along which we can measure the consequences of particular actions. By specifying such a performance measure we lay the groundwork for later comparison and evaluation of actions. Although much of our coverage deals with models that focus on a single criterion, we recognize that in some problems there may be several important outcomes. Therefore, we introduce some models that can measure performance along several dimensions. We also recognize that decision making involves intangible factors. As we will discuss later, we do not advocate ignoring intangible considerations, nor do we suggest measuring them. Instead, we emphasize measuring those factors that we can quantify.

Finally, models create structures for thinking about decision situations. The purpose of a problem structure is first to organize the parts of the problem and then to trace the causal relationships between decisions and outcomes. The problem structure thus attempts to connect choices with consequences. In order to establish this connection, a model must reflect the definitions and rules operating within the problem. With this organization in place, the model helps us to anticipate the implications of a decision.

In this chapter we introduce some basic terms and concepts in order to provide a background for the chapters that follow. The simple structure in Figure 1.1 suggests how the modeling approach relates to decision making. The

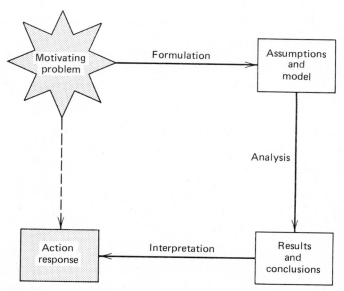

FIGURE 1.1

process begins with a decision problem for which a management response is needed. In principle, there exist a number of possible responses, and we seek the one with the most desirable consequences. The objective in building a model is to find a conceptual framework for dealing with the problem that will permit us to evaluate possible responses and to develop a logical basis for selecting a particular response. We could proceed directly from recognition of the problem to choosing a response (along the dashed arrow in Figure 1.1). However, this method of dealing with the problem is unstructured and may be unproductive. Instead, the first step in the modeling approach is to develop a model to describe the problem. This process is usually called **formulation** and involves the abstract representation of the problem's important features. The next step is to study the properties of the model and to draw conclusions about the specific consequences of different responses. This process is called **analysis** and involves deductive examination of the model. The final step is to apply the results of the deductive study. This is a process of **interpretation** and involves a realistic assessment of the conclusions drawn from the model as they relate to the actual problem. In the discussion to follow we will look more closely at these fundamental steps.

FORMULATING MODELS

Model formulation is the process of describing a problem in formal terms, so that we can deal with it in an organized fashion. The formal description defines the problem by identifying its elements, delineating its boundaries, and specifying the relationships that exist within it. A key factor in this process is **simplification.** Part of the value of a model comes from its ability to represent the essential features of a problem, usually under a set of simplifying assumptions, so that decision making focuses on the most important issues and ignores the irrelevant ones. At this stage the goal is to provide the decision maker with an understanding of the vital cause-and-effect logic in the situation being faced. A specification of this logic relates environmental conditions, potential actions, and eventual consequences.

In mathematical models, these three components are usually associated with specialized terminology. For instance, environmental conditions are those that are beyond the decision maker's control. It is convenient to summarize the status of environmental conditions in certain quantitative measures, which appear in models as **parameters.** Examples of parameters include the market price of a particular product, the amount of a scarce resource available to a firm, or the productivity of a repair crew. In contrast, potential decisions consist of those actions that are subject to the decision maker's influence. Quantitative descriptions of *potential* decisions are often called **decision variables.** Examples of decision variables include the length of a production run, the quantity of finished goods to be shipped from a particular warehouse to a particular customer, or the size of a repair crew. Finally, the eventual consequences in a problem depend on both the parameters and the decision variables. When a specific single measure of performance guides decision making, we call that measure a criterion, or **objective function.** Examples of criteria include the profit to the firm from a particular sale, the length of time a customer waits for service, or the proportion of time a repair crew is idle.

In short, the elements in a model are typically the measurable aspects of a decision situation: parameters, variables, and criteria. Model formulation is the process of describing the relationships among these elements. In essence, model formulation amounts to the use—either directly or indirectly—of mathematical **equations.**

Table 1.1 summarizes the elements of decision models by listing the mathematical term associated with each element, along with corresponding informal terminology.

Our ability to formulate problems is enhanced by certain skills in classifying problem elements. These skills help us to make formulations more effective by enabling us to be specific about the nature of problem elements. Perhaps the very first step in model formulation is to classify the problem elements according to some of the schemes associated with modeling.

For example, models can be **deterministic** or **probabilistic.** In deterministic situations we assume that we know all parameters and relationships with certainty, but in probabilistic situations we introduce uncertainty as a distinctive feature of the problem. Most real-world situations involve some degree of uncertainty, but it may not be necessary to reflect that uncertainty in the model. For example, in scheduling a routine production process, it is reasonable to suppress the randomness in modeling actual productivities if the scheduling decision is concerned with long-run average performance. On the other hand, the sales volume for the product may depend on unpredictable economic and competitive

TABLE 1.1

Elements of Decision Models	Mathematical Terminology	Informal Terminology
Decisions	Decision variables	Choices Possible actions Controllable variables
Data	Parameters	Information Environmental conditions Uncontrollable variables
Outcomes	Objective function	Criterion Eventual consequences Performance measure
Structure	Equations	Logic Relationships Cause-and-effect

factors, reflecting a degree of uncertainty that is vital in describing the market. In such a case, a probabilistic representation is much more convincing.

On another dimension, models can be **static** or **dynamic.** Static situations call for a single action or a number of actions simultaneously, and the focus is on one-time consequences. On the other hand, dynamic situations have a relevant time element, so that future conditions and actions depend on actions taken previously. For example, the initial stock level for a weekly newsmagazine, along with its weekly sales, will influence the cash position at the end of the week. As a result, we can treat this ending cash position as a static outcome. Because a new magazine is produced each week, we cannot sell the final stock since the old magazines lose their value when the new issue arrives. By contrast, for a product with ongoing sales, the stock level at the end of the week affects the sales and replenishment possibilities in the future. To deal with continuing sales, we must recognize the dynamic relationships.

On still another dimension, models can be **discrete** or **continuous.** Discrete phenomena involve a process of counting, or at least measurement on an integer scale, and continuous phenomena typically involve time intervals or distance, and measurement on a continuous scale. For example, describing the number of customers arriving at a ticket window involves counting (using integers) and lends itself to a discrete representation. But describing a particular customer's waiting time at the ticket window involves a time interval, which is most conveniently represented as continuous.

Differences between discrete and continuous models (as well as between static and dynamic models or deterministic and probabilistic models) often are more conceptual than real. In principle, the decision maker desires a model that reflects enough aspects of reality to make the problem understandable. Also, the model should be sufficiently simple to permit analysis of the possible choices. Thus, the selection of a particular model (a discrete model in preference to a continuous model, or a static model in preference to a dynamic one, or a deterministic model in preference to a probabilistic one) should make it possible to represent the essence of the problem faithfully and to exploit any relevant analytic capability. There is seldom one best way to achieve these objectives, for model building is somewhat of an individualistic art. Like an effective artist the effective decision maker should be prepared to treat problems in alternative ways, according to what is most suitable. The "art" of building a model often lies in determining what features of the problem are essential (that is, what features are truly relevant to the decision at hand) as well as how to express them in abstract form.

ANALYZING MODELS

The process of formulation determines the relationships in the model. These relationships comprise model structure, and we can think of them as describing the rules of operation of the model. The process of model analysis systematically examines how specific decisions interact with these rules to produce distinct results. In complicated models, our goal may simply be to develop an understanding of how decisions and the problem structure account for performance. In other situations, a more ambitious goal would be to identify optimal decisions.

A common element of decision making deals with the problem of achieving a balance or **trade-off** between two conflicting tendencies. In the simplest cases there is one decision variable, and the problem is essentially deterministic. For example, in inventory control the choice of a replenishment order quantity (or lot size) affects both ordering costs and inventory carrying costs. An ordering cost is incurred with each replenishment order, and the larger the lot size, the smaller the number of orders placed in a year. As a consequence, the annual ordering cost tends to be smaller as the lot size gets larger. But inventory carrying costs are proportional to the average inventory carried, and the larger the lot size, the greater the average inventory. Thus, the annual carrying cost tends to be larger as the lot size gets larger. The choice of a lot size to minimize total costs requires a balance between ordering costs, which decrease with larger lot sizes, and carrying costs, which increase with larger lot sizes. Achieving a minimum total cost requires an optimal balance of these two conflicting tendencies.

A more complicated case involves a deterministic problem with several decision variables. For example, the problem of allocating scarce resources among competing activities requires a decision about the level of each activity. One activity might consume small amounts of resource A and large amounts of resource B, while another activity might consume large amounts of A and small amounts of B. Rather than dealing with only one activity, however, a typical planning problem might involve a decision regarding which of the *two* activities to use or which combination of both activities to use. This decision must recognize the relative costs of the respective activities and also the amounts of the resources available. When there are several activities and several resources, achieving a minimum total cost requires an optimal balance among several conflicting tendencies.

A different sort of trade-off is encountered in problems in which probabilistic elements are significant. For example, consider a firm that is ready to launch a new product. Depending on the market response there may be a possibility of making considerable profit, but there also may be a possibility of sustaining substantial losses. The firm must determine whether to launch the product in the face of such uncertainty or to maintain the status quo and do nothing. In this case there is, in a sense, a need to achieve a trade-off between profit outcomes and their probabilities. This type of problem can be even more complicated when there is no single criterion to guide decision making. Indeed, some individuals are attracted to the possibility of earning a large profit even when there is a low probability of doing so, while others would prefer a smaller potential profit if the probability is higher. In the face of uncertainty, it is sometimes possible to deal with averages so that the focus can be on the cost or profit trade-off. In other circumstances, the role of individual preferences renders the problem somewhat more complicated.

The role of analysis in the study of trade-offs is to determine how performance measures increase or decrease, and by how much, as a result of particular decisions. Furthermore, analysis involves the search for improvements in a performance measure and ultimately for decisions that optimize the performance measure.

Optimization may take several forms. The most elementary form of optimization uses model relationships (such as formulas) to calculate directly the measured outcome for each possible decision and then to select the best outcome from this list. However, in some models there is an extremely large number of alternatives, and direct calculation may be inefficient or impossible. A more sophisticated approach is to follow an **algorithm,** or computational procedure, which evaluates only selected alternatives and utilizes information gained during the evaluation process to guide the way logically and efficiently toward an optimum. A more general approach is to derive a mathematical expression for the optimal decision in terms of the parameters and relationships of the problem.

Optimization literally means finding the best—for example, finding the lowest cost, the highest profit, or the maximum efficiency. Most forms of optimization or even the less ambitious processes of analysis aimed at finding an improvement rely on the specification of one objective function. This commitment to a specific criterion must be kept in perspective, however, for the criteria in actual problem settings are rarely so simple. The real, unsimplified decision problem is likely to involve more than one criterion, and several intangible factors may also be present. The best that a mathematical model can do is deal clearly with the tangible, objective factors. This model may be an incomplete representation of the entire problem. However, it should still be of some help, because it makes the decision maker aware of the sacrifice in **objective** terms implied by a decision based on **subjective** grounds to pursue a different (nonoptimal) course of action. In this sense, model analysis brings the subjective components into sharper relief by providing complete and precise quantitative information about the objective components.

If we can view model formulation as something of an art, then we can think of model analysis as a science. In particular, the process of analysis operates logically within the boundaries of the relationships assumed in the model. It begins with the premises of the model, and in deductive fashion reveals the conclusions that follow. By tracing the consequences of different decisions, analysis reveals the spectrum of possible outcomes; and in the process of optimization, analysis reveals the best possible value for the chosen criterion.

INTERPRETING MODELS

Once we carry out the analysis of a model, the next step in the modeling approach is to apply the results of that analysis to the real problem situation. In this context, the process of interpretation requires a judicious use of the conclusions drawn from the analysis. It is important to remember that analysis can determine which action or actions are desirable for the *model,* but that does not necessarily mean that the same action will be as desirable in the actual problem situation. The reason for the difference is that a model is not a complete representation of reality but only an abstract representation based on certain simplifying assumptions. Because of this difference, the validity of the conclusions depends on the realism of the assumptions used in the model.

Although it is often easy to see how conclusions follow from the deductive process of analyzing a model, the relationship between conclusions and assumptions is more difficult to recognize. Figure 1.2 suggests where this relationship fits into our scheme of formulation-analysis-interpretation, which was given earlier. The process of establishing a direct link between assumptions and conclusions is called **sensitivity analysis,** or **sensitivity testing.** The terms suggest an investigation of the extent to which conclusions are affected by changes in assumptions. In Figure 1.2, the additional dashed line at the right is symbolic of the link provided by studies of sensitivity.

As we noted previously, a model is based on simplifying assumptions, normally involving the elements, relationships, and criteria in a problem situation. If these assumptions are not valid for representing the important features of the actual situation, the conclusions themselves will have little value to the decision maker. In sensitivity analysis, rather than examine the validity of model assumptions directly, we sometimes ask how we might alter the assumptions without changing the conclusions. For example, the specification of a mathematical

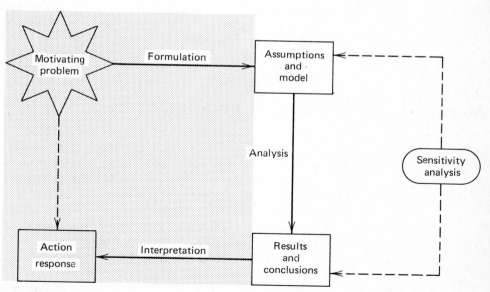

FIGURE 1.2

model typically requires the use of numerical values for certain parameters. For the purposes of analyzing the model, we assume that we know these values when, in fact, we may not know them with much precision. In sensitivity testing we ask: If we were to alter the particular value of a parameter, how would we affect the results of the analysis? Stated another way: For what alternative values of a certain parameter would the conclusions of the model remain exactly the same? This set of values is called a **range of validity** for the parameter under study. In other words, the conclusions drawn from the analysis are valid as long as the actual parametric value falls within its range of validity. When a parameter's range of validity is quite small, we say the conclusions are quite **sensitive** to the parametric value; whereas we say the conclusions are relatively **insensitive** when the range of validity is large.

When we do not know the value of a parameter with precision, we must think about whether the conclusions are sensitive to the value assumed in the model. If the results of analysis are relatively insensitive to the value of the parameter, we need not have much concern about our lack of precision. But if the results are sensitive to the parametric value, we may wish to devote some effort to obtaining more precise knowledge, perhaps through research or statistical sampling. At the very least, we should be aware of the implications of different parametric values for the results of analysis when we recommend or make a decision.

An investigation of **parametric validity** contemplates the impact on the conclusions if assumptions about certain parameters are altered. On a different level, sensitivity analysis may also involve an investigation of **structural validity,** which contemplates the impact on the conclusions if assumptions about portions of the model's structure are altered. These two types of investigations alert us to specific areas where we may have to temper the conclusions drawn from model analysis.

MANAGEMENT SCIENCE IN ORGANIZATIONS

Decision models can provide people with insight and understanding, but the greater challenge is often to convert this understanding into action within a real organization. In its broadest sense, management science deals not only with model-based analysis but also with the process of implementing the results of that analysis in a particular organizational setting.

The **implementation** of management science analyses has received considerable attention in recent years, first by practitioners who lamented the fact that good analysis did not always influence organizations, and later by researchers who began to notice some general patterns in implementation failures and successes. Although a comprehensive treatment of this topic is beyond the scope of this book, we at least want to highlight some of the important principles as we lay the groundwork for studying models.

The practical motivation for studying the implementation process is a simple one: implementation failures are costly. There are two kinds of costs that organizations incur when a modeling initiative fails. In the short run a failed modeling initiative involves a lost opportunity. Specifically, by ignoring the insights that modeling can provide, a manager may take an action that is ineffective, and thus there is a foregone improvement. In the long run there is a more damaging effect, for an implementation failure will often produce negative attitudes toward the process of using models. Once an initial failure becomes visible, future attempts at using management science approaches are less likely to work. For this reason, an implementation failure may diminish a firm's subsequent ability to exploit management science.

As practitioners and researchers have learned more about the topic of implementation, some general patterns have become more clear. For a start, we can think of there being two levels—technical and organizational—at which critical factors may contribute to the success or failure of a management science project. In what follows, we outline some of the factors that frequently arise.

TECHNICAL ISSUES

A first step in a management science project is problem definition. At early stages, we might be able to describe a problem only in terms of its symptoms, but eventually we move toward a clearer delineation of the problem's scope. This process involves an identification of controllable and uncontrollable variables (or "choices" and "givens," as we called them earlier) and the performance measures that are of interest. Problem definition may also involve classifying the problem or developing some initial assumptions, thus laying the groundwork for modeling.

Just as the problem needs to be defined at an early stage, so does the modeling project itself need direction and scope. This is especially true if the modeling is being done by a consulting group, or a staff group, in support of line management. But it is also important for the decision maker to specify the scope of the project, its objectives, and the tangible products expected from it.

Once a model-building effort is under way, it is important to recognize what requirements the model will have for data gathering and analysis. Some thought must be given to the resources and skills necessary to acquire data for a model.

A key design choice relates to the simplicity or complexity of the model. Several arguments exist for building a simple model rather than a complex one: It is cheaper and faster to build, easier to debug, less demanding of data, and easier to maintain for repeated use. Simpler models are usually easier for their users to understand, and they facilitate more effective training if it is required. On the other hand, complex models are more realistic and more complete. The technical art of model building involves the ability to incorporate sufficient complexity for the model to be useful without sacrificing the virtues of simplicity.

An important step in developing a model is validating it. This step is essentially a means of testing the model to determine how well it represents the problem. Depending on the setting, validation might involve reproducing historical performance or just showing logical qualitative responses to changes in parameters.

Finally, when the model-building activity is carried out by people who will ultimately pass the model on to other users, it is important to document the model well. Good documentation exhibits a certain degree of "user friendliness" so that the model does not remain dependent on its innovator.

ORGANIZATIONAL ISSUES

Entirely apart from the technical capability in a management science study there are several "process" factors that influence implementation success. We can think of the use of a model as one form of organizational change. As we anticipate how to deal with resistance to change we are putting in place some safeguards that increase the probability of success in implementation.

A major factor in successful change is participation by those in the organization affected by the change. In the case of models, this means that the ultimate users of model analysis should be involved in developing the model. By involving users in the model-building phase, a project team increases user understanding, allays fears about the impact of the model, and builds commitment to the model-based approach.

The prototype is one widely used mechanism for enhancing communication between model builders and model users (assuming they are different populations). An early attempt to create a prototype of the final model can open an important dialogue. With a prototype, model builders reveal their formal definition of the problem and describe their need for data. Model users can provide feedback on the problem definition, finding mistakes or bugs, and they can indicate where the model will need refinements. Thus the prototype becomes a tangible point of discussion early in the project, as a device for shaping future model development.

A prominent factor in the implementation process is the role of top management. Support from top management is widely cited as a major factor in successful implementation. This support can take many forms, such as helping to define the problem realistically, providing suitable resources for the model-building effort, and introducing a reward structure that promotes model use. Management's commitment, in terms of people and funding, provides the entire organization with an important signal. When those in management treat the problem as important and the results of modeling as useful, they greatly enhance the longer run prospects for successful implementations.

These technical and organizational issues suggest many of the main themes in management science implementation. The important point is that beyond the ability to develop effective models, which we shall emphasize in this book, there are many considerations that account for successful use of such models.

A PREVIEW

In the next four chapters of this book we deal with deterministic models and emphasize optimization as the form of analysis. "The Transportation Model" introduces the subject of linear programming by examining a special kind of distribution model. This special case affords us an early opportunity to cover concepts of model formulation, optimization procedure, and sensitivity analysis. In "Linear Programming" we show the full generality of these concepts in modeling and sensitivity analysis, emphasizing graphical methods and computer techniques for performing the optimization. In "The Simplex Method" we focus on the mathematics of the optimization technique itself and demonstrate how it provides information for sensitivity analysis as a by-product of solving the typical linear programming problem. "Integer Programming" deals with an important extension of linear programming, in which integer requirements arise on certain decision variables. In this chapter we emphasize both formulation and optimization concepts.

In "Network Models for Project Scheduling" we study the use of a simple graphical approach for describing and analyzing the progress of a complex project. The graphical approach leads to a network structure that facilitates scheduling analysis. We also adapt the basic deterministic analysis so that we can answer questions related to probabilistic factors in scheduling.

The next two chapters deal with fundamental concepts of decision making in probabilistic environments. In "Decision Analysis" we study basic modeling notions, relying on graphs and tables and emphasizing the role of criteria in the various models. "Trade-off Models for Surplus and Shortage" treats an important special case, involving the balance of supply and demand, that allows us to exploit a more powerful form of analysis.

The chapter on "Forecasting Models" deals with a critical step in acquiring data. We concentrate on time-series information and on the measurement of forecast errors.

Our chapter on "Inventory Models" examines a collection of model structures that have proven useful in understanding the behavior of inventories. Although our basic model is deterministic and contains only one decision variable, we explore questions of structural validity by reformulating the basic model to fit a variety of situations involving inventory management.

In "Queueing Models" we study a family of model structures that are useful for understanding the phenomenon of congestion in service systems. We emphasize the role of parameters and criteria in representing the dynamic behavior of waiting lines, and we look briefly at some basic design trade-offs.

In the "Simulation" chapter we describe a very flexible modeling technique. We begin with a deterministic and static emphasis, and we show how to incorporate probabilistic and dynamic considerations. The methods of analysis depend heavily on statistical concepts, and the role of the computer is critical in large-scale simulations.

In every situation we begin with the description of a decision-making problem that is amenable to analysis using the concepts of the chapter. Then, we discuss appropriate modeling approaches and illustrate how they help us to deal with the problem. Thus, we motivate the general modeling discussion with specific, realistic examples.

Chapter 2
THE TRANSPORTATION MODEL

The Piedmont Power Company

Each week the Piedmont Power Company (PPC) must decide how to transport coal from its mines to its generating plants. By the middle of this week, for example, its mining operations will have produced the following quantities ready to be shipped from each location:

Source	Quantity Available
Mine 1	40 tons
Mine 2	50 tons
Mine 3	60 tons

PPC has also determined that next week the requirements for coal at each of its generating plants will be the following:

Source	Quantity Required
Plant 1	30 tons
Plant 2	20 tons
Plant 3	45 tons
Plant 4	55 tons

Because it is possible to ship from each mine to any of the plants, there are 12 possible supply routes, and PPC must decide which routes to use and how much to ship along each one. Fortunately, there is precisely enough coal available to meet next week's requirements, but PPC must also consider the costs associated with using various routes. The table below shows the dollar cost per ton for shipping coal on each of the possible routes:

	P1	P2	P3	P4
M1	9	4	6	6
M2	10	5	7	8
M3	4	7	3	5

PPC has determined that these unit costs are accurate for any shipment size of up to 100 tons. The problem facing PPC is to determine how to allocate deliveries among possible supply routes in order to meet requirements at minimum cost.

In this chapter we shall study a systematic technique for analyzing allocation problems of the type facing the Piedmont Power Company. This type is known as a **transportation problem.** One of the important considerations in the problem faced by Piedmont Power is that *some* allocation is certain to be made for next week's coal deliveries. If, with the investment of a little time and effort, Piedmont Power can find the most efficient allocation, then it is certainly worth the trouble to do so. The primary role of a model in such a situation is to provide a convenient means of determining the minimum-cost delivery schedule. In this case the problem is already well defined, and there exists an appropriate procedure for finding an optimal solution. A substantial portion of the chapter deals with this solution technique and illustrates the kind of information that the analysis of a model can develop. As it happens, this technique is a special case of the simplex method for linear programs, which is covered elsewhere in the book. Thus, this chapter affords us an opportunity to learn about some of the features of the simplex method, at least to the extent that its features are reflected in the solution of transportation problems.

In a broader sense, a model provides a systematic structure for thinking about a problem and for specifying its properties. An understanding of this structure, in turn, forms the basis for dealing with a variety of managerial issues that arise in conjunction with the problem. This chapter discusses how the model of Piedmont Power Company's problem can help find answers to important managerial questions.

In building a model for the Piedmont Power situation we recognize three main elements:

1. There are three sources for coal shipments, each with a known supply quantity.
2. There are four destinations for coal shipments, each with a known demand quantity.
3. There are 12 possible shipment routes, each with a known unit cost of shipping.

TABLE 2.1

9	4	6	6	40
10	5	7	8	50
4	7	3	5	60
30	20	45	55	

There are several ways in which we might organize these elements into a model. One way involves the format shown in Table 2.1. In this format each row corresponds to a source of supply and each column corresponds to a destination. The cells in the body of the table contain the unit costs for each supply route. Eventually, they will also contain the shipment allocations. Across each row these allocations must add to the number shown at the right, and down each column they must add to the number shown underneath. (These sums must be equal to the row and column requirements in this example because there is sufficient total supply to meet demand exactly.) Furthermore, we can compute the total cost of a shipment schedule by multiplying the unit cost by the allocation in every cell and then adding these 12 products.

Although the table format will be the basis for our subsequent treatment, we can illustrate another model structure that has more general usefulness. This structure is algebraic, and it uses the following definition of a shipment allocation:

x_{ij} = quantity shipped from source i to destination j

There are 12 x_{ij} values, comprising the unknown variables of the algebraic model. Our objective is to minimize total cost *(TC)*, and we write our criterion as follows:

$$TC = 9x_{11} + 4x_{12} + 6x_{13} + 6x_{14} + 10x_{21} + 5x_{22} + 7x_{23} \\ + 8x_{24} + 4x_{31} + 7x_{32} + 3x_{33} + 5x_{34}$$

One type of restriction in the problem is the requirement that the shipment quantities that leave Mine 1 must add to 40 tons. We express this requirement with the following algebra:

$$x_{11} + x_{12} + x_{13} + x_{14} = 40$$

Similar equations apply to Mine 2 and Mine 3. Another type of restriction is the requirement that the shipment quantities that reach Plant 1 must add to 30 tons. Stated algebraically,

$$x_{11} + x_{21} + x_{31} = 30$$

Similar equations apply to the other plants. Finally, we add the obvious requirement that shipment allocations must be positive or 0. Then, we write our complete model as follows:

minimize

$$TC = 9x_{11} + 4x_{12} + 6x_{13} + 6x_{14} + 10x_{21} + 5x_{22}$$
$$+ 7x_{23} + 8x_{24} + 4x_{31} + 7x_{32} + 3x_{33} + 5x_{34}$$

subject to

$$
\begin{aligned}
x_{11} + x_{12} + x_{13} + x_{14} &= 40 \quad &(M1 \text{ supply}) \\
x_{21} + x_{22} + x_{23} + x_{24} &= 50 \quad &(M2 \text{ supply}) \\
x_{31} + x_{32} + x_{33} + x_{34} &= 60 \quad &(M3 \text{ supply}) \\
x_{11} + x_{21} + x_{31} \phantom{+ x_{14}} &= 30 \quad &(P1 \text{ demand}) \\
x_{12} + x_{22} + x_{32} \phantom{+ x_{14}} &= 20 \quad &(P2 \text{ demand}) \\
x_{13} + x_{23} + x_{33} \phantom{+ x_{14}} &= 45 \quad &(P3 \text{ demand}) \\
x_{14} + x_{24} + x_{34} \phantom{+ x_{14}} &= 55 \quad &(P4 \text{ demand}) \\
\text{all } x_{ij} &\geq 0 &
\end{aligned}
$$

Before we analyze the Piedmont Power Company example, it will be helpful to think about the general form of these two model structures. The transportation problem deals with a situation in which a product is stored at several supply points (sources) and must be shipped to several demand points (destinations). For purposes of notation, let

a_i = quantity available at source i ($i = 1, 2, \ldots, m$)

b_j = quantity required at destination j ($j = 1, 2, \ldots, n$)

c_{ij} = unit cost of transportation from source i to destination j

where m denotes the number of sources and n the number of destinations. The quantities a_i and b_j and the costs c_{ij} are **parameters** of the model and represent given information. The allocation quantities x_{ij}, which represent **decision variables,** are unknown.

For the time being, we shall assume that the total quantity available at all sources (the sum of the a_i terms) is precisely enough to meet the total quantity required at all destinations (the sum of the b_j terms). Thus, we have

$$\sum_{i=1}^{m} a_i = \sum_{j=1}^{n} b_j$$

Later we shall see how to deal with situations in which this relationship does not hold.

To write total cost mathematically, note that for a given allocation the term $c_{ij}x_{ij}$ represents the cost of transportation along the route from source i to destination j. The total transportation cost will be the sum of these terms for all routes, or combinations of i and j:

$$TC = \sum_{i=1}^{m} \sum_{j=1}^{n} c_{ij}x_{ij}$$

This expression represents an **objective function;** it measures the total cost for any particular allocation. Clearly we wish to minimize this total cost.

One restriction or **constraint** in the problem is that the quantities shipped along routes leaving source i and going to all destinations j must add to a_i, or

$$\sum_{j=1}^{n} x_{ij} = a_i, \qquad \text{for each source } i$$

There are m constraints of this type. They are equality constraints because it is physically impossible to ship *more* product from a source than is actually available and (since total supply equals total demand) we would fail to meet demand if we were to ship *less*. Similarly, the quantities arriving at destination j from all sources i must add to b_j, or

$$\sum_{i=1}^{m} x_{ij} = b_j, \qquad \text{for each destination } j$$

There are n constraints of this type. As in the case of the supply constraints above, these demand constraints must be expressed as equalities. Finally, our approach assumes the obvious restriction that the amount shipped must be either positive or 0:

$$x_{ij} \geq 0, \qquad \text{for each route } (i, j)$$

In concise form, the model is

minimize

$$TC = \sum_{i=1}^{m} \sum_{j=1}^{n} c_{ij} x_{ij}$$

subject to

$$\sum_{j=1}^{n} x_{ij} = a_i \qquad i = 1, 2, \ldots, m$$

$$\sum_{i=1}^{m} x_{ij} = b_j \qquad j = 1, 2, \ldots, n$$

$$x_{ij} \geq 0 \qquad \text{all } (i, j)$$

In this form we can see the delivery problem involves optimization under constraints; in particular, the problem is to find the minimum transportation cost subject to supply and demand restrictions. Alternatively, the problem can be displayed in table format, as shown in Table 2.2. In the table format each row corresponds to a source and each column corresponds to a destination. The cells in the body of the table contain the unit costs, c_{ij}, and the decision variables. Along each row these allocations must add to the number shown at the right, and down each column they must add to the number shown underneath. Table 2.1 was just the specific form of this table for the Piedmont Power problem.

TABLE 2.2

	Destinations			
c_{11}	c_{12}	$\cdots$	c_{1n}	a_1
c_{21}	c_{22}	$\cdots$	c_{2n}	a_2
$\vdots$	$\vdots$	$\cdots$	$\vdots$	$\vdots$
c_{m1}	c_{m2}	$\cdots$	c_{mn}	a_m
b_1	b_2	$\cdots$	b_n	

Sources

To summarize, the transportation problem lends itself to both a tabular model and an algebraic model, with m supply points and n demand points. The transportation **algorithm** is a solution technique for finding a minimum-cost allocation for this model.

ELEMENTS OF THE ANALYSIS

This section introduces the building blocks in our solution approach. From these elements we shall be able to develop a systematic procedure for solving transportation problems.

AN INITIAL SOLUTION

Our first building block is a routine that constructs a transportation schedule satisfying the supply and demand equations. Such a schedule is called a **feasible** solution. Because there are many ways to construct a feasible schedule, we suggest a simple routine that uses the unit costs as a guide. Our routine is based on the intuitive notion that we should ship as much product as possible along the cheapest route. The steps are as follows:

1. Identify the cell in the table with the smallest unit cost. (Break ties arbitrarily.)
2. Without altering any existing allocations, allocate the maximum possible amount to this cell.
3. If the allocation in Step 2 has satisfied a row (supply) constraint, remove this row from further consideration. If the allocation has satisfied a column (demand) constraint, remove this column from further consideration. Return to Step 1 until all requirements have been met.

When we use the routine in the example of Table 2.1, the first step allocates as much as possible to cell (3, 3), which has the smallest unit cost in the table. The maximum quantity we can allocate to this route at Step 2 is 45 tons, which satisfies the demand requirement at Plant 3. According to Step 3, we need not consider column 3 any further. Returning to Step 1, there is now a tie for the smallest unit cost, between cells (1, 2) and (3, 1). After arbitrarily breaking the tie in favor of cell (3, 1), we next allocate 15 tons to that cell, since the 15-ton amount is the most we are permitted to allocate without altering the previous allocation. Now we have satisfied the supply constraint for Mine 3, and we need not consider row 3 any further. Returning again to Step 1, we next identify cell (1, 2) as having the smallest cost, and we allocate 20 tons there, meeting the demand in column 2. If we continue following the steps of our routine, we eventually construct the solution shown in Table 2.3, with a total cost of $825. This solution is feasible, but as we shall see, it is not optimal.

TABLE 2.3

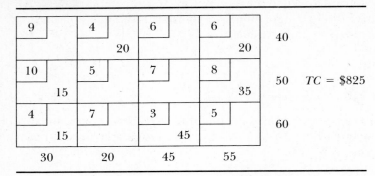

$TC = \$825$

Our solution routine typically requires $m + n - 1$ allocations. This number relates to the fact that the model contains $m + n$ equations. One equation, however, depends on the others because total supply must equal total demand. This leaves $m + n - 1$ independent equations. The theory for systems of equations tells us that we need the values of only $m + n - 1$ variables to satisfy these equations. Our routine usually produces just that number of allocations. (Later we shall deal with the exceptional cases in which there are fewer allocations.)

TOURS

The second building block in our approach relates to the configuration of cell allocations. For each cell without an allocation there is a single closed loop formed by alternating horizontal and vertical movements in the table, starting with the unallocated cell and turning only at allocated cells. The allocated cells that are turning points on this path form a **tour,** and each unallocated cell has its own unique tour. For example, in Table 2.3, the tour for the unallocated cell

TABLE 2.4

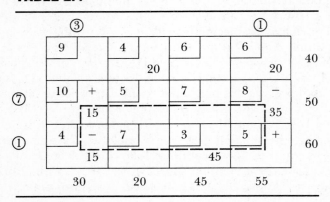

TABLE 2.5

9	4	6	6	40
	20		20	
10	5	7	8	50
15			35	
4	7	3	5	60
15		45		

| 30 | 20 | 45 | 55 |

(3, 4) consists of the allocated cells (3, 1), (2, 1), and (2, 4). The dashed lines in Table 2.4 show the corresponding loop. Note that cell (3, 3) is not part of the tour because no turn is made there. The tour for the unallocated cell (3, 2), shown in Table 2.5, is a little more complicated. It consists of the cells (3, 1), (2, 1), (2, 4), (1, 4), and (1, 2). The direction of the tour has no important significance. For cell (3, 2) we could specify the tour in reverse order by making a vertical movement first. The important point is that as a result of our initial solution routine, and at every succeeding stage in our procedure, there will be a unique tour for each unallocated cell.

The tour plays a key role when we look for cost improvements. If we decide to make a shipment along a route corresponding to an unallocated cell, the tour identifies the existing allocations that must be revised for us to preserve feasibility. For example, if we make an allocation in cell (3, 4) in Table 2.4, we shall have to revise the existing allocations so that the shipments still satisfy the supply and demand constraints. In Table 2.4 we label cell (3, 4) with a "+" sign to signify that its allocation will increase. Then we label the cells on its tour with alternating "−" and "+" signs, as shown in Table 2.4. By increasing the allocations in the "+" cells and decreasing those in the "−" cells by the same amount we can preserve feasibility (at least, if the amount we reallocate is no more than 15 tons).

The cell labels also help us evaluate whether such a reallocation is economically desirable. If we make an allocation of 1 ton into cell (3, 4) of Table 2.4, the direct cost for this shipment is 5, which is the unit cost of transportation along this route. Next we need to determine whether the savings from making the necessary reallocations along the tour will offset this additional cost. Because positive savings occur on routes with reduced shipments, we associate *positive* savings with "−" cells, and *negative* savings with "+" cells. On the tour for cell (3, 4) we obtain

$$\text{Cost savings} = c_{31} - c_{21} + c_{24} = 4 - 10 + 8 = 2$$

Comparing this incremental benefit to the incremental direct cost, we obtain

Incremental cost	= 5 per ton
Incremental benefit	= 2 per ton
Net incremental cost	= 3 per ton

In other words, the incremental benefit is less than the incremental cost, and we would increase TC by 3 if we were to reallocate 1 ton in this fashion. Similarly, a reallocation of q tons would raise costs by $3q$. Thus, we cannot reduce TC by utilizing the (3, 4) route and making compensating adjustments in the existing allocations.

In principle, we could use a similar procedure to evaluate the desirability of reallocating into any cell that has no allocation in our initial solution. We would find the cell's tour and label it; then we would find the net incremental cost of the reallocation by subtracting the incremental benefit from the incremental direct cost. If this difference turned out to be positive, as we found for cell (3, 4), we would know that the reallocation would be undesirable. On the other hand, if the difference turned out to be negative, the reallocation would be economically attractive. In our example, we would find that costs could be reduced by reallocating either to cell (2, 2) or to cell (2, 3).

ROW AND COLUMN EVALUATORS

The tour evaluation approach outlined above is reliable, but tedious. Our third building block provides a more efficient approach. In Table 2.4, suppose we were to reallocate 1 ton into cell (3, 4). We know that the incremental direct cost of doing so is 5. Our procedure requires us to compute the incremental benefit of making the necessary reallocation. Suppose that we arbitrarily guess that this incremental benefit will be 1, and let us record this guess in a circle at the side of row 3, which contains the cell we are evaluating. Now we can begin to evaluate the accuracy of our guess by proceeding in that row along the tour for cell (3, 4). The next cell we encounter on the tour is (3, 1). Its label is "−" and its unit cost is 4, which indicates a benefit of 4 when we reallocate 1 ton. Thus, our guess has so far underestimated the tour's benefit by 3. In particular, we have

Original guess	= 1 per ton
Cumulative benefit	= 4 per ton
Difference (underestimate)	= (3) per ton

We record this underestimate in a circle at the top of column 1, since the tour turns along column 1 at this point.

The next cell we encounter on the tour is (2, 1). Its label is "+" and its unit cost is 10, which indicates a cost of 10 when we reallocate. At this stage, our cumulative net benefit is −6, which means that our original guess has so far overestimated the tour's benefit by 7. In particular, we have

Original guess	= 1 per ton
Cumulative benefit	= −6 = 4 − 10 per ton

Difference (overestimate) = 7 per ton

We record this overestimate in a circle at the side of row 2, where the tour turns next.

Proceeding along the tour, we encounter cell (2, 4). Its label is "−" and its unit cost is 8, bringing our tour's net benefit to 2. We have

Original guess	= 1 per ton
Cumulative benefit	= 2 = 4 − 10 + 8 per ton

Difference (underestimate) = (1) per ton

Now our original guess is an underestimate of 1, which we place in a circle at the top of column 4.

At this stage our tour returns to its starting point, cell (3, 4). We now know the incremental benefit along this tour: it is equal to 2, our original guess (1) adjusted for our cumulative underestimate (1). Note that these two numbers have been assigned to the row and column pair that identify cell (3, 4). If our original guess had been 0, the adjustment would have been 2. If our original guess had been 5, the adjustment would have been −3. For any original guess, the process would have led us to a **row evaluator** for row 3 and a **column evaluator** for column 4 such that the sum of the two evaluators would equal the incremental benefit of reallocating along the designated tour.

Because the tour's direction has no significance, we could have followed the tour in the reverse direction, starting out along column 4. In this case we would have recorded our initial guess as the evaluator for column 4. Ultimately, the evaluator for row 3 would have provided the proper adjustment, and the two evaluators would still have added to 2.

Stated in general terms, when we start out along the row, our first row evaluator is our initial guess for the incremental benefit in a reallocation. We can interpret each subsequent row evaluator as the cumulative overestimate in our guess and each column evaluator as the cumulative underestimate. The reverse is true when we start out along the column. In either event, two properties hold: (1) If we choose a cell on the tour, the sum of its row evaluator and its column evaluator will equal its unit cost; and (2) for the unallocated cell where we began the tour, the sum of its row evaluator and its column evaluator will equal the incremental benefit along the tour. This second property allows us to determine whether a reallocation is desirable; by comparing the incremental direct cost in the unallocated cell to the incremental benefit along the tour we can determine whether total cost will decrease when we reallocate.

Thus far, the method of using row and column evaluators may not seem very efficient compared to the previous method of calculating the net cost change. However, there is another useful property of row and column evaluators: We can use a single set of evaluators to determine the incremental benefit for *all* unallocated cells. We require only that the sum of the row evaluator and the column evaluator equal the unit cost in every allocated cell. In symbols let

$$R_i = \text{evaluator for row } i \qquad (i = 1 \text{ to } m)$$
$$K_j = \text{evaluator for column } j \qquad (j = 1 \text{ to } n)$$

Then we need to find a set of evaluators satisfying

$$R_i + K_j = c_{ij}, \qquad \text{for every allocated cell } (i, j)$$

Fortunately, there are many sets of evaluators that are satisfactory. We can choose one of the R_i values (or K_j values) arbitrarily; all the remaining values will then be unique.

In our example, suppose we begin by setting $R_2 = 2$. Because (2, 1) is an allocated cell, we must have

$$R_2 + K_1 = c_{21}, \qquad \text{giving } K_1 = 8$$

Similarly, since (2, 4) is an allocated cell we must have $K_4 = 6$. Now using the fact that $K_4 = 6$ and the fact that (1, 4) is an allocated cell, we find that $R_1 = 0$. Continuing in this fashion we eventually produce the set of evaluators shown in Table 2.6. Instead of starting with $R_2 = 2$, we could have started by setting $K_4 = 29$ (or any other number); and we would eventually have produced an equally valid set of R_i and K_j values. In general, a reasonable procedure is to set $R_1 = 0$ and then solve for the remaining values of R_i and K_j.

In summary, our three building blocks provide a procedure for getting started (an initial solution), a procedure for changing the solution (using tours),

TABLE 2.6

	⑧	④	⑦	⑥	
⓪	9	4 — 20	6	6 — 20	40
②	10 — 15	5	7	8 — 35	50
⓪−4	4 — 15	7	3 — 45	5	60
	30	20	45	55	

and a procedure for determining where improvements exist (using evaluators). In the next section we combine these procedures into a complete solution method.

A SOLUTION ALGORITHM

This section describes a specific procedure to determine the minimum transportation cost and the allocations that achieve it. This procedure is known as the **transportation algorithm,** and it relies on the building blocks we have introduced. We discuss how to use the alogrithm by applying it to the Piedmont Power example.

The general form of the solution procedure is outlined as Algorithm 2.1 in the accompanying box. In essence, it consists of three parts: Initial Solution, Optimality Check, and Improvement Routine. The Initial Solution routine con-

ALGORITHM 2.1
Solution Procedure for the Transportation Problem

A. INITIAL SOLUTION

A1 Identify the cell in the table with the smallest unit cost. (Break ties arbitrarily.)

A2 Without altering any existing allocations, allocate the maximum possible amount to this cell.

A3 If the allocation in Step 2 has satisfied a row (supply) constraint, remove this row from further consideration. If the allocation has satisfied a column (demand) constraint, remove this column from further consideration. Return to Step 1 until all requirements have been met.

B. OPTIMALITY CHECK

B1 Be sure that $(m + n - 1)$ allocations appear in the table.

B2 Find a row evaluator, R_i, for each row and a column evaluator, K_j, for each column so that for each allocated cell (i, j) these evaluators satisfy $R_i + K_j = c_{ij}$.

B3 If $R_i + K_j \leq c_{ij}$ on all unallocated cells, stop; the allocation is optimal. If $R_i + K_j > c_{ij}$ on any unallocated cell, the current allocation is not optimal; proceed to the Improvement Routine.

C. IMPROVEMENT ROUTINE

C1 Choose any (unallocated) cell for which $R_i + K_j > c_{ij}$. Label this cell "+," and label the cells at the corners of its tour alternately "−" and "+."

C2 Find the minimum quantity allocated in cells labeled "−." Add this amount to the cells labeled "+" and subtract it from the cells labeled "−." Return to the Optimality Check.

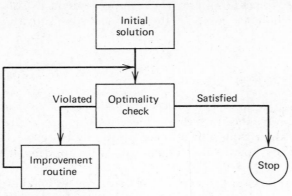

FIGURE 2.1

structs a feasible allocation that serves as a starting point. The Optimality Check determines whether the current allocation is optimal (whether it minimizes total cost), and if not, it identifies a desirable adjustment. When an adjustment is needed, the Improvement Routine produces a new and better allocation, and the algorithm returns to the Optimality Check. The algorithm repeats the Optimality Check and Improvement Routine until it constructs an optimal allocation. The logical flow of the algorithm's three parts is shown in Figure 2.1. We next examine these steps in greater detail.

The Initial Solution routine produces the allocations shown in Tables 2.4 to 2.6, with a total cost of $825. This routine relies on our previously discussed guideline that, at each stage of the allocation process, we should ship as much as possible along the cheapest route. Although this is a plausible way of making allocations, it is not a method that always leads to the minimum cost. As we pointed out earlier, there is room for improvement in the initial solution for our example problem.

The Optimality Check uses a set of row and column evaluators, such as those in Table 2.6, to determine whether total cost is at its minimum. For each unallocated cell we can compare incremental cost with incremental benefit to determine whether a desirable reallocation exists. For the solution in Table 2.6 we obtain the following results:

Cell (i, j)	Cost c_{ij}	Benefit $R_i + K_j$	Net Benefit $R_i + K_j - c_{ij}$	Improvement Potential
1, 1	9	8	-1	No
1, 3	6	7	1	Yes
2, 2	5	6	1	Yes
2, 3	7	9	2	Yes
3, 2	7	0	-7	No
3, 4	5	2	-3	No

TABLE 2.7

9	4	6	6	40
	20		20	
10 −	5	7 +	8	50
15			35	
4 +	7	3 −	5	60
15		45		
30	20	45	55	

If the incremental benefit were never as large as the incremental cost, there would be no room for improvement, and the solution would be optimal. However, we see that there are three unallocated cells in which incremental benefit exceeds incremental cost. This means that we can achieve a better total cost if we allocate into one of these three cells.

Proceeding to the Improvement Routine, Step C1 permits us a choice if there are two or more cells in which incremental benefit exceeds incremental cost. As a rule of thumb, we shall choose the cell for which incremental benefit exceeds incremental cost by the greatest amount. (This rule usually leads us to an optimum in the smallest number of steps.) In our example, we choose cell (2, 3), and we label its tour in the usual manner. (See Table 2.7.) The tour for cell (2, 3) identifies the existing allocations that must be revised in order to preserve feasibility.

We know that when we add 1 ton to the "+" cells and subtract 1 ton from the "−" cells we shall preserve feasibility. We also know that this reallocation will reduce total cost by 2. Similarly, a reallocation of 1 more ton will reduce total cost by 2 more, and we can continue in this fashion. Specifically, we can make this reallocation until no allocation remains in one of the "−" cells. (If we went any further, we would create a negative shipment, which our problem structure does not allow.) We identify this limit in Step C2, and in our example this limit is 15 tons, which is the minimum quantity allocated in the cells labeled "−." By adding 15 to the "+" cells and subtracting 15 from the "−" cells, we produce the solution shown in Table 2.8, with a total cost of $795.

Next we return to the Optimality Check to determine whether this improved solution is optimal. We still have six allocations in the table, but because the pattern of allocations has changed, our previous set of row and column evaluators is no longer valid. Table 2.9 displays a new set.

At Step B3 we again check the optimality conditions by comparing incremental benefit and incremental cost on each unallocated cell. We find that only for cell (2, 2) does the incremental benefit (6) still exceed the incremental cost (5); so we proceed to the Improvement Routine.

TABLE 2.8

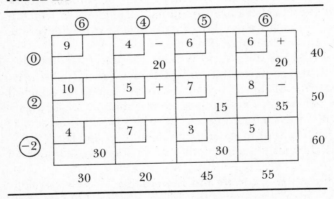

9	4	6	6	40
	20		20	
10	5	7	8	50
		15	35	
4	7	3	5	60
30		30		
30	20	45	55	

$TC = \$795$

TABLE 2.9

	⑥	④	⑤	⑥	
⓪	9	4 −	6	6 +	40
		20		20	
②	10	5 +	7	8 −	50
			15	35	
−2	4	7	3	5	60
	30		30		
	30	20	45	55	

TABLE 2.10

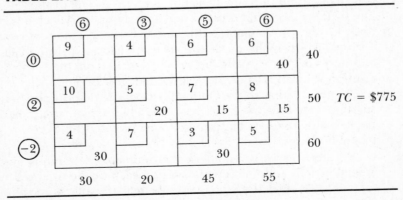

	⑥	③	⑤	⑥	
⓪	9	4	6	6	40
				40	
②	10	5	7	8	50
		20	15	15	
−2	4	7	3	5	60
	30		30		
	30	20	45	55	

$TC = \$775$

At Step C1 there is only cell (2, 2) to consider, and in Table 2.9 we label this cell and the cells of its tour. At Step C2 we identify the reallocation quantity to be 20, and by making the reallocation we arrive at the solution shown in Table 2.10, with a cost of $775.

Once more we return to the Optimality Check, but this time we find that the optimality conditions are satisfied. Table 2.10 displays a set of row and column evaluators, and we can verify the optimality conditions:

$$R_i + K_j \leq c_{ij}, \qquad \text{for all unallocated cells } (i, j)$$

Thus the minimum transportation cost is $775, and the solution in Table 2.10 is the corresponding transportation schedule.

DEGENERACY

In order to complete the exposition of the algorithm, we must consider the situation in which fewer than $(m + n - 1)$ cells have allocations. This condition can occur during either the Initial Solution or the Improvement Routine stages of the algorithm. Table 2.11 shows such a configuration (called a **degenerate** solution) for a modification of our example problem, in which we have altered the requirements at Plants 2 and 4. It is necessary to have six allocated cells to execute the algorithm; otherwise, we shall not be able to find a tour for each unallocated cell (consider cell (2, 1), for example). The remedy is a simple one: For the purposes of executing the algorithm we treat one additional cell as an allocated cell even though there is no physical shipment on the corresponding route. In the table, we designate such a cell by an allocation of 0, as in Table 2.12; we may select for this role any unallocated cell that does not already have a tour. The algorithm essentially treats the quantity 0 as a positive allocation, but one that is negligible compared to any physical allocation that already appears in the table.

TABLE 2.11

9		4		6		6		40
	30		10					
10		5		7		8		50
							50	
4		7		3		5		60
			15		45			
	30		25		45		50	

In Table 2.12 the cells (2, 1) and (3, 4) are among those in which the optimality conditions are violated. Suppose that we invoke the Improvement Routine for (2, 1). In Step C2 we add the quantity 30 to cells (2, 1) and (1, 4) and subtract it from cells (1, 1) and (2, 4). The allocation that emerges is shown in Table 2.13. The 0 that was previously in cell (1, 4) disappears because it is negligible in comparison to the allocation of 30 in that cell. At this stage no degeneracy remains: There are $(m + n - 1)$ allocations, and the algorithm proceeds in normal fashion.

Suppose instead that we invoke the Improvement Routine for cell (3, 4) in Table 2.12. Because we identify the quantity 0 at Step C2 as the minimum allocation in the cells labeled "$-$," the net effect of the Improvement Routine is to move the 0 allocation from cell (1, 4) to (3, 4), as shown in Table 2.14. Here, we ignore the effect of the 0 allocation in cells (1, 2) and (3, 2) because the quantity is negligible in comparison to the allocations that already exist in those two cells. In this case the Improvement Routine does not remove the degeneracy from the table, nor does it yield an actual reduction in total cost; but it does find a solution from which we can make subsequent improvements.

The above discussion has examined only the simplest case of dengeneracy—that in which we add one 0 allocation to a solution having $(m + n - 2)$ allocations. Clearly, we can modify this process to deal with more complex situations in which we have to use more than one 0 allocation. However, it is important to ensure that we add the 0s in such a way that it is still possible to identify a unique tour for every unallocated cell in the table.

Having elaborated on the details of Algorithm 2.1, we have described a solution procedure that will solve any transportation problem that fits the mathematical model formulated earlier.

COMPUTER SOLUTION

Specialized computer software for solving transportation problems is certainly available, even on personal computers. Because the transportation model is quite specific, it is straightforward to provide the data for a particular example to a computer program. Figure 2.2 shows how this might be done for a BASIC program. The essential information consists of

Problem size

Supply and demand quantities

Unit cost matrix

Figure 2.2 also shows how the program might take this information and produce an optimal solution.

In practice, there is a need for considerable sensitivity analysis of optimal solutions. In addition, specific applications sometimes require additional conditions that supplement the basic structure of the transportation model. For these

TABLE 2.12

	30	25	45	50	
40	9 — 30	4 — 10	6	6 — 0	40
50	10	5	7	8 — 50	50
60	4	7 — 15	3 — 45	5	60
	30	25	45	50	

TABLE 2.13

	30	25	45	50	
40	9	4 — 10	6	6 — 30	40
50	10 — 30	5	7	8 — 20	50
60	4	7 — 15	3 — 45	5	60
	30	25	45	50	

TABLE 2.14

	30	25	45	50	
40	9 — 30	4 — 10	6	6	40
50	10	5	7	8 — 50	50
60	4	7 — 15	3 — 45	5 — 0	60
	30	25	45	50	

```
LIST 5000-5010
5000 REM *** PIEDMONT POWER EXAMPLE***
5001 REM   PROBLEM SIZE (ORIGINS, DESTINATIONS)
5002 DATA 3,4
5003 REM   SUPPLIES
5004 DATA 40,50,60
5005 REM   DEMANDS
5006 DATA 30,20,45,55
5007 REM   TABLE OF UNIT COSTS
5008 DATA 9,4,6,6
5009 DATA 10,5,7,8
5010 DATA 4,7,3,5


RUN

OPTIMAL SOLUTION

    0            0            0           40
    0           20           15           15
   30            0           30            0

        OBJECTIVE FUNCTION =         775
```

FIGURE 2.2

reasons, it is often convenient to obtain computer solutions to transportation problems by utilizing a general-purpose linear programming package, such as the one we describe in the next chapter.

FURTHER CONSIDERATIONS IN THE SOLUTION ALGORITHM

Although the algorithm described in the preceding section will solve any transportation problem, some additional observations are worth examining.

AN ALTERNATE CALCULATION OF TOTAL COST

The most direct way to calculate total cost involves substituting into the cost expression $TC = \Sigma \Sigma c_{ij}x_{ij}$. It is sometimes helpful to check the arithmetic with an alternate calculation. Using the mathematical theory underlying the transportation algorithm, it is possible to show that

$$TC = \sum_{i=1}^{m} R_i a_i + \sum_{j=1}^{n} K_j b_j$$

where R_i and K_j are any valid set of row and column evaluators. In the Piedmont Power Company solution shown in Table 2.10, this calculation takes the form:

$$TC = 0(40) + 2(50) - 2(60) + 6(30) + 3(20) + 5(45) + 6(55) = \$775$$

In addition to providing a check on the cost calculation, this form also provides some insight that might not otherwise be so readily available. For example, this calculation reveals whether it may be possible to reduce total cost by increasing both one of the supplies and one of the demands. Specifically, if $R_i + K_j < 0$ for a source-destination pair (i, j), then total cost may be reduced by increasing both a_i and b_j.

PROHIBITING THE USE OF A PARTICULAR ROUTE

Sometimes it is impossible to ship between a particular source and a particular destination. In other situations operating policy may dictate specifically that a certain route be avoided, or the planning staff may be interested in the effect of excluding a specified route. In terms of the transportation model, this means restricting one of the allocations to 0. Explicitly including this capability in the algorithm would require a few modifications, but a relatively simple tactic will work without any change in the algorithm: Assign to the prohibited cell a cost large enough to make any positive allocation in that cell economically undesirable in the search for minimum total cost. In the formulation of a problem, we typically denote such a unit cost with the symbol M, signifying a large positive number. When implementing the algorithm by hand, it suffices to write the unit cost as M and to treat it as a large number in the steps of the algorithm. However, when implementing the algorithm on a computer, it is necessary to specify a numerical value. Although it is sometimes a subtle problem to choose an appropriate value, it will normally be possible to examine the unit cost data in a particular example and to choose a value for M that is large enough to give allocations of 0 where desired.

ALTERNATE OPTIMA

In some transportation problems there is more than one optimal solution; that is, more than one set of allocations exists that will provide the minimum total cost. If an alternate optimal allocation exists, it can be recognized in the optimal solution by the existence of an unallocated cell (i, j) for which $R_i + K_j = c_{ij}$. In Table 2.10, no such unallocated cell exists. Therefore, there are no other transportation plans that achieve a cost of \$775.

In order to illustrate alternate optima, consider the slightly modified problem for which an optimal solution is shown in Table 2.15. (It only differs from Table 2.10 in that $c_{34} = 4$ instead of $c_{34} = 5$). In this example we have an

TABLE 2.15

	⑥	③	⑤	⑥	
⓪	9	4	6	6 40	40
②	10	5 20	7 + 15	8 − 15	50
−②	4 30	7	3 − 30	4 +	60
	30	20	45	55	

unallocated cell for which the incremental benefit precisely matches the incremental cost. Specifically,

$$R_3 + K_4 = c_{34}$$

This condition indicates that alternate optima exist. If we allocate 1 ton to cell (3, 4) and make compensating adjustments in the cells of its tour, we find no change in the total cost of $775. Similarly, we could reallocate a second and a third ton this way and continue as if we were performing Step C2 of the algorithm, allocating up to 15 tons to cell (3, 4). In principle, we could also reallocate fractions of tons in this manner so that there would actually be an infinite number of distinct allocations, all of which would have attained the optimal cost.

In general, we can state the following:

1. The optimal allocation is unique if $R_i + K_j < c_{ij}$ for all (i, j) unallocated.
2. The optimal allocation is not unique and an infinite number of alternate optima exist if $R_i + K_j = c_{ij}$ for at least one (i, j) unallocated.

When there are alternate optima, we may use secondary criteria in order to choose among several schedules with the minimum transportation cost. For example, we may want to consider the timing of shipments or the reliability of certain routes in distinguishing among alternate optima.

EXCESS SUPPLY OR EXCESS DEMAND

Thus far we have dealt only with the case in which total availabilities equal total requirements (i.e., $\Sigma a_i = \Sigma b_j$). Clearly the transportation model would seldom be useful unless it also could deal with cases in which there is excess supply ($\Sigma a_i > \Sigma b_j$) or excess demand ($\Sigma a_i < \Sigma b_j$). The following more general representation of the model captures an excess in supply:

minimize

$$\sum_{i=1}^{m} \sum_{j=1}^{n} c_{ij} x_{ij}$$

subject to

$$\sum_{j=1}^{n} x_{ij} \leq a_i \qquad i = 1, 2, \dots, m$$

$$\sum_{i=1}^{m} x_{ij} \geq b_j \qquad j = 1, 2, \dots, n$$

This representation reflects the idea that the a_i are the *maximum* available supplies, and that the b_j are the *minimum* demands. Fortunately such cases can be handled with a slight reformulation of the model.

Suppose that in the Piedmont Power example there are 60 tons available at each of the three mines. Because the total requirements are only 150 tons, this means that 30 tons need not be shipped. We can think of this situation as requiring that we ship 30 tons to a destination called "Nowhere." This interpretation is the key to reformulating the problem. To the original table we simply add a column corresponding to the destination Nowhere. We also set the requirement at this destination equal to 30 tons, so that in the modified problem we again find that total supply equals total demand. Physically, of course, the 30 tons allocated in this column will not move at all; therefore, the appropriate unit cost of transportation to assess on these "routes" is likely to be 0, as shown in Table 2.16. (On the other hand, if surplus coal is actually transported a short distance to storage then the costs assigned to the surplus column can reflect this fact.)

TABLE 2.16

9	4	6	6	0	60
10	5	7	8	0	60
4	7	3	5	0	60
30	20	45	55	30	

We would use a symmetric approach in handling the case of excess demand. Instead of an extra column for excess supply, there would have to be an extra row for excess demand. Allocations in this row would correspond to unmet demand, and the unit costs in the cells of this row would presumably reflect any penalty costs involved.

SENSITIVITY ANALYSIS

In general, our use of the term "sensitivity analysis" refers to the study of changes in the model and their impact on the conclusions drawn from analysis. One facet is the study of **parametric validity,** which involves changes in the parameters of the model and their impact on the solution. The motivation for this type of study relates to questions that commonly arise about the validity of a model's parameters. In the transportation model, the specific reasons for such questions may involve data errors, forecast uncertainty, or policy alternatives. For example, data errors may occur because of mistakes in gathering data or because a portion of the information system is out of date. Forecast uncertainty may be a factor in the demand figures because they represent predictions of future requirements. Policy initiatives can alter productivities and thereby affect unit costs or supply quantities. Thus, there are many reasons why we may want to know not only the optimal solution but also whether it will remain optimal if a certain parameter is subject to change.

When we use optimization techniques to determine desirable patterns of resource allocation, we can carry out studies of parametric validity once we gain an understanding of the optimization procedure. It is not necessary to learn any new concepts. To assess the impact of a particular change we simply ask what impact the change will have on our solution. Specifically, we choose a particular parameter and consider whether the optimal solution (or its cost) will change if we alter that parameter.

In the transportation model there are two kinds of model parameters. First, there are unit costs. We shall find that the form of parametric analysis used differs according to whether the unit cost corresponds to an allocated cell in the optimal solution. Second, there are supply and demand quantities. For the purpose of sensitivity analysis these parameters play identical roles, but we shall find it useful to distinguish between two cases according to whether or not there is a surplus.

UNIT COSTS IN UNALLOCATED CELLS

First we will consider the analysis of a cost parameter in a cell that does not contain an allocation in the optimal solution. At the outset we can anticipate the qualitative form of this analysis. For an unallocated cell the current unit cost must be too high to provide an incentive to use the corresponding route. Clearly, if we made the unit cost even higher without changing anything else, there would still be no incentive to use the route. On the other hand, if we made the unit cost lower, we could expect that at some point the incentive would occur, and we would want to modify the optimal solution.

Stated more formally, consider the unit cost c_{ij}, corresponding to an unallocated cell in the optimal solution. Recall that this unit cost satisfies the optimality condition, $R_i + K_j \leq c_{ij}$. Because we know the R_i and K_j values when we find an optimum, this condition is equivalent to a condition for c_{ij}. As long as c_{ij} obeys this condition, there will be no incentive to alter the existing optimal allocation. Further, if we determine that $R_i + K_j = c_{ij}$, we will know that the existing optimal allocation is just one of a number of optimal allocations. In such a case there is still no incentive to reallocate. In general, we refer to a **range of validity** for the parameter c_{ij}. This range is defined as the set of values for which the optimal solution remains valid.

As an example, consider cell (1, 1) in the optimal solution to the Piedmont Power problem. From Table 2.10 we see that the inequality $R_1 + K_1 \leq c_{11}$ becomes $6 \leq c_{11}$. As long as c_{11} stays above 6 per ton, the incremental cost exceeds the incremental benefit of using the route from Mine 1 to Plant 1. Of course, $c_{11} = 9$ at present, but the analysis indicates that even if the unit cost were to drop to 7 per ton (as might happen if an independent shipper offered a discount for using the route) there would still be no incentive to alter the existing allocation. If c_{11} were equal to 6 we could change the existing allocation, but such a change would not improve the value of the objective function. Only for $c_{11} < 6$ is there an incentive to reallocate. In that case, we can determine exactly how the reallocation should be made by invoking the Improvement Routine.

UNIT COSTS IN ALLOCATED CELLS

Next we consider the analysis of a cost parameter for an allocated cell. In this situation the unit cost is already sufficiently attractive for its route to be used in the optimal solution. Intuitively, we can expect that if we make this unit cost higher, the route will become less desirable. In this case the allocation will drop or possibly even vanish. But if we make the unit cost lower, the allocation will be at least as large and can possibly rise. However, there is usually an interval around the original value of the unit cost in which there is no incentive to modify the allocation at all.

When we perform sensitivity analysis for the unit cost of an allocated cell, we must keep in mind that the values of R_i and K_j depend on the unit costs of allocated cells. If we wish to treat one unit cost as a parameter, we must also express the R_i and K_j values in terms of that parameter. Then we can proceed as before to examine the optimality conditions. For example, consider cell (2, 3) in Table 2.10. If we treat c_{23} as a variable and reconstruct the row and column evaluators starting with $R_1 = 0$, we obtain the set shown in Table 2.17. No matter what value we choose for the parameter c_{23}, the circled numbers in Table 2.17

TABLE 2.17

	$c_{23}-1$	③	$c_{23}-2$	⑥	
⓪	9	4	6	6 / 40	40
②	10	5 / 20	7 / 15	8 / 15	50
$5-c_{23}$	4 / 30	7	3 / 30	5	60
	30	20	45	55	

will comprise a valid set of row and column evaluators. In particular, when we substitute $c_{23} = 7$ in Table 2.17, we obtain precisely the evaluators displayed in Table 2.10.

Next we write the optimality condition for each cell. For cell (1, 1) we have

$$R_1 + K_1 \le c_{11}$$
$$0 + (c_{23} - 1) \le 9$$
$$c_{23} \le 10$$

Note that this inequality imposes a condition on c_{23}, the parameter in which we are interested. As long as $c_{23} \le 10$, the incremental cost of using the route from Mine 1 to Plant 1 exceeds its incremental benefit, and the optimality condition for cell (1, 1) continues to hold. For cell (1, 2) we have

$$R_1 + K_2 \le c_{12}$$
$$0 + 3 \le 4$$

This inequality does not involve c_{23} at all, so the optimality condition for cell (1, 2) does not impose any condition on c_{23}. Continuing with the other unallocated cells, we have

For cell (1, 3): $c_{23} \le 8$
For cell (2, 1): $c_{23} \le 9$
For cell (3, 2): $c_{23} \ge 1$
For cell (3, 4): $c_{23} \ge 6$

In order to preserve the optimal allocation in Table 2.17, the value of c_{23} must satisfy *all* of these inequalities, each one of which provides either a lower limit or upper limit on the interval of possible changes. The tightest lower limit is $c_{23} \ge 6$, and the tightest upper limit is $c_{23} \leq 8$. Thus, we must have $6 \leq c_{23} \leq 8$ for no change to occur. In this range of validity we have no incentive to modify the allocation.

If c_{23} assumes a value outside this range, then such an incentive will exist. Moreover, we can trace the effect of this incentive by using the Improvement Routine. For example, suppose the unit cost along the route from Mine 2 to Plant 3 rises above 8. Reviewing the list of conditions above, we recall that when $c_{23} > 8$, the optimality condition for cell $(1, 3)$ no longer holds. The specific calculations of the Improvement Routine reveal that as we reallocate shipments into cell $(1, 3)$, the allocation in cell $(2, 3)$ will vanish. Similarly, if the unit cost c_{23} drops below 6, then the allocation in cell $(2, 3)$ will increase. Both of these effects are consistent with the intuitive reasoning given earlier.

SURPLUS SUPPLY PARAMETER

To illustrate the analysis of a supply quantity corresponding to a surplus in the optimal solution, we deal with a model in which there is originally excess supply. Table 2.18 displays the optimal solution to the excess-supply model formulated in Table 2.15. Consider the impact of a change in the 60-ton supply predicted for Mine 2. In the optimal solution we plan to ship only 30 tons of this available quantity. Therefore, if we had more than 60 tons available, we would still expect to ship 30 tons and have a larger surplus in our optimal solution. Similarly, if we had fewer than 60 tons available, but at least 30 tons, then we would expect to have a smaller surplus. In either case, the actual pattern of physical shipments would remain the same, as would the optimal transportation cost of $740. Therefore, a change in the supply available at Mine 2, as long as it does not reduce the total supply by more than 30 tons, would not affect the shipping plan or the optimal cost. This change would simply be reflected in a change of the allocation in cell $(2, 5)$. A reduction of more than 30 tons would violate the feasibility of the shipping plan shown in Table 2.18, and would require a new solution.

TABLE 2.18

	⑧	⑤	⑦	⑦	⓪	
⊖1	9	4	6 / 5	6 / 55	0	60
⓪	10	5 / 20	7 / 10	8	0 / 30	60 $TC = \$740$
⊖4	4 / 30	7	3 / 30	5	0	60
	30	20	45	55	30	

In general, we can expect that a change in a surplus supply quantity will, at the margin, have no effect on the optimal schedule or its total cost.

SCARCE SUPPLY PARAMETER

We say a supply quantity is **scarce** when it is entirely shipped and no excess remains in the optimal transportation plan. We can think of such a supply quantity as a scarce economic resource. If we obtain more of a scarce resource, our economic intuition tells us that we can expect total cost to improve. But if we have less of a scarce resource, we can expect total cost to rise. The effects on the optimal shipping plan of altering a scarce supply quantity, however, are less obvious than the effects on cost. We must draw on insights from our solution procedure in order to carry out this kind of parametric analysis.

In the solution shown in Table 2.18, the 60-ton availability at Mine 1 is a scarce supply, because the entire supply quantity is allocated to Plants 3 and 4 as part of the optimal plan. Suppose that there is uncertainty about this parameter because a key piece of equipment at Mine 1 is old and prone to breakdowns. Although an allowance for breakdowns has already been taken into consideration, the actual downtime is somewhat uncertain. As a result, we may think of the availability at Mine 1 as $60 + Q$, where Q represents an error in predicted supply. (Note that Q could be either positive or negative.)

If we revise the model to reflect a supply quantity of $60 + Q$ at Mine 1, then we also need to revise the requirement in the column corresponding to excess supply. Because total supply must equal total demand in the model, the requirement in column 5 becomes $30 + Q$, as shown in Table 2.19.

First, suppose that the quantity Q is positive. We can think of the allocation in Table 2.19 as representing a partial solution, with Q additional tons still to be scheduled. One simple alternative is then to allocate the quantity Q to cell $(1, 5)$, which links the supply and demand quantities we have revised. Because $c_{15} = 0$, the incremental cost of this allocation is 0. Nevertheless, it is important to remember that cell $(1, 5)$ was unallocated in the optimal solution. This result

TABLE 2.19

9	4	6 $\;+$ 5	6 55	0	$60 + Q$
10	5 20	7 $\;-$ 10	8	0 $\;+$ 30	60
4 30	7	3 30	5	0	60
30	20	45	55	$30 + Q$	

indicates that the incremental cost of using cell (1, 5) has exceeded the incremental benefit of using its tour. Therefore, in accommodating the quantity Q we should prefer to use the allocated cells corresponding to the tour for cell (1, 5). This tour is designated in Table 2.19 with signs corresponding to $Q > 0$. Thus, the addition of Q to the total quantity available in row 1 leads us to increase one of the existing allocations in row 1. Similarly, the addition of Q to the total quantity required in column 5 leads us to increase the existing allocation in column 5. Furthermore, since we want no net addition in row 2 or column 3, we can decrease the existing allocation in cell (2, 3) to make the compensating adjustment.

In Table 2.19 we can add Q to the "+" cells and subtract Q from the "−" cells. This adjustment will yield an optimal solution to the modified problem, provided we maintain feasibility. Because we have assured feasibility in the sense that row allocations add to the corresponding availabilities and column allocations add to the corresponding requirements, we need only ensure that our modified allocations are nonnegative. We require the following conditions:

For cell (1, 3): $5 + Q \geq 0$ or $Q \geq -5$

For cell (2, 3): $10 - Q \geq 0$ or $Q \leq 10$

For cell (2, 5): $30 + Q \geq 0$ or $Q \geq -30$

Therefore, although we have treated Q as a positive quantity, we find that our modification will work as long as

$$-5 \leq Q \leq 10$$

because no allocation will be negative when Q is in this range. This interval corresponds to a range of validity for the supply at Mine 1 of 55 to 70 tons. We conclude that as long as the supply at Mine 1 is in this range there will be no change in the pattern of routes in the optimal shipping plan. However, within this range the actual quantities shipped along the routes corresponding to cells (1, 3) and (2, 3), and the actual surplus at Mine 2, will depend on the precise supply quantity at Mine 1.

We can also confirm the economic intuition suggested earlier. For a change Q in the supply at Mine 1, the signs in Table 2.19 indicate that the impact on total cost will be

$$\Delta TC = +6Q - 7Q + 0Q = -Q$$

In other words, total cost will drop by 1 per ton for every additional ton Q available at Mine 1, and it will rise by 1 for each unavailable ton. This dollar-per-ton value holds for the range $-5 \leq Q \leq 10$.

In general, this type of analysis begins by altering a particular supply quantity (by an amount Q) and then making a corresponding change in the total requirement in the excess column. The next step is to accommodate these changes by using only the allocations already present in the optimal transportation plan and making suitable modifications. The main idea is that the row and column evaluators continue to hold for small modifications of this sort. By "small" we mean small enough so that we do not lose feasibility.

To illustrate this idea as it extends to demand parameters as well as to supply parameters, consider the forecast for a demand of 55 tons at Plant 4. In Table 2.20 we show that if we modify this demand by Q, we must also modify the surplus requirement by an opposite amount. We then look for a set of changes in existing allocations that will

Increase the amount allocated in column 4.

Reduce the amount allocated in column 5.

Make no net changes of the allocations in other columns.

Make no net changes of the allocations in the rows.

The signs in Table 2.20 indicate the one set of modifications that will work. From the signs in Table 2.20 we can determine the effect on total cost:

$$\Delta TC = -6Q + 7Q + 6Q - 0Q = 7Q$$

Thus cost will change by 7 per ton in the direction of the change in the demand at Plant 4. Furthermore, feasibility conditions for this change also follow from the information in Table 2.20:

For cell $(1, 3)$: $5 - Q \geq 0$ or $Q \leq 5$

For cell $(2, 3)$: $10 + Q \geq 0$ or $Q \geq -10$

For cell $(1, 4)$: $55 + Q \geq 0$ or $Q \geq -55$

For cell $(2, 5)$: $30 - Q \geq 0$ or $Q \leq 30$

Thus the analysis is valid for $-10 \leq Q \leq 5$, corresponding to Plant 4 demands between 45 and 60 tons.

This brief introduction to sensitivity analysis in the transportation model

TABLE 2.20

9		4		6	−	6		0		60
					5		55			
10		5		7	+	8		0	−	60
			20		10				30	
4		7		3		5		0		60
	30				30					
30		20		45		$55 + Q$		$30 - Q$		

should suggest that the information available in an optimal solution transcends the specifics of the given problem. A review of the sensitivity analyses will reveal the following:

1. Within the range of validity for a unit cost on an unallocated route there is no change in the optimal cost or in the optimal allocation quantities.
2. Within the range of validity for a unit cost on an allocated route there is no change in the optimal allocation quantities, but the total cost will depend on the modification to the unit cost.
3. Within the range of validity for a supply or demand parameter there is no change in the pattern of allocations; however, there may be a change in both the total cost and the optimal allocation quantities.

In particular, we have focused on one-at-a-time analysis, in which we have considered only one of the parameters at a time as a variable for the purpose of sensitivity analysis. This is the simplest case but often the most valuable, since it isolates the role of each given parameter in the problem's solution. The analysis can be generalized to two or more at a time, but at the expense of greater complexity and perhaps less illumination.

SUMMARY

In the previous sections we have studied a process that exemplifies the problem-solving approach outlined in Chapter 1. The first phase of this process involves formulation of the problem, that is, the translation of a verbal description of the decision problem into a specific mathematical model. In terms of the transportation model, the task of formulation need not be too difficult. Once we perceive that the transportation model may be a valid representation of the problem at hand, the following questions must be answered:

What are the sources and destinations?

What are the availabilities at the sources and the requirements at the destinations?

What are the unit costs associated with each source-destination pair?

In problems arising in physical distribution systems, the sources and destinations are usually easy to identify, although the specification of unit costs might present some difficulties. But the model is also useful in problems involving the planning and scheduling of systems that (at least at first glance) do not correspond to physical distribution. For example, the destinations may represent different points in time instead of different physical locations. In these situations, the process of formulation is much less routine and much more of an art. Nevertheless, the rationale is the same: The model can provide valuable insights into the nature of the problem.

The second phase of the process involves analysis of the model, in this case by means of an optimizing algorithm for transportation problems. The procedure used for analysis—the transportation algorithm—is actually a special case of a more general method for linear optimization known as the simplex method. The algorithm is remarkably simple in its basic structure: initialize, check for optimality, improve, and repeat. It is powerful enough to produce an optimal set of decisions in any transportation problem, and when it is implemented on a computer it can solve some fairly large problems. Furthermore, the technique lends itself readily to sensitivity analysis, which is a characteristic that is of vital importance in the implementation phase.

Our treatment of the transportation model highlights many factors that become important in the third phase of the process, in which analysis is converted to decision making. Perhaps the most important feature of the transportation problem as a mathematical model is that it is specific. Its data requirements are explicit and easily understood, and the solution it provides by means of optimization has direct implications for the individual responsible for taking action. The model is also quite specific with regard to its criterion: the minimization of transportation-related costs. The result of the analysis is to determine the best set of decisions (at least, the best set of decisions for the model) in terms of a particular measure of performance.

Another important aspect of the transportation model is that it is deterministic, all parameters having been assumed known. The model is therefore specific in the sense that it assumes that the environment in which the decision is to be made can also be perfectly known. Clearly the real problem is unlikely to be so well-specified; nevertheless, the value of sensitivity analysis is to show which assumptions about the environment are most critical to the actions implied by the optimal solution. Specifically, one-at-a-time parametric analysis can trace the relation between changes in a parameter of the model and resulting changes in decisions or costs. When the range of validity is small, we say that the results are relatively sensitive to the value of the corresponding parameter. In this case, the parameter should be scrutinized closely (to assure that accurate values are being used) because the actions recommended depend crucially on the parametric values assumed. If, upon more careful study, assumed values fail to hold, then the optimization technique imbedded in sensitivity analysis provides a starting point for finding ways to respond appropriately.

As we mentioned earlier, the transportation model and its analysis are special cases of a more general approach, one that we shall examine in the chapters on linear programming. These same themes involving model formulation, optimization, and sensitivity analysis will be prominent again in our treatment of that subject.

EXERCISES

SOLUTION ALGORITHM

1 The Fine Products Company faces the problem of scheduling the shipment of 135 boxes of dishes from four warehouses, where the supply is stored, to four retail stores, where the demand has occurred. The parameters of Fine's problem are given below:

	Unit costs			Supply
6	12	5	7	25
5	10	4	2	20
2	8	9	5	40
3	7	6	5	50
Demand				
36	24	48	27	

Find a minimum-cost shipment schedule.

2 The Levitan Linen Company has five manufacturing plants that produce the firm's best-selling line of towels. Each plant has the capacity to produce 12,000 towels next month. The output of 60,000 units must be shipped to the firm's three regional warehouses, whose managers have already ordered replenishment supplies. The unit transportation costs (in dollars per thousand towels) are shown below, together with the warehouse orders.

		From plant					Orders
		1	2	3	4	5	(thousands)
To	1	4	6	5	6	8	10
warehouse	2	3	8	6	4	7	20
	3	5	8	3	7	6	30

Find a transportation plan that will allocate the production output to the various warehouses and minimize total transportation costs.

3 The Novick Razor Blade Company (NRBC) has designed a new blade and plans to test market it next month. The blades are presently stocked in warehouses in Asheville, Boston, and Cleveland in the following quantities:

Warehouse	Cartons in Stock
A	25
B	30
C	50

Four test markets have been chosen: Denver, Eugene, Flint, and Greensboro. Distributors in these cities have requested the following quantities for the test period:

Distributor	Cartons
D	45
E	15
F	25
G	20

The cost (in dollars per carton) of shipping the blades from warehouses to distributors is given below:

	D	E	F	G
A	8	10	6	3
B	9	15	8	6
C	5	12	5	7

Determine how NRBC should plan its distribution of blades for the test-market period in order to minimize transportation costs.

4 Faced with a court order to desegregate its schools, the Cargile County School Board plans to redistribute its minority students by means of busing. The plan calls for busing 50 students from each of three towns (Easton, Centerville, and Weston) to four regional high schools (Northeast, Southeast, Northwest, and Southwest). For satisfactory desegregation the high schools should enroll 20, 40, 30, and 60 minority students, respectively. The distance in miles between the towns and the schools is given in the table.

	NE	SE	NW	SW
E	14	12	10	8
C	18	14	6	12
W	16	16	14	6

Find an allocation of students that meets the redistribution requirements and minimizes the total number of student-miles driven.

5 The Cooper Furniture Company faces the problem of planning the shipment of 115 truckloads of furniture from its three production facilities, where the supply exists, to four warehouses, where demand has been recorded. The parameters of the distribution problem are given below.

	Unit costs			Supply
6	9	7	9	25
7	4	4	8	40
5	6	7	3	50

Demand	30	40	30	15

Find an optimal allocation for the problem.

6 Review Exercise 5.

a Calculate the optimal total cost using the alternate calculation to verify the minimum value.

b Give two allocations, different from the one in (a), which also achieve minimum total cost.

c Suppose route (2, 3) were prohibited. By how much would total cost rise?

7 Review the solution to Exercise 1.

   a Show that it is possible to increase the supply available at one of the sources and (by the same quantity) the demand required at one of the destinations so that there is a reduction in total cost. (*Hint:* Notice that supplies and demands can be related to total cost by means of the alternate calculation of total cost.)

   b Without introducing allocations on unused routes, what is the limit on the cost reduction that can be made in (a)?

8 Determine whether alternate optima exist in Exercise 3.

9 Determine whether alternate optima exist in Exercise 4.

EXCESS SUPPLY

10 Review the problem facing the Novick Razor Blade Company (Exercise 3). Suppose that supply conditions change and that each warehouse has 50 cartons available. Determine how much of an improvement could be achieved in total transportation cost.

11 The Coleman Appliance Company manufactures three types of ovens at its major plant. Coleman has a contract to deliver ovens to a large retailer during the next three months, following the schedule shown in the table.

Oven Type	1	2	3
Month 1	75	60	30
Month 2	60	110	75
Month 3	105	80	120

The ovens are all produced on the same assembly line. Under existing schedules for production of its own brand-name products and for preventive maintenance, only a limited amount of capacity is available at the assembly line, although some overtime can be utilized. The number of hours available each month is shown below.

Capacity	Regular Time	Overtime
Month 1	80	80
Month 2	100	80
Month 3	150	100

The amount of time required per oven is 20 minutes for type 1, 30 minutes for type 2, and 40 minutes for type 3. The variable cost of operating the assembly line is $4 per hour at regular time and $6 per hour at overtime. Ovens stored in the warehouse from one month to the next awaiting delivery incur a carrying charge of $1.20 per oven.

Find a production schedule that meets delivery requirements at minimum cost. (*Hint:* Convert demand data into hours required.)

12 A firm has openings for each of five job categories, A, B, C, D, and E, and it would like to fill as many positions as possible. They have 25, 10, 5, 15, and 20 vacancies, respectively, in the five categories.

The personnel department has screened applicants into eight personnel qualification descriptions. The following table shows the number of applicants fitting each qualification description and the jobs for which they are qualified:

Personnel qualification descriptions	1	2	3	4	5	6	7	8
Number of applicants	10	15	25	10	5	15	15	5
Job qualifications	A,E	A,D	B,E	B,D	C,D,E	C,E	D,E,	E

Maximize the number of openings filled with qualified personnel.

13 Review Exercise 5. Suppose the supply at each source is increased to 60. By how much will this alter optimum total cost?

SENSITIVITY ANALYSIS

14 Review Exercise 1. Suppose that route (3, 1) closes down. By how much will total cost increase?

15 For the optimal solution to the problem in Exercise 2:

a Perform a sensitivity analysis for the cost c_{22}.

b Perform a sensitivity analysis for the cost c_{31}.

16 Consider the optimal solution to the problem in Exercise 10.

a The Boston-Eugene route is not used in the optimal solution. By how much would its unit cost have to be decreased before there would be a cost incentive to use the route?

b Suppose the requirement for the Denver market (destination 1) were increased to 48 cartons. What would be the incremental cost of supplying these additional cartons?

17 Review Exercise 11. Suppose that a change in the maintenance schedule for month 2 makes an additional 20 hours available at regular time. By how much can the costs be reduced?

CONCEPTUAL ISSUES

18 a Suppose that a constant is subtracted from every unit cost in one row of a transportation tableau. Show that any allocation that was optimal for the original problem will also be optimal for the problem containing revised unit costs.

b Suppose that the constant α_i is subtracted from the unit costs in row i and that the constant β_j is subtracted from the unit costs in column j. Show that any allocation that was optimal for the original problem will also be optimal for the problem containing revised unit costs.

19 Describe an algorithm for finding the maximum total cost in a transportation problem. (Such an algorithm would be useful where c_{ij} represents unit profit on an amount transported.)

Chapter 3

LINEAR PROGRAMMING

Sherwood Furniture Company

Recently Sherwood Furniture Company has been interested in developing a new line of stereo speaker cabinets. In the coming month, Sherwood expects to have excess capacity in its Assembly and Finishing departments and would like to experiment with two new models. One model is the Standard, a large, high-quality cabinet in traditional design that can be sold in virtually unlimited quantities to several manufacturers of audio equipment. The other model is the Custom, a small, inexpensive cabinet in a novel design that a single buyer will purchase on an exclusive basis. Under the tentative terms of this agreement, the buyer will purchase as many Customs as Sherwood produces, up to 32 units. The Standard requires 4 hours in the Assembly Department and 8 hours in the Finishing Department, and each unit contributes $20 to gross profit. The Custom requires 3 hours in Assembly and 2 hours in Finishing, and each unit contributes $10 to profit. Current plans call for 120 hours to be available next month in Assembly and 160 hours in Finishing for cabinet production, and Sherwood desires to allocate this capacity in the most economical way.

The problem facing Sherwood Furniture is one of allocating a set of limited resources among competing activities. In particular, Sherwood's resources are the available capacity in its Assembly and Finishing departments, and the competing activities are production of Standards and production of Customs. The company will "solve" its allocation problem by determining the quantity of each model to produce. These quantities are the decision variables in the problem. Furthermore, in selecting a set of decision variables, Sherwood Furniture must recognize certain constraints, which take the form of capacity limitations and a ceiling on the output of Custom models. These restrictions force Sherwood to consider only those values of the decision variables that will meet its constraints. Finally, the selection of decision variables is guided by a clear-cut objective function: the total profit contribution from the production of cabinets. A more formal description of the allocation problem might be

maximize total profit contribution subject to

assembly hours allocated $\leq$ assembly hours available

finishing hours allocated $\leq$ finishing hours available

custom models produced $\leq$ market ceiling

In order to translate this word model into a mathematical model, let x_1 denote the number of Standards to be produced and let x_2 denote the number of Customs. The problem statement then becomes

maximize

$$20x_1 + 10x_2$$

subject to

$$4x_1 + 3x_2 \leq 120 \tag{3.1}$$
$$8x_1 + 2x_2 \leq 160 \tag{3.2}$$
$$x_2 \leq 32 \tag{3.3}$$
$$x_1 \geq 0 \quad x_2 \geq 0$$

We have added the last constraints to show that the production quantities cannot be negative.

The allocation problem described above illustrates the type of problem amenable to analysis by the methods of linear programming (LP). The general LP problem contains the same elements as the Sherwood Furniture problem: decision variables, constraints, and an objective function. In what is usually called **standard form,** the general linear program contains n decision variables and m upper-bound (less-than-or-equal-to) constraints:

maximize

$$c_1x_1 + c_2x_2 + \cdots + c_nx_n$$

subject to

$$a_{11}x_1 + a_{12}x_2 + \cdots + a_{1n}x_n \leq b_1$$
$$a_{21}x_1 + a_{22}x_2 + \cdots + a_{2n}x_n \leq b_2$$
$$\vdots \qquad \vdots \qquad \qquad \vdots$$
$$a_{m1}x_1 + a_{m2}x_2 + \cdots + a_{mn}x_n \leq b_m$$
$$x_1 \geq 0, x_2 \geq 0, \ldots, x_n \geq 0$$

Although LP techniques are not restricted to the analysis of allocation problems literally involving limited resources and competing activities, it is still helpful to keep that basic scenario in mind when studying LP models. Thus, the following interpretation usually accompanies the notation for the standard form:

x_j = number of units of the jth activity (i.e., jth activity level)

c_j = profit contribution per unit of the jth activity

b_i = available capacity of the ith resource (i.e., ith upper bound)

a_{ij} = consumption of the ith resource per unit of the jth activity

In terms of their role in the mathematical structure of an LP problem, the x_j are called **decision variables,** the c_j are **objective function coefficients,** the b_i are **constraint constants** (or **right-hand-side constants**), and the a_{ij} are **constraint coefficients.** In general, a linear program is a problem in optimization subject to constraints. The constraints are relationships that restrict the decision variables to certain admissible values. We express them as linear inequalities involving the decision variables. Any set of x values that satisfies all constraints corresponds to a feasible or possible course of action and represents what we call a **feasible solution.** We measure the attractiveness of a feasible solution by the objective function, which itself is a linear function of the decision variables.

In addition, LP models have important characteristics that are worth mentioning at the outset. Linear models involve **proportionality.** In the case of the objective function, this means that the profit contribution from a given activity is strictly proportional to the activity level. (See Figure 3.1.) In the Sherwood Furniture example, proportionality means that when we double the output of Standard models we double the total profit they generate. Similarly, consumption of a particular resource by a given activity is also strictly proportional to the activity level. In economic terms, this behavior is known as **constant returns to scale.**

Second, linear models involve **additivity.** This means that the respective profit contributions (or resource consumptions) of two activities are independent: If the level of one activity is increased, there will be no effect on the unit profit contribution from the other activity or on its unit resource consumption. For Sherwood Furniture, additivity means that when we alter the output of Standard models there is no effect on the profit generated by Custom models.

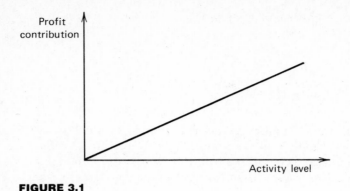

FIGURE 3.1

Third, linear models involve **divisibility.** In effect, this permits activity levels to be fractional and assumes that decision variables make sense when expressed as fractions. In our example, we are able to interpret the output levels as monthly rates. Thus, if a solution to our model were to call for production of 7.5 Custom models, we would interpret that result to mean that we should produce an average of 7.5 Customs per month. Because Sherwood Furniture is not likely to sell half a cabinet in a given month, we would translate the 7.5 into a plan for 15 Customs every 2 months.

Although LP models have wide applicability, these three assumptions are still somewhat restrictive. Taken literally, for example, the requirement of proportionality prevents the model from representing economies or diseconomies of scale in resource consumption. The requirement of additivity prevents the model from capturing interdependence among activities. The requirement of divisibility prevents the model from describing allocation models in which only integer-valued decision variables are possible. Keep in mind, however, that the essence of building mathematical models is to simplify, and LP models can have considerable practical value even when these three requirements are not met.

In some cases the assumptions of proportionality and additivity may provide very good approximations of reality in the region of interest for decision making. For example, we may know that production costs are nonlinear, especially when economies of scale are involved. Nevertheless, if there is good reason to believe that the optimal production quantities will inevitably be close to capacity, it may be reasonable to assume linearity in that region. In addition, the assumption of divisibility may not be crucial when the model's data are somewhat imprecise, for we may be willing to round off any fractional values and accept an approximate solution. Further, although divisibility may prohibit literal interpretations of some LP solutions, other reasonable interpretations may still be possible. For example, in an LP model for scheduling telephone operators the solution may call for two-fifths of an operator somewhere in the schedule. This capability may then actually be supplied by a part-time employee who works only 2 days a week instead of the normal 5 days. Thus the requirements of linearity do not necessarily limit the practical application of LP analysis, although the art of adapting such analysis to a nonlinear reality requires common sense and some practical insights.

Perhaps the most important—and most difficult—skill in the practical application of linear programming is the ability to translate a problem description into a valid mathematical model. Sometimes this step is aided by the construction of a word model, as illustrated in the Sherwood Furniture example, but the development of such a skill requires considerable practice with a variety of structures. In a later section we describe situations that often lend themselves to analysis with LP models, but first we discuss solutions to simple linear programming problems.

GRAPHICAL SOLUTION TECHNIQUE

We can use a graphical technique to solve linear programs containing two variables, such as the Sherwood Furniture problem. This section discusses the graphical solution approach and illustrates the technique for the Sherwood Furniture example. However, the importance of the graphical approach does not lie in its value as a solution procedure. Instead, by studying the geometry of LP problems in the two-variable case, we can gain some visual and algebraic insights that will help us understand the solution of problems with many more variables.

The graphical method begins by constructing $x_1 - x_2$ axes and representing each of the inequalities in the set of constraints. Because we constrain x_1 and x_2 to be nonnegative we shall be interested only in the graph's first quadrant, that is, the region above and to the right of the origin. To represent one of the inequalities we must sketch the straight line associated with it and then determine which side of the line contains satisfactory values of x_1 and x_2. For example, the constraint dealing with assembly hours is

$$4x_1 + 3x_2 \leq 120$$

or, equivalently,

$$x_2 \leq 40 \; - \frac{4}{3}x_1$$

In the latter form, we see that points (x_1, x_2) satisfying the constraint must lie on or below the line $x_2 = 40 - 4x_1/3$. Note that when we write this expression in terms of x_2, the slope of the line is just the coefficient of x_1. Thus, the straight line associated with the first constraint has a slope of $-4/3$. This line is sketched in Figure 3.2, and the nonnegative points that satisfy the constraints are repre-

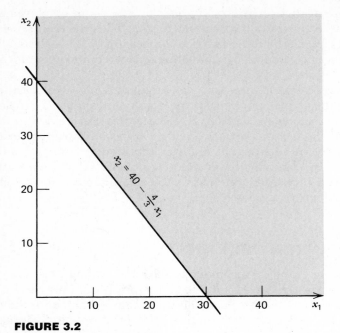

FIGURE 3.2

sented by the unshaded triangle bounded by this line and the axes ($x_1 = 0$ and $x_2 = 0$). Similarly, we can sketch the other two inequalities, each time shading the region of points that do not satisfy the constraint. Figure 3.3 shows the resulting diagram.

The unshaded region that remains is a graphical representation of the feasible region. This two-dimensional polygon contains all pairs (x_1, x_2) that correspond to production quantities of Standards and Customs that simultaneously satisfy all of the constraints. Thus each point in the feasible region is a geometric representation of a possible course of action. Furthermore, each point in the feasible region has associated with it a total profit contribution, which we calculate by substituting the values of x_1 and x_2 into the objective function expression, $20x_1 + 10x_2$. The problem now is to find the point in the feasible region where the objective function attains the greatest value; this will represent the most profitable decision.

Let z denote the value of the objective function, so that

$$z = 20x_1 + 10x_2 \qquad\qquad (3.4)$$

or

$$x_2 = .1z - 2x_1$$

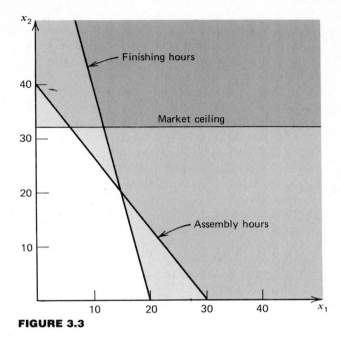

FIGURE 3.3

For a particular choice of z, we can represent equation (3.4) as a straight line on the graph. In fact, equation (3.4) describes a family of straight lines with a slope of -2, where we identify a particular member of the family by specifying a particular value of z. Figure 3.4 shows three lines in this family (corresponding to $z = 160$, 240, and 320). As the sketch makes evident, the family of objective function lines is a set of parallel lines, and in this case lines associated with larger z values lie in the direction indicated by the arrow in Figure 3.4. Because we desire to maximize Sherwood's profit, we wish to push a line with a slope of -2 as far as possible in the direction of the arrow without leaving the feasible region. Further analysis reveals that we reach this limit for the line corresponding to $z = 500$, which just touches the feasible region at the point ($x_1 = 15$, $x_2 = 20$). We interpret this result to mean that if we want to maximize profit contribution we should produce $x_1 = 15$ Standards and $x_2 = 20$ Customs, leading to a total contribution of $500. (See Figure 3.5.)

By substituting $x_1 = 15$ and $x_2 = 20$ in the original constraints, it becomes evident that this production plan consumes all the capacity in Assembly and Finishing. We say that the first two constraints of the problem are therefore **binding** on the optimal decisions. (Alternate names for this condition are **tight, active,** or **effective.**) As graphed, the optimal point lies on the boundary lines for both the Assembly hours constraint and the Finishing hours constraint. By comparison, we note that the Market constraint is not binding on the optimal deci-

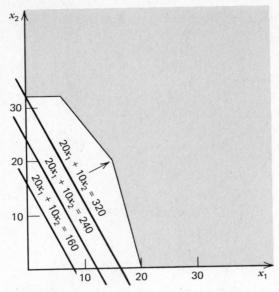

FIGURE 3.4

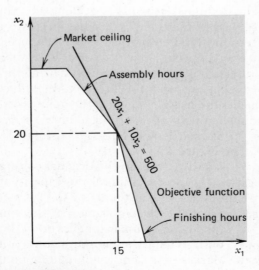

FIGURE 3.5

sion, since the desired production of 20 Customs is less than the ceiling of 32 units.

In general, we should expect to encounter certain properties whenever we use the graphical method for solving two-variable LP problems. For example, the feasible region is usually a polygon in two dimensions, although it could also be a line or even a single point. Of course, it is mathematically possible for there to be no feasible region at all, if there is no solution that can satisfy all of the constraints of the problem. This type of inconsistency typically occurs in practice only when the problem formulation misrepresents reality—when the model itself contains a flaw—or else when the graph is drawn incorrectly.

In addition, the feasible region has some visible corner points, called **extreme** points, which occur at the intersection of the region's boundary lines. We can determine the values of the decision variables at the extreme points by simultaneously solving the equations of the boundary lines that intersect. For example, the values $x_1 = 15$ and $x_2 = 20$ at the optimal point result from the solution of the pair of equations

$$4x_1 + 3x_2 = 120 \qquad \text{(the Assembly hours boundary line)}$$

and

$$8x_1 + 2x_2 = 160 \qquad \text{(the Finishing hours boundary line)}$$

Extreme points play an important role in the solution of linear programs. The theory of linear programming states that when an optimal solution exists, it can always be found at an extreme point. The significance of this result is that it enables us to limit attention to a finite number of points on the boundary of the feasible region. In the Sherwood Furniture problem, for example, we could simply evaluate the five corner points in Figure 3.3 and choose the best one. The theory also provides one way of recognizing an optimal extreme point: If we find an extreme point that has a better value of the objective function than all adjacent (neighboring) extreme points, then it is optimal. In two-variable LP problems, each extreme point has two neighbors, each connected to it by a straight line on the boundary of the feasible region. For example, in the Sherwood Furniture problem, once we reached the point $(15, 20)$ and verified that it achieved a higher total profit contribution than either of its neighbors, we could then terminate our evaluation of extreme points with assurance that we had found the best one.

In the next chapter we describe the **simplex method,** which is a systematic approach for finding optimal solutions in this way, especially for problems containing more than two variables. The simplex method is based on the procedure suggested by the properties mentioned above:

1. Start with a feasible extreme point solution.
2. Check to see whether a neighboring extreme point is better.
3. If not, stop; otherwise move to that better neighbor and return to Step 2.

ALTERNATE OPTIMA

In the Sherwood Furniture example there was a single optimal solution. In some situations the optimal solution will not be unique. Consider, for example, what happens in the Sherwood Furniture problem if we change the objective function to:

$$z = 16x_1 + 12x_2$$

The graphical method yields the solution described in Figure 3.6, in which the optimal profit contribution is \$480. Note that there are two extreme points for which $z = 480$: $(15, 20)$ and $(6, 32)$. Moreover, *any* point on the line $16x_1 + 12x_2 = 480$ between these two corner points is optimal, since that line segment forms part of the boundary of the feasible region. For example, one such point $(10.5, 26)$, is the midpoint of the straight line between $(15, 20)$ and $(6, 32)$. Thus there are two **alternate optima** corresponding to the extreme points and an infinite number of alternate optima along the line segment connecting them.

If a linear programming problem has an optimal solution then it will have either a single optimal solution (as in Figure 3.5) or else an infinite number of optimal solutions (as in Figure 3.6). When multiple optima exist, the decision maker should be indifferent to the alternatives in this set, at least on objective grounds. At such times, it is possible to respond to subjective criteria without sacrificing the value of the objective function. The ability to recognize alternate

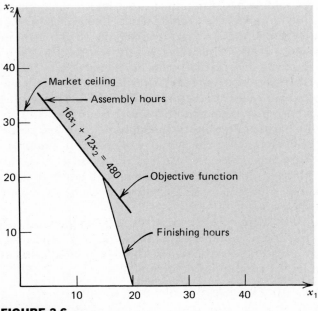

FIGURE 3.6

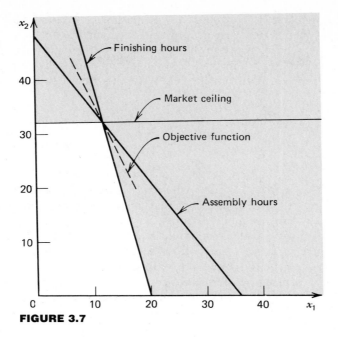

FIGURE 3.7

optima is therefore the ability to identify opportunities to incorporate qualitative preferences into LP analysis without compromising the basic thrust of the analysis.

DEGENERACY

In our example, corner points always occurred at the intersection of two constraint lines. In some situations corner points can occur at the intersection of three (or more) constraint lines. For example, consider what happens in the Sherwood Furniture problem when there are 144 Assembly hours available. The graph for this modification is shown in Figure 3.7. Note that the three constraint lines all pass through the point (12, 32), which is the optimal solution. If we pick any two of the constraint lines and locate their intersection, we find the intersection occurs at (12, 32), which also lies on the third constraint line. Assembly capacity would be binding if the available hours were reduced below 144, but it would be nonbinding if the available hours were increased above 144.

INCONSISTENT AND UNBOUNDED PROBLEMS

Mathematically, there are two situations in which a linear programming problem does not have an optimal solution. In practice, these situations seldom apply to a well-formulated LP model, but they may arise during the attempt to construct a valid formulation. We can study these two cases graphically.

An **inconsistent** LP problem has no feasible solutions at all; its constraints are logically inconsistent. In graphical terms, such a problem has no feasible region. For example, suppose that the Sherwood Furniture problem does not have a market ceiling but instead has an agreement to deliver at least 45 cabinets to the buyer of the Custom model. With this new condition the constraints become

$$4x_1 + 3x_2 \leq 120$$
$$8x_1 + 2x_2 \leq 160$$
$$x_2 \geq 45$$

Figure 3.8 shows what happens when we shade the infeasible regions: no unshaded region remains. This means that there is no set of values of x_1 and x_2 that simultaneously satisfies all constraints.

We can imagine that a firm could negotiate a set of contracts that leave no feasible course of action. (Indeed, an LP framework might be the best way to detect such a problem.) However, infeasible formulations more often result from misrepresenting parameters or constraints. When we encounter an infeasible problem we should check carefully for errors of this sort before we begin thinking about changing the conditions of the problem.

An **unbounded** LP problem has no limit on the value of its objective function in the direction of optimization. There is no upper limit on a unbounded maxi-

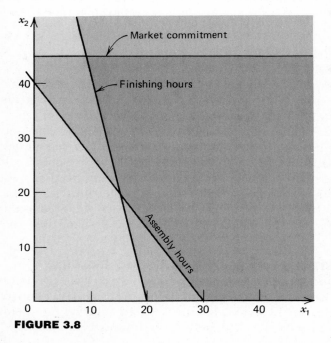

FIGURE 3.8

mization problem, and no lower limit on an unbounded minimization problem. For example, suppose the Sherwood Furniture problem has only the following two constraints: There must be at least 45 Custom models, and the number of Standard models must be less than or equal to half the number of Customs. With the same objective function, our formulation becomes

maximize

$$20x_1 + 10x_2$$

subject to

$$x_2 \geq 45$$
$$x_1 - .5x_2 \leq 0$$

Figure 3.9 shows what happens when we shade the infeasible region. Recall from Figure 3.4 that we wish to push our objective function line as far as possible in the direction of the arrow. In Figure 3.9 there is no upper limit on the value of the objective function that we can achieve.

As this small example suggests, an unbounded formulation may result from

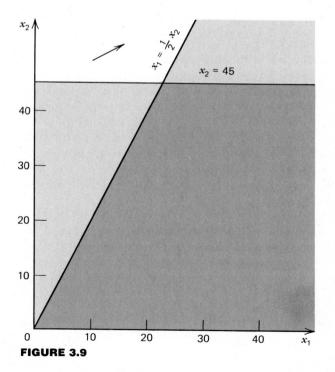

FIGURE 3.9

recognizing some, but not all, of a problem's constraints. As in the case of inconsistent formulations, unbounded problems can also result from misrepresenting parameters or constraints, and in practice the same error-checking advice applies.

In summary, there are two special cases in which LP formulations do not lead to optimal solutions. These cases are mostly of mathematical interest, since well-conceived LP modeling seldom, if ever, encounters infeasible or unbounded situations. Aside from these cases, an LP formulation will always have an optimal solution, and either it is unique or else there are multiple optima. In this section we have seen graphical interpretations of these concepts.

SENSITIVITY ANALYSIS WITH THE GRAPHICAL TECHNIQUE

Once we have identified the optimal solution it is possible to determine how the solution would change if the problem parameters were changed. For example, consider the following two questions:

1. If we fix the profit contribution of Customs at $10 per unit, for what range of values of the Standard's contribution (now $20 per unit) is the current solution optimal?
2. Would there be any benefit if Sherwood could increase the number of Assembly hours from 120 to 128?

To deal with the first question refer to Figure 3.5. We see that the optimal extreme point occurs at the intersection of the boundary lines for the Assembly hours and Finishing hours constraints. In addition, we know that a change in the contribution of Standards will change the slope of the objective function. Figure 3.5 shows us that the current extreme point will be optimal as long as the objective function line lies within the feasible region only at the point (15, 20) or possibly also along one of the boundary lines that meet at that point. This condition amounts to a requirement that the slope of the objective function be bracketed by the slopes of the two lines that intersect to form the optimal extreme point. Here, we see that the current objective function slope of -2 is bracketed by the Assembly hours constraint slope of $-4/3$ and the Finishing hours constraint slope of -4. Furthermore, the point (15, 20) will be optimal for *any* objective function whose slope falls between $-4/3$ and -4.

Recalling our standard form, we let c_1 represent the Standard's unit contribution. Then we can express the objective function slope as $-c_1/10$. Given this information, we can write the required relation among the slopes as

$$-4 \leq \frac{-c_1}{10} \leq -\frac{-4}{3}$$

or

$$\frac{40}{3} \leq c_1 \leq 40$$

We call this set of values the **range of validity** for the parameter c_1.

Let us investigate the boundaries of this range. If $c_1 = 40/3$ the objective function has a slope of $-4/3$, and the situation corresponds to Figure 3.10. In this case there are multiple optima, one of which is the current optimal solution (15, 20), and another of which is a different extreme point (6, 32). If instead we set $c_1 = 40$, the objective function and the boundary line for the Finishing hours constraint have the same slope, -4. (See Figure 3.11). Again this identifies a case of multiple optima. Clearly, between these two extremes there is only the single optimal solution (15, 20).

Consider what would happen if the Standard's contribution fell outside the range from 40/3 to 40. If we return to graphical analysis, we find that the set of binding constraints changes so that a different extreme point becomes optimal. For example, if we decrease c_1 to 5, the new optimal point will be (6, 32). If instead we increase c_1 to 50, then the optimal point becomes (20, 0).

With the same type of analysis we can also establish that the optimal solution does not change as long as we fix the Standard's contribution at \$20 and ensure that c_2, the Custom's contribution, satisfies the relationship

$$5 \leq c_2 \leq 15$$

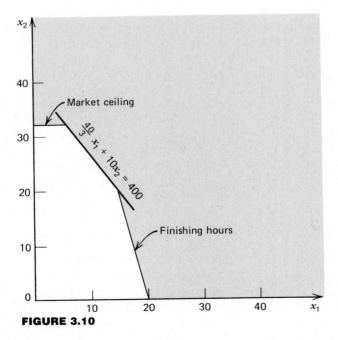

FIGURE 3.10

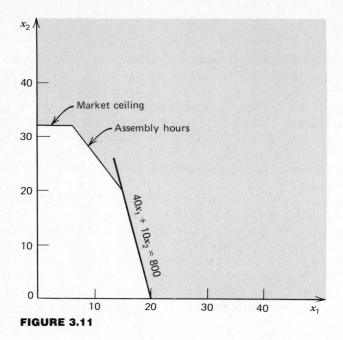

FIGURE 3.11

Notice in both cases that when we vary the objective function coefficient within its range of validity, the optimal values of the decision variables do not change from (15, 20). On the other hand, the optimal value of the objective function does vary. In the first case, when we vary only c_1, the objective function value is $c_1(15) + 10(20) = 200 + 15c_1$, and in the second case, when we change only c_2, the value is $20(15) + c_2(20) = 300 + 20c_2$.

Now consider the second question, dealing with the effects of raising the number of available Assembly hours from 120 to 128. To examine this change in our graphical context we will need to have a new boundary line for the Assembly hours constraint. This new line will be parallel to the old one, but will be slightly farther away from the origin. (See Figure 3.12.) Additional analysis will show that the binding constraints will be the same as before—Assembly hours and Finishing hours—and that the new extreme point will be different. The values of the decision variables at this point are ($x_1 = 14$, $x_2 = 24$), resulting from the simultaneous solution of the two equations

$$4x_1 + 3x_2 = 128 \quad \text{(the new Assembly hours boundary line)}$$
$$8x_1 + 2x_2 = 160 \quad \text{(the Finishing hours boundary line)}$$

Given this solution, we find that the new value of the objective function is

$$z = 20(14) + 10(24) = 520$$

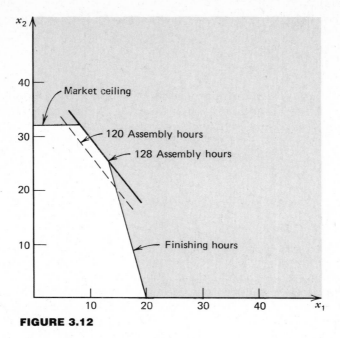

FIGURE 3.12

Now we can determine the effects of the change. The increase in the objective function is $520 - 500$, or 20, and the increase in the constraint right-hand side is $128 - 120$, or 8. If we examine the ratio

$$\frac{\text{change in objective function}}{\text{change in constraint right-hand side}}$$

we find that its value is 2.5 and that its dimensions are dollars per hour. If we were now to investigate the effect of adding another additional hour by making 129 hours available in Assembly, we would find that the ratio would still be \$2.50 per hour.

We usually call this ratio a **shadow price** (or **dual variable**). We can interpret it as measuring the effect on the objective function of changing the right-hand side of a constraint by a small amount. In other words, the shadow price tells us the rate of change of the optimal objective function value as the right-hand side changes.

We can also determine the shadow price by solving the boundary equations parametrically. If we define Δb as the change in Assembly hours from the original capacity of 120, we find the optimal corner point by solving the following two equations:

$$4x_1 + 3x_2 = 120 + \Delta b$$
$$8x_1 + 2x_2 = 160$$

Simultaneously solving these two equations we obtain the point

$$\left(15 - \frac{\Delta b}{8}, 20 + \frac{\Delta b}{2}\right)$$

Thus, for example, we can substitute $\Delta b = 8$ and verify that the optimal point becomes (14, 24). In addition, when we substitute the parametric solution into the objective function we obtain

$$20x_1 + 10x_2 = 20\left(15 - \frac{\Delta b}{8}\right) + 10\left(20 + \frac{\Delta b}{2}\right)$$

$$= 300 - 5\frac{\Delta b}{2} + 200 + 5\Delta b$$

$$= 500 + 2.5\Delta b$$

In this form we can see how the shadow price (2.5) measures the impact on the objective function of a small change (Δb) in the Assembly capacity.

An appropriate question is whether the improvement at this stage in the analysis measured by the shadow price could continue forever. In principle, it would seem that eventually we might run into another restriction. In this example we saw in Figure 3.12 that our move from 120 to 128 hours allowed us to decrease the output of Standards from 15 to 14 units and to increase the output of Customs from 20 to 24 units. In addition, a move from 128 hours to 129 hours would yield a further change of -0.125 unit for Standards and $+0.5$ unit for Customs. Given that x_1 cannot become negative and that x_2 cannot exceed 32, at some point we would reach a limit.

Using the parametric solution we can examine two different cases according to whether Δb is positive or negative. In each case we will consider the remaining constraints for the problem:

$$x_2 \leq 32 \qquad x_1 \geq 0 \qquad x_2 \geq 0$$

For the situation when Δb is positive, the third condition will always hold, so we must investigate the effect of the other two. The first condition becomes

$$x_2 \leq 32$$

or

$$20 + \frac{\Delta b}{2} \leq 32$$

or

$$\Delta b \leq 24$$

The second condition becomes

$$x_1 \geq 0$$

or

$$15 - \frac{\Delta b}{8} \geq 0$$

or

$$\Delta b \leq 120$$

Here we find the first condition (the market ceiling) is more constraining, since it limits the positive change to $\Delta b = 24$. Thus our optimal point is still defined by the intersection of the Assembly constraint and the Finishing constraint as long as we have no more than $120 + \Delta b = 144$ Assembly hours. Figure 3.13 shows the graph for the situation of 144 Assembly hours. The situation is identical to the case of degeneracy we previously encountered in Figure 3.7. If we were to increase the number of Assembly hours above 144, the optimal point would no

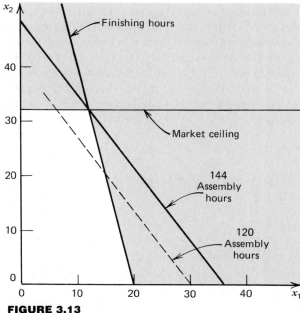

FIGURE 3.13

SOLID BLACK

longer be given by the intersection of the Assembly and Finishing constraints. (In fact, this intersection point would no longer be feasible). In other words, the number of Assembly hours would no longer be binding above 144. In that case, we would not consume all of the available capacity. We can interpret this fact to mean that a further increase in the Assembly capacity would provide no additional profit contribution. Therefore the shadow price for Assembly hours would drop to 0.

For the situation when Δb is negative, only the third of our three conditions will provide a limit:

$$x_2 \geq 0$$

or

$$20 + \frac{\Delta b}{2} \geq 0$$

or

$$\Delta b \geq -40$$

Here the nonnegativity of x_2 limits the negative change to $\Delta b = -40$. Thus our optimal point is still defined by the intersection of the Assembly and Finishing constraints as long as we have at least $120 + \Delta b = 80$ Assembly hours. Figure 3.14 shows the graph for the limiting case. We again see a form of degeneracy: Three constraints, rather than just two, intersect at the optimal point. If we were to reduce the number of Assembly hours below 80, the optimal point would no longer be given by the intersection of the Assembly and Finishing constraints. (Instead, the nonnegativity constraint on x_2 would become active.) In that case the shadow price would actually be greater than $2.50 per hour.

We can use this same form of analysis for the Finishing hours constraint to find that the shadow price is $1.25 per hour when

$$112 \leq \text{finishing hours available} \leq 240$$

and is 0 above this range. In addition, for the market ceiling constraint the shadow price is 0 for

$$20 \leq \text{market ceiling}$$

In both derivations we would again find that the shadow price changes outside of the range of validity, and also that the optimal solution is degenerate at the end of the range.

Although we have investigated only one example, all of the approaches we

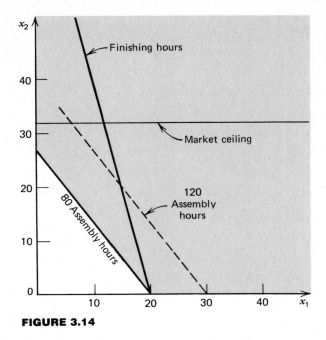

FIGURE 3.14

have used are applicable to any two-variable LP problem. The important features of linear programming analysis always have a convenient and simple graphical interpretation.

THE USE OF A COMPUTER PROGRAM

It is not possible to use the two-dimensional graphical method to solve linear programming problems with more than two variables. Instead, we use computer programs to perform the detailed calculations. This section describes the use of a computer program, called LINDO, which is representative of the many LP codes that presently exist. The LINDO system is designed to run on a variety of mainframe computers. Recently, it has also been adapted for use on the IBM Personal Computer.[1]

For the purposes of illustrating the program, we use a variation of the Sherwood Furniture example. Suppose that, in addition to producing Standard and Custom models, we can also produce a Portable model, which requires 5 hours of Assembly time, 6 hours of Finishing time, and for which the unit profit

[1] LINDO was developed by Professor Linus Schrage of the University of Chicago. Its user's manual is listed in our bibliography.

contribution is \$18. If x_3 denotes the number of Portable cabinets scheduled for production, we can write the linear program in standard form as follows:

maximize

$$20x_1 + 10x_2 + 18x_3$$

subject to

$$
\begin{aligned}
4x_1 + 3x_2 + 5x_3 &\leq 120 \\
8x_1 + 2x_2 + 6x_3 &\leq 160 \\
x_2 &\leq 32 \\
x_1 \geq 0, \ x_2 \geq 0, \ x_3 &\geq 0
\end{aligned}
\tag{3.5}
$$

In order to use LINDO, the first step is to specify the LP formulation. Figure 3.15 reproduces the portion of the program in which we specify the formulation of the Sherwood Furniture example. The program LINDO contains a number of user options, or **commands,** which tell the program to perform certain tasks; these are entered in response to a colon printed by LINDO. For example, the option MAX in Figure 3.15 prepares the program to accept information describing a maximization problem. Then, taking advantage of the program's capability to work with names for variables, we specify the objective function as:

```
20 STD + 10 CUS + 18 POR
```

Next, we enter ST to tell the program that information about the constraints will follow. In response to LINDO's question marks we enter each of the constraints of our model, finishing with END. The variable names STD, CUS, and POR stand for x_1, x_2, and x_3 in our model, and they provide some convenience in interpreting the results later.

At this point the computer program has a complete specification of the problem to be solved. In order to verify the problem statement, LINDO permits

```
:MAX 20 STD + 10 CUS + 18 POR
?ST
?4 STD + 3 CUS + 5 POR <= 120
?8 STD + 2 CUS + 6 POR <= 160
?        CUS           <=  32
?END


:
```

FIGURE 3.15

```
:LOOK ALL

MAX       20 STD + 10 CUS + 18 POR
SUBJECT TO
   2)     4 STD + 3 CUS + 5 POR <=    120
   3)     8 STD + 2 CUS + 6 POR <=    160
   4)       CUS <=    32
END
```

FIGURE 3.16

the user to examine the formulation with the option LOOK, as shown in Figure 3.16 (The command LOOK ALL asks for the entire formulation; other variations of the command ask for portions of the formulation.) Notice that LINDO automatically numbers the rows in the model, using a convention in which the objective function is row 1 and the first constraint is row 2. This listing displays the problem data in a systematic form, as an aid to checking on the information supplied during the specification of the problem. We can use a special edit command to correct any errors discovered at this point.

The GO command finds the optimal solution and displays the results, as shown in Figure 3.17. First we see the value of the objective function in the

```
:GO
     LP OPTIMUM FOUND   AT STEP     2


             OBJECTIVE FUNCTION VALUE

   1)          500.000000

   VARIABLE         VALUE          REDUCED COST
     STD          15.000000            .000000
     CUS          20.000000            .000000
     POR            .000000           2.000000

      ROW     SLACK OR SURPLUS      DUAL PRICES
      2)            .000000           2.500000
      3)            .000000           1.250000
      4)          12.000000            .000000

   NO. ITERATIONS=        2

    DO RANGE(SENSITIVITY) ANALYSIS?
   ?
```

FIGURE 3.17

example; this value is 500. Next follows a list of variables and their values in the optimal solution. In the example, the report lists the three decision variables: STD = 15, CUS = 20, and POR = 0.

Below the list of variables is a list of row numbers, starting with row 2. In this list we can identify binding constraints because they have no slack or surplus. In Figure 3.17, the solution report indicates that rows 2 and 3, corresponding to the Assembly and Finishing constraints, are binding, while there is slack of 12 in the market constraint. The report also contains information about reduced costs and dual prices. We discuss the significance of this information in the next section.

The program LINDO has some flexibility associated with the capabilities illustrated thus far. For example, the program can minimize the value of an objective function rather than maximize it. (The command for this purpose is MIN in place of MAX.) In addition, the problem formulation need not involve only upper-bound constraint types; it is possible to include equations and lower-bound constraints as well. For example, Sherwood Furniture might decide that its monthly plan should contain at least 30 cabinets. This requirement could be reflected in the problem formulation by the following constraint:

$$x_1 + x_2 + x_3 \geq 30$$

Had LINDO solved the problem with this constraint included, the program would have reported a surplus of 5 for this row in the optimal solution.

In addition to identifying the optimal solution to a problem, a computer code can detect inconsistent and unbounded formulations. When LINDO encounters an inconsistent set of constraints, it reports

NO FEASIBLE SOLUTION

and when it discovers the problem to be unbounded, it reports

UNBOUNDED SOLUTION

In summary, a computer program requires the specification of an LP formulation in terms of the number and type of constraints, the number of variables, and the numerical data in the constraints and objective function. The program can then maximize or minimize the objective function and either identify problems of formulation or print out a summary of the optimal solution.

SENSITIVITY ANALYSIS WITH COMPUTER OUTPUT

Recall that in the Sherwood Furniture example our tentative schedule, based on the LP solution in Figure 3.17, involves 20 Standard cabinets, 15 Customs, and no Portables. This schedule consumes all Assembly and Finishing capacity available. Now consider the following:

1. The Marketing Department indicates that it can increase the selling price of Portable cabinets, raising the unit contribution to $19. Should some Portable cabinets be produced?
2. The Assembly Department foreman learns that it is possible to lease a machine that will expand the department's available capacity to 140 hours. The monthly leasing cost for this machine is $85. Will the firm benefit from leasing the machine?

Questions such as these can be answered with the help of sensitivity analyses.

In the context of LP, sensitivity analysis involves the systematic evaluation of changes in the model as they affect the optimal decisions and the optimal value of the objective function. As we illustrated in our graphical example, most sensitivity analyses are directed toward the parameters of the LP model, such as objective function coefficients and constraint constants. The approach is to seek a **range of validity** for the parameter in question, that is, to find an interval of values for the parameter over which the optimal solution is unaltered (in a way to be specified).

The computer solution of an LP problem provides much more than just a set of optimal decisions. Indeed, it is often said that the major value of LP analysis lies not in the optimal solution but in the information produced as a by-product of identifying the optimal solution. This information, obtained from sensitivity analyses, provides some quantitative help in evaluating possible responses to changes in the environment that can occur after the original model is solved.

The questions posed above lend themselves to the use of range-of-validity information. In general, alterations in an objective function coefficient may occur as a result of changes in the cost of input materials, renegotiation of a labor contract, errors discovered in the data, revisions in tax laws, or changes in the market. Alterations in a constraint constant may occur as a result of improvement in forecasts, discovery of a new supply source, changes in regulatory codes, or modifications in administrative policy. Armed with the information produced by sensitivity analysis, the decision maker is in a position to respond quickly and logically to such changes. We now consider each type of sensitivity analysis using the output of LINDO as a framework.

REDUCED COSTS

Recall that LINDO provides a reduced cost for each variable. We can interpret the reduced cost as the minimum amount by which its objective function coefficient must improve in order for the variable to become positive. (In some cases, an even larger improvement will be necessary.) By definition, the positive variables always have reduced costs equal to 0. Also, in the absence of alternate optima and degeneracy, variables that are 0 in the optimal solution will have a nonzero reduced cost.

Now consider the situation in which the unit profit contribution for Portable cabinets increases. In Figure 3.17 we see that the reduced cost for the unused variable POR is equal to 2. This means that the unit contribution must grow by at least 2 from its current value (from 18 to 20) before there can be an incentive to include Portable cabinets in the schedule. An increase of less than 2 will not provide a sufficient incentive to change the optimal product mix. In particular, a raise to 19 is not enough to make the production of Portable cabinets attractive.

A nonzero reduced cost also represents the rate at which the objective function will deteriorate if the corresponding variable is introduced into the optimal solution at a positive level (assuming that adjustments in other variables are made to preserve feasibility). Thus, in the original formulation for our example the profit contribution will drop by 2 for each Portable model included in the schedule.

SHADOW PRICES

As we have found with our graphical example, we can interpret the shadow price (or dual price, in LINDO terminology) as the rate at which the objective function improves if a small change is made in the right-hand side of the corresponding constraint. Shadow prices are always 0 for constraints that are not binding, because a small change in the constraint constant will simply be absorbed by the existing slack or surplus.

Now consider the situation in which leasing a new machine expands Assembly capacity. In Figure 3.17 the report tells us that the shadow price associated with row 2 is 2.5. This means that an additional hour of Assembly capacity allows us to increase total profit contribution by 2.50. Similarly, an additional 20 hours could increase profits by 20 times as much, or 50. Therefore, the leasing possibility remains unattractive because it costs 85 to increase the value of the production output by 50. Unless Sherwood can negotiate a leasing cost of less than 50, the cost of the additional capacity will outweigh its economic benefit. In other words, only prices of up to 2.50 per hour will be attractive for additional units of the binding resource. This is the interpretation that gives rise to the term "shadow price."

To be precise, we are actually assuming that the cost of the resource is not already part of the objective function. In the example, this means that the hourly cost of Assembly capacity is not imbedded in the expression for profit contribution. When that is the case, an additional hour of Assembly capacity raises profit contribution by 2.50, and to provide a net benefit, the cost of that capacity must be less than 2.50 per hour.

On the other hand, it might be the case that machinery is already being leased at a cost of 5 per hour and that this cost is recognized as a variable cost in the calculation of profit contributions for the various models of cabinets. In this case, the variable cost of Assembly time would be 20 per Standard cabinet (i.e., 4 Assembly hours required per cabinet, multiplied by $5 per Assembly hour). Similarly, the variable cost of Assembly time would be 15 for a Custom and 25 for a Portable. In this situation, an additional Assembly hour would raise the total profit contribution by 2.50, beyond the resource cost (5 per hour) already reflected in the objective function. Then the cost of that additional capacity must be less than 7.50 per hour to provide a net benefit.

We can hypothesize these two different cases only because we were not precise in our original problem statement about the composition of the contribution coefficients. However, our definition of a shadow price is precise: It is the rate at which the objective function improves when a small change is made in the right-hand side of the corresponding constraint.

This evaluation of the leasing alternative assumes that the shadow price of 2.50 per hour continues to hold for all 20 hours of additional capacity. Based on the information produced thus far by LINDO, we cannot know whether the shadow price will hold over this range. (Later on, when we study the program's ranging analysis, we shall see that it holds.) However, we do know that the shadow price will not increase with additional capacity. Thus, we can be certain that 20 additional hours of Assembly capacity are worth *at most* 50. In general, linear programs have the property that the shadow price for a scarce resource will stay the same or else decrease as the resource becomes more plentiful. In the study of economics this property is called **decreasing returns to scale** or **diminishing marginal returns.**

In Figure 3.17, the report tells us that row 4 has a shadow price of 0. This result is consistent with the fact that the Custom ceiling is not a binding constraint in the optimal solution. The production of 20 Custom cabinets leaves a slack of 12 in the market constraint; if the ceiling increases or decreases by one unit, the slack quantity simply changes accordingly, and there is no change in the objective function.

RANGING

A computer program can also calculate the ranges of validity for the objective function coefficients and the constraint constants. In LINDO we obtain this information by answering YES to the question that follows the optimal solution. Figure 3.18 shows the ranging summary for the Sherwood Furniture example. The ranging report furnished by the program is based on one-at-a-time analyses. We suppose that one of the parameters in the formulation is changed and we ask, What range of values could this parameter take without altering the optimal solution?

The cost ranging summary shows that the range of validity for the unit contribution of the Standard model extends from 16 (an allowable decrease of 4) to 40 (an allowable increase of 20). The value of this parameter is 20 in the formulation, but it can be increased by 20 or decreased by 4 without altering the optimal product mix of 15 Standard and 20 Custom cabinets. If the unit contribution for Standard cabinets were changed within its range of validity then, of

```
DO RANGE(SENSITIVITY) ANALYSIS?
?YES


   RANGES IN WHICH THE BASIS IS UNCHANGED

                           OBJ COEFFICIENT RANGES
VARIABLE         CURRENT       ALLOWABLE      ALLOWABLE
                  COEF         INCREASE       DECREASE
  STD          20.000000      20.000000       4.000000
  CUS          10.000000       5.000000       2.000000
  POR          18.000000       2.000000       INFINITY

                          RIGHTHAND SIDE RANGES
   ROW           CURRENT       ALLOWABLE      ALLOWABLE
                  RHS          INCREASE       DECREASE
    2          120.000000      24.000000      40.000000
    3          160.000000      80.000000      48.000000
    4           32.000000      INFINITY       12.000000
:
```

FIGURE 3.18

course, the optimal value of the objective function would necessarily change, since Standard cabinets constitute part of the optimal product mix. In particular, the objective function would take the form:

$$c_1(15) + 10(20) = 15c_1 + 200$$

where c_1 is the unit contribution for standard cabinets.

For the variable CUS the ranging report shows that the range of validity for its objective function coefficient extends from 8 to 15. For example, when the discovery of a data collection error indicates the coefficient should be changed from 10 to 8.50, the ranging information tells us that there will be no change in the optimal schedule.

For the Portable cabinets the ranging information is consistent with the reduced cost interpretation we mentioned earlier: If the objective function coefficient is not increased by more than 2, then the variable POR will remain at 0 in the optimal solution. Thus, the range of validity is from $-\infty$ to 20. Within this range there is no change either in the optimal product mix or in the optimal value of the objective function.

The right-hand side ranging summary shows that the range of validity for Assembly capacity is from 80 to 144 hours. The value of this parameter is 120 in row 2 of the model, and its range allows an increase of 24 or a decrease of 40. The associated shadow price of 2.5 holds throughout this range. (Earlier, we assumed as much when evaluating the attractiveness of leasing the machine; the ranging summary provides confirmation.) We also know (as we found in the graphical example) that within this range the value of the objective function is $500 + 2.5\Delta b$, where Δb represents the change in the number of Assembly hours.

The ranging report contains the same kind of information for the other constraints. The information about row 4 illustrates the fact that the range of validity for the right-hand side of a nonbinding constraint will always be open ended. In particular, for the market constraint there is positive slack in the optimal schedule, and the report in Figure 3.18 shows that the corresponding range of validity extends from 20 to $+\infty$.

Within the range of validity for a constraint constant the shadow prices remain unchanged. Also, the optimal solution is said to remain unchanged in a particular fashion: the set of variables that are positive remains unchanged, even though their values and the optimal value of the objective function do change. At the limit of a right-hand-side range, at least one of the positive variables becomes 0.

SIMULTANEOUS RANGING

As a rule, computer codes for LP provide one-at-a-time ranging analysis for each objective function coefficient and for each constraint constant. They do not analyze what happens when we vary two or more parameters simultaneously. However, it is possible to perform some simultaneous ranging based only on the one-at-a-time results.

Consider first the objective function coefficients of zero-valued variables. For any one of these coefficients we can make a change within its range of validity without affecting the optimal solution. In essence, the coefficient does not become sufficiently attractive to give us an incentive to make the corresponding variable positive. If we simultaneously vary two such coefficients within their ranges of validity, then neither one will give us such an incentive. Similarly, we can simultaneously vary any number of coefficients of zero-valued variables within their respective ranges of validity without altering the optimal solution.

An analogous situation exists with respect to the right-hand-side constants of nonbinding constraints. We can simultaneously vary any number of those constants within their respective ranges of validity without altering the optimal decision variables or the objective function. Of course, slack or surplus quantities will vary to reflect the changes in right-hand sides.

Such reasoning does not necessarily apply when we simultaneously vary the objective function coefficients of two positive variables. In general, there is no guarantee that the optimal decisions remain the same when we vary two objective function coefficients simultaneously even though they remain within their respective ranges of validity. We can, however, make a slightly more restrictive guarantee. Suppose that we choose to vary two (or more) objective function coefficients simultaneously and we specify the amount by which each parameter will change. For each parameter we can measure this amount as a fraction of the largest allowable change in the parameter for its one-at-a-time ranging analysis. If the sum of these fractions does not exceed 1, then the optimal solution will be preserved. This condition is sometimes called the **100% rule.**

In the Sherwood Furniture problem, suppose that we consider decreasing the profit contribution of Standards (c_1) from its original value of 20 toward the lower end of its range of validity, which is 16. Because the actual change is ($20 - c_1$) and the maximum change is ($20 - 16$), the fractional change we make is ($20 - c_1$)/($20 - 16$). Suppose that we consider simultaneously increasing the profit contribution of Customs (c_2) from its original value of 10 toward the upper end of its range of validity, which is 15. Here the fractional change is ($c_2 - 10$)/($15 - 10$). Then we can say that the optimal product mix remains unchanged as long as the sum of the fractional changes is less than 1:

$$\frac{20 - c_1}{20 - 16} + \frac{c_2 - 10}{15 - 10} \leq 1$$

For example, if we set $c_1 = 18$ and $c_2 = 12$ then the fractional changes are 0.5 for c_1 and 0.4 for c_2. Because

$$0.5 + 0.4 \leq 1$$

the 100% rule tells us that this change will not alter the optimal solution of $x_1 = 15, x_2 = 20$. (The optimal value of the objective function will change, in this case, from 500 to 510.)

An analogous result applies to right-hand-side constants of binding constraints. Suppose we make simultaneous changes in two (or more) of the constraint constants, in specified directions. We can measure the amount that each constant changes as a fraction of the maximum allowable change in its range of validity. Again, if the sum of these fractions does not exceed 1, then the optimal solution remains unchanged. As in the case of one-at-a-time ranging, this means that the shadow prices and the set of positive variables will not change.

In the Sherwood Furniture example, suppose that we increase both the number of Assembly hours and the number of Finishing hours. Assembly capacity rises from 120 to b_1, with an upper limit of 144; thus, the fractional change is ($b_1 - 120$)/($144 - 120$). Finishing capacity rises from 160 to b_2, with an upper limit of 240; thus, its fractional change is ($b_2 - 160$)/($240 - 160$). Our two-at-a-time range of validity becomes

$$\frac{b_1 - 120}{144 - 120} + \frac{b_2 - 160}{240 - 160} \leq 1$$

Suppose we wanted to know how many hours of additional capacity we could simultaneously add to both departments without altering the shadow prices in our optimal solution. If Δb represents the size of this increment, then the 100% rule yields

$$\frac{\Delta b}{24} + \frac{\Delta b}{80} \le 1$$

or

$$\Delta b \le \frac{240}{13} = 18.46$$

Thus we could add about 18 hours to each department's capacity without altering the optimal shadow prices. An increase of 18 hours in each department would therefore increase the optimal profit contribution by

$$18(2.50 + 1.25) = 67.50$$

because we could apply the individual shadow prices of 2.50 per hour and 1.25 per hour, for Assembly and Finishing capacity, respectively.

To understand why the 100% rule works, think of the range of validity as defining an allowance that is available for parameter changes. As long as the total amount of this allowance is not used up by a combination of changes, then the form of the solution will not change.

ADDITIONAL TOPICS

In the previous section we covered the main points concerning the use of a computer program for obtaining LP solutions: specifying the formulation for the program, recognizing the solution, and interpreting the sensitivity analyses. This section deals with some detailed points and additional topics that will complete our treatment of computer solutions to LP problems.

DEGENERACY

A degenerate solution occurs when the right-hand-side constant of a constraint lies at one end of its range of validity. We encountered this property when we studied ranging analysis graphically. (See Figures 3.13 and 3.14.) It is important to be able to recognize degeneracy, because certain properties that hold for nondegenerate solutions may not be true when the solution is degenerate. For example, suppose we are interested in the range of validity for an objective function coefficient corresponding to a zero-valued variable. If the solution is nondegenerate, we can always determine this range from the reduced cost. We have illustrated this point in connection with the contribution coefficient of the variable POR, for which the reduced cost was 2.

```
:ALT
ROW:
2
VAR:
RHS
NEW COEFFICIENT:
?176
:LOOK ALL

MAX      20 STD + 10 CUS + 18 POR
SUBJECT TO
   2)     4 STD + 3 CUS + 5 POR <=    176
   3)     8 STD + 2 CUS + 6 POR <=    160
   4)       CUS <=    32
END

:GO
    LP OPTIMUM FOUND   AT STEP       3


            OBJECTIVE FUNCTION VALUE

  1)        608.000000

VARIABLE          VALUE              REDUCED COST
   STD           .000000                 .000000
   CUS         32.000000                 .000000
   POR         16.000000                 .000000

   ROW        SLACK OR SURPLUS       DUAL PRICES
   2)             .000000             1.500000
   3)             .000000             1.750000
   4)             .000000             2.000000


NO. ITERATIONS=        3

 DO RANGE(SENSITIVITY) ANALYSIS?
?YES


   RANGES IN WHICH THE BASIS IS UNCHANGED


                         OBJ COEFFICIENT RANGES
VARIABLE        CURRENT      ALLOWABLE       ALLOWABLE
                COEF         INCREASE        DECREASE
   STD        20.000000      4.000000        4.000000
   CUS        10.000000      INFINITY        2.000000
   POR        18.000000      2.000000        3.000000
```

FIGURE 3.19

```
                         RIGHTHAND SIDE RANGES
        ROW       CURRENT        ALLOWABLE          ALLOWABLE
                    RHS          INCREASE           DECREASE
         2       176.000000       .000000          32.000000
         3       160.000000      64.000000           .000000
         4        32.000000      16.000000           .000000
:
```

FIGURE 3.19 (Continued)

Similar reasoning could fail in the case of a degenerate solution. Suppose we alter the Sherwood Furniture example by changing the Assembly capacity to 176 hours. In Figure 3.19 we make this change with the ALT command, which allows us to alter parameters in the original model. When we optimize, the solution turns out to be degenerate because at least one right-hand-side constant lies at the end of its range of validity. (As it happens, all three constraint constants exhibit this property.) Note that the variable STD has both a value of 0 and a reduced cost of 0. However, we cannot deduce its coefficient's range of validity from the reduced cost. Instead, we must consult the ranging analysis to see that the range extends from 16 to 24.

ALTERNATE OPTIMA

A linear program has alternate optima if there is more than one set of decision variables that attains the best possible value of the objective function. We can easily detect alternate optima in nondegenerate solutions by looking for an objective function coefficient that lies at one end of its range of validity.

An example of a solution involving alternate optima is shown in Figure 3.20, where we have restored the Assembly capacity to 120 hours. We have also set the unit profit contribution of Standard cabinets to 16 and the unit profit contribution of Customs to 12. With this modification we find that the optimal profit is $480 and the optimal product mix remains the same as in the original formulation. Notice, however, that c_1 and c_2, the coefficients of STD and CUS, both lie at one end of their ranges. In particular, there is no allowable decrease in the range for c_1 and no allowable increase in the range for c_2. This condition indicates that there is another set of decision variables that attains $480 in total profit. It turns out that this set is 6 Standard and 32 Custom cabinets. (Because Portable cabinets are not involved in these product mixes, we can refer to the two-variable version of the example in Figure 3.6 as a reminder of the geometry of alternate optima.)

The LINDO system has some advanced features that help us find the alternate optimum directly. However, we can also utilize the features already introduced. Because the contribution coefficient for CUS is 12, and the ranging analysis tells us that there is no allowable increase in the range of validity, suppose we alter the original model so that the coefficient becomes 12.01. As Figure 3.21 demonstrates, this manipulation generates the decision variables of the alternate

```
:LOOK ALL

MAX      16 STD + 12 CUS + 18 POR
SUBJECT TO
    2)    4 STD + 3 CUS + 5 POR <=   120
    3)    8 STD + 2 CUS + 6 POR <=   160
    4)      CUS <=   32
END
:GO
      LP OPTIMUM FOUND  AT STEP      2


          OBJECTIVE FUNCTION VALUE

  1)        480.000000


VARIABLE         VALUE           REDUCED COST
  STD          15.000000            .000000
  CUS          20.000000            .000000
  POR            .000000           2.000000


  ROW      SLACK OR SURPLUS      DUAL PRICES
  2)            .000000           4.000000
  3)            .000000            .000000
  4)          12.000000            .000000


NO. ITERATIONS=        2
 DO RANGE(SENSITIVITY) ANALYSIS?
?YES



    RANGES IN WHICH THE BASIS IS UNCHANGED

                      OBJ COEFFICIENT RANGES
VARIABLE      CURRENT      ALLOWABLE      ALLOWABLE
               COEF        INCREASE       DECREASE
  STD        16.000000     32.000000        .000000
  CUS        12.000000       .000000       2.000000
  POR        18.000000      2.000000       INFINITY

                      RIGHTHAND SIDE RANGES
  ROW        CURRENT      ALLOWABLE      ALLOWABLE
               RHS        INCREASE       DECREASE
    2       120.000000     24.000000      40.000000
    3       160.000000     80.000000      48.000000
    4        32.000000     INFINITY       12.000000
  :
```

FIGURE 3.20

```
:LOOK ALL

MAX       16 STD + 12.01 CUS + 18 POR
SUBJECT TO
   2)     4 STD + 3 CUS + 5 POR <=    120
   3)     8 STD + 2 CUS + 6 POR <=    160
   4)      CUS <=    32
END
:GO
     LP OPTIMUM FOUND  AT STEP     3


               OBJECTIVE FUNCTION VALUE

    1)        480.320000


VARIABLE          VALUE          REDUCED COST
   STD          6.000000            .000000
   CUS         32.000000            .000000
   POR           .000000           2.000000

    ROW     SLACK OR SURPLUS     DUAL PRICES
    2)            .000000         4.000000
    3)          48.000000          .000000
    4)            .000000          .010000


NO. ITERATIONS=        3

 DO RANGE(SENSITIVITY) ANALYSIS?
?YES


   RANGES IN WHICH THE BASIS IS UNCHANGED

                       OBJ COEFFICIENT RANGES
VARIABLE        CURRENT        ALLOWABLE        ALLOWABLE
                 COEF          INCREASE         DECREASE
   STD        16.000000         .013334         1.600000
   CUS        12.010000        INFINITY          .010000
   POR        18.000000        2.000000         INFINITY

                       RIGHTHAND SIDE RANGES
    ROW        CURRENT        ALLOWABLE        ALLOWABLE
                 RHS          INCREASE         DECREASE
     2        120.000000      24.000000        24.000000
     3        160.000000      INFINITY         48.000000
     4         32.000000       8.000000        12.000000
:
```

FIGURE 3.21

optimum. (The shadow prices and the objective function are slightly misleading unless we adjust for the extra cent in the contribution coefficient.)

When at least one alternate optimum occurs in an LP solution there will always be an infinite number of alternate optima. To see why this property is true, consider the two sets of decision variables in our example that yield $480 in total profit:

Solution 1:	STD = 15	CUS = 20	POR = 0
Solution 2:	STD = 6	CUS = 32	POR = 0

Any product mix that is a weighted average of these two solutions will be feasible and will also yield a total profit of $480. We construct such a weighted average in the form

$$\alpha(\text{Solution 1}) + (1 - \alpha)(\text{Solution 2})$$

where $0 \leq \alpha \leq 1$. For example, if $\alpha = 1/3$ then we obtain

$$\frac{1}{3}(15 \text{ Standards, } 20 \text{ Customs, } 0 \text{ Portables})$$

$$+\frac{2}{3}(6 \text{ Standards, } 32 \text{ Customs, } 0 \text{ Portables})$$

$$\overline{\phantom{+\frac{2}{3}}(9 \text{ Standards, } 28 \text{ Customs, } 0 \text{ Portables})}$$

We can easily verify that a product mix containing 9 Standard and 28 Custom cabinets is feasible and yields $480 in total profit. As graphed in the two-variable example of Figure 3.6, the solution ($x_1 = 9$, $x_2 = 28$) corresponds to a point that lies on the boundary line segment that connects the corner points (6, 32) and (15, 20). Assuming that the decision variables are infinitely divisible, there are an infinite number of choices for α and, consequently, an infinite number of alternate optima in this example.

It is important to remember that our condition for identifying alternate optima (a coefficient at one end of its range) relies on nondegeneracy. If we discover the same condition in a degenerate solution, there may or may not be a different set of decisions that achieve the same optimal value of the objective function. Only further exploration will reveal whether alternate optima exist.

PARAMETRIC ANALYSIS

We said earlier that within the range of validity for a constraint constant the corresponding shadow price remains the same. Suppose we are dealing with a maximization problem and a binding upper-bound constraint. As the constant on the right-hand side of this constraint changes, the optimal value of the objective function will increase or decrease in straight-line fashion. Furthermore, the slope of this straight line will be exactly the shadow price corresponding to the constraint being modified. This straight-line behavior holds throughout the range of validity.

In some cases we may be interested in treating the constraint constant as a parameter and allowing it to vary beyond its range of validity. A description of the impact of this sort of change is called **parametric** analysis. To illustrate some of the information that a parametric analysis might generate, let us look specifically at the Sherwood Furniture example. Figure 3.22 shows a graph of optimal profit as a function of the number of hours of Finishing capacity. The arrow points to the optimal solution of the original problem, the point (160, 500). In the vicinity of this point, a 1-hour change in Finishing capacity leads to a 1.25 change in the objective function. This is the shadow price on the Finishing capacity constraint, and it is also the slope of the line in the vicinity of 160 Finishing hours. More specifically, this slope holds between 112 and 240 Finishing hours, which is just the range of validity we encountered in Figure 3.18.

In order to extrapolate beyond this range of validity, we can rerun the problem with, for instance, 100 Finishing hours. In this case the shadow price on Finishing capacity is reported as 1.75 and the ranging option gives the corresponding range of validity as 92.8 to 112 hours. We can continue this process, selectively modifying the Finishing capacity, to construct the graph in Figure 3.22.

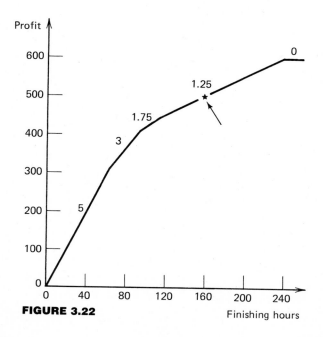

FIGURE 3.22

Looking at the graph as a whole, we see that the optimal profit consists of linear segments with slopes of 5, 3, 1.75, 1.25, and 0. For instance, the graph tells us that if we were to reduce the number of Finishing hours to 60, then the best possible profit would be $300, and there would be a 5 shadow price for Finishing hours. The graph also tells us that Finishing capacity is no longer scarce once 240 hours are made available. Beyond this level the optimal profit remains at $600 no matter how many Finishing hours are available.

Instead of several reruns, the LINDO system has a more convenient way of generating the information for parametric analysis. In Figure 3.23 we use the command PARA to identify a row for which the right-hand side will be varied. Because LINDO performs the parametric analysis in one direction at a time, it requests a new right-hand-side value. This value establishes the direction of the analysis and also the interval over which the parameter will be varied. We first vary the number of Finishing hours in the direction of 0, then in the direction of 1000. The column RHS VAL provides values for the horizontal axis of Figure 3.22, and the column OBJ VAL provides values for the vertical axis. When we connect these points with straight line segments, we construct the graph as shown in Figure 3.22.

In general, we can make the following statements about parametric analysis of constraint constants:

1. Loosening an inequality constraint will never hurt the objective function; if it helps the objective function the benefits will exhibit diminishing marginal returns.

2. Tightening an inequality constraint will never help the objective function; if it hurts the objective function the costs will exhibit increasing marginal costs.

Here, by "loosening" we refer to decreasing the right-hand-side of a lower-bound constraint or to increasing the right-hand-side of an upper-bound constraint. Similarly, "tightening" refers to increasing the right-hand-side of a lower-bound constraint and decreasing it for an upper-bound constraint.

When we couple these results with the two types of objectives, we find four possible graphs of the relationship between the objective function and a right-hand-side constant. Figure 3.24 depicts these relationships.

When we examine equality constraints in parametric analysis we can apply the same principles. It is helpful to think of an equality constraint as composed of two inequality constraints. For example, suppose that in the Sherwood Furniture problem we needed to produce *exactly* 32 Customs. Although it would be cumbersome to do so, we could represent this requirement by keeping the original constraint

$$x_2 \leq 32$$

and adding another constraint

$$x_2 \geq 32$$

```
:PARA
ROW:
3
NEW RHS VAL=
0
```

VAR OUT	VAR IN	PIVOT ROW	RHS VAL	DUAL VARIABLE	OBJ VAL
SLK4	POR	4	112.000	1.25000	440.000
STD	SLK2	3	92.8000	1.75000	406.400
POR	SLK4	4	64.0000	3.00000	320.000
CUS	ART	2	.000000	5.00000	.000000

```
:GO
     LP OPTIMUM FOUND  AT STEP    3
```

OBJECTIVE FUNCTION VALUE

```
   1)        500.000000
```

VARIABLE	VALUE	REDUCED COST
STD	15.000000	.000000
CUS	20.000000	.000000
POR	.000000	2.000000

ROW	SLACK OR SURPLUS	DUAL PRICES
2)	.000000	2.500000
3)	.000000	1.250000
4)	12.000000	.000000

```
NO. ITERATIONS=       3

 DO RANGE(SENSITIVITY) ANALYSIS?
?NO
:
:PARA
ROW:
3
NEW RHS VAL=
1000
```

VAR OUT	VAR IN	PIVOT ROW	RHS VAL	DUAL VARIABLE	OBJ VAL
CUS	SLK3	2	240.000	1.25000	600.000
ART	ART	0	240.000	.000000	600.000

```
:
```

FIGURE 3.23

Based on this consideration we should expect that parametric analysis of equality constraints in a maximization problem would combine the relationships shown in Figures 3.24a and 3.24b. Similarly, parametric analysis of equality constraints in a minimization problem would combine the relationships shown in Figures 3.24c and 3.24d. Thus for equality constraints we usually find the relationships shown in Figure 3.25a for maximization, and Figure 3.25b for minimization.

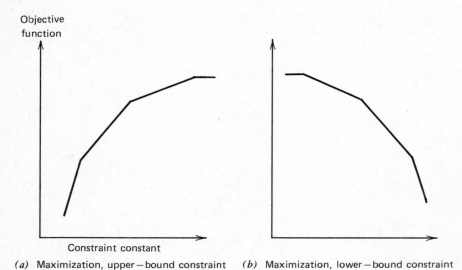

(a) Maximization, upper—bound constraint   (b) Maximization, lower—bound constraint

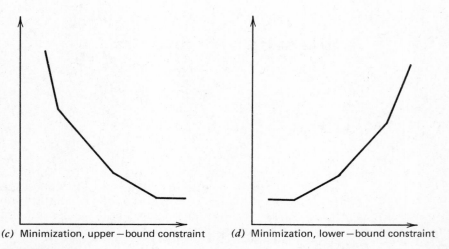

(c) Minimization, upper—bound constraint   (d) Minimization, lower—bound constraint

FIGURE 3.24

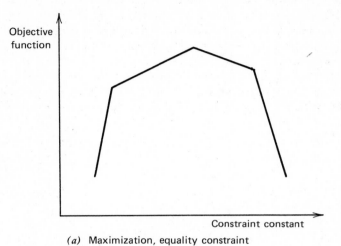

(*a*) Maximization, equality constraint

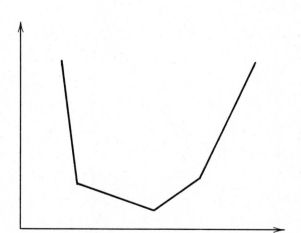

(*b*) Minimization, equality constraint

FIGURE 3.25

Some situations may arise, however, in which one "half" of the equality constraint is never active; in such cases one of the graphs in Figure 3.24 will apply.

We can also draw piecewise linear graphs to show the relationship of the decision variables to the Finishing capacity parameter. Within each of the same five ranges of validity that appear in Figure 3.22 the number of Custom cabinets, for example, will be a straight-line function of the number of Finishing hours.

We can perform similar analysis with respect to changes in the value of objective function coefficients. For example, consider Figure 3.26, which is a graph of optimal profit as a function of the Standard's contribution. As in Figure 3.22, the arrow points to the optimal solution of the original problem, the point (20, 500). Near this point a $1 change in the Standard's contribution leads to a

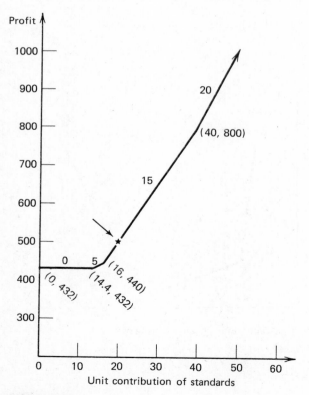

FIGURE 3.26

$15 change in the objective function. The value 15 represents the optimal number of Standards produced and is also the slope of the line in the vicinity of a 20 unit contribution. This slope holds between unit contributions of 16 and 40, the range of validity for c_1 which we identified in Figure 3.16.

In Figure 3.26 we also see that the optimal profit has linear segments with slopes of 0, 5, 15, and 20. Examining one extreme of the range, we see that if we increase the Standard's contribution to 40, the total profit rises to $800. In addition, for any Model contribution above $c_1 = 40$, the total profit is $20c_1$. This result occurs because for $c_1 \geq 40$ the optimal solution is to produce only 20 Standards and neither of the other models. If we examine the other extreme, we see that for $c_1 \leq 14.4$ the optimal profit remains at $432 independent of the Standard's contribution. This result occurs because we produce only 18 Portable models and no Customs or Standards.

For parametric analysis of objective function coefficients we can make the following general statements:

1. In a maximization problem, increasing the profitability of an activity will never reduce the optimal level of that activity.
2. In a minimization problem, reducing the cost of an activity will never reduce the optimal level of that activity.

These statements also help us to anticipate the shape of the relationship between the optimal objective function and the value of an objective function coefficient. For example, in a maximization problem the slope of this relationship must remain the same or increase as a unit contribution increases. Similarly, in a minimization problem the slope must remain the same or decrease as a unit cost decreases. These concepts lead us to conclude that there are only two possible graphs depicting the relationship between the value of the objective function and the value of one of its coefficients. Figure 3.27 shows these graphs.

Parametric analysis of constraint constants and objective function coefficients is a user option on many computer programs for LP, enabling the user to look beyond the original ranges of validity for broader information on sensitivity analysis. It is helpful to think in graphical terms in carrying out parametric analysis. In particular, when a parameter of the model takes on a value somewhere outside its range of validity, these graphs can help the user determine bounds on the possible effect on the objective function.

MODEL STRUCTURES

This section describes some of the problem settings in which LP is applicable and presents the basic structures that accompany them. As we said earlier, the formulation of LP models is an art, and it requires some practice. A good first step, however, is a study of some of the structural elements that model builders have

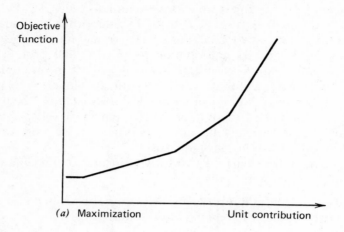

(a) Maximization   Unit contribution

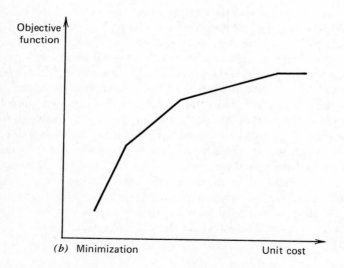

(b) Minimization   Unit cost

FIGURE 3.27

often found helpful. In what follows, we highlight a number of these structures, in connection with some simplified problem scenarios.

RESOURCE ALLOCATION

Perhaps the most common type of model for LP application involves the allocation of limited resources. We alluded to this scenario when we introduced the elements of LP models. In this type of model we identify the resources available (machine time, employees, material, etc.) and the products or activities that consume these resources. We build a model to maximize profit subject to upper-bound constraints on resource capacities.

Suppose that a firm can manufacture two products and that the bottleneck resources are labor hours and machine hours. The following table describes the consumption of these resources per unit of production:

	Product 1	*Product 2*
Labor hours/unit	5	3
Machine hours/unit	4	6

Now suppose there are 100 labor hours and 200 machine hours available. Suppose also that Products 1 and 2 generate profits of 22 per unit and 26 per unit, respectively. Then our LP model is

maximize

$$22x_1 + 26x_2$$

subject to

$$5x_1 + 3x_2 \leq 100$$
$$4x_1 + 6x_2 \leq 200$$
$$x_1 \geq 0 \qquad x_2 \geq 0$$

where x_1 and x_2 give the output quantities of Products 1 and 2, respectively. Our model assumes that there is only one manufacturing facility with limited resources (or that we can aggregate over all facilities), and it distinguishes between labor and machine resources. By contrast, the Sherwood Furniture example distinguished between two facilities (the Assembly and Finishing departments) but recognized only one kind of limited resource (hours).

In general, the format of a resource allocation model involves a profit criterion:

maximize

$$c_1 x_1 + c_2 x_2 + \cdots + c_n x_n$$

where x_j represents the output quantity of product j, and c_j represents the corresponding unit profit. A generic constraint in the model takes the form

$$a_{i1} x_1 + a_{i2} x_2 + \cdots + a_{in} x_n \leq b_i$$

where b_i is the capacity of the ith resource and a_{ij} is the amount of that resource consumed by the jth product. As usual, all of the decision variables (x_j) must be nonnegative.

PRODUCT MIX

The product mix model is an extension of the resource allocation model with demand information included. A common way to reflect demand conditions is to use upper and lower demand limits. For example, there may be an upper limit U_j on the demand for product j that can be sold in the firm's market. (Such a condition appeared in the Sherwood Furniture problem as a market ceiling for Customs.) In addition, there may be a lower limit L_j on the demand for product j, as a result of delivery contracts already negotiated. For product j, the market constraints would simply reflect these limits:

$$x_j \leq U_j$$
$$x_j \geq L_j$$

We form the product mix model by adding these limits to the resource allocation model.

INVENTORY RELATIONSHIPS

In multiperiod production models, inventory plays an important role. As an illustration, we can re-examine our two-product example as a two-period planning model. Suppose that we have the following delivery commitments:

	Product 1	Product 2
Period 1	5	10
Period 2	12	15

Assume that we have available 100 labor hours and 200 machine hours in each period. Note that these amounts are insufficient for us to meet our delivery commitments directly from production in period 2. However, we also can meet demand from inventory if we build more product in period 1 than we need immediately. Now let x_{1t} and x_{2t} represent the production of product 1 and product 2, respectively, in period t (where $t = 1$ or $t = 2$). Also let y_{1t} and y_{2t} represent the ending inventory of product 1 and product 2, respectively, in period t. Assuming that inventory charges are 2 per period on either product, our objective function becomes

maximize

$$22x_{11} + 26x_{21} - 2y_{11} - 2y_{21} + 22x_{12} + 26x_{22} - 2y_{12} - 2y_{22}$$

The constraints of our model are the following:

$$
\begin{array}{llll}
5x_{11} + 3x_{21} & & \leq 100 \\
4x_{11} + 6x_{21} & & \leq 200 \\
& 5x_{12} + 3x_{22} & \leq 100 \\
& 4x_{12} + 6x_{22} & \leq 200 \\
x_{11} + x_{21} + x_{12} + x_{22} & & = 42 \\
x_{11} - y_{11} & & = 5 \\
x_{21} - y_{21} & & = 10 \\
y_{11} + x_{12} - y_{12} & & = 12 \\
y_{21} + x_{22} - y_{22} & = 15 \\
\end{array}
$$

The last constraint, for instance, comes from the fundamental accounting equation for inventory:

Ending inventory this period = ending inventory last period
+ production this period − sales this period

or, for period 2

$$y_{22} = y_{21} + x_{22} - 15$$

By rearranging terms so that all the variables appear on the left of the equals sign, with the constant on the right, we obtain the equation in our model. (If we wish to prohibit ending inventories, then we can remove y_{12} and y_{22} from the formulation.)

The generic inventory constraint expresses the relationship in our accounting equation

new inventory = old inventory + production − shipments

In general, "production" may have several components, and the constraint can contain several variables in this role. For example, there may be both a regular production quantity and an overtime production quantity, which together comprise "production." However, these components would be kept separate in the model because the profit contributions for regular production and overtime production are different. Similarly, "shipments" may also have several components if we distinguish among modes of shipment or different destinations. The important modeling step is to start with the accounting equation and determine the variables or the constants to go with each element of the equation.

POSITIVE AND NEGATIVE VARIABLES

In our example we assumed implicitly that inventories would not be negative ($y_{it} \geq 0$ in the model above). This assumption is equivalent to assuming that we meet delivery commitments on time. In some situations, however, it might make sense to meet some demands late. This possibility allows for negative inventories, or **backorders.** To model negative inventories it is not enough simply to allow our inventory variables to be negative, because the impact on the objective function is likely to be different for positive inventories than for negative inventories. We would like to be able to separate the "positive part" of the inventory variable from the "negative part." To implement this idea, we define two separate variables:

$$u_{it} = \text{(positive) inventory of product } i \text{ in period } t$$
$$v_{it} = \text{backorders for product } i \text{ in period } t$$

Then, everywhere that our model would have contained a variable y_{it} for the inventory of product i in period t, we make the substitution

$$y_{it} = u_{it} - v_{it}$$

In our two-product example, suppose that backorders are permitted only for product 1, and that the unit cost of a backorder is 3 in any period. Then we modify our model in the following way:

maximize

$$22x_{11} + 26x_{21} - 2u_{11} - 3v_{11} - 2y_{21} + 22x_{12} + 26x_{22} - 2u_{12} - 3v_{12} - 2y_{22}$$

subject to

$$5x_{11} + 3x_{21} \qquad\qquad\qquad\qquad\qquad \leq 100$$
$$4x_{11} + 6x_{21} \qquad\qquad\qquad\qquad\qquad \leq 200$$
$$\qquad\qquad\qquad 5x_{12} + 3x_{22} \qquad\qquad \leq 100$$

$$
\begin{array}{llllllll}
& & & 4x_{12} & + & 6x_{22} & & \le 200 \\
x_{11} + & x_{21} & & + & x_{12} + & x_{22} & & = 42 \\
x_{11} & & - u_{11} + v_{11} & & & & & = 5 \\
& x_{21} & & - y_{21} & & & & = 10 \\
& & u_{11} - v_{11} & + & x_{12} & - u_{12} + v_{12} & & = 12 \\
& & y_{21} & & + & x_{22} & - y_{22} = & 15
\end{array}
$$

Note that we account separately for inventories and backorders of product 1 in our objective function.

In general, we may encounter a situation in which we wish to treat the positive part of a variable x differently from its negative part. The modeling strategy is to make the substitution $x = u - v$ everywhere that x would normally appear. We do this because the positive part of x and the negative part of x have different influences in the objective function. By creating the two parts explicitly we can construct an objective function that represents these influences.

When we make this substitution and solve the LP, we will find that one of three situations occurs:

1. $x > 0$ (In this case $u = x$ and $v = 0$)
2. $x < 0$ (In this case $u = 0$ and $v = -x$)
3. $x = 0$ (In this case $u = 0$ and $v = 0$)

We never find that both $u > 0$ and $v > 0$. This result should make sense if we recognize that the objective function provides an incentive to make either u or v equal to 0. In our example, suppose that the optimal plan involved backorders for six units of product 1 in period 1 ($y_{11} = -6$). In principle, there are an infinite number of feasible representations of this value in our model, such as

$$
\begin{array}{lll}
u_{11} = 0 & \text{with} & v_{11} = 6 \\
u_{11} = 1 & \text{with} & v_{11} = 7 \\
u_{11} = 10 & \text{with} & v_{11} = 16
\end{array}
$$

and so on. However, notice that in our objective function, profits are reduced by \$2 for each positive unit of u_{11} and by \$3 for each unit of v_{11}. Therefore, when we optimize the objective function with $y_{11} = -6$, the best solution will set $u_{11} = 0$ and $v_{11} = 6$. Other feasible combinations of u_{11} and v_{11} that differ by -6 will have a lower profit and will therefore be unattractive.

COVERING

We turn now to some problem structures in which the objective function involves minimization. In the basic covering model we are faced with a set of demands to cover by deploying certain people or resources. We build a model to minimize the cost of deployment subject to constraints on meeting demand.

For example, consider a firm that provides personnel for security checks at a busy airport. Although some check lines must operate around the clock, the need for personnel varies during the day. The firm has been given the following set of requirements:

	#1	#2	#3	#4	#5	#6
Period:	(2 A.M.– 6 A.M.)	(6 A.M.– 10 A.M.)	(10 A.M.– 2 P.M.)	(2 P.M.– 6 P.M.)	(6 P.M.– 10 P.M.)	(10 P.M.– 2 A.M.)
Minimum personnel:	20	50	60	75	60	30

People employed as security personnel work 8-hour shifts and can be scheduled to work any two consecutive 4-hour periods in the table of requirements. The firm is interested in minimizing the total size of its work force while meeting this schedule of requirements. Its LP model takes the following form:

minimize

$$x_1 + x_2 + x_3 + x_4 + x_5 + x_6$$

subject to

$$
\begin{aligned}
x_1 \quad\quad\quad\quad\quad\quad + x_6 &\geq 20 \\
x_1 + x_2 \quad\quad\quad\quad\quad &\geq 50 \\
x_2 + x_3 \quad\quad\quad\quad &\geq 60 \\
x_3 + x_4 \quad\quad &\geq 75 \\
x_4 + x_5 \quad &\geq 60 \\
x_5 + x_6 &\geq 30
\end{aligned}
$$

Here $x_j \geq 0$ represents the number of personnel who will be scheduled to start work at the beginning of period j. The objective function measures the total work-force size, and each constraint assures that the number of people scheduled is at least as large as the requirement in the corresponding period. For example, the first constraint shows that the requirement for at least 20 people in period 1 can be met either by people who start work in period 1 or by people who start in the preceding period, 6.

In the general covering model each activity will cover a subset of the demands, and a_{ij} indicates how much of the ith demand is covered by the jth resource. In addition, c_j denotes the unit cost of deploying the jth resource, and b_i represents the amount of the ith demand. If x_j represents the amount of the jth resource deployed then the cost criterion becomes

minimize

$$c_1 x_1 + c_2 x_2 + \cdots + c_n x_n$$

and a generic constraint takes the form

$$a_{i1}x_1 + a_{i2}x_2 + \cdots + a_{in}x_n \geq b_i$$

Again, the decision variables (x_j) are assumed to be nonnegative.

BLENDING

A common variation on the covering model involves the optimal blending of components. Suppose a firm's marketing staff decides to introduce a new fruit punch with the following specifications (per 8-ounce serving):

Sugar: at least 30 grams
Protein: at least 16 grams
Vitamin C: at least 25% of the Recommended Daily Allowance (RDA)

The fruit punch will be manufactured as a blend of five natural fruit juices. Each of these natural ingredients has its distinctive composition of sugar, protein, and Vitamin C, and, of course, its own cost. This information appears in the table below:

Ingredient	1	2	3	4	5
Sugar	36	30	25	20	25
Protein	18	20	15	16	20
Vitamin C	20	25	50	35	40
Cost	3.5	3.6	4.0	2.8	3.0

In this table the sugar and protein content is measured in grams per serving; the Vitamin C content appears as RDA percentage per serving; and the cost is in cents per serving.

Let x_j denote the proportion of ingredient j in a serving of the blend. Then we construct a minimum-cost blend with the following model:

minimize

$$3.5x_1 + 3.6x_2 + 4.0x_3 + 2.8x_4 + 3.0x_5$$

subject to

$$36x_1 + 30x_2 + 25x_3 + 20x_4 + 25x_5 \geq 30$$
$$18x_1 + 20x_2 + 15x_3 + 16x_4 + 20x_5 \geq 16$$
$$20x_1 + 25x_2 + 50x_3 + 35x_4 + 40x_5 \geq 25$$
$$x_1 + x_2 + x_3 + x_4 + x_5 = 1$$

where

$$x_j \geq 0$$

Our final constraint forces the blend to be made up of only the five ingredients. If we were willing to add water, we could change the final constraint into an upper-bound constraint and find a cheaper solution.

This type of model is sometimes called the **diet problem.** In the generic diet model there are several possible ingredients, each with its own cost. If x_j denotes the amount of ingredient j in the blend and c_j denotes the unit cost of ingredient j, then the cost minimization criterion becomes

minimize

$$c_1 x_1 + c_2 x_2 + \cdots + c_n x_n$$

The generic constraint in the diet model takes the form

$$a_{i1} x_1 + a_{i2} x_2 + \cdots + a_{in} x_n \geq b_i$$

where b_i is the minimum requirement for the ith nutritional component and a_{ij} represents the nutritional contribution of ingredient j toward this ith component. Although our example contained only minimum requirements, we can easily imagine a ceiling on certain nutritional components. A ceiling would give rise to an upper-bound constraint in the model

$$a_{i1} x_1 + a_{i2} x_2 + \cdots + a_{in} x_n \leq b_i$$

Finally, if the ingredient quantities are actually proportions for the ultimate blend, there will be a requirement that these proportions add to one:

$$x_1 + x_2 + \cdots + x_n = 1$$

A slightly different blending problem arises when supplies of the ingredients are limited. Suppose a coffee company has access to green coffee beans each week in the following quantities:

Brazilian   6000 pounds
Colombian   3000 pounds
Mexican   2000 pounds

Each type of bean has its own characteristics. For blending purposes, the most important of these properties are acidity, caffeine content, and body. The table below summarizes these properties:

Ingredient:	Brazilian	Colombian	Mexican
Acidity	4	5	3
Caffeine (%)	0.03	0.02	0.05
Body	9	7	8
Cost ($/lb)	1.25	1.60	1.00

Acidity and body are measured on a standard scale of 1 to 10, and caffeine content is expressed as a percentage. Suppose the firm wishes to market two blends, named House Blend and Special Blend, with the requirements tabulated below:

	House	*Special*
Acidity (maximum)	4.5	4.0
Acidity (minimum)	3.5	—
Caffeine (maximum)	0.04	—
Body (minimum)	—	8.6

The House Blend will sell for 2.75 per pound, and the Special Blend will be priced at 3.50. To form the model we let x_{ij} denote the number of pounds of ingredient i used in blend j. Assume that our criterion is to maximize net revenue (revenue minus cost). For each item, the net revenue per pound is as follows:

Item	*Net Revenue*
11	$2.75 - 1.25 = 1.50$
12	$3.50 - 1.25 = 2.25$
21	$2.75 - 1.60 = 1.15$
22	$3.50 - 1.60 = 1.90$
31	$2.75 - 1.00 = 1.75$
32	$3.50 - 1.00 = 2.50$

Thus, for all combinations of ingredients and blends, the objective is

maximize

$$1.50x_{11} + 2.25x_{12} + 1.15x_{21} + 1.90x_{22} + 1.75x_{31} + 2.50x_{32}$$

For the acidity of the Special Blend, we can write the requirement temporarily in terms of p_j, the proportion of ingredient j in the blend:

$$4p_1 + 5p_2 + 3p_3 \leq 4$$

However, we know these proportions in terms of our decision variables. In particular. $p_1 = x_{12}/(x_{12} + x_{22} + x_{32})$. Thus, in terms of x_{ij}, this constraint becomes

$$\frac{4x_{12}}{(x_{12} + x_{22} + x_{32})} + \frac{5x_{22}}{(x_{12} + x_{22} + x_{32})} + \frac{3x_{32}}{(x_{12} + x_{22} + x_{32})} \leq 4$$

or

$$4x_{12} + 5x_{22} + 3x_{32} \leq 4(x_{12} + x_{22} + x_{32})$$

Moving all variables to the left-hand side, we obtain

$$x_{22} - x_{32} \le 0$$

In a similar fashion, the acidity constraints for the House Blend take the forms

$$-0.5x_{11} + 0.5x_{21} - 1.5x_{31} \le 0$$
$$0.5x_{11} + 1.5x_{21} - 0.5x_{31} \ge 0$$

When we include caffeine, body, and supply constraints, the full model becomes

maximize

$$1.5x_{11} + 2.25x_{12} + 1.15x_{21} + 1.9x_{22} + 1.75x_{31} + 2.5x_{32}$$

subject to

$$
\begin{array}{rrrrrrl}
x_{11} + & x_{12} & & & & & \le 6000 \\
& & x_{21} + & x_{22} & & & \le 3000 \\
& & & & x_{31} + & x_{32} & \le 2000 \\
-0.5x_{11} & & + 0.5x_{21} & & - 1.5x_{31} & & \le\ 0 \\
0.5x_{11} & & + 1.5x_{21} & & - 0.5x_{31} & & \ge\ 0 \\
& & & x_{22} & & - x_{32} & \le\ 0 \\
-0.01x_{11} & & - 0.02x_{21} & & + 0.01x_{31} & & \le\ 0 \\
& 0.4x_{12} & & - 1.6x_{22} & & - 0.6x_{32} & \ge\ 0 \\
\end{array}
$$

where all $x_{ij} \ge 0$.

The key insight in this type of formulation is that we can use linear inequalities to express blending constraints among ingredients, using weighted averages. Furthermore, we can express the weighted averages in linear form even when the total amount of product is itself a variable.

NETWORK FLOWS

Suppose that a firm has a distribution system with three plants, two warehouses, and four distribution centers. The plants have known capacities (measured in units of output per month):

Plant	P1	P2	P3
Capacity	250	350	200

The distribution centers are responsible for supplying customer demand in their respective regions. Demand forecasts for the month are as follows:

Region	R1	R2	R3	R4
Demand	225	150	240	180

The warehouses (W1 and W2) have unlimited capacity, but all products must flow from a plant to a warehouse, for assembly and test operations, prior to being shipped to a distribution center. The unit cost of production and/or shipment between relevant points in the system is well-documented:

From/to	W1	W2	R1	R2	R3	R4
P1	6	3	—	—	—	—
P2	8	6	—	—	—	—
P3	5	10	—	—	—	—
W1	—	—	12	11	16	10
W2	—	—	10	15	13	12

As a start in building an LP model to find a minimum-cost distribution schedule, it is helpful to visualize a diagram of product flows. (See Figure 3.28.) In our diagram there is a circle, or **node,** for each point in the distribution system. The plants, which we can view as **origins** of product flow, are shown with an input arrow showing the amount of product that initiates its flow at each one. The distribution centers, which we can view as **destinations** of product flow, are shown with an output arrow showing the amount of product that terminates its flow at each one. The warehouses do not have product flow either initiating or terminating, although there can be product flowing through them.

We can associate a unit cost with each point-to-point route, or **arc,** in the network; the flow along that route is a decision variable. In Figure 3.28 we have numbered the 14 routes for identification. The system incurs cost on the plant-to-warehouse routes and also on the warehouse-to-distribution center routes. Let x_j denote the flow along route j. The unit cost corresponding to x_j can be found in the cost table above. Our criterion for the system is

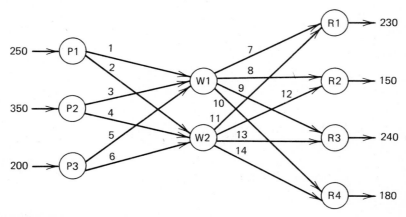

FIGURE 3.28

minimize

$$6x_1 + 3x_2 + 8x_3 + 6x_4 + 5x_5 + 10x_6 + 12x_7 + 11x_8 + 16x_9$$
$$+ 10x_{10} + 10x_{11} + 15x_{12} + 13x_{13} + 12x_{14}$$

The constraints on product flow are of three types: capacity at the plants, demand at the distribution centers, and conservation at the warehouses. (**Conservation** means that the output flow must equal the input flow.) Actually, we can simply use the conservation condition to express all of these constraints. Under conservation we require that output flow equals input flow at any node in the system. Hence

	Input		*Output*
(P1)	250	=	$x_1 + x_2$
(P2)	350	=	$x_3 + x_4$
(P3)	200	=	$x_5 + x_6$
(W1)	$x_1 + x_3 + x_5$	=	$x_7 + x_8 + x_9 + x_{10}$
(W2)	$x_2 + x_4 + x_6$	=	$x_{11} + x_{12} + x_{13} + x_{14}$
(R1)	$x_7 + x_{11}$	=	230
(R2)	$x_8 + x_{12}$	=	150
(R3)	$x_9 + x_{13}$	=	240
(R4)	$x_{10} + x_{14}$	=	180

When we move the variables to the left-hand side of each equation, and the constants to the right-hand side, we obtain a set of equations that make up the constraints of our model:

$$
\begin{array}{l}
-x_1 - x_2 = -250 \\
\quad - x_3 - x_4 = -350 \\
\qquad - x_5 - x_6 = -200 \\
x_1 \quad + x_3 \quad + x_5 \quad - x_7 - x_8 - x_9 - x_{10} = 0 \\
\quad x_2 \quad + x_4 \quad + x_6 \quad - x_{11} - x_{12} - x_{13} - x_{14} = 0 \\
x_7 \quad + x_{11} = 230 \\
x_8 \quad + x_{12} = 150 \\
x_9 \quad + x_{13} = 240 \\
x_{10} \quad + x_{14} = 180
\end{array}
$$

As usual, $x_j \geq 0$. In addition, we can multiply the first three equations by -1 to avoid negative constraint constants, if that seems convenient for interpretation. However, the form above illustrates three generic properties of network models as linear programming problems:

1. Each constraint is an equation.
2. The sum of all right-hand-side constants is 0.

3. Each variable appears in exactly two constraints, once with a coefficient of $+1$ and once with a coefficient of -1.

As we illustrated, the network LP model can be constructed in a logical fashion by first drawing a diagram of flows and then representing the conservation condition for each node in the network. Thus, there will be one constraint for each node and one variable for each arc.

We can also add arcs and nodes to the diagram when the addition makes sense. For example, if total capacity had exceeded total demand in our problem, we could have introduced a tenth node to capture excess capacity. The tenth node would appear with a demand equal to this excess and with arcs from each of the plants. With this modification we would again have a diagram in which the sum of node inputs would be equal to the sum of node outputs, satisfying condition 2 above.

Network models are important special cases of LP models because their special structure makes it possible to develop extremely efficient solution procedures. Moreover, their structural analogy with systems involving product flow makes them valuable in modeling large production and distribution planning problems.

SUMMARY

Linear programming is a widely used approach in modeling decision problems. This chapter began by introducing the elements of LP models—decision variables, constraints, and an objective function—and discussing the formal assumptions of proportionality, additivity, and divisibility. We covered the graphical method for LP in order to provide a glimpse of the procedure for finding optimal solutions to linear programs. The next chapter gives a more complete and formal treatment of this procedure.

The solution of a linear programming problem yields several pieces of useful information:

1. The optimal value of the objective function.
2. The optimal values of the decision variables.
3. An identification of which constraints are binding.
4. A shadow price for each constraint.

We can think of the optimal value of the objective function and the optimal values of the decision variables as **tactical** information. In other words, if we accept as given the conditions and parameters of the problem, then the LP solution tells us the best performance measure we can achieve and the decisions that will achieve it. On the other hand, the identification of binding constraints and their shadow prices provides **strategic** information. In other words, if we want to change the given conditions and parameters, then the LP solution tells us the economic value of certain changes at the margin.

We studied the graphical method for two-variable problems in order to develop a visual sense of LP concepts. However, computerized methods are clearly the best means of solving larger linear programs in practice. The widespread availability of general-purpose computer programs for LP has made it possible to obtain solutions quickly and easily for a variety of large LP problems that arise in practical applications. This does not mean that the use of LP models is always easy. There are often difficult conceptual problems in formulating LP models and severe practical problems in obtaining the data required by the formulation; however, the solution phase itself is made easier by the use of computer programs.

We underscored the importance of the computer's role in using LP by illustrating the use of the LINDO program. We showed how to give the program a description of decision variables, constraint relationships, and an objective function; and we illustrated the type of reporting and analysis the program offers.

We dealt with sensitivity analysis and described how to interpret ranges of validity. In linear programming models, the ranges of validity behave in a special way. Within the range of validity for an objective function coefficient there is no change in the optimal decisions; within the range of validity for a constraint constant there is no change in the shadow prices. Furthermore, the relative size of the range of validity provides some indication of how precise our data collection needs to be. When the range of validity is relatively small, we say that the optimal solution is sensitive to the value of the corresponding parameter. In this situation we would like to have a precise value for the parameter. On the other hand, when the range of validity is relatively large, we can get by with less precise information.

The exercises following this chapter focus on two important skills. One is **formulating** LP models, a process that requires taking a description of a situation and converting it into a formal LP structure for analysis. The second skill is that of **interpreting** the solutions to LP models. This means not only translating the solution into terms that relate to the original situation, but also using sensitivity analysis to answer additional decision-oriented questions that may arise in conjunction with the original analysis.

EXERCISES

GRAPHICAL SOLUTIONS

1 A manufacturer of engine parts produces valves and pistons at its main plant. Both parts are processed by the Machining Department and by the Finishing Department. Each valve requires 0.4 hours of machining time and 0.3 hours of finishing time, and each piston requires 0.3 hours of machining and 0.5 hours of finishing. The production process also requires 2 pounds of steel for each part.

In drawing up a schedule for the coming month the plant manager knows that 300 hours of production time will be available in the Machining Department and 400 hours will be available in the Finishing Department. In addition, existing contracts provide for the delivery of 1800 pounds of steel during the month.

The market for valves and pistons is competitive, and the company can sell all the parts it produces during the month. At current prices the gross profit on each valve sold is $3, while for each piston sold the gross profit is $4. The plant manager would like to find a production plan for the month that will maximize profits.

Determine the optimal plan and the maximum possible profit.

2 A firm is currently manufacturing a line of hardware with a daily production of 30 units for Model X and 180 units of Model Y. The vice-president of manufacturing wants to know if profits can be increased by changing the product mix between the two models. The following information has been compiled about the hours required to build each model and the capacities of the departments in the plant.

	Hours Required		Department Capacity (Hours per Day)
	Model X	Model Y	
Department 1	2	0	300
Department 2	0	3	540
Department 3	2	2	440
Department 4	1	1.5	300
Contribution/unit	$50	$40	

a Determine the optimum product mix, assuming that 180 units of X and 180 units of Y can be sold daily.

b By how much would the profit contribution increase if the optimum mix were used?

3 The Arnett Lumber Company cuts raw timber—oak and pine logs—into 2 × 4 boards. Two steps are required to produce the rough boards from logs. The first step involves stripping bark from the logs. For this step, 2 hours are required to remove the bark from every 1000 feet of oak logs, while 3 hours are required for every 1000 feet of pine. The second step involves cutting the stripped logs into boards. The cutting process requires 2.4 hours per 1000 feet of oak logs and 1.2 hours per 1000 feet of pine logs. The bark-removing machine can operate up to 60 hours a week, but the older cutting machine requires more maintenance and provides only 48 productive hours per week. Existing agreements with suppliers permit the company to buy up to 18,000 feet of newly harvested oak logs and 16,000 feet of newly harvested pine logs each week. The lumber company's profit on the processed logs is $360 per 1000 feet of oak and $360 per 1000 feet of pine. How many feet of each type of log should be purchased each week?

4 During a recent fire a 20-acre section of Pine Mountain National Forest was destroyed. The U.S. Forest Service is planning to reseed this section with a minimum of 5000 seedlings. Regulations require that at least 50% of the seedlings be white pine and that the remainder be yellow pine. White pine seedlings cost $4 per 100 and yellow pine seedlings cost $3 per 100. The cost of planting the white pine is $10 per 100; the cost of planting the yellow pine is $9.50 per 100. The Forest Service has been allocated $700 to reseed this area, of which only $300 may be used to purchase seedlings. Determine how many trees of each type should be planted if the Forest Service wishes to minimize costs.

5 An investor has $100 to invest in Stocks S and T. The annual return on investment on Stock S is 15% and on Stock T 10%. The investment is restricted by a rule that any investment in S must be accompanied by an investment at least one-fourth as great in T. In addition, a $60 limit is prescribed for any investment in a stock. How should the funds be invested in order to maximize the return?

6 The Burnett Agency wants to devise an advertising strategy for a new line of food products. The agency has decided that TV and newspaper advertisements will be most effective, and they have identified three major target audiences. By intelligent choice of a morning newspaper and late-night TV commercials, Burnett believes that it can reach nonoverlapping segments of each audience. Each TV minute will cost $2000, and each newspaper page will cost $1200. The table below shows the average number of exposures (per minute or per page) in each of the three target audiences, together with the total number of exposures Burnett has committed to achieve in each one.

Audience	TV	Paper	Total
1	2000	8000	40,000
2	5000	6000	45,000
3	6000	3000	30,000

What mix of advertising will minimize the cost of providing the desired exposures?

7 A food products company is planning to introduce a new brand of soup that will appeal to consumers on the basis of its nutritional value. The soup will contain two newly developed chemical additives. Additive A costs $4 per ounce and Additive B costs only $2 per ounce. The marketing department has specified that each can of soup must, at a minimum, contain 5 grams of protein, 4 grams of B-vitamins, and 3 grams of minerals. The composition of each additive is shown in the table below.

	A	B
Protein	4 grams/ounce	6 grams/ounce
Vitamins	7	3
Minerals	2	5

Fortunately, varying the mix of additives will not affect the appearance or taste of the soup.

Determine a minimum-cost blend of additives for the soup.

8 An oil refinery utilizes two grades of crude oil and produces two grades of gasoline and motor oil as output. From each barrel of grade-1 crude they obtain 0.5 barrel of high-grade gasoline, 0.3 barrel of low-grade gasoline, and 0.1 barrel of motor oil. From each barrel of grade-2 crude they obtain 0.2 barrel of high-grade gasoline, 0.3 barrel of low-grade gasoline, and 0.4 barrel of motor oil. Grade-1 crude costs $40 per barrel. Grade-2 crude costs $32 per barrel. Each day 3000 barrels of high-grade gasoline and 2700 barrels of low-grade gasoline must be produced. No minimum output level for motor oil is set, but all quantities produced can be sold. Determine how many barrels of each type of crude should be purchased to minimize total crude costs and fulfill the production requirements.

GRAPHICAL SENSITIVITY ANALYSIS

9 Review Exercise 1.

   a Suppose the gross profit of valves will increase if a price change is approved. By how much would the unit price have to rise in order to provide an incentive to alter the product mix?

   b At the margin, what is the value of additional pounds of steel?

   c What is the range for which the value in (b) continues to hold?

   d What is the range of validity for Machining capacity? Finishing capacity?

10 Review Exercise 2.

   a What is the range of validity for the unit contribution of Model X? Model Y?

   b What is the shadow price on capacity for each of the departments?

   c Over what ranges do the shadow prices in (b) continue to hold?

11 Review Exercise 6.

   a Suppose that the goal for Audience 3 is increased to 32,000. What will be the impact on total cost?

b Suppose instead that the goal for Audience 2 is reduced to 36,000. What will be the impact on total cost?

c Suppose instead that the TV station offers a reduced price for its commercials. How much of a reduction would it need to offer before Burnett will have an incentive to buy additional commercials?

COMPUTER SOLUTIONS TO LP PROBLEMS

12 *Savings Investment.* In deciding on a savings plan for your money you have a choice between a 1-year certificate, which returns 12% per year, and a 2-year certificate, which returns 30% after 2 years.

a How should you invest your money if you wish to liquidate your investment with the maximum return after 3 years?

b How should you invest your money if you wish to liquidate your investment with the maximum return after 5 years?

13 *Alloy Blending.* A company desires to blend a new alloy of 30% lead, 20% zinc, and 50% tin from several available alloys having the following properties:

			Alloy		
Property	1	2	3	4	5
Percentage Lead	30	10	50	10	50
Percentage Zinc	60	20	20	10	10
Percentage Tin	10	70	30	80	40
Cost per pound	$8.5	$6.0	$8.9	$5.7	$8.8

The objective is to determine the proportions of these alloys that should be blended to produce the new alloy at a minimum cost.

14 *Commodity Warehousing.* Gottstein Commodities, Inc., buys and sells corn for cash. The company owns a warehouse with a capacity of 5000 bushels, and as of December 31 it has 1000 bushels of corn in the warehouse. Market analysts at the company have estimated corn prices per bushel for the next quarter as follows:

Month	January	February	March
Buy price	$2.85	$3.00	$2.90
Sell price	3.10	3.15	3.00

Corn is bought and delivered to the warehouse during the first 5 days of the month and is sold later in the month. All transactions are made on a cash basis, and as of December 31 the company expects to have $10,000 available for purchases. Determine a plan for buying and selling that will maximize net revenues for the quarter and leave at least 500 bushels in the warehouse at the end of March.

15 *Warehouse Leasing.* A company needs to lease warehouse storage space for 5 months at the start of the year. The materials manager knows just how much space will be required in each of these months. However, since the space requirements fluctuate, it may be most economical to lease only the amount needed each month on a month-by-month basis. On the other hand, the monthly cost for leasing space for additional months is much less than for the first month, so it may be less expensive to lease the maximum amount needed for the entire 5 months. Another option is the intermediate approach of changing the total amount of space leased (by adding a new lease and/or having an old lease expire) at least once but not every month.

The space requirement and the leasing costs for the various leasing periods are:

Month	Required Space	Lease Period (Months)	Cost per 1000 Square Feet Leased
January	15,000	1	$280
February	10,000	2	450
March	20,000	3	600
April	5,000	4	730
May	25,000	5	820

Two or more leases for different periods can begin at the same time. Determine the leasing schedule that provides the required amounts of space at a minimum cost.

16 *Nurse Scheduling.* The operations manager of McLain Hospital is examining the current method of staff scheduling. Demand for nurses varies throughout the day, but an analysis of demand data indicates the number of nurses required to handle all emergencies 99% of the time is the following:

Hour	1	2	3	4	5	6	7	8	9	10	11	12
Staff	4	3	2	2	3	4	6	6	9	10	10	10

Hour	13	14	15	16	17	18	19	20	21	22	23	24
Staff	12	12	8	6	8	9	7	6	5	4	4	4

Hour 1 refers to the period from midnight to 1 A.M.; hour 2 is from 1 A.M. to 2 A.M., and so on.

Nurses can be assigned to any one of six (overlapping) shifts, with salary costs as shown below:

Shift	2 A.M.– 10 A.M.	6 A.M.– 2 P.M.	10 A.M.– 6 P.M.	2 P.M.– 10 P.M.	6 P.M.– 2 A.M.	10 P.M.– 6 A.M.
Cost/day	$60	$48	$48	$54	$54	$60

Find a shift allocation that will provide the number of nurses required and also minimize salary costs.

17 *Process Scheduling.* A coffee manufacturer blends four component coffee beans into three final blends of coffee. The table below summarizes the very precise recipes for the final coffee blends, the cost and availability information for the four components, and the wholesale price per pound of the final blends. The percentages in the body of the table indicate the percentage of each component to be used in each blend.

	Final Blend (%)			Cost Per Pound	Maximum Availability Each Week (pounds)
	1	2	3		
Component					
1	20	35	10	$0.60	40,000
2	40	15	35	0.80	25,000
3	15	20	40	0.55	20,000
4	25	30	15	0.70	45,000
Wholesale price per pound	$1.25	$1.50	$1.40		

Weekly capacity for the processor's plant is 100,000 pounds, and the company wishes to operate at capacity. There is no problem in selling the final blends, although there is a requirement that minimum production levels of 10,000, 25,000, and 30,000 pounds, respectively, be met for blends 1, 2, and 3. Determine the number of pounds of each component which should be used in each blend so as to maximize total weekly profit.

18 *Production Scheduling.* The Seaboch Tire Company currently produces four lines of tires, the economy, glass-belted, snow tire, and the steel radial. Recent recessionary trends have caused a decline in demand, and the company is laying off workers and discontinuing its third shift.

The problem it faces is that of rescheduling production during the first and second shifts for the remaining quarter of the year. The production process primarily involves the use of vulcanization, fabrication, and plastometer machines. However, the limiting resource in production is the availability of machine hours on the vulcanization machines. The economy, glass-belted, snow tire, and steel radial require, 4, 5, 5, and 7 hours, respectively, of vulcanizing time.

The sales manager has forecast the expected sales for each of the four tires in the last quarter of the year. These estimates are shown in the following table:

		Forecast Sales		
Month	Economy Tire	Glass-belted Tire	Snow Tire	Steel Radial Tire
October	8000	18,000	4,000	6000
November	7000	16,000	15,000	5000
December	6000	18,000	15,000	8000

The production capacity in terms of vulcanizing hours available is expressed by month and shift in the next table:

	Vulcanizing Hours Available	
Month	Shift 1	Shift 2
October	110,000	100,000
November	130,000	120,000
December	120,000	115,000

The labor cost of operating the vulcanizing machines is $10 per hour during the first shift. The shift differential requires that the wages be $12 per hour during the second shift. The other relevant cost is storage: It costs $4 per month to store a tire, regardless of its type, if production exceeds demand.

Assuming that the company wishes to produce exactly as many tires as the sales manager has forecast, determine a production schedule that will meet demand at minimum total cost.

19 *Make-Buy.* A sudden increase in the demand for smoke alarms has left a major supplier of household smoke detectors with insufficient capacity to meet demand. The company has seen monthly demand for its electronic and battery-operated models rise to 20,000 and 10,000, respectively. The relevant quantitative data for the production process are summarized below.

Department	Monthly Hours Available	Hours/Unit (Electronic)	Hours/Unit (Battery)
Fabrication	2000	0.15	0.10
Assembly	4200	0.20	0.20
Shipping	2500	0.10	0.15
Variable cost/unit		$18.00	$16.00
Retail price		$29.50	$28.00

Additional units can be obtained from a subcontractor, who has offered to supply up to 20,000 units per month in any combination of electronic and battery-operated models, at a charge of $21.50 per unit. Determine how the manufacturer should allocate its in-house capacity and how it should utilize the subcontractor in order to meet all demand and maximize total profit.

20 *Financial Planning.* The treasurer of Trefny's department store is performing his financial planning for the next 6 months, September through February. Because of the holiday season Trefny's will need large amounts of cash during October, November, and December, while a large cash inflow is expected after the first of the year when customers pay off their holiday bills. The following table summarizes the predicted net cash flows (in thousands) from operations.

	September	October	November	December	January	February
Surplus	$20	—	—	—	30	150
Deficit	—	30	60	90	—	—

The treasurer has three sources of short-time funds to meet the store's needs. These are

a *Pledge Accounts Receivable.* A local bank will loan Trefny's funds on a month-by-month basis against a pledge on the accounts receivable balance as of the first day of a particular month. The maximum loan is 75% of the balance, and the cost of the loan is 1.5% per month, assessed on the amount borrowed. The predicted balances (in thousands) for the planning period are shown below:

	September	October	November	December	January	February
Balance	$70	50	70	110	100	50

b *Stretch Payment of Purchases.* Payment of all or part of purchases can be delayed 1 month. All bills for purchases come due on the first of the month, but payments can be delayed 1 month. When payments are delayed this way, Trefny's loses the 2% discount it normally receives for prompt payment. The predicted payment schedule (in thousands) is shown below:

	September	October	November	December	January	February
Payment	$80	90	100	60	40	50

c *Take Short-Term Loan.* A bank is willing to loan Trefny's any amount from $40,000 to $100,000 for 6 months, starting September 1. The principal would be paid back at the end of February, and Trefny's would not be permitted to pay off part of the loan, or add to it, during the 6-month period. The cost of the loan is 1% per month, payable at the end of each month.

In any month, excess funds can be transferred to Trefny's short-term investment portfolio, where the funds can earn 0.5% per month.

Determine a plan for the treasurer that will allow him to meet the firm's cash needs at minimum cost.

21 *Portfolio Selection.* The Sargent Insurance Company has developed a list of seven investment alternatives for a 10-year investment horizon. These investments, and their corresponding financial factors, are presented below. In the table, the meaning of the various financial factors is as follows. The length of investment is the expected number of years required for the annual rate of return to be realized taking into account the possibility of reinvestment. The annual rate of return is the expected rate of return over the 10-year investment horizon. The risk coefficient is a subjective, dimensionless estimate representing the portfolio manager's appraisal of the relative safety of each alternative, based on a scale of 10. The growth potential, expressed as a percentage, is again a subjective estimate representing the portfolio manager's appraisal of the potential increase in the value of the investment alternative for the 10-year period.

Investment Alternative	Length of Investment (Years)	Annual Rate of Return (%)	Risk Coefficient	Growth Potential (%)
Treasury bills	4	6	1	0
Common stock	7	15	5	18
Corporate bonds	8	12	4	10
Real estate	6	24	8	32
Growth mutual fund	10	18	6	20
Savings and loan	5	9	3	7

The Sargent Insurance Company wants to maximize the return on its portfolio of investments, subject to the following restrictions on the selection of the portfolio.

The average length of the investment for the portfolio should not exceed 7 years.

The average risk coefficient for the portfolio should not exceed 5.

The average growth potential for the portfolio should be at least 10%.

The investment in real estate should be no more than twice the investment in stocks and bonds.

Determine how the funds should be allocated to investments. What is the optimal return and the corresponding average risk coefficient?

22 *Production Planning.* The Devlin Manufacturing Company produces an item that is subject to wide seasonal fluctuations in sales. The fluctuations in the demand for this product are illustrated by the sales table (below) for the forthcoming year.

January	1,000	July	10,000
February	2,000	August	10,000
March	5,000	September	7,000
April	7,000	October	4,000
May	8,000	November	6,000
June	9,000	December	2,000

The firm must always meet the monthly demand requirements or risk the possibility of losing customers. It can fulfill individual demands either by producing the required amount during the particular month or by producing only part of the required amount and making up the difference by using the overproduction (inventory) from previous months.

There are many different production schedules that the company could consider. For example, it could produce the exact number of units required by the sales forecast for each month. But this would involve a widely fluctuating production pattern that would be costly to maintain because of overtime costs and hiring costs in high-production months, and because of layoff costs (personnel and machinery) during low-production months. Another alternative available to Devlin would be to overproduce in periods of low requirements, store the surplus, and use the excess in periods of high requirements. This would result in a rather stable production pattern, but perhaps a costly one because of the cost of storing the surplus. Such a solution would be most undesirable if it yielded relatively large monthly surpluses. Neither of these extreme cases would be satisfactory to management since its objective is to determine a production schedule that minimizes the sum of the costs due to output fluctuations and to inventories.

The cost accounting department has estimated that on a one-time basis it costs approximately $1.00 to increase output by 1 unit from one month to another and $0.50 to reduce output by 1 unit from one month to another. The monthly cost of storing one unit of product is $0.65. The production schedule for the month of December in the current year calls for the production of 1000 units, and the firm estimates that the inventory level on this January 1 will be 2000 units. Also, it desires to have an inventory level of no more than 2000 units next January 1 as well.

Find an optimal production plan for the 12-month period.

INTERPRETING COMPUTER OUTPUT

23 A manufacturer of office furniture has recently received a number of inquiries about its interest in producing desks, bookcases, and filing cabinets for several new customers. The production process requires essentially three stages: fabrication, painting, and assembly, with several work stations at each stage. An initial contract has already been signed, committing the firm to 250 filing cabinets. A summary of available information is given below.

Item	D	B	F
Maximum demand	1000	600	700
Minimum demand	—	—	250
Profit contribution	$75	$80	$36

Stage/Item	D	B	F	Hours Available
Fabrication	0.1 hrs	0.2	0.5	450
Painting	0.5	0.4	0.2	400
Assembly	0.3	0.2	0.3	600

In order to help understand the allocation decisions at stake, the firm's analyst had developed the LP model shown below (see Exhibit 3.1 for computer output).

maximize

$75x_1 + 80x_2 + 36x_3$

subject to

$$0.1x_1 + 0.2x_2 + 0.5x_3 \leq 450$$
$$0.5x_1 + 0.4x_2 + 0.2x_3 \leq 400$$
$$0.3x_1 + 0.2x_2 + 0.3x_3 \leq 600$$
$$x_1 \leq 1000$$
$$x_2 \leq 600$$
$$x_3 \leq 700$$
$$x_3 \geq 250$$

Consider each of the following questions separately.

a Identify the binding constraints in the optimal solution.

b Suppose that 30 hours of overtime could be scheduled in the plant in order to increase the available hours at one or more of the stages. How should this overtime be utilized most productively?

c What increment to total profit contribution would result if the maximum demand for bookcases could be expanded by 50?

d Suppose that the selling price of bookcases had to be reduced to meet competition. How much of a reduction could be absorbed without altering the allocation?

EXHIBIT 3.1

```
MAX    75 X1 + 80 X2 + 36 X3
SUBJECT TO
   2)    0.1 X1 + 0.2 X2 + 0.5 X3 <= 450
   3)    0.5 X1 + 0.4 X2 + 0.2 X3 <= 400
   4)    0.3 X1 + 0.2 X2 + 0.3 X3 <= 600
```

EXHIBIT 3.1 (*Continued*)

```
  5)    X1 <= 1000
  6)    X2 <= 600
  7)    X3 <= 700
  8)    X3 >= 250
END

   LP OPTIMUM FOUND AT STEP 5

      OBJECTIVE FUNCTION VALUE

   1)    75886.9500

VARIABLE       VALUE      REDUCED COST
   X1        60.869570     .000000
   X2       600.000000     .000000
   X3       647.826000     .000000

      ROW     SLACK OR SURPLUS     DUAL PRICES
      2)          .000000          13.043480
      3)          .000000         147.391300
      4)       267.391300            .000000
      5)       939.130400            .000000
      6)          .000000          18.434780
      7)        52.173950            .000000
      8)       397.826000            .000000

NO. ITERATIONS=     5

   RANGES IN WHICH THE BASIS IS UNCHANGED

              OBJ COEFFICIENT RANGES
VARIABLE     CURRENT      ALLOWABLE     ALLOWABLE
              COEF        INCREASE      DECREASE
   X1       75.000000    15.000000     67.800000
   X2       80.000000    INFINITY      18.434780
   X3       36.000000    70.666660      6.000000

              RIGHTHAND SIDE RANGES
ROW       CURRENT       ALLOWABLE     ALLOWABLE
           RHS          INCREASE      DECREASE
  2      450.000000     24.000020    183.000000
  3      400.000000    432.000000     28.000000
  4      600.000000     INFINITY     267.391300
  5     1000.000000     INFINITY     939.130400
  6      600.000000     87.500000    200.000100
  7      700.000000     INFINITY      52.173950
  8      250.000000    397.826000     INFINITY
```

Chapter 4

THE SIMPLEX METHOD

Sherwood Furniture Company (Revisited)

Recently Sherwood Furniture Company has been interested in developing a new line of stereo speaker cabinets. In the coming month, Sherwood expects to have excess capacity in its Assembly and Finishing departments and would like to experiment with two new models. One model is the Standard, a large, high-quality cabinet in traditional design that can be sold in virtually unlimited quantities to several manufacturers of audio equipment. The other model is the Custom, a small, inexpensive cabinet in a novel design that a single buyer will purchase on an exclusive basis. Under the tentative terms of this agreement, the buyer will purchase as many Customs as Sherwood produces, up to 32 units. The Standard requires 4 hours in the Assembly Department and 8 hours in the Finishing Department, and each unit contributes $20 to gross profit. The Custom requires 3 hours in Assembly and 2 hours in Finishing, and each unit contributes $10 to profit. Current plans call for 120 hours to be available next month in Assembly and 160 hours in Finishing for cabinet production, and Sherwood desires to allocate this capacity in the most economical way.

In the previous chapter we focused on the formulation and computer solution of LP problems. Although we did not present details of the general solution algorithm, our use of the graphical method provided a glimpse of a structured procedure for finding solutions. In this chapter we describe in detail the main steps of the simplex method for solving linear programs.

ALGEBRAIC ELEMENTS OF LINEAR PROGRAMMING

The standard form of an LP problem, which we presented earlier, involves maximizing the objective function subject to a set of upper-bound constraints together with nonnegativity conditions on the decision variables. Using summation notation, we write the standard form as

maximize

$$z = \sum_{j=1}^{n} c_j x_j$$

subject to

$$\sum_{j=1}^{n} a_{ij} x_j \leq b_i \qquad (i = 1, 2, \ldots, m)$$

$$x_j \geq 0$$

When analyzing LP problems it is generally more convenient to work with equations than with inequalities. This is because the mathematics involving systems of equations is relatively powerful and easily understood. To illustrate the use of equations we return to the original Sherwood Furniture example, which we solved by the graphical technique in the previous chapter. In each constraint we insert a new variable and create an equation so that the problem statement becomes

maximize

$$z = 20x_1 + 10x_2 + 0x_3 + 0x_4 + 0x_5$$

subject to

$$
\begin{aligned}
4x_1 + 3x_2 + x_3 &&&= 120 \\
8x_1 + 2x_2 &&+ x_4 &= 160 \\
x_2 &&+ x_5 &= 32 \\
\end{aligned}
$$

$$x_1 \geq 0 \quad x_2 \geq 0 \quad x_3 \geq 0 \quad x_4 \geq 0 \quad x_5 \geq 0$$

(4.1)

The new variables x_3, x_4, and x_5 are **slack** variables. For example, x_3 represents the number of unallocated assembly hours under a particular choice of decision variables x_1 and x_2. Similarly, x_4 and x_5 represent slack quantities in the Finishing and Market constraints, respectively. In addition, we can include the slack variables in the objective function with 0 coefficients, as shown above, because they do not affect the objective function directly.

In general the standard form becomes

maximize

$$z = \sum_{j=1}^{n} c_j x_j + \sum_{i=1}^{m} 0 x_{n+i}$$

subject to

$$\sum_{j=1}^{n} a_{ij} x_j + x_{n+i} = b_i \qquad (i = 1, 2, \ldots, m) \tag{4.2}$$

$$x_j \geq 0 \qquad \text{and} \qquad x_{n+i} \geq 0 \qquad (i = 1, 2, \ldots, m; j = 1, 2, \ldots, n)$$

In this form the linear program contains n original variables $(x_1, x_2, \ldots, x_n)$ and m slack variables $(x_{n+1}, x_{n+2}, \ldots, x_{n+m})$. The constraints are essentially a system of m equations in $m + n$ (nonnegative) unknowns. From the theory of simultaneous equations we know that such a system can potentially have an infinite number of solutions. Among these solutions, we seek a feasible solution (one in which all variables are nonnegative) that maximizes the value of the objective function.

We can exploit most effectively the theory of solving simultaneous equations by working with m independent equations in m unknowns, a system that will have a unique solution. Therefore, our approach will be to treat n of the variables as constants rather than as unknowns. This will leave a system of m equations and m unknowns to be solved and analyzed.

When we solve a system of m independent equations in $m + n$ unknowns for the unique values of m of the variables (in terms of the remaining n, which are constants), we call these m variables **basic** variables. Furthermore, if we set the remaining n nonbasic variables to 0 and the resulting values of the basic variables are nonnegative, then they constitute what we call a **basic feasible solution**, since all of the variables satisfy the problem's original constraints. These concepts are important because the simplex method for solving LP problems involves the systematic evaluation of basic feasible solutions.

When solving a problem by the simplex method it is convenient to express the problem in **canonical form**. We say that the LP problem is in canonical form with respect to a given set of basic variables when the objective function is expressed as an equation and when

1. Each basic variable appears in only one constraint equation and appears with a coefficient of 1.
2. Each constraint equation contains one basic variable.
3. Each basic variable has a 0 coefficient in the objective function.

To illustrate this definition let us reconstruct the Sherwood Furniture objective function in (4.1) to read

$$z - 20x_1 - 10x_2 = 0$$

As it happens, the rest of the constraint equations are in canonical form with respect to the set of basic variables $\{x_3, x_4, x_5\}$, for we can verify the three conditions of canonical form in the problem statement below:

maximize

$$z - 20x_1 - 10x_2 + 0x_3 + 0x_4 + 0x_5 = 0 \qquad\qquad \text{(R0)}$$

subject to

$$
\begin{aligned}
4x_1 + \ 3x_2 + \ x_3 \qquad\qquad\ &= 120 &\text{(R1)}\\
8x_1 + \ 2x_2 \qquad + \ x_4 \qquad\ &= 160 &\text{(R2)}\\
x_2 \qquad\qquad + \ x_5 &= \ 32 &\text{(R3)}
\end{aligned}
$$

We omit the explicit listing of nonnegativity conditions, as these will always be implicit whenever we use canonical form.

Canonical form has certain advantages for solving LP problems. First, it permits us to find the details of a basic feasible solution by inspection. For the system of equations (R0) to (R3) above, notice that when we set the nonbasic variables x_1 and x_2 equal to 0, we see that the values of the remaining variables and the value of the objective function are

$$x_3 = 120 \qquad x_4 = 160 \qquad x_5 = 32 \qquad \text{and} \qquad z = 0$$

Thus the right-hand-side constants of the canonical form equations represent the value of the objective function and the values of the basic variables. The basic solution is feasible (and the values of the original variables satisfy the original constraints) as long as the right-hand-side constants in the equations are nonnegative.

A second advantage of canonical form is that it shows whether we can improve the objective function by increasing any of the nonbasic variables from 0 to a positive value. By inspecting (R0), for example, we can see that z will increase if we increase either x_1 or x_2, because both variables have negative coefficients and (R0) remains an equation.

A third advantage of canonical form is that we can specify a complete solution to the constraint equations for any set of values assigned to the nonbasic variables. In the example problem, we determine this solution by rewriting (R1) to (R3) with only the basic variables on the left-hand side, as follows:

$$x_3 = 120 - 4x_1 - 3x_2$$
$$x_4 = 160 - 8x_1 - 2x_2$$
$$x_5 = 32 - x_2$$

For any set of values assigned to the nonbasic variables, we simply substitute on the right-hand side to compute the values of the basic variables that complete the solution.

To summarize, when we view an LP problem in canonical form we are quickly able to (1) specify the corresponding basic feasible solution, (2) evaluate the potential for improvement in the objective function from increasing a non-basic variable, and (3) trace the effect on the basic variables of increasing the value of a nonbasic variable. If, as a result of such an evaluation, we decide that it is desirable to examine a different set of basic variables, we need to be able to produce the canonical form with respect to this new set.

Construction of a new canonical form requires that we look at the same equations in a different format. In this new format the set of equations must be *equivalent* to the original equations in the sense that any solution to the new set is a solution to the original set, and vice versa. We carry out the transformation of one set of equations to another, equivalent set by means of **elementary row operations.** Two types of elementary row operations are permissible:

1. Transform an equation by multiplying it by a constant.
2. Transform an equation by adding to it a multiple of another equation.

In order to illustrate such transformations, suppose that we specify the **basis** (i.e., the set of basic variables) in the Sherwood Furniture example to be $\{x_2, x_3, x_4\}$. The system of equations (R0) to (R3) does not yet meet the definition of canonical form with respect to this basis because the basic variable x_2 appears in more than one equation and also has a nonzero coefficient in the objective function. Variables x_3 and x_4, however, satisfy the requirements for canonical form. Therefore, it seems appropriate to eliminate x_2 from equations (R0), (R1), and (R2). For instance, we can eliminate the variable x_2 from (R2) by subtracting two times (R3) from (R2) and replacing (R2) with the result. If we denote the replacement equation by (R2'), we obtain

$$(R2') = (R2) - 2(R3)$$

or

$$8x_1 + x_4 - 2x_5 = 96$$

We can then obtain the canonical form we seek by eliminating x_2 from (R0) and (R1), yielding the following system of equations:

maximize

$$z - 20x_1 + 0x_2 + 0x_3 + 0x_4 + 10x_5 = 320 \ (R0') = (R0) + 10(R3)$$

subject to

$$4x_1 \qquad + \; x_3 \qquad - \quad 3x_5 = \quad 24 \; (R1') = (R1) - \; 3(R3)$$
$$8x_1 \qquad\qquad\quad + \; x_4 - \; 2x_5 = \quad 96 \; (R2') = (R2) - \; 2(R3)$$
$$x_2 \qquad\qquad\quad + \quad x_5 = \quad 32 \; (R3') = (R3)$$

Now if we set the nonbasic variables x_1 and x_5 equal to 0, the system of equations yields

$$x_2 = 32 \qquad x_3 = 24 \qquad x_4 = 96 \qquad \text{and} \qquad z = 320$$

This is another basic feasible solution, and obviously one with a better profit contribution than the previous solution.

In order to see the relationship between the graphical approach and the algebraic approach to LP problems, refer to Figure 4.1 and notice that extreme points on the graph of the feasible region are basic feasible solutions. In particular, each boundary line in the feasible region of the graph corresponds to setting $x_j = 0$, where x_j is one of the variables that appear in the canonical form of the problem. In the Sherwood Furniture example the relationships are as follows:

Variable	Boundary Line
$x_1 = 0$	Vertical (x_2) axis
$x_2 = 0$	Horizontal (x_1) axis

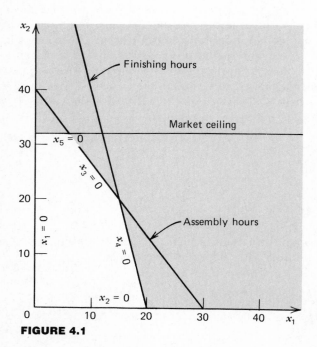

FIGURE 4.1

$x_3 = 0$ Equation for Assembly hours constraint

$x_4 = 0$ Equation for Finishing hours constraint

$x_5 = 0$ Equation for Market ceiling

At each extreme point on the graph a pair of boundary lines meet; at this point two variables are equal to 0. Canonical form then reduces to three equations in three unknowns, and the solution of this system of equations will yield the values of the basic variables.

The process of eliminating one basic variable in favor of a nonbasic variable, while maintaining feasibility, has been illustrated above by interchanging the roles of x_2 and x_5 in the example. This interchange of one basic variable and one nonbasic variable constructs a neighboring extreme point. In effect, we keep one of the nonbasic variables at 0 (i.e., we maintain one of the boundary lines) while we replace the other nonbasic variable in the process of interchange (i.e., a different boundary line accounts for the intersection). In Figure 4.1, the interchange allowed us to move along the vertical axis, from the point $(x_1 = 0, x_2 = 0)$ to the point $(x_1 = 0, x_2 = 32)$. The algebraic approach thus provides a different perspective on the graphical solution procedure. However, since the algebraic approach adapts easily to several variables, it provides the more useful context for developing a general solution technique. In the next section we study the essential steps in this technique.

THE SIMPLEX ALGORITHM

The heart of the simplex algorithm is based on two conclusions from the theory of linear programming, which we mentioned in conjunction with the graphical solution method. We restate these results below and then formalize them in the discussion that follows.

Property 1
Whenever an optimal solution to an LP problem exists, at least one optimum will occur at an extreme point. (Therefore, in searching for an optimum, a procedure need examine only basic feasible solutions.)

Property 2
An extreme point is optimal if no improvement potential exists at any of its neighboring extreme points. (Therefore, in searching for an optimum, a procedure need evaluate only neighbors of a basic feasible solution in order to determine whether to continue the search.)

When we express a problem in canonical form, we can determine the potential for improvement by examining the coefficients in the objective function equation. In the original canonical form for the Sherwood Furniture example, the objective function was

$$z - 20x_1 - 10x_2 = 0$$

Evidently, if we could increase the value of x_1 (x_1 is 0 at this point), then we would also increase z; the same conclusion holds for x_2. In general, for a *maximization* problem a *negative* objective equation coefficient indicates that we can obtain an improvement by increasing the value of the corresponding variable. Consequently, in a maximization problem, any basic feasible solution in which all objective function coefficients are nonnegative must be an optimal solution.

In the example problem, negative coefficients in the objective function indicate the potential for improvement. In particular, the value of the objective function will increase by 20 for each unit increase in x_1 and by 10 for each unit increase in x_2. When we are faced with alternative ways of improving a solution, our rule of thumb will be to work with the variable having the largest coefficient (in this case, x_1). Now a greater increase in x_1 is more desirable at this stage than a smaller increase, so one question is: How large can x_1 become? To answer this question we must examine the equations of canonical form (4.1), rewritten as follows:

$$x_3 = 120 - 4x_1 - 3x_2$$
$$x_4 = 160 - 8x_1 - 2x_2 \tag{4.3}$$
$$x_5 = 32 - x_2$$

Because x_2 remains a nonbasic variable, its value stays at 0. As we increase x_1, however, we must keep in mind the requirement that all variables remain nonnegative. Thus, the equations in (4.3) imply

$$x_3 = 120 - 4x_1 \geq 0$$
$$x_4 = 160 - 8x_1 \geq 0$$
$$x_5 = 32$$

The requirement that x_3 and x_4 remain nonnegative gives rise to inequalities on x_1 as follows:

$$x_1 \leq \frac{120}{4} \text{ or } x_1 \leq 30$$

$$x_1 \leq \frac{160}{8} \text{ or } x_1 \leq 20$$

The second of these is the tighter of the constraints on x_1 and dictates its new value. We conclude that we can increase x_1 up to 20, at which point we will have reduced x_4 to 0. At this limit, x_1 and x_4 will also have changed roles: x_1 will become positive (basic) and x_4 will become 0 (nonbasic). For this reason, x_1 is called the **entering** variable and x_4 is the **leaving** variable, in the formation of the new basis $\{x_1, x_3, x_5\}$.

The next step is to construct a revised canonical form, with respect to the new basis. This step can be accomplished using the elimination method described in the previous section, in which we form a new equation by subtracting from the original a multiple of another equation. Because x_3 and x_5 already appear in only one equation and with a coefficient of 1, the elimination process must rewrite the equations so that x_1 appears only in (R2) (the equation currently associated with x_4) with a coefficient of 1. This equation, in which the entering and leaving variables both appear, is called the **pivot** equation. We can put it into the desired form by dividing by the coefficient of the entering variable. In the example, since x_1 has a coefficient of 8, we divide (R2) by 8. The result is

$$x_1 + \tfrac{1}{4}x_2 + \tfrac{1}{8}x_4 + 20 \qquad\qquad\qquad\text{(R2')}$$

We revise the other equations to eliminate x_1 by adding or subtracting a suitable multiple of (R2'). The revised canonical form is

$$
\begin{aligned}
z \quad - 5x_2 \quad\;\; + \tfrac{5}{2}x_4 &= 400 \;\; \text{(R0')} = \text{(R0)} + 20\text{(R2')} \\
2x_2 + x_3 - \tfrac{1}{2}x_4 &= \;\;40 \;\; \text{(R1')} = \text{(R1)} - 4\text{(R2')} \\
x_1 + \tfrac{1}{4}x_2 \quad\;\; + \tfrac{1}{8}x_4 &= \;\;20 \;\; \text{(R2')} = \tfrac{1}{8}\text{(R2)} \\
x_2 \quad\quad\quad\;\; + x_5 &= \;\;32 \;\; \text{(R3')} = \text{(R3)}
\end{aligned}
$$

This canonical form allows us to evaluate the solution corresponding to the basis $\{x_1, x_3, x_5\}$ to see whether we can make any further improvements.

A more general description of the procedure is given as Algorithm 4.1, which summarizes the process just illustrated. The notation follows the general canonical form represented by (4.2), with primes to denote values obtained after conversion to the new basis.

Continuing with the Sherwood Furniture example, we follow the same steps with respect to the basis $\{x_1, x_3, x_5\}$ and the canonical form given above. At Step I2, we identify the variable x_2 as the entering variable (i.e., $k = 2$) since $c_j < 0$ only for $j = 2$. At Step F2, the three ratios are 20, 80, and 32; and we identify x_3 as the leaving variable (i.e., $r = 1$). The new basis will therefore be $\{x_1, x_2, x_5\}$, and we derive the corresponding canonical form in Steps E1 and E2:

$$
\begin{aligned}
z \quad\;\; + \tfrac{5}{2}x_3 + \tfrac{5}{4}x_4 &= 500 \;\; \text{(R0')} = \text{(R0')} + 5\text{(R1')} \\
x_2 + \tfrac{1}{2}x_3 - \tfrac{1}{4}x_4 &= \;\;20 \;\; \text{(R1')} = \tfrac{1}{2}\text{(R1)} \\
x_1 - \tfrac{1}{8}x_3 + \tfrac{3}{16}x_4 &= \;\;15 \;\; \text{(R2')} = \text{(R2)} - \tfrac{1}{4}\text{(R1')} \\
- \tfrac{1}{2}x_3 + \tfrac{1}{4}x_4 + x_5 &= \;\;12 \;\; \text{(R3')} = \text{(R3)} - \text{(R1')}
\end{aligned}
$$

Upon returning to Step I1 we find that no improvement potential exists because all objective function coefficients are nonnegative. To interpret the final canonical form, we set the nonbasic variables x_3 and x_4 equal to 0, yielding

$$x_1^* = 15 \qquad x_2^* = 20 \qquad x_5^* = 12 \qquad z^* = 500$$

where the (*) notation designates the optimal values.

Looking back at the basic feasible solutions we have encountered, and referring to Figure 4.1, we can see that we began at the origin ($x_1 = 0$, $x_2 = 0$) and moved to a neighboring extreme point ($x_1 = 20$, $x_2 = 0$) with our first improvement. Then we moved to a new neighboring extreme point ($x_1 = 15$, $x_2 = 20$) when we discovered improvement potential still existed. At this point we stopped, because no further improvement was possible.

ALGORITHM 4.1
Steps in the Simplex Algorithm for Maximization (A basic feasible solution is assumed to be available at the outset.)

A. IMPROVEMENT

I1 Examine the objective function coefficients. If all coefficients are nonnegative then stop: The current solution is optimal.

I2 Otherwise choose the (nonbasic) variable corresponding to the objective function coefficient that is most negative as the entering variable. Let k denote the index of this variable, that is,

$$c_k = \min_j \{c_j | c_j < 0\}$$

B. FEASIBILITY

F1 Identify the equations containing positive coefficients for the entering variable ($a_{ik} > 0$).

F2 For each of these equations calculated the ratio b_i/a_{ik} and find the equation that yields the minimum ratio. The basic variable in this equation becomes the leaving variable. Let r denote the equation in which this variable appears, that is,

$$\frac{b_r}{a_{rk}} = \min_i \left\{ \frac{b_i}{a_{rk}} \middle| a_{ik} > 0 \right\}$$

C. ELIMINATION

E1 Divide the pivot equation by a_{rk}. Thus

$$a'_{rj} = \frac{a_{rj}}{a_{rk}} \qquad \text{and} \qquad b'_{rj} = \frac{b_r}{a_{rk}}$$

E2 Eliminate x_k from the other equations including the objective function. Thus for $i \neq$

$$a'_{ij} = a_{ij} - a_{ik} a'_{rj} \text{ and } b'_i = b_i - a_{ik} b'_r$$

E3 A new basis and a new canonical form has been created. Return to Step I1.

The evaluation and improvement cycle in Algorithm 4.1, in which we replace a basic feasible solution by a better neighbor, is called a **pivot step,** or sometimes a **simplex iteration.** The Improvement steps check for optimality, but if improvement potential exists a rule of thumb is used to select the entering variable. This selection provides the largest possible increase in the objective function per unit increase in the entering variable. The Feasibility steps determine how large a value we can give to the entering variable without violating feasibility. Finally, the Elimination steps construct the canonical form for the neighboring basic feasible solution.

We mention in passing that the rule of thumb used in selecting an entering variable does not guarantee that the *total* increase in the objective function will be as large as possible at each iteration. In practice, however, the choice of an entering variable to make the *unit* increase as large as possible tends to minimize the number of iterations required to reach an optimal solution.

The steps in Algorithm 4.1 will find optimal solutions to LP problems, provided there is a convenient way to initiate the algorithm with a starting basic feasible solution. We discuss this initiation step and some additional aspects of the procedure more fully in the next section.

We should make one final observation about the effect of a sucession of pivot steps on the original canonical form. A single iteration adds to each equation a multiple of the pivot equation. Therefore, a sequence of iterations adds to each original equation a multiple (possibly 0) of every equation. Although the specific multiples involved will be significant later when we examine more advanced topics, it is enough at this point to think of the pivot step as a technique for restating the original equations in a way that clarifies how improvements can be made. In this fashion, the simplex method systematically finds improvements until it identifies the best solution. At that stage, the simplex method has changed each original equation only by adding to it multiples of all the other equations.

SPECIAL SITUATIONS IN THE SIMPLEX ALGORITHM

The example problem used in the previous section to illustrate the execution of the simplex method may have been deceptively simple. Certain variations may occur during the solution of LP problems that prevent us from implementing the simplex algorithm exactly as we illustrated it in the example. In this section we deal with those variations, and we show how to adapt the algorithm appropriately. Thus, we provide the capability to solve any small LP problem by hand.

MINIMIZATION

In order to solve an LP problem in which the objective is minimization, one possible approach is to multiply the coefficients in the objective function by -1 and then maximize. However, we can take a more direct approach by appropriately modifying the conditions for improvement. As indicated in Algorithm 4.1, the signal for improvement potential in a maximization problem is a negative coefficient in the objective function equation. In a *minimization* problem the opposite is true: The signal for improvement potential is a *positive* coefficient in the objective function equation. Similarly, when all coefficients in the objective function equation are 0 or negative in a minimization problem, the corresponding solution is optimal. To solve a minimization problem, we adapt our solution algorithm by modifying only the improvement steps. In the case when several coefficients in the objective function equation are positive, the rule of thumb for selecting an entering variable is to choose the variable with the largest positive coefficient.

ALTERNATE OPTIMA

As suggested by the discussion of graphical methods in LP problems, it is possible for more than one basic feasible solution to be optimal. The signal for this condition is that a nonbasic variable in an optimal solution has a 0 coefficient in the objective function equation. For example, if the original objective function in the Sherwood Furniture example were $z = 16x_1 + 12x_2$, one optimal basis would be $\{x_1, x_2, x_5\}$, corresponding to the point ($x_1 = 15$, $x_2 = 20$) and to the following canonical form

$$
\begin{aligned}
z \quad + 3x_3 \qquad\qquad\qquad &= 480 \\
x_2 + \tfrac{1}{2}x_3 - \tfrac{1}{4}x_4 \qquad &= 20 \\
x_1 \quad - \tfrac{1}{8}x_3 + \tfrac{3}{16}x_4 \qquad &= 15 \\
- \tfrac{1}{2}x_3 + \tfrac{1}{4}x_4 + x_5 &= 12
\end{aligned}
$$

The 0 coefficient in the objective function equation for the nonbasic variable x_4 signals the condition for alternate optima. This condition indicates that we could treat x_4 as the entering variable with no increase or decrease in the value of the objective function. Steps F1 and F2 of the simplex algorithm reveal that it is possible to increase x_4 up to 48 without jeopardizing feasibility. Because x_3 remains nonbasic, the corresponding changes in the original variables then become

$$
\begin{aligned}
x_1 &= 15 - \tfrac{3}{16}x_4 \\
x_2 &= 20 + \tfrac{1}{4}x_4
\end{aligned}
\tag{4.4}
$$

When x_4 reaches its upper limit of 48, the point on the graph moves to

$(x_1 = 6, x_2 = 32)$ and the corresponding canonical form becomes

$$
\begin{aligned}
z && + 3x_3 && && &&= 480 \\
&& x_2 && && + x_5 &&= 32 \\
x_1 && + \tfrac{1}{4}x_3 && && - \tfrac{3}{4}x_5 &&= 6 \\
&& - 2x_3 && + x_4 &&+ 4x_5 &&= 48
\end{aligned}
$$

In between these extreme points, the locus of optimal points described in (4.4) is part of the straight-line segment between (15, 20) and (6, 32) as sketched in Figure 4.2. Because there are an infinite number of possible values of x_4 in the interval $0 \leq x_4 \leq 48$, there are correspondingly an infinite number of optimal solutions (x_1, x_2) as given by (4.4).

DEGENERACY

A basic feasible solution is degenerate if one or more of the basic variables has a value of 0. This situation may arise at intermediate pivot steps as well as in the optimal solution. The simplex algorithm will usually proceed without difficulty at intermediate pivot steps as long as the basic variables are not treated as nonbasic.

One additional theoretical consideration arises in this situation. At a simplex

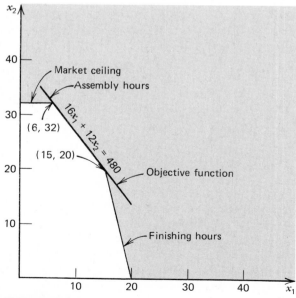

FIGURE 4.2

iteration, if the leaving variable has a value of 0 then the entering variable will also be 0 in the new basis. The effect of such a pivot step would be to interchange the roles of the entering and leaving variable without altering the value of the objective function. In theory, a succession of such interchanges could occur, eventually leading back to the basis at which degeneracy first arose. The simplex algorithm would then cycle indefinitely, repeating the same sequence of interchanges. However, sophisticated modifications of the simplex method will prevent cycling. Perhaps more significantly, instances of cycling in practical LP solutions appear to be quite rare; therefore, the problem of potential cycling should not create much concern in practical applications of the simplex method.

ARTIFICIAL VARIABLES

For LP problems in which every constraint is an upper-bound constraint, there is seldom any difficulty in finding an initial basic feasible solution. When we add one slack variable to each constraint, the full set of slack variables forms a convenient, feasible set of basic variables, provided the right-hand side of the inequality is a nonnegative constant. However, when the constraint constant is negative, or when other kinds of original constraints are involved, the starting steps are not so straightforward.

In order to illustrate a fool-proof method of starting, consider the following maximization problem:

maximize

$$8x_1 + 4x_2$$

subject to

$$3x_1 + 2x_2 \leq 48$$
$$x_1 \qquad \geq 10$$
$$x_2 \geq 6$$
$$x_1 \geq 0 \qquad x_2 \geq 0$$

This LP model could represent an allocation problem involving two products competing for a single limited-capacity resource. Each box of the first product consumes three units of capacity and contributes \$8 to profit, and each box of the second product consumes two units of capacity and contributes \$4 to profit. Delivery commitments already call for 10 boxes of product 1 and 6 boxes of product 2, but additional boxes can be sold if more can be produced from the 48 units of capacity that are available.

The first constraint in this model is an upper-bound inequality, and we can transform it into an equation in the usual way by adding a slack variable. The second constraint is a lower-bound inequality, and here our approach is to insert a **surplus** variable in order to form an equation. We insert another surplus variable in the third constraint; and, with z again denoting the value of the objective function, our model becomes

maximize

$$z - 8x_1 - 4x_2 \qquad = 0$$

subject to

$$
\begin{aligned}
3x_1 + 2x_2 + x_3 \quad &= 48 \\
x_1 \qquad\qquad - x_4 \quad &= 10 \\
x_2 \qquad - x_5 &= 6
\end{aligned}
\qquad (4.5)
$$

In this system of equations, x_3 denotes the unused amount of capacity. The surplus variable x_4 measures the amount by which the quantity of product 1 exceeds the delivery commitment of 10 boxes. Similarly, the surplus variable x_5 measures the excess product-2 quantity above its own delivery commitment of six boxes. As usual, all five variables are required to be nonnegative.

The system of equations (4.5) is not in canonical form. If we want to create canonical form with respect to the set of slack and surplus variables $\{x_3, x_4, x_5\}$ then we must multiply the last two constraint equations by -1, since this modification will at least provide us with one basic variable in each constraint equation with a coefficient of $+1$, as required by the definition of canonical form. However, once we multiply by -1 the constraint constants become negative. Thus, we are unable to form a *feasible* solution with the basic set $\{x_3, x_4, x_5\}$. This means we are unable to get started with Algorithm 4.1 because it requires that we begin with a feasible basic solution. In principle, one way to deal with this situation is to search by trial and error for a basic solution without negative variables. A more systematic approach, which we will describe below, is to use **artificial** variables.

To form a convenient basic feasible solution, we would like to have had slack variables in the equations of (4.5), or at least one variable in each equation having a coefficient of $+1$ and appearing in no other equation. Suppose we insert such a variable (x_6) in the second constraint equation. The equation becomes

$$x_1 - x_4 + x_6 = 10$$

The nonnegativity requirement on x_6 is equivalent to the requirement that $x_1 - x_4 \le 10$, which does not convey the information in our original constraint. In fact, the only value of x_6 that preserves the information originally in the constraint is the value $x_6 = 0$. Here lies the key to our approach. We shall add x_6 temporarily, only as an aid to starting the algorithm. In addition, we shall make certain that x_6 is forced to equal 0 in the optimal solution to our problem, thus ensuring feasibility. Similarly, we shall add another variable (x_7) to the third constraint equation and make certain that it, too, is driven to 0 in the optimal solution. At this point our model takes the following form:

maximize

$$z - 8x_1 - 4x_2 = 0$$

subject to

$$3x_1 + 2x_2 + x_3 = 48$$
$$x_1 - x_4 + x_6 = 10$$
$$x_2 - x_5 + x_7 = 6$$

The next step is to think of our solution procedure as having two phases. The purpose of Phase I is to force our artificial variables (x_6 and x_7) to take on values of 0. At the end of Phase I we shall have a basic feasible solution; the purpose of Phase II is to proceed from that point to an optimal solution.

In order to implement Phase I we simply adopt a new objective: minimizing the sum of the artificial variables. In symbols, our criterion for minimization is $x_6 + x_7$, and when this sum is reduced to 0 we shall know that Phase I has been completed. Now our model takes the following form:

minimize

$$v - x_6 - x_7 = 0$$

maximize

$$z - 8x_1 - 4x_2 = 0$$

subject to

$$3x_1 + 2x_2 + x_3 = 48$$
$$x_1 - x_4 + x_6 = 10$$
$$x_2 - x_5 + x_7 = 6$$

Our model contains two objective functions, one denoted v for Phase I, and the other denoted z (as usual) for Phase II. In Phase I we shall use only v as an objective function and apply the optimality check for minimization. At this stage we can observe that our Phase I objective function is not yet in canonical form with respect to the basic set $\{x_3, x_6, x_7\}$. We must add each of the last two constraint equations to the first objective function to give us canonical form:

minimize

$$v + x_1 + x_2 \qquad - x_4 - x_5 \qquad = 16$$

maximize

$$z - 8x_1 - 4x_2 \qquad\qquad\qquad = 0$$

subject to

$$3x_1 + 2x_2 + x_3 \qquad\qquad\qquad = 48$$
$$x_1 \qquad\qquad - x_4 \qquad + x_6 \qquad = 10$$
$$x_2 \qquad\qquad - x_5 \qquad + x_7 = 6$$

Now we can begin Phase I, using v as an objective function and using the simplex algorithm, adapted for minimization. Following the Improvement steps in Algorithm 4.1, we find that the objective function coefficients are nonoptimal for x_1 and x_2. Furthermore, these two coefficients are equal, and our rule of thumb allows us to break such ties arbitrarily. Suppose we choose x_1 to be the entering variable. Then x_6 becomes the leaving variable, and the Elimination steps yield the next canonical form:

minimize

$$v + x_2 \qquad\qquad - x_5 - x_6 \qquad = 6$$

maximize

$$z - 4x_2 \qquad - 8x_4 \qquad + 8x_6 \qquad = 80$$

subject to

$$2x_2 + x_3 + 3x_4 \qquad - 3x_6 \qquad = 18$$
$$x_1 \qquad\qquad - x_4 \qquad + x_6 \qquad = 10$$
$$x_2 \qquad\qquad - x_5 \qquad + x_7 = 6$$

The v function is still not optimal, and in the next pivot step x_2 becomes the entering variable and x_7 the leaving variable. Thus the next canonical form is the following:

minimize

$$v \qquad\qquad\qquad - x_6 - x_7 = \quad 0$$

maximize

$$z \qquad - 8x_4 - 4x_5 + 8x_6 + 4x_7 = 104$$

subject to

$$x_3 + 3x_4 + 2x_5 - 3x_6 + 2x_7 = \quad 6 \qquad\qquad (4.6)$$
$$x_1 \quad - x_4 \qquad + x_6 \qquad\qquad = 10$$
$$x_2 \qquad - x_5 \qquad\qquad\qquad = \quad 6$$

We can make a number of observations about the system of equations in (4.6). First, v has been minimized: The optimality conditions are satisfied in the first objective function, and the optimal value of $x_6 + x_7$ is 0. Therefore, Phase I is complete. Notice that in (4.6) we have constructed a basic feasible solution:

$$x_1 = 10 \qquad x_2 = 6 \qquad x_3 = 6$$

The artificial variables have served their purpose by directing the simplex method to a basic feasible solution. We might have eventually discovered this same solution by a trial-and-error search, but such a search might have been very time-consuming.

At the completion of Phase I we can ignore the first objective function, v, and we can also delete the artificial variables from our model. Neither the Phase I objective function nor the artificial variables are necessary to find an optimum in Phase II; however, it also does no harm to maintain the full model in each of the simplex iterations of Phase II. We simply focus on the second objective function, z, and use the appropriate optimality conditions (for maximization, in this example) as we proceed.

To summarize, artificial variables provide a general device for systematically finding an initial basic feasible solution. They can be introduced when the use of slack or surplus variables in the initial basic set would lead to an infeasibility. In addition, they can be inserted into equality constraints, where no slack or surplus variables are permitted.

INFEASIBLE AND UNBOUNDED PROBLEMS

Another advantage of the method of artificial variables is that it provides a systematic test for feasibility. If Phase I cannot drive all artificial variables to 0, then no basic feasible solution can exist. Computer codes for the simplex method thus make a check at the end of Phase I, when v has been minimized. If some artificial variable remains positive (or, equivalently, if the optimal value of v is positive) then the constraints are inconsistent, and the program prints a message that the formulation is infeasible.

Returning to the canonical form (4.6) we find that improvement potential still exists, and our rule of thumb identifies x_4 as the next entering variable. In Algorithm 4.1, Step F1 requires that we examine ratios b_i/a_{i4} only for $a_{i4} > 0$. Now we can see why this restriction applies. Because any positive value of x_4 will improve the value of the objective function, its entry into the basis at a positive amount is limited only by the requirement of feasibility for the other variables. Note what happens in the equations where a_{i4} is not positive. From the second constraint equation we obtain

$$x_1 - x_4 = 10$$

or

$$x_1 = 10 + x_4 \geq 0$$

Here we do not jeopardize the nonnegativity constraint on x_1 by increasing x_4, since x_1 will increase by a like amount. From the third constraint equation we obtain

$$x_2 - x_5 = 6$$

or

$$x_2 = 6$$

Here we can ignore x_5, since it is nonbasic. Clearly the value of x_2 is unaffected by increasing x_4, so again nonnegativity is not jeopardized. Only in the first constraint is the preservation of nonnegativity (for x_3) an issue, and the limit on x_4 is $b_1/a_{14} = 2$. Therefore, the neighboring extreme point at which improvement occurs corresponds to the basic set $\{x_1, x_2, x_4\}$. (This extreme point happens to be optimal.)

Consider what happens if we choose an entering variable x_k and there is no $a_{ik} > 0$. This condition indicates that it is possible to increase x_k indefinitely without jeopardizing feasibility at all. Because the choice of x_k as the entering variable depends only on the sign of its objective function coefficient c_k, it follows that we can increase the value of the objective function without limit. Such a condition therefore signifies an unbounded problem. Computer codes for the simplex method thus make a check during Step F1 to see whether all the coefficients in the entering column are nonpositive. If so, the program prints out a message that the formulation is unbounded.

To summarize, we have seen that the simplex method can deal not only with "well-behaved" formulations, but also with inconsistent or unbounded formulations in the natural execution of a series of pivot steps.

THE SIMPLEX TABLEAU

After using the simplex algorithm along with canonical form to represent LP problems, it becomes evident that it is possible to display the essential information in each step more compactly than in canonical form. The simplex **tableau** is a compact representation, in tabular form, of the relevant information in an LP problem. The tableau contains the coefficients and constants that appear in canonical form. The top row of the tableau corresponds to the objective function, R0, and the last column corresponds to the right-hand side of the canonical form equations. The general structure of the tableau is shown in Table 4.1, in which we assume that the formulation has m constraints, n original variables (x_1 through x_n), and t additional variables (x_{n+1} through x_{n+t}). We have seen that the number of additional variables (slack, surplus, or artificial) may be greater than the number of constraints; hence $t \geq m$.

In Table 4.2 we illustrate the use of a tableau for displaying the results of applying the simplex algorithm to the Sherwood Furniture problem. In Step I1 we scan the top row for negative values of the coefficients c_j in the objective function equation. In Step I2, we choose x_1 as the entering variable. In Steps F1 and F2 we identify equation (R2) as the pivot row and circle the coefficient a_{12} of the entering variable in the pivot row.

The necessary information is now available to construct the tableau corresponding to the new basis, and we write this tableau just below the initial tableau in Table 4.2. We can use the elimination procedure described earlier to derive the entries in the new tableau, or we can calculate them directly by the pivot formulas reproduced below. Here, unprimed values denote values in the old tableau (not necessarily the initial tableau) and primes denote values in the new tableau, as a result of the pivot step:

pivot row ($i = r$):

$$a'_{rj} = \frac{a_{rj}}{a_{rk}}$$

TABLE 4.1 The Simplex Tableau

x_1	x_2	—	x_{n+t}		
$-c_1$	$-c_2$	—	$-c_{n+t}$	z	R0
a_{11}	a_{12}	—	$a_{1,n+t}$	b_1	R1
a_{21}	a_{22}	—	$a_{2,n+t}$	b_2	R2
.	.		.		.
.	.		.		.
.	.		.		.
a_{m1}	a_{m2}	—	$a_{m,n+t}$	b_m	Rm

TABLE 4.2 Tableau Solution of the Example Problem

	x_1	x_2	x_3	x_4	x_5		
	-20	-10	0	0	0	0	R0
Tableau 1	4	3	1	0	0	120	R1
	⑧	2	0	1	0	160	R2
	0	1	0	0	1	32	R3
	0	-5	0	$\frac{5}{2}$	0	400	R0
Tableau 2	0	②	1	$-\frac{1}{2}$	0	40	R1
	1	$\frac{1}{4}$	0	$\frac{1}{8}$	0	20	R2
	0	1	0	0	1	32	R3
	0	0	$\frac{5}{2}$	$\frac{5}{4}$	0	500	R0
Tableau 3	0	1	$\frac{1}{2}$	$-\frac{1}{4}$	0	20	R1
	1	0	$-\frac{1}{8}$	$\frac{3}{16}$	0	15	R2
	0	0	$-\frac{1}{2}$	$\frac{1}{4}$	1	12	R3

and

$$b'_r = \frac{b_r}{a_{rk}}$$

other rows ($i \neq r$):

$$a'_{ij} = a_{ij} - \frac{a_{ik}a_{rj}}{a_{rk}}$$

and

$$b'_i = b_i - \frac{a_{ik}b_r}{a_{rk}}$$

To streamline the process of filling in the new tableau at each iteration, notice that the column corresponding to each basic variable will contain all 0s and a single 1 in the equation where it appears. These columns can be filled in first; the remaining entries can then be calculated from the pivot formulas.

The second iteration in the example problem produces a third tableau, as shown below the others in Table 4.2. When we scan the top row of this tableau, all entries are nonnegative, indicating an optimal solution. Thus, the entries in Table 4.2 are just the coefficients and the constants encountered in canonical form, displayed in a compact and systematic tabular arrangement.

From our analysis of the Sherwood Furniture example in the previous chapter we note that the entries in the top row of the tableau (excluding the value of the objective function, which appears in the right-hand column) are reduced costs. The requirements of canonical form guarantee that these entries are 0 for the basic variables; for nonbasic variables the reduced cost is simply the corresponding objective function coefficient. The definition of reduced cost explains its interpretation in the optimal solution. It is the amount by which the objective function deteriorates when we increase the corresponding variable by one unit.

Also from our previous analysis of the Sherwood Furniture example, we recognize that the shadow prices appear in the top row of the tableau. In general, for a maximization problem in which there is a slack variable in each constraint, the shadow price will always appear in the optimal tableau as the reduced cost of the corresponding slack variable.

AN AGGREGATE VIEW OF THE SIMPLEX ALGORITHM

We said earlier that it is possible to view the simplex algorithm as a sequence of pivot steps, in which each pivot step consists of

1. Adding a multiple of original constraint equation r to the objective function equation.
2. Adding a multiple of original constraint equation r to each of the constraint equations.

The proper choice of equation r at each iteration, as well as the proper choice of multiples, leads the algorithm ultimately to the canonical form of an optimal solution. In this section we interpret the aggregate effect of this sequence of pivot steps on the original canonical form, as a prelude to presenting the algebra of sensitivity analysis. First, we derive relationships between the numbers in the initial canonical form and the numbers in the optimal canonical form. Using these relationships, we shall then be able to determine how changes in the initial parameters might alter (or preserve) the original optimal solution. In this manner we can establish ranges of validity for the model parameters.

Although the concepts are completely general, we illustrate them here for the familiar standard form case, with extensions to other cases left as exercises. Thus, we make the following assumptions:

Assumption 1
The original LP problem is in standard form; that is, it is a maximization problem subject to upper-bound constraints in which all constraint constants are nonnegative.

Assumption 2
The initial canonical form contains a slack variable in each constraint.

We can represent the canonical form of the original problem by separating the n decision variables from the m slack variables and writing (4.2) as follows:

maximize

$$z - \sum_{j=1}^{n} c_j x_j + \sum_{i=1}^{m} 0 x_{n+i} = 0$$

subject to (I)

$$\sum_{j=1}^{n} a_{ij} x_j + x_{n+i} = b_i \qquad (i = 1, 2, \ldots, m)$$

Similarly, we can represent the canonical form of an optimal solution as follows:

maximize

$$z + \sum_{j=1}^{n} c_j^* x_j + \sum_{j=n+1}^{m} c_j^* x_j = z^*$$

subject to (II)

$$\sum_{j=1}^{n} a_{ij}^* x_j + \sum_{j=n+1}^{n+m} a_{ij}^* x_j = b_i^* \qquad (i = 1, 2, \ldots, m)$$

where asterisks denote the values at optimality. In addition, optimality requires nonnegative coefficients in the objective function, and feasibility requires non-negative constraint constants. Stated in symbols

$$
\begin{aligned}
c_j^* &\geq 0 \qquad (j = 1, 2, \ldots, n + m) \\
b_i^* &\geq 0 \qquad (i = 1, 2, \ldots, m)
\end{aligned}
$$
(4.7)

Associated with an optimal solution is a set of basic variables, denoted B. Its complement, the set of nonbasic variables, is denoted B'. Because in canonical form the objective function coefficients of the basic variables are equal to 0, they will always satisfy the requirement in conditions (4.7). What remains is an optimality condition that requires nonnegative coefficients of the nonbasic variables: $c_j^* \geq 0$ for $j \in B'$.

Now define $(z_j - c_j) = c_j^*$ for $j = 1, 2, \ldots, n$ and define $y_i = c_{n+i}^*$ for $i = 1, 2, \ldots, m$. Using this notation for the optimal objective function coefficients, substitution in canonical form (II) yields

maximize

$$z + \sum_{j=1}^{n} (z_j - c_j) x_j + \sum_{i=1}^{m} y_i x_{n+i} = z^*$$

subject to (III)

$$\sum_{j=1}^{n+m} a_{ij}^* x_j = b_i^* \qquad (i = 1, 2, \ldots, m)$$

For the slack variables (i.e., tableau columns $j > n$), it may also be convenient to use $(z_{n+i} - c_{n+i})$ to denote the objective function coefficient in place of y_i.

The quantities $(z_j - c_j)$, as we have pointed out, are simply the reduced costs. This term derives from the fact that c_j (the original objective function coefficient of x_j) is reduced by the amount z_j during the course of the simplex iterations. Notice, however, that we originally enter this coefficient as $-c_j$ in the initial tableau, corresponding to form (I), and we finish with the coefficient as $(z_j - c_j)$ in the final tableau, corresponding to form (III). Thus, in the final tableau z_j represents the amount by which the simplex method has increased the coefficient of x_j as it appears in the objective function equation of canonical form.

In order to interpret the quantity y_i, compare forms (I) and (III). Notice that the objective function coefficients of x_{n+i} changed from 0 in form (I) to y_i in form (III). Furthermore, note that x_{n+i} appears in the original canonical form (I) only in the ith constraint equation. Because we form the final objective function equation by adding multiples of the original constraint equations to the original objective function equation, we conclude

> y_i is the multiple of original constraint equation i added to the original objective function equation during the simplex algorithm.

This conclusion has important consequences for all of the coefficients of the final objective function.

If we examine the objective function, we note that its value is 0 in the original form (I), whereas its value is z^* in the final form (III). The difference between these values, z^*, must have come from a process of multiplying each original constraint equation i by y_i and adding it to the original objective function. Because the right-hand side of original equation i is b_i, this process means adding the term $y_i b_i$ to the original objective function equation value. However, the final objective function value of z^* comes from carrying out this process for *each* constraint. As a result, we obtain

$$z^* = \sum_{i=1}^{m} b_i y_i \qquad (4.8)$$

In the Sherwood Furniture example these multiples are $y_1 = 2.5$, $y_2 = 1.25$, and $y_3 = 0$. They are, of course, the shadow prices for the three constraints. To verify the definition of y_i, start with the original objective function equation and add 2.5 times constraint equation 1 and 1.25 times constraint equation 2, as follows:

$$
\begin{array}{lll}
z - 20x_1 - 10x_2 & = & 0 \\
+ \quad 10x_1 + 7.5x_2 + 2.5x_3 & = & 300 \\
+ \quad 10x_1 + 2.5x_2 \quad\quad + 1.25x_4 & = & 200 \\
\hline
z \quad\quad\quad\quad\quad + 2.5x_3 + 1.25x_4 & = & 500
\end{array}
$$

Clearly, the result is the objective function of the final canonical form. Then, for this example, equation (4.8) yields

$$z^* = b_1y_1 + b_2y_2 + b_3y_3 = 120(2.5) + 160(1.25) + 32(0) = 500$$

Let us now consider other implications of this process. If we examine the objective function equations of forms (I) and (III) we see that for each of the n decision variables the term $-c_jx_j$ appears in both objective function equations, whereas the term z_jx_j appears in form (III) but not in form (I). Following the reasoning we used for the objective function value, the difference between forms (I) and (III) is

$$\sum_{j=1}^{n} z_jx_j$$

and this difference must have been created by the process of adding multiples of the original constraint equations to the original objective function equation.

To be consistent with our definition of y_i, we conclude that z_j is the multiple of x_j added to the original objective function equation during the simplex method. However, we already know that we have multiplied each constraint i (in which x_j also appears with the coefficient a_{ij}) by the term y_i. We couple these considerations in the finding

$$z_j = \sum_{i=1}^{m} a_{ij}y_i \qquad (j = 1, 2, \ldots, n) \tag{4.9}$$

In fact, this definition also holds for the slack variables, corresponding to tableau columns $j = n + 1$ to $j = n + m$. For these columns $c_j = 0$ and y_i has a coefficient of 1 in constraint i and 0 otherwise. As a result, equation (4.9) reduces to $z_{n+i} = y_i$.

As an example of this result, return to the Sherwood Furniture problem. We know that $y_1 = 2.5$ and $y_2 = 1.25$, and that the matrix of a_{ij} values is

$$a_{11} = 4 \qquad a_{12} = 3$$
$$a_{21} = 8 \qquad a_{22} = 2$$
$$a_{31} = 0 \qquad a_{32} = 1$$

For the two values of j we can calculate

$$z_1 = a_{11}y_1 + a_{21}y_2 + a_{31}y_3 = 4(2.5) + 8(1.25) + 0(0) = 20$$
$$z_2 = a_{12}y_1 + a_{22}y_2 + a_{32}y_3 = 3(2.5) + 2(1.25) + 1(0) = 10$$

Then, when we couple the z_j terms with the c_j terms (20, 10) we obtain the following:

$$z_1 - c_1 = 20 - 20 = 0$$
$$z_2 - c_2 = 10 - 10 = 0$$

Also, we know that

$$z_3 = y_1 = 2.5$$
$$z_4 = y_2 = 1.25$$
$$z_5 = y_3 = 0$$

and that $c_3 = c_4 = c_5 = 0$. Thus

$$z_3 - c_3 = 2.5$$
$$z_4 - c_4 = 1.25$$
$$z_5 - c_5 = 0$$

These results duplicate the values of the reduced costs identified in the final tableau of Table 4.2.

We can now apply the same form of analysis to the constraints in the final canonical form. To interpret the constraint coefficients, compare forms (I) and (III). Notice that the coefficient of x_{n+k} in the ith equation ($k \neq i$) changed from 0 in form (I) to $a^*_{i,n+k}$ in form (III). In addition, recall that x_{n+k} appears in the original canonical form only in the kth constraint equation. Because the final ith constraint is formed by adding multiples of the original constraint equations to the original ith constraint, we conclude

$a^*_{i,n+k}$ is the multiple of original constraint equation k incorporated in the original ith constraint during the simplex algorithm.

In the special case $i = k$ the coefficient of x_{n+i} in the ith equation changed (by multiplication) from 1 in form (I) to $a^*_{i,n+i}$ in form (III).

Based on this information we can think of the right-hand side of equation i as being formed by multiplying its original value by $a^*_{i,n+i}$ and adding the multiples $a^*_{i,n+k}$ of the right-hand sides of the other original equations k. In symbols this relationship is

$$b^*_i = \sum_{k=1}^{m} b_k a^*_{i,n+k} \tag{4.10}$$

To illustrate this last point, in the Sherwood Furniture example we form the first equation ($i = 1$) in the optimal tableau by adding the multiples $a^*_{1,n+1}$, $a^*_{1,n+2}$, and $a^*_{1,n+3}$ of the original three constraint equations. We know that $a^*_{1,3} = \frac{1}{2}$, $a^*_{1,4} = -\frac{1}{4}$, and $a^*_{1,5} = 0$. Then, from (4.10) we find that the right-hand side of the first equation is

$$b^*_i = b_1\left(\frac{1}{2}\right) + b_2\left(-\frac{1}{4}\right) + b_3(0) = 120\left(\frac{1}{2}\right) + 160\left(-\frac{1}{4}\right) + 32(0) = 20$$

Similarly, we find

$$b^*_2 = b_1\left(-\frac{1}{8}\right) + b_2\left(\frac{3}{16}\right) + b_3(0) = 120\left(-\frac{1}{8}\right) + 160\left(\frac{3}{16}\right) + 32(0) = 15$$

and

$$b^*_3 = b_1\left(-\frac{1}{2}\right) + b_2\left(\frac{1}{4}\right) + b_3(1) = 120\left(-\frac{1}{2}\right) + 160\left(\frac{1}{4}\right) + 32(1) = 12$$

With the new information and notation, we can rewrite the optimality and feasibility conditions (4.7):

$$z_j - c_j \geq 0 \qquad (j \in B') \tag{4.11}$$

$$\sum_{k=1}^{m} b_k a^*_{i,n+k} \geq 0 \qquad (i = 1, 2, \ldots, m) \tag{4.12}$$

As a result of the derivations that led to conditions to (4.11) and (4.12), we are now able to state the optimality and feasibility conditions in terms of the objective function coefficients c_j and the constraint constants b_k of the *original* model. This form permits us to determine directly the ranges of validity for these parameters.

OBJECTIVE FUNCTION RANGING ANALYSIS

In order to determine the range of validity for a particular objective function coefficient, c_k, consider what happens in the simplex method if we modify the original value of this coefficient by an amount Δc. In symbols, we shall use primes to represent parameter values in the modified problem, so that in this case $c_k' = c_k + \Delta c$. If we perform the same pivot steps—that is, if the multiples of equation r added at each pivot step are the same as in the solution to the original problem—then the final solution will still be optimal if we preserve the optimality conditions (4.11) and (4.12) when we replace c_k with c_k'. Because the parameter c_k plays a role only in the set of conditions (4.11), the requirement is

$$z_j - c_j' \geq 0 \qquad (j \in B') \tag{4.11'}$$

In this inequality the original objective function coefficients, except for the kth coefficient, remain unchanged:

$$c_k' = c_k + \Delta c$$
$$c_j' = c_j \qquad (j \neq k)$$

There are two cases for us to examine, depending on whether the variable is basic.

COEFFICIENT OF A NONBASIC VARIABLE

If x_k is a nonbasic variable then condition (4.11') will not be affected for $j \neq k$, since the only result for modifying c_k is to change the objective function coefficient of x_k in the final solution from $z_k - c_k$ to $z_k - c_k'$. Therefore, condition (4.11') for optimality becomes the single condition

$$z_k - (c_k + \Delta c) \geq 0$$

or

$$z_k - c_k - \Delta c \geq 0$$

or

$$\Delta c \leq z_k - c_k \tag{4.13}$$

Stated in words, condition (4.13) says that we can improve the contribution coefficient by an amount up to the corresponding reduced cost without violating the optimality of the current solution. As long as Δc satisfies this inequality, the change in c_k will have no effect on the optimal value of either the decision variables or the objective function.

COEFFICIENT OF A BASIC VARIABLE

If x_k is a basic variable, it is necessary to reconstruct the canonical form before examining the optimality conditions. Because x_k is basic, this means that its objective function coefficient in the optimal solution to the original problem is 0, as required of basic variables in canonical form

$$z_k - c_k = 0$$

When we follow the same pivot steps in the modified problem, the coefficient of x_k in the final objective function equation will be

$$z_k - c_k' = z_k - (c_k + \Delta c) = (z_k - c_k) - \Delta c = -\Delta c$$

We reconstruct canonical form by multiplying the constraint equation in which x_k appears by Δc and adding the result to the objective function equation. Suppose that x_k appears in constraint equation t. This equation takes the form

$$\sum_{j \in B'} a_{tj}^* x_j + x_k = b_t^* \qquad (4.14)$$

Note that the sum is taken over only the nonbasic variables because basic variables other than x_k do not appear in the equation. Similarly, we can write the objective function equation as

$$z + \sum_{j \in B'} (z_j - c_j) x_j - \Delta c x_k = z^* \qquad (4.15)$$

where we use the notation $(z_j - c_j)$ to denote the objective function coefficient for x_j, even if x_j is a slack variable. Multiplying equation (4.14) by Δc and adding to equation (4.15) yields

$$z + \sum_{j \in B'} (z_j - c_j + \Delta c a_{tj}^*) x_j = z^* + \Delta c b_t^* \qquad (4.16)$$

Because the requirement for optimality is that the coefficient of x_j must be nonnegative, we find

$$z_j - c_j + \Delta c a_{tj}^* \geq 0 \qquad (j \in B') \qquad (4.17)$$

As long as Δc satisfies this set of inequalities, the change in c_k will have no effect on the optimal decision variables. As can be seen in equation (4.16), however, the value of the objective function changes by an amount equal to $(\Delta c) b_t^*$, which is equal to the change in unit profit contribution multiplied by the value of the decision variable x_k.

TABLE 4.3 Tableau Solution of the Example Problem

	x_1	x_2	x_3	x_4	x_5	x_6		
	-20	-10	-18	0	0	0	0	R0
Tableau 1	4	3	5	1	0	0	120	R1
	8	2	6	0	1	0	160	R2
	0	1	0	0	0	1	32	R3
	0	-5	-3	0	$\frac{5}{2}$	0	400	R0
Tableau 2	0	2	2	1	$-\frac{1}{2}$	0	40	R1
	1	$\frac{1}{4}$	$\frac{3}{4}$	0	$\frac{1}{8}$	0	20	R2
	0	1	0	0	0	1	32	R3
	0	0	2	$\frac{5}{2}$	$\frac{5}{4}$	0	500	R0
Tableau 3	0	1	1	$\frac{1}{2}$	$-\frac{1}{4}$	0	20	R1
	1	0	$\frac{1}{2}$	$-\frac{1}{8}$	$\frac{3}{16}$	0	15	R2
	0	0	-1	$-\frac{1}{2}$	$\frac{1}{4}$	1	12	R3

As an example, consider the modified version of the Sherwood Furniture problem, in which production of Portable cabinets is an alternative. Recall from the previous chapter that the LP formulation in standard form is

maximize

$$z = 20x_1 + 10x_2 + 18x_3$$

subject to

$$4x_1 + 3x_2 + 5x_3 \le 120$$
$$8x_1 + 2x_2 + 6x_3 \le 160$$
$$x_2 \qquad\qquad \le 32$$

Table 4.3 gives the simplex tableau data for the solution of this problem. Below we find the range of validity for each of the unit contribution coefficients.

k = 1 The variable x_1 is basic in the final solution and appears in constraint equation $t = 2$. Hence the range of validity for c_1 is given by (4.17).

$$z_j - c_j + \Delta c a_{1j}^* \ge 0, \qquad j \in B'$$
$$(j = 3) \quad 2 + \Delta c(\tfrac{1}{2}) \ge 0, \qquad \text{or} \quad \Delta c \ge -4$$

$$(j = 4) \quad \tfrac{5}{2} + \Delta c(-\tfrac{1}{8}) \quad \geq 0, \qquad \Delta c \leq 20$$
$$(j = 5) \quad \tfrac{5}{4} + \Delta c(\tfrac{3}{16}) \quad \geq 0, \qquad \Delta c \geq -\tfrac{20}{3}$$

Thus, the limiting range is $-4 \leq \Delta c \leq 20$, and the range of validity for c_1 is therefore $16 \leq c_1 + \Delta c \leq 40$.

k = 2 The variable x_2 is also basic and appears in constraint equation $t = 1$. Hence the range of validity for c_2 is given by (4.17):

$$z_j - c_j + \Delta c a_{1j}^* \quad \geq 0, \quad j \in B'$$
$$(j = 3) \quad 2 + \Delta c(1) \quad \geq 0, \quad \text{or} \quad \Delta c \geq -2$$
$$(j = 4) \quad \tfrac{5}{2} + \Delta c(\tfrac{1}{2}) \quad \geq 0, \qquad \Delta c \geq -5$$
$$(j = 5) \quad \tfrac{5}{4} + \Delta c(-\tfrac{1}{4}) \quad \geq 0, \qquad \Delta c \geq \quad 5$$

Here the limiting range is $-2 \leq \Delta c \leq 5$, and the range of validity for c_2 is $8 \leq c_2 + \Delta c \leq 15$.

k = 3 The variable x_3 is nonbasic in the final solution. Hence the range of validity for c_3 is given by condition (4.13):

$$\Delta c \leq z_3 - c_3 = 2$$

and the range of validity for c_3 is therefore $c_3 \leq 20$. These results match those generated in the computer analysis discussed in the previous chapter.

MINIMIZATION

It is important to remember that the key formulas, (4.13) and (4.17), are based on Assumption 1, which involves maximization. Suppose instead that we were dealing with a **minimization** problem. If we trace the logic of our derivation in the previous section, we find that this change would be reflected in condition (4.11), in which the optimality condition becomes $z_j - c_j \leq 0$ for nonbasic values of j. Therefore, the ultimate effect of changing to minimization would be reversing the direction of the inequalities in conditions (4.13) and (4.17). Thus, for minimization, the range of validity formulas for c_k can be stated as follows:

For x_k nonbasic

$$\Delta c \geq z_k - c_k \qquad \text{(4.13, minimization)}$$

For x_k basic

$$z_j - c_j + \Delta c a_{tj}^* \le 0 \qquad (j \in \mathbf{B}') \qquad\qquad\qquad \text{(4.17, minimization)}$$

where, as before, x_k appears in constraint equation t.

CONSTRAINT RANGING ANALYSIS

In order to determine the range of validity for a particular constraint constant b_t consider what happens in the simplex method if we replace the original value of this constant by $b_t' = b_t + \Delta b$. If we perform the same pivot steps as in the original problem, then the final solution will still be optimal as long as we preserve the optimality conditions (4.11, 4.12) when we replace b_t by b_t'. Because the parameter b_t plays a role only in the set of conditions given by (4.12), the requirement is

$$\sum_{k=1}^{m} b_k' a_{i,n+k}^* \ge 0 \qquad (i = 1, 2, \ldots, m) \qquad\qquad\qquad (4.12')$$

In these conditions the original right-hand-side constants, except for the one in constraint t, remain unchanged:

$$b_t' = b_t + \Delta b$$
$$b_k' = b_k \qquad (k \ne t)$$

As in objective function ranging, here are two cases to examine, depending on whether the constraint is binding.

RIGHT-HAND SIDE OF A NONBINDING CONSTRAINT

If constraint t is a nonbinding constraint in the optimal solution, then the slack variable in constraint t must be basic. This means that $a_{t,n+t}^* = 1$. The feasibility conditions (4.12') become

$$\sum_{k=1}^{m} b_k a_{i,n+k}^* = b_i^* \ge 0 \qquad \text{for } i \ne t$$

and

$$\sum_{k \ne t}^{m} b_k a_{i,n+k}^* + (b_t + \Delta b) a_{t,n+t} = b_t^* + \Delta b \ge 0 \qquad \text{for } i = t$$

Clearly, there is no change in the feasible values of b_i^* except for $i = t$, so that the optimality condition reduces to

$$b_t^* + \Delta b \geq 0$$

or

$$\Delta b \geq -b_t^* \tag{4.18}$$

As long as Δb satisfies this inequality, the change in b_t will have no effect on either the optimal value of the original decision variables or the optimal value of the objective function. Only the slack variable in constraint t will be affected.

RIGHT-HAND SIDE OF A BINDING CONSTRAINT

If constraint t is binding in the optimal solution, it is not possible to simplify the optimality condition. In this case we preserve optimality if $\Sigma_k b_k' a_{i,n+k}^* \geq 0$ for all i. We can rewrite these inequalities as follows:

$$\sum_{k=1}^{m} b_k a_{i,n+k}^* + \Delta b a_{i,n+t}^* \geq 0 \qquad (i = 1, 2, \ldots, m)$$

or

$$b_i^* + \Delta b a_{i,n+t}^* \geq 0 \qquad (i = 1, 2, \ldots, m) \tag{4.19}$$

As long as Δb satisfies this set of inequalities, the change in b_t will have no effect on the feasibility of the optimal set of basic variables. Their specific values, and the value of the objective function, will vary with Δb.

As an example, we return to the solution tableau in Table 4.3 and find the range of validity for each of the constraint constants, using conditions (4.18) or (4.19).

$t = 1$ Constraint 1 is binding in the final solution. Hence the range of validity for b_1 is given by condition (4.19):

$$b_i^* + \Delta b a_{i,n+t}^* \geq 0$$

$(i = 1)$	$20 + \Delta b(\tfrac{1}{2}) \geq 0,$	or $\Delta b \geq -40$
$(i = 2)$	$15 + \Delta b(-\tfrac{1}{8}) \geq 0,$	or $\Delta b \leq 120$
$(i = 3)$	$12 + \Delta b(-\tfrac{1}{2}) \geq 0,$	or $\Delta b \geq 24$

The limiting range on Δb is $-40 \leq \Delta b \leq 24$, and thus, the range of validity for b_1 is $80 \leq b_1 + \Delta b \leq 144$.

$t = 2$ Constraint 2 is binding in the final solution. Hence the range of validity for b_2 is given by condition (4.19).

$$b_i^* + \Delta b a_{i,n+t}^* \geq 0$$

$(i = 1)$ $20 + \Delta b(-\tfrac{1}{4}) \geq 0$,   or $b \leq 80$

$(i = 2)$ $15 + \Delta b(\tfrac{3}{16}) \geq 0$,   or $b \geq -80$

$(i = 3)$ $12 + \Delta b(\tfrac{1}{4}) \geq 0$,   or $b \geq -48$

Here the limiting range is $-48 \leq \Delta b \leq 80$, and the range of validity for b_2 is therefore $112 \leq b_2 + \Delta b \leq 240$.

t = 3 Constraint 3 is not binding in the final solution. Hence the range of validity for b_3 is given by condition (4.18):

$$\Delta b \geq -b_t^*$$
$$\Delta b \geq -12$$

The range of validity for b_3 is therefore $20 \leq b_3 + \Delta b$.

From the sensitivity analysis above we conclude, for example, that if the Finishing department has only 144 hours available instead of 160, then the optimal set of basic variables will remain unchanged, since 144 lies within the range of validity for b_2. This means production of Standard and Custom cabinets, but no Portable cabinets, as in the original plan. The output quantities will change, however, due to the reduced availability of a binding resource (i.e., Finishing hours). The revised output quantities are given by equation (4.10):

$$b_1^* = \sum_{k=1}^{m} b_k' a_{1,n+k}^* = 120\left(\frac{1}{2}\right) + 144\left(-\frac{1}{4}\right) + 32(0) = 24 \quad (x_2^* = 24)$$

$$b_2^* = \sum_{k=1}^{m} b_k' a_{2,n+k}^* = 120\left(-\frac{1}{8}\right) + 144\left(\frac{3}{16}\right) + 32(0) = 12 \quad (x_1^* = 12)$$

$$b_3^* = \sum_{k=1}^{m} b_k' a_{3,n+k}^* = 120\left(-\frac{1}{2}\right) + 144\left(\frac{1}{4}\right) + 32(1) = 8 \quad (x_6^* = 8)$$

As these calculations indicate, there is sufficient information in the final tableau to calculate the values of all variables within the range of validity of any one of the constraint constants.

LOWER-BOUND CONSTRAINTS

Again, it is important to recognize that the key formulas, (4.18) and (4.19), are based on Assumption 1, which involves maximization subject to upper-bound constraints, and Assumption 2, which specifies a slack variable in each constraint equation. Suppose instead that we were dealing with **lower-bound** constraints, so that there would be a surplus variable in each constraint. Tracing the logic of our earlier comments, we would have to conclude the following:

> $-y_i$ is the multiple of original constraint equation i added to the original objective function equation during the simplex algorithm

and

> $-a_{i,n+k}^*$ is the multiple of original constraint equation k added to the original ith constraint equation $(k \neq i)$ during the simplex algorithm.

The source of the minus sign in these definitions is essentially the coefficient of the surplus variable in any original constraint. This change requires us to replace $a_{i,n+k}^*$ by $(-a_{i,n+k}^*)$ in (4.10) and (4.12) and ultimately in (4.18) and (4.19). Thus, for lower-bound constraints the range of validity formulas for b_t can be stated as follows:

For b_t nonbinding

$$\Delta b \leq b_i^* \tag{4.18, L-B}$$

For b_t binding

$$b_i^* - \Delta b a_{i,n+t}^* \geq 0 \qquad (i = 1, 2, \ldots, m) \tag{4.19, L-B}$$

Furthermore, when b_t is altered within its range of validity, the revised optimal values of the decision variables are given by

$$b_i^* = \sum_{k=1}^{m} b_k(-a_{i,n+k}^*) \tag{4.10, L-B}$$

SHADOW PRICES

Assume, as we did originally, that we have used the simplex algorithm to solve a problem in maximization subject to upper-bound constraints. By virtue of the optimality conditions for maximization, all objective function coefficients must be nonnegative in the canonical form of the optimal solution. Suppose that the coefficient y_i of the ith slack variable is strictly positive. The ith slack variable must therefore be nonbasic (zero-valued), and so the ith constraint must be binding. Stated in symbols

$$y_i > 0$$

implies

$$\sum_{j=1}^{n} a_{ij}x_j = b_i$$

Now suppose we increase the right-hand constant in the ith constraint by one unit. If this change does not alter the optimal basis then the value of y_i is unaffected, and it follows from equation (4.8) that the increase in the optimal value of the objective function will be precisely y_i. Thus, y_i measures the increase in z^* per unit increase in b_i. This fact allowed us to interpret y_i as a shadow price.

Conversely, suppose that the ith constraint is not binding. Then the ith slack variable must be positive (basic) in the optimal solution, and so its coefficient must be 0 in the objective function. Stated in symbols

$$\sum_{j=1}^{n} a_{ij}x_j < b_i$$

implies

$$y_i = 0$$

In this case, the 0 shadow price correctly reflects the fact that a unit change in b_i (assuming this change lies within its range of validity) will not have any impact on the value of z^*.

The main point of the foregoing summary is to clarify where the shadow prices are located in the computations of the simplex method: They are simply objective function coefficients. In particular, when we solve a maximization problem subject to upper-bound constraints, shadow prices occur as objective function coefficients of the slack variables.

Now consider the interpretation of shadow prices of lower-bound constraints in a maximization problem. The generic lower-bound constraint can be written

$$\sum_{j=1}^{n} a_{ij}x_j \geq b_i \qquad (4.20)$$

Note that we add a surplus variable to this constraint when we create canonical form. Suppose the objective function coefficient y_i of this variable is positive in the optimal solution. (Remember that we cannot have $y_i < 0$ in any optimal solution.) We might ask how to interpret the value of y_i as a shadow price.

In order to answer this question, consider what happens when we increment b_i by 1 unit. The ith constraint becomes

$$\sum_{j=1}^{n} a_{ij}x_j \geq b_i + 1 \qquad\qquad (4.21)$$

Note that any set of decision variables that is feasible in (4.21) will also be feasible in (4.20). The reverse is, however, not true. Some decision variables feasible in (4.20) could fail to satisfy (4.21). Therefore, by increasing the right-hand side of a lower-bound constraint, we have reduced the feasible region. If this change has any impact on the optimal value of the objective function, it must be to reduce z^*. Thus a unit increase in b_i leads to a reduction in z^*. The value of y_i in the optimal simplex tableau is *positive,* yet most computer codes will report the shadow price as *negative* in this case, to reflect the fact that the optimal value of the objective function deteriorates as the constraint constant increases.

To carry the sign convention one step further, consider the case of minimization problems. The objective function coefficient y_i corresponding to a slack or surplus variable must be nonpositive by virtue of the optimality conditions for minimization. If y_i is strictly negative, its interpretation as a shadow price still depends on the type of constraint with which it is associated. For a binding upper-bound constraint, an increase in the right-hand side extends the feasible region and yields a lower value of the objective function. In this case we would report the shadow price as *positive* (i.e., as $-y_i$) because an increase in the constraint constant produces an improvement in the objective function. On the other hand, for a binding lower-bound constraint, we treat the shadow price as *negative* because an increase in the constraint constant produces a deterioration in the objective function.

The sign convention for shadow prices is consistent with LINDO and many other computer codes; however, some codes may adopt different conventions. The main point is that the numerical value of the shadow price can be found in the simplex tableau. The interpretation of its sign should be intuitive, following the prescription we gave in the preceding chapter: Loosening an inequality constraint will never hurt the objective function, and tightening an inequality constraint will never help the objective function.

SUMMARY

In this chapter we have studied the simplex method from an algebraic point of view. As we saw in the previous chapter, it is possible to solve linear programming problems with the use of a general purpose LP computer code, which is a resource widely available to business, education, and government organizations. An explicit knowledge of the simplex method is not essential for solving LP programs. Why then do we even study the simplex method?

The first and most important reason is that the study of the solution procedure affords us a better understanding of the information produced in the analysis. For example, someone who solves many LP problems with a computer program might wonder why it is that only a certain number of decision variables are ever positive in LP solutions, while many variables are typically 0. Perhaps intuition suggests that the best solution could be obtained by making all variables positive, but an understanding of the algebra of the simplex method gives us some insight into why this need not be the case. Furthermore, the definitions of shadow prices and ranges of validity that we encounter in the simplex procedure provide a deeper understanding of those terms and enhance our ability to use the concepts of sensitivity analysis.

A second reason for studying the simplex method is that it is often a building block in solution methods for more complicated types of problems, most notably for integer programming. The simplex method, or at least some of the insight it provides, is also important to the study of solution procedures for network optimization, nonlinear programming, and decomposition models as well.

Third, the study of the simplex method leads to insights about solution algorithms in general. The simplex algorithm illustrates such common facets as initializing the procedure, improving on existing solutions, deciding when to stop, detecting special cases (infeasible constraints or unbounded objective functions), and providing the information for sensitivity analysis. As a systematic and comprehensive solution procedure, the simplex method provides an excellent paradigm for structuring other kinds of optimization algorithms.

Specifically, we have seen in this chapter how we can harness the ability to solve systems of equations in finding optimal solutions to LP problems. Three modules comprised the algorithm: specifying an initial basic feasible solution, checking for optimality, and improving the solution if improvement potential exists. Algorithm 4.1 described the improvement, feasibility, and elimination steps that check for optimality and improve the solution. We also introduced the method of artificial variables to show how to carry out the initializing module.

Once we specified the steps in the simplex method, we were able to interpret the entire procedure as a sequence of pivot steps that transformed initial coefficients into final coefficients. An aggregate view of this transformation enabled us to specify how a change in an initial coefficient might alter the solution, and this perspective allowed us to derive the principal results in sensitivity analysis for linear programs.

EXERCISES

SOLUTION BY THE SIMPLEX METHOD

1 The Arnett Lumber Company cuts raw timber—oak and pine logs—into 2×4 boards. Two steps are required to produce the rough boards from logs. The first step involves stripping bark from the logs. For this step, 2 hours are required to remove the bark from every 1000 feet of oak logs, while 3 hours are required for every 1000 feet of pine. The second step involves cutting the stripped logs into boards. The cutting process requires 2.4 hours per 1000 feet of oak logs and 1.2 hours per 1000 feet of pine logs. The bark-removing machine can operate up to 60 hours a week, but the older cutting machine requires more maintenance and provides only 48 productive hours per week. Existing agreements with suppliers permit the company to buy up to 18,000 feet of newly harvested oak logs and 16,000 feet of newly harvested pine logs each week. The lumber company's profit on the processed logs is $360 per 1000 feet of oak and $360 per 1000 feet of pine. The decision problem is to determine how many feet of each type of log should be purchased each week.

2 As a toy manufacturer, employing 50 laborers and running on a 40-hour workweek, you find that your best-selling item is a line of stuffed St. Bernard dogs. These dogs come in three sizes: miniature, regular, and large. Stuffing, covering, and labor is required in the manufacturing of these dogs. Your distributor informs you that a retailer is having a grand opening sale in 1 week. The retailer has agreed to buy as many dogs as you can supply in that time provided the number of miniatures is at least twice the number of regulars and large combined. Your inventory records show that you have 800 pounds of stuffing and 1000 square yards of covering available for this order. The table indicates the amount of raw materials used for each size dog and the selling price per unit.

Size	Pounds Stuffing	Square Yards Covering	Man-Hours Labor	Selling Price
Miniature	2	1	5	$2
Regular	4	2	8	$4
Large	8	4	10	$7

You want to find an output plan that will maximize total revenue.

3 The Blackburn Brewing and Bottling Company, because of faulty planning, was not prepared for a long weekend coming up. There was to be a big party at the university, and Blackburn's manager knew that he would be called upon to supply the refreshments. However, the raw materials required had not been ordered and could not be obtained before the weekend. He took an inventory of the available supplies and found the following:

Malt   500 units
Hops   250 units
Yeast   250 units

Blackburn produces three types of drinks: light beer, dark beer, and malt liquor, with the following specifications:

	Requirements per Gallon		
	Malt	Hops	Yeast
Light beer	2	1	2
Dark beer	4	3	2
Malt liquor	7	2	2

The light beer brings $1/gallon profit, the dark beer $2/gallon profit, and the malt liquor $3/gallon profit. Knowing the students will buy whatever is made available, how should production be planned in order to maximize total profit?

4 Cochrane's Gourmet Products, Inc., markets three blends of oriental tea: premium, fine, and regular. The firm uses three types of tea leaves in the production process, from Korea, Japan, and Taiwan. The following lists the composition of the three blends:

Leaves	Blend:	Premium	Fine	Regular
Korean		40%	30	20
Japanese		20%	30	40
Taiwanese		40%	40	40

The firm's net profit per pound for each blend is: premium, $0.50; fine, $0.30; and regular, $0.20. The firm's regular weekly supplies of the Korean and Japanese tea leaves are 20,000 and 22,000 pounds, respectively, while the supply from Taiwan is virtually unlimited. The marketing research department reports that there is almost an unlimited market for the premium and fine blends. However, the maximum expected sale for the regular blend is 2000 pounds. Determine the optimal product mix to maximize total profit.

5 An electric appliance manufacturer makes irons, toasters, and frying pans. The table below shows the production rates for each product in each major department, along with the number of hours available next month and the profit contributions for each item.

Department	Irons	Toasters	Pans	Hours Available
Stamping	10/hour	10/hour	20/hour	50
Casting	10	10	5	40
Assembly	8	10	8	30
Profit	$8	$10	$15	

The firm wishes to determine how many of each product should be produced next month in order to maximize the total profit contribution.

6 A furniture dealer has 1500 square feet of floor space in his showroom reserved for purchases of new styles. The pieces of furniture available to him are the following:

Piece	Square Feet per Unit	Selling Price	Cost
Chair	10	$110	$ 60
Sofa	40	300	180
Bed	50	270	120
Dresser	10	300	150

Because customers usually buy only items shown on the floor, the dealer would like to stock a set of pieces that will maximize profit potential. He wishes to have the same number of dressers as beds and at least as many chairs as sofas. Moreover, he has a budget of $4200 for these purchases. Determine how this money should be used.

7 A survey company has undertaken a job requiring both personal and telephone interviews: The client has specified the following requirements:

At least 1000 interviews must be scheduled, of which at least half must be personal interviews.

At least 30% of the interviews must be scheduled at night.

At most 60% of the daytime interviews can be by telephone.
The direct costs to the survey company are $3 per telephone interview and $5 per personal interview; night interviews involve a premium of 40%. How should the survey company schedule interviews to minimize costs?

8 The local police department has the following daily requirements schedule for officers on patrol:

Period	Time of Day	Officers Required
1	00–04	20
2	04–08	70
3	08–12	80
4	12–16	120
5	16–20	90
6	20–00	30

Each officer works 8 consecutive hours and can begin work at the start of any one of the six periods. The department would like to find a schedule that meets the requirements with the smallest possible number of officers. Find the optimum size force and determine a corresponding work-force schedule.

SENSITIVITY ANALYSIS

9 Refer to Exercise 1.

a What are the optimal purchase quantities and optimal total profit in the problem?

b Specify a range of validity for each contribution coefficient and a range of validity for each constraint constant.

c Suppose that a promotion initiative reduced the profit on pine logs to only $150 per 1000 feet. How would the optimal product mix be altered? What would be the optimal total profit?

d Suppose instead that an overhaul of the cutting machine could yield 52 hours of productive time per week. What would be the value of this additional capacity?

10 Refer to Exercise 2.

a What is the optimal output plan and the corresponding revenue?

b Suppose the price of the large size stuffed dog were to rise. How much of an increase in its price would be necessary to provide an incentive for changing the quantity in the plan of (a)?

c Suppose instead that an inventory check were to reveal the actual inventory of covering to be 900 square yards (rather than 1000, as originally assumed.) What impact will this discovery have?

d How much should you, as the manufacturer, be willing to pay for additional stuffing?

11 Refer to Exercise 3.

a What quantities of the three types of drinks produce the most profit?

b What is the unit value of an additional supply of malt? Of hops? Of yeast?

c Determine the range for which each of the values in (b) will hold.

d Compute the range of validity for the unit contributions of each of the three drinks.

12 Refer to Exercise 4.

a What is the optimal product mix?

b What would be the marginal impact on total profits of expanding the market of the regular blend beyond 2000 pounds?

c What would be the marginal impact on total profits of expanding the supply of Korean tea?

d What would be the marginal impact on total profits of expanding the supply of Japanese tea?

e Determine ranges of validity for your answers to b, c, and d.

f Determine ranges of validity for the net profit per pound of each blend.

13 Refer to Exercise 5.

    a What are the output quantities in the optimal plan, and what is the maximum profit contribution?

    b Determine a range of validity for each objective function coefficient.

    c Suppose that competition in the toaster market is about to cause a drop in toaster prices. How much of a reduction in the unit contribution of toasters could be absorbed before there is an incentive to change the output mix?

    d Determine a range of validity for each constraint constant.

    e Suppose that a more careful study leads to the conclusion that the number of Casting hours available will actually be 34. What is the impact of this change on the optimal output plan?

14 Refer to Exercise 6.

    a What is the optimal plan for the furniture dealer?

    b At what interest rates would it be desirable for the dealer to borrow funds (thereby expanding his budget), assuming that any pieces of furniture he buys are certain to be sold within 6 months?

    c How much money should the dealer be willing to borrow under the conditions of (b)?

    d To which of the objective function coefficients is the solution in (a) most sensitive?

15 Refer to Exercise 7.

    a What is the cost-minimizing schedule of interviews?

    b What would be the cost of 10 additional interviews?

    c Suppose the premium on night telephone interviews could be reduced. How much of a reduction would be necessary to change the optimality of the schedule in (a)?

16 Refer to Exercise 8.

    a What is the optimal size force?

    b In which periods is there no slack in matching the optimal patrol coverage to patrol requirements?

    c In which periods of the day would an increase in the patrol requirements require an increase in the size of the force?

ALTERNATE OPTIMA AND DEGENERACY

17 Refer to the solution to Exercise 2.

a Is the solution degenerate? Why?

b Do alternate optima exist? If so, construct an alternate optimal solution.

18 Refer to the solution to Exercise 3.

a Is the solution degenerate? Why?

b Do alternate optima exist? Why?

19 Refer to the solution to Exercise 8.

a Is the solution degenerate? Why?

b Do alternate optima exist? Why?

INTERPRETING THE SIMPLEX TABLEAU

20 A manufacturer of plywood panels is developing a production schedule for the next month. The firm has a product line of five items, and there is reason to believe that the company will be able to sell whatever it chooses to produce. Production is limited by the inventory of wood (12,000 units of fir, 15,000 of pine, and 6000 of spruce), the capacity of the drying operation (60,000 minutes), and the availability of space for finished panels (10,000 panels). The firm has five kinds of panels it can produce, and a linear program is used for planning purposes. In the LP shown in Exhibit 4.1, the decision variables are x_j = thousands of panels of type j to be manufactured next month (for $j = 1$ to 5) and the criterion is maximum profit contribution (in thousands of dollars) from the panels produced.

Answer each of the following questions about this planning problem, relying on the information given in the simplex tableaus of Exhibit 4.1.

a What is the firm's maximum profit contribution under the assumed conditions?

b How many panel types are produced in the optimal product mix?

c Is the optimal product mix unique or do alternate optima exist?

d Find the range of validity for the unit profit contribution of Type 5 panels and interpret its meaning.

e Find the range of validity for the inventory of pine and interpret its meaning.

f Suppose additional space for finished panels could be leased in a public warehouse. In particular, space for an extra 400 panels could be leased for $2750. Would the firm improve its profits by leasing some (or all) of this extra space?

EXHIBIT 4.1

x_1	x_2	x_3	x_4	x_5	x_6	x_7	x_8	x_9	x_{10}	
2	0	2	1	1	1	0	0	0	0	12 (Fir)
0	2	1	2	1	0	1	0	0	0	15 (Pine)
1	1	0	0	1	0	0	1	0	0	6 (Spruce)
5	7	4	5	6	0	0	0	1	0	60 (Drying)
1	1	1	1	1	0	0	0	0	1	10 (Space)
-7	-10	-12	-12	-8	0	0	0	0	0	0 (Objective function)

Initial Tableau

x_1	x_2	x_3	x_4	x_5	x_6	x_7	x_8	x_9	x_{10}	
2	0	1	0	1	0	-1	0	0	2	5
-2	0	0	1	-1	1	2	0	0	-4	2
0	0	0	0	0	1	1	1	0	-3	3
0	0	0	0	0	2	1	0	1	-9	9
1	1	0	0	1	-1	-1	0	0	3	3
3	0	0	0	2	2	2	0	0	6	114

Optimal Tableau

g Suppose instead that the market price for Type 1 panels rises by $4 per panel. What is the effect on the optimal product mix?

21 A company manufactures a variety of small kitchen appliances in several factories. One of its factories is set up to produce meat slicers, food choppers, and blenders. Each product is made up of steel and plastic components that are fabricated in the Forming department, put together in the Assembly department, and then subjected to a series of quality control tests in the Standards department. Although the firm expects to be able to sell whatever it manufactures next month, it has limited resources in the form of available hours in each department (800 in Forming, 1000 in Assembly, and 2000 in Standards). For planning purposes, a linear program is being used. In the LP reproduced in Exhibit 4.2, the decision variables are x_j = number of items produced, where $j = 1$ for slicers, $j = 2$ for choppers, and $j = 3$ for blenders. The criterion is maximum total profit contribution.

Answer each of the following questions about this planning problem, relying on the information given in the simplex tableaus of Exhibit 4.2.

a What is the firm's maximum profit contribution under the assumed conditions?

b Which products are produced in the optimal product mix?

EXHIBIT 4.2

x_1	x_2	x_3	x_4	x_5	x_6	
1	2	1	1	0	0	800 (Forming hours)
1	1	2	0	1	0	1000 (Assembly hours)
2	1	1	0	0	0	2000 (Standards hours)
−30	−45	−35	0	0	0	0 (Objective function)

Initial Tableau

x_1	x_2	x_3	x_4	x_5	x_6	
1	3	0	2	−1	0	600
0	−1	1	−1	1	0	200
0	−4	0	3	1	1	600
0	10	0	25	5	0	25,000

Optimal Tableau

c Is the optimal allocation unique or do alternate optima exist?

d Find the range of validity for the unit profit contribution of choppers and interpret its meaning.

e Find the range of validity for the capacity in the Forming department and interpret its meaning.

f Suppose additional hours in the Assembly department can be produced by scheduling some overtime work. Under the existing union contract a minimum of 400 overtime hours would have to be scheduled. Beyond the material, labor, and overhead costs already included in the profit contribution figures, the additional costs to the firm for this amount of overtime would amount to $2400. Should the production manager plan on scheduling overtime?

g Suppose instead that the market price for choppers increases by $12 per unit. What would be the resulting effect on the optimal product mix?

CONCEPTUAL EXERCISES

22 Discuss the effects of (a) alternate optima and (b) degeneracy on ranging analysis for the objective function and for constraint constants.

23 Describe how to compute shadow prices for equality constraints.

Chapter 5
INTEGER PROGRAMMING

Mansfield Insulated Products

The plant manager at Mansfield Insulated Products is preparing to schedule the main production line which produces two types of insulation material known as Type 1 and Type 2. He schedules Mansfield's output in terms of standard containers, which hold approximately 5000 pounds of insulation and which can hold only one type of insulation. Only 50 hours of time are available each week at the bottleneck machine on the main production line. One container of Type 1 material requires 3 hours of machine time, and one container of Type 2 requires 6 hours. Because of the chemical properties of the insulation material, company policy prohibits the storage of partially filled containers over the weekend. The trucking firm used by Mansfield has contracted for up to 10 trips per week, in which each trip delivers a single standard container of insulation. Because the trucks have special racks designed to hold the containers, it is not possible to ship containers of smaller than standard size. The plant realizes a profit of $300 on each Type 1 container and $400 on each Type 2 container produced, although at present its distributors will take no more than eight Type 1 containers per week. How should the manager schedule the production line to maximize profit?

In the chapter on linear programming we mentioned that divisibility was one of the essential characteristics of LP models. This characteristic allows us to assume that the decision variables are continuous—that they make sense when expressed as fractions. In some situations all of the linear programming assumptions *except* divisibility are satisfied. In these cases the decision variables have to be integers.

The Mansfield Insulated Products problem illustrates a situation in which circumstances require an integer solution. Let x_1 denote the weekly production of containers of Type 1 insulation, and let x_2 denote the production of Type 2 containers. The problem statement then becomes

maximize

$$z = 300x_1 + 400x_2$$

subject to

$$
\begin{aligned}
3x_1 + \quad 6x_2 &\leq 50 \\
x_1 \qquad\quad &\leq \quad 8 \\
x_1 + \quad x_2 &\leq 10 \\
x_1 \geq 0, \quad x_2 &\geq 0 \text{ and integer}
\end{aligned}
\tag{5.1}
$$

Although this problem has the appearance of a linear program, when we prohibit mixed containers and weekend storage of partially filled containers, we are requiring that the decision variables take integer values. As a result, the Mansfield example is an **integer programming** (IP) problem.

For our purposes, integer programs are linear programs with the additional requirement that some or all of the variables must be integer valued. For some applications it is no more difficult to formulate an IP problem than it is to formulate an LP problem. The Mansfield example falls into this category. In such cases we develop an LP structure while recognizing that certain of the decision variables are constrained to be integers. If all of the variables are constrained to be integers, as in the Mansfield example, the problem is often called a **pure integer program.** On the other hand, if some of the variables are required to be integers, and the remaining variables are continuous, we call the problem a **mixed integer program (MIP).** Actually, we can think of the pure integer programming problem as a special case of an MIP in which there are no continuous variables.

Another distinction is helpful when we look at the integer variables of an MIP. In many cases it is convenient to work with variables that can assume only the values 0 and 1. Such integer variables are called **binary** or **zero-one** variables, and they make it possible to model "all-or-nothing" or "go/no go" alternatives. When all the integer variables in an integer program are binary variables, the special case is called a zero-one programming problem. Although we can think of a zero-one programming problem as just a special case of an MIP in which all integer variables have an upper bound of 1, this is an extremely important special case when it comes to applications of integer programming. The use of binary variables allows us to model many kinds of relationships that on the surface may not resemble linear programming structures at all.

In this chapter we shall study the formulation and solution of integer programming problems. We first discuss the use of binary variables in order to illustrate the potential of zero-one programs. We also describe some common IP formulations. Then we return to the Mansfield example and show how to find an optimal solution. When solving a mixed integer program our intuitive first thought might be that the LP optimum, together with some kind of simple round-off procedure, should provide the IP solution. However, the optimal solution of IP problems is considerably more difficult than it may seem. As we shall see, rounding schemes are not reliable, and we will need a more sophisticated approach. In developing the solution to the example problem we illustrate a powerful technique that is general enough to handle mixed integer programs as well.

USING BINARY VARIABLES

As we mentioned earlier, binary variables are permitted to be either 0 or 1. A binary variable allows us to think of a decision as a "switch" that we can turn on or off. In what follows we discuss some typical uses of these variables.

ALL-OR-NOTHING VARIABLES

We can use a binary variable to represent an activity that must be either completely accepted or else rejected. We sometimes refer to this type of activity as a project, in the sense that no fraction of the activity can be implemented. If we let y denote the binary variable, then

$$y = 1 \quad \text{if the activity is accepted}$$
$$= 0 \quad \text{if the activity is rejected}$$

As an example, suppose that it is possible at the Mansfield company to schedule a second shift for the bottleneck machine. The second shift provides 35 effective hours of extra capacity per week, and under the terms of Mansfield's labor agreement it is not possible to schedule a partial shift. Above the costs normally included in the variable profit contributions of the two products, the use of a second shift would result in an additional cost of $550 due to second shift premiums. Let the binary variable y indicate whether to schedule a second shift ($y = 1$ if so; $y = 0$ if not). The model in (5.1) becomes

maximize

$$z = 300x_1 + 400x_2 - 550y$$

subject to

$$3x_1 + 6x_2 - 35y \leq 50$$
$$x_1 \qquad\qquad \leq 8$$
$$x_1 + x_2 \qquad \leq 10$$

$x_1 \geq 0$ and integer; $x_2 \geq 0$ and integer

$y = 0$ or 1

In comparison to the constraints in (5.1) only the first constraint, for machine hours, is different. We have essentially changed the number of machine hours available for manufacturing the two products to $50 + 35y$, where the value of y will be determined by solving the IP problem. If $y = 1$ (the second shift is scheduled), then 85 hours are available, and if $y = 0$ (the second shift is not scheduled), then only 50 hours are available. We also incorporate the cost of the second shift in the objective function.

Now suppose that Mansfield also has the option to schedule a third shift, with a capacity of 28 machine hours at the bottleneck and a premium cost of $620. A similar extension of the original model becomes

maximize

$$z = 300x_1 + 400x_2 - 550y_1 - 620y_2$$

subject to

$$3x_1 + 6x_2 - 35y_1 - 28y_2 \leq 50$$
$$x_1 \qquad\qquad\qquad\quad \leq 8$$
$$x_1 + x_2 \qquad\qquad\quad \leq 10$$
$$x_1 \geq 0 \text{ and integer}; x_2 \geq 0 \text{ and integer}$$
$$y_1 = 0 \text{ or } 1; y_2 = 0 \text{ or } 1$$

The variables y_1 and y_2 indicate whether the second shift and the third shift, respectively, will be scheduled. An additional consideration is that the third shift can be scheduled only if there is a second shift. To represent this requirement we add the constraint

$$y_1 - y_2 \geq 0 \qquad\qquad\qquad\qquad\qquad\qquad\qquad (5.2)$$

Thus if $y_1 = 0$ (there is no second shift), then $y_2 = 0$ (there cannot be a third shift), and if $y_2 = 1$ (there is a third shift), then $y_1 = 1$ (there must be a second shift). Also, if $y_1 = 1$ (there is a second shift), then $y_2 = 0$ or 1 (a third shift is possible but not required). This type of inequality is usually called a **contingency** constraint, because it expresses the fact that the implementation on a third shift is contingent on the existence of a second shift.

It is possible to use an alternative structure to represent this situation. Let y_1 indicate whether a second shift is scheduled (providing 35 more hours and costing $550), and let y_2 indicate whether both additional shifts are scheduled (providing $35 + 28 = 63$ more hours and costing $550 + 620 = \$1170$). We can formulate the problem as follows:

maximize

$$z = 300x_1 + 400x_2 - 550y_1 - 1170y_2$$

subject to

$$3x_1 + \quad 6x_2 - \quad 35y_1 - \quad 63y_2 \le 50$$
$$x_1 \qquad\qquad\qquad\qquad \le \quad 8$$
$$x_1 + \quad x_2 \qquad\qquad\qquad \le \quad 10$$

$x_1 \ge 0$ and integer; $x_2 \ge 0$ and integer

$y_1 = 0$ or 1; $y_2 = 0$ or 1

In this model there is no contingency relation, but rather a **mutually exclusive** relation between the two project variables. To represent this requirement we add the constraint

$$y_1 + y_2 \le 1 \tag{5.3}$$

This "either-or" constraint expresses the fact that y_1 or y_2, but not both, can assume a value of 1.

STARTUP VARIABLES

In some problems there are decisions about the scale of an activity that permit the use of a continuous variable but that also involve startup conditions. In such cases it may be possible to use a binary variable, along with the continuous variable, to model the startup relationship.

For example, the Mansfield company might have a policy on minimum batch sizes in weekly production. In particular, if containers of a given type are scheduled at all, then the economics of the situation dictate that at least three containers of that type should be produced. In order to represent this condition let

$y_j = 1,$ if Type j insulation is scheduled
    $= 0,$ if Type j insulation is not scheduled

Then, for $j = 1$ and $j = 2$ we include the following constraints in the model:

$$x_j - 3y_j \ge 0 \tag{5.4}$$
$$x_j - 99y_j \le 0 \tag{5.5}$$
$$y_j = 0 \text{ or } 1$$

Here the role of the binary variable y_j is a switch that indicates whether or not Type j insulation appears in the schedule. If so, then $y_j = 1$ and constraint (5.4) enforces the startup condition that $x_j \ge 3$. Meanwhile, constraint (5.5) imposes no effective limit on x_j, since we already know from the trucking constraint that $x_j \leq 10$. We selected the coefficient 99 to be larger than any possible value of x_j. Therefore, when $y_j = 1$ this constraint will not interfere with the choice of x_j. On the other hand, when $y_j = 0$, constraint (5.5) forces $x_j = 0$. Meanwhile, constraint (5.4) imposes no effective limit on x_j. In effect, the binary variable y_j is a startup switch that changes the information in constraints (5.4) and (5.5). In summary, the switch works as follows:

	$y_j = 1$	$y_j = 0$
switch:		
constraint (5.4):	$x_j \geq 3$	$x_j \geq 0$
constraint (5.5):	$x_j \leq 99$	$x_j \leq 0$

Incorporating the minimum batch size constraints into the Mansfield model, we obtain

maximize

$$z = 300x_1 \qquad + 400x_2$$

subject to

$$
\begin{aligned}
3x_1 \quad + \quad 6x_2 \quad &\leq 50 \\
x_1 \quad\quad &\leq 8 \\
x_1 - 3y_1 \quad &\geq 0 \\
x_1 - 99y_1 \quad &\leq 0 \\
x_2 - 3y_2 \quad &\geq 0 \\
x_2 - 99y_2 \quad &\leq 0 \\
x_1 \quad + \quad x_2 \quad &\leq 10
\end{aligned}
$$

$x_1 \geq 0$ and integer; $x_2 \geq 0$ and integer

$y_1 = 0$ or 1; $y_2 = 0$ or 1

We could also streamline the model by removing the second inequality and changing 99 to 8 in the fourth inequality. In any event, the important characteristic of startup conditions is that the binary variables appear in constraints with the continuous variables that are involved in the startup condition. This was not the case with project variables.

FIXED COSTS

The minimum batch size constraint is an example of a startup condition that affects the values of certain variables. Another important startup effect involves costs. In particular, there are many situations in which the decision to use an activity incurs a **fixed cost.** To reflect such costs in a model we can use binary variables in the objective function.

We can look at the modeling of fixed costs as requiring a contingency constraint: Payment of the fixed charge is contingent on the activity level. If the activity level is positive, then we incur the fixed charge, but if the activity level is 0, then we do not. In the absence of other startup conditions we may want to deal with a cost function of the form

$$\text{activity cost} = f + cx \quad \text{if} \quad x > 0$$
$$= 0 \quad \text{if} \quad x = 0$$

Here x represents an activity level to be determined, c is a linear cost rate, and f is the fixed charge incurred when $x > 0$. Figure 5.1 shows the graph of this cost structure. As we illustrated above, we use a binary variable in this situation:

$$y = 0 \quad \text{if} \quad x = 0$$
$$= 1 \quad \text{if} \quad x > 0$$

Then, in the objective function we include the total activity costs as follows:

$$\text{cost} = fy + cx \tag{5.6}$$

With this representation, we incur the fixed charge in the objective function only when y equals 1.

The formulation problem does not end here, because the binary variable does not yet appear in the problem constraints. Specifically, we have not repre-

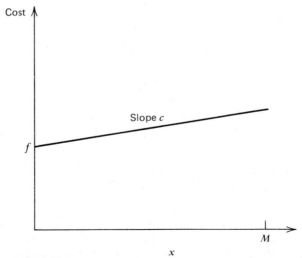

FIGURE 5.1

sented the contingency requirement that a fixed charge is incurred (that is, $y = 1$) whenever there is a positive activity level (that is, $x > 0$). We next identify a constant M that exceeds the largest possible value of the decision variable x. Then we represent the contingency constraint by the requirement that

$$x \leq My \qquad\qquad (5.7)$$

This constraint will force $y = 1$ if there is any activity; in turn this value incurs the fixed cost in equation (5.6). When $y = 0$ we avoid the fixed cost in equation (5.6). At the same time we do not permit any activity because constraint (5.7) reduces to $x \leq 0$.

An additional issue arises when $x = 0$. Constraint (5.7) will then permit y to be either 0 or 1. This ambiguity is resolved, however, by the nature of the objective function. Specifically, the IP optimization algorithm will choose $y = 0$, the value of the decision variable producing the smallest (least expensive) value of the objective function.

As an example, suppose that in the one-shift version of the Mansfield problem there is still a minimum batch size requirement, as expressed in equations (5.4) and (5.5). In addition, suppose that there is also a fixed cost of \$250 for any production run of Type 1 insulation and a fixed cost of \$325 for any production run of Type 2 insulation. Because we have already introduced y_1 and y_2 as startup indicators, it is a simple matter to reflect these costs in the objective function. Our full model becomes

maximize

$$z = 300x_1 - 250y_1 + 400x_2 - 325y_2$$

subject to

$$
\begin{aligned}
3x_1 \quad\quad + \quad 6x_2 \quad\quad &\leq 50 \\
x_1 - 3y_1 \quad\quad\quad\quad\quad &\geq 0 \\
x_1 - 8y_1 \quad\quad\quad\quad\quad &\leq 0 \\
x_2 - 3y_2 &\geq 0 \\
x_2 - 99y_2 &\leq 0 \\
x_1 \quad\quad + \quad x_2 \quad\quad &\leq 10
\end{aligned}
$$

$x_1 \geq 0$ and integer; $x_2 \geq 0$ and integer

$y_1 = 0$ or 1; $y_2 = 0$ or 1

The foregoing discussion suggests how we can use binary variables to describe fairly complicated relationships. In fact, the major role of binary variables is to help deal with noncontinuous logical structures. The benefit of formulating these problems with binary variables is that we can find solutions using any standard IP algorithm.

COMMON IP FORMULATIONS

In this section we describe some well-known IP models. These models illustrate how to apply the concepts of the previous section, and they also suggest the settings in which IP approaches have proven fruitful.

CAPITAL BUDGETING

A company is considering a set of investment proposals from its two divisions. Proposal j has an estimated present value, denoted v_j, along with requirements for floor space (s_j), work-force expansion (w_j), and capital expenditures in the current year (c_j). The company has available a certain amount of floor space (S), a known potential for work-force expansion (W), and a budget for capital expenditures (C). Suppose that there are seven proposals available, three from Division 1 and four from Division 2. We might formulate the project selection problem as the following IP:

maximize

$$\sum_{j=1}^{7} v_j y_j$$

subject to

$$\sum_{j=1}^{7} s_j y_j \leq S$$

$$\sum_{j=1}^{7} w_j y_j \leq W \tag{5.8}$$

$$\sum_{j=1}^{7} c_j y_j \leq C$$

where $y_1 - y_3$ are binary variables representing the accept/reject decisions for the Division 1 proposals and $y_4 - y_7$ are binary variables for the Division 2 proposals. We can imagine that there might be a number of additional constraints that arise either from technological considerations or from company policy. These are illustrated below, along with the constraints that would be added to the model:

1. Proposals 3 and 5 are contingent on Proposal 2.

$$y_2 - y_3 \geq 0 \quad \text{and} \quad y_2 - y_5 \geq 0$$

2. At least one proposal must be accepted from Division 1.

$$y_1 + y_2 + y_3 \geq 1$$

3. Proposals 2, 4, and 6 duplicate certain capabilities, and only one of them can be implemented.

$$y_2 + y_4 + y_6 \leq 1$$

4. Proposals 4 and 5 must be done together or else not at all.

$$y_4 - y_5 = 0$$

5. Exactly two of the Division 2 proposals should be accepted.

$$y_4 + y_5 + y_6 + y_7 = 2$$

KNAPSACK PROBLEM

A special case of the capital budgeting model contains just one constraint. Such a model is called the **knapsack** problem. The name comes from the decision faced by a hiker who wants to load a knapsack in the best possible way. Each item that could go into the knapsack has a given value (v_j) to the hiker and also a given weight (w_j). The problem is to maximize the value of the knapsack's contents (maximize $\Sigma\, v_j y_j$) subject to the knapsack's limited weight capacity ($\Sigma\, w_j y_j \leq W$).

WAREHOUSE LOCATION

The warehouse location model generalizes the transportation model by allowing selection of the sources (warehouse locations). In addition to a variable cost for shipment along any source-destination route there is also a fixed cost for scheduling activity in any warehouse.

If we define f_i as the fixed cost for using source i, the problem becomes

minimize

$$\sum_i \sum_j c_{ij} x_{ij} + \sum_i f_i y_i$$

subject to

$$\sum_{j=1}^{n} x_{ij} \leq a_i \qquad \text{for} \qquad i = 1, 2, \ldots, m \tag{5.9}$$

$$\sum_{i=1}^{m} x_{ij} \geq b_j \qquad \text{for} \qquad j = 1, 2, \ldots, n \tag{5.10}$$

$$x_{ij} \leq M y_i \qquad \text{for all } (i,j) \tag{5.11}$$

$$x_{ij} \geq 0$$

$$y_i = 0 \text{ or } 1 \text{ and integer}$$

Note that the first set of terms in the objective function represents the variable costs, and the second set represents the total fixed charges. In addition, constraints (5.9) limit the supply at source i, constraints (5.10) specify the demand at destination j, and constraints (5.11) reflect the fixed charge contingency relationships. Once we have formulated the problem in this way, we can economize on the total number of constraints by replacing (5.9) and (5.11) with the constraint

$$\sum_{j=1}^{n} x_{ij} \leq a_i y_i \qquad \text{for} \qquad i = 1, 2, \ldots, m \tag{5.12}$$

FIXED CHARGE TRANSPORTATION PROBLEM

Another variation of the transportation model contains fixed costs and variable costs for each route. For example, the trucking cost along a particular route may consist of a fixed charge (for the truck driver's fee) and a variable cost (for the tonnage carried). In the general model we use a binary variable y_{ij} to denote whether the route from location i to destination j is used. The model takes the following form:

minimize

$$\sum_{i} \sum_{j} c_{ij} x_{ij} + \sum_{i} \sum_{j} f_{ij} y_{ij}$$

subject to

$$\sum_{j=1}^{n} x_{ij} \leq a_i \qquad \text{for} \qquad i = 1, 2, \ldots, m \tag{5.13}$$

$$\sum_{i=1}^{m} x_{ij} \geq b_j \qquad \text{for} \qquad j = 1, 2, \ldots, n \tag{5.14}$$

$$x_{ij} \leq M y_{ij} \qquad \text{for all } (i,j) \tag{5.15}$$

In this model we cannot condense the contingency relationships in equation (5.15) as we did with equation (5.11).

INCREMENTAL QUANTITY DISCOUNTS

A fixed cost is a special case of a more general structure in which costs are piecewise linear and show economies of scale. As an illustration of this general structure, consider a problem that involves ordering from a supplier who offers a quantity discount. In particular, there is a $500 charge for servicing the order, along with a unit price of $6 for the first 100 units, $4 for the next 200 units, and $3 for the next 200 units. The supplier does not accept orders greater than 500 units.

The ordering cost function is shown in Figure 5.2. The graph reflects a cost function with three linear segments and with marginal costs that improve as the order quantity increases. In this function the slopes of the three segments are 6, 4, and 3. We can think of this function as a combination of three component functions, each having its own fixed cost and its own variable cost. The first component function has a fixed cost of $500 and a variable cost of $6 per unit. The second component function has a fixed cost of $700 and a variable cost of $4 per unit. We find this fixed cost by taking the middle segment of Figure 5.2 and extrapolating it toward a quantity of 0, as shown by a dotted line in the figure. To

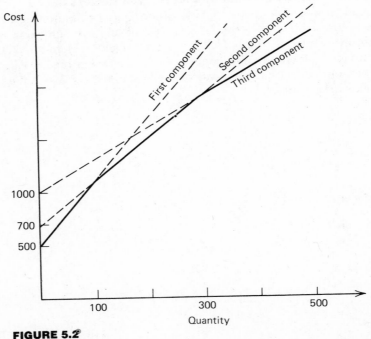

FIGURE 5.2

find the intercept, we require that the first component function and the second component function cross

$$f_2 + 4x = 500 + 6x$$

Because the crossing point occurs at $x = 100$, we obtain

$$f_2 + 4(100) = 500 + 6(100)$$

or

$$f_2 = 700$$

Similarly, the third component function has a fixed cost of $1000 and a variable cost of $3 per unit. We find the intercept by using the fact that the second and third component functions cross at the point $x = 300$.

Now we can think of the overall cost function as comprised of the three component functions and a three-way contingency constraint. In other words, if we order up to 100 units, we shall use the first component function; if we order more than 100 but no more than 300 units, we shall use the second component function; and if we order more than 300 units we shall use the third component function. To represent this structure in the model we define two new variables, y_i and z_i, in the following way:

$y_i = 1$, if x corresponds to the ith component function
   $= 0$ otherwise

$z_i = x$, if x corresponds to the ith component function
   $= 0$ otherwise

Then the model contains the following structure:

minimize

$$500y_1 + 700y_2 + 1000y_3 + 6z_1 + 4z_2 + 3z_3$$

subject to

(other problem constraints)

$$z_1 \leq 100y_1 \tag{5.16}$$

$$z_2 \leq 300y_2 \tag{5.17}$$

$$z_3 \leq 500y_3 \tag{5.18}$$

$$y_1 + y_2 + y_3 \leq 1 \tag{5.19}$$

$$z_i \geq 0 \qquad \text{for all } i$$

$$y_i = 0 \text{ or } 1 \qquad \text{for all } i$$

This formulation effectively replaces the activity level x with the term $(z_1 + z_2 + z_3)$ anywhere x would appear in the formulation. Note that the binary variables y_i perform two functions. First, due to constraint (5.19), they ensure that at most one z_i is positive while the others are 0. Second, due to the three-way contingency in equations (5.16) to (5.18), they ensure that the objective function correctly represents the cost structure.

Here, again, there is an additional issue worth noticing. When $y_3 = 1$, it is feasible in the constraints to have an order quantity of 50 (that is, $x = z_3 = 50$). From Figure 5.2 we see that at $x = 50$, the third component function overstates the actual ordering cost. Fortunately, the optimization implied in the objective function would never select this value, because we would prefer to have $y_1 = 1$ instead. Then costs would be evaluated on the first component function, with $x = z_1 = 50$ and $y_3 = z_3 = 0$.

SUBSETS OF CONSTRAINTS

At times, a firm may decide to satisfy only some of a group of constraints. To illustrate the modeling approach that might capture such a requirement, suppose we are working with a situation that contains the transportation model constraints (5.9) and (5.10), among others. First, suppose that we would be satisfied if at least $n - 2$ of the n demand constraints were met. (This might be the case if we were willing to permit lost sales at two demand locations.) Let

$z_j = 1$, if the jth demand constraint is met
$\quad = 0$ otherwise

Then we could write our demand constraints as follows:

$$\sum_{i=1}^{m} x_{ij} \geq b_j z_j \tag{5.20}$$

together with the additional requirement:

$$\sum_{j=1}^{n} z_j \geq n - 2 \tag{5.21}$$

Constraint (5.21) requires that at least $n - 2$ of the demand constraints be met. When $z_j = 1$, constraint (5.20) reduces to the original demand constraint (5.10). On the other hand, when $z_j = 0$, constraint (5.20) will not restrict the quantity shipped to destination j.

Similarly, suppose we would be satisfied if at least $m - 3$ of the m supply constraints were met. (This might be the case if we could expand the work force at up to three supply locations in order to provide additional capacity.) Let

$u_i = 1$, if the ith supply constraint is met
$\quad = 0$ otherwise

Then we could write our supply constraints as follows:

$$\sum_{j=1}^{n} x_{ij} \le a_i u_i + M(1 - u_i) \tag{5.22}$$

together with the additional requirement:

$$\sum_{i=1}^{m} u_i \ge m - 3 \tag{5.23}$$

Constraint (5.23) requires that at least $m - 3$ of the supply constraints be met. When $u_i = 1$, constraint (5.22) reduces to the original supply constraint (5.9). On the other hand, when $u_i = 0$, constraint (5.22) will not limit the quantity shipped from source i as long as M is an arbitrary large number, such as the sum of all demands.

THE STRUCTURE OF IP PROBLEMS

We can gain some insight into the differences between IP and LP problems by approaching the original Mansfield example (5.1) as we would approach an LP. Because there are only two variables in the problem, we can use a graphical technique to solve the LP version of the model, ignoring the integer requirements. This version is called the **LP relaxation** of the IP problem. Figure 5.3 depicts the feasible region for the LP relaxation. Using the graphical technique for LP, we find that the optimal solution occurs at the intersection of the production and trucking constraints. We can easily verify that this intersection corresponds to the solution

$$x_1 = \frac{10}{3} \text{ (or 3.33)} \qquad x_2 = \frac{20}{3} \text{ (or 6.67)} \qquad z = \frac{11{,}000}{3} \text{ (or 3667)}$$

Clearly this solution, which is optimal for the LP relaxation, is not even feasible for the IP problem because neither decision variable is an integer.

In order for a solution to be feasible in the IP problem, the decision variables must satisfy the LP constraints and also be integers. In other words, feasible solutions to the IP problem occur only at the integer points (sometimes called **lattice points**) that fall within the LP feasible region. Figure 5.4 shows the lattice

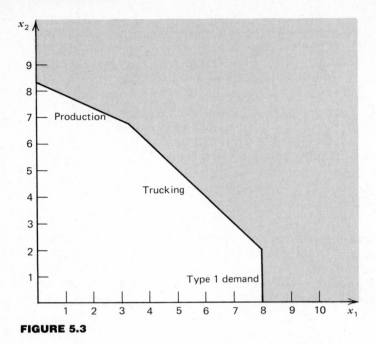

FIGURE 5.3

points for our example problem. In what follows we use our example to illustrate several basic approaches to solving IP problems.

ROUNDING THE LP OPTIMUM

One logical idea for solving IP problems is to round the optimal LP solution to the nearest integer value, or lattice point. If we try this idea in the Mansfield example we produce the solution

$$x_1 = 3 \qquad x_2 = 7 \qquad z = 3700$$

The difficulty with this approach is that the solution is infeasible even for the LP relaxation: It requires a production capacity of 51 hours, but only 50 hours are available.

To deal with this infeasibility, we might in general try to round the LP optimum in a way that preserves feasibility. For the Mansfield problem we could achieve this goal by rounding *down* to produce the solution

$$x_1 = 3 \qquad x_2 = 6 \qquad z = 3300$$

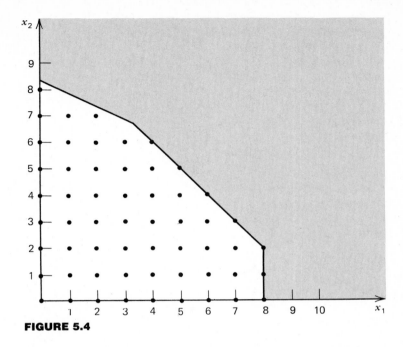

FIGURE 5.4

One problem with rounding to preserve feasibility is that there is no guarantee of optimality. In the Mansfield problem, for example, it turns out that the optimal IP solution attains a better profit than 3300. A second problem with rounding to preserve feasibility is that there may be no way to round the LP optimum to produce a point that is feasible for the IP problem. Figure 5.5 shows the graph of a feasible region with this characteristic. In more complicated problems, rounding may not lead to *any* feasible solution to the IP problem. Nevertheless, rounding may still be attractive in spite of the possibility that it will produce infeasible or suboptimal solutions. Rounding is relatively simple and convenient. Moreover, empirical observation suggests that the effect of rounding, especially for mixed integer programs, is often small. However, this result does not apply to binary integer programs.

Based on our example we can see some important differences between IP problems and LP problems. First of all, the approach of rounding the LP optimum may not preserve feasibility; even if it does, the resulting feasible solution may not be optimal. Second, the IP optimal solution can, and often does, fall in the interior of the LP feasible region. As a result, it is not possible to use a solution technique (such as the simplex method) that examines only the corner points on the boundary of the LP feasible region. Third, the IP problem has only a finite number of feasible points, whereas the LP relaxation has an infinite number of feasible points.

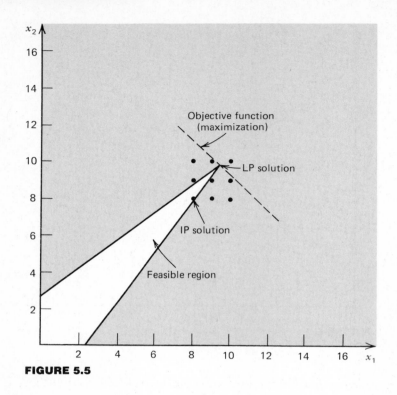

FIGURE 5.5

COMPLETE ENUMERATION

Intuition may suggest that we can solve IP problems more easily than LP problems because integer programs have only a finite number of feasible solutions. For example, in the Mansfield problem we could calculate the value of the objective function for each of the 57 lattice points that satisfy the LP constraints. Then we could identify the IP optimal solution by finding the lattice point that has the highest value of the objective function. Looking at the graph in Figure 5.4, we find that this does not seem to be a very difficult task.

Unfortunately the two-dimensional representation may mislead us. Most practical IP problems have many more than two integer variables, and the number of feasible lattice points grows rapidly as the number of variables increases. For example, if we encountered an IP problem with only 10 variables that could each take on 12 possible values, there could be as many as 12^{10} feasible lattice points. Suppose we could design a computer program to evaluate 100,000 lattice points per second (which is fairly ambitious given the record-keeping that would be necessary). Then complete enumeration of all feasible solutions could require our program to run for roughly 620,000 seconds, or more than a week. As a result, complete enumeration is not a practical solution approach, except in relatively small problems.

CUTTING PLANES

Because of the difficulty of solving IP problems using complete enumeration, some other, more efficient approach is necessary. Although rounding the LP optimum may not work, we can design an effective approach based on intelligent use of LP. One such approach is the cutting plane method.

In the cutting plane method we modify the LP relaxation to remove noninteger LP optima from the LP feasible region. Specifically, we add a constraint to the LP relaxation that excludes the noninteger LP optimum but does not exclude any integer points. Figure 5.6 shows the **cutting plane** constraint that we add to the Mansfield problem to exclude the LP optimum of $x_1 = 3.33$, $x_2 = 6.67$, $z = 3667$. It is not necessary here to discuss the technical details of this approach. All we need to say is that it is fairly easy to generate the appropriate cutting plane while guaranteeing that no lattice points are excluded from the feasible region.

By adding a new constraint to the LP relaxation, we have changed the LP feasible region. As a result, we can solve the new, modified LP problem. We continue this process of adding additional cutting plane constraints and solving the modified problem until the optimal LP solution is integer. This solution is then the optimal solution to the original IP problem.

The cutting plane method is attractive because it relies on the power of linear programming. In practice, however, it is often necessary to solve a large number of LP problems before the modified LP solution has the required inte-

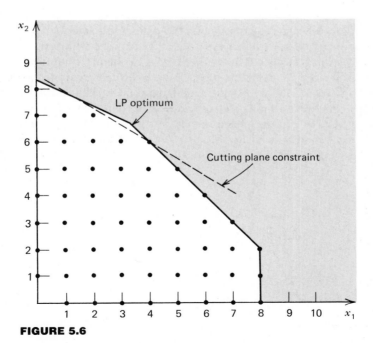

FIGURE 5.6

ger values. Therefore, few commercially available IP algorithms rely on the cutting plane approach.

THE BRANCH AND BOUND TECHNIQUE

In the previous section we mentioned complete enumeration as a possible solution approach, but we indicated that it might be impractical for problems with many variables. One potential difficulty in complete enumeration is the design of an efficient means of generating those combinations of variables that are feasible. Even if we could resolve this difficulty, a related problem is that when there are many feasible solutions the examination of each distinct combination might be prohibitively time-consuming. In this section we show how to resolve these difficulties.

The most effective general methods for solving integer programming problems are various forms of a technique known as **branch and bound.** This technique relies on a tree-structured search procedure and attacks the original problem with a "divide-and-conquer" strategy. It divides the original problem into subproblems and solves a modified version of each subproblem. Then it uses the information in these solutions to shorten the task of identifying an optimum.

BRANCHING

In branch and bound, the **branching** step creates subproblems according to a particular tree-search strategy. In the branching scheme we shall illustrate, information from the solution of the LP relaxation will determine how to create subproblems. Recall that in the Mansfield problem the optimal values for the LP relaxation were $x_1 = 3.33$ and $x_2 = 6.67$. We shall create subproblems by adding inequality constraints on one of the fractional variables, for example, x_1. In one subproblem we add the constraint $x_1 \geq 4$, while in the other subproblem we require $x_1 \leq 3$. These constraints use as upper and lower limits on x_1 the integer values on either side of its value (3.33) in the LP solution.

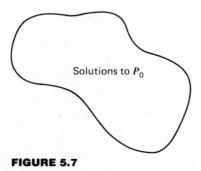

Solutions to P_0

FIGURE 5.7

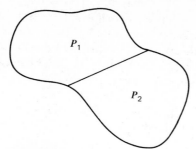

FIGURE 5.8

We can visualize the creation of subproblems with the aid of a simple diagram. In Figure 5.7 we represent the set of all feasible solutions to the original IP problem, labeled P_0. In Figure 5.8 we "divide" P_0 into two subproblems, labeled P_1 and P_2. The figure shows that P_1 and P_2 do not overlap and that together they replace all of P_0. Moreover, since P_1 and P_2 are smaller than P_0, they should be easier to "conquer." The task that remains is to solve P_1 and P_2. The better of their solutions will be the best solution to P_0.

Earlier we alluded to the branch and bound procedure as a tree-structured search. We pursue this idea in Figure 5.9. At the top of the tree shown in Figure 5.9, the node for P_0 represents the original Mansfield problem. Two branches emanate from the top node, each corresponding to the addition of a single

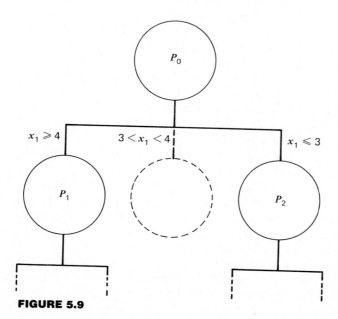

FIGURE 5.9

constraint to P_0. In problem P_1 we have the original IP, along with the requirement $x_1 \geq 4$. In problem P_2 we have the original IP, along with the requirement $x_1 \leq 3$. Note that these two requirements are **mutually exclusive,** which means that there is no overlap between the condition $x_1 \leq 3$ and the condition $x_1 \geq 4$. Moreover, these two requirements are **exhaustive,** which means that no other possibilities exist. (In principle, there could be a branch corresponding to the condition $3 < x_1 < 4$, as we show in Figure 5.9; but there would be no feasible solutions to the IP in this case because no integer values of x_1 would be permitted. Therefore, this third branch could not even lead to a feasible solution to the original problem, let alone an optimal one.) We refer to P_0 as **level 0** in the tree, and we refer to P_1 and P_2 as comprising **level 1.**

We should think of the two problems on level 1 as IP problems in their own right. They are each smaller than P_0 in the sense that their feasible regions are contained within the feasible region of the original problem. For this reason they are subproblems of P_0. Furthermore, as noted above, we can solve P_0 by solving both P_1 and P_2 and then choosing the better of the two solutions. Thus, we can think of P_1 and P_2 as replacing P_0 in our search for an optimal solution. Because they, too, are IP problems, we may ultimately want to replace them with their own subproblems in the course of our search.

BOUNDING

After the branching step of branch and bound replaces an IP problem with two smaller problems, the **bounding** step produces for each subproblem a bound guaranteed to be at least as good as the subproblem's optimal solution. One reasonable way to obtain such a bound is to use the optimal value of the objective function in the subproblem's LP relaxation.

In general terms, we can compute a bound by relaxing at least one of the problem requirements (in this case the requirement that certain variables must be integers) and solving the relaxed problem. The process of relaxing a requirement may help but cannot hurt the objective function. As a result, the optimal value of the objective function will be at least as good after relaxation as before. Hence, it serves as a valid bound.

To see how this principle works in the case of an IP problem, consider the diagram in Figure 5.10. As the figure indicates, the set of feasible solutions for the LP relaxation of P_0 contains the set of IP feasible solutions. Therefore, the optimal solution to the LP relaxation must be at least as good as the optimal solution to the corresponding IP. In fact, there are two cases. In Figure 5.10, our diagram indicates that the LP optimum (z_{LP}^*) does not lie in the set of IP feasible solutions. In this case, the LP optimum provides only a bound for the IP problem. In Figure 5.11, by contrast, the LP optimum happens to be IP feasible. In this case we obtain not only a bound but also an optimal solution to the IP.

In order to anticipate how bounds can help us solve an IP problem, let us take P_0 to be the IP problem whose feasible solutions are represented in Figure

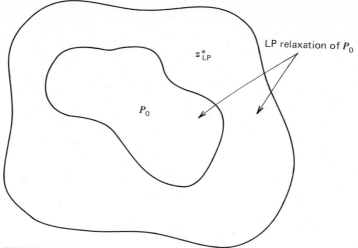

FIGURE 5.10

5.10. As in the Mansfield example, suppose P_0 is a maximization problem. Once we divide P_0 into subproblems P_1 and P_2, we may still face a formidable search because P_1 and P_2 are both IP problems, and they may be difficult to solve. Assume, however, that their LP relaxations, denoted LP_1 and LP_2, are easy to solve. Suppose that when we solve LP_1 we happen to obtain an integer solution with an optimal objective function value of z_1^*. In Figure 5.12 we see that z_1^* lies

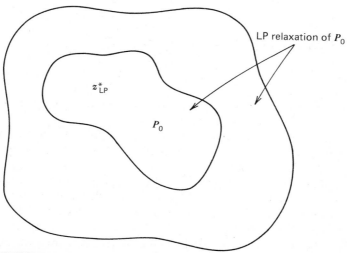

FIGURE 5.11

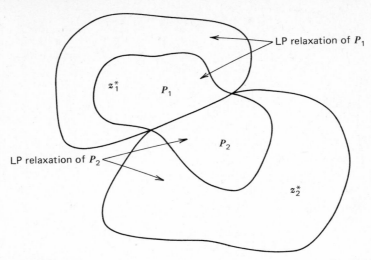

FIGURE 5.12

inside the IP feasible region for P_1. Suppose also that when we solve LP_2 we obtain a noninteger solution with a value of z_2^* that is less than z_1^*. Again, considering Figure 5.12 we see that z_2^* lies outside the IP feasible region for P_2. Because z_2^* is a bound on the optimal solution of P_2, we know that no solution of P_2 could ever be better than z_2^*. Because $z_2^* < z_1^*$, no solution of P_2 could be as good as z_1^*, which is the value of a feasible solution already on hand. Therefore, although we have not yet solved the integer program P_2, the information in its bound tells us we do not need to solve it, for its best solution cannot be as good as the solution we have already found.

TREE-STRUCTURED SEARCHING

The branching step creates two integer programs to be solved in place of the original IP. As we indicated earlier, we solve the original problem by solving the two subproblems and choosing the better of the two solutions. However, because both of the subproblems are themselves IP problems, we may want to solve them with the aid of further branching.

We will deal with each subproblem in one of three ways. First, when solving its LP relaxation we may encounter an integer solution. In that case we will have solved an IP with only LP effort. Second, we may encounter an infeasible LP. In that case we will know that no integer solution to the subproblem can exist. Third, we may encounter an LP relaxation with a noninteger optimum. In that case we will have to create its subproblems and investigate them, or else discover a good reason to drop the problem from consideration. Until we deal with a subproblem in one of these three ways, we call it an **active** subproblem. In the tree diagram, we refer to the corresponding node as an **active node.**

Algorithm 5.1 outlines the steps in the branch and bound procedure. For the time being assume that we are solving a maximization problem. Therefore, when we solve an LP relaxation, its optimal objective function value will be at least as large as that of the corresponding IP. For this reason, we refer to it as an *upper* bound. In what follows we illustrate the steps in Algorithm 5.1 by solving the Mansfield example.

ALGORITHM 5.1
The Branch and Bound Procedure for Maximization Problems

1. INITIAL BOUND
Calculate an upper bound for the problem. Use the optimal value for the LP relaxation of the original IP problem. If the solution to the LP problem is feasible, stop; the solution is optimal.

2. BRANCH
Select an active node. Choose a (fractional) variable at this node, and divide its possible values into two mutually exclusive and exhaustive sets. Create a new branch and node in the tree to correspond to each set.

3. BOUND
Calculate an upper bound for each new node created in Step 2, using the optimal value for its LP relaxation.

4. UPDATE
Set the lower bound equal to the best objective function value of all feasible integer solutions obtained so far.

5. PRUNE
Delete an active node from the tree if

a. Its LP relaxation produces a feasible integer solution
b. Its LP relaxation is infeasible
c. Its upper bound is lower than the lower bound calculated at Step 4

6. CHECK
Stop if all nodes have been pruned. The optimal solution is the best solution obtained so far. If some nodes have not been pruned, return to Step 2.

Step 1: Initial Bound We have already seen how to calculate an upper bound for the Mansfield problem. The solution to the LP relaxation of the original IP problem (Problem P_0) is $x_1 = 3.33$ and $x_2 = 6.67$, with a profit of $z = 3667$. As a result, 3667 is an upper bound on the optimal solution to the IP problem. If we had been fortunate, the solution to problem P_0 would have contained integer values. In this case we could have stopped, because the LP relaxation would have produced an optimal solution to the IP problem. Because our solution does not have integer values, we proceed.

Step 2: Branch We shall branch on variables that have fractional values. If there are several fractional variables, we arbitrarily choose the variable closest to being an integer. In Problem P_0 both x_1 and x_2 have fractional values, and both are equally close to an integer value. Here we break the tie arbitrarily and select x_1 for branching. As we discussed earlier, we need to consider only two different subproblems, one corresponding to $x_1 \geq 4$ and the other to $x_1 \leq 3$. We denote these problems P_1 and P_2, respectively. Their specific formulations are as follows:

Problem P_1
maximize

$$z = 300x_1 + 400x_2$$

subject to

$$
\begin{aligned}
3x_1 + 6x_2 &\leq 50 \\
x_1 &\leq 8 \\
x_1 + x_2 &\leq 10 \\
x_1 &\geq 4 \\
x_1, x_2 &\geq 0 \text{ and integer}
\end{aligned}
\tag{5.24}
$$

Problem P_2
maximize

$$z = 300x_1 + 400x_2$$

subject to

$$
\begin{aligned}
3x_1 + 6x_2 &\leq 50 \\
x_1 &\leq 8 \\
x_1 + x_2 &\leq 10 \\
x_1 &\leq 3 \\
x_1, x_2 &\geq 0 \text{ and integer}
\end{aligned}
\tag{5.25}
$$

Step 3: Bound We can immediately calculate upper bounds for P_1 and P_2 by solving their LP relaxations. Figures 5.13 and 5.14 show these problems graphically. The solution to the LP relaxation of P_1 is

$$x_1 = 4 \qquad x_2 = 6 \qquad z = 3600$$

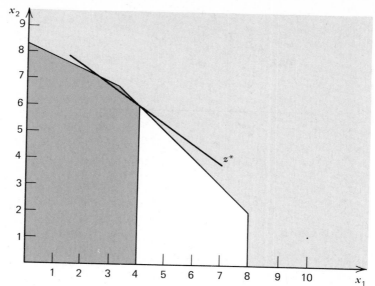

FIGURE 5.13

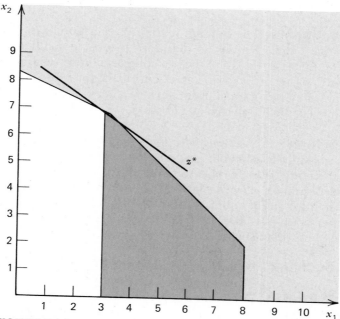

FIGURE 5.14

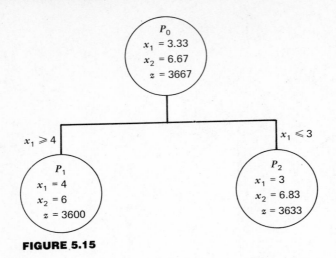

FIGURE 5.15

and the solution to the LP relaxation of P_2 is

$$x_1 = 3 \qquad x_2 = 6.83 \qquad z = 3633$$

Thus, all solutions to P_1 have a profit of 3600 or less, and all solutions to P_2 have a profit of 3633 or less. The solutions to the LP relaxations are recorded in the nodes of the tree in Figure 5.15.

Step 4: Update The solution to the LP relaxation of P_1 has integer values of the decision variables and is therefore a feasible solution to the original IP problem. Because this is also the best integer solution obtained so far (in fact, the only one), we record its value as a benchmark for subsequent comparisons. We now know that the optimal profit must be at least as large as 3600. As a result, we can interpret this value as a *lower* bound.

Step 5: Prune Continuing with P_1, we know that the solution to its LP relaxation is not only feasible but also optimal for P_1. Therefore, we do not need to enumerate any other feasible solutions of P_1. Instead, we can **prune** the tree at P_1, which means that we can avoid the portion of the tree emanating from P_1 in our search for an optimum. On the other hand, we cannot prune the tree at P_2. Its upper bound of 3633 indicates that there *may* be an integer solution with a profit greater than the best feasible value found so far.

Step 6: Check We have not pruned the tree at problem P_2, so we proceed.

Step 2: Branch There is one node (P_2) from which to branch. Examining the solution to the LP relaxation of P_2, we see that only x_2 takes on a fractional value

(6.83). We branch by adding inequalities that constrain x_2 above or below this value. Thus, we create two new subproblems from P_2, one corresponding to $x_2 \geq 7$ and the other to $x_2 \leq 6$. (We ignore the set of solutions in which $6 < x_2 < 7$ because it cannot contain an integer solution.) We denote these problems P_3 and P_4, respectively. Their specific formulations are as follows:

Problem P_3
maximize

$$z = 300x_1 + 400x_2$$

subject to

$$
\begin{aligned}
3x_1 + 6x_2 &\leq 50 \\
x_1 &\leq 8 \\
x_1 + x_2 &\leq 10 \\
x_1 &\leq 3 \\
x_2 &\geq 7 \\
x_1, x_2 &\geq 0 \text{ and integer}
\end{aligned}
\tag{5.26}
$$

Problem P_4
maximize

$$z = 300x_1 + 400x_2$$

subject to

$$
\begin{aligned}
3x_1 + 6x_2 &\leq 50 \\
x_1 &\leq 8 \\
x_1 + x_2 &\leq 10 \\
x_1 &\leq 3 \\
x_2 &\leq 6 \\
x_1, x_2 &\geq 0 \text{ and integer}
\end{aligned}
\tag{5.27}
$$

Step 3: Bound In Figure 5.16 we find that the LP relaxation of P_3 produces the solution

$$x_1 = 2.67 \quad x_2 = 7 \quad z = 3600$$

and in Figure 5.17 we find that the LP relaxation of P_4 produces the solution

$$x_1 = 3 \quad x_2 = 6 \quad z = 3300$$

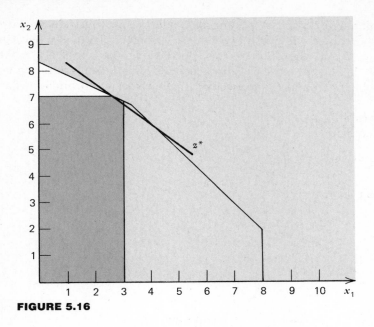

FIGURE 5.16

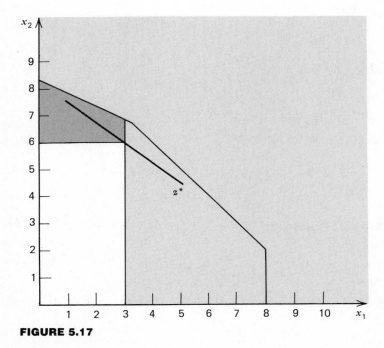

FIGURE 5.17

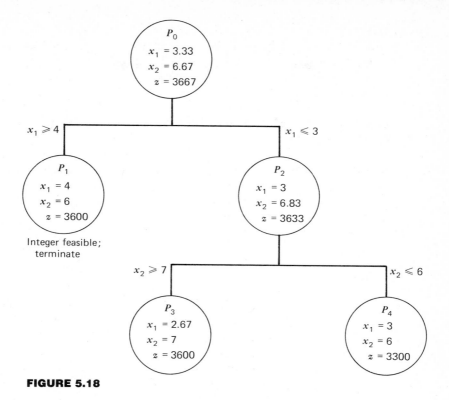

FIGURE 5.18

Thus, all solutions to P_3 have a profit of 3600 or less, and all solutions to P_4 have a profit of 3300 or less. The status of the tree search is displayed in Figure 5.18.

Step 4: Update The solution to the LP relaxation of P_4 has integer values of the decision variables. However, this integer solution has a profit of 3300, which is less than 3600, the profit of the best solution found so far. Therefore, there is no need to update the lower bound.

Step 5: Prune We next consider pruning the tree at P_3. If we were looking for only one optimal solution, pruning would be possible. To see why this is so, recall that we earlier encountered a feasible solution with a profit of 3600. We also know that no solution to P_3 could achieve a profit greater than 3600. (We learned this fact from solving its LP relaxation.) Therefore, it would be unnecessary for us to enumerate the feasible solutions of P_3 if we want to find only one optimum. Suppose, however, that in addition to determining the optimal profit we want to find all alternate optima. In this case, we shall have to consider P_3 further, because at this point its bound tells us that there *may* be a feasible solution to P_3 with a profit of 3600. Therefore, we cannot prune the tree at P_3.

With respect to P_4, the situation is different. The LP relaxation of P_4 produced an upper bound of 3300. This means that no feasible solution of P_4 achieves a profit greater than 3300. It follows that no feasible solution of P_4 can be optimal because we already know that the optimal profit is at least 3600. Therefore, we can prune the tree at P_4.

Step 6: Check As discussed above, we did not prune the tree at subproblem P_3, so we proceed.

Step 2: Branch Examining the solution to the LP relaxation of P_3 we see that only x_1 takes on a fractional value, 2.67. We branch by adding the constraints $x_1 \geq 3$ to form P_5 and $x_1 \leq 2$ to form P_6. (Again, we ignore the set of solutions for which $2 < x_1 < 3$, because it cannot contain an integer solution.) The specific formulations are as follows:

Problem P_5
maximize

$$z = 300x_1 + 400x_2$$

subject to

$$
\begin{aligned}
3x_1 + 6x_2 &\leq 50 \\
x_1 &\leq 8 \\
x_1 + x_2 &\leq 10 \\
x_1 &\leq 3 \\
x_2 &\geq 7 \\
x_1 &\geq 3 \\
x_1, x_2 &\geq 0 \text{ and integer}
\end{aligned}
\tag{5.28}
$$

Problem P_6
maximize

$$z = 300x_1 + 400x_2$$

subject to

$$
\begin{aligned}
3x_1 + 6x_2 &\leq 50 \\
x_1 &\leq 8 \\
x_1 + x_2 &\leq 10 \\
x_1 &\leq 3 \\
x_2 &\geq 7
\end{aligned}
\tag{5.29}
$$

$$x_1 \quad\quad \leq \; 2$$
$$x_1, x_2 \quad \geq \; 0 \text{ and integer}$$

Step 3: Bound Figure 5.19 shows that the LP relaxation of P_5 is infeasible. Therefore, there is no feasible solution to P_5. Meanwhile, Figure 5.20 shows that the LP relaxation of P_6 produces the following solution:

$$x_1 = 2 \quad\quad x_2 = 7.33 \quad\quad z = 3533$$

Thus, all solutions to P_6 have a profit of 3533 or less. Figure 5.21 shows the status of the tree search.

Step 4: Update Since neither of our LP relaxations produced an integer feasible solution, there is no basis for updating the best integer solution we have found so far.

Step 5: Prune As indicated above, we can prune the tree at P_5 because it contains no feasible solutions. We can also prune the tree at P_6 because its upper bound (3533) is smaller than the lower bound (3600).

Step 6: Check We have no active subproblems left to examine. All feasible solutions other than the ones we have explicitly encountered lie in portions of the tree that we have pruned. Hence, the optimal solution is the best integer

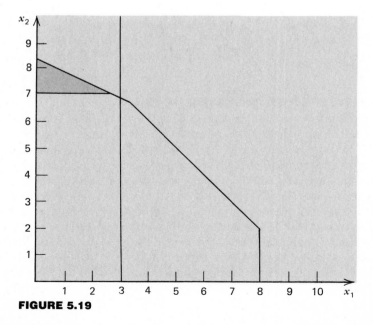

FIGURE 5.19

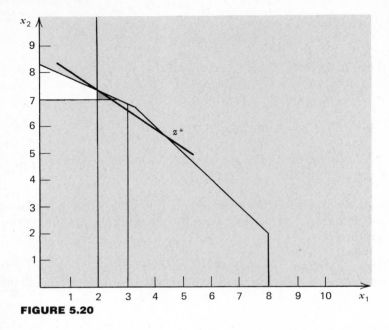

FIGURE 5.20

solution we encountered:

$$x_1 = 4 \qquad x_2 = 6 \qquad z = 3600.$$

Although we sought alternate optima, none were present in this example. Notice that in finding the optimal solution we investigated only seven nodes. That number was sufficient to implicitly compare all 57 feasible solutions.

OVERVIEW OF BRANCH AND BOUND

In the example we observe two different effects. First, as we move deeper into the tree the bounds for the subproblems tend to get worse (lower). This trend occurs because we move deeper into the tree by adding more constraints to the problem and reducing the size of the feasible region. We know that adding constraints can never help the objective function and may hurt it; consequently, the bounds tend to get worse. Second, we observe that the value of the best on-hand feasible solution never gets worse as we move deeper into the tree. Because we find more feasible solutions as we move deeper into the tree, the lower bound may remain unchanged, as it did in our example, or it may actually improve as we encounter better solutions. From these effects we conclude that as we move deeper into the tree the upper bounds move closer to the value of the lower bound. The branch and bound process stops when no remaining upper bound exceeds the lower bound.

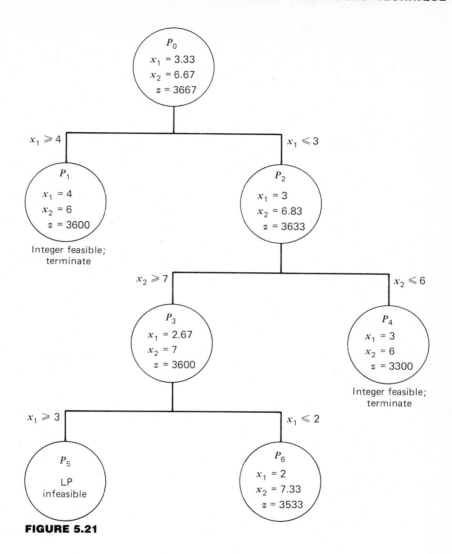

FIGURE 5.21

COMPUTER SOLUTION

Several general purpose computer codes are available for solving integer programming problems. Typically these codes rely on a branch and bound technique, sometimes enhanced by other procedures. Certain computer codes have the capability of solving mixed integer programming problems, while other codes are limited to zero-one programming problems. This may not be a severe limitation for two reasons. First, many of the most practical applications of integer programming are actually zero-one programs. Our earlier discussion of the use of binary variables in IP models reinforces the significance of zero-one programs. Second, it is possible to reformulate any mixed integer program into a zero-one program. Therefore, in principle, we can use a computer code for zero-one problems to solve any mixed integer problem. We elaborate on this point below.

To illustrate the process of reformulating a mixed integer program as a zero-one program we focus on one particular variable x, which is an integer variable in the original model, but which is not a binary variable. We assume that there is a known upper bound U for the variable x. This upper bound may appear explicitly in the model as the inequality $x \leq U$. Alternatively, the upper bound may be implied by broader inequalities in the model. For example, suppose that a model contains the following constraint:

$$3r + 2x + 4s \leq 10$$

This constraint implies $x \leq 5$, so we may take $U = 5$ as an implied upper bound.

Having identified the upper bound U, we set k to be the integer that satisfies the following condition:

$$2^{k-1} \leq U < 2^k \tag{5.30}$$

We then define k zero-one variables $x_1, x_2, \ldots, x_k$; and we make the following substitution:

$$x = x_1 + 2x_2 + 4x_3 + \cdots + 2^{k-1}x_k \tag{5.31}$$

In other words, wherever the variable x appears in the original mixed integer program, we substitute the sum on the right-hand side of equation (5.31). This substitution creates a zero-one program that is logically equivalent to the original, because any feasible value of x can be represented uniquely by a suitable combination of 0's and 1's for the variables x_1 through x_k.

As an example, consider the original Mansfield problem (5.1). Notice that the first constraint implicitly requires $x_2 \leq 8$, and the second constraint explicitly requires $x_1 \leq 8$. Thus, we can replace x_1 by

$$x_{11} + 2x_{12} + 4x_{13} + 8x_{14} \tag{5.32}$$

and we can replace x_2 by

$$x_{21} + 2x_{22} + 4x_{23} + 8x_{24} \tag{5.33}$$

Notice that we can achieve any integer value from 0 to 8 with these substitutions, as shown for x_1 in Table 5.1.

TABLE 5.1

x_1	x_{11}	x_{12}	x_{13}	x_{14}
0	0	0	0	0
1	1	0	0	0
2	0	1	0	0
3	1	1	0	0
4	0	0	1	0
5	1	0	1	0
6	0	1	1	0
7	1	1	1	0
8	0	0	0	1

The reformulation is shown below:

maximize

$$z = 300x_{11} + 600x_{12} + 1200x_{13} + 2400x_{14} + 400x_{21} + 800x_{22} + 1600x_{23} + 3200x_{24}$$

subject to

$$3x_{11} + 6x_{12} + 12x_{13} + 24x_{14} + 6x_{21} + 12x_{22} + 24x_{23} + 48x_{24} \leq 50$$
$$x_{11} + 2x_{12} + 4x_{13} + 8x_{14} \leq 8$$
$$x_{11} + 2x_{12} + 4x_{13} + 8x_{14} + x_{21} + 2x_{22} + 4x_{23} + 8x_{24} \leq 10$$
$$x_{jk} = 0 \text{ or } 1$$

The computer program LINDO, which we discussed in connection with solving linear programs, has the capability to solve zero-one programs, even on a personal computer. Figure 5.22 shows the relevant portion of LINDO output for the solution of the Mansfield example. Notice that the optimal values of x_{1k} imply $x_1 = 4$, and the optimal values of x_{2k} imply $x_2 = 6$. In addition, the output indicates that the optimal value of the objective function is 3600. Thus, LINDO produces a solution to the zero-one reformulation that matches the solution we developed earlier using branch and bound.

As we said earlier, it is possible to reformulate any mixed integer program as a zero-one program. The Mansfield example indicates that we can accomplish this conversion only at the expense of having many more variables than in the original IP formulation. If there is a large number of variables in the original model, or if the upper bound on several variables is quite high, then the reformulation may require an extremely large number of variables. In such cases it would be easier to solve the problem using a computer code for mixed integer programs. Thus, there are practical reasons for using a mixed integer code in preference to a zero-one code.

```
                 OBJECTIVE FUNCTION VALUE

    1)              3600.00000

VARIABLE              VALUE              REDUCED COST
    X11              .000000             100.000000
    X12              .000000             200.000000
    X13             1.000000             400.000000
    X14              .000000             800.000000
    X21              .000000               .000000
    X22             1.000000               .000000
    X23             1.000000               .000000
    X24              .000000               .000000

    ROW          SLACK OR SURPLUS        DUAL PRICES
    2)             2.000000                .000000
    3)             4.000000                .000000
    4)              .000000             400.000000
```

FIGURE 5.22

VARIATIONS OF BRANCH AND BOUND

Having demonstrated the branch and bound process, we can discuss a number of variations of the technique. Among these are an adaptation of the procedure to minimization problems and some different tactical alternatives in its implementation.

MINIMIZATION

Although our exposition of branch and bound has assumed that we are dealing with a maximization problem, we need to make only minor modifications to handle minimization. First, the bounds we calculate from the LP relaxation are *lower* bounds in minimization, rather than upper bounds. Second, we prune a subproblem when its bound is *higher* than the value of an on-hand feasible solution. Finally, the value of the best feasible solution found so far becomes an *upper* bound. With these changes in implementation, Algorithm 5.1 applies to minimization as well as maximization.

TACTICAL ALTERNATIVES

Although Algorithm 5.1 provides a framework for branch and bound, there are still several tactical issues that arise when we implement the procedure. In this section we discuss some of the tactical choices.

One tactical choice involves **initialization** of the algorithm. As our example problem demonstrated, we can exploit an on hand feasible solution to prune portions of the tree. The better the feasible solution, the more pruning we can do. This fact suggests that it is desirable to find a good feasible solution at the outset. In our example problem we encountered a good (in fact, optimal) feasible solution very early in the tree search, but we cannot always be so fortunate. In other problems we run the risk of creating many nodes in the tree before we encounter a feasible solution at all. To reduce this risk we can try to find a good feasible solution initially, and then proceed with Algorithm 5.1. One possibility, for example, would be an attempt to round off the solution obtained from the LP relaxation in Step 1. As we discussed earlier, rounding the LP optimum is not a reliable means of generating a feasible solution; but if our attempt does achieve feasibility, then we at least have a basis for pruning.

We can also extend this idea to Step 3, for each bound we obtain. Ideally, we want the LP relaxation to yield a bound that allows us to prune the tree at the corresponding node. This situation occurred for subproblem P_1. If the LP relaxation yields a noninteger solution that does not allow pruning, then we can again try rounding the LP optimum to produce a good feasible solution. If this attempt succeeds, we might be able to utilize the resulting feasible solution to prune other portions of the tree.

Another tactical choice involves the **node selection rule.** Each time we execute the check at Step 6 and discover that we must do more branching, we usually have a choice of which subproblem to attack next. Two possible rules are the following:

1. Select a subproblem from the highest numbered level of the tree at which branching is possible.
2. Select the subproblem with the best bound. (In a maximization problem, this means the largest bound.)

Rule 1 tends to select subproblems that are relatively close to being solved in the sense that subproblems at levels with high numbers include many constraints added by branching steps. Therefore, their feasible regions tend to be relatively small, and we have a good chance of dealing with them easily, either by finding a feasible solution or by discovering an infeasibility. A common name for Rule 1 is **depth-first search,** because the search thrusts deep into a particular portion of the tree before moving elsewhere. Rule 1 exhibits some computational efficiencies because it keeps the search focused in one area of the tree and thus on subproblems with very similar structures.

The advantage of Rule 2 is that it tends to create fewer subproblems than Rule 1. Because it is continually branching from the node with the best bound, Rule 2 tends to create better feasible solutions than Rule 1; consequently, it does more pruning. Rule 2 is commonly called **best-bound search.** For solving problems by hand, we recommend Rule 2. However, for computer implementation, Rule 2 may require a substantial amount of record-keeping to track progress as it moves from one portion of the tree to another. Rule 2 also requires more computer storage. Therefore, many computer codes rely on Rule 1, especially in solving large IP problems.

A related tactical choice involves the **variable selection rule.** Given that we have decided to branch from a particular subproblem, we must select a variable on which to branch. It seems sensible to branch on variables that have fractional values in the solution to the LP relaxation. Among such variables, several selection rules are still available, such as the following:

1. Select the first noninteger variable in the LP solution.
2. Select the noninteger variable closest to an integer value.
3. Select the noninteger variable farthest from an integer value.

Rule 1 clearly involves the least effort. Rule 2 would appear most likely to produce a good feasible value for one of the resulting subproblems, but Rule 3 should produce a bound in one of the subproblems most likely to lead to pruning. Because the likelihood of pruning, the likelihood of feasibility, and the ease of implementation are all desirable characteristics, we do not have a specific rule to endorse. We reiterate, however, that the choice is a tactical one, and it may affect the computational effort required in any particular IP problem.

We also mention the possibility that we can calculate bounds by methods other than solution of the LP relaxation. In small or specially structured IP problems, we might be able to obtain an optimal solution to the LP relaxation by means other than LP. This idea has been implemented successfully in a number of optimization problems that could be solved by IP but lend themselves readily to more specialized methods. Similarly, in very large IP problems, the solution of the LP relaxation might itself be prohibitively time-consuming, and there may be an incentive to solve a problem that is simpler than the LP relaxation in order to calculate a bound. We can think of this bound as arising from a feasible (but not necessarily optimal) solution to the LP relaxation. In such cases we might prefer to calculate bounds more quickly (but less effectively) and spend more time in the tree search.

Finally, we consider the possibility of using different **pruning rules.** In our example we used a rule that calls for pruning a subproblem when its bound is worse than the value of the best feasible solution yet found. This rule will identify all optimal solutions. A slight variation calls for pruning a subproblem when its bound is no better than the value of the best feasible solution yet found. This rule will find only one optimal solution, even if several exist.

For many practical problems, however, it may be desirable to find only a *nearly* optimal solution rather than the *exact* optimal solution. This idea derives from empirical observations that branch and bound often identifies the best solution early in the search process but then spends a great deal of time verifying its optimality. This situation was illustrated in the Mansfield problem, in which we found the optimal solution at the second node and then examined five more nodes before we knew we had found an optimum. In some cases we may choose to avoid this extra effort, recognizing that we do so at the cost of not knowing the optimal solution.

Fortunately, once we have found a feasible solution in the branch and bound process, we can determine the maximum improvement we can obtain from further branching and bounding. Let B denote the best bound among all active nodes and let F denote the best feasible solution yet found. Define the quantities Δz_1 and Δz_2 as follows:

$$\Delta z_1 = |B - F| \tag{5.34}$$

$$\Delta z_2 = \left| \frac{B - F}{B} \right| \tag{5.35}$$

where the use of the brackets $|\ |$ denotes the absolute value function. We note that Δz_1 is the maximum possible *absolute* improvement, and Δz_2 is the maximum possible *percentage* improvement that can be achieved by further branching. In both cases we can actually attain the maximum improvements only if B is the optimal value.

To demonstrate the use of the terms Δz_1 and Δz_2, consider the Mansfield problem at Level 1 in the tree. Here we know that P_1 is feasible with an objective function value of $z = 3600$, and P_2 has $z = 3633$ but is not feasible. At this point in the tree we can prune the node for P_1, so that we have only one active node, that for P_2. Thus, we have $F = 3600$ and $B = 3633$. Therefore, we calculate

$$\Delta z_1 = |3633 - 3600| = 33$$

$$\Delta z_2 = \left| \frac{3633 - 3600}{3633} \right| = 0.009$$

The value of B signifies that there may exist a feasible solution with a value as much as 33 greater than the value of the best solution obtained so far. In this case if we stopped and implemented the best feasible solution yet obtained, Δz_1 tells us that we might be as much as 33 worse than optimal, and Δz_2 tells us that we might be as much as 0.9% worse than optimal. Thus, the terms Δz_1 and Δz_2 represent **error bounds** in the branch and bound process.

As an aside, we could also use the terms Δz_1 and Δz_2 to determine the effects of rounding an LP optimum to preserve feasibility in an IP problem. In the original analysis of the Mansfield problem we first solved the LP relaxation and obtained the solution $x_1 = 3.33$, $x_2 = 6.67$, and $z = 3667$. Thus, we found $B = 3667$. Then we rounded this solution and produced the integer feasible solution $x_1 = 3$, $x_2 = 6$, and $z = 3300$. Thus, we obtained $F = 3300$. As a result, our error bounds from rounding were

$$\Delta z_1 = |3667 - 3300| = 367$$

$$\Delta z_2 = \left| \frac{3667 - 3300}{3667} \right| = 0.10$$

In other words, we know that our rounded solution could be suboptimal by no more than \$367, or 10%.

In general, we can terminate the branch and bound process (and accept the best on-hand feasible solution) if we are willing to tolerate the possible suboptimality indicated by the error bounds. Many commercial IP programs allow the user to specify such limits at the outset. In effect, they use a pruning rule that calls for pruning a subproblem when Δz_1 is within a prespecified absolute limit, or else when Δz_2 is within a prespecified percentage limit. The larger the limit, the more suboptimality we permit, but the earlier the search process will stop.

SUMMARY

LP problems in which some of the decision variables must have integer values are called integer programming (IP) problems. Although any IP model has integer requirements, it may fall into one of two main classes of integer programming, depending on the types of variables present. In mixed integer programming models some of the variables must be integers, and others may be continuous. A special case of such models is a pure IP problem, in which all of the variables are integers. In binary IP models the integer variables are restricted to the values 0 and 1.

It is possible to use integer programming models to describe complicated problem situations, particularly with the use of binary variables. In constraints these variables can help represent complex relationships among activities, and in the objective function they can represent nonlinear criteria.

If we drop the integer requirements of an IP problem we obtain its LP relaxation. Solutions to IP problems occur only at the integer points within the feasible region of the LP relaxation. One attractive solution approach for IP models is to round the solution of the LP relaxation to the nearest integer value. However, rounding the LP optimum may not preserve feasibility, and even if it does, the resulting feasible solution may not be optimal for the IP problem. The cutting plane approach modifies the LP relaxation to remove noninteger LP optima from the feasible region. Such methods rely on the power of linear programming but can be extremely time-consuming.

Because IP problems have only a finite number of feasible points, it is possible to use total enumeration to solve an IP problem. However, such a methodology is not practical because the number of feasible values grows rapidly as the number of integer variables increases. Thus, total enumeration can have enormous computational requirements.

The most effective solution method, branch and bound, uses a tree-structured enumeration procedure. It divides the set of all possible solutions into subsets; this division is called branching. Then the subsets are evaluated to determine whether they are promising in terms of leading to an optimal solution; this evaluation is called bounding. Only the promising subsets need be examined in order to obtain an optimal solution. We can think of branching as the process of working with smaller problems (with smaller feasible regions) and bounding as the process of working with easier problems (with no integer requirements).

Branch and bound has many variations involving different branching schemes to divide the problem and various bounding approaches for evaluating subsets. Also, in branch and bound it is possible to specify criteria for stopping the process early before identifying the optimal solution. Thus, branch and bound is not a single solution procedure for IP problems. Instead it is a general approach that can have many forms.

EXERCISES

FORMULATION OF INTEGER PROGRAMS

1 Baggage handlers at Metropolis Airport are scheduled for work tours under the terms of an agreement between their union and the agency that manages the airport. This agreement specifies that employees are entitled to 2 consecutive days off each week and also that employees are assigned to the same shift all the time. (There are three nonoverlapping work shifts at the airport: day, evening, and night.)

The airlines tend to operate on fixed schedules, and the operations engineer at the airport has determined the following requirements schedule for the day shift:

Day	Requirement
Monday	16
Tuesday	11
Wednesday	17
Thursday	13
Friday	15
Saturday	19
Sunday	14

How many baggage handlers should be assigned to the day shift in order to meet these requirements?

2 Steel mills, pulp and paper plants, and aluminum sheet manufacturers usually have one problem in common: They produce long continuous sheets of a standard width that are made into rolls of a standard size. These standard rolls must be cut into different widths as required by customers. It is not uncommon for a plant to deliver its products in hundreds of different specifications as orders vary, but the manufacturer must face the fact that most combinations of desired widths produce trim loss.

A mill of the Williams Paper Company produces so-called liner board in jumbo reels having a standard width of 68 inches. (Each reel has a fixed length.) The company's customers, however, order reels having smaller widths (and the same fixed length as the larger reel). Today's orders are for 110 reels of 22-inch width, 120 reels of 20-inch width, and 80 reels of 12-inch width. These smaller widths are to be cut from the larger standard size reel.

For example, the company can decide to slit a jumbo into two reels each 22 inches wide, and one reel 20 inches wide; this leaves 4 inches of trim waste from the 68-inch jumbo. Several other combinations of cuts can be made from each jumbo reel, and the production scheduler wants to select the cuts for today's orders so as to minimize total trim waste. Find a schedule of combinations that will meet demand with minimum waste.

3 The Murdough Petroleum Company is faced with the problem of allocating a fixed capital budget among five competing projects. The nature of these projects, their estimated net present value (NPVs), and anticipated cash flows are summarized below. The company wishes to maximize the NPV of its investment portfolio, but is constrained to limit its expenditures to $65

Project Characteristics (Millions of Dollars)

Project Number	Nature of Project	NPV	Cash Expenditures	
			Year 1	Year 2
1	Renovation of Essex refinery; this proposal will increase capacity by 500 barrels per day	$10	$20	$20
2	Construction of new refinery to replace Essex refinery; this proposal will increase capacity by 1000 barrels per day	20	30	15
3	Construction of new pipeline to the contemplated new refinery; this proposal will increase capacity by an additional 100 barrels per day	5	15	5
4	Construction of a new pipeline to the Essex refinery; this proposal will increase capacity by 50 barrels per day	3	10	7
5	Purchase of a tanker to transport oil to another existing refinery; this proposal will increase capacity by 20 barrels per day	2	5	4

million in the first year and $46 million in the second year. Furthermore, management has determined that an increase in capacity of at least 500 barrels per day and no more than 1100 barrels per day is required. It is clear (from information above) that projects 1 and 2 are mutually exclusive, and that the acceptance of project 3 is contingent upon the acceptance of project 2. Which projects should the firm undertake?

4 The Spencer Shoe Company manufactures a line of inexpensive shoes in one plant in Pontiac and now distributes to five main distribution centers: Milwaukee, Dayton, Cincinnati, Buffalo, and Atlanta, from which the shoes are shipped to retail shoe stores. To meet increased demand, the company has decided to build at least one new plant with a capacity of 40,000 pairs of shoes per week. General surveys have narrowed the choice to three locations: Cincinnati, Dayton, and Atlanta. Distribution costs include freight, handling, and warehousing costs. As expected, production costs would be low in the Atlanta plant, but distribution costs are relatively high compared to the other two locations. Other data are as follows:

Distribution Costs per Pair, Handling, Warehousing, and Freight

Distribution Centers	Plants				Forecast Weekly Demand in Pairs
	Pontiac	Cincinnati	Dayton	Atlanta	
Milwaukee	$0.42	$0.46	$0.44	$0.48	10,000
Dayton	0.36	0.37	0.30	0.45	15,000
Cincinnati	0.41	0.30	0.37	0.43	16,000
Buffalo	0.39	0.42	0.38	0.46	19,000
Atlanta	0.50	0.43	0.45	0.27	12,000
Normal weekly plant capacity, pairs of shoes	27,000	40,000	40,000	40,000	
Unit production costs	$2.70	$2.64	$2.69	$2.62	
Weekly fixed cost	$7,000	$4,000	$6,000	$7,000	

The Spencer Shoe Company desires to choose the plant locations that will minimize the total costs, including production, distribution, and fixed costs.

5 California Products Company has the capability of producing and selling three products. Each product has an annual demand potential (at current pricing and promotion levels), a variable contribution, and an annual fixed

cost. The fixed cost can be avoided if the product is not produced at all. This information is summarized below.

Product	Demand	Contribution	Fixed Cost
I	240,000	$1.20	$ 60,000
J	160,000	1.80	200,000
K	80,000	2.30	110,000

Each product requires work on three machines. The standard productivities and capacities are given below.

Machine	Hours per 100 Units			Hours Available
	Product I	Product J	Product K	
A	3.205	3.846	7.692	1750
B	2.747	4.808	6.410	1750
C	1.923	3.205	9.615	1750

Assume that the California Products Company wishes to plan its activity to maximize profits for the year. Determine which products should be produced and how much of each should be produced, and determine the maximum profit contribution from these operations.

6 In 1976 the U.S. government began to sell crude oil from its Naval Petroleum Reserve in sealed bid auctions. There are typically six items to be sold in the auction, corresponding to the crude oil at the six major production and shipping points. A "bid package" from a potential buyer consists of (a) a number indicating an upper limit on how many barrels the buyer is willing to buy overall in this auction and (b) any number of "product bids." Each product bid consists of a product name and three numbers representing respectively the bid price per barrel of this product, the minimum acceptable quantity of this product at this price, and the maximum acceptable quantity of this product at this price. The government usually places an arbitrary upper limit, such as 20%, on the percentage of the total barrels over all six products that one firm is allowed to purchase.

To illustrate the principal ideas let us simplify slightly and suppose there are only two supply sources/products which are denoted by A and B. There are 17,000 barrels available at A and 13,000 barrels at B. Also, there are only two bidders, the Mobon and the Exxil companies. The government arbitrarily decides that either one can purchase at most 65% of the total available crude. The two bid packages are as follows:

Mobon   Maximum desired = 16,000 barrels, total.

Product	Bid/barrel	Minimum Barrels Accepted	Maximum Barrels Wanted
A	43	9000	16,000
B	51	6000	12,000

Exxil   Maximum desired = No limit

Product	Bid/barrel	Minimum Barrels Accepted	Maximum Barrels Wanted
A	47	5000	10,000
B	50	5000	10,000

What is the best allocation for the seller?

7 The following problem is known as a segregated storage problem. A feed processor has various amounts of four different commodities that must be stored in seven different silos. Each silo can contain at most one commodity. Associated with each commodity and silo combination is a loading cost. Each silo has a finite capacity so some commodities may have to be split over several silos. The following table contains the data for this problem. Formulate a model for finding the minimum cost storage plan.

Loading Cost per Ton

Silo	1	2	3	4	5	6	7	Amount of Commodity to Be Stored (Tons)
Commodity A	1	2	2	3	4	5	5	75
B	2	3	3	3	1	5	5	50
C	4	4	3	2	1	5	5	25
D	1	1	2	2	3	5	5	80
Silo capacity in tons	25	25	40	60	80	100	100	

8 You are the scheduling coordinator for a small but growing airline. You must schedule *exactly one* flight out of Chicago to each of the following cities: Atlanta, Los Angeles, New York, and Peoria. The available departure slots are 8 A.M., 10 A.M., and 12 P.M. Your airline has only two departure lounges so at most two flights can be scheduled per slot. Demand data suggest the following expected profit contribution (PC) per flight as a function of departure time:

Expected PC (in 1000s)

	Time		
Destination	8	10	12
Atlanta	10	9	8.5
Los Angeles	11	10.5	9.5
New York	17	16	15
Peoria	6.4	2.5	−1

Formulate a model for solving this problem.

9 A company currently has a warehouse in cities A through E. These warehouses supply six customer regions throughout the United States. There is some feeling that the company is "overwarehoused"; that is, it may be able to save substantial fixed costs by closing some warehouses without unduly increasing transportation and service costs. Relevant data have been collected and assembled on a monthly basis and are displayed below. What is the optimal warehouse configuration?

Cost per Ton Matrix		Demand Region						Monthly Capacity (Tons)	Monthly Fixed Cost
		1	2	3	4	5	6		
Supply location	A	$1675	$ 400	$ 685	$1630	$1160	$2800	18	$7650
	B	1460	1940	970	100	495	1200	24	3500
	C	1925	2400	1425	500	950	800	27	5000
	D	380	1355	543	1045	665	2321	22	4100
	E	922	1646	700	508	311	1797	31	2200
Monthly demand in tons		10	8	12	6	7	11		

SOLUTION BY BRANCH AND BOUND

10 A company must supply warehouses 1, 2, 3, and 4 with 80, 90, 110, 160 units per month, respectively. Plants may be built in locations A, B, and/or C at monthly fixed costs of $600, $120, and $1200, respectively. The unit production plus shipping costs are given in the following matrix:

To From	1	2	3	4
A	42	48	38	37
B	40	49	52	51
C	39	38	40	43

Assume that overtime is not allowed and that there are no capacity limitations on the plants. Use the branch and bound method to determine the optimal solution by hand and specify

a Which plants should be open.

b The allocation of destinations to plants.

c The monthly cost of the solution.

11 A company wishes to schedule TV advertisements for a new product. The project requires advertising exposure in two audiences: urban and rural. Demographic data indicate that an advertisement on a certain game show will yield 3 million exposures in the urban audience and 2 million exposures in the rural audience. Alternatively, an advertisement on a certain public affairs program will yield 4 million urban exposures and 1 million rural exposures. Each advertisement costs $10,000, and only 30-second advertisements are available. The goal is to achieve 12 million urban exposures and 6 million rural exposures by a combination of advertisements. The company seeks a minimum cost advertising schedule. Formulate this problem as an IP and find the optimal solution by hand, using the branch and bound method.

12 Review the formulation in Exercise 1. Solve the IP by the branch and bound method, using a computer code to solve the LP relaxations and performing the tree search by hand.

13 Review the formulation in Exercise 3. Solve the IP by the branch and bound method, using a computer code to solve the LP relaxations and performing the tree search by hand.

Chapter 6

NETWORK MODELS FOR PROJECT SCHEDULING

Watkins Architects and Consultants, Inc.

Watkins Architects and Consultants, Inc. recently won a contract to prepare plans and specifications for the construction of an office building for health care professionals. As founder and president of the firm, Mr. Watkins has had experience with this kind of project. He anticipates that in order to fulfill the requirement of the contract his firm will have to carry out the individual activities listed below:

Prepare preliminary sketches of the building

Outline the physical specifications for the building

Compose detailed drawings of the building

Write detailed engineering specifications

Draft the project report

Print the detailed drawings

Print tables of engineering specifications

Prepare the final project report

Mr. Watkins can estimate the time it will take to perform each of these activities, but he is wondering whether the firm can complete the entire project in 16 weeks. Also, since the firm will be exploring other projects during this period, Mr. Watkins would like to know which of the activities deserve his closest attention in order to keep the project on schedule.

From time to time managers are faced with the problem of planning and scheduling a major project. The project might be a one-of-a-kind undertaking for the firm, such as the installation of a computer system, the construction of a building, or the introduction of a new product. The project could also be an activity that is repeated only infrequently, such as the overhaul of major equipment or the development of a large firm's annual budget. Major projects of either type consist of a large number of individual activities, some of which must be carried out in a special sequence, while others can be carried out concurrently.

The planning and control of a large-scale project is a complex managerial task. Network models can give the manager some valuable assistance in dealing with this type of problem. First, network models of the scheduling problem provide a graphical representation that helps users understand the logical relationships involved. In this role the model can facilitate communication about various aspects of a project. Moreover, the model can provide a structure for reporting and monitoring progress. Second, network models link the completion schedule of the entire project to the timing of individual activities. With this framework the project manager can conveniently assess the impact on project completion of changes in the scheduling of certain activities. In particular, the analysis of a network model yields information that helps answer the following managerial questions:

When will the project be complete?

What are the planned start and finish times for each activity?

Which activities are critical in determining the project length?

How much delay can be tolerated in noncritical activities?

The basic form of a project network model involves some simplifying assumptions about the scheduling problem:

Assumption 1
The project can be broken down into distinct activities, each having an identifiable start and finish.

Assumption 2
Once an activity is initiated, it will progress directly through to completion, regardless of the status of other activities.

Assumption 3
The entire list of activities and the logical relationships among them are known in advance.

In the case of the Watkins project, the activities have been identified and listed, but the logical relationships remain to be determined.

Logical relations (or **precedence** relations) involve the sequencing requirements of certain pairs of activities. For example, in the process of building a house, the roof cannot be put on until the walls are built. The activity "build

TABLE 6.1

Activity Code	Activity Description	Predecessor List	Estimated Duration (Weeks)
A	Prepare sketches	—	4
B	Outline specifications	—	3
C	Compose drawings	A	5
D	Write specifications	A,B	4
E	Print drawings	A,C,D	5
F	Draft report	C,D	4
G	Print tables	D	3
H	Prepare final report	F,G	2

walls" is said to *precede* the activity "install roof." In other words, the roof activity cannot begin until the wall activity is complete. For this relation we call the wall activity the **predecessor** and the roof activity the **successor.** Many precedence relations are fairly obvious. For example, delivery of materials precedes processing of the materials, and assembly of a prototype precedes final testing of the prototype. Other precedence relations are less obvious and need to be determined by knowledgeable people associated with the project. For instance, in the Watkins project, Mr. Watkins knows that the report cannot be drafted until the drawings are composed and the detailed specifications written.

In order to compile the necessary information to build a network model, Mr. Watkins must specify all logical relations in the project and estimate a time for each activity. Table 6.1 shows this information.

NETWORK DIAGRAMS

We use the information about logical relations and time estimates of each activity to construct a network diagram, which is a graphical model for analysis of the scheduling problem. Although all diagrams use nodes (circles) and arcs (arrows), there are two ways to construct a diagram.

ACTIVITY-ON-NODE DIAGRAM

In the most simple approach for hand calculation each node represents an activity, and each arc shows logical precedence. This approach is most commonly used with the Critical Path Method (CPM). CPM was developed in 1957 by the Sperry Rand Corporation to help the Du Pont Corporation schedule the construction, maintenance, and shutdown of their chemical plants.

The method is an activity-on-node (AON) approach. To demonstrate the AON method, consider the Watkins project. The portion of a network shown in

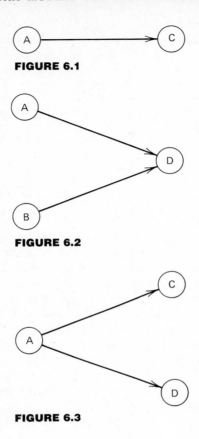

FIGURE 6.1

FIGURE 6.2

FIGURE 6.3

Figure 6.1 represents the logical relationship between activity A (preparing sketches) and activity C (composing drawings). The arrow shows that A precedes C.

An activity may have more than one predecessor, which means that it cannot start until two or more other activities are completed. This is the situation for activity D (writing specifications), which depends on the completion of both activity A (preparing sketches) and activity B (outlining specifications). The way to model this relationship is shown in Figure 6.2.

An activity may also have more than one successor in the project. This is the case for the Watkins project, in which activity A (preparing sketches) precedes both activity C (composing drawings) and activity D (writing specifications). Figure 6.3 shows how to represent this type of relationship.

Figures 6.1 to 6.3 show the building blocks for network diagramming: single predecessors, multiple predecessors, and multiple successors. From these basic structures we can develop network diagrams for large, complicated projects. We usually follow two conventions in constructing the diagram, especially in con-

PROCEDURE 6.1
Network Drawing Procedure

1 At the left of the page, draw a single node called START.

2 Moving slightly to the right, draw a node (and its appropriate code) for each activity that has no predecessors, and draw an arrow from START to each node.

3 Moving slightly to the right, draw a node (and its appropriate code) for each activity whose immediate predecessors are all shown in the diagram. (Do not draw nodes for activities whose predecessors are *not* all present.) For each precedence relationship, draw an arrow leading from the predecessor node to the appropriate successor node. It is permissible for arrows to cross other arrows.

4 Repeat Step 3 for each activity whose predecessor nodes are all present. Again, it is permissible for arrows to cross other arrows.

5 When all activities in the project have been represented as nodes in the diagram, draw a node called FINISH slightly to the right of all other nodes. Look for all nodes corresponding to activities without successors, and add arrows to connect them to the FINISH node.

6 Look for ways to clean up the diagram: Eliminate any redundant arrows, and try to reduce the number of arrows that cross.

7 Inside each node add the estimate of the corresponding activity time. (For START and FINISH the activity time is 0.)

junction with computerized analysis. First, only one node should represent a particular activity. Second, the diagram should have a single start node and a single finish node. Given these rules, the steps for drawing a network are outlined in Procedure 6.1.

For the Watkins project the steps are discussed in conjunction with Figure 6.4, which illustrates the use of Procedure 6.1 in developing the network.

(*a*) We create a START node, as prescribed by Step 1.

(*b*) In Step 2 the two activities without predecessors are A and B. We create their nodes and connect them each to START with arrows.

(*c*) We add nodes for activities C and D in Step 3, since they depend on A or B or both. Then we draw the arrows corresponding to their predecessors.

(*d*) We add nodes for activities E, F, and G, since they depend only on the activities already in the diagram and we draw their arrows.

(*e*) Next we add activity H, with arrows connecting it to F and G.

(*f*) Now that all activities in the project have been represented by nodes, we follow Step 5 and add a FINISH node. Then we find the activities without successors (E and H), and we connect them to the FINISH node.

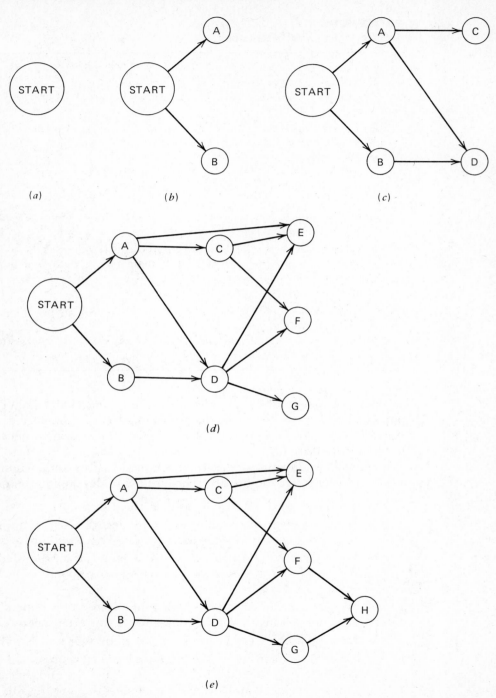

(a) (b) (c)

(d)

(e)

FIGURE 6.4

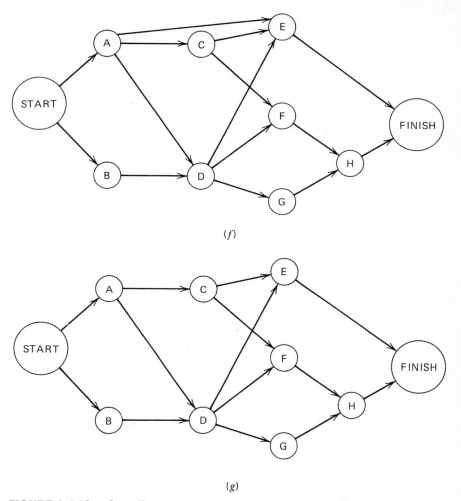

(f)

(g)

FIGURE 6.4 (Continued)

(g) As suggested by Step 6 we can remove the redundant arrow from A to E, since the arrows from A to C and from C to E imply that A precedes E. As a result, we can eliminate A as an immediate predecessor of E.

(h) Finally, in Figure 6.5, we write inside each node the corresponding activity time.

For the Watkins project Figure 6.5 shows the complete network diagram that satisfies all of the rules given above. Each arrow shows a precedence relationship, and each node contains Mr. Watkins' estimate of the activity time. (Note that the START and FINISH nodes do not consume any time.) As a result, the network represents a complete translation of the information from Mr. Watkins' list into a network model for the project.

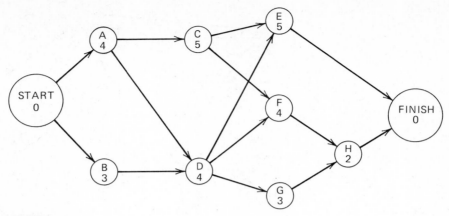

FIGURE 6.5

ACTIVITY-ON-ARROW DIAGRAM

Another way of representing the project activities and their precedence relationships is to represent activities as arrows. This is called the activity-on-arrow (AOA) method. This method is most commonly used with the Project Evaluation and Review Technique (PERT). PERT was developed in 1958 by the U.S. Navy to help plan and control the activities in building the Polaris Fleet Ballistic Missile Submarine.

In the AOA approach an arrow also shows the direction of a corresponding precedence relation. The technique uses nodes to symbolize events, which represent milestones in the progress of the project, such as the start or completion of a certain activity. Figure 6.6 depicts the AOA network for the Watkins project. As before, we index the activities with letters and also show the activity times. Now, however, we number the nodes to show milestones in the project. For example, node 6 represents the event "activities F and G are both finished."

A complication of the AOA approach is that **dummy activities** may be necessary. A dummy activity, represented by a dashed arrow in the diagram, does not correspond to any task in the project. It simply helps us represent precedence information concisely. For example, in Figure 6.6 we use dashed arrows twice. In the first case (from node 2 to node 3) the dummy shows that activity D has both A and B as predecessors, and activity C has only A as a predecessor; in the second case (from node 4 to node 5) the dummy shows that activities E and F both have C and D as predecessors, and activity G has only D as a predecessor. Without dummies we would have to represent some activities more than once in the network diagram. Thus, dummies permit the diagram to represent activities uniquely while modeling the logical relationships accurately.

The difference between the AON and AOA methods is that the activity-on-node method focuses on activities, while the activity-on-arrow method focuses on milestones. By representing milestones as nodes, the AOA diagram identifies

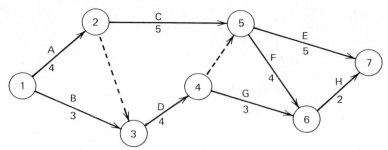

FIGURE 6.6

places where decisions might occur. The AOA network can also be time-scaled, with the length of the arrows proportional to activity duration. The AON diagram is simpler to construct, since a distinct arrow will correspond to each precedence relation, and it requires no dummy activities. Because neither method dominates the other, both are common.

For convenience, we rely on the simpler AON approach in our analysis of the Watkins project. However, either method will allow us to answer the managerial questions we posed earlier.

CRITICAL PATH ANALYSIS

Critical path calculations provide information on the completion of the project and on the timing of individual activities. In this section we examine the definitions, procedures, and results of critical path analysis.

A **path** is a sequence of connected activities in the network diagram, following a set of precedence arrows from the start of the project to its completion. In the diagram of Figure 6.5 there are eight distinct paths:

ACE	ADE	ADGH	BDFH
ACFH	ADFH	BDE	BDGH

Because of precedence relations, the activities on any particular path must be done in sequence. Because the activities on a path cannot overlap, the project must be at least as long as the total time required to carry out the activities along any path. In fact, the length of the longest path dictates the length of the project, assuming that there are sufficient resources available to perform each activity as soon as its predecessors are complete.

The longest path in a network is called the **critical path.** It determines the project length in the sense that precedence relations permit no earlier completion of the project. The activities along a critical path are called **critical activities,** because a delay in any one of them will cause a delay in the completion of the entire project. By contrast, it may be possible to absorb some delay in the noncritical activities without affecting the project completion.

In order to identify the critical path we could compile an exhaustive list of the different paths and sum the activity durations along each one, ultimately finding the longest path. However, in very large networks the number of distinct paths can be prohibitively large, and a more systematic method is available. The method has two parts.

First, we determine the earliest time at which each activity can begin, given the precedence relationships. For each activity we define the following times:

Early Start Time (*ES*):   The earliest time at which the activity can begin.

Early Finish Time (*EF*):   The earliest time at which the activity can be completed.

For the START node we define the early start time as 0. This means that the project begins at time 0.

To compute the early start time and early finish time of any other activity (or node), we perform some simple computations. In general, an activity's *EF* is just its *ES* plus its duration. For activity *i*

$$EF_i = ES_i + D_i \tag{6.1}$$

where D_i denotes the duration of activity *i*.

To compute the early start time, we must recognize that an activity cannot start until all of its predecessors are complete. In other words, it cannot begin until the latest (or maximum) finish time of all its predecessors. Thus, we have

$$ES_i = \max[EF \text{ of activity } i\text{'s predecessors}] \tag{6.2}$$

With these definitions, the *ES* and *EF* calculations proceed systematically from left to right, from the START node to the FINISH node of the network.

In the Watkins example, for the START node we have $ES_{ST} = 0$ and $EF_{ST} = ES_{ST} + D_{ST} = 0 + 0 = 0$. Then, for activity A we have $ES_A = 0$ (the *EF* of START, its only predecessor), and $EF_A = ES_A + D_A = 0 + 4 = 4$. Similarly, activity B has $ES_B = 0$ (the *EF* of START, its only predecessor) and $EF_B = 3$, and activity C has $ES_C = 4$ (the *EF* of A, its only predecessor) and $EF_C = 9$.

For activity D, the analysis is more complicated, because it has two predecessors, A and B. Activity D cannot start at time 3, when B is finished, but instead must wait until time 4, when *both* A and B are finished. Using equation (6.2) for activity D we obtain the same result:

$$ES_D = \max[EF_A, EF_B] = \max[4, 3] = 4$$

Then, using equation (6.1) we find

$$EF_D = ES_D + D_D = 4 + 4 = 8$$

Proceeding in this manner for the rest of the network, we find the following:

Activity	ES Calculation	EF Calculation
E	max $[EF_C, EF_D] = 9$	$ES_E + D_E = 9 + 5 = 14$
F	max $[EF_C, EF_D] = 9$	$ES_F + D_F = 9 + 4 = 13$
G	$EF_D = 8$	$ES_G + D_G = 8 + 3 = 11$
H	max $[EF_F, EF_G] = 13$	$ES_H + D_H = 13 + 2 = 15$
FINISH	max $[EF_E, EF_H] = 15$	$ES_{FIN} + D_{FIN} = 15 + 0 = 15$

Figure 6.7 shows the early start time and early finish time for each activity, with the pair *ES/EF* given at each node.

The important result is that the early finish time for FINISH represents the earliest time at which the project can be completed. Thus, the Watkins project can be finished by time 15 at the earliest.

In the second part of the procedure we determine how late each activity can begin without delaying completion of the project. In this analysis, we define the following times:

Late Finish Time (*LF*): The latest time at which the activity can finish without delaying the project.

Late Start Time (*LS*): The latest time at which the activity can begin without delaying the project.

Initially we will use the project's earliest completion time as the project deadline. Thus, we equate the late finish time for the FINISH node to its early finish time. Later we will discuss a more general approach.

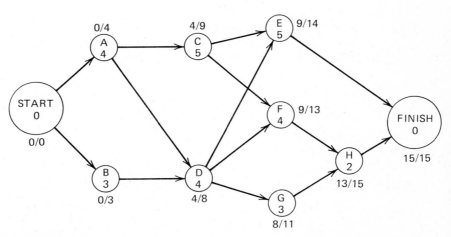

FIGURE 6.7

To compute the late start time and late finish time of other activities we use a relationship analogous to equation (6.1). For activity i we have

$$LS_i = LF_i - D_i \tag{6.3}$$

To compute the late finish time, we recognize that an activity must finish before any of its successors can start. In other words, it must be complete by the earliest (or minimum) start time of all its successors. Thus, we have

$$LF_i = \min LS \text{ of activity } i\text{'s successors} \tag{6.4}$$

The calculations of LS and LF proceed right to left, beginning with the FINISH node. For the FINISH node in our example, we have $LF_{FIN} = LS_{FIN} = 15$. Then, considering activity H, we find $LF_H = 15$ (the LS of its only successor, FINISH) and $LS_H = 15 - 2 = 13$. This calculation makes sense: We know that to avoid delaying the project we must complete activity H by time 15; and, given an activity duration of 2 weeks, this means that we must start the activity by time 13. Similarly, we find the following:

Activity	LF Calculation	LS Calculation
E	$LS_{FIN} = 15$	$LF_E - D_E = 15 - 5 = 10$
G	$LS_H = 13$	$LF_G - D_G = 13 - 3 = 10$
F	$LS_H = 13$	$LF_F - D_F = 13 - 4 = 9$

When we consider activity D, however, we encounter a complication because it has three successors—E, F, and G. Applying equation (6.4) we find

$$LF_D = \min[LS_E, LS_F, LS_G] = \min[10, 9, 10] = 9$$

Notice that we cannot permit D to finish at time 10 because we would then have to start F at time 10. As a result, we would delay the start of H until time 14; and we would then complete the project at time 16. In other words, delaying the finish time for D beyond time 9 would delay the project.

Proceeding with the Watkins project we obtain the following results:

Activity	LF Calculation	LS Calculation
D	$\min[LS_E, LS_F, LS_G] = \min[10, 9, 10] = 9$	$EF_D - D_D = 9 - 4 = 5$
C	$\min[LS_E, LS_F] = \min[10, 9] = 9$	$EF_C - D_C = 9 - 5 = 4$
B	$LS_D = 5$	$EF_B - D_B = 5 - 3 = 2$
A	$\min[LS_C, LS_D] = \min[4, 5] = 4$	$EF_A - D_A = 4 - 4 = 0$
START	$\min[LS_A, LS_B] = \min[0, 2] = 0$	$EF_{ST} - D_{ST} = 0 - 0 = 0$

Figure 6.8 shows the late finish time and late start time for each activity, with the pair LS/LF given at each node.

The important result is that the LS for START represents the latest time at

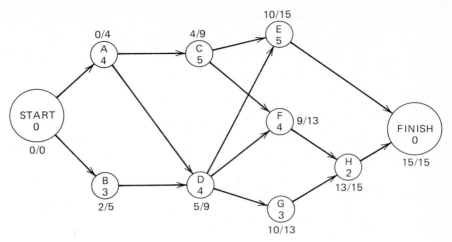

FIGURE 6.8

which we can begin the project without delaying its completion. Thus, we must begin the Watkins project at time 0. For the Watkins project the four activity times are summarized in Table 6.2.

These four activity times provide very useful information about a project. In the Watkins project, the writing of detailed specifications (activity D) requires the services of the firm's planning engineer, who is currently working on another project. From the information produced by network analysis, the ES for activity D is time 4. Therefore, Mr. Watkins knows that the engineer will have at least 4 weeks to complete his present assignment before he will be needed on the construction project. Also, the analysis reveals that the LS for activity D is time 5. Therefore, Mr. Watkins knows that the engineer must be made available to the construction project before 5 weeks pass, otherwise the project completion will be delayed to at least time 16. The analysis also reveals that the late finish time

TABLE 6.2

Activity	ES	EF	LF	LS
A	0	4	4	0
B	0	3	5	2
C	4	9	9	4
D	4	8	9	5
E	9	14	15	10
F	9	13	13	9
G	8	11	13	10
H	13	15	15	13

for drafting the report (activity F) is time 13. If Mr. Watkins discovers that the people working on the draft might not be able to finish it by the end of the thirteenth week, he might schedule some overtime work on this activity in order to avoid a delay in the entire project.

Recall that our goal was to determine the critical path for the project, since it determines the project length. One way to identify the critical path is to find a path with a length equal to the early finish time of the FINISH node. In the network for the Watkins project the path ACFH is critical, since it is the only path with a length of 15 weeks. Note that this path contains only activities for which $ES = LS$ (and, therefore, $EF = LF$).

MEASURES OF SLACK

Another way to find the critical path is to consider a measure of scheduling flexibility called **total slack:**

Total Slack (TS): The allowable delay in an activity's start time that can be absorbed without delaying the project, assuming that all other activities begin as early as possible.

This definition means that the total slack for an activity is the difference between its early and late start times, or, equivalently, between its early and late finish times. For activity i,

$$TS_i = LS_i - ES_i$$
$$= LF_i - EF_i \tag{6.5}$$

Table 6.3 summarizes the calculation of total slack times for the example project.

Such a table will quickly help us identify the critical activities as those with total slack equal to 0. In general, the condition $TS = 0$ indicates that we could not absorb any delay in an activity's start time without delaying the project. On the other hand, positive TS values identify activities for which some scheduling flexibility exists. In the example, activity B has a total slack of 2 weeks. This means that a delay in the completion of activity B of up to 2 weeks would not

TABLE 6.3

Activity	ES	EF	LF	LS	TS	FS
A	0	4	4	0	0	0
B	0	3	5	2	2	1
C	4	9	9	4	0	0
D	4	8	9	5	1	0
E	9	14	15	10	1	1
F	9	13	13	9	0	0
G	8	11	13	10	2	2
H	13	15	15	13	0	0

delay the project. Such a delay might occur prior to the start of the activity, or it might be caused by unforeseen circumstances that cause activity B to require a total of 5 weeks. These two situations, along with the planned early start schedule, are shown in the sketches of Figure 6.9.

The partial schedules displayed in Figure 6.9 also show why total slack should sometimes be viewed as a "shared" measure of flexibility. In the example, once activity B is delayed 2 weeks there is no longer any flexibility in the scheduling of activity D, for the late start time of activity D is time 5. Thus, the total slack along the path B–D is only 2 weeks, even though the sum of the total slacks for activities B and D is 3 weeks. We interpret total slack as a measure of scheduling flexibility along a particular path, since in general the flexibility available in scheduling one activity depends on how other activities are scheduled.

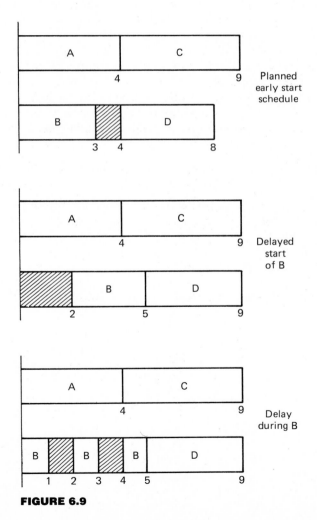

FIGURE 6.9

We can generalize these concepts to the case in which a project deadline is specified beforehand. In the basic form of critical path analysis we set $LF = EF$ for the project's FINISH node. However, when a deadline has been specified beforehand, the late finish time of the FINISH activity is by definition the deadline itself. For this case in order to initialize the procedure for calculating LF values the late finish time for FINISH is taken to be the project deadline. If the deadline is different from the length of the critical path, then there may not be any activities with total slack of 0. For example, if the Watkins project is assigned a deadline of time 17, then the four critical activities (A, C, F, and H) and the START activity will all have $TS = 2$, which will be the minimum total slack among the activities in the project. On the other hand, if the deadline is time 12, then these five activities will all have $TS = -3$. Therefore, the general result is that the critical activities—those on the longest path—will have the minimum total slack in the project. The value of their total slack will be 0 only if the deadline matches the length of the longest path.

Critical path analyses can be complicated by the existence of multiple critical paths in a network. In such cases there are several paths through the network, each of which has a length equal to the longest path. When there are several critical paths, each activity on any of the critical paths is a critical activity. A delay in any one of these activities will delay the entire project.

Another measure of scheduling flexibility is called **free slack** and is defined as follows:

Free Slack (FS):   The allowable delay in an activity's start time that can be absorbed without delaying another activity.

The free slack for an activity is the difference between its earliest finish time and the earliest of the start times of its immediate successors. Thus, we have for activity i

$$FS_i = \min[ES \text{ of activity } i\text{'s successors}] - EF_i \tag{6.6}$$

In the Watkins project we have the following results:

Activity	FS Calculation
A	$\min[ES_C, ES_D] - EF_A = 4 - 4 = 0$
B	$ES_D - EF_B = 4 - 3 = 1$
C	$\min[ES_E, ES_F] - EF_C = \min[9, 9] - 9$ $= 9 - 9 = 0$
D	$\min[ES_E, ES_F, ES_G] - EF_D = \min[9, 9, 8] - 8$ $= 8 - 8 = 0$
E	$ES_{FIN} - EF_E = 15 - 14 = 1$
F	$ES_H - EF_F = 13 - 13 = 0$
G	$ES_H - EF_G = 13 - 11 = 2$
H	$ES_{FIN} - EF_H = 15 - 15 = 0$

Examining the network diagram, we can see how these results arise. For example, A is the only predecessor of C; if we delay the start of A we automatically delay the start of C. Thus, A has no free slack. The same observation applies to D, which is the only predecessor of G.

On the other hand, activity B is one of two predecessors of D; and we could delay its start by 1 week without delaying the start of D. Thus, activity B has a free slack of 1 week. This situation occurs because to start D we must wait until time 4, when both A and B are complete.

In general, there are two important characteristics of free slack. First, an activity's free slack is less than or equal to its total slack. Second, free slack occurs only when a successor has multiple predecessors. One of these predecessors must have no free slack because it limits the start of the activity. The other predecessors may or may not have free slack, depending on the actual times involved and the structure of precedence relations. This is the situation for A (with $FS = 0$) and B (with $FS = 1$), which are predecessors of D.

In contrast to total slack, free slack is not shared by groups of activities. Instead, it is a measure of scheduling flexibility for a particular activity. Thus, an activity has two slack measures, total slack and free slack. Table 6.3 summarizes these measures for the Watkins project. The total slack and free slack for Activity B tell us the following:

1. We can delay B by 2 weeks without delaying the project.
2. We can delay B by 1 week without delaying any other activity.

Clearly, these two measures are of great value to a project scheduler. The total slack measure helps indicate the overall criticality of an activity, and thus indicates the relative degree of attention it should receive. On the other hand, the free slack measure shows how much individual flexibility is available for the detailed scheduling of the project.

UPDATING

The critical path analysis is appropriate before the start of a project. In addition, however, there are many situations in which it would be desirable to update the analysis once the project is under way. Fortunately, it is easy to accomplish this task. We simply revise the earliest time calculations (that is, the calculations moving through the network from START to FINISH) by substituting actual times for activities that are complete and otherwise using the best estimates of times for incomplete activities. It is not necessary to modify the latest time calculations. The information produced by such updating is useful because it may reveal critical paths that did not previously exist, or it may show new areas of scheduling flexibility.

To summarize, critical path analysis assumes that the precedence relations and activity times in a project can be specified in advance and that sufficient resources are available to carry out any of the activities as early as precedence requirements permit. Under these conditions critical path analysis provides responses to the relevant managerial questions in deterministic fashion. To determine how long the project will take, the analysis finds the length of the longest path in the network. To establish a project schedule, the analysis supplies early start times and early finish times for each activity. To determine which activities bear the most careful attention in scheduling, the analysis identifies the critical path, which accounts for the project length. To describe the flexibility that exists in the project schedule, the analysis provides such quantities as late start times, late finish times, total slack, and free slack. Finally, it is possible to update the analyses once the project has started.

TIME/COST TRADE-OFFS

In some situations critical path analysis may yield a project length that is not acceptable, perhaps because of contractual or resource limitations. For such problems, it is possible that the use of more resources can reduce some of the activity times. For example, additional people or equipment might be able to accelerate an activity. However, these additional resources cost money. As a result, the decision maker's problem may be to reduce the project duration with a minimum increase in cost.

This problem may have many complicating factors. For example, the reduction in time might not be proportional to the cost of additional resources, or there might be upper and lower limits on the activity time. For such situations, a typical curve of cost versus time is shown in Figure 6.10.

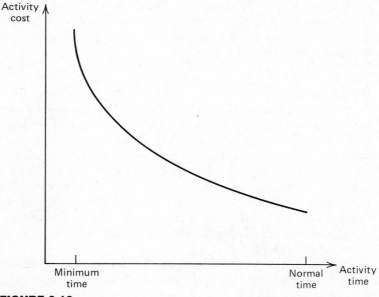

FIGURE 6.10

Analyzing situations such as this can be difficult if the cost curves are not linear. Most solution approaches make the problem easier by using a linear approximation of actual costs, as shown in Figure 6.11. More generally, these approaches accommodate cost functions with several linear segments. However, for purposes of illustration we shall use only one linear segment. Thus, we represent the time/cost trade-off for any activity with the notation shown in Figure 6.12.

Suppose that Mr. Watkins would like to complete the project in 11 weeks and that the actual parameters for the Watkins project are as follows:

Activity	Normal Situation		Minimum Time Situation	
	Time (weeks)	Cost ($000s)	Time (weeks)	Cost ($000s)
A	4	10	3	15
B	3	11	2	14
C	5	4	5	4
D	4	2	3	5
E	5	3	2	9
F	4	6	1	18
G	3	9	3	9
H	2	4	1	9

We can illustrate the nature of this problem by using Procedure 6.2. At each stage of this procedure we find the minimum incremental cost per unit to accelerate the project. To implement Procedure 6.2 we begin by creating a table of cost changes, such as the following:

	ΔC (Cost of Minimum Time − Cost of Normal Time)	ΔT (Normal Time − Minimum Time)	$\Delta C/\Delta T$
A	5,000	1	5,000
B	3,000	1	3,000
C	0	0	—
D	3,000	1	3,000
E	6,000	3	2,000
F	12,000	3	4,000
G	0	0	—
H	5,000	1	5,000

Note that the $\Delta C/\Delta T$ ratio is just the slope of the line (actually the negative of the slope) in Figure 6.12. It tells us the cost of achieving a 1-week reduction in the duration of any activity. Now we can apply the cost reduction procedure.

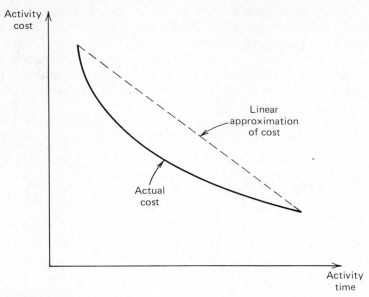

FIGURE 6.11

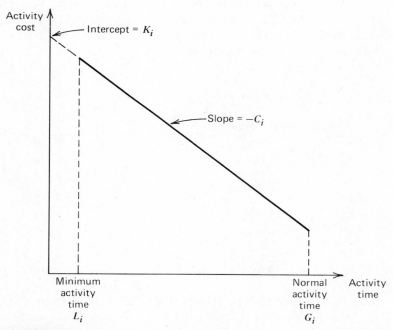

FIGURE 6.12

PROCEDURE 6.2
Simple Procedure for Reducing Project Length.

1 Use the normal times to find the critical path.

2 Reduce the critical path in time increments of one unit by finding the activity or group of activities that accomplishes the reduction at the smallest cost. In the event of ties, break them arbitrarily. When multiple critical paths occur, each path must be reduced.

3 Repeat Step 2.

4 Stop when the desired project length has been achieved.

To start, the critical path is ACFH, with a length of 15 weeks. Our goal is to reduce the project length and thus, the critical path by 1 week (from 15 weeks to 14 weeks). The only candidates for reduction are those activities on the critical path: A, C, F, and H. From our table, we see that activity F is the least expensive choice. Thus, we reduce F to 3 weeks at an additional cost of $4000. When we make this reduction, the path ACFH is shortened to 14 weeks. At this point, the total cost of the project is $53,000: the original cost of $49,000 plus the extra cost of $4000. However, path ACE also has a length of 14 weeks. As a result it, too, is a critical path.

As before, we want to reduce the project duration by 1 week (this time from 14 weeks to 13 weeks). Our problem, however, is that reducing one of the critical paths and not the other will not shorten the project. Thus, we have to reduce each critical path.

Considering path ACFH, the least expensive action is still to reduce F, at an additional cost of $4000. Similarly, the least expensive way to shorten path ACE by 1 week is to reduce E, at an additional cost of $2000. Note, however, that this action is *not* the overall least expensive action. Instead of reducing both F and E at a total cost of $6000 we could reduce only A, which is on both paths, at a cost of only $5000. Clearly, this alternative is preferable. Thus, we reduce A to 3 weeks at an additional cost of $5000. Now the project costs $58,000.

At this stage both paths ACFH and ACE are critical, and the project duration is 13 weeks. We would like to obtain an additional reduction, this time from 13 weeks to 12 weeks. However, we cannot reduce A any further, because it is at its minimum time of 3 weeks. As a result, our only recourse is to reduce F (to 2 weeks) and E (to 4 weeks) at an additional cost of $6000. This gives us a new total cost of $64,000.

With the new times, we have a project duration of 12 weeks, but now there are three critical paths: ACFH, ACE, and BDGH. To obtain a 1-week reduction in the project length, we again have to shorten *each* path. Here the analysis becomes more complicated. First, for path ACE the only candidate for further reduction is E, because A and C are already at their minimum times. This reduction costs an additional $2000. Second, considering the other two paths, the least expensive alternative is to reduce H, which is on both paths, at a cost of $5000. Thus, we reduce E to 3 and H to 1 at a total additional cost of $7000; the total cost is now $71,000.

As expected, we have reduced the project duration to 11 weeks. Now, however, there are *four* critical paths: ACFH, ACE, BDGH, and ADGH. To achieve the duration of 11 weeks, Mr. Watkins must spend a total of $71,000. Clearly, we could continue with the analysis to achieve an additional reduction of 1 week. However, the form of the analysis is clear. By doing the analysis incrementally, just 1 week at a time, we can identify additional paths that become critical.

One interesting result of the analysis is the plot of total project cost versus project time. Figure 6.13 shows such a plot for the Watkins project. Note that the curve is composed of linear segments that get steeper as we reduce the project duration. In general, the curve exhibits the characteristic of **increasing marginal costs:** Each additional reduction costs more than its predecessors when activity costs are linear.

THE LINEAR PROGRAMMING MODEL

For a large project it would not be practical to use the incremental approach for determining the minimum cost increase. Furthermore, the incremental ap-

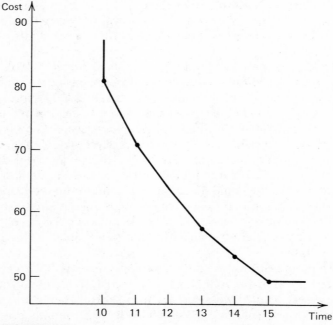

FIGURE 6.13

TABLE 6.4

DEFINITIONS

ES_i = early start time of activity i

D_i = duration (activity time) for i

PD = project deadline or project duration

B = amount of funds budgeted for the project

L_i = lowest activity time for i (see Figure 6.12)

G_i = greatest activity time for i (see Figure 6.12)

K_i and C_i = intercept and negative slope for i (see Figure 6.12)

OBJECTIVE

Minimize B subject to meeting fixed PD.

Here $B = \sum_i (K_i - C_i D_i)$

CONSTRAINTS

1. $ES_i + D_i \leq PD$	for all activities that have no successors	
2. $ES_j + D_j \leq ES_i$	for all pairs of activities i and j in which j is a predecessor of i	
3. $L_i \leq D_i \leq G_i$	for all activities	
4. $ES_i \geq 0$	for all activities	

proach does not always provide the optimal solution. Fortunately, it is possible to formulate the problem as a linear program. Table 6.4 shows the overall LP formulation of the problem, which is to minimize cost subject to meeting the constraint on project duration.

In the formulation, note that the term $(K_i - C_i D_i)$ represents the total cost of activity i. Thus, by summing over all activities, the objective is to minimize the total project cost. The constraints are as follows:

Constraint 1 assures that the project is completed by its deadline. Here $(ES_i + D_i)$ is just the finish time of a "dead-end" activity.

Constraint 2 assures that the start time of an activity satisfies the precedence relations. Note that $(ES_j + D_j)$ is just the finish time of activity j, which is a predecessor of activity i.

Constraint 3 assures that activity times fall within their appropriate lower and upper bounds.

Constraint 4 assures that all activities start no earlier than time 0.

To illustrate the general approach, the following is the formulation of the problem for Mr. Watkins:

minimize

$$
\begin{aligned}
\text{cost} = 49{,}000 \\
+ 5000(4 - D_A) + 3000(3 - D_B) + 3000(4 - D_D) \\
+ 2000(5 - D_E) + 4000(4 - D_F) + 5000(2 - D_H)
\end{aligned}
$$

subject to

1. $ES_E + D_E \leq 11$

   $ES_H + D_H \leq 11$

2. $ES_A + D_A \leq ES_C$ $ES_C + D_C \leq ES_F$

   $ES_A + D_A \leq ES_D$ $ES_D + D_D \leq ES_F$

   $ES_B + D_B \leq ES_D$ $ES_D + D_D \leq ES_G$

   $ES_C + D_C \leq ES_E$ $ES_F + D_F \leq ES_H$

   $ES_D + D_D \leq ES_E$ $ES_G + D_G \leq ES_H$

3. $3 \leq D_A \leq 4$

   $2 \leq D_B \leq 3$

   $5 \leq D_C \leq 5$

   $3 \leq D_D \leq 4$

   $2 \leq D_E \leq 5$

   $1 \leq D_F \leq 4$

   $3 \leq D_G \leq 3$

   $1 \leq D_H \leq 2$

4. $ES_i \geq 0$ $i = A, \ldots, H$

The objective function contains several pieces of information: The cost of 49,000 represents the cost of the project using normal times, the multiplier of each quantity in parentheses is just the $\Delta C / \Delta T$ ratio we calculated, and the quantity in parentheses represents the amount of reduction in an activity time. Also, activities C and G are omitted because it is not possible to reduce their times. Finally, we can simplify the objective function to read

$$
\begin{aligned}
\text{minimize cost} = 126{,}000 - 5000D_A - 3000D_B - 3000D_D \\
- 2000D_E - 4000D_F - 5000D_H
\end{aligned}
$$

Furthermore, we can eliminate the constant cost of 126,000 because it is not part of the optimization. Notice that there is a separate constraint for each predecessor relationship in the form of either constraints 1 or 2. If we solve this LP problem for the Watkins project we obtain the same results as we did performing calculations by hand. Specifically, we find that when the project is completed in 11 weeks the minimum total cost is $71,000.

In the example we illustrated a problem of minimizing cost subject to meeting a constraint on the project duration. Although this type of LP problem occurs frequently, it is possible to encounter other variations of the LP problem. For example, one possibility is to minimize the project length subject to a constraint on cost. Another variation recognizes the existence of fixed overhead costs per unit time. In this problem both the activity durations and the total project length are variable. The objective function is to minimize cost, including both the costs of accelerating activities and the cost of overhead. The constraints are similar to those in Table 6.4, but with the project length as a variable instead of being fixed.

For large projects the LP formulation could have an extremely large number of variables and constraints. Fortunately, there are algorithms available that efficiently solve problems of this type. One additional benefit of using the LP formulation is the flexibility it gives us to include other realistic considerations. For example, we may encounter situations in which we have limited labor or machine resources available for the project. As long as we can represent these resource limits with linear relationships, we can add them to the basic LP formulation. These changes may require use of binary variables, and, thus, may produce an IP problem. Nevertheless, the use of the basic LP framework is extremely helpful.

PROBABILISTIC ANALYSIS

One of the crucial assumptions in critical path analysis is that all activity times are known with certainty. Such an approach is particularly open to question in the scheduling of a one-of-a-kind project. Furthermore, we are not likely to be so knowledgeable about activities that have never even been attempted before, such as in the installation of a new computer system or the relocation of a hospital. Therefore, there are situations in project planning in which it makes sense to recognize the uncertain nature of activity times. Probabilistic analysis of project networks extends the concepts of a critical path analysis to confront issues of uncertainty. However, a formulation of the network scheduling problem in probabilistic terms leads to a more complicated form of analysis.

Perhaps the most widely used form of probabilistic analysis is associated with the methods of PERT. The PERT approach comprises three major steps in the analysis of a project:

1. Recognize uncertainty in activity time forecasts
2. Estimate the mean project length
3. Describe the project length in probabilistic terms

At the outset, we remark that the PERT methodology does not represent a strict application of probability theory to network analysis. In fact, PERT avoids some theoretical complexities in favor of a simpler, more practical resolution of the difficulties in probabilistic analysis. Furthermore, the PERT model represents a framework within which it is possible to address the more penetrating theoretical issues. We shall return to some of these considerations after examining the PERT methodology in detail.

UNCERTAINTY IN ACTIVITY TIMES

In the PERT approach the time required to carry out a particular activity is uncertain, and, in principle, we can describe any activity time by specifying its probability distribution. This step is difficult for several reasons. First, in novel projects there may be no history on which we can base such a specification. Further, if we use subjective probability distributions, we must obtain them from people who are knowledgeable about the activities. However, these people may not be inclined to express their knowledge in terms of probability models. Also, large projects require an extensive effort to obtain probability judgments for the many activities that occur. This kind of effort might well be considered too expensive a means of determining probability information.

The PERT approach provides a simpler alternative. For each activity, it utilizes the following three descriptive parameters:

a = an optimistic estimate of the activity duration

b = a pessimistic estimate of the activity duration

m = an estimate of the most likely activity duration

The optimistic estimate is usually considered to be the activity time under the most favorable circumstances. That is, if all conditions on which the activity time depends turn out to be favorable, then the activity will be completed in its optimistic time. Analogously, the pessimistic estimate is usually considered to be the activity time under the least favorable circumstances. The third estimate is literally the activity time believed to be most likely to occur.

From the three parameters (a, m, and b), the PERT approach prescribes the calculation of the mean μ and the standard deviation σ of the activity time distribution from the following formulas:

$$\mu = \frac{a + 4m + b}{6} \tag{6.7}$$

$$\sigma = \frac{b - a}{6} \tag{6.8}$$

For example, in the Watkins project, suppose that a technical illustrator assigned to the preparation of drawings (activity C) estimates that under favorable conditions the activity will take 3 weeks, under unfavorable conditions it might take up to 11 weeks, and it is most likely to take 4 weeks. In the notation of PERT we have

$$a = 3 \qquad m = 4 \qquad b = 11$$

and

$$\mu = \frac{3 + 4(4) + 11}{6} = 5$$

$$\sigma = \frac{11 - 3}{6} = \frac{4}{3}$$

One simple rationale for the formulas in equation (6.7) is that μ can be interpreted as a weighted average of the most likely estimate and the midpoint of the range of the estimate, with weights of $\frac{2}{3}$ and $\frac{1}{3}$, respectively. Here, the midpoint is the average of the optimistic and pessimistic extremes. Stated in symbols:

$$\mu = \frac{2}{3} \text{ (most likely)} + \frac{1}{3} \text{ (midpoint)}$$

$$= \frac{2}{3}(m) \qquad\qquad + \frac{1}{3}\left(\frac{a + b}{2}\right)$$

$$= \frac{a + 4m + b}{6}$$

Furthermore, the range of six standard deviations in the distribution ($b - a = 6\sigma$) in equation (6.8) is consistent with the behavior of a normal distribution, for which six standard deviations span virtually the entire distribution.

AN ESTIMATE OF THE PROJECT LENGTH

Given these definitions, the next step in the analysis is to describe the length of the project. In the probabilistic model, because the individual activity times are uncertain, the length of the project is also uncertain. However, it is quite difficult to rigorously derive the properties of the random variable that represents the project length.

The PERT method associates with each activity its mean time, calculated from equation (6.7). The method then proceeds with critical path analysis using only the mean time for each activity and suppressing the random aspects of activity durations. This approach gives rise to a form of critical path analysis in which mean activity times play the role of deterministic activity times. As in the deterministic case, the analysis reveals the length of the longest path and identifies the critical activities. In the PERT method, the length of the longest path in the network is taken as an estimate of mean project length. Although we said earlier that the AOA approach is most commonly used with PERT, the AON approach can also be used.

A PROBABILITY MODEL FOR THE PROJECT LENGTH

Having estimated the length of the project and having identified a set of critical activities, the PERT method builds a probabilistic interpretation. For any path in the network it is possible to compute the mean and variance of the path length. The mean of the path length is the sum of the activity means. If we assume that the times are independent, the variance of the path length will be the sum of the activity variances. Stated in symbols:

$$\mu_{\text{path}} = \sum_i \mu_i \tag{6.9}$$

$$\sigma^2_{\text{path}} = \sum_i \sigma^2_i \tag{6.10}$$

where the summation is taken for all activities on the given path. PERT also assumes that the probability model for the length of the path is a normal distribution with mean μ_{path} and variance σ^2_{path}. Although this calculation could apply to all paths, PERT analysis is most concerned with the critical path. For the critical path we will use μ_* and σ^2_* to denote the mean and variance of the path length.

To illustrate the PERT methodology, suppose that the activity times of the Watkins project are described in terms of the following optimistic, pessimistic, and most likely estimates:

Activity	a	m	b	μ	σ^2
A	3	4	5	4	$\frac{1}{9}$
B	2	3	4	3	$\frac{1}{9}$
C	3	4	11	5	$\frac{16}{9}$
D	2	4	6	4	$\frac{4}{9}$
E	3	5	7	5	$\frac{4}{9}$
F	1	3	11	4	$\frac{25}{9}$
G	3	3	3	3	0
H	1	2	3	2	$\frac{1}{9}$

The first step in the PERT method is to calculate the μ value and σ value implied by formulas (6.7) and (6.8) for each activity, as shown in the table. Then we perform critical path analysis using the μ values. In this example, the μ values agree with the activity times in Figure 6.5, so that the estimated length of the project is 15 weeks and the critical activities are A, C, F, and H. For this set of activities we have

$$\mu_* = \mu_A + \mu_C + \mu_F + \mu_H = 4 + 5 + 4 + 2 = 15$$

$$\sigma_*^2 = \sigma_A^2 + \sigma_C^2 + \sigma_F^2 + \sigma_H^2 = \frac{1 + 16 + 25 + 1}{9} = \frac{43}{9} = 4.78$$

$$\sigma_* = \sqrt{4.78} = 2.19$$

Thus, we model the length of the Watkins project as following a normal distribution with a mean of 15 and a standard deviation of 2.19 weeks. Figure 6.14 depicts this distribution. Applying this probability model we can calculate the probability that the project will be complete within 18 weeks:

$$P(\text{project length} \le 18) = P\left(z \le \frac{18 - 15}{2.19}\right)$$

where z is the standard normal variate. Using the normal probability table we find

$$P\left(z \le \frac{18 - 15}{2.19}\right) = P(z \le 1.37) = 0.91$$

Therefore, the probability is 0.91 that the project will be completed within 18 weeks.

In this fashion we can begin to recognize the uncertain nature of the project schedule when making statements about the time required to complete the project. The advantage of the PERT method is that it provides a basis for incorporating uncertainty in the analysis of the project. Nevertheless, the PERT model rests on certain assumptions and simplifications that bear close scrutiny. We address these issues later.

COMPUTER SOLUTION

Many computer programs are available, even on personal computers, for analyzing a project planning problem. Most of these programs are flexible enough to

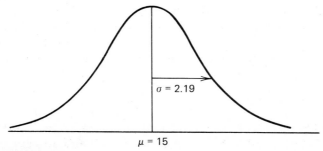

$\sigma = 2.19$

$\mu = 15$

FIGURE 6.14

```
9000 DATA 8
9010 DATA A,5,4,3,START
9020 DATA B,4,3,2,START
9030 DATA C,11,4,3,A
9040 DATA D,6,4,2,A,B
9050 DATA E,7,5,3,C,D
9060 DATA F,11,3,1,C,D
9070 DATA G,3,3,3,D
9080 DATA H,3,2,1,F,G
```

WATKINS ARCHITECTS AND CONSULTANTS, INC.

ACTIVITY	MEAN	STD DEV	EARLY START	EARLY FINISH	LATE START	LATE FINISH	TOTAL SLACK	FREE SLACK
A	4.0	0.3	0.0	4.0	0.0	4.0	0.0	0.0
B	3.0	0.3	0.0	3.0	2.0	5.0	2.0	1.0
C	5.0	1.3	4.0	9.0	4.0	9.0	0.0	0.0
D	4.0	0.7	4.0	8.0	5.0	9.0	1.0	0.0
E	5.0	0.7	9.0	14.0	10.0	15.0	1.0	1.0
F	4.0	1.7	9.0	13.0	9.0	13.0	0.0	0.0
G	3.0	0.0	8.0	11.0	10.0	13.0	2.0	2.0
H	2.0	0.3	13.0	15.0	13.0	15.0	0.0	0.0

TOTAL TIME TO COMPLETION 15

FIGURE 6.15

be able to deal with both the deterministic and probabilistic forms of the problem. The essential information for such programs includes

Number of activities
Precedence relationships
Activity times

Figure 6.15 shows how to provide a BASIC program with the data for the Watkins project. The figure also shows the type of information provided by the program. Note that the inputs and outputs of the program are the same as those of our analyses. The only difference is that the structure of the program makes it possible to deal with projects having hundreds or even thousands of activities.

ISSUES IN PROBABILISTIC ANALYSIS

By examining the assumptions and simplifications of the PERT method we can appreciate some of the limitations of the method and also get an idea of how to apply the method judiciously in situations that do not match the assumptions.

There are three important areas to consider:

1. The probability model for activity times
2. The estimate of mean project length
3. The probability model for project length

We deal with each of these areas in the material that follows.

THE PROBABILITY MODEL FOR ACTIVITY TIMES

As mentioned earlier, there is an intuitive rationale for formulas (6.7) and (6.8) to provide the mean and variance of an activity time distribution. There is also a more formal justification of the formulas. Formulas (6.7) and (6.8) actually apply to a family of special cases of the **beta distribution,** which is often believed to be a good model for representing the uncertain behavior of activity times. In general, a beta distribution is described by a specification of three parameters: a minimum a, a maximum b, and a mode m as shown in Figure 6.16. Unlike some other distributions, the beta distribution has a finite lower limit and a finite upper limit. For a certain special family of beta distributions, the mean and variance are related to the three parameters by the simple formulas (6.7) and (6.8).

There may be a question as to whether the beta distributions adequately represents the subjective distributions ideally sought, but the beta model will at least be a plausible one in many situations. In any event, the key idea is that to proceed with the analysis PERT requires a mean and a variance for the distribution of each activity time. Furthermore, PERT provides a reasonable substitute for direct inquiry about means and variances.

THE ESTIMATE OF MEAN PROJECT LENGTH

As we discussed previously, the PERT method utilizes the longest mean path length as an estimate of mean project length. This estimate has a systematic bias in it and will always tend to underestimate the actual mean, assuming that all parameters are accurate. To suggest why this is the case, consider the very simple network in Figure 6.17. In this project there are two independent activities, A and B, and the project length is the time of A or the time of B, whichever is

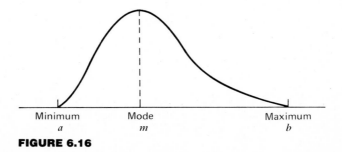

FIGURE 6.16

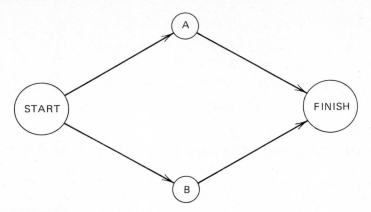

FIGURE 6.17

larger. Furthermore, assume that the probability models for activity times are as follows:

A time	8	9	10	11	12
Probability	0.4	0.1	0.3	0.1	0.1

B time	10
Probability	1

The time for A is random with a mean of 9.4 weeks, and the time for B is 10 weeks with certainty (this is a special kind of probability model). If we use the PERT method for this project, the estimate of the mean project length is 10. In essence, the critical path analysis compares the mean time of A with the mean time of B and finds B to be larger. However, in this simple model we can see that, because the time of B is certain, the project will take 10, 11, or 12 weeks depending only on the actual time of A. When we collect the corresponding probabilities, we obtain the following discrete distribution for the project length:

Project length	10	11	12
Probability	0.8	0.1	0.1

Obviously, because of the fixed time for B, the project length can never be less than 10. Note that the B time is limiting 80% of the time (when A is 10 or less) and the A time is limiting 20% of the time (when A is 11 or 12). Using the basic definition of mean value we obtain

mean project length = 0.8(10) + 0.1(11) + 0.1(12) = 10.3

Thus, the true mean of the project length distribution is 10.3 weeks, slightly larger than the 10 weeks estimated by the PERT method.

Although this example is quite simple, it does suggest the reason for bias in the PERT estimate. Because PERT uses the mean time along a particular path as an estimate, it fails to recognize that other paths may have some probability of actually being longer than the path with the longest mean length. Therefore, to the extent that alternative paths exist, and to the extent that they have significant probabilities of being the longest, the PERT method will underestimate the true mean of the project length. However, when one particular path is almost certain to be the longest, there will be little bias in the PERT estimate.

A related issue involves the determination of critical activities. The PERT method does identify one path as critical, but the procedure simply classifies activities as either critical or noncritical. In the case of probabilistic activity times, the notion of criticality is more complex. Note that even in the simple network of Figure 6.16 it is misleading to say (as the PERT method, strictly interpreted, would say) that activity B is critical while activity A is not. In fact, given the probability models for the two activity times, there are three possibilities:

A is critical and B is not   (with a probability of 0.2)
B is critical and A is not   (with a probability of 0.5)
A and B are both critical   (with a probability of 0.3)

Stated another way, activity A has a probability of 0.5 of being critical and B has a probability of 0.8 of being critical.

Thus, in the probabilistic case, it may be more meaningful to find the probability that a given activity will be critical than to label the activity as either critical or noncritical, as PERT does. In more complicated networks, it is difficult to derive these probabilities theoretically, as we did for the simple network above. However, it is possible to use simulation techniques to obtain reliable estimates of these probabilities.

For example, suppose that the activity times in the Watkins project follow a beta distribution, with the parameters (a, m, b) given earlier. Given this information, the PERT method still identifies ACFH as the critical path. However, a simulation study might yield estimates of the probability of being critical such as the following:

Activity	A	B	C	D	E	F	G	H
Probability	0.91	0.09	0.86	0.14	0.22	0.74	0.04	0.78

As these results suggest, it is possible that different activities along the PERT critical path will exhibit different probabilities of being critical. Here again, the PERT method for identifying critical activities is valid when there are few alternative paths that could actually be the longest path or when all paths but one have very small probabilities of being the longest.

THE MODEL FOR PROJECT LENGTH

The PERT method focuses on the properties of a particular path—the path identified as having the largest mean length. To determine the mean and variance of the length of this path it is valid to add the means and the variances of the activity times on the path, as PERT does, only if these activity times are independent random variables.

In many situations, independence would be a plausible assumption, but there are cases in which independence is not justified. For example, in a large construction project in which the progress of several activities depends on the weather or on the productivity of a particular work crew there would be good reason to expect the independence assumption to be violated. Specifically, bad weather or low productivity would lengthen all of these activities, but good weather or high productivity would shorten them. Thus, it would not be realistic to assume that the times are independent, since they are affected by the same factors.

Even if independence can safely be assumed, the next issue is whether the sum of the activity times along a path tends to follow a normal distribution. Here the PERT rationale usually appeals to the Central Limit Theorem of probability theory, which states that the sum of a number of random variables approaches normal behavior in the limit, as the number of random variables in the sum gets quite large.

Although this probability model might be plausible for the length of a particular path, we must keep in mind that the PERT method substitutes this model of the behavior of a particular path length for the actual behavior of the project length. Once again, this substitution is reasonable when there is only one path with any significant probability of being the longest path, but the method is certainly questionable otherwise. When there are several paths that could turn out to be critical, the normal model and the PERT calculation of σ_*^2 are unlikely to be valid. In such cases a strict application of the PERT method should not be accepted without caution, for there may be a considerable gap between the existing conditions and the conditions assumed in the PERT analysis.

SUMMARY

Network diagrams are graphical models that capture logical information about the activities in a project. The typical network diagram is a fairly simple model that describes precedence relationships but does not convey information about uncertainty in activity time estimates or about the resources that may actually be required to execute certain activities. Thus, the simplification involved in building the network model allows attention to be focused on the sequencing and timing aspects of the project.

Although their roles are less explicit in network models than in most other models, we can still identify parameters, variables, and criteria. Activity times are the main parameters, and activity start times are the main decision variables in project scheduling. Although activity start times are not explicit variables in critical path analysis, the calculations yield early start times and late start times, which provide a range within which the scheduled start times must lie. Once the start times are set, completion times are determined by activity durations. When the activity times are treated explicitly as random variables, the interpretation of critical path analysis must be modified appropriately.

The implicit criterion in most network analyses is to complete the project as efficiently as possible, which usually means in minimum time. For critical activities there is no latitude in scheduling: Any delay in the start of a critical activity will delay the entire project. For noncritical activities, by contrast, some scheduling flexibility exists. The extent of this flexibility is measured by such quantities as an activity's total slack. The total slack is usually viewed as a measure of how much latitude exists in the assignment of a start time to a particular activity. From another viewpoint, the total slack calculation is also a form of sensitivity analysis, because it measures the increase in a specific parameter (the activity time) that could be absorbed without affecting the criterion (the length of the project). A similar argument applies to free slack.

Also, we saw that it is possible to modify critical path analysis to consider time/cost trade-offs. In such analyses we encounter several realistic modeling phenomena, such as increasing marginal costs. Furthermore, it is helpful to use linear programming in dealing with these time/cost trade-offs. Linear programming also enables us to include other realistic considerations, such as resource limits.

In its simplest form, critical path analysis assumes a deterministic version of the network model; but, as we have seen, the analysis can adapt to a probabilistic interpretation by using the PERT methodology. Also, the basic form of critical path analysis is static, as if the start times will remain unchanged once they are determined. In the midst of carrying out a project, however, conditions might change; the project deadline might be revised or activity times might turn out to be different from those assumed. It is possible to update critical path analysis in the middle of such a project, by deleting portions of the project that have been completed and by revising the parameters that describe what remains. This approach, in which the decision variables might change as the project progresses, is more nearly a dynamic form of critical path analysis.

EXERCISES

CRITICAL PATH ANALYSIS

1 A new product has been designed and test marketed. The task now is to prepare for its full-scale introduction. The production manager is responsible for the activities described below, leading to an 8-week production run.

a Determine the length of the project.

b Find the critical path.

c Construct a table showing the quantities ES, EF, LF, TS, and FS for each activity.

Activity	Predecessors	Weeks
A. Prepare bill of materials	—	1
B. Design assembly line	—	3
C. Order and await delivery of equipment	B	5
D. Order and await delivery of materials	A	6
E. Determine inspection procedures	A	3
F. Install assembly line	C	2
G. Install inspection stations	E	1
H. Hire work force	B	9
I. Train work force	H, D, G	2
J. Assemble product	F, I	8

2 An aerospace company has received a contract for the final assembly of a space module for an upcoming mission. A team of engineers has determined the activities, precedence constraints, and time estimates given below.

a Determine the length of the project.

b Find the critical path.

c Construct a table showing the quantities ES, EF, LF, LS, TS, and FS for each activity.

Activity	Preceding Activities	Time Estimate (Days)
A. Construct shell of model	—	30
B. Order life support system and experimentation package from same supplier	—	15
C. Order components of control and navigational system	—	25
D. Wire module	A	3
E. Assemble control and navigational system	C	7
F. Give a preliminary test of life support system	B	1

Activity	Preceding Activities	Time Estimate (Days)
G. Install life support system in module	D, F	5
H. Install scientific experimentation package in module	D, F	2
I. Conduct a preliminary test of control and navigational system	E, F	4
J. Install control and navigational system in module	H, I	10
K. Final testing and debugging	G, J	8

3 A project consisting of the introduction of a firm's new product consists of the activities represented in the table and chart below. The chart is a technician's rendering of the logical relationships among the project activities.

a Draw the AOA network diagram for this project.

b Find the length of the project.

c Identify the critical path.

d Calculate the total slack and free slack for each activity.

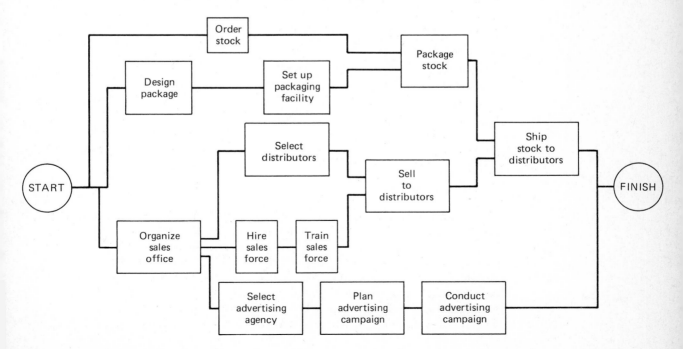

Activity	Description	Weeks
A	Organize sales office	6
B	Hire sales force	4
C	Train sales force	7
D	Select advertising agency	2
E	Plan advertising campaign	4
F	Conduct advertising campaign	10
G	Design package	2
H	Set up packaging facilities	10
I	Package initial stocks	6
J	Order stock from manufacturer	13
K	Select distributors	9
L	Sell to distributors	3
M	Ship stock	5

4 Metropolis General Hospital has decided to install a computer to record and collate patient bills. It has been projected that the hospital will save $900 per day with the new system. The following is the list of activities and other appropriate information.

Activity	Immediate Predecessors	Activity Time (Days)	Required Labor
A. Build a raised floor	None	4	Carpenter
B. Wire office to feed results into computer	C	5	Electrician
C. Wire computer room	None	6	Electrician
D. Install air conditioning	G, B	2	Electrician
E. Wait for delivery of computer	None	See below	Administrator
F. Install computer	D, E	10	Electrician
G. Build vents	A	3	Carpenter
H. Hook up to office	F	4	Electrician

The computer is expected to arrive by the end of day 14. All other activities can be speeded up by using overtime labor. The electricians are employed by the hospital at the rate of $15 per hour for a normal 8-hour day. They may work overtime at an *additional* cost of $120 per hour for the four-person crew. The carpentry work is done by contract. This crew (of three people) may work overtime at a cost of $60 per hour for the crew for a maximum of 4 hours per day. The electricians can only work a maximum of 4 hours of overtime per day. In both cases 1 hour of overtime is equivalent to 1 hour of regular time, so that 8 hours of overtime would be required to speed up an activity by 1 day.

a Draw a network diagram. Calculate *ES*, *EF*, *LS*, *LF*, and *TS* for each activity. Identify the critical path.

b Should the hospital use overtime labor? If not, why not? If so, how many hours of overtime for what activity? What savings result?

5 Furillo's Pizza, a fast-food chain, has prepared a construction plan for a new location and the construction contract has been let. The plan is summarized in Exhibit 2. The original plan called for completion of the project in 20 weeks, but that looked impossible when the project description was first compiled. Subsequently, however, it has been discovered that several of the activities can be completed earlier than initially estimated. (See Exhibit 1.) Note that the time to complete some activities cannot be shortened at all. Only those activities that are listed can be shortened. Some can be shortened by just 1 week, but others can be shortened by 4 weeks. For example, activity M can be shortened by 1 or 2 weeks. The cost to shorten it by 2 weeks, however, is more than double the cost of shortening it by 1 week.

a Draw the network diagram for the project.

b Assuming that no speedup is scheduled:

   1 How long will it take to complete the project?

   2 Which activities are critical?

c Assuming that the project should be planned to complete in 20 weeks:

   1 What is the minimum cost of achieving the speedup?

   2 Which activities should be scheduled for speedup?

   3 Which activities are critical?

EXHIBIT 1 Activity Expediting

Activity	Number of Weeks Reduction	Cost of Reduction
B	1	$ 500
G	1	400
	2	800
	3	1300
	4	2000
H	1	200
	2	350
J	1	400
M	1	500
	2	1200

EXHIBIT 2 Activities and Predecessors

In the first week of the project the final blueprints can be started and the excavation for the foundation can begin.

After the blueprints are drawn, the lumber and building materials can be ordered. At that same time it will also be possible to order the kitchen equipment.

Once the excavation for the foundation has been completed, the foundation can be poured.

The delivery of the lumber and building materials is an activity that follows the ordering of these materials. After the lumber is delivered and the foundation poured, the frame construction can begin.

After the frame is constructed, two activities can begin: first, plumbing and electrical work and, second, exterior finishing.

Following the placement of the order for kitchen equipment, the delivery of the equipment must take place. After the equipment is delivered and both the plumbing and electrical work are completed, the kitchen equipment can be installed.

The interior finishing must wait until the kitchen equipment finish work is completed.

Landscaping and parking facilities must wait until the exterior finish work is completed.

Once the landscape and interior finish work is completed, the project is finished.

These activities and their estimated completion times are given below.

Activity	Estimated Completion Time in Weeks
A. Make up final blueprints	3
B. Excavate foundation	2
C. Order lumber and building materials	1
D. Order kitchen equipment	3
E. Deliver lumber and materials	2
F. Pour foundation	1
G. Construct frame	8
H. Finish exterior	5
I. Do electrical and plumbing work	3
J. Install kitchen	3
K. Deliver kitchen equipment	5
L. Do landscaping and parking	3
M. Finish interior	4

6 In 1981, Kirven Construction Company (KCC) had received a fixed price contract to construct a missile launching site for the National Bureau of Aeronautics (NBA). By the fall of 1982 work was nearly complete on the main launch site. However, it was apparent that work on a special remote-control building would have to be finished earlier than originally planned if the contract were to be completed on time.

The field supervisor of KCC met with the firm's project engineer to restudy the network diagram for the construction of the remote-control building, in an effort to determine the shortest possible time in which the job could be done without spending more money than necessary. The original diagram for the remote-control building is shown in Exhibit 3. It was, of course, considerably simpler than the similar diagrams for the entire missile site construction job.

Using data from the cost table (Exhibit 4) for this project, it was apparent that the critical path for this project followed the sequence of activities A–D–G and would require 12 weeks. The original project cost was estimated at $61,000.

a What is the minimum cost required to shorten the project to 10 weeks?

b What is the minimum cost required to shorten the project to 9 weeks?

c What is the minimum cost required to complete the project at the earliest possible date?

d Suppose KCC were proceeding on a 10-week schedule and it became obvious that it would take not 2 weeks but 5 weeks to prepare the necessary data for the request for NBA approval and that this step alone would now cost $7000. What steps would you take to keep on schedule? What would be your new critical path or paths? What would happen to project costs?

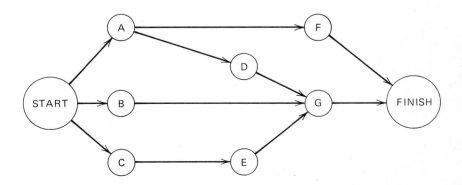

EXHIBIT 4 Cost Table for Remote Control Building Project

| Activity | Normal Duration | | Crash[a] Duration | | Cost Slope Dollars/Week |
	Weeks	Dollars	Weeks	Dollars	
A	3	$ 5,000	2	$ 10,000	$5,000[b]
B	6	14,000	4	26,000	6,000
C	2	2,500	1	5,000	2,500
D	5	10,000	3	18,000	4,000
E	2	8,000	2	8,000	—
F	7	11,500	5	17,500	3,000
G	4	10,000	2	24,000	7,000
Total		$61,000		$108,500	

[a] Crash weeks shown represent the minimum possible time for the given activity.

[b] This is the cost of gaining 1 week over the normal time by use of "crash" methods.

PROBABILISTIC ANALYSIS

7 Review Exercise 1. Suppose that a subsequent study produces the time estimates shown in the table below. Using the PERT method

a Calculate the mean project length.

b Identify the critical path.

c Compute the probability that the production run will be complete within 22 weeks.

Activity	Optimistic Estimate	Most Likely Estimate	Pessimistic Estimate
A	1	1	3
B	2	3	4
C	2	4	10
D	3	6	7
E	1	3	11
F	2	2	6
G	1	1	2
H	2	10	12
I	1	2	3
J	6	8	16

8 Review Exercise 2. Suppose that a more detailed study produces the time estimates shown in the table below. Using the PERT method

a Calculate the mean project length.

b Identify the critical path.

c Compute the probability that the project will be complete within 65 days.

Activity	Optimistic Estimate	Most Likely Estimate	Pessimistic Estimate
A	25	30	45
B	10	15	20
C	20	25	35
D	3	3	5
E	5	7	12
F	1	1	1
G	4	5	7
H	2	2	3
I	4	4	6
J	8	10	14
K	6	8	15

9 The KSM Distribution Company has obtained nationwide exclusive rights for distribution of a new expensive breakfast cereal. The project manager in charge of planning its introduction has done a PERT analysis and has found that the critical path contains the following tasks and that their times are as shown.

	Time Estimates (Weeks)		
Task	Optimistic	Most Likely	Pessimistic
A. Laboratory tests	3	4	5
B. Home tests	7	7	7
C. Test marketing in a small region	5	10	21
D. Making a decision as to whether to continue	2	5	8

a What is the estimated time for completion of the critical path, and what is the standard deviation of that estimate?

b What is the probability of completing the critical path in 30 weeks?

c By how much must you shorten the critical path to achieve a 90% probability of completion within 27 weeks?

10 Consider the machine setup project described below, and the associated costs of reducing the mean time. Assume that the variance of activity times does not change when the mean time is reduced.

Activity	Immediate Predecessor Event(s)	Optimistic Time (days)	Pessimistic Time (days)	Most Likely Time (days)
A	—	2	4	3
B	—	2	6	4
C	A	3	5	4
D	B	6	10	6.5
E	C	4	8	6
F	D	2	4	3
G	E	4	10	5.5
H	A, F	1	3	2
I	G	3	7	5
J	H	4	10	7
K	I, J	2	4	3

Total Cost of Reduction of Mean Time by Days (dollars)

Activity	A	B	C	D	E	F	G	H	I	J	K
Cost of 1-day reduction	10	15	15	15	20	*	20	20	30	30	20
Additional cost to achieve another 1-day reduction	30	30	40	40	35	*	35	60	65	65	30

* Cannot be reduced.

a Determine the critical path and the expected completion time.

b Estimate the probability that the setup will be done within 25 days.

c What is the least expensive action that the company can take to increase the probability of completion within 25 days to 0.50? What is the cost?

ISSUES IN PROBABILISTIC ANALYSIS

11 In the project model shown below, each activity time is random. Furthermore, there are three possible activity time outcomes for each activity in the network, and these occur with equal probabilities of $\frac{1}{3}$. (The outcomes are shown on the diagram.)

a Determine the probability distribution for the project length. That is, list the possible outcomes for the project length together with their respective probabilities.

b Calculate the mean and the variance of the project length and compare them to the figures produced by the PERT method.

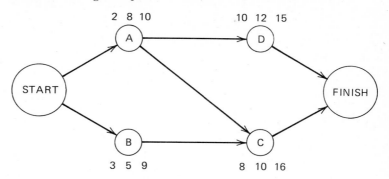

12 In the project shown below, each activity time follows a Normal distribution. The parameters (μ, σ^2) are given on the diagram.

a What is the mean and the variance for the length of path AB?

b What is the mean and the variance for the length of path CD?

c What is the probability that path CD will be longer than path AB?

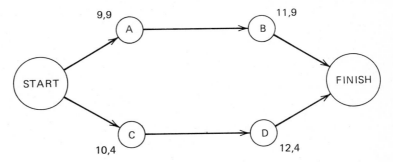

Chapter 7
DECISION ANALYSIS

Foster Textile Company

Foster Textile Company has developed a synthetic insulation material and is considering the introduction of a new line of winter sports clothing. If the firm chooses to go into production, one option requires a small-scale investment in modified facilities for producing winter jackets. Another option needs a large-scale investment in expanded facilities with production lines for gloves, hats, slacks, and sweaters. The sales manager envisions two types of market responses—"very favorable" or "relatively indifferent"—and a study by the planning staff has compiled profitability estimates for each response. The study predicts that the large-scale option will yield net profits of $4 million over the life of the investment, if the market response is favorable. On the other hand, the study predicts a $5 million loss if the response is indifferent. For the small-scale option the study predicts a net profit of $1 million for a favorable response, but a loss of $2 million for an indifferent response. The president, aware that a third option is simply not to go into production at all, is evaluating all the options.

The Foster Textile Company example illustrates a situation in which the decision maker faces conditions of uncertainty. Here we use the word "uncertainty" in a broad, nontechnical sense to mean that conditions neither are predetermined nor are they controllable. Specifically, under these conditions a decision maker cannot predict the exact consequences of each possible action. Moreover, this lack of precise knowledge is such an important feature in the situation that any analysis should capture it explicitly. The subject of **decision analysis** includes a number of principles and techniques for the systematic study of decision making with uncertain conditions.

In this chapter we shall focus on monetary outcomes—the economic consequences of an action as measured by profits or costs. Even with such a definite yardstick, it is not always easy to find a suitable criterion to guide decision making. Under conditions of certainty, monetary outcomes are predictable. This means that we can associate a single profit or cost measure with each possible action. Furthermore, we can expect two people to agree on whether one action is better than another because each action is unambiguously associated with a monetary outcome.

In the face of uncertainty, however, the association between action and outcome is not as dependable. The same two people might not agree about a particular decision, even though after the fact they can agree whether its outcome has been good. We refer to the assessment of an outcome as an **ex post** evaluation. The more important problem is the evaluation of a decision **ex ante,** before its consequences are known. Because there are differences among individuals in their ex ante evaluations, it is difficult to find a simple, all-encompassing criterion. As a result, we approach decision making under uncertainty in an individualized manner, relying on the concept of a single decision maker. In some cases, the responsibility for a particular decision may actually rest with a group, but it can be helpful to imagine that we are in the role of a single decision-making agent facing the problem.

In this context a **decision** is the choice of one action from a number of available actions. We assume that the consequences of a decision are measurable and refer to their monetary value as a **payoff.** Finally, we deal with situations in which the outcome of a decision depends on uncertain conditions in the environment, called **states of nature.** We will use probability models to describe this uncertainty. Although it is not necessary to rely on probability models (and we shall briefly examine some nonprobabilistic approaches), it is often convenient and persuasive to do so.

To summarize, we are concerned with the payoff associated with the action we select, and this payoff depends on both the action (which is controllable) and the state of nature that occurs (which is uncontrollable). The key feature of decision analysis is that we must select an action *before* we have an opportunity to learn the state of nature.

One way to describe such a problem involves a table of payoffs. Let row i of the table correspond to action i, and let column j of the table represent state j. Thus, each action-state pair corresponds to a single entry in the table, Z_{ij}, which denotes the payoff achieved with action i when state j occurs. This **payoff table** forms part of the model for a decision problem.

To clarify these ideas, let us examine the specific problem facing the president of Foster Textile Company. In the example we can immediately recognize three actions and two states of nature:

	Actions		States
$i = 1$:	Large-scale (LS)	$j = 1$:	Favorable response (F)
$i = 2$:	Small-scale (SS)	$j = 2$:	Indifferent response (I)
$i = 3$:	Do nothing (DN)		

Associated with each action-state pair is a payoff for the company. The table of payoffs in millions of dollars is as follows:

	State	
Action	F	I
LS	4	−5
SS	1	−2
DN	0	0

Now that we have identified the monetary consequences of different actions, we can consider how we may reach a decision.

DECISION CRITERIA AND OPTIMAL DECISIONS

In our basic model we face a choice among several actions, in which each action leads to one of many different outcomes depending on the state of nature. To resolve the problem of selecting an action, it would be convenient if we could use a single number to describe the possible outcomes for each action. Then we could make a decision simply by selecting the action with the best value. Unfortunately, it is not an easy matter to reduce a set of potential outcomes to a single summary value, and there are several ways to proceed. First, we will examine procedures that do not use probability judgments.

NONPROBABILISTIC CRITERIA

Perhaps the boldest approach to this problem is to select the action that potentially yields the largest payoff. For Foster Textile Company this philosophy leads to the selection of action 1, since only the large-scale strategy has the potential to gain a payoff as large as $4 million. Clearly, this decision is implicitly optimistic about the state of nature that will occur; if the indifferent response should occur, this action would appear less desirable.

We use the term **maximax** to describe this decision approach, because it selects the action that maximizes the maximum possible payoff. Conceptually, this means calculating the maximum payoff attainable for each action and then selecting the action with the largest maximum. Stated in symbols

$$V_i = \text{maximum possible payoff for action } i = \max_j \left\{Z_{ij}\right\}$$

$$V^* = \text{maximax payoff} = \max_i \left\{V_i\right\}$$

TABLE 7.1

Action	State F	I	Summary Value
LS	4	−5	$V_1 = 4$
SS	1	−2	$V_2 = 1$
DN	0	0	$V_3 = 0$
			$V^* = 4 \ (i^* = 1)$

Here, the summary value for each action is the maximum possible payoff. In the case of the maximax strategy the optimal action i^* yields the maximum value of V_i. For example, for the Foster Textile Company the maximax strategy dictates $i^* = 1$, with $V^* = 4$, as shown in Table 7.1.

As indicated above, the maximax strategy is a bold one. However, there are many situations in which we might prefer to be more cautious. One way to be conservative is to assume that, whichever action we select, the least favorable state of nature will occur. Conceptually, this means calculating the minimum possible payoff for each action and then selecting the action with the highest minimum. We call this conservative strategy the **maximin** strategy, because it selects the action that maximizes the minimum possible payoff. In this situation the summary value for a particular action is the minimum possible payoff. In symbols, we have

$$V_i = \text{minimum possible payoff for action } i = \min_j \left\{ Z_{ij} \right\}$$

$$V^* = \text{maximin payoff} = \max_i \left\{ V_i \right\}$$

Under the maximin strategy the optimal action i^* is the choice that maximizes the value of V_i. For the Foster Textile Company the maximum strategy dictates $i^* = 3$, with $V^* = 0$, as shown in Table 7.2.

TABLE 7.2

Action	State F	I	Summary Value
LS	4	−5	$V_1 = -5$
SS	1	−2	$V_2 = -2$
DN	0	0	$V_3 = 0$
			$V^* = 0 \ (i^* = 3)$

Although the maximin approach is obviously a conservative one, there is another conservative strategy to consider. This approach relies on the notion that relative payoffs are more significant than absolute payoffs. In particular, once we commit ourselves to a specific action and observe the state of nature, we remain aware of the payoff we might have earned had we chosen differently. In our example problem, suppose that the president of Foster Textile Company were to choose action 3 (do nothing) and state 1 (favorable response) were to occur. Even though the resulting zero payoff would be the best that could happen with action 3, the president would nevertheless feel a twinge of regret because the company could have earned a payoff of $4 million in state 1. On the other hand, if state 2 were to occur, the president would feel no such regret because the choice of action 3 is the best action for state 2.

In this spirit we can define **regret** for any action-state pair as the difference between the corresponding payoff and the best possible payoff for that state of nature. In symbols, regret is defined by

$$R_{ij} = \max_k \{Z_{kj}\} - Z_{ij}$$

The quantity R_{ij} is also called an **opportunity loss** or an **opportunity cost,** and it is always defined to be nonnegative. For the Foster Textile Company we begin the analysis by deriving a **regret table** of R_{ij} values from the original payoff table:

Action	State	
	F	I
LS	0	5
SS	3	2
DN	4	0

In general, the regret table has at least one 0 value (corresponding to the best outcome for the state) in every column.

In this context a conservative approach is to choose the action that minimizes the maximum possible regret, and we call this approach the **minimax regret** strategy. Thus, the summary value for a particular action is the maximum possible regret. Stated in symbols

$$V_i = \text{maximum possible regret for action } i = \max_j \{R_{ij}\}$$

$$V^* = \text{minimax regret} = \min_i \{V_i\}$$

Under the minimax regret strategy the optimal action i^* is the choice that minimizes the value of V_i. In our example, the minimax regret strategy dictates $i^* = 2$, with $V^* = 3$, as shown in Table 7.3.

The example thus illustrates that the two conservative strategies, maximin and minimax regret, may lead to different decisions. As stated earlier, the differ-

TABLE 7.3

Action	State F	State I	Summary Value
LS	0	5	$V_1 = 5$
SS	3	2	$V_2 = 3$
DN	4	0	$V_3 = 4$
			$V^* = 3\ (i^* = 2)$

ence is caused by considering absolute payoffs for maximin and relative payoffs for minimax regret.

INCLUDING PROBABILITY INFORMATION

The three approaches we have just examined represent optimistic and pessimistic criteria that supply useful benchmarks for selecting among possible actions. However, they do not use information about the relative likelihoods of the different states of nature. If we are prepared to assess the probability that each state will occur, then we can also incorporate those assessments into our decision-making strategy. To do so, we specify a probability of occurrence for each state:

$$P_j = P(\text{state } j \text{ will occur})$$

Sometimes we can use historical frequencies to construct a probability distribution for the states of nature. However, when historical data are unavailable, we rely on subjective probability assessments. Viewed as a subjective judgment, the value of P_j reflects the degree to which we believe that state j will actually occur. For action i it follows that P_j represents the probability that payoff Z_{ij} will occur.

In many cases a particular approach to decision making may affect many decisions, and its effectiveness is reflected in the outcomes produced by numerous decision opportunities. As a result, the strategy that leads to the largest total payoff in the long run will be the strategy that leads to the largest average payoff per opportunity. In this situation a decision maker can achieve the largest total payoff from many decisions by maximizing the expected payoff (or mean payoff) on each decision.

Equivalently, we can use the expected payoff as the summary value for each action and then select the action with the largest expected value. Stated in symbols

$$V_i = \sum_j P_j Z_{ij} = \text{expected payoff for action } i$$

$$V^* = \max_i \{V_i\} = \text{maximum expected payoff}$$

Under a strategy aimed at maximizing expected payoff, the optimal action i^* is the choice that maximizes the value of V_i. As it happens, we could just as well use a strategy aimed at minimizing expected regret. With this approach we would let

$$V_i = \sum_j P_j R_{ij} = \text{expected regret for action } i$$

$$V^* = \min_i \{V_i\} = \text{minimum expected regret}$$

Here, we define the optimal action i^* as the choice that minimizes expected regret, but this will always be the same action that maximizes expected payoff.

In the Foster Textile Company example suppose that the president (with advice from the sales manager) arrives at the following subjective probability distribution for the states of nature:

State j	1	2
Probability P_j	0.7	0.3

For this distribution the expected payoff takes the form

$$V_i = P_1 Z_{i1} + P_2 Z_{i2} \tag{7.1}$$

Thus, for example, we have

$$V_1 = 0.7(4) + 0.3(-5) = 1.3$$

Table 7.4 summarizes the remaining calculations, showing that $i^* = 1$, with $V^* = 1.3$.

Notice that the expected payoff does not necessarily correspond to an actual payoff under one of the states of nature. In particular, action 1 has an expected payoff of 1.3; yet when we choose action 1, there is no state of nature that can lead to an actual payoff of 1.3. Thus, the summary value does not have to represent an achievable outcome.

TABLE 7.4

Action	State (Probability) F(0.7)	I(0.3)	Summary Value
LS	4	−5	$V_1 = 1.3$
SS	1	−2	$V_2 = 0.1$
DN	0	0	$V_3 = 0.0$
			$V^* = 1.3 \ (i^* = 1)$

We reiterate that the criterion of maximum expected payoff is appropriate for situations in which one criterion guides many decisions. Over the long run the payoff will be maximized by maximizing the expected payoff, even though in a single instance such an action might not produce the best outcome. In our example, when we choose action 1 on the basis of maximum expected payoff, it is still possible that state 1 will occur and we will not achieve the best outcome for that state. If we face many decisions resembling the one in our example, however, the favorable state will occur often enough that our total payoff from all outcomes will be maximized by using the expected payoff criterion. The same concept applies for the approach of minimizing expected regret.

If we use expected regret as the criterion in our example, the summary value takes the form

$$V_i = P_1 R_{i1} + P_2 R_{i2} \tag{7.2}$$

Table 7.5 summarizes the analysis, showing that $i^* = 1$, with $V^* = 1.5$.

The example calculations illustrate a general point—that either criterion (maximum expected payoff or minimum expected regret) will identify the same optimal *action*. However, the optimal *values* corresponding to this action will usually differ, because in one approach we measure absolute payoffs, and in the other we measure relative payoffs.

We have said that in many cases an expected value approach is appropriate. However, there are some circumstances in which it may not be justified. For example, if the magnitude of the payoffs were so great that the survival of the firm were potentially at stake, a more plausible strategy would be one that confronts the possibility of extinction. In such a case, we might ignore probability assessments entirely, and we might adopt one of the conservative criteria introduced earlier. Alternatively, we might recognize the risk of extinction in our probabilistic analysis. Later in the chapter we shall return to considerations of risk in decision making.

The common thread in these approaches is converting information about the possible consequences of a particular action into a single summary value. So

TABLE 7.5

| | State (Probability) | | Summary |
Action 2	F(0.7)	I(0.3)	Value
LS	0	5	$V_1 = 1.5$
SS	3	2	$V_2 = 2.7$
DN	4	0	$V_3 = 2.8$
			$V^* = 1.5 \ (i^* = 1)$

long as each summary value reflects our relative preference for the action's consequences, we can use the summary values to identify the most desirable action. The challenge, however, is to find an effective way to translate information about a probability distribution of payoffs into a summary measure that reflects our decision-making preferences.

DECISION TREES

Having examined some basic approaches for decision making under uncertainty, we introduce a modeling device known as a decision tree. A decision tree is a graphical aid for displaying the problem elements, for organizing the analysis, and for describing the problem and its analysis to another person. The basic structure, depicted in Figure 7.1 for the Foster Textile Company, consists of branches emerging, left to right, from blocks (squares) or from nodes (circles). A block represents a decision point, and the branches emerging from it correspond to alternative courses of action. A node represents the occurrence of a state of nature. Drawing the tree left to right, with decision blocks preceding nodes, helps to emphasize the fact that we must make the decision before we know the state of nature.

In order to label a decision tree we begin by identifying the payoff for each action-state pair and writing the payoff at the end of the corresponding state

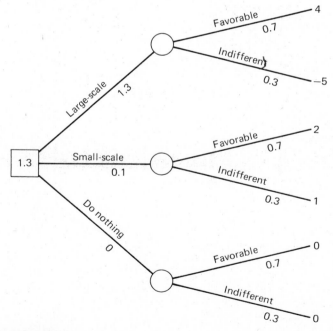

FIGURE 7.1

branch. Then we place state probabilities on the branches emerging from nodes. We proceed by calculating the expected payoff for each action using equation (7.1) and writing the expected payoff on the corresponding action branch. Finally, we label the decision block with the maximum expected payoff and mark the action branch on which it occurs. Labeling the tree from right to left, with calculations for states preceding the selection of an action, helps to emphasize the fact that all possible outcomes must be anticipated in order to determine the best course of action.

Figure 7.2 shows the general form of the decision tree, with m possible actions and n states of nature. State j has probability P_j, and action-state pair (i,j) has payoff Z_{ij}. We combine these two sets of values to form the expected payoff

$$V_i = \sum_j P_j Z_{ij} \tag{7.3}$$

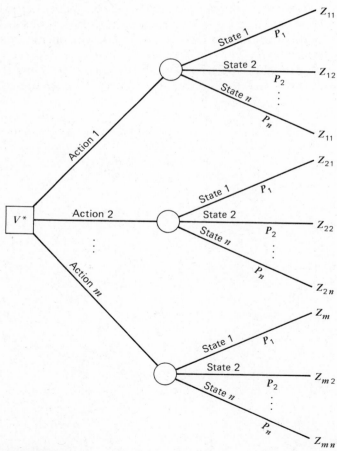

FIGURE 7.2

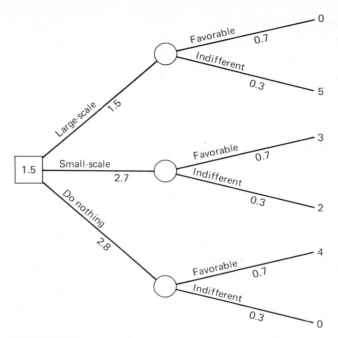

FIGURE 7.3

The values of V_i are recorded along the corresponding branches, and the best value (V^*) is recorded in the decision block.

Alternatively, we could use the decision tree to minimize expected regret. For this purpose we would replace the payoff labels Z_{ij} with regret labels R_{ij}. Then we would combine regret values and probabilities to form the expected regret for each action:

$$V_i = \sum_j P_j R_{ij} \tag{7.4}$$

We would then identify the minimum expected regret and enter it in the decision block.

For the Foster Textile example a decision tree for the analysis of expected regret is shown in Figure 7.3. This decision tree has the same structure as the one in Figure 7.1, but we label it differently. The calculations shown in Figure 7.3 correspond to those given in Table 7.5.

SENSITIVITY ANALYSIS

In decision problems involving uncertainty we are seldom able to specify with precision all payoff outcomes and state probabilities. This lack of precision makes it important to examine how a change in one of the parameters could

TABLE 7.6

Action	State F	I	Summary Value
LS	4	Z_{12}	$V_1 = \min(4, Z_{12})$
SS	1	-2	$V_2 = -2$
DN	0	0	$V_3 = 0$

affect the optimal solution. This type of study, in which we investigate **parametric validity,** is relatively straightforward in the case of payoff values but more complicated in the case of probabilities.

In the Foster Textile Company example, suppose that we treat Z_{12} as a parameter. Then our payoff table takes the form shown in Table 7.6.

Suppose that we are pursuing a maximin strategy. Then, as shown in Table 7.6

$$V_1 = \min(4, Z_{12}) \qquad V_2 = -2 \qquad V_3 = 0$$

Clearly, the maximin strategy dictates action 3 when $V_3 \geq V_1$ and action 1 otherwise. Also, it is easy to see that the point of indifference, when $V_3 = V_1$, occurs for $Z_{12} = 0$. Given this result, we have

for $Z_{12} \leq 0$ select action 3; $V^* = 0$

for $Z_{12} > 0$ select action 1: $V^* = \min(4, Z_{12})$

This result shows how changes in Z_{12} could affect both the optimal action and the optimal value of the criterion. Suppose instead that we are pursuing a strategy of maximizing the expected payoff. For this criterion the summary values are given in Table 7.7.

Here the expected payoff criterion dictates action 1 when $V_1 \geq V_2$ and action 2 otherwise. Here, to find the point of indifference, when $V_2 = V_1$, we must solve

TABLE 7.7

Action	State (Probability) F(0.7)	I(0.3)	Summary Value
LS	4	Z_{12}	$V_1 = 2.8 + 0.3Z_{12}$
SS	1	-2	$V_2 = 0.1$
DN	0	0	$V_3 = 0$

the equation

$$0.1 = 2.8 + 0.3Z_{12}$$

The solution is

$$Z_{12} = -9$$

As a result, we have

for $Z_{12} \leq -9$ select action 2; $V^* = 0.1$
for $Z_{12} > -9$ select action 1; $V^* = 2.8 + 0.3Z_{12}$

Thus, if we are fairly confident about all the parameters except Z_{12}, the decision to select action 1 reflects our confidence that $Z_{12} > -9$. In addition, notice that the change of criterion from maximin payoff to expected payoff has changed not only the range of Z_{12} over which action 1 is optimal, but also the pair of actions that are candidates for optimality when we vary Z_{12}.

We can alter a probability parameter in an analogous fashion. In the case of discrete states of nature, however, we cannot hold constant all but one of the state probabilities, because all of the state probabilities must add to 1. Nevertheless, we can still perform some single-parameter sensitivity analysis. In the Foster Textile Company example, suppose that we let P denote the probability that state 1 occurs. Because there are only two states of nature, this means the probability that state 2 occurs must be $1 - P$. The expected payoffs of the three actions are shown in Table 7.8. Utilizing these three expressions, we conclude that action 1 is optimal for

$$
\begin{array}{ccc}
V_1 \geq V_2 & \text{and} & V_1 \geq V_3 \\
9P - 5 \geq 3P - 2 & & 9P - 5 \geq 0 \\
6P \geq 3 & & 9P \geq 5 \\
P \geq 0.5 & \text{and} & P \geq 0.56
\end{array}
$$

TABLE 7.8

Action	State (Probability)		Summary Value
	F(P)	I(1 − P)	
LS	4	−5	$V_1 = 9P - 5$
SS	1	−2	$V_2 = 3P - 2$
DN	0	0	$V_3 = 0$

Combining the information, we conclude that action 1 is optimal when $P \geq 0.56$. Similar calculations show that action 3 is optimal when $P \leq 0.56$. Interestingly enough, this parametric study also reveals that action 2 is not optimal for any value of P.

It is helpful to look at a graphical interpretation of this result. Because the focus is on the relationship between the expected payoffs V_i and the probability parameter P, we construct a graph of these relationships, as shown in Figure 7.4. In this example the graph consists of three straight lines ($V_3 = 0$ is the horizontal axis). For any particular value of P, the line that is highest on the graph offers the best expected payoff. We can see from the graph that V_1 is best when $P \geq 0.56$, and V_3 is best when $P \leq 0.56$. Because the V_2 line lies below at least one of the others for every value of P, action 2 does not provide the highest expected payoff for any value of P.

Returning to our example, we had previously thought that P was 0.7. Given our analysis, we could have a reasonable amount of confidence about our choice of action 1, because we now know that action 1 would be optimal even if P were as small as 0.56. In other words, P could fall by about 20% of its original value without changing the decision.

In the situations described above, we can think of both the optimal decision and the associated payoff as a function of a single parameter. In such cases we can specify a **range of validity** for the parameter, in which the optimal decision remains unchanged. This range is important because it tells us whether the optimal decision is sensitive to the parameter being studied. When the range is

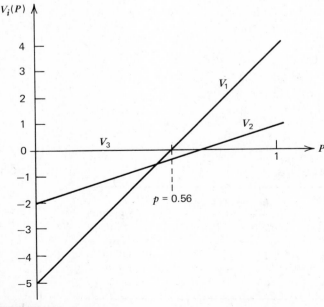

FIGURE 7.4

small, or when the parameter is close to one endpoint of its range, we should be alert to the fact that the optimal decision could change with a slight change in the parameter. On the other hand, when the range is large, we can have confidence in the optimality of the decision, even if we lack confidence in the precise estimate of the parameter.

PERFECT INFORMATION

In our example, suppose that before choosing an action the president of Foster Textile Company discovers that it is possible to hire a local consulting agency to determine in advance whether consumer reaction will be favorable or indifferent. The value of such a service is considerable, because if the president knows in advance exactly how the market will respond tó the new material, then it will be easy to select the proper action. In particular, it will be possible to consult the payoff table and to select the action that maximizes payoff. In the example the president will select either action 1 (for a profit of $4 million) or action 3 (for a payoff of 0) depending on the consulting agency's information. The only problem then will be to negotiate a price for the agency's service.

A reliable prediction, which provides advance knowledge about the state of nature, removes uncertainty from the problem. With such foreknowledge, our decision rule is obvious: Given the state of nature that will occur, we select the action that maximizes payoff in that state. Because this decision is based on reliable rather than uncertain information, and because we can achieve the maximum possible payoff under the circumstances, the advance knowledge about the state of nature is called **perfect information.** In order to evaluate the worth of such information we must determine how it will alter the decision. Specifically, we must compare the decisions made with and without perfect information.

Suppose that the consulting agency learns that the consumer reaction will be favorable. For this state of nature ($j = 1$) the best action is the large-scale alternative ($i = 1$). However, this is also the optimal action for the original problem, in which we believed there was a 0.7 probability of favorable reaction. The agency's information induces no change in the decision; therefore, in monetary terms this information has no value. On the other hand, suppose the consulting agency learns that consumer reaction will be indifferent. For this state of nature ($j = 2$) the best action is to do nothing ($i = 3$). Therefore, this particular information induces a change from the previous optimal decision, and a corresponding improvement in payoff from −$5 million to $0. In monetary terms the value of this information is therefore $5 million. To summarize, let VPI_j denote the value of perfect information for state j. Then $VPI_1 = 0$ and $VPI_2 = 5$.

Recall that the company had already assessed the probability of favorable or indifferent responses. These are probability assessments of the occurrence of different states of nature, but we can also interpret them as probabilities of the different values for perfect information. Thus, we can think of the value of perfect information (*VPI*) as a random variable with different outcomes associated with the different states of nature. In our example, the distribution of *VPI* is a simple one:

	State j	
	1	2
P_j	0.7	0.3
VPI_j	0	5

and the mean of this distribution is $1.5 million.

The availability of perfect information about which state of nature will occur induces a change from action i^*, the decision that maximizes expected payoff, to the action with the best payoff in the given state. Stated in symbols:

$$VPI_j = \max_i (Z_{ij}) - Z_{i^*j}$$

Moreover, the expected value of perfect information (*EVPI*) is the mean of the *VPI* distribution, or

$$EVPI = \sum_j P_j VPI_j = \sum_j P_j[\max_i (Z_{ij}) - Z_{i^*j}] \tag{7.5}$$

The expected value of perfect information is exactly equal to the minimum expected regret, since equation (7.5) is equivalent to equation (7.4). We can think of *EVPI* as a measure of the value of being able to select a decision *after* learning the state of nature rather than before. The important concept here is that we can place a monetary value on information by tracing its effects on decisions and determining the monetary consequences of reacting to the information. In the case of decision making under uncertainty, this process recognizes the probabilities involved and values the information in expected-value terms.

In our example the calculation of *EVPI* provides us with a value for the consulting agency's services. In this case that value is $1.5 million. If the agency can indeed produce perfect information, then Foster Textile should be willing to pay up to this amount for the service. To the extent that Foster Textile can negotiate a price less than $1.5 million for the service, then the company will have come out ahead. However, if the agency's information is less than perfect, we can expect that the price for its service will be less than $1.5 million. We consider the case of imperfect information in the next section.

ADDITIONAL INFORMATION

Thus far we have studied decision making in an uncertain environment, where we model uncertainty by using a probability distribution for the possible states of nature. These probability assessments are usually called **prior probabilities,** and they represent our best judgment about the relative likelihoods of potential outcomes. In other words, they represent our *incomplete* knowledge about the environment in which we must select an action. We have also studied the concept of perfect information, as a characterization of the other end of the spectrum, where we work with *complete* knowledge about the environment and where no elements of uncertainty remain in the analysis.

At intermediate points in this spectrum, we can sometimes obtain additional information to improve our analysis. This information supplements our prior probabilities and may induce us to revise our original probability assessments. Such information will nevertheless be imperfect, leaving us with some degree of uncertainty about the environment. In this section we examine a framework for incorporating additional information into decision analysis and for measuring the value of such information.

In formal terms, the revision of prior probabilities in light of additional information is accomplished by means of **Bayes' rule** for conditional probability. Let I_t represent a specific type of additional information that is available. The revised probability assessment we seek is the probability that state j will occur given that we know I_t. In symbols, we write this as $P(j|I_t)$. From elementary probability theory, the definition of this conditional probability is

$$P(j|I_t) = \frac{P(j \text{ and } I_t)}{P(I_t)}$$

Bayes' rule rewrites the numerator as

$$P(j \text{ and } I_t) = P(I_t|j)P_j$$

and the denominator as

$$P(I_t) = P(\text{state } 1 \text{ and } I_t) + P(\text{state } 2 \text{ and } I_t) + \cdots + P(\text{state } n \text{ and } I_t)$$

$$= \sum_{k=1}^{n} P(\text{state } k \text{ and } I_t) = \sum_{k=1}^{n} P(I_t|k)P_k$$

Thus, we have

$$P(j|I_t) = \frac{P(I_t|j)P_j}{\sum_{k=1}^{n} P(I_t|k)P_k} \tag{7.6}$$

In this formula, P_j symbolizes the *prior* probability for each possible state of nature, and $P(I_t|j)$ symbolizes a computable probability, called the **likelihood,** of obtaining the additional information I_t given that state j is true. Combining these probabilities as prescribed by equation (7.6) yields the revised or **posterior probabilities** represented by the conditional probabilities $P(j|I_t)$. Having sought additional information, and having revised the initial probability assessments in accordance with equation (7.6), we can then follow the basic steps of decision analysis to find an optimal action, using posterior probabilities.

As an example, suppose that the president of Foster Textile Company is still pondering the fate of the firm's new synthetic material knowing that the consulting agency has surveyed consumer attitudes to help get a better idea about the overall market response. Suppose that the agency had done similar surveys in the past for a number of new products, and although its predictions were not always perfect, its track record was reasonably good. The table below summarizes the agency's performance on previous surveys:

| | | Actual Response | |
		Favorable	Indifferent
Agency	Positive	12	2
Report	Negative	8	8

The interpretation is that for the 14 times the agency had given a positive report, the actual response turned out favorable 12 times and indifferent 2 times. Similarly, for the 16 situations having a negative report, the actual response turned out favorable in 8 and indifferent in 8. Also suppose that Foster had hired the agency weeks ago (for $40,000) to do a survey on the new material; their response has just arrived, and it contains a negative report.

In this example we can calculate the posterior probabilities from the information available. Recall that the elements of the example problem are the following:

Actions	States	Information
($i = 1$) Large-scale (LS)	($j = 1$) Favorable (F)	(I_1) Positive report (P)
($i = 2$) Small-scale (SS)	($j = 2$) Indifferent (I)	(I_2) Negative report (N)
($i = 3$) Do nothing (DN)		

As we know, the president's prior probabilities are

$$P_1 = 0.7 \qquad P_2 = 0.3$$

Based on the table describing the consulting agency's past performance, the likelihoods are

$$P(I_1|1) = \frac{12}{20} = 0.6 \qquad P(I_1|2) = \frac{2}{10} = 0.2$$

$$P(I_2|1) = \frac{8}{20} = 0.4 \qquad P(I_2|2) = \frac{8}{10} = 0.8$$

The likelihoods show, for example, that favorable responses had positive agency reports 60% of the time and negative reports the other 40% of the time. Given the negative report I_2 produced this time by the agency, the appropriate posterior probabilities are

$$P(1|I_2) = \frac{P(I_2|1)P_1}{P(I_2|1)P_1 + P(I_2|2)P_2} = \frac{(0.4)(0.7)}{(0.4)(0.7) + (0.8)(0.3)} = 0.5385$$

and

$$P(2|I_2) = 1 - P(1|I_2) = 0.4615$$

In essence, the report from the consulting agency induces the president to lower the assessment of the probability of a favorable response from 0.7 to 0.5385. This change occurs due to the agency's partial ability to detect indifferent markets. Using the posterior probabilities in place of the prior probabilities for states 1 and 2, the calculations yield new values for V_i, the expected payoff for action i. In particular

$$V_1 = 0.5385(4) + 0.4615(-5) = -0.154$$
$$V_2 = 0.5385(1) + 0.4615(-2) = -0.384$$
$$V_3 = 0.5385(0) + 0.4615(0) = 0$$

In this case the action that maximizes expected payoff is action 3. Hence, the impact of the consultant's report is to change the decision from action 1 (large-scale) to action 3 (do nothing), given the payoffs and probabilities involved.

Had the agency's report been positive (I_1), the situation would have been different. In this case the posterior probabilities would have become

$$P(1|I_1) = \frac{P(I_1|1)P_1}{P(I_1|1)P_1 + P(I_1|2)P_2} = \frac{(0.6)(0.7)}{(0.6)(0.7) + (0.2)(0.3)} = 0.875$$

and

$$(P(2|I_1) = 1 - P(1|I_1) = 0.125$$

With these revised probabilities, the expected payoff calculations yield the following expected payoffs:

$$V_1 = 0.875(4) + 0.125(-5) = 2.875$$
$$V_2 = 0.875(1) + 0.125(-2) = 0.625$$
$$V_3 = 0.875(0) + 0.125(0) = 0$$

In this case the action that maximizes expected payoff turns out to be action 1, just as it was when prior probabilities were used in the original analysis. Therefore, the agency's positive report would reinforce the original decision.

THE VALUE OF ADDITIONAL INFORMATION

We have already seen that additional information alters the original decision problem. When we compare the analyses before and after the use of additional information, we find that there may be changes in (a) the state probabilities, (b) the expected payoffs, and (c) the optimal decision. The change in the state probabilities occurs because we combine additional information with prior probabilities (using equation (7.6) for Bayes' rule) in order to produce posterior probabilities. Then, the expected payoffs depend on the probability assessments, and so it is necessary to recalculate them. In turn, these changes may ultimately lead to a different choice for the action that maximizes expected payoff. Thus, additional information may alter the optimal decision, although in some instances the optimal decision remains unchanged.

In this context the value of specific additional information I_t is the value of altering the optimal decision. A convenient way to measure this value is to calculate the difference between the expected payoff for the revised decision and the expected payoff for the original decision. To describe this calculation more formally, let $i*$ denote the action that maximizes expected payoff in the original problem and let r denote the action that maximizes expected payoff in the revised problem. Accordingly, let

$$V_{i*t} = \text{expected payoff for original decision} = \sum_{j} P(j|I_t)Z_{i*j}$$

$$V_{rt} = \text{expected payoff for revised decision} = \sum_{j} P(j|I_t)Z_{rj}$$

Note that we use the posterior probabilities in both calculations. Therefore, $V_{rt} \geq V_{i*t}$, and we define the value of additional information (VAI_t) as the difference between these two expected payoffs

$$VAI_t = V_{rt} - V_{i*t}$$

For example, in the Foster Textile example the original optimal action is action 1 ($i* = 1$). However, the revised optimal action given I_2, the consultant's negative report, is action 3 ($r = 3$). Thus, we have

$$V_{i*t} = V_{12} = -0.154$$
$$V_{rt} = V_{32} = 0$$
$$VAI_2 = V_{32} - V_{12} = 0.154$$

As a result, the value of the consultant's information is $154,000.

Notice that the calculation of the value of additional information is actually an ex post evaluation. Specifically, VAI_t is a function of the information acquired, and we can compute it only *after* observing the information outcome. Moreover, different information outcomes lead to different calculations of VAI_t. In the Foster Textile Company example, suppose instead that the consultant's report is positive, so we have information I_1. Then, as we noted earlier, the optimal action in the revised problem is still action 1. Therefore, since $r = i*$, we have

$$VAI_1 = V_{r1} - V_{i*1} = 0$$

Thus, a positive consultant's report is a form of additional information with 0 value in an ex post evaluation.

Our intuition probably tells us that a positive consultant's report should have *some* positive value, even if it is only the value of reaffirming the original analysis. The suggestion that VAI could be 0 in this case is counterintuitive mainly because our intuition confuses ex post evaluations with ex ante evaluations, and we must be careful to keep the distinction in mind. Although it is true that a positive consultant's report is valueless, given the way we measure the value of additional information, we must remember that the decision to utilize the consultant's service had to be made ex ante, before the contents of the report were known. The problem of evaluating information outcomes ex ante is precisely what decision analysis addresses.

In fact, we can even construct a decision-tree model for the analysis of the uncertain information outcomes by thinking of I_1 and I_2 as alternative information states and by thinking of VAI_t in each case as the corresponding information payoff. Moreover, the probability that an information state will occur, $P(I_1)$ or $P(I_2)$, has already been identified as the denominator of equation (7.6). Specifically

$$P(I_2) = P(I_2|1)P_1 + P(I_2|2)P_2 = (0.4)(0.7) + (0.8)(0.3) = 0.52$$
$$P(I_1) = P(I_1|1)P_1 + P(I_1|2)P_2 = (0.6)(0.7) + (0.2)(0.3) = 0.48$$

The decision-tree model for the evaluation of information outcomes is shown in Figure 7.5, where we see that the expected value of the information payoffs is $80,000.

This value is called the **expected value of additional information** (*EVAI*). In symbols, the definition is

$$EVAI = \sum_t VAI_t P(I_t)$$

Obviously, a decision maker operating with an expected profit criterion would decline to seek additional information where $EVAI$ is 0. Nevertheless, even in the case where $EVAI$ is positive, the cost of securing the information is also relevant; and the same decision maker should also decline to seek additional information when its expected value fails to offset its cost. In the Foster Textile Company example the $EVAI$ of $40,000 exceeds the consultant's fee of $40,000, and the

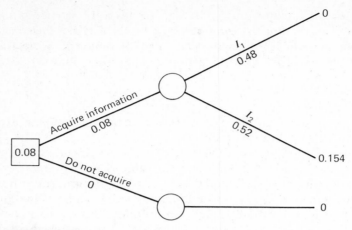

FIGURE 7.5

firm would appear to have come out ahead (in terms of an ex ante evaluation) by approximately $40,000.

DECISION TREES

The option to seek additional information complicates the structure of the original decision problem, but we can still accommodate it in our decision-tree model. Figure 7.6 shows a complete decision tree for the Foster Textile Company example. Conceptually, the alternatives facing the company begin with the decision box on the far left—the decision whether to obtain additional information. For the decision not to seek it (the lower branch), the subtree that results is identical to the decision tree for the original problem. Recall that the analysis of expected payoffs in the original problem identified action 1 as the optimal decision, with an expected payoff equal to $1.3 million. The decision to hire the consultant (the upper branch) leads to a node at which there are two possible outcomes corresponding to the possible reports turned in by the consultant. For each of these outcomes, the subtree reproduces the structure of the original problem, since each of the three original actions is still possible at this stage.

Although we conceptualize the structure of the problem by building the decision tree from left to right, we perform the analysis most conveniently from right to left, in a process called **folding back** the decision tree. For each three-action subtree, we enter the payoff values corresponding to each action-state pair at the extreme right. In the upper two subtrees we label the final branches with posterior probabilities, and we enter prior probabilities in the subtree corresponding to the original problem without additional information. We then analyze each subtree independently to find **conditional** optimal expected payoffs. This analysis produces a set of optimal actions (called conditional actions)

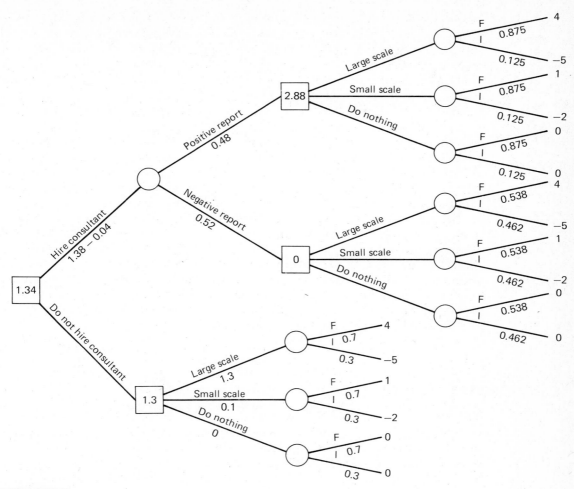

FIGURE 7.6

that depend on the additional information obtained:

Form of Additional Information	Conditional Action	Conditional Expected Payoff
I_1 (positive report)	A_1 (large-scale)	2.88
I_2 (negative report)	A_3 (do nothing)	0.0
None sought	A_1 (large-scale)	1.3

Once the analysis shows how to proceed optimally following any additional information outcome, we can view the conditional expected payoff figures as the payoff measures associated with the information outcomes. We then label the branch corresponding to each information outcome with the appropriate probability, and we calculate the expected payoff for additional information. At the left-hand decision box we adjust this value for the cost of acquiring additional information and compare it to the expected payoff without additional information, to determine whether seeking additional information is desirable. Notice that the $40,000 cost of obtaining additional information has been incorporated in the final calculation, leading to an optimal expected payoff of $1.34 million.

The important feature of the process of folding back the decision tree is that we first analyze later decisions, thus identifying conditional actions and payoffs. Once we know how to select an action given each information outcome, we can determine the expected payoff for each information outcome and thereby determine the *EVAI*. We call this evaluation procedure **preposterior analysis,** and its aim is to assess the desirability of seeking additional information.

In Figures 7.5 and 7.6 we have seen two different views of essentially the same analysis. In conjunction with Figure 7.5 we evaluated the *EVAI* as $80,000. Considering the $40,000 cost of the information, we concluded that the firm was better off by $40,000 for obtaining the information. In Figure 7.6, when we examined actual payoffs rather than only information payoffs, we found that the optimal expected payoff was $1.34 million with the consultant's report and only $1.30 million without it. The difference is the same $40,000 that measures the net expected payoff to the firm for obtaining additional information.

SEQUENTIAL DECISIONS

The inclusion of additional information in decision analysis gives rise to a new consideration in decision trees: the occurrence of decisions in sequence. In the model for decision analysis with additional information we can distinguish two stages of decision making. First comes the question of whether to seek additional information, and then (assuming that such information is desirable) comes the question of what course of action to follow for each possible information outcome. In between these two decisions is the uncontrollable event that produces information. As we saw in connection with the analysis of Figures 7.5 and 7.6, each possible information state gives rise to its own subproblem, which itself can be represented by a decision tree. More generally, we can conceive of a sequence of decisions to be made in this fashion, where each decision gives rise to possible information states. We analyze such a sequence by **multistage** decision techniques, a generalization of the methods we have been studying.

To illustrate the analysis of sequential decisions, consider the following situation faced by a real estate agent who specializes in commercial property. The agent's client was interested in selling three separate properties at the following prices:

Property	Price
Land	$ 50,000
Garage	$100,000
Store	$200,000

The agent was to receive a 4% commission on the sales, but the client also laid down some conditions. The agent would first get an opportunity to sell the land. If she could not find a buyer within 1 month the whole deal would be terminated. If the land were sold within the month, the agent would get a commission and could elect either to stop there or to handle one of the other properties on the same basis. That is, the agent would get 1 month to sell either one of the two remaining properties; if she could sell the property, then she would have the option to handle the third property, otherwise the deal would end.

After giving the matter some thought, the agent estimated the probabilities of selling each of the properties within 1 month, along with anticipated commissions and out-of-pocket costs for handling each one:

Property	Probability	Cost	Commission
Land	0.7	$1600	$2000
Garage	0.6	400	4000
Store	0.5	800	8000

As a first step in the analysis, the agent drew a decision tree (Figure 7.7) to determine whether to proceed with the deal, at least as far as attempting to sell the land. Note that she receives a benefit of $400 ($2000 commission less $1600 cost) if she can sell the land, whereas she incurs a cost of $1600 if she cannot sell the land. From these numbers, there is no cost or benefit if she foregoes the deal, but there is an expected loss of $200 if she attempts to sell the land. Viewed this

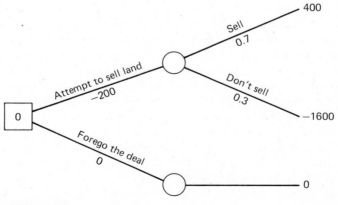

FIGURE 7.7

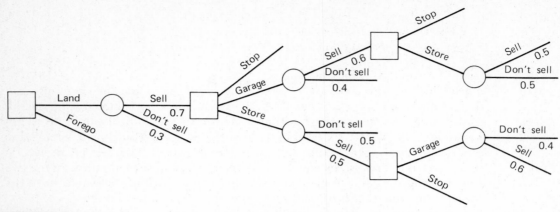

FIGURE 7.8

way, the decision tree seems to indicate that she should pass up the deal. However, the analysis is incomplete because it neglects the opportunity to proceed further. We can assess this value by additional decision-tree analysis.

Suppose that the agent could sell the land. She then would face the choice among three possible actions:

1. Attempt to sell the garage.
2. Attempt to sell the store.
3. Terminate the deal.

The third action has 0 payoff, but the others have different payoffs with probabilities that have already been estimated. Again, a decision-tree analysis is possible, but it is important to reflect in the analysis the value of the opportunity to proceed, in the case that a sale is made.

We display the entire decision tree in Figure 7.8. The figure depicts three stages, corresponding to the three potential decisions. As in the simpler decision trees studied earlier, we evaluate the various decisions using the process of folding back the tree starting from the end of the sequence. As we evaluate each subtree, we compute the expected payoff under the optimal action for each decision node. This quantity measures the value of the opportunity to proceed beyond the corresponding decision. Thus, when we evaluate the second stage actions, we augment the payoff by the value of a subsequent opportunity, wherever it exists.

Figure 7.9 shows the entire stage-by-stage process of folding back the tree. In Figure 7.9a we see that in either case (the "store" decision or the "garage" decision) it is desirable to attempt to sell the property. Then, in Figure 7.9b the quantities in parentheses (+3200 for "garage-sell" and +2000 for "store-sell") represent the values of these subsequent opportunities. The analysis of Figure 7.9b indicates that the "store-garage" sequence (expected value of $4200) is

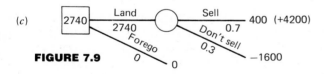

(a)

(b)

(c)

FIGURE 7.9

preferable to the "garage-store" sequence (expected value of $3920). Then in Figure 7.9c the quantity in parentheses (+4200) shows the value of the remaining opportunities. Finally, we see that it is preferable to attempt to sell the land (and then to undertake the "store-garage" sequence if the land is sold) because the expected value is $2740. Note here that the correct analysis of Figure 7.9 shows that the agent should proceed with the deal, whereas the incomplete analysis of Figure 7.7 shows incorrectly that she should not proceed.

In essence, we measure the value of an opportunity to proceed to a future stage as an expected value—in particular, the expected payoff for proceeding optimally from that point. This value summarizes the prospective payoffs in much the same way that the model for the decision analysis with additional information uses conditional payoffs to summarize the prospective payoffs after we observe an information state.

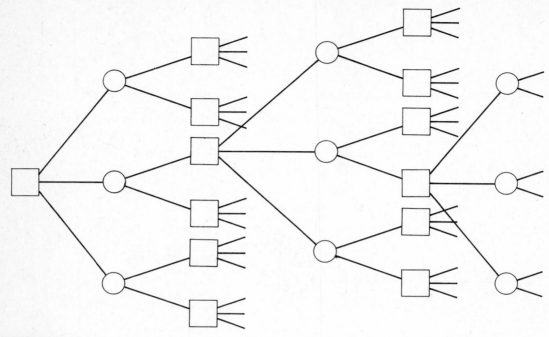

FIGURE 7.10

Finally, we indicate in Figure 7.10 the general structure of multistage analysis with probabilistic states of nature. Notice that at each stage every decision block has an associated subtree and that once we determine the value of this subtree (i.e., as an expected payoff) this quantity represents the value of an opportunity to proceed for some previous subtree. Figure 7.10 also makes it abundantly clear that there can be considerable computational effort involved in folding back a multistage decision tree. Methods for making these calculations in an efficient manner are the subject of **dynamic programming,** a modeling and optimization technique that is beyond the scope of our present treatment.

ATTITUDES TOWARD RISK

The use of an expected value to summarize the payoffs and probabilities associated with a particular action may not always capture decision-making preferences. As we mentioned earlier, the expected value criterion is most appropriate for frequent decisions involving only a small portion of the resources available to the firm. In other settings, if there is a one-time choice or the chance of a major loss, the expected value approach may be inadequate.

As an example, imagine that you were offered the following proposition. A

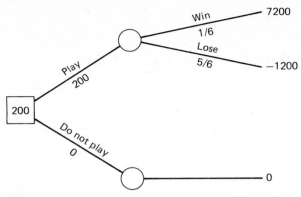

FIGURE 7.11

single die will be tossed, and if it lands on 6 you win $7200; otherwise you lose $1200. Would you be willing to play this game once?

Figure 7.11 shows the simple decision tree for the game. As the figure indicates, the maximum expected payoff occurs for the "Play" action. Nevertheless, we could easily find people who would choose not to play, even though the game has an expected payoff of $200.

This example illustrates that decision-making preferences may not always be consistent with the logic of selecting the maximum expected payoff. However, by re-examining the example, we can begin to understand the factors that might account for inconsistency. For one thing, the "Do not play" action results in a payoff of 0 with certainty, and the "Play" action can result in either a profit or a loss. Clearly, the consequences of the "Play" action are more variable. This lack of certainty might help to explain why some people would choose not to play the game.

In practice, management's planning is complicated by the lack of certainty about the consequences of a particular action. Facing variable outcomes, we develop contingency plans, and we might have to delay various other decisions until outcomes are known. With certainty, however, the future is more clear. Certainty eliminates the need for delay or for hedging tactics. Thus, decision makers may prefer a more certain set of outcomes to a more variable set of outcomes, even when the expected payoff is lower for the more certain outcomes.

Another factor in our hypothetical game is the possibility, for the "Play" action, that there will be a loss of $1200. The decision maker who chooses to play could wind up poorer by $1200 as a result, whereas the choice not to play protects the decision maker from exposure to any losses.

In practice, decision makers are usually concerned about exposure to an economic setback. Beyond the fact that economic outcomes typically influence managers' personal rewards, we can imagine that economic losses restrict future decisions by reducing the resources available to them. More seriously, losses may threaten the continued existence of the manager's job, or the viability of the organization itself. Thus, decision makers may prefer an action with little exposure to one with the possibility of great losses, even when the expected payoff is lower for the action with limited exposure.

To summarize, two qualitative factors at work in decision problems are variability and exposure. These factors may account for decision preferences that are not consistent with expected payoff measurements. In other words, an expected value measure provides no insight into variability or exposure as factors in the decision. By condensing a set of payoffs and their probabilities into a single summary value, the expected payoff criterion masks some of the important features of the problem. To reach beyond this simplification we need an approach that recognizes the role of variability and exposure—in short, an approach that recognizes attitudes toward risk.

To help us elaborate on the concept of risk, we expand the Foster Textile example. Our original model, with only two states of nature, is fairly coarse, although it may be a useful first step in the analysis. Suppose that, upon further study, the firm's planning staff concludes that there are four discernible market responses: enthusiastic (E), favorable (F), mild (M), and indifferent (I), with respective probabilities of 0.2, 0.4, 0.3, and 0.1. In addition, suppose that this closer look results in the detailed payoffs shown in Table 7.9. As the table shows, the large-scale option provides the largest expected payoff, $1.2 million. The payoff table also provides us with an opportunity to consider various ways to measure risk.

MEASURING VARIABILITY

One logical approach derives from the fact that the standard deviation of a probability distribution summarizes the degree of variability in the possible outcomes. Thus, one theory is that the decision maker weighs both the mean and the standard deviation of the payoff distribution. Pursuing this idea, we may hypothesize that the summary measure for action i can take the form

$$V_i = \mu_i - w\sigma_i \tag{7.7}$$

TABLE 7.9

Action	State (Probability)				Expected Payoff
	E(0.2)	F(0.4)	M(0.3)	I(0.1)	
Large-scale (LS)	6	2	−1	−5	$V_1 = 1.2$
Small-scale (SS)	2	1	0	−2	$V_2 = 0.6$
Do nothing (DN)	0	0	0	0	$V_3 = 0.0$

where μ_i represents the mean payoff for action i, and σ_i represents the standard deviation of the payoff for action i. Also, w represents a positive weighting factor that reflects the relative influence of variability on the decision maker's preferences.

In the example of Table 7.9, suppose we take $w = 0.3$, and use equation (7.7) to calculate the summary measure. Our results are

Action (i)	μ_i	σ_i	V_i
LS(1)	1.2	3.19	0.243
SS(2)	0.6	1.11	0.267
DN(3)	0	0	0

In this case, the optimal action is the small-scale option, although some additional calculations will suggest that this result is somewhat sensitive to the choice of the weighting factor w. In any event, the use of a summary measure such as equation (7.7) could suggest why a decision maker may prefer the small-scale action, even though the large-scale action yields the largest expected payoff.

Although the trade-off of mean and standard deviation may be intuitively plausible, there are practical and conceptual problems with its use. One practical problem is how to determine the weighting factor. We would expect this weighting factor to vary across decision makers. It could even vary for a particular individual in different settings. A conceptual problem relates to the fact that the standard deviation fails to discriminate between "downside" variation and "upside" variation. Considerable upside variation may lead to a high standard deviation, but this may not be a reason to reduce the summary measure, as prescribed by equation (7.7). In other words, the standard deviation is a measure that is blind to the direction of variability. For this reason we may prefer an approach that deals more directly with downside risk.

MEASURING EXPOSURE

In response to the shortcoming described previously, we could take an approach that focuses on the possibility of negative outcomes. For example, as we saw earlier, nonprobabilistic criteria such as the maximin strategy or the minimax regret strategy represent conservative approaches that protect against worst-case outcomes. To incorporate probabilities, a related approach might be to define a particular undesirable payoff outcome Z_0 as the **exposure level.** We could then minimize the probability of obtaining a payoff that is less than or equal to Z_0. Stated in symbols, the summary measure is $V_i = P(Z_{ij} \leq Z_0)$.

As an illustration, suppose we designate as an exposure level the loss of \$2 million for the Foster Textile example. In terms of the payoffs in Table 7.9, this means $Z_0 = -2$. For the three actions described in the table, we obtain the following:

Action (i)	$P(Z_{ij} \leq -2)$
LS(1)	0.1
SS(2)	0.1
DN(3)	0.0

Thus, the do-nothing option is best. Note, however, that if we wish to minimize the probability of not making any profit (equivalently, setting $Z_0 = 0$), then we obtain

Action (i)	$P(Z_{ij} \leq 0)$
LS(1)	0.4
SS(2)	0.4
DN(3)	1.0

In this case we reach the opposite conclusion: The do-nothing option is worst.

The exposure level approach is an analog of the maximin criterion that reflects probabilities as well as the direction of the outcome. Nevertheless, by focusing on the outcomes in the downside direction (and not incorporating the expected payoff) the exposure-level approach may be criticized for ignoring information in the payoff distribution. Ideally, we would like to have an approach that explicitly recognizes expected payoff, variability, and exposure. In the next section we discuss an approach that at least recognizes those factors *implicitly.*

ELEMENTS OF UTILITY THEORY

A full discussion of utility theory and its principles lies beyond the scope of this chapter, but we can appreciate its perspective by means of a brief introduction. We begin with two basic concepts. The first concept is that of a **lottery,** which is essentially a simple probability distribution. Specifically, a lottery is a chance event with two possible payoffs, Z_1 and Z_2. The outcome Z_1 occurs with probability p, and Z_2 occurs with probability $1 - p$. The expected value of this lottery is

$$EV = pZ_1 + (1 - p)Z_2$$

It is possible for lotteries to represent chance events with more than two possible outcomes, but for now it is sufficient to work with the concept of a two-payoff lottery. We denote this lottery $L(p, Z_1, Z_2)$.

The second basic concept involves a **certainty equivalent.** The certainty equivalent is a payoff Q such that the decision maker is indifferent between the payoff Q for certain and the lottery $L(p, Z_1, Z_2)$. In our earlier example we described a game corresponding to a lottery with an expected payoff of $200. Suppose an individual had no preference between playing that game and receiving a payoff of $50. Then we have $EV = 200$ and $Q = 50$.

The difference $(EV - Q)$ provides some insight into the decision maker's attitude toward risk. In particular, this difference is called the **risk premium,** which we interpret as the amount the decision maker is willing to pay in order to avoid the uncertainty inherent in a lottery. Equivalently, it is the minimum amount that the decision maker will have to be offered as a successful inducement to choose the lottery in favor of a certain outcome. When people exhibit positive risk premiums, we call them **risk averse** decision makers. The risk premium exists because factors such as variability and exposure influence decision makers.

Utility theory hypothesizes that any lottery has associated with it a certainty equivalent such that the decision maker will be indifferent to a choice between the two. In this case the certainty equivalent serves as the summary value in decision making. At this point we might ask how to discover an individual's certainty equivalents and how to describe them.

UTILITY FUNCTIONS

We add two plausible axioms from utility theory. First, given a payoff Q and given a lottery $L(p, Z_1, Z_2)$, with $Z_2 < Q < Z_1$, we can always choose p such that Q is the certainty equivalent of the lottery. This is called the **continuity** axiom. Second, given a lottery $L(p, Z_1, Z_2)$ with $Z_2 < Z_1$, and another lottery $L(p', Z_1, Z_2)$, we will prefer the second lottery if $p' > p$. This is called the **monotonicity** axiom.

With these two axioms we can conceive of constructing a decision maker's **utility function** $U(Z)$ for a given payoff Z. Utility functions always have an arbitrary scale, so we can fix $U = 0$ to correspond to Z_2 (the smaller payoff) and $U = 1$ to correspond to Z_1 (the larger payoff). These points are plotted in Figure 7.12. The axioms of continuity and monotonicity imply that the utility function must be a smooth function, rising steadily in some fashion from 0 at Z_2 to 1 at Z_1.

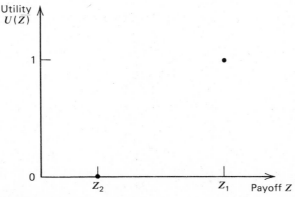

FIGURE 7.12

The aim of utility theory is to permit us to apply expected value logic to utilities (rather than monetary payoffs) when analyzing choices. This means that the expected utility of the payoffs in a lottery must be equal to the utility of the corresponding certainty equivalent.

The expected utility EU of the payoffs in our lottery is

$$EU = pU(Z_1) + (1 - p)U(Z_2) = p$$

If Q is the corresponding certainty equivalent, then we must have

$$U(Q) = EU = p$$

Thus, we begin constructing the utility function as follows. We specify a payoff Q between Z_1 and Z_2, and we ask the decision maker what value of p would make Q the certainty equivalent for the lottery $L(p, Z_1, Z_2)$.

Suppose that there is no risk premium. In this case the decision maker would be **risk neutral,** and we would have $Q = EV$. Thus

$$U(Q) = U(EV)$$
$$p = U[pZ_1 + (1 - p)Z_2]$$

This relationship corresponds to a straight line connecting the points $(0, Z_2)$, and $(1, Z_1)$, as shown in Figure 7.13.

Now suppose there is a positive risk premium, so that $Q < EV$. This means that the risk averse decision maker would associate with the certainty equivalent Q a utility equal to the utility that a risk neutral decision maker would associate with the lottery leading to EV. In Figure 7.14 we set $U(Q)$ for the risk averse individual equal to $U(EV)$ for the risk neutral individual. This step identifies a third point on the curve of the utility function. By drawing a smooth curve through the three points thus identified, we can approximate the utility function, as shown in Figure 7.15. Of course, we can improve the approximation if we propose some other values of Q and determine the corresponding values of p.

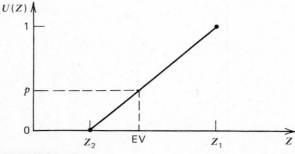

FIGURE 7.13

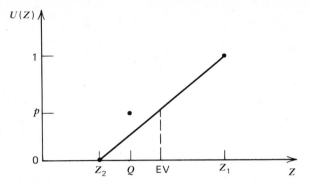

FIGURE 7.14

To suggest how utility functions might be used in the Foster Textile example, suppose we look only at the two payoff extremes, $Z_1 = 6$ and $Z_2 = -5$. We assign utilities of 1 and 0, respectively, to these values:

$U(6) = 1$

$U(-5) = 0$

Now suppose we tell Foster's president about a lottery in which the outcomes are winning \$6 million and losing \$5 million. Then we ask at what probability of winning would the president just be willing to enter the lottery, and suppose we find that the answer is a probability of 0.75. We conclude that the president is risk averse, since we have

$Q = 0$

$EV = 0.75(6) + 0.25(-5) = 3.25 > Q$

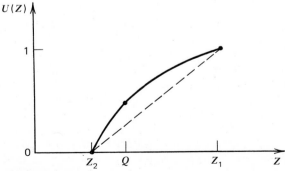

FIGURE 7.15

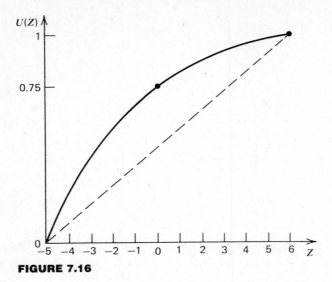

FIGURE 7.16

Figure 7.16 shows a sketch of the corresponding utility function. Based on the sketch, we estimate the following values:

Payoff	6	2	1	0	-1	-5
Utility	1	0.88	0.83	0.75	0.62	0

Now we can replace the table of payoffs (Table 7.9) with a table of utilities (Table 7.10). As the new table shows, when we take expected values we find that the small-scale option maximizes expected utility.

TABLE 7.10

	State (Probability)				Summary
Action	E(0.2)	F(0.4)	M(0.3)	I(0.1)	Value
LS	1	0.88	0.62	0	$V_1 = 0.738$
SS	0.88	0.83	0.75	0.62	$V_2 = 0.795$
DN	0.75	0.75	0.75	0.75	$V_3 = 0.750$
					$V^* = 0.795$

To be entirely rigorous in our example, utility theory would require us to extend these concepts from a two-outcome lottery to a multioutcome lottery, which more closely resembles the structure in Table 7.9. Although the details of this generalization are beyond our scope here, the two-outcome case should provide the key insight. Specifically, it is possible to convert a set of monetary outcomes into a measure of utility, by means of a utility function. This conversion allows us to use expected value concepts in decision analysis while still incorporating individual attitudes toward risk.

SUMMARY

The elementary framework of decision analysis illustrates our general modeling approach by recognizing several features of a single decision. Most fundamentally, the decision-tree model distinguishes between controllable and uncontrollable factors in a problem. We represent the controllable possibilities as actions and the uncontrollable possibilities as states of nature. The choice of a particular action, together with the occurrence of a particular state, results in a particular outcome. We reflect the measured consequences of each outcome in the corresponding payoff.

We use probability models to describe the uncontrollable factors in a decision problem. Thus, there are two types of parameters essential to the description of a decision problem: payoffs, which describe measured outcomes, and probabilities, which describe uncertainty about outcomes. In general, we combine payoff and probability information into a summary preference value for each action. This value serves as a criterion for selecting the most preferred decision. In this chapter we have emphasized an expected-value approach, which uses expected payoff or expected regret as an indicator of preference. Although other measures are possible, the expected-value approach is appealing because it maximizes the long-run total payoff from a series of opportunities. Also, because the expected value is a logical way of combining payoff and probability information, it represents a reasonable first cut at the analysis, even when other criteria are relevant.

We examined the expected-value approach in some detail, and we illustrated sensitivity analysis of payoff and probability parameters in order to suggest the form that studies of parametric validity might take. We also introduced the concept of perfect information and investigated how the "cost of uncertainty" might be assessed in economic terms. The extension of this notion suggested that a decision maker might rely on two sources when modeling the uncertain elements in a decision problem. One source is prior information, which may reflect a subjective or historical perspective and which may be fairly general in its applicability. The other source is additional information, which is specific to the problem at hand. The analysis of decision problems with additional information relies on Bayes' formula for combining the two types of information to yield an updated probability model. This formula dictates that additional information should be structured in the form of likelihoods, expressed as conditional probabilities. This additional information can influence decision making through its effect on probability assessments. After revising probability assessments to include additional information, we might find it necessary to alter a decision that we had determined based only on prior probability assessments.

Preposterior analysis permits us to assess the economic value of additional information in advance, in order to determine whether its cost is offset by the benefit of reduced uncertainty in the problem. This approach actually prescribes a two-stage process of decision making. At the first stage we evaluate the additional information, using preposterior analysis. If the information is desirable, we collect it and then revise our probability assessments. At the second stage, we use these revisions to make the ultimate choice among alternative actions.

We can view preposterior analysis as a special case of a more general decision problem in which we have an opportunity to make a sequence of decisions. Here the key point is to recognize at each stage the value of the opportunity to proceed to the next stage.

Finally, we examined the measurement of risk and its role in decision analysis. Expected value criteria do not completely account for the preferences that a manager exhibits. It is important to understand how attitudes toward risk will influence an individual's choices.

To the extent that a decision maker wants to be cautious in a risky situation, it is possible to use nonprobabilistic criteria, such as the maximin payoff. However, since risk in part reflects probabilities, it seems important to incorporate probabilities in the criterion. In this spirit, we explored the exposure-level measure as a probabilistic analog of maximin payoff. Ultimately, we examined the basic ideas of utility theory in order to see how to accommodate the notion of risk within an expected value framework.

EXERCISES

PAYOFF TABLES AND DECISION TREES

1 Wertz Game and Toy Company is introducing a new line of plastic animals, and the firm is considering whether to bring out a full, partial, or minimal product line. They have broadly identified three levels of market response and have estimated the probabilities of occurrence. The firm expects to have about a 1-year lead time before competitors will be able to react, and the objective is to maximize profits during this period. The following table gives their predicted 1-year profits (in thousands of dollars) for various combinations.

| | Market Response | | |
Product Line	Good	Fair	Poor
Full	300	100	−80
Partial	250	80	−30
Minimal	100	40	−10
Probability	0.2	0.4	0.4

a Construct a regret table for the problem.

b Find the maximax, maximin, and minimax regret strategies for the company.

c Draw a decision tree for the problem.

d What action maximizes expected profit?

e An advertising campaign costing $30,000 could be expected to raise the probabilities of "Fair" and "Good" each by 0.1. Would the campaign be worthwhile?

2 The McNeill Manufacturing Company is about to produce 1000 roof panels for use in an auto assembly line. The facility requires a lengthy setup, and if this is carried out thoroughly the process will produce an average of 1% defectives. Nevertheless, two types of mistakes could be made during the setup. One type (a minor error) yields a process that produces an average of 5% defectives, while the other type (a major error) increases the average proportion defective to 8%. The production manager has three options:

(i) Perform a quality control "check." This will cost $500 in inspection labor and delays and will detect only a minor setup error if it exists. In that case the proportion defective can be reduced to 1%.

(ii) Perform a quality "audit." This will cost $2500 but will detect either type of setup error and guarantee 1% defectives.

(iii) Do nothing.

Based on past experience, the production manager believes that the probabilities of the setup errors are as follows:

Result	No Error	Minor Error	Major Error
Probability	0.7	0.1	0.2

The items are sold at a profit of $10 each, so that total profits equal $10,000 on the good items. Each unit produced costs $50 and defectives must be scrapped at a complete loss.

a Construct a payoff table for the production manager's problem.

b Construct the regret table for the production manager's problem.

c Find the maximax, maximin, and minimax regret strategies for the company.

d What action maximizes expected profit?

3 Ramage Sporting Goods (RSG) is planning to sell backyard swing sets for the outdoor season. Its manager is considering the quantity discount schedule that has been offered by the manufacturer of a swing set that will be sold at a retail price of $60. The cost schedule, which permits RSG to order one of three lot sizes, is shown below:

Lot Size	Unit Cost	Total Cost
Small (20 sets)	$50	$1000
Medium (50 sets)	40	2000
Large (100 sets)	35	3500

At the same time RSG's manager is concerned about the effect of the economy on this season's sales. Her forecasts for demand are as follows:

Inflation rate	Increases	Stabilizes	Decreases
Demand	25	60	100

The manager also expects that any surplus sets left at the end of the season will eventually have to be discounted to $20 in order to clear out inventory and make room for ski equipment.

a Construct a payoff table for RSG's ordering decision.

b Construct a regret table for RSG's ordering decision.

c Find the maximax, maximin, and minimax regret strategies for the firm.

d Given the following probability distribution for inflation behavior in the coming year, determine the optimal expected payoff.

Inflation rate	Increases	Stabilizes	Decreases
Probability	0.3	0.5	0.2

4 The Cooper Furniture Company has received a special order for 60,000 contemporary-style lighting fixtures from a large hotel chain. Using the old production machinery, the fixtures could be produced at a cost of $8 each. Years of experience with the old equipment indicate that the fixture could be manufactured with 5% rejects. Informal discussions with another firm indicate that the fixtures can be purchased on a subcontracting arrangement at $8.40 each, with defectives replaced free of charge. In addition, an engineer has recently proposed a design for a new, custom process that would speed up the manufacture of the fixtures and reduce the unit cost to $6.50. He also estimates the cost of new equipment to be $60,000. However, there is one potential problem with the proposal: The engineer is uncertain about the proportion of the fixtures that would turn out to be defective. The engineer has come up with the following distribution for the reject rate.

Reject rate (%)	5	10	15	25
Probability	0.2	0.4	0.3	0.1

Assume that all in-house defectives are scrapped and that the cost of the new equipment will be entirely allocated to the 60,000 fixtures. Compute the expected total cost under each alternative and determine which is preferred on economic grounds.

5 The manager of Huntington Foods must decide on the production volume of a specific product for the coming year. In this industry, volumes are determined prior to the harvest season in order to arrange supply levels with vendors and to set capacity. The production period is relatively short, and finished goods are stored for marketing and distribution throughout the year. Unsold food is valueless at the end of the year.

Three possible market volumes are anticipated: low (40,000 cases), medium (60,000 cases), and high (80,000 cases). As it happens, these are also convenient lengths for production runs. Production costs consist of a fixed cost of $100,000 and a variable cost of $5 per case. Each case is sold for $8, and the penalty cost for lost sales is taken to be $1 per case. In the manager's estimation, there is a 50% chance that the medium market volume will occur; the other two volumes are equally likely.

a Verify the following payoff table (all entries in thousands of dollars):

Production Level	Market Volume		
	Low	Medium	High
Low	20	0	−20
Medium	−80	80	60
High	−180	−20	140

b What is the maximin payoff?

c What is the minimax regret?

d What is the maximum expected payoff?

SENSITIVITY ANALYSIS

6 Review Exercise 1.

a Suppose the criterion is minimax regret. Perform a sensitivity analysis of Z_{21} (the payoff for a partial line when the market response is good). In other words, for each possible value of Z_{21} specify the value V^* of the minimax regret and specify which action is optimal.

b Repeat (a) for the criterion of expected regret.

7 Review Exercise 1.

a Consider the following parametric probability model for the states of nature:

State	Good	Fair	Poor
Probability	P	0.4	$0.6 - P$

Perform a sensitivity analysis of P when the criterion is expected payoff. In other words, for each possible value of P specify the value V^* of the optimal expected payoff and specify which action achieves it.

b Repeat (a) for the following model, performing a sensitivity analysis for P_1 and P_2 when the criterion is expected payoff.

State	Good	Fair	Poor
Probability	P_1	$1 - P_1 - P_2$	P_2

PERFECT INFORMATION

8 Review Exercise 1. Calculate the *EVPI*.

9 Review Exercise 2. Calculate the *EVPI*.

10 Review Exercise 3. Calculate the *EVPI*.

11 Review Exercise 5. Calculate the *EVPI*.

ADDITIONAL INFORMATION

12 Review Exercise 1. The marketing department at the Wertz Game and Toy Company has designed a brief test-marketing program, costing $5000, which will enable them to classify consumer attitudes as "favorable" or "unfavorable." The historic data on favorable outcomes in such test market efforts suggest the following relation to eventual market response levels.

Market response level	Good	Fair	Poor
Probability of favorable outcome	0.75	0.60	0.20

a Draw a decision tree for the problem and identify conditional actions for favorable and unfavorable test-market outcomes.

b Evaluate the desirability of the test-market program.

13 Fisk Electronics Corporation is a small company that obtains most of its revenues from subcontracts with larger manufacturing firms. One of its current subcontracts calls for the production of a miniature heating device for an aircraft manufacturer. Experience with the existing production process has shown that 30% of the devices are faulty. The flaw, which occurs in a basic component, cannot be detected by current inspection procedures and can be discovered only when the device is fully assembled and tested. When tests indicate the existence of a flaw, the device is disassembled, corrected, and reassembled. The cost of this repair is $60; and, under the terms of the contract, this cost is charged to Fisk.

One possibility that has been suggested involves the addition 1 a new inspection and repair operation to the production process. This operation would increase the cost per unit by $12 on all devices but would correct any faulty components continuing to assembly.

Another possibility involves a brief test of the questionable component. This test would add only $4 to the unit cost but would not provide perfect discrimination between defective components and nondefectives. Specifically, the test registers positive, neutral, or negative results, and experiments with the test have indicated the following probabilities:

	State of Component	
Test Result	Good	Defective
Positive	0.50	0.10
Neutral	0.30	0.30
Negative	0.20	0.60
	1.00	1.00

Thus, the test results are not completely reliable indicators of the quality of the questionable component.

How should Fisk redesign its production process to reduce its costs?

14 Review Exercise 2. Before making a decision, the production manager notices that he has some scrap material available from which he can make some sample panels. Although the composition of the scrap renders it inadequate for the batch of panels, setup errors will lead to the same proportion of defectives on scrap input as on the actual production run.

a Suppose there is enough scrap to sample two panels. Calculate the *EVAI* for a sample of two items, and specify the conditional actions associated with sampling outcomes.

b Suppose there is enough scrap to sample three panels. Calculate the *EVAI* for a sample of three items, and specify the conditional actions associated with sampling outcomes.

15 Review Exercise 5. At Huntington Foods there have been several previous attempts at predicting market volumes by the Forecasting Department, which predicts whether the market will be good, mediocre, or bad. The history of these predictions is summarized in the probabilities below:

	Low	*Medium*	*High*
Good	0.05	0.25	0.70
Mediocre	0.20	0.60	0.20
Bad	0.70	0.25	0.05

a What is the conditional action corresponding to each possible prediction?

b What is the economic value of the Forecasting Department's prediction?

MULTISTAGE DECISIONS

16 During the season of peak demands for power the turbines at the Susac River Power Plant are inspected at the end of each day. Roughly speaking, a turbine is classified as (1) operating smoothly, (2) operating roughly, or (3) not operating. If it is operating smoothly, there is no need for maintenance. If it is operating roughly, the turbine can be serviced for maintenance at a cost of $400 to restore it to efficient operation by the beginning of the next day. The turbine can also be left alone, although its condition may deteriorate. If it is not operating, the turbine can be serviced for overhaul at a cost of $1100, restoring the turbine to smooth operation by the beginning of the next day, or else it can be serviced for repair at a cost of $750 to restore it to rough operation by the beginning of the next day.

Aside from the maintenance, repair, and overhaul charges, there are incremental costs of power generation that depend on the turbine's state. When a turbine is found to be operating roughly during inspection there is an associated operating cost averaging $300 per day, due to underutilization. When a turbine is found to be inoperable, however, there is a cost averaging $1250, primarily due to the need to draw on auxiliary power sources.

The operating status of the turbine may deteriorate in the course of a day, according to the probability model described in the table below.

		End-of-Day Status		
		Operating Smoothly	*Operating Roughly*	*Not Operating*
Start of day Status	Operating smoothly	0.8	0.15	0.05
	Operating roughly	0.0	0.75	0.25

a Find a plan for maintaining the turbine over a 3-day period that will minimize expected cost.

b Repeat (a) for a 4-day period.

17 A small manufacturer requires the use of a delivery van for a 5-year period. A new, specially equipped van can be purchased for $10,000. As the van gets older, its annual operating and maintenance expenses increase, but its resale value declines. Thus, the company may decide to replace the van with a new one in any year. Furthermore, since the van will be exposed to heavy use, there is a probability of a breakdown in any year. The cost and probability parameters are given in the table below.

Year of Operation (t)	Expenses C(t)	Resale Value R(t)	Breakdown Probability P(t)
1	1500	7000	0.1
2	2000	5000	0.2
3	3000	4000	0.4
4	4500	2000	0.5
5	6000	500	0.8

Assume that when a van breaks down it can be used through the end of the year, after which it must be replaced by a new one. Also, the resale value of a broken-down van can be taken as 0.

Find a replacement policy that will minimize the expected value of all costs and revenues associated with the 5-year operation of the van.

18 The Rogers Manufacturing Company produces component parts for heavy machinery and equipment. Typically, its parts are subjected to a series of three quality tests, and a part must pass all three tests before being shipped. If it fails any one of the tests it is sent back for rework.

Because the tests are expensive, engineers at RMC have questioned whether there is an "optimal" test sequence, that is, a sequence that will minimize the expected cost of performing the tests. Figures on the cost of each test have been compiled from the cost accounting department and the engineers have developed subjective assessments for the probability that a part will fail each of the tests. This information is reproduced below.

Test	Cost/unit	Failure Probability
Fracture	$11.00	0.175
X-ray	$12.50	0.10
Vibration	$15.00	0.20

a Based on this information determine the optimal test sequence.

b What is the average testing cost per item tested?

c What is the average testing cost per item shipped?

19 Review Exercise 18. One of the engineers has proposed that the failure probabilities are not completely independent. In other words, the probability of failure on the second test should not be assumed independent of the outcome of the first test; instead, the relevant probability should be viewed as dependent on the outcome of the first test. Thus, the appropriate probability in that instance would be the conditional probability of failure on the second test given success on the first test.

With a view to developing the pertinent conditional probabilities, the quality control manager had a random sample of 2000 items subjected to all three tests. Here are the results:

Vibration	Pass Fracture Test		Fail Fracture Test	
	Pass X-ray Test	Fail X-ray Test	Pass X-ray Test	Fail X-ray Test
Pass Vibration test	1500	30	40	30
Fail Vibration test	100	20	160	120

a Determine the optimal test sequence.

b What is the average testing cost per item tested?

c What is the average testing cost per item shipped?

ATTITUDES TOWARD RISK

20 Review Exercise 1. Suppose that decision makers at Wertz Game and Toy Company prefer to evaluate decisions based on the mean and standard deviation of payoffs, using the formula $V_i = \mu_i - w\sigma_i$.

a For $w = 0.25$, which action maximizes V_i?

b For what values of w does the minimal product line maximize V_i? The partial line? The full line?

21 Review Exercise 1. Suppose that Wertz Game and Toy adopts the following utility function for the range of payoffs they anticipate

$$U(x) = \left(\frac{x}{300}\right)^{1/2} \quad \text{if} \quad x \geq 0$$

$$= -\left(\frac{x}{80}\right)^2 \quad \text{if} \quad x < 0$$

where x represents profit in thousands of dollars. Which action maximizes expected utility?

22 Review Exercise 5. Suppose that Huntington Foods' manager prefers to evaluate decisions based on the mean and standard deviation of payoffs, using the formula $V_i = \mu_i - w\sigma_i$.

a For $w = 0.4$, which action maximizes V_i?

b For $w = 0.8$, which action maximizes V_i?

23 Review Exercise 5. Suppose the manager at Huntington Foods decides to use an exposure level Z_0 in the determination of an optimal action. For each of the following values of Z_0 (in thousands), determine which action maximizes expected profit, subject to the condition that there is at most a 10% chance that profit will be less than Z_0.

a $Z_0 = -100$

b $Z_0 = -50$

c $Z_0 = 0$

24 Review Exercise 5. To develop a suitable utility function for the manager of Huntington Foods, suppose that the following values are specified

$$U(x) = 1 \quad \text{for} \quad x = 140$$
$$= 0 \quad \text{for} \quad x = -180$$

where $x = 140$ and $x = -180$ are the extreme values in the original payoff table. Next, suppose the manager considers the possibility of entering a lottery with payoffs of 140 and -180 and decides that the lottery would be attractive if the probability of winning (i.e., obtaining 140) were at least 0.65. Sketch a utility function for the manager based on this observation, and determine the expected utility for each action.

Chapter 8

TRADE-OFF MODELS FOR SURPLUS AND SHORTAGE

The Hinman News and Supply Company

Newsboys who work for the Hinman News and Supply Company sell daily newspapers at streetcorner newsstands. Under the company's rules, each newsboy is required to purchase his daily stock of newspapers from the company at a cost of $0.05 each, for eventual sale at a price of $0.20 each. The rules also stipulate that if the newsboy runs out of papers during the day he cannot obtain a replenishment supply. Furthermore, if the newsboy finishes the day with a surplus he will not be permitted to return any of the excess for a refund. In view of the fact that daily demand at a typical newsstand is random, how many newspapers should the newsboy stock?

A common type of management decision problem involves the trade-off of surplus and shortage outcomes in an uncertain environment. Such a problem is frequently called a **newsboy** problem, after the simple trade-off posed in the Hinman Company scenario. We could analyze the newsboy problem using the techniques of decision analysis introduced in the previous chapter. However, we can gain additional insights by studying the problem's special structure. This chapter explores that special structure in order to demonstrate the use of newsboy analysis in decision making and to identify the information needed to support the analysis.

At the outset it is important to understand how the newsboy problem lends itself to a decision analysis approach. Notice that

1. Each potential supply quantity can be interpreted as a possible action.
2. Each potential demand outcome can be interpreted as a possible state of nature.

317

3. The supply quantity must be chosen before the demand outcome can be observed.

4. The newsboy's profit for the day is an appropriate payoff measure.

No intrinsic aspect of the newsboy problem dictates a criterion for decision making, but the lessons of decision analysis still apply. If we interpret the newsboy scenario literally, as a repeating daily problem, then an appropriate objective is the maximization of long-run profits. An equivalent objective is to maximize expected daily profit. Alternatively, we may want to apply the same concepts to a scenario in which the decision is a one-time problem rather than a repeating one. In either event, an important first step is to investigate the maximization of expected payoff. Therefore, we shall begin the analysis using a criterion of expected daily profit. This approach will emphasize the similarity between the newsboy problem and the material covered in our previous treatment of decision analysis.

First of all, we can develop a decision-tree model for the newsboy's problem. For example, suppose that the demand is known to be between 12 and 15 papers per day. Then the newsboy will need to consider only four possible actions, each of which is associated with four possible demand outcomes, as shown in Figure 8.1. In the figure we use c to denote the unit cost, and we use r to denote the unit price. Then, in the spirit of the decision theory approach, we can use this decision tree as a basis for determining the newsboy's optimal order quantity. However, imagine how the tree would look instead if we knew demand would be between 1200 and 1500. Then there would be 301 possible actions and 301 states of nature for each action, and the expected payoff calculations would be quite time-consuming. To avoid these lengthy calculations we can take an algebraic approach. Not only does this approach allow us to compute solutions much more quickly than with the decision tree, but it also helps us understand the key factors in the newsboy problem.

In order to develop the general analysis of newsboy models we define

y = initial supply (the decision variable)
X = demand
S = sales quantity
P = newsboy's profit

where capital letters denote random variables. We represent profit by an equation that states simply that profit equals revenue minus cost:

$$P = rS - cy \tag{8.1}$$

Here the sales quantity, S, is the minimum of the initial supply and the demand:

$$S = \min\{X, y\} \tag{8.2}$$

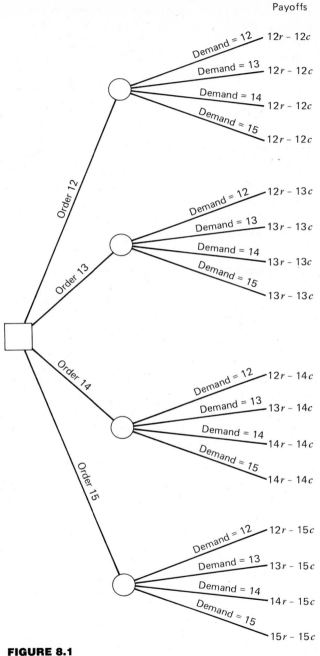

FIGURE 8.1

The newsboy's objective is to maximize expected profit. In light of equation (8.1), this means that the criterion is to maximize

$$E[P] = E[rS - cy] = rE[S] - cy \tag{8.3}$$

In the next section we examine the policies that allow us to maximize this criterion.

ANALYSIS OF OPTIMAL POLICIES

The analysis of the criterion (8.3) differs slightly according to whether a discrete model or a continuous model represents demand. There is no essential difference in the conclusions drawn from these two cases, but treating them separately serves to illustrate how we might apply different mathematical concepts in analyzing a particular situation.

THE DISCRETE VERSION OF THE MODEL

In the discrete case, we represent the demand for newspapers using P_k, the probability mass function for X. We define P_k as the probability that exactly k papers will be demanded:

$$P_k = P(X = k)$$

Also, we define the **cumulative distribution function** (cdf) for demand to be

$$F(y) = P(X \le y) = \sum_{k=0}^{y} P_k$$

Stated in words, $F(y)$ denotes the probability that demand is less than or equal to the initial supply. Using the probability model for demand we can write expected sales as follows:

$$\begin{aligned}
E[S] = E[\min\{X, y\}] &= \sum_{k=0}^{\infty} \min\{k, y\}P_k \\
&= \sum_{k=0}^{y} kP_k + \sum_{k=y+1}^{\infty} yP_k \\
&= \sum_{k=0}^{y} kP_k + y \sum_{k=y+1}^{\infty} P_k
\end{aligned}$$

Then equation (8.3) yields

$$E[P] = r \sum_{k=0}^{y} kP_k + ry \sum_{k=y+1}^{\infty} P_k - cy$$

To emphasize the fact that this expected payoff depends on the decision variable y, we define $G(y) = E[P]$, so that

$$G(y) = r \sum_{k=0}^{y} kP_k + ry[1 - F(y)] - cy \qquad (8.4)$$

A typical graph of this function is shown in Figure 8.2.

Notice that the function shown in Figure 8.2 is defined only for integer values of y. For each value of y, representing the number of papers stocked, the height $G(y)$ is the expected profit for the newsboy. Furthermore, as the graph shows, $G(y)$ first increases as y increases and then eventually decreases as y increases. The turning point is the value of y at which $G(y)$ is maximized. For the turning point itself, $G(y)$ will be higher than $G(y - 1)$ and higher than or equal to $G(y + 1)$. Therefore, the value of y that maximizes expected profit is defined by

$$G(y) - G(y - 1) > 0 \qquad (8.5)$$
$$G(y + 1) - G(y) \leq 0 \qquad (8.6)$$

Upon substituting equation (8.4) into equation (8.5) we obtain

$$r \sum_{k=0}^{y} kP_k + ry[1 - F(y)] - cy - r \sum_{k=0}^{y-1} kP_k - r(y - 1)[1 - F(y - 1)] + c(y - 1) > 0$$

$$r \left(\sum_{k=0}^{y} kP_k - \sum_{k=0}^{y-1} kP_k \right) + ry[-F(y) + F(y - 1)] + r[1 - F(y - 1)] - c > 0$$

$$r(yP_y) - ry[F(y) - F(y - 1)] + r - rF(y - 1) - c > 0$$

$$ryP_y - ry[P_y] + r - c - rF(y - 1) > 0$$

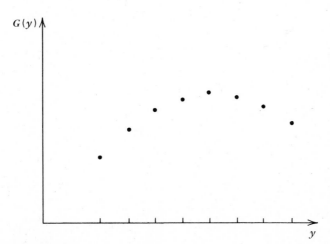

FIGURE 8.2

Collecting terms, we obtain

$$rF(y - 1) < r - c$$

$$F(y - 1) < \frac{r - c}{r}$$

Similarly, substitution of equation (8.4) into equation (8.6) yields

$$F(y) \geq \frac{r - c}{r}$$

Thus, the optimal stock level, which we denote y^*, satisfies the condition

$$F(y^* - 1) < \frac{r - c}{r} \leq F(y^*) \tag{8.7}$$

Stated in words, y^* is the smallest value of y for which the cumulative distribution function equals or exceeds the ratio $(r - c)/r$. Conceptually, we can determine y^* from a graph of the function $F(y)$. For a discrete probability model, $F(y)$ is a step function that takes on values between 0 and 1 (see Figure 8.3). The ratio $(r - c)/r$ is a number between 0 and 1, and we can plot it on the vertical axis of the graph. Then y^* is simply the first y value for which $F(y)$ equals or exceeds this height, as sketched in Figure 8.3. However, $F(y)$ is the probability that demand is less than

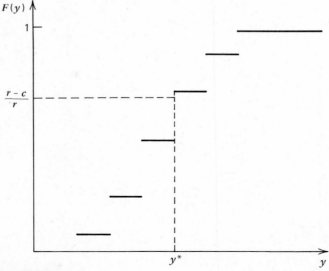

FIGURE 8.3

or equal to supply, or, equivalently, the probability that the supply quantity y is sufficient to meet all demand. Thus, we can interpret the result in equation (8.7) as identifying y^* to be the smallest possible stock level that will guarantee a probability $(r - c)/r$ of meeting all demand.

An important factor in our newsboy analysis involves the information necessary to determine an optimal stock level. Specifically, the rule (8.7) for selecting an optimal action requires information about costs and revenues and a probabilistic description of demand. In particular, if this description is available in the form of a cdf, we can use the method illustrated in Figure 8.3 to identify y^* immediately.

As an example, suppose the newsboy purchases his stock at a unit cost of $c = 5$ and sells them for a price of $r = 20$. Suppose also that demand for newspapers follows the discrete distribution shown below:

Demand	k	12	13	14	15	16	17	18
Probability	P_k	0.05	0.10	0.30	0.25	0.15	0.10	0.05
cdf	$F(k)$	0.05	0.15	0.45	0.70	0.85	0.95	1.00

In this case the ratio $(r - c)/r$ equals $(20 - 15)/20$, or 0.75, and the optimal supply quantity is the first point at which the cumulative distribution function equals or exceeds this level. Therefore, the optimal supply quantity is 16, since

$$F(15) < 0.75 \leq F(16)$$

We calculate the expected profit for the optimal decision from equation (8.4), which takes the form

$$G(16) = r \sum_{k=0}^{16} kP_k + r(16)[1 - F(16)] - c(16)$$

Substituting the cost and price parameters, this expression becomes

$$G(16) = 20 \sum_{k=0}^{16} kP_k + 20(16)[1 - F(16)] - 5(16)$$

Then, using the probabilities in the table, we obtain

$$\begin{aligned}
G(16) &= 20[12(0.05) + 13(0.10) + 14(0.30) + 15(0.25) + 16(0.15)] \\
&\quad + 20(16)[1 - 0.85] - 5(16) \\
&= 20[12.25] + 320[0.15] - 80 \\
&= 213
\end{aligned}$$

TABLE 8.1

k	P_k	$F(k)$	k	P_k	$F(k)$
0	0.0000	0.0000	17	0.0934	0.6593
1	0.0000	0.0000	18	0.0830	0.7423
2	0.0000	0.0000	19	0.0699	0.8122
3	0.0001	0.0001	20	0.0559	0.8682
4	0.0003	0.0004	21	0.0426	0.9108
5	0.0010	0.0014	22	0.0310	0.9418
6	0.0026	0.0040	23	0.0216	0.9633
7	0.0060	0.0100	24	0.0144	0.9777
8	0.0120	0.0220	25	0.0092	0.9869
9	0.0213	0.0433	26	0.0057	0.9925
10	0.0341	0.0774	27	0.0034	0.9959
11	0.0496	0.1270	28	0.0019	0.9978
12	0.0661	0.1931	29	0.0011	0.9989
13	0.0814	0.2745	30	0.0006	0.9994
14	0.0930	0.3675	31	0.0003	0.9997
15	0.0992	0.4667	32	0.0001	0.9999
16	0.0992	0.5660	33	0.0001	0.9999

As another example, let us again use $c = 5$ and $r = 20$. However, this time suppose that on the basis of experience the newsboy believes that demand can be modeled by a Poisson distribution with a mean of 16. The ratio $(r - c)/r$ is again 0.75, and to find the optimal supply quantity we must consult a table of cumulative Poisson probabilities for a mean of 16. Table 8.1 is an excerpt from the Poisson table in the Appendix. Examination of the table reveals that the optimal supply quantity is 19, because

$$F(18) < 0.75 \le F(19)$$

In other words, the cumulative distribution function first equals or exceeds the level 0.75 at $F(19) = 0.8122$. In order to calculate the expected profit for the optimal policy we must again calculate directly from equation (8.4):

$$
\begin{aligned}
G(19) &= r \sum_{k=0}^{19} kP_k + r(19)[1 - F(19)] - c(19) \\
&= 20[0P_0 + 1P_1 + 2P_2 + \cdots + 19P_{19}] + 20(19)[1 - F(19)] - 5(19) \\
&= 20[11.88] + 380[1 - 0.8122] - 95 \\
&= 213.96
\end{aligned}
$$

THE CONTINUOUS VERSION OF THE MODEL

Sometimes it is convenient to treat the elements of the newsboy model as continuous rather than discrete. A continuous model would be particularly appropriate if we have a very large number of possible supply actions and demand states. In the continuous case we describe the random variable X with a continuous probability model, by specifying either its cumulative distribution function, $F(x)$, or else its probability density function, $f(x)$. The form of the expected profit criterion remains unchanged:

$$G(y) = E[P] = rE[S] - cy \qquad (8.8)$$

Here, the graph of $G(y)$ is not a discrete function, as was the case in Figure 8.2, but a smooth curve, as shown in Figure 8.4. As y increases, this function increases, reaches a peak, and then decreases.

With the use of calculus, it is possible to show that the optimal stock level y^* satisfies the condition

$$F(y^*) = \frac{r - c}{r} \qquad (8.9)$$

Notice that this result is just the continuous analog of the result in equation (8.7). In graphical terms, we solve equation (8.9) by plotting the function $F(y)$ and locating the point at which its height equals $(r - c)/r$, as shown in Figure 8.5. As the figure also indicates, another way to interpret this result is that the area under the density function to the left of y must be equal to $(r - c)/r$.

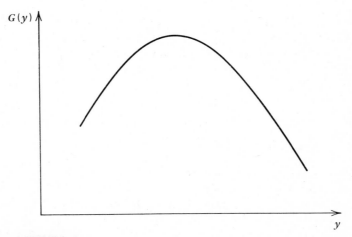

FIGURE 8.4

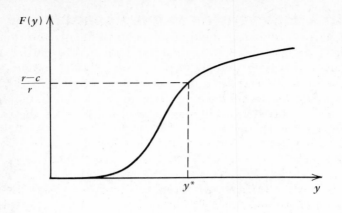

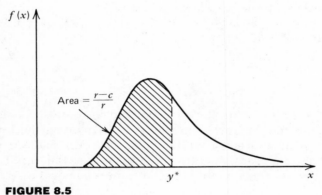

FIGURE 8.5

As an example let $c = 15$ and $r = 20$, and suppose that demand follows a uniform distribution from 100 to 300. In other words, mean demand is 200 and demand is equally likely to be any quantity between 100 and 300. More formally, the cumulative distribution function for demand will then be

$$F(y) = \begin{cases} 0 & y \leq 100 \\ \dfrac{y - 100}{200} & 100 \leq y \leq 300 \\ 1 & y \geq 300 \end{cases}$$

Here the ratio $(r - c)/r$ is equal to $(20 - 15)/20$ or 0.25. The procedure illustrated in Figure 8.5 calls for this ratio to be set equal to $F(y^*)$. We have

$$\frac{y^* - 100}{200} = 0.25$$

$$y^* = 150$$

Notice that the uniform demand distribution characterizes demand as occurring in the range 200 ± 100, with equally likely outcomes in this range. However, the optimal supply level does not lie at the center of this interval. In this case the relative values of unit cost and unit profit dictate a supply quantity less than the mean of the distribution.

If we think of the quantity 200 as a forecast, and the tolerance of ± 100 as representing a confidence interval around that forecast, we can see why it is logical to make a decision different from a forecast simply because of the cost structure that applies to forecast errors. Specifically, forecast errors that lead to a shortage will cost the newsboy \$0.05 per paper in lost profit. On the other hand, forecast errors that lead to a surplus will cost \$0.15 per paper in excess purchases. Because the cost is greater for surplus than for shortage, it makes sense to bias the decision toward providing more protection against the risk of surplus. The newsboy achieves this result by supplying a quantity less than the forecast.

As another example, suppose again that $c = 15$ and $r = 20$, but this time suppose that demand follows a normal distribution with mean $\mu = 200$ and standard deviation $\sigma = 50$. The ratio $(r - c)/r$ is again 0.25, but we cannot implement the procedure implied by Figure 8.5 by solving equation (8.9) for y^*. Here we must rely on normal tables because the function $F(y)$ cannot be written in explicit form for the normal distribution. The height $F(y)$ represents the area under a normal curve to the left of y. We convert the value y^* to the scale of the standard normal distribution via the relationship

$$z = \frac{y^* - \mu}{\sigma} = \frac{y^* - 200}{50}$$

In this case the z value associated with a left-hand tail area of 0.25 is $z = -0.675$, yielding

$$-0.675 = \frac{y^* - 200}{50}$$

$$y^* = 166$$

In order to calculate the expected profit for this policy we utilize a special formula for the normal case:

$$G(y) = r(\mu - y)F(y) - r\sigma f(y) + (r - c)y \tag{8.10}$$

where $f(y)$ denotes the height of the normal curve at y. To determine $f(y)$ we calculate the z value corresponding to y and find the height of the standard normal density function in the table given in the Appendix. In our example, we have $z = -0.675$, so that $f(166) = 0.3166$. We also have $F(166) = 0.25$, as we determined earlier, and thus

$$G(166) = 20(200 - 166)F(166) - 20(50)f(166) + (20 - 15)(166)$$
$$= 20(34)(0.25) - 20(50)(0.3166) + 5(166)$$
$$= 683.40$$

QUANTITY DISCOUNTS

Our understanding of the basic newsboy problem and its analysis can help us solve some more complicated variations of the basic version. To illustrate this point we consider the effects of price discounts in the purchase of the newsboy's stock.

In particular, we examine the structure of an "all-units" quantity discount, in which the discount applies to every unit in the purchase lot. For example, if there are two price breaks, we might write the unit cost schedule as follows:

$$c(y) = \begin{cases} c_1 y & \text{if} & y < b_1 \\ c_2 y & \text{if} & b_1 \le y < b_2 \\ c_3 y & \text{if} & y \ge b_2 \end{cases} \tag{8.11}$$

Here the function $c(y)$ represents the total cost of supplying y items. The cost per unit is c_1 if the supply level is less than the first break point, or $y < b_1$. When the supply level reaches b_1 the unit cost drops to c_2, where $c_2 < c_1$. This unit cost applies until we reach the second break point, b_2. At a supply level of b_2 or above the unit cost drops to c_3, where $c_3 < c_2$. Thus, the total cost for y units is equal to $c_1 y$, or $c_2 y$, or $c_3 y$, depending on the size of y. In essence, the newsboy facing the prospect of such a quantity discount must determine whether the possible savings in purchase cost will offset the added risk of surplus if the supply quantity is raised.

When the quantity discount is available, the newsboy's criterion is a variation of equation (8.8), which incorporates the cost schedule in equation (8.11):

$$G(y) = rE[S] - c(y) \tag{8.12}$$

For the purposes of illustration, we assume that a continuous probability model applies, so that for a given unit cost the graphical shape of $G(y)$ will resemble Figure 8.4. However, our arguments apply to the discrete case without modification. If there are two price breaks, as in the cost schedule of equation (8.11), then there are three possible unit costs: c_1, c_2, or c_3. For each unit cost there is a corresponding version of $G(y)$ that we write as follows:

$$G_i(y) = rE[S] - c_i y \qquad (i = 1, 2, 3)$$

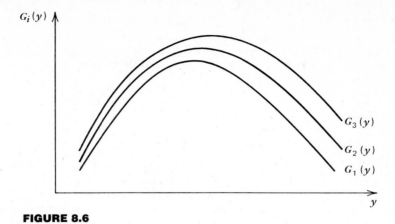

FIGURE 8.6

Figure 8.6 shows a graph of the functions $G_i(y)$. There are two features of this graph to notice. First, the three curves $G_i(y)$ do not intersect. To see why this is true, choose any supply level y. At this level we must have

$$G_1(y) < G_2(y) < G_3(y)$$

since $c_1 > c_2 > c_3$. Therefore, the function $G_1(y)$ always lies below $G_2(y)$, which always lies below $G_3(y)$.

Now let y_i denote the supply level where $G_i(y)$ reaches its peak. The second point to notice is that $y_1 < y_2 < y_3$. This observation follows from the fact that the critical ratio increases as the unit cost decreases:

if

$$c_1 > c_2 > c_3$$

then

$$\frac{r - c_1}{r} < \frac{r - c_2}{r} < \frac{r - c_3}{r}$$

Because $G_i(y)$ peaks at the supply level y_i corresponding to the critical ratio $(r - c_i)/r$, then an increase in the critical ratio must lead to an increase in y_i.

Although there are three expected profit functions in Figure 8.6, we must be careful when we interpret them. The function $G_1(y)$ applies to the smaller purchase quantities, $y < b_1$. For a purchase quantity as large as $y = b_2$, the unit cost is c_2. In Figure 8.6, this unit cost moves us to the curve for

$G_2(y)$, which is higher (more profitable) than $G_1(y)$, as we noted earlier. For a purchase quantity as large as $y = b_3$, we can move to the highest curve, $G_3(y)$. Thus, any one of the three curves $G_i(y)$ might be a possible representation of expected profit, following the schedule shown below:

$$G(y) = \begin{cases} G_1(y) & \text{if} & y < b_1 \\ G_2(y) & \text{if} & b_1 \leq y < b_2 \\ G_3(y) & \text{if} & y \geq b_2 \end{cases}$$

Depending on the location of b_1 and b_2, the maximum value of $G(y)$ could conceivably lie at one of five points, as shown in the graphs of Figure 8.7.

In Figure 8.7a we have $y_3 > b_2$. In this case the supply y_3 attains the maximum expected profit on the topmost curve, and clearly no other y value can yield a larger expected profit. In Figure 8.7b, we have $y_3 < b_2$, so that it is not feasible to obtain a supply of y_3 at a unit cost of c_3. The feasible portion of $G_3(y)$ lies to the right of y_3. In this interval, $G_3(y)$ is decreasing, hence the largest feasible expected profit on the curve occurs at $y = b_2$. The graph depicts a case in which $G_3(b_2) > G_2(y_2)$. In other words, the best feasible supply quantity for the unit price c_3 leads to a better expected profit than the best possible supply quantity for the unit price c_2. The situation could be reversed, however, as Figure 8.7c indicates. Here we have $G_2(y_2) > G_3(b_2)$, so that the optimal supply quantity is y_2. In Figure 8.7d we find that neither y_3 nor y_2 is feasible. For unit costs c_3 and c_2 the best feasible supply quantities are b_1 and b_2, respectively. In the case of Figure 8.7(d) we have $G_2(b_1) > G_3(b_2)$ and $G_2(b_1) > G_1(y_1)$, so that the optimal supply is $y = b_1$. Finally, Figure 8.7e shows a situation in which the optimal supply level is y_1, since $G_1(y_1) > G_2(b_1)$ and $G_1(y_1) > G_3(b_2)$.

In general, we can find the optimal supply level by comparing the best feasible supply quantity for each curve. For $G_i(y)$, if the peak value y_i is feasible (i.e., if $y_i \geq b_{i-1}$), then the best supply quantity on that curve is y_i. If $y_i < b_{i-1}$, then the feasible portion of $G_i(y)$ will be a decreasing function, and the best supply level on that curve will be the smallest feasible supply quantity, or $y = b_{i-1}$. Once we identify the best feasible supply quantity on each curve, we can compare the best expected profit on each curve and select the largest. This comparison will reveal the optimal supply level.

As an illustration we examine the effect of a quantity discount on a scenario considered earlier: Demand for papers follows a Poisson distribution with a mean of 16. We again take the selling price as $r = 20$, and we suppose the following discount schedule applies:

$c_1 = 5$ for $y < 12$

$c_2 = 4$ for $12 \leq y < 24$

$c_3 = 3$ for $y \geq 24$

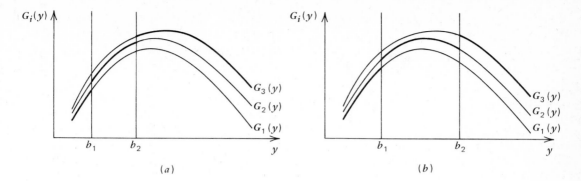

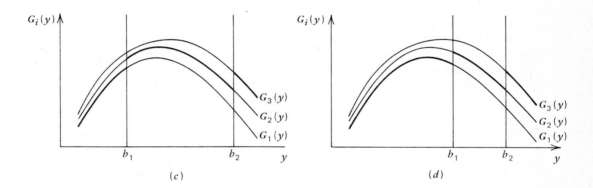

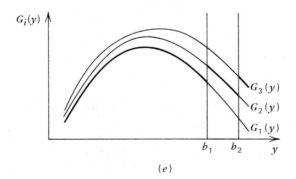

FIGURE 8.7

For this problem the expected profit functions are

$$G_i(y) = 20 \sum_{k=0}^{y} P_k + 20y[1 - F(y)] - c_i y \qquad (8.13)$$

First we consider the uppermost "curve," corresponding to the unit cost $c_3 = 3$. For this curve, the critical ratio is $(20 - 3)/20 = 0.85$ and from Table 8.1 we see that the peak expected profit on this curve occurs at $y_3 = 20$. Because the unit cost $c_3 = 3$ is not feasible for supply levels below 24, the best expected profit for the top curve must be $G_3(b_2)$, or $G_3(24)$. We substitute in equation (8.13):

$$G_3(24) = 20[0P_0 + 1P_1 + 2P_2 + \cdots + 24P_{24}] + 20(24)[1 - 0.9777] - 3(24)$$
$$= 308.28 + 10.70 - 72$$
$$= 246.98$$

Next we examine the middle curve, for which $c_2 = 4$. This unit cost implies a critical ratio of $16/20 = 0.80$. The peak expected profit occurs at $y_3 = 19$. Because the unit cost $c_2 = 4$ is feasible at this supply level, the best expected profit for the middle curve must be $G_2(y_2)$ or $G_2(19)$. From equation (8.13) we obtain

$$G_2(19) = 20[0P_0 + 1P_1 + 2P_2 + \cdots + 19P_{19}] + 20(19)[1 - 0.8122] - 4(19)$$
$$= 237.60 + 71.36 - 76$$
$$= 232.96$$

Finally, we could find the best expected profit on the lowest curve, but in this situation the calculation would not be necessary. We know that the best value on the lowest curve cannot be larger than the peak value on the middle curve, which we calculated above as 232.96. Thus, we have

$$G_3(24) = 246.98$$
$$G_2(19) = 232.96$$
$$G_1(y_1) < 232.96$$

and we conclude that the optimal supply level is $y = 24$. In this case the discount schedule provides an incentive to take the largest discount.

As a second example, we illustrate the continuous version of the analysis by returning to the normal distribution considered earlier. We assume that $\mu = 200$ and $\sigma = 50$ and, as before, $r = 20$. Suppose the following discount schedule applies:

$$
\begin{array}{llll}
c_1 = 15 & \text{for} & y < 200 \\
c_2 = 14 & \text{for} & 200 \le y < 250 \\
c_3 = 13 & \text{for} & y \ge 250
\end{array}
$$

In addition, we adapt equation (8.10) to evaluate various points on the curves $G_i(y)$, and we obtain

$$G_i(y) = r(\mu - y)F(y) - r\sigma f(y) + ry - c_i y \qquad (8.14)$$

As before, $f(y)$ denotes the height of the normal density function at y, and $F(y)$ represents the area to the left of y under the density function for demand.

First we evaluate the options on the top curve. For $c_3 = 13$ the critical ratio is $(20 - 13)/20 = 0.35$, implying $y_3 = 181$. Because this quantity is infeasible, the best feasible value will be found at $y = b_2 = 250$. Using equation (8.14) we obtain

$$G_3(250) = 20(-50)(0.8413) - 20(50)(0.2420) + 20(250) - 13(250) = 666.7$$

On the middle curve, $c_2 = 14$, and the critical ratio is $(20 - 14)/20 = 0.30$, implying $y_2 = 174$. Because this quantity is also infeasible, the best feasible value will be found at $y = b_1 = 200$. Using equation (8.14) we obtain

$$G_2(200) = 20(0)(0.5) - 20(50)(0.3989) + 20(200) - 14(200) = 801.1$$

Therefore, the best expected profit available at a unit cost of 14 exceeds the best expected profit available at a unit cost of 13. Finally, on the lowest curve, $c_1 = 15$, and the critical ratio is 0.25, implying $y_1 = 166$. This quantity is feasible, and from equation (8.14) we obtain

$$G_1(166) = 20(34)(0.25) - 20(50)(0.3166) + 20(166) - 15(166) = 683.4$$

We conclude that the optimal supply quantity is 200.

The case of quantity discounts illustrates how we can analyze some modifications of the purchase cost in the basic newsboy model. At the heart of this analysis is the critical ratio, which is used repeatedly in the calculations that accompany the expected profit functions sketched in Figure 8.5.

GENERALIZATIONS

The quantity $(r - c)/r$ which appears in the optimality condition of the newsboy analysis is often called the **critical ratio.** This ratio has a general interpretation that arises even in somewhat different situations, such as those characterized by salvage costs or penalty costs.

In general, we can define the concept of a **unit shortage cost** as the answer to the following question. Suppose that demand exceeds supply ($X > y$); then how much better off would the newsboy have been by stocking one unit more? In the basic problem the answer is $(r - c)$, since he would have to pay c for the additional paper in order to realize the added revenue of r.

We can also define a **unit surplus cost** in a similar fashion. Suppose that supply exceeds demand ($y > X$); then how much better off would the newsboy have been by stocking one unit less? Here the answer is c, since he would have saved the amount of this purchase while revenues would not have been affected. Thus, we conclude that

unit shortage cost $= r - c$

unit surplus cost $\quad = c$

and we interpret the critical ratio (CR) as follows:

$$CR = \frac{\text{unit shortage cost}}{\text{unit shortage cost} + \text{unit surplus cost}}$$

Then, in the discrete case, the optimality condition becomes

$$F(y^* - 1) < CR \leq F(y^*) \tag{8.15}$$

and in the continuous case we have

$$F(y^*) = CR \tag{8.16}$$

This structure is characteristic of all newsboy-type models when the criterion involves maximizing the expected payoff.

For example, suppose that we modify the newsboy's problem so that at the end of the day he can return unsold papers for a salvage value of s per paper, where we assume $s < c$. In this situation we can identify the unit shortage and surplus costs by answering the two questions suggested above. We conclude:

unit shortage cost $= r - c$

unit surplus cost $\quad = c - s$

Here the surplus cost reflects the fact that the newsboy pays an amount c for each unsold paper but receives an amount s for each unsold paper he returns. Then the critical ratio becomes

$$CR = \frac{r - c}{r - s}$$

For instance, if $c = 5$, $r = 20$, and $s = 3$, and demand follows a Poisson distribution with mean 16, then the critical ratio is

$$CR = \frac{r - c}{r - s} = \frac{20 - 5}{20 - 3} = \frac{15}{17} = 0.8824$$

Upon examining the table of cumulative Poisson probabilities (Table 8.1), we find that $y^* = 21$ in this case (as compared to $y^* = 19$ when there was no salvage value.)

To trace the relationship between this result and the elements of decision analysis, consider how to calculate regrets (or opportunity losses) in the newsboy problem. Recall that for a given state and action the regret is equal to the difference between the payoff for that state and action and the payoff under the best action for that state. In the newsboy context, the best action for a demand-state equal to X is the supply-action $y = X$. We can define the regret for demand X and supply y to be $R(X, y)$, where

$$R(X, y) = [(r - c)X] - [r \min\{X, y\} - cy]$$

When $X = y + 1$ the regret is

$$R(y + 1, y) = (r - c)(y + 1) - ry + cy = r - c$$

Similarly, when $X = y - 1$ the regret is

$$R(y - 1, y) = (r - c)(y - 1) - r(y - 1) + cy = c$$

Thus, the unit shortage cost is $R(y + 1, y)$, the regret for a shortage of one item, and the unit surplus cost is $R(y - 1, y)$, the regret for a surplus of one item.

Once we set the stock level y, the regret is a function of X. In fact, this regret function is the V-shaped function shown in Figure 8.8. For simplicity, let α

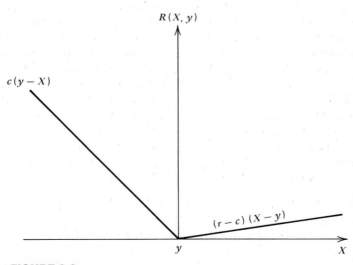

FIGURE 8.8

denote the unit shortage cost and let β denote the unit surplus cost. We interpret α as the slope of the regret function for shortage and β as the slope for surplus. The optimal supply quantity is given (in the continuous case) by

$$F(y^*) = \frac{\alpha}{(\alpha + \beta)} \tag{8.17}$$

This result suggests a way of solving newsboy-type problems with linear cost structures involving components other than just unit price and unit cost. First identify the unit shortage and surplus costs; then utilize equation (8.17) to determine y^*.

As an example, think of a large bank that centrally processes the checks received from all of its branches. Checks are routinely picked up by couriers and brought to the central processing office throughout the day. The problem is to determine how large a staff to employ for processing checks. In this scenario the random variable is demand for the check processing service. From company records on check processing it should be possible to develop a satisfactory probability model for the daily demand for staff. The decision to employ a particular staff size must recognize the risks of too small or too large a staff:

The unit surplus cost (for too large a staff) involves the wages and fringe benefits paid to idle staff members.

The unit shortage cost (for too small a staff) involves the premiums paid to staff members who work overtime to complete the processing task.

Thus, we can calculate the optimal staff size y^* from equation (8.17) where α represents the hourly overtime premium and β represents the hourly regular payroll cost, while $F(y)$ represents the cdf for the demand for staff.

As another example, consider a mining company that purchases a large, specialized piece of drilling machinery, with plans to use the machinery extensively for several years. Because of the heavy use, there will likely be a need to replace the electric motor one or more times during the life of the equipment. After the initial purchase, however, the manufacturer will charge a premium for replacement motors. The problem for the mining company is to determine how many spare motors to buy initially, at the lower price. In this scenario the random variable is the demand for replacement motors. The mining company would want to develop a probability distribution for the number of spares needed over the life of the equipment. The decision to purchase spares initially must recognize the risks of oversupply and undersupply.

The unit surplus cost (oversupply) is the initial cost of a spare, possibly mitigated by its salvage value several years later.

The unit shortage cost (undersupply) is the difference between the premium replacement cost and the initial cost of a spare.

Thus, we could derive the optimal number of spares from equation (8.11), where α represents the additional premium in the price of a replacement motor and β represents the initial price less salvage value, while $F(y)$ represents the cdf for the number of replacement motors needed over the life of the equipment.

THE NEWSBOY'S RISK

Thus far, our analysis has focused on the criterion of maximizing expected profit. This criterion is appropriate in the newsboy problem because the decision problem is a recurring one, and expected daily profit is equivalent to long-run average daily profit. Similarly, when we encounter recurring decision problems involving the trade-off between shortage and surplus in an uncertain environment, we can appropriately use a criterion of maximum expected payoff, for that will be consistent with maximizing long-run payoffs. However, if the decision problem is a one-time situation rather than a recurring one, it may also be relevant to consider risk.

To suggest how to confront exposure to risk in the general problem, let us return to a newsboy scenario in which the newsboy might be concerned about the chances of suffering a loss. We can clarify this concern with the help of some additional analysis.

For a supply quantity of y papers the cost is cy. The newsboy will just break even if $rX = cy$. Let x_0 denote the breakeven demand outcome, so that $rx_0 = cy$ or $x_0 = cy/r$. It follows that

If $X \le x_0$ the newsboy realizes no profit.

If $X > x_0$ the newsboy realizes a profit.

The newsboy's probability of making a profit is

$$P(X > x_0) = 1 - P(X \le x_0) = 1 - F(x_0) = 1 - F(cy/r) \tag{8.18}$$

As we might expect, this is a decreasing function of the decision variable y. The probability of making a profit decreases as y increases, although we saw earlier that the expected profit peaks at some intermediate value. For a continuous probability model this relationship takes the form shown in Figure 8.9. It is clear from the graph that the newsboy may be faced with a trade-off of expected profit and the probability of realizing a profit. If he is dissatisfied with the probability of realizing a profit at y^*, he can increase the probability only by sacrificing expected profit.

As an example, let $c = 15$ and $r = 20$ and suppose that demand follows a normal distribution with mean $\mu = 200$ and standard deviation $\sigma = 50$. We saw earlier that in this situation the optimal supply quantity is $y^* = 166$ and the

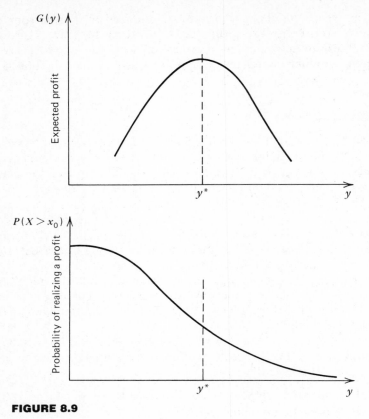

FIGURE 8.9

optimal expected profit is $G(y^*) = 683$. From equation (8.18) we can also calculate the probability of realizing a profit:

$$1 - F(cy^*/r) = 1 - F[15(166)/20] = 1 - F(125) = 0.933$$

The newsboy may not be entirely satisfied with a 93.3% chance of making a profit, but if he wants to increase this value he will have to tolerate a decrease in the expected profit. The table below shows some representative supply quantities to illustrate the trade-off.

Supply y	Expected Profit $G(y)$	Profit Probability $P(X > x_0)$
166	683	0.933
157	677	0.95
131	617	0.975
112	544	0.99

A more formal way to deal with risk in this situation is to view the newsboy's problem as one of constrained optimization:

maximize expected profit
subject to achieving a probability P of earning a profit.

In symbols, this is

maximize

$G(y)$

subject to

$$1 - F(cy/r) \geq P$$

Using the information in Figure 8.9, we can find a solution to the constrained problem by the method of Algorithm 8.1. Thus, one fundamental way to accommodate the trade-off between risk and expected value is to pose the newsboy's problem in terms of constrained optimization. The role of the constraint is to limit the probability of realizing no profit. In general, we could define an exposure level Z_0 and then impose a constraint to limit the probability that the outcome fails to exceed Z_0.

ALGORITHM 8.1
A Solution Method for the Constrained Newsboy Problem

1. Determine y^*, the value that maximizes $G(y)$.

2. Test the probability constraint to determine whether $1 - F(cy/r) \geq P$.

3. If so, stop; the risk constraint is not active and y^* is the solution. Otherwise, proceed; the risk constraint will determine the solution.

4. A smaller supply quantity is needed to satisfy the risk constraint. Because $G(y)$ decreases as y decreases, the supply level should be reduced only enough to meet the constraint. Therefore, determine an optimal y value from $F(cy/r) = 1 - P$.

SENSITIVITY ANALYSIS

In the newsboy model, it is possible to examine the sensitivity of the solution to changes in the cost parameters by varying the critical ratio. For example, in the continuous case, changes in r or c lead to an observable change in y^* via the

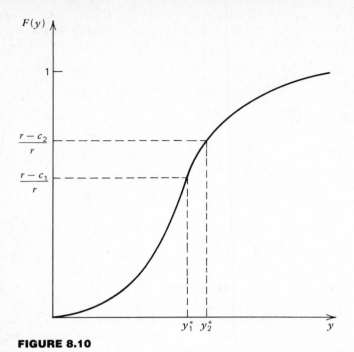

FIGURE 8.10

relationship $F(y^*) = (r - c)/r$. This effect is displayed in Figure 8.10. It is easy to see graphically that y^* increases as c decreases. In particular, suppose that the unit cost is changed from c_1 to a smaller value, c_2. As we observed previously, this change leads to an increase in the value of the critical ratio which, in turn, leads to an increase in the optimal supply quantity from y_1^* to y_2^*. The direction of this change should be intuitive: The lower unit cost implies both a larger unit shortage cost and a smaller unit surplus cost. These changes induce the newsboy to stock a larger number of papers.

In general, we can use a graph such as the one in Figure 8.10 to trace the effects of changes in the cost structure, via their impact on the critical ratio. In addition, we can use the same type of graph to trace the effects of changes in the demand distribution.

An additional facet of sensitivity analysis arises in newsboy-type problems. When supply is inadequate to meet demand, certain customer requests go unfilled, causing customer dissatisfaction. This type of reaction accounts for intangible costs that add to the tangible costs of shortage. Intangible penalty costs, such as the loss of customer goodwill, are obviously quite difficult to measure, but they can sometimes be measured indirectly.

Let b denote the intangible penalty cost facing the newsboy. This means that the cost structure consists of

unit shortage cost = $r - c + b$

unit surplus cost = c

and the form of the optimal decision is given by

$$F(y^*) = \frac{r - c + b}{r + b}$$

From this relationship we can determine the value of b that would justify any particular stock level y^*. Conversely, if the newsboy can specify a stock level that he believes will properly account for the intangible costs involved, we can calculate the implied value of b. This approach allows for an indirect calculation of the intangible cost, and the parameter value determined this way is sometimes called an **imputed** cost.

As an example, let $c = 15$ and $r = 20$ and suppose that demand follows a normal distribution with mean $\mu = 200$ and standard deviation $\sigma = 50$. From our earlier analysis we know that without a penalty cost the optimal order quantity is $y^* = 166$. Now, however, let us suppose that the newsboy believes that a stock level of $y^* = 200$ is necessary to account for the intangible shortage costs. Because the mean of the demand distribution is 200, we know that $F(y^*) = 0.50$. Thus, we know

$$\frac{r - c + b}{r + b} = 0.50$$

or

$$\frac{20 - 15 + b}{20 + b} = 0.50$$

or

$$b = 10$$

In other words, the choice of $y^* = 200$ as the stock level implies an intangible shortage cost of $0.10 per paper.

We can get some insight into questions of structural validity in sensitivity analysis with an alternative interpretation of the newsboy model, emphasizing forecasting. The mean of the demand distribution in the newsboy's problem may be viewed as a forecast for demand, and the difference between this value and actual demand may be viewed as a forecast error. Thus, the newsboy model represents a general class of problems in which an unknown quantity is to be estimated and in which opportunity costs (regrets) are proportional to estimation errors. In the basic model the form of the cost function $R(X, y)$ is linear on either side of actual demand:

$$\begin{aligned} R(X, y) &= \alpha(y - X) & \text{if} \quad X \leq y \\ &= \beta(X - y) & \text{if} \quad X > y \end{aligned}$$

From this perspective, the newsboy recognizes the possibility of a forecast error and selects a supply level y^* that may differ from the demand forecast $E[X]$. The difference between y^* and $E[X]$ reflects the nature of the forecast distribution and also the structure of the cost function. Specifically, if the distribution of forecast errors is symmetric with a mean of 0 and if the cost function $R(X, y)$ is also symmetric, then the optimal supply level will always match the forecast. However, if there is asymmetry either in the distribution of forecast errors or in the cost function, then the optimal supply may well differ from the demand forecast.

In the elementary newsboy problem the cost function is linear, but more generally, the cost function may be nonlinear. In large companies, major operating decisions are driven by forecast data, but in such complicated problems it may not be logical to assume that costs due to forecast errors follow a linear structure. The two variations below suggest some possible alternative structures.

QUADRATIC LOSSES

$$\begin{aligned} R(X, y) &= \alpha(y - X)^2 & \text{if} \quad X \leq y \\ &= \beta(X - y)^2 & \text{if} \quad X > y \end{aligned}$$

Here the marginal cost due to a forecast error increases with the size of the error, and large errors are penalized relatively more heavily than small errors.

LUMP-SUM LOSSES

$$\begin{aligned} R(X, y) &= \alpha(y - X) & \text{if} \quad X \leq y \\ &= \gamma + \beta(X - y) & \text{if} \quad X > y \end{aligned}$$

Here a lump-sum cost, or **fixed charge,** is associated with any shortage; otherwise the cost function is linear.

We can utilize the same algebraic approach that yielded an optimal policy for the newsboy model to determine analogous results for the nonlinear models above. A comparison of such results can demonstrate the effect of a change in the structure of the cost function on the optimal policy.

SUMMARY

A common management problem requires a supply decision to be made in the face of uncertain demand. An analogous problem arises where planning decisions are based on forecast information, but where the forecast is subject to error. This kind of problem often contains the special structure of a newsboy model for the trade-off of surplus and shortage outcomes under uncertainty.

In this trade-off the important decision variable is the supply quantity. The economic parameters in the problem describe purchase or production costs, sales revenues, salvage values, and shortage penalties. In addition, an essential feature is a probability model to describe our uncertainty about demand. In practical applications of newsboy analysis there are two possible sources of information from which it is possible to build this probability model. First, there is historical data. If the demand process has been observed in the past there is at least some statistical information available. In this case it might be possible to fit a theoretical model to existing data (using statistical techniques for distribution fitting), or to use the data to construct a frequency distribution. On the other hand, historical data may not exist. If the demand process has not been observed, or if new conditions apply, then the most appropriate approach might be to develop a subjective probability model based on the perceptions of those people most knowledgeable about demand prospects.

In any event, the development of a probability distribution is a crucial step. As the analysis of the model indicates, information about the distribution is vital to the determination of a decision that maximizes expected payoffs. The same kind of information is also vital to considerations of risk versus return. Therefore, one valuable lesson from the analysis of the model is that the appropriate information to be gathered in specifying the problem should include distribution information to describe uncertainty.

Optimization in the model leads to a simple rule for selecting a supply quantity. Sometimes this rule can be expressed as a formula, in which case it is easy to trace the impact of parameters on the ultimate decision. In other cases the rule can be interpreted conveniently with the aid of tables and graphs, but the role of parameters is still easily traced. The rule for determining an optimal decision demonstrates how cost structure information and probability information are combined in order to select an action. The analysis also shows that planning decisions might consciously be made above or below a given forecast, depending on the shortage and surplus costs at stake and on the relative likelihoods of potential outcomes. Finally, the model and the analysis lend themselves well to sensitivity studies involving questions of parametric validity and also, to some extent, questions of structural validity.

EXERCISES

NEWSBOY ANALYSIS

1 Jeff's Bakery sells a special cheesecake on Saturdays as its *piecè de resistance*. Jeff bakes the cheesecakes late Friday night for the next day, but does not have time to bake additional ones on Saturday if he runs out. Because of the special ingredients in the recipe, and Jeff's unwillingness to freeze leftovers for the next week, surplus pastries are simply thrown away Saturday night (or eaten by the staff). The ingredients in the recipe cost a total of $2.50, and Jeff sets the selling price at $6.00. The data collected so far suggests that demand for the cheesecake follows a Poisson distribution with a mean of 10.

   a How many cheesecakes should Jeff bake each Friday night?

   b What is the expected profit each week under this policy?

2 A news shop stocks copies of foreign newspapers for interested customers. One particular weekly edition is purchased for $0.15 each and sold locally for $1.25. Demand for this particular paper appears to follow the geometric distribution shown below:

$$P_j = (1 - \theta)\theta^{j-1} \quad j = 1, 2, \ldots$$

where $\theta = 0.4$.

   a What is the optimal number of papers for the store to stock?

   b Under the optimal policy, what is the store's expected profit?

3 While at home for Christmas vacation, Pete Levinson, an enterprising college student, decides to sell Christmas trees to make some extra money. He plans to buy trees from a local forest products company for $5 each, and he expects to sell them for $15 each. Pete can order a number of trees to be delivered on December 18 so that we will have 1 week to sell them, but he will not be able to reorder if he runs out. He will also be stuck with any surplus that remains at the end of the week. Pete's assessment is that demand for his trees will follow a normal distribution with $\mu = 60$ and $\sigma = 10$.

   a How many trees should he buy in order to maximize his expected profit?

   b What is the expected profit for the policy in (a)?

   c For the order quantity in (a), what is the probability that Pete will make a profit?

4 Review Exercise 3. Suppose that the forest products company offers Pete a quantity discount. If he purchases 75 or more trees, the unit cost will be only $4 each.

   a If Pete's objective is to maximize expected profit, how does the quantity discount opportunity change his order?

b For the order quantity in (a), what is the probability that Pete will make a profit?

5 The campus student union normally sells beer on Friday afternoon, but for March 17 this year, the management has decided to offer "Green Grog." This special drink will contain $0.10 worth of ingredients in a pint, which will sell for $0.20. Green Grog must be made the day before it is to be sold, but it spoils so quickly that any surplus will have to be thrown away. Demand for Green Grog is difficult to anticipate, since the weather will be a critical factor, as will be campus morale after midterm exams. The bartender believes that the day's demand for drinks can adequately be modeled as following an exponential distribution with a mean of 200. For this distribution, $F(x) = 1 - e^{-x/200}$

a How many pints of Green Grog should be made to maximize the student union's expected payoff?

b Given the policy determined in (a), what is the probability that demand will not be completely met?

c How many pints should be made in order to reduce the probability in (b) by half?

SHORTAGE/SURPLUS ANALYSIS

6 Review the Christmas tree problem, Exercise 3. Suppose Pete discovers someone who agrees to purchase any surplus trees after Christmas for $3 each.

a How many trees should Pete buy in this case?

b Calculate his expected profit under the policy in (a).

7 A travel agency offers its customers a special deal on round-trip excursion flights to Europe. For a service charge of $50 per ticket the agency will book them on an affinity group flight and in return they will be able to save over $100 on the fare. For his part, the travel agent is required to reserve a block of at least 10 seats well in advance of the flight to qualify for the reduced fare. He also must give the airline a deposit of $25 per seat, which he loses for each reserved seat he fails to sell. Based on prior experience, the travel agent has concluded that for each offering the demand for his affinity group deal is Poisson-distributed with a mean of 12. How many seats should he reserve in order to maximize his expected profits? (The agency receives no income for this service other than the service charge.) What is the maximum expected profit?

8 A large printing company wishes to determine how many extra rollers to purchase with its new printing presses. In the event that the machine breaks down and there are no extra rollers, the downtime would cost $20,000. The cost of an additional roller at the time the presses are purchased is $500. Subsequent to this, however, a roller would cost $1500. The probability distribution of roller failures during the lifetime of the presses is given by the manufacturer as follows:

Number of Failures	Probability
0	0.73
1	0.12
2	0.07
3	0.04
4	0.02
5	0.015
6	0.005

How many rollers should be purchased with the presses in order to minimize total costs?

9 The Merritt Computer Company has decided to enter the market for home computers. Although there is considerable uncertainty about how large this market will be, the firm has space available for up to six assembly lines on which the computers can be manufactured. According to engineering estimates, each assembly line has the capacity to produce 1000 units during the coming year. In addition, the marketing department has produced the following probability distribution to describe the firm's demand for the year:

Units	1000	2000	3000	4000	5000	6000
Probability	0.1	0.2	0.3	0.2	0.1	0.1

The fixed cost to the company of setting up an assembly line is $15,000. Furthermore, if too few lines are set up, the company will incur penalty costs due to lost sales estimated to be $40 per unit.

a How many lines should be set up if the firm's objective is to minimize the expected total cost (fixed cost plus penalty cost)?

b Actually, the cost accountant is not confident that his $15,000 figure is a precise estimate of the fixed cost. For what values of the fixed cost would the policy determined in part (a) remain optimal?

c For part (a) calculate the *EVPI*.

10 The Customer Service Department of the Piedmont Power Company is responsible for processing all payments of utility bills by retail customers served by PPC. The department faces a great deal of paperwork each week, and one important issue is how large a clerical staff to maintain. If too large a staff is hired, PPC essentially pays clerical employees (whose average salary is $200 per week) for nonproductive time. On the other hand, if the staff size is too small, PPC must pay time-and-a-half overtime rates to perform the work on time.

A time study indicates that a staff member processes 320 bills per week, on the average. PPC has a "rolling invoice" system that generates a rather stable weekly load of paperwork. Existing records suggest that the number of bills that arrive in a typical week follows a normal distribution with mean $\mu = 16,000$ and standard deviation $\sigma = 2000$. The policy at PPC is to process in a given week all payments that arrive during the week, even if overtime is required. (This policy has been dictated by the Finance Department, which is concerned about the opportunity cost of interest foregone on customer payments that have been received but not yet processed.)

Formulate the problem of determining an appropriate number of clerical employees in the Customer Service Department, and recommend a specific staff size.

SENSITIVITY ANALYSIS

11 Toppin's Candy Store plans to stock a number of chocolate bunnies for the Easter season. The store's proprietor, Ms. Toppin, must place an order with the manufacturer of the chocolate bunnies several weeks in advance and will not be able to obtain an additional supply if the original order fails to meet demand. On the other hand, if there is a surplus she plans to simply donate the leftovers to charity, since there is little demand for chocolate bunnies after Easter and there is limited shelf space in her small store. The chocolate bunnies are purchased for $0.50 each and sell for $1.50 each. At the time the order must be placed, Ms. Toppin believes that demand at her store can be modeled as following a normal distribution with parameters $\mu = 250$ and $\sigma = 40$.

a What would be the optimal order size for maximizing expected profit on the bunnies?

b What would be the expected profit under the policy in (a)?

c Ms. Toppin has tentatively decided on an order size of 350 bunnies. She reasons that there is actually an intangible good-will cost for any customer who cannot buy a bunny because of a stockout, and she knows that a stock level of 350 provides a very high probability that all demand will be met. Suppose there were a penalty cost of Q per unit for shortages. What would the value of Q have to be in order to justify an optimal order of 350?

12 Review Exercise 3. Suppose that Pete feels certain he can find someone willing to buy his surplus trees but he is not sure what the salvage price will be. What unit price on surplus trees will justify a purchase of 75 trees?

13 Review Exercise 7. Suppose that the travel agent decides that the reputation of the agency will suffer if customer demands cannot be accommodated, and potential future sales will be lost. For this reason the agent decides to reserve 22 seats. What is the imputed cost per unit of customer ill-will produced by shortages?

CONCEPTUAL ISSUES

14 In the general problem of trading-off shortage and surplus outcomes, suppose that the following regret functions are specified:

$$R(X, y) = \alpha(X - y) \quad \text{if} \quad X \geq y$$
$$= \beta(y - X) \quad \text{if} \quad X \leq y$$

Derive the form of the optimal action y^* for minimizing expected regret. In other words show that y^* is defined by

$$F(y^* - 1) < \frac{\alpha}{\alpha + \beta} \leq F(y^*)$$

15 Derive an expression for the probability that the newsboy's profit exceeds p^*. Verify that equation (8.18) holds for the special case $p^* = 0$.

16 Using graphical arguments, describe how to solve the following constrained optimization version of the newsboy problem:

Maximize the probability of realizing a profit subject to achieving an expected profit of at least p^*.

Chapter 9
FORECASTING MODELS

Mason Appliances Company

Mason Appliances Company sells radios, television sets, air conditioners, and other electric appliances to customers in a large urban area. Recently its financial manager has become concerned about the increasing amounts of money required to support the firm's unique "Lay-A-Way" credit program. Next week she will be renegotiating Mason's line of credit with a local bank. Before dealing with the bank she would like to know the firm's expected sales by product line for each of the next 12 months. With this information and her knowledge of the product mix, unit prices, and the percentage of units bought on credit she will be able to estimate the total cash requirements of the "Lay-A-Way" program. Fortunately, she has the following information for the past 2 years of sales:

Period	Radio	TV	Air Conditioner	Period	Radio	TV	Air Conditioner
1	34	17	4	13	30	48	5
2	44	19	2	14	42	57	4
3	42	24	5	15	32	62	11
4	30	22	8	16	38	59	13
5	46	25	11	17	54	59	18
6	44	27	13	18	44	70	22
7	56	30	18	19	46	78	27
8	50	33	15	20	34	65	23
9	38	36	9	21	32	59	17
10	44	41	6	22	40	76	12
11	46	60	5	23	46	79	13
12	36	45	4	24	38	82	9

TABLE 9.1

Type	Use	Function	Time Horizon
Market forecast	Guide R&D planning and facilities	Top-management Planning	1–20 years
Financial forecast	Estimate future profits, cash flow, and capital requirements	Finance Accounting	1 month–3 years
Sales forecast	Plan sales campaigns, promotions, and other market strategies	Marketing	1 month–1 year
Operations forecast	Plan capacity utilization and inventory levels, schedule production, determine work-force size and number of shifts	Operations	1 week–1 year

The problem facing Mason Appliances involves forecasting. Specifically, Mason's financial manager has information about the past 24 months of demand for radios, televisions, and air conditioners. Given these data, she would like to have an estimate of monthly sales for these product lines for the next year. She needs a forecasting model that will take the past 24 values of demand and produce an estimate of the next value and all future values.

In general, forecasts provide useful inputs for the planning activities in the operations, marketing, and financial functions of a firm. Many surveys of large companies have shown that forecasting is believed to be either "critical" or "important" to the success of the companies. Other surveys have shown that forecasting techniques are the most widely used of all quantitative methods.

There are many uses of forecasts in today's business environment. Table 9.1 illustrates some different types of forecasts for various functions. It also shows some of the different forecasting time horizons—that is, how far into the future the forecasts must predict.

Table 9.1 also helps point out a major difference between forecasting models and the other models we have studied—the use of the model's results. In other situations we have discussed the use of models to aid in decision making. In those situations the model's output influences decisions directly. Here we will discuss forecasting models, which may not be as useful by themselves. Instead, they provide useful inputs for other models. Thus, the output of the forecasting model influences the decision indirectly, through other models. For Mason Appliances the sales forecasts will be used in the company's financial model to help plan the firm's cash-flow requirements. Elsewhere, we might use forecasting models to predict demands, arrival rates, service rates, machine efficiencies, activity times, purchase costs, or labor productivities.

Before discussing specific forecasting models it is useful to point out that these models are only part of a larger forecasting system, such as that illustrated in Figure 9.1. Note that there are three main activities in the system: forecast generation, management judgment, and forecast monitoring. In this system forecasts for a future event are generated using quantitative and/or qualitative techniques. These forecasts *may* be modified using management judgment to produce a modified forecast or prediction that is used for planning purposes. This approach may be based on a sequence of past observations of the quantity to be forecasted, that is, a **time series,** or on forecasts for external data about the economy, competitors, or the weather. Another important component of the forecasting system is the continual monitoring of the forecasting performance. The monitoring activity involves comparing the actual value that occurred with what had been predicted. The size and direction of these differences are helpful in adjusting the forecast generation process and in influencing managerial judgment.

In this chapter we examine several general approaches to forecast generation. We concentrate on the techniques of time series analysis, which extrapo-

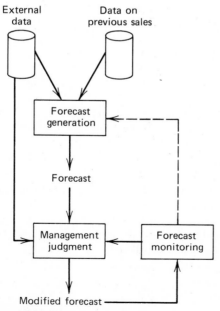

FIGURE 9.1

lates historical data into the future. Within the area of time series analysis, we focus primarily on the methods of exponential smoothing, which is a simple but powerful approach to short-term forecasting. Finally, we examine two important methods for monitoring and controlling forecasts.

GENERAL APPROACHES TO FORECASTING

There are three general classes of techniques for forecasting: qualitative, causal, and time series. The characteristics of the methods are described below.

Qualitative techniques are most useful when historical information does not exist, is not representative, or is too expensive to gather and analyze. In such cases qualitative techniques essentially substitute human judgment for historical data. The objective of these procedures is to bring together in a logical, unbiased, and systematic way all relevant information about future behavior of the item for which forecasts are required. Such information obviously includes the opinions of experts. Some typical qualitative techniques include sales-force composites, Delphi or panel methods, and historical analogies. Although such techniques can yield good results, a drawback is that they can take a great deal of time to implement and can be quite costly.

If adequate historical data exist, then it is possible to use a quantitative forecasting technique. Many such techniques are available, ranging from very sophisticated methods containing hundreds of equations and variables to very simple "quick-and-dirty" approaches that are easy to implement. Both causal techniques and time series methods fall in the category of **quantitative** forecasting approaches.

Causal procedures attempt to use knowledge about one or more known factors (called independent variables) to predict the value of another factor (called a dependent variable). For example, the demand for a product might be forecasted on the basis of its price, advertising and promotion levels, quality control expenditures, disposable personal income, or other variables. Causal techniques often rely on statistical regression methods to determine the relationship between the dependent variable and the independent variables. Causal approaches are useful for investigating policy questions, since in addition to providing a forecast they show relationships among variables. For example, the use of a regression method makes it possible to explore the impact of different advertising expenditures on a product's demand. These techniques typically require significant amounts of data and can also be expensive and time consuming. Further, the predictions of future values of the dependent variable rely on predictions of each of the independent variables. Thus, we can think of a causal technique as a two-stage procedure in which we must first forecast the values of the independent variables and then use these forecasts to produce the forecast of the dependent variable.

A **time series** is a set of data arranged in chronological order; a good example is monthly sales for each of the three product lines at Mason Appliances

Company. Time series methods rely solely on the analysis of historical data and its extrapolation into the future. They differ from the causal techniques because they do not consider relationships among variables. Such techniques are relatively simple to use and can be quite accurate for short-range forecasting. As a result, they are extremely useful in an operations setting where it is necessary to produce forecasts for hundreds or even thousands of items.

In what follows we concentrate on the techniques of time series analysis. The reason for doing so is one of practicality. For a large number of situations time series analysis is simple to implement and has sufficient accuracy so that it is the forecasting method of choice.

OVERVIEW OF TIME SERIES METHODOLOGY

The process of developing a time series model for some item of interest is depicted in Figure 9.2. It consists of the following steps:

1. Analysis of historical data.
2. Identification of a forecasting technique.
3. Estimation of parameters.

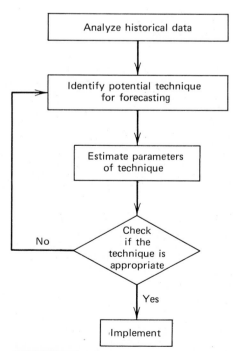

FIGURE 9.2

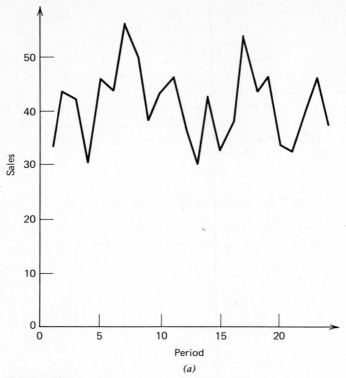

FIGURE 9.3

4. Checks of the model's appropriateness.
5. Implementation of the model.

The process begins with the analysis of representative historical data. This step assists in hypothesizing the form of a model for the data and thus in selecting an appropriate time series method. This analysis is typically done by plotting the data and examining it to identify the underlying components of the pattern, including **base level, trend, seasonal variation, cyclicals,** and **randomness.**

The base level represents the relatively constant behavior of the time series. Figure 9.3*a* depicts such a pattern for the sales of radios at Mason Appliances. Note that the pattern is not completely level—it is somewhat obscured by random fluctuations. As a result, an appropriate model for this pattern might be

$$d_t = a + e_t \tag{9.1}$$

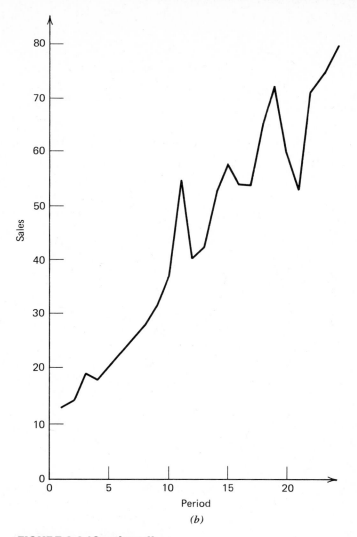

FIGURE 9.3 (Continued)

where

> d_t = actual observation in period t
>
> a = base level
>
> e_t = random fluctuation in period t

In this case, the analysis of historical data would attempt to separate the systematic behavior of the data (the base level, a) from the random behavior (also

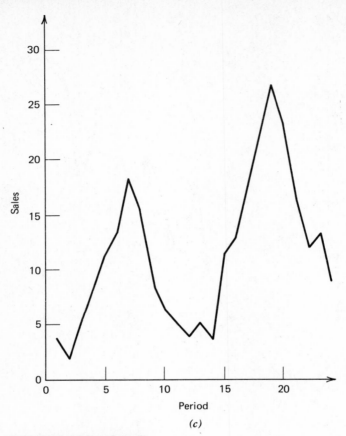

FIGURE 9.3 (Continued)

called **noise**). If the fluctuation around the base level is completely random, it cannot be predicted. Thus, an appropriate forecasting method would track the constant pattern without the noise.

Trend refers to long-term growth or decline in the time series. Figure 9.3*b* shows that the sales of televisions at Mason Appliances have such a pattern. In fact, the pattern seems to be linear. Because the sales of televisions also seem to include both a constant amount and random fluctuations, the appropriate model might be

$$d_t = a + bt + e_t \qquad (9.2)$$

where

d_t = actual observation in period t

a = base level

b = trend factor per period

e_t = random fluctuation in period t

As with the previous case, we still want to separate the systematic behavior of the time series from the random behavior. For televisions, however, this analysis of historical data is more complicated. Now there are two components of the systematic pattern—base level and trend. For such a pattern an appropriate forecasting method would track the constant and trend without the noise.

Seasonal fluctuations of the time series recur at regular, periodic intervals. From Figure 9.3c we find that such a situation exists for air conditioner sales at Mason Appliances. In this time series December (periods 12 and 24) has a low demand, while June (periods 6 and 18) has a high demand. Because this pattern repeats itself every 12 periods, we say that it has a 12-period seasonal cycle.

For the time series of Figure 9.3c we observe that a slight trend is also apparent: air conditioner sales in periods 13–24 are greater than their counterparts 12 periods earlier. Thus, our model to incorporate trend, seasonality, and a base level might be

$$d_t = (a + bt)s_t + e_t \qquad (9.3)$$

where

d_t = actual observation in period t

a = base level

b = trend factor per period

s_t = multiplicative seasonal factor for period t

e_t = random fluctuation in period t

An alternative model (with an additive seasonal factor, s_t) might be

$$d_t = a + bt + s_t + e_t \qquad (9.4)$$

In either case we would use the same approach as before: separate the systematic behavior from the noise. This time, however, the systematic behavior includes three components (base level, trend, and seasonals).

Cyclical fluctuations differ from seasonals because the length of time between fluctuations and the size of the fluctuations do not remain constant. Also, since cyclical fluctuations tend to occur at a much slower rate than seasonals, they may have large long-term effects but negligible short-term effects. Because time series analysis is much more concerned with the short term than with the long term, it does not attempt to deal with cyclicals.

As we have seen, analyzing historical data leads directly to the next step of identifying a potential forecasting technique. Based on the data analysis, we hypothesize a model (or several possible models) of the data, and this suggests a particular forecasting method or methods. For example, the analysis of television sales at Mason Appliances suggests there is an upward trend with no seasonality. As a result, we would want to select a forecasting technique that is appropriate for trend without seasonality.

It should be clear from this discussion of models that all time series techniques are based on the assumption that existing patterns will continue into the future. This assumption is more likely to be correct over the short term than it is over the long term. For this reason, time series techniques provide reasonably accurate forecasts for the immediate future, but they may do poorly further into the future.

In the third step of time series analysis we use historical data to estimate the parameters (the values of a, b, or s_t) in the formula for the technique to be tested. Then we prepare forecasts using the technique, and we compare these forecasts to actual values for some or all of the historical data by computing summary measures of the forecast errors. Based on this computation we evaluate the appropriateness of the method chosen. By "appropriate" we mean that the differences between predicted and actual values behave like random fluctuations. If the method is appropriate, we then implement it. If it is not appropriate, however, we can identify and test a new technique. Conceptually, this trial-and-error process continues until we find an appropriate method.

SIMPLE FORECASTING TECHNIQUES

There are many time series techniques for forecasting. In this section we describe some of the most simple ones: last period, arithmetic average, and moving average. These techniques would be logical when the time series has the constant behavior described in equation (9.1), although it is also important to consider how the techniques would respond to other models of behavior.

LAST PERIOD

The last-period technique simply forecasts for the next period the level that occurred in the latest period. No calculations are required, and forecasted values lag behind actual data by one period. Mathematically, we express this as

$$F_{t+1} = d_t \qquad\qquad (9.5)$$

where

F_{t+1} = forecast made at end of period t for period $t + 1$

d_t = actual observation in the previous period

Table 9.2*a* shows how this approach is implemented for the first five periods of data for Mason Appliances. For example, after period 1 our forecast for

TABLE 9.2a

Radios

Period	1	2	3	4	5
Forecast		34	44	42	30
Actual	34	44	42	30	46

Televisions

Period	1	2	3	4	5
Forecast		17	19	24	22
Actual	17	19	24	22	25

Air Conditioners

Period	1	2	3	4	5
Forecast		4	2	5	8
Actual	4	2	5	8	11

period 2 sales would be 34 radios, 17 televisions, and 4 air conditioners. Similarly, after period 2, our period 3 forecasts would be 44 radios, 19 televisions, and 2 air conditioners.

The advantage of the last-period technique is its simplicity. In addition, if we assumed the constant behavior of equation (9.1) and in reality there were trends or seasonal behaviors, we would find that the last-period technique would track these behaviors but with a lag. The main disadvantage of the last-period technique is that it does not separate random influences from systematic behavior. Because it reacts to random fluctuation, it has a high degree of variation.

ARITHMETIC AVERAGE

To avoid the variation inherent in the last-period technique we might use an averaging approach. The arithmetic average arrives at a forecast by taking the average of all past data. Mathematically we have

$$F_{t+1} = \frac{1}{t} \sum_{i=1}^{t} d_i \tag{9.6}$$

where

F_{t+1} = forecast made at end of period t for period $t + 1$

d_i = actual observation in period i

t = number of time periods in the data, a variable

TABLE 9.2b

			Radios		

Period	1	2	3	4	5
Forecast		$\dfrac{34}{1} = 34.0$	$\dfrac{34 + 44}{2} = 39.0$	$\dfrac{34 + 44 + 42}{3} = 40.0$	$\dfrac{34 + 44 + 42 + 30}{4} = 37.5$
Actual	34	44	42	30	46

			Televisions		

Period	1	2	3	4	5
Forecast		$\dfrac{17}{1} = 17.0$	$\dfrac{17 + 19}{2} = 18.0$	$\dfrac{17 + 19 + 24}{3} = 20.0$	$\dfrac{17 + 19 + 24 + 22}{4} = 20.5$
Actual	17	19	24	22	25

			Air Conditioners		

Period	1	2	3	4	5
Forecast		$\dfrac{4}{1} = 4.0$	$\dfrac{4 + 2}{2} = 3.0$	$\dfrac{4 + 2 + 5}{3} = 3.7$	$\dfrac{4 + 2 + 5 + 8}{4} = 6.3$
Actual	4	2	5	8	11

Table 9.2b shows how this approach is implemented for Mason Appliances. After period 1 we know only one period of data, so that our forecasts for period 2 are 34 radios, 17 televisions, and 4 air conditioners. After period 2 we have two periods of history. Thus, our forecasts for period 3 (of 39, 18, and 3, respectively) represent the average of two periods of data. Similarly, our forecasts for period 4 at the end of period 3 represent the average of three periods of data, and so on. By the end of period 24, our forecasts for period 25 are based on the average of all 24 previous values. The number of terms included in the average will continue to grow.

The advantage of the arithmetic average is that it separates random fluctuations from systematic behavior. It does so by "smoothing out" randomness in the averaging process: positive errors (when actual exceeds forecast) tend to cancel negative errors (when forecast exceeds actual). This cancellation removes most of the random behavior. On the other hand, this smoothing process may remove some systematic behavior as well, if there is seasonality in the time series. Another disadvantage of the arithmetic average is its poor response to trends. For example, after period 23 the arithmetic average forecast for period 24 television sales at Mason was 47.4 units, while the actual value was 82 units. The problem here seems to be that the arithmetic average method is too stable; it takes too little account of recent data and is not responsive to changes in the pattern of data.

MOVING AVERAGE

To avoid the overstability in the arithmetic average as well as the volatility of the last-period technique, some compromise seems reasonable. The moving average technique generates the next period's forecast by averaging the actual data for the last N time periods, where N is fixed.

Stated mathematically

$$F_{t+1} = \frac{1}{N} \sum_{i=1}^{N} d_{t+1-i} \tag{9.7}$$

where

F_{t+1} = forecast made at end of period t for period $t + 1$

d_{t+1-i} = actual observation in period $t + 1 - i$

N = number of time periods included in moving average

Table 9.2c depicts use of a two-period moving average for Mason Appliances. Note that this approach has several differences from the last-period and arithmetic average methods. First of all, we must wait until we have at least N periods (here two periods) of data to begin forecasting. Second, unlike with

TABLE 9.2c

			Radios		
Period	1	2	3	4	5
Forecast			$\frac{34 + 44}{2} = 39.0$	$\frac{44 + 42}{2} = 43.0$	$\frac{42 + 30}{2} = 38.0$
Actual	34	44	42	30	46

			Televisions		
Period	1	2	3	4	5
Forecast			$\frac{17 + 19}{2} = 18.0$	$\frac{19 + 24}{2} = 21.5$	$\frac{24 + 22}{2} = 23.0$
Actual	17	19	24	22	25

			Air Conditioners		
Period	1	2	3	4	5
Forecast			$\frac{4 + 2}{2} = 3.0$	$\frac{2 + 5}{2} = 3.5$	$\frac{5 + 8}{2} = 6.5$
Actual	4	2	5	8	11

arithmetic averages, there is a fixed number of periods averaged to produce the forecast. Thus, we average the data for periods 1 and 2 to forecast for period 3, we average the data for periods 2 and 3 to forecast for period 4, and so on. The key point is that whenever we acquire new information, the data for period t, we discard the oldest information, the data for period $t - N$.

With the moving average approach we have a great deal of flexibility in choosing the parameter N, the number of periods included in the averaging process. If N is 1, the moving average forecasts behave like last-period forecasts. On the other hand, if N is a large number, the moving average forecasts will resemble arithmetic average forecasts. Thus, the moving average is a compromise between the two extremes of last period and arithmetic average. In either case, however, we have to implement an averaging process, and we must store N data points.

The actual choice of N should be determined by experimentation. The general objective is to include a sufficient number of periods of data to smooth out random fluctuations but also to include a small enough number of periods to discard irrelevant information. Thus, given a data set, the choice of N might involve a trial-and-error process: we would pick a value of N, simulate how the forecasting process behaves for that value, and evaluate the results. Then we would continue the process of trying different values of N until the results appeared satisfactory.

In general, the moving average approach is attractive. It gives us the capability of smoothing, that is, allowing random fluctuations to cancel, while still maintaining some response to changes. However, although it discards old data, it gives equal weight to all of the data points included in the average. This characteristic still violates our intuition that the older a data point is, the less weight it should have. Finally, our examples from Mason Appliances show that the method has limited ability to deal with trend and seasonals.

Based on our discussion of simple forecasting techniques we can list several desirable properties. They are as follows:

1. *Advantages of Moving Averages.* A moving average will smooth random fluctuations while maintaining some responsiveness to change. In addition, moving averages have a great deal of flexibility because it is possible to use different values of N, the number of periods included in the moving average. It would be good to have this flexibility in any forecasting technique

2. *Greater Emphasis on More Recent Data.* As we discussed earlier, this characteristic is suggested by our intuition. Certainly the financial manager at Mason Appliances would agree that recent sales of radios, televisions, and air conditioners are much more indicative of future sales than are sales of 10 years ago.

3. *Small Computational Requirements.* Although this feature might not be necessary in some situations, it would be attractive in cases where it is periodi-

cally necessary to produce forecasts for hundreds or thousands of items. Furthermore, in any forecasting environment simple calculations are desirable.

4. *Small Storage Requirements.* As with calculations, data storage requirements would be important to consider when there is a need to produce a great many forecasts on a regular basis.

5. *Wide Range of Use.* The forecasting technique should have the capability to deal with both trend and seasonals.

6. *Logical Response to Errors.* The forecasting method should be easy to understand, and it should include a sensible way of updating forecasts as new observations become available.

As we shall see, the general technique of exponential smoothing has all of these properties. To explain the technique we will first ignore trend and seasonals; later we will include the capability to deal with them.

SIMPLE EXPONENTIAL SMOOTHING

As we observed earlier, the demand for radios at Mason Appliances exhibits constant behavior with some random fluctuations, and equation (9.1) is an appropriate model for this process. For the purpose of illustration, suppose that we are using a 5-month moving average for forecasting radio demand at Mason Appliances. Thus, our estimate of the base-level parameter a is the average of demand for the past five time periods. Let us call this A_t. Here the subscript t denotes that we compute the average *after* observing the data for period t.

Our forecast for period 25 follows equation (9.7). Furthermore, our use of equation (9.1) as our model of demand indicates our belief that demand follows only a constant base level with some random fluctuations. As a result, our forecast of next period's demand also represents our forecast of demand for *any* future period. Thus, if we define

F_{24+k} = forecast made at end of period 24 for period $24 + k$

then

$$F_{24+k} = A_{24} \qquad k = 1, 2, 3, \ldots$$

As a result, we find

$$F_{24+k} = A_{24} = \frac{34 + 32 + 40 + 46 + 38}{5}$$
$$= 38.0$$

When we learn d_{25}, the actual demand in month 25, we can update our estimate of a. Then in our moving average process we discard the oldest data point, the demand of 34 in period 20, and include d_{25}, the latest data point. Thus,

$$F_{25+k} = \text{forecast made at the end of period 25 for period } 25 + k$$
$$= A_{25}$$
$$= \frac{32 + 40 + 46 + 38 + d_{25}}{5}$$

We can rewrite this forecast as

$$F_{25+k} = \frac{4}{5}\left(\frac{32 + 40 + 46 + 38}{4}\right) + \frac{1}{5}(d_{25})$$
$$= \frac{4}{5}(39.0) + \frac{1}{5}(d_{25})$$

Stated in words, the components of this forecast are

$$F_{25+k} = \frac{4}{5}\binom{\text{old average}}{\text{for four periods}} + \frac{1}{5}\binom{\text{new}}{\text{data point}} \tag{9.8}$$

Note that equation (9.8) separates the moving average into two parts. The first part represents what we might call "old" information, while the second part represents "new" information.

The main advantage of this partitioning is that it suggests how we might change the relative emphasis we give to old information versus new information. Specifically, if we wanted to emphasize new information more than old, we might use a formula where the weight on new data was larger than $\frac{1}{5}$ and the weight on old data was smaller than $\frac{4}{5}$. For example, we might have

$$F_{25+k} = \frac{3.5}{5}\binom{\text{old average}}{\text{for four periods}} + \frac{1.5}{5}\binom{\text{new}}{\text{data point}} \tag{9.9}$$

Conversely, to decrease the emphasis on new information we might use weights like $\frac{4.5}{5}$ and $\frac{0.5}{5}$. In both cases we would like the weights to add to $\frac{5}{5}$ so that the forecasts would not be biased.

It is certainly possible to accomplish such an adjustment with the moving average approach. However, this kind of adjustment is built into the technique of **simple exponential smoothing.** In this technique, we use the formula

$$A_t = \alpha d_t + (1 - \alpha)A_{t-1} \qquad \text{where } 0 \le \alpha \le 1 \tag{9.10}$$

In equation (9.10), A_t is a weighted average of the actual observation in period t and the old average. The weight given to the most recent observation is α, the **smoothing constant.** Then, as with the moving average approach, the forecast for all future periods is equal to the forecast for the next period:

$$F_{t+k} = A_t \qquad k = 1, 2, 3, \ldots \tag{9.11}$$

Note that equation (9.10) takes the same basic form as equation (9.8). This means that simple exponential smoothing also takes the approach of partitioning our information into an old part and a new part. Also, we see that our choice of the smoothing constant α gives us the capability of changing our relative emphasis on old information versus new information.

We can rewrite equation (9.10) as

$$A_t = A_{t-1} + \alpha(d_t - A_{t-1}) \tag{9.12}$$

Since $F_t = A_{t-1}$, the term $(d_t - A_{t-1})$ represents the forecast error in period t; it is the difference between what actually occurred and what had been forecasted one period previously. This means that exponential smoothing gives us the capability of incorporating "learning" into our calculation of A_t, which is our estimate of a in equation (9.1). Specifically, equation (9.12) shows us that whenever we receive a new piece of information (d_t), we "learn" from it by taking our old information and adding to it a fraction (α) of the error. Our choice of α, the smoothing constant, indicates how much we want our new forecast to be influenced by the size of the error.

Let us explore the implications of these ideas by calculating some forecasts for radio sales at Mason Appliances. Suppose we know that $A_{24} = 38.0$ and that we are using $\alpha = 0.2$. Also, suppose that Mason sells 33 radios in period 25. Thus, using equation (9.10) we find

$$
\begin{aligned}
A_{25} &= \alpha d_{25} + (1 - \alpha)A_{24} \\
&= 0.2(33) + 0.8(38.0) \\
&= 37.0
\end{aligned}
$$

From equation (9.11) our forecast for period 26 (and all future periods) is

$$F_{25+1} = A_{25} = 37.0$$

In this situation the actual demand in period 25 ($d_{25} = 33$) was below the period 24 forecast for period 25 ($A_{24} = 38$). Because the actual was below the forecast, it is only logical that our new forecast, F_{25+1}, would drop slightly in an attempt to find a better estimate of the average of the demand-generating process. This is exactly what occurs mathematically. In addition, we can use equation (9.12) and our knowledge that $\alpha = 0.2$ to see how this happens. Specifically, our forecast error is -5 (demand of 33 minus forecast of 38). Also, our choice $\alpha = 0.2$ indicates our desire to respond to only 20% of the forecast error. We see that 20% of the error is -1.0; and so from equation (9.12) we obtain

$$
\begin{aligned}
A_{25} &= A_{24} + 0.2(d_{25} - A_{24}) \\
&= 38.0 - 0.2(5.0) \\
&= 38.0 - 1.0 \\
&= 37.0
\end{aligned}
$$

This is exactly the mathematical result produced by the simple approach of equation (9.10).

Now, let us go one more period, and suppose that during period 26 Mason actually sells 47 radios. Again, using equation (9.10) we find

$$
\begin{aligned}
A_{26} &= \alpha d_{26} + (1 - \alpha)A_{25} \\
&= 0.2(47) + 0.8(37.0) \\
&= 39.0
\end{aligned}
$$

and thus, from equation (9.11) our forecast for period 27 (and all future periods) is

$$
F_{26+1} = A_{26} = 39.0
$$

This time the actual demand is above the forecast, so the updating process produces a new forecast, F_{26+1}, which is slightly larger than the previous forecast. In equation (9.12), this time the error is 10 units (demand of 47 minus forecast of 37), 20% of which is 2, and as a result, the new forecast ($F_{26+1} = A_{26} = 39.0$) is larger by 2 than the old one ($F_{25+1} = A_{25} = 37.0$).

Notice that we can expand equation (9.10) as follows:

$$
A_t = \alpha d_t + (1 - \alpha)A_{t-1}
$$

but

$$
A_{t-1} = \alpha d_{t-1} + (1 - \alpha)A_{t-2}
$$

so that

$$
A_t = \alpha d_t + (1 - \alpha)[\alpha d_{t-1} + (1 - \alpha)A_{t-2}]
$$

or

$$
A_t = \alpha d_t + \alpha(1 - \alpha)d_{t-1} + (1 - \alpha)^2 A_{t-2}
$$

However,

$$A_{t-2} = \alpha d_{t-2} + (1 - \alpha)A_{t-3}$$

so that after collecting terms we find

$$A_t = \alpha d_t + \alpha(1 - \alpha)d_{t-1} + \alpha(1 - \alpha)^2 d_{t-2} + (1 - \alpha)^3 A_{t-3}$$

When we continue substituting and also recognize that $F_{t+k} = A_t$, we obtain

$$F_{t+k} = A_t = \alpha d_t + \alpha(1 - \alpha)d_{t-1} + \alpha(1 - \alpha)^2 d_{t-2} \qquad (9.13)$$
$$+ \cdots + \alpha(1 - \alpha)^x d_{t-x} + \cdots$$

Thus, A_t (and hence F_{t+k}) is an average of all previous observations. Figure 9.4 shows how the weights decline *exponentially* for previous data points. From the figure it is easy to see the origin of the term "exponential smoothing."

Note that while the weights of past data decline exponentially they never

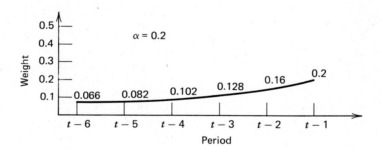

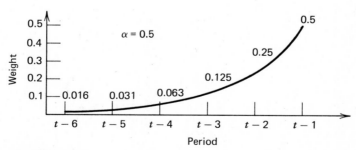

FIGURE 9.4

reach 0; some weight is placed on every past observation; hence A_t summarizes *all* past observations. The higher the value of α, the faster the weights on the past decline, or in other words, the smaller the average age in the forecast. Figure 9.4 shows the weights for two different values of the smoothing constant ($\alpha = 0.2$ and $\alpha = 0.5$).

Although a higher smoothing constant is analogous to a smaller number of periods in a moving average, there is no smoothing constant that will always yield forecasts that match those given by an N-period moving average. However, we can equate the average age of the data by setting

$$\alpha = \frac{2}{N + 1} \tag{9.14}$$

Thus, if $N = 9$ in a moving average, the comparable smoothing constant is $\alpha = 0.2$.

One advantage that exponential smoothing has over the moving average (and many other methods) is that it is necessary to store only one piece of data, the current average, at each period of time. This is one reason why exponential smoothing is so commonly used when there is a need for thousands of separate forecasts.

It is important to recognize the effects of different values of α, the smoothing constant. Table 9.3 shows the results of applying exponential smoothing to the first 12 months of data for radio sales at Mason Electronics using two

TABLE 9.3

Month	Observation	$\alpha = 0.1$ A_t	Forecast	$\alpha = 0.5$ A_t	Forecast
0	Initial value = 40			40	
1	34	39.40	40	37.00	40
2	44	39.86	39.40	40.50	37.00
3	42	40.07	39.86	41.25	40.50
4	30	39.07	40.07	35.63	41.25
5	46	39.76	39.07	40.81	35.63
6	44	40.18	39.76	42.41	40.81
7	56	41.77	40.18	49.20	42.41
8	50	42.59	41.77	49.60	49.20
9	38	42.13	42.59	43.80	49.60
10	44	42.32	42.13	43.90	43.80
11	46	42.69	42.32	44.95	43.90
12	36	42.02	42.69	40.48	44.95
13			42.02		40.48

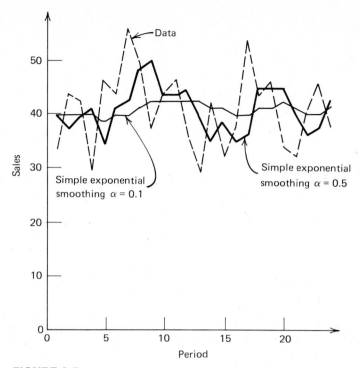

FIGURE 9.5

smoothing constants: $\alpha = 0.1$ and $\alpha = 0.5$. In order to start this process we must supply an initial value for the average. Here we arbitrarily use the value 40.0. The initial value may be subjective or based on the average of the first part of the time series. Figure 9.5 is a plot of the smoothed values from Table 9.3 (and also from the next year of observations) for the two smoothing constants. Note that the higher smoothing constant ($\alpha = 0.5$) results in more movement in the averages. It appears that the higher smoothing constant ($\alpha = 0.5$) fits the observations better than the lower one ($\alpha = 0.1$). We should not be misled into thinking that the higher value of α will give better forecasts. The average at time t is the forecast for time $t + 1$ (as shown in columns 4 and 6 of Table 9.3). For many summary measures of forecast error it turns out that the forecasts from $\alpha = 0.1$ are better.

A way to select α is to take the one that produces the most accurate forecasts. However, we should be cautious about using an equation with an α higher than about 0.5. If the most accurate forecast is for an α greater than this value, it is often the case that a better model exists. In the next section we give an example of how to modify the method when there is a trend in the data.

Now that we have examined simple exponential smoothing, which is appropriate only for a constant time series model, it is possible to consider two additional exponential smoothing methods—for time series models that have linear trend and for those that have seasonal components. These methods are extensions of simple exponential smoothing. Both methods rely on the basic approach of simple exponential smoothing expressed in the formula

$$\text{new forecast} = \left(\begin{matrix}\text{smoothing}\\\text{constant}\end{matrix}\right)\left(\begin{matrix}\text{actual}\\\text{observation}\end{matrix}\right) + \left(1 - \begin{matrix}\text{smoothing}\\\text{constant}\end{matrix}\right)\left(\begin{matrix}\text{old}\\\text{forecast}\end{matrix}\right)$$

EXPONENTIAL SMOOTHING FOR LINEAR TREND MODELS

If the historical data have a trend in it, such as the demand for televisions at Mason Appliances, simple exponential smoothing will not provide good forecasts. As long as this upward linear trend lasts, the forecast will lag (always be less than) the actual. In fact, the value of α that minimizes forecast error in this case is $\alpha = 1.0$. This is equivalent to the last-period forecasting technique. By accounting for the trend pattern in the data, however, we can produce better forecasts. To do so, we will use the linear trend model of equation (9.2).

As in simple exponential smoothing, we would like to estimate the parameter a using the averaging process. In addition, we would like to estimate b using a separate averaging process based on the trend. The Holt method uses the following equations.

$$L_t = \alpha d_t + (1 - \alpha)(L_{t-1} + T_{t-1}) \qquad 0 \le \alpha \le 1 \tag{9.15}$$
$$T_t = \beta(L_t - L_{t-1}) + (1 - \beta)T_{t-1} \qquad 0 \le \beta \le 1 \tag{9.16}$$

At time t, L_t is the estimate of a and T_t is the estimate of b in equation (9.2). Furthermore, α is the smoothing constant used for the level, and β is the smoothing constant used for the trend.

Note that equation (9.15) is not the same as equation (9.10). Figure 9.6 helps

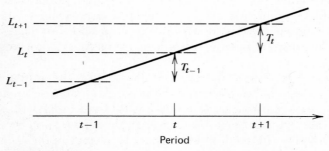

FIGURE 9.6

TABLE 9.4

$Month_t$	$Observation_t$	L_t	T_t	Forecast (made in $t-1$)
0		15.0	3.0	
1	17	17.90	2.97	18.0
2	19	20.68	2.91	20.87
3	24	23.64	2.93	23.60
4	22	26.11	2.79	26.56
5	25	28.51	2.67	28.90
6	27	30.76	2.55	31.18
7	30	32.98	2.45	33.31
8	33	35.18	2.37	35.42
9	36	37.40	2.33	37.56
10	41	39.86	2.37	39.73
11	60	44.00	2.90	42.22
12	45	46.71	2.84	46.90
13				49.55

show why. Specifically, the forecasting process is similar to climbing a ramp. At time t we are standing at level L_t, and the height of the next step is T_t. Similarly, when we are standing at L_{t-1} the term $(L_{t-1} + T_{t-1})$ represents our forecast of where on the ramp we shall be at time t. In other words, $(L_{t-1} + T_{t-1})$ is the forecast of the demand level in period t which is made at the end of period $t-1$. This change from equation (9.10) to equation (9.15) eliminates any lag in forecasting and brings the level up in accordance with the slope of the trend line. In equation (9.16) the difference in levels (which is the most recent observation of trend) is combined with the old trend estimate to construct a new estimate of the trend. In this case, the smoothing constant β is used for the trend, and it can be the same as or different from the constant α used for the level. To get started, the model requires initial estimates, L_0 and T_0. These estimates can be based either on judgment or on past data.

Using the above values, we can compute forecasts for the future. The procedure is slightly different from simple exponential smoothing, because a constant trend is assumed in the time series. The forecast made at the end of period t for period $t + k$, k periods in the future, is therefore

$$F_{t+k} = L_t + (T_t)k \qquad k = 1, 2, 3, \ldots \tag{9.17}$$

In this equation we add one unit of trend for each future period we consider.

In Table 9.4 we apply Holt's method to forecasting the first 12 months of television sales for Mason Appliances. In the table we use $\alpha = 0.1$ and $\beta = 0.3$. Also, let us assume $L_0 = 15$ and $T_0 = 3$. For example, at time 0, we calculate the forecast for k months into the future from equation (9.17):

$$F_{0+k} = L_0 + (T_0)k$$
$$= 15 + 3k$$

Thus, a forecast for month 1 ($k = 1$) is

$$F_{0+1} = 15 + (3)1 = 18$$

In month 1 the actual demand (d_1) was 17. So the level and trend values are updated according to equations (9.15) and (9.16):

$$L_1 = \alpha d_1 + (1 - \alpha)(L_0 + T_0)$$
$$= 0.1(17) + (1 - 0.1)(15 + 3)$$
$$= 17.90$$
$$T_1 = \beta(L_1 - L_0) + (1 - \beta)T_0$$
$$= 0.3(17.90 - 15) + (1 - 0.3)3$$
$$= 0.3(2.90) + 0.7(3)$$
$$= 2.97$$

The actual value in period 1 ($d_1 = 17$) was below the forecast value for period 1 ($L_0 + T_0 = 18.0$). As a result, L_1 (17.90) is lower than what we had forecasted for the level, and T_1 (2.97) is below what we had forecasted for the trend ($T_0 = 3.0$). As in simple exponential smoothing, when the actual observation is lower than the old forecast, the new forecast is also lower.

At the end of month 1 we calculate forecasts from equation (9.17) as follows:

$$F_{1+k} = L_1 + (T_1)k$$
$$= 17.90 + 2.97k$$

Thus, a forecast for month 2 ($k = 1$) is

$$F_{1+1} = 17.90 + (2.97)1 = 20.87$$

Note, that if at the end of month 1 we desire a forecast for month 5 (four periods into the future), then $k = 4$ and

$$F_{1+4} = F_5 = 17.90 + (2.97)4 = 29.78$$

The next-period forecasts from the Holt method are shown in Figure 9.7 along with forecasts from a simple exponential smoothing model.

A special case of the Holt method uses the same smoothing constant for smoothing both the level and the trend. We call this version the **trend-adjusted model.** The advantage of this method is that there is only a single smoothing constant to worry about. The disadvantage is that the method may not produce

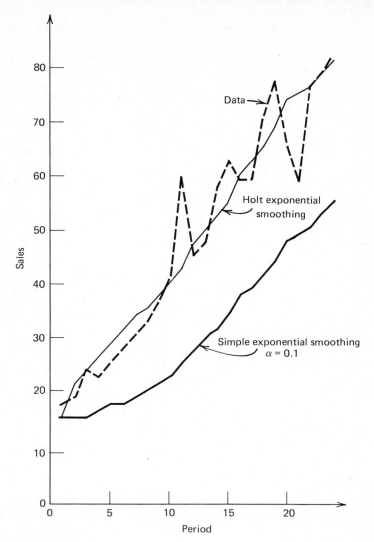

FIGURE 9.7

forecasts that are as accurate as those produced by Holt's method, which uses two smoothing constants. This difference in accuracy may result because there is no reason why the smoothing constant for the level should always equal the smoothing constant for the trend.

Other smoothing methods use nonlinear models of trend (e.g., quadratic trend) for short-term forecasting. These may not do any better than Holt's method, because over short horizons a linear trend may be a good approximation of any trend. However, more complicated trend models may be useful for forecasting over longer horizons.

EXPONENTIAL SMOOTHING FOR TREND AND SEASONALITY

As we stated earlier, seasonality is a repeating pattern with a fixed number of periods in its cycle. The seasonal cycle for monthly data is typically 12 periods long (as we see for Mason Appliances sales of air conditioners), for quarterly data four periods long, and so on. However, some exceptions may occur. For example, monthly demand for fashion goods that come out in two lines a year (winter and summer) may have a seasonal cycle of six periods.

One way to handle seasonality is to first **deseasonalize** the data and then use any of the models we discussed previously. For example, if December sales have historically been 180% of average monthly sales and January sales have historically been 70% of average sales, then we could divide December sales by 1.8 and January sales by 0.7 to deseasonalize the data. Then we could use any time series model on the deseasonalized data to forecast next month's sales. However, this would be a deseasonalized forecast. We **reseasonalize** it by multiplying by the appropriate seasonal factor (e.g., 1.8 if the forecast is for December, or 0.7 if it is for January).

The commonly used Winters method comes from the model of demand in equation (9.3). It is similar to Holt's method but uses another equation and with it an additional smoothing constant:

$$L_t = \alpha \frac{d_t}{S_{t-C}} + (1 - \alpha)(L_{t-1} + T_{t-1}) \tag{9.18}$$

$$T_t = \beta(L_t - L_{t-1}) + (1 - \beta)T_{t-1} \tag{9.19}$$

$$S_t = \gamma \frac{d_t}{L_t} + (1 - \gamma)S_{t-C} \tag{9.20}$$

where C is the length of the seasonal cycle, S_t is the seasonal factor (such as 1.8 or 0.7), and γ is the smoothing constant for the seasonal factor. Equation (9.18) differs from equation (9.15) only in that d_t is divided by S_{t-C}, the estimate of the seasonal factor for period t calculated one complete seasonal cycle prior to t. Therefore, the level computed in equation (9.18) is for deseasonalized data. The trend is then updated according to equation (9.19), which is identical to equation (9.16). Finally, the seasonal factor is updated in equation (9.20). The ratio (d_t/L_t), which represents the most recent observation of the seasonal ratio, is combined with S_{t-C}, the old seasonal ratio, to produce a new seasonal factor.

Note that there are C seasonal ratios, one for each period in the seasonal cycle. If the data are monthly and the seasonal cycle repeats on an annual basis, then $C = 12$. Each month, one of the seasonal ratios will be updated to a new value, along with the trend and level. The model requires estimates of L_0, T_0, and each of the C seasonal factors. These initial estimates can be based on judgment or data, if available.

Typical ranges for the smoothing constants will vary depending upon the nature of the item being forecasted. For each smoothing constant, the higher the value is, the more weight is placed on the most recent observation. For example, Winters found the following weights gave the best results:

Item	α	β	γ
Cooking utensils	0.2	0.2	0.6
Paint	0.2	0.4	0.4
Prefab homes	0.4	0.0	0.0

In general, if the best value of α or β is greater than 0.5, we should probably question the validity of using Winters' method. Higher values for γ are not unexpected since the seasonal factors are revised only once per cycle, whereas the level and trend are updated every period.

Using the Winters method, the equation of the forecast for k periods into the future is

$$F_{t+k} = [L_t + (T_t)k]S_{t+k-C} \qquad k = 1, 2, 3, \ldots \tag{9.21}$$

The index $t + k - C$ on the seasonal term requires some additional explanation. It is simply an accounting device to keep track of the seasonal terms—if we desire a forecast for January, we should use January's seasonal factor, and so on. The first part of the index, $t + k$ shows that we want to use the appropriate seasonal factor for period $t + k$, the period for which we are forecasting. For example, if $t = 0$ corresponds to January and we want to forecast for May, then $k = 4$, because May is 4 months later than January. Thus, $t + k = 0 + 4 = 4$. The second part of the index, $-C$, merely shows that our latest estimate of this factor was produced one cycle (C periods) previously. If we have 12-period seasonality, then $C = 12$. As a result, $t + k - C = 0 + 4 - 12 = -8$. The index thus tells us that we should use the seasonal factor for the period 8 months earlier than the current one. This corresponds to the updated seasonal factor as of May in the prior year. This approach is logical: first, our forecast for May should use May's seasonal, and second, the seasonal to use is the one we produced most recently for the appropriate period.

To illustrate this approach, consider forecasting for sales of air conditioners at Mason Appliances as of the end of period 12. Our first problem is to estimate L_{12}, T_{12}, and S_1 through S_{12}. We can proceed as follows.

A reasonable estimate of L_{12} is just the average demand for the first 12 periods. Because 100 air conditioners are sold during this time, we have

$$L_{12} = \frac{100}{12}$$

$$= 8.33$$

Now a reasonable estimate of T_{12} is harder to find, but we can start with a naive assumption of no trend. Thus, we have

$$T_{12} = 0$$

Finally, a good way to produce the 12 seasonal factors is to take the ratio of the period's demand to the average demand per period (8.33). We find

$$S_1 = \frac{d_1}{8.33}$$

$$= \frac{4}{8.33}$$

$$= 0.48$$

$$S_2 = \frac{d_2}{8.33}$$

$$= \frac{2}{8.33}$$

$$= 0.24$$

and so on:

$$S_3 = 0.60$$
$$S_4 = 0.96$$
$$S_5 = 1.32$$
$$S_6 = 1.56$$
$$S_7 = 2.16$$
$$S_8 = 1.80$$
$$S_9 = 1.08$$
$$S_{10} = 0.72$$
$$S_{11} = 0.60$$
$$S_{12} = 0.48$$

Note that we have a simple explanation of these factors. For example, demand in period 1 is only 60% of the average monthly demand, while demand in period 7 is 216% of the average.

Now we can proceed with updating, using the values $\alpha = 0.2$, $\beta = 0.1$, and $\gamma = 0.5$. First of all, we use equation (9.21) to forecast for the future as of the end of period 12. Specifically, we have for period 13 ($k = 1$):

$$F_{12+1} = [L_{12} + (T_{12})1]S_{12+1-12}$$
$$= [L_{12} + T_{12}]S_1$$
$$= [8.33 + 0]0.48$$
$$= 4.0$$

Notice that since we have a 12-period cycle, period 13 is the first period in a new cycle. For period 14 ($k = 2$) we have

$$
\begin{aligned}
F_{12+2} &= [L_{12} + (T_{12})2]S_{12+2-12} \\
&= [L_{12} + (T_{12})2]S_2 \\
&= [8.33 + 0]0.24 \\
&= 2.0
\end{aligned}
$$

These results replicating d_1 (of 4) and d_2 (of 2) should not be surprising, because our initial expectation is that there is no trend present. As a result, it is only logical that future forecasts should exactly replicate the past.

Suppose that one period passes. During period 13 Mason Appliances actually sells five air conditioners. Then we can go through the updating process according to equations (9.18), (9.19), and (9.20):

$$
\begin{aligned}
L_{13} &= \alpha\, \frac{(d_{13})}{S_{13-12}} + (1 - \alpha)(L_{12} + T_{12}) \\
&= \alpha \left(\frac{d_{13}}{S_1}\right) + (1 - \alpha)(L_{12} + T_{12}) \\
&= 0.2 \left(\frac{5}{0.48}\right) + 0.8(8.33 + 0) \\
&= 8.75
\end{aligned}
$$

$$
\begin{aligned}
T_{13} &= \beta(L_{13} - L_{12}) + (1 - \beta)T_{12} \\
&= 0.1(8.75 - 8.33) + 0.9(0) \\
&= 0.04
\end{aligned}
$$

$$
\begin{aligned}
S_{13} &= \gamma \left(\frac{d_{13}}{L_{13}}\right) + (1 - \gamma)S_{13-12} \\
&= \gamma \left(\frac{d_{13}}{L_{13}}\right) + (1 - \gamma)S_1 \\
&= 0.5 \left(\frac{5}{8.75}\right) + 0.5(0.48) \\
&= 0.53
\end{aligned}
$$

Note that the actual demand in period 13 ($d_{13} = 5$) was higher than the forecast ($F_{12+1} = 4$). Just as with simple exponential smoothing, the appropriate parameters increase: L_{13} is greater than ($L_{12} + T_{12}$), T_{13} is greater than T_{12}, and S_{13} is greater than S_1.

With these new values, we can again use equation (9.21) to forecast into the future:

$$
\begin{aligned}
F_{13+1} &= [L_{13} + (T_{13})1]S_{13+1-12} \\
&= [L_{13} + T_{13}]S_2 \\
&= [8.75 + (0.04)1]0.24 \\
&= 2.11
\end{aligned}
$$

and so on. Our new forecast for period 14 ($F_{13+1} = 2.11$) is higher than our old forecast for period 14 ($F_{12+2} = 2.00$) because of the effects of actual demand in period 13 being larger than expected.

Suppose that another month passes, and we observe $d_{14} = 4$. The updating process using equations (9.18), (9.19), and (9.20) yields

$$L_{14} = 10.37$$
$$T_{14} = 0.20$$
$$S_{14} = 0.31$$

Again these values have been changed upward because demand was higher than the old forecast. With these new values we can, once again, forecast into the future.

The next-period forecasts from Winters' method are shown in Figure 9.8. Note that the forecast and actual values for the first 12 months are identical; this

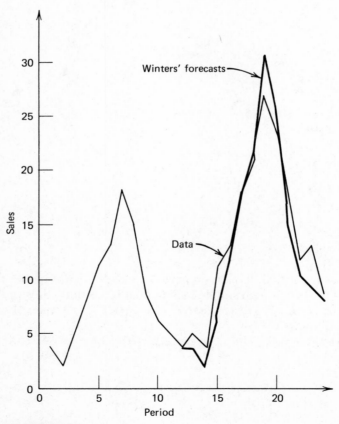

FIGURE 9.8

occurs because we used the first 12 periods of data to initialize the Winters model.

If there is no trend, Winters' method can also be used with seasonal factors alone. In this case, the trend equation (9.19) and T_t values are simply dropped from the method. Similarly, if there is no seasonality, the seasonal equation (9.20) and S_t values can be dropped, resulting in the Holt method previously discussed. Finally, with neither trend nor seasonality we can drop both equations and their values. What remains is just equation (9.10) for simple exponential smoothing. This means that the Winters method is general enough to deal with a constant demand model, with or without trend, and with or without seasonality. This fact explains why the method is used widely in industry.

USE OF THE COMPUTER

Many computer programs are now available to perform the forecasting calculations that we have demonstrated. In fact, some of these programs can be run on a personal computer. For such programs it is necessary to provide the choice of the model to be used, the number of periods to use in estimating the initial values of the model components, the values of the smoothing constants (or the choice of N for a moving average model), and the data.

Figure 9.9 shows the output from a BASIC program that applies Winters' method to sales of air conditioners at Mason Appliances. As expected, these results are the same as ours. Notice that the program has the ability to simulate the behavior of the next-period forecasting process—it forecasts for period 13 as of the end of period 12, simulates the passage of one period and acquisition of the period 13 observation, updates the model, forecasts for period 14 as of the end of period 13, and so on. Such simulations allow the user to compare the performances of the model with different smoothing constants and thus permit an intelligent choice of smoothing constants.

MEASURING FORECAST ACCURACY

In principle, the quality of a forecast should be evaluated on how well it performs in the application for which the forecasts are used. In most business settings this translates into how much profit or loss results from the use of the forecast. In many applications, however, it is difficult if not impossible to calculate the profit or loss associated with a particular forecast. For example, if Mason Appliances underforecasts and lost sales occur, it is difficult to specify a cost for such a result. Instead, we rely on surrogate measures. It is possible to classify these measures into two categories: **bias** and **precision.** These are discussed subsequently.

In evaluating a set of forecasts using these two categories, some general guidelines are important. First, we should not decide whether a forecasting method is appropriate on the basis of just one or two observations. Instead, we

```
INITIALIZATION BASED ON DATA FROM FIRST 12 PERIODS
INITIAL PERMANENT COMPONENT=          8.33
INITIAL TREND COMPONENT=        0.00
INITIAL SEASONAL FACTOR FOR PERIOD  1 = 0.480
INITIAL SEASONAL FACTOR FOR PERIOD  2 = 0.240
INITIAL SEASONAL FACTOR FOR PERIOD  3 = 0.600
INITIAL SEASONAL FACTOR FOR PERIOD  4 = 0.960
INITIAL SEASONAL FACTOR FOR PERIOD  5 = 1.320
INITIAL SEASONAL FACTOR FOR PERIOD  6 = 1.560
INITIAL SEASONAL FACTOR FOR PERIOD  7 = 2.160
INITIAL SEASONAL FACTOR FOR PERIOD  8 = 1.800
INITIAL SEASONAL FACTOR FOR PERIOD  9 = 1.080
INITIAL SEASONAL FACTOR FOR PERIOD 10 = 0.720
INITIAL SEASONAL FACTOR FOR PERIOD 11 = 0.600
INITIAL SEASONAL FACTOR FOR PERIOD 12 = 0.480


SIMULATION OF ONE PERIOD AHEAD FORECASTING
THE SMOOTHING CONSTANTS ARE SPECIFIED AS
ALPHA=    0.2000     BETA=     0.1000     GAMMA=     0.5000
```

PERIOD	OBSERVATION	LEVEL	TREND	SEASONAL	FORECAST	ERROR
t	t	t	t	t	made in t-1	t
13	5.00	8.75	0.04	0.53	4.00	1.00
14	4.00	10.37	0.20	0.31	2.11	1.89
15	11.00	12.12	0.35	0.75	6.34	4.66
16	13.00	12.69	0.38	0.99	11.97	1.03
17	18.00	13.18	0.39	1.34	17.24	0.76
18	22.00	13.67	0.40	1.58	21.16	0.84
19	27.00	13.76	0.37	2.06	30.39	-3.39
20	23.00	13.85	0.34	1.73	25.42	-2.42
21	17.00	14.50	0.37	1.13	15.33	1.67
22	12.00	15.23	0.41	0.75	10.71	1.29
23	13.00	16.84	0.53	0.69	9.38	3.62
24	9.00	17.65	0.55	0.49	8.34	0.66

FORECASTS FOR THE FUTURE AS OF THE END OF PERIOD 24

PERIOD	FORECAST
25	9.57
26	5.87
27	14.56
28	19.71
29	27.42
30	33.24
31	44.38
32	38.21
33	25.49
34	17.49
35	16.29
36	12.03

FIGURE 9.9

should include several observations in the evaluation. Second, we cannot evaluate a technique in absolute terms. Instead, we should compare its forecasts to those produced by some other technique, so that the evaluation is made in relative terms.

FORECAST BIAS

Bias refers to whether forecasts are consistently higher or lower than the actual observations. Ideally a forecast should be unbiased; that is, the positive errors should cancel out the negative ones in the long run. Fortunately, most forecasting techniques often exhibit this characteristic.

There are three primary statistics for measuring bias: the average error ($\bar{E}$), the mean percentage error (MPE), and the smoothed error (SE_t). They are all based on the following definitions:

$$E_t = d_t - F_t = \text{error in period } t$$

$$\%E_t = 100\left(\frac{E_t}{d_t}\right) = \text{percentage error in period } t, \text{ assuming } d_t \neq 0$$

The three measures of bias are then

$$\bar{E} = \sum_{i=1}^{t} \frac{E_i}{t} = \text{average error} \tag{9.22}$$

$$MPE = \sum_{i=1}^{t} \frac{\%E_i}{t} = \text{mean percentage error} \tag{9.23}$$

and

$$SE_t = \delta E_t + (1 - \delta)SE_{t-1} = \text{smoothed error} \tag{9.24}$$

where δ is a smoothing constant between 0 and 1. The average error and smoothed error are measured in the same units as the forecast, such as dollars or units of demand, while the mean percentage error is expressed as a percentage. If no bias is present, all of these measures are exactly 0.

One of the measures might have some drawbacks in certain situations. For example, when the actual or forecast data are very small, the mean percentage error may be misleadingly large. On the other hand, when the data are seasonal, the MPE is a better measure than $\bar{E}$ since it adjusts the errors relative to the actual size of the observations.

Note that equation (9.24) for the smoothed error takes the same form as equation (9.10) for simple exponential smoothing. As a result, it has the same attractive features as exponential smoothing: updating the error term is simple, minimal data storage is required, and the older error terms are given less weight.

Thus, the smoothed error measure is often used instead of the average error. In many cases the smoothing constant, δ, takes on a small value, such as 0.1 and 0.2.

FORECAST PRECISION

Even if forecasts are unbiased, they may still be imprecise. Precision is a measure of variability in the forecast error. The four principal measures of forecast precision are the standard deviation (SD), mean absolute deviation (MAD), mean absolute percentage error ($MAPE$), and smoothed mean absolute deviation ($SMAD_t$). These are defined below:

$$SD = \sqrt{\frac{\Sigma(E_i - \bar{E})^2}{(t - 1)}} \tag{9.25}$$

$$MAD = \sum_{i=1}^{t} \frac{|E_i|}{t} \tag{9.26}$$

$$MAPE = \sum_{i=1}^{t} \frac{|\%E_i|}{t} \tag{9.27}$$

$$SMAD_t = \delta|E_t| + (1 - \delta)SMAD_{t-1} \tag{9.28}$$

where again δ is a smoothing constant between 0 and 1. The $|\ |$ symbol used in equations (9.26) to (9.28) indicates the absolute value—that is, we ignore the sign of the error. Here the standard deviation, mean absolute deviation, and smoothed mean absolute deviation are in the same units as the forecast, while the mean absolute percentage error is expressed in percent.

Using the standard deviation as a measure reflects an attitude that larger errors (e.g., twice as large) are much worse than smaller errors (e.g., four times as bad). The standard deviation is also very useful in inventory systems. Historically, the mean absolute deviation has been used in inventory systems because it is easily understood and computed. Also, when the error terms follow a normal distribution it has been shown that

$$SD = 1.25MAD \tag{9.29}$$

As a result, the standard deviation and mean absolute deviation are often used interchangeably. The smoothed mean absolute deviation again follows the exponential smoothing approach and, thus, is more convenient to use. Finally, since the mean absolute percentage error is a relative measure, it is useful for comparing forecasts that have different units (such as dollars and yen). Although these measures are not equivalent, they will usually rank different forecasting methods in the same order.

Table 9.5 shows an example in which each of the measures in equations (9.22) to (9.28) has been computed for a comparison of two methods over six

TABLE 9.5

Forecasting Method A

Time Period	Actual Data	Forecast	Error	Absolute Error	Percentage Error	Absolute Percentage Error
1	18	15	3	3	16.7	16.7
2	12	18	-6	6	-50.0	50.0
3	20	16	4	4	20.0	20.0
4	22	18	4	4	18.2	18.2
5	18	18	0	0	0	0
6	8	13	-5	5	-62.5	62.5
Total			0	22	-57.6	168.0

Forecasting Method B

Time Period	Actual Data	Forecast	Error	Absolute Error	Percentage Error	Absolute Percentage Error
1	18	20	-2	2	-11.1	11.1
2	12	15	-3	3	-25.0	25.0
3	20	20	0	0	0	0
4	22	20	2	2	9.1	9.1
5	18	20	-2	2	-11.1	11.1
6	8	12	-4	4	-50	50
Total			-9	13	-88.2	106.3

	Method A	Method B
$\bar{E}$	0	-1.5
MPE	-9.6%	-14.7%
$SE_6(\delta = 0.1)$	-0.10	-0.73
SD	4.5	2.2
MAD	3.67	2.17
MAPE	28%	17.7%
$SMAD_6(\delta = 0.1)$	1.69	1.06

observations. In this example, we prefer Method B to Method A because it is superior on all measures of precision. It is true that the bias of Method B is higher, but it is easy to adjust for bias. For example, if we subtracted 1.5 from every forecast of Method B, the average error would drop to 0. On the other hand, there is no simple adjustment to fix precision errors. Bias is a systematic error for which compensation can be made, whereas lack of precision is erratic and is much harder to repair.

In actual practice, the smoothed error and the smoothed mean absolute deviation are calculated each time an observation becomes known. The value of the smoothing constant δ affects how rapidly the estimate responds to changes. To utilize SE_t and $SMAD_t$, it is necessary to have an initial estimate of each, SE_0 and $SMAD_0$. The customary assumption is that $SE_0 = 0$ and $SMAD_0 = 0$. If the user has a lot of confidence in the estimate of SE_0 and $SMAD_0$, then δ should be set at a low value, say, 0.1 or 0.2. On the other hand, if the estimate of SE_0 or $SMAD_0$ is being built on historical data, then a larger value may be more appropriate until several periods have passed.

MONITORING FORECASTS

This section discusses mechanisms for controlling and monitoring forecasts and for automatically adjusting to shifts in the quantity being forecast. These concepts are most useful in computer-based systems, when there are many items to forecast and considerable reason to suspect that some of the basic patterns of data will change.

In order to monitor a forecast and test for whether there has been a change in the data pattern, we need to have an estimate of what the typical errors are. For all practical purposes, if an appropriate forecasting technique is being used, it is safe to assume that e_t, the forecast error in period t, is normally distributed. Empirically this is almost always true, and even when the error is not normal, correct decisions will often be made by assuming normality. Given that e_t is normally distributed, we need to estimate only the mean and standard deviation of errors to completely describe the distribution. This can be done by using historical data about forecast errors.

An important use of information about forecast errors is for automatic monitoring of the forecasting system. This monitoring is done through two control tests that are designed to detect changes in the underlying data-generating process.

DATA FILTER

This test is meant to detect unusual occurrences such as clerical errors or sudden large changes in the actual observation such as unforecast promotions. The test is as follows: accept the hypothesis that the process is "in control" if

$$|d_t - F_t| = |e_t| < z(SD) \tag{9.30}$$

where z is a constant chosen to give an acceptable degree of sensitivity. In words, this test asks if the absolute value of the forecast error in period t is less than z times the standard deviation of forecast error. In a computerized system this test is implemented by testing the forecast error and printing out an exception message if the error is too large.

Theoretically, we can choose the constant z by using the result that the errors are normally distributed. For example, if $z = 1.96$ and we know the standard deviation of forecast errors, then there is only a 5% chance of printing out an exception report when the forecasting process is actually "in control" and the forecast error is random. In practice, we may know the standard deviation of errors because we use either the mean absolute deviation or smoothed mean absolute deviation as a measure of forecast precision. If this is the case, we use equation (9.29) or the approximate result that

$$SMAD = MAD$$

to arrive at the following two equations, which are equivalent to equation (9.30):

$$|d_t - F_t| = |e_t| < (1.25z)(MAD) \tag{9.31}$$

or

$$|d_t - F_t| = |e_t| < (1.25z)(SMAD) \tag{9.32}$$

and by choosing a value of z that generates a tolerable number of exception messages. It is, of course, possible to select different values of z for different items depending upon their importance.

TRACKING SIGNAL

A major concern in forecasting is possible bias in the forecast. The primary objective of the tracking signal is to provide a monitoring device that will signal a basic change in the data pattern or a change in its coefficients. Normally, limits are set that when exceeded by the tracking signal (referred to as **tripping**) provide an alarm that something has changed. If the tracking signal is tripped on two or three successive observations, there is clear indication that something is wrong with the forecasting model. Conceptually, the tracking signal is given by

$$\frac{\text{sum of errors}}{\text{standard deviation of errors}}$$

In practice, this statistic creates problems because it has no natural upper or lower bounds. A preferable measure is given by

$$TS_t = \frac{SE_t}{SMAD_t} \tag{9.33}$$

where TS_t is the tracking signal and SE_t and $SMAD_t$ are the smoothed error and smoothed mean absolute deviation defined by equations (9.24) and (9.28), respectively.

Note that if the tracking signal is defined in this way, it can never be greater than 1 or less than -1 because the average error can never be greater than the mean absolute error. If the forecast errors are consistently positive, then the tracking signal will get closer to $+1$, whereas if the errors are consistently negative, the tracking signal will approach -1.

The tracking signal, TS, is a measure of whether there is significant bias in the forecasting system. The rationale of this approach is that if the forecast is good, then the smoothed error will tend to be near 0. The smoothed error may be positive at one point; however, shortly a negative error will occur that will decrease the smoothed error. If there is a change in the data process, for example, from a constant model to a model with upward trend, then the forecast will lag behind the actual. Thus, the errors will tend to all be positive, and hence the smoothed error will tend to grow.

Figure 9.10 shows two different examples. In Figure 9.10a the data pattern seems to change from a constant to one with a downward trend. The tracking signal initially fluctuates around 0, but as the forecast errors continue to be negative, the tracking signal gets closer to -1, and eventually the lower limit is violated. This violation of the lower limit is a signal that the model and data should be examined to determine if a change has occurred. In Figure 9.10b, the

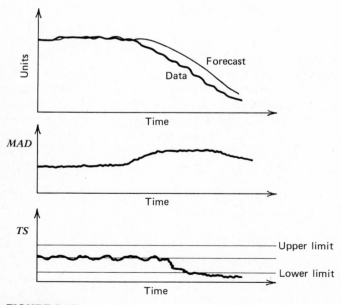

FIGURE 9.10

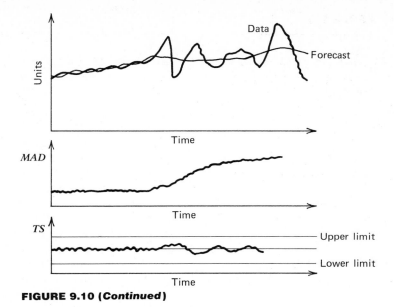

FIGURE 9.10 (Continued)

variability in the data pattern increases significantly. This will cause the standard deviation (and thus *SMAD*) to increase; however, the tracking signal will not increase or decrease because the average error will remain close to 0. Thus, the tracking signal limits are not violated, and there is no signal suggesting that the data and model should be investigated.

As another example, suppose a simple exponential smoothing model is being used to forecast with $A_0 = 100$ and $\alpha = 0.1$. From past experience the following estimates are made:

$$\delta = 0.15$$
$$SE_0 = 0$$
$$SD = 2.5$$

Note that from *SD* we can estimate the initial smoothed mean absolute deviation as $SMAD_0 = 0.8SD = 2.0$. Table 9.6 shows the actual, forecast error, smoothed average error, smoothed mean absolute deviation, and tracking signal for six periods. Notice that toward the end of this interval a trend occurs. As a result, the tracking signal grows quite large, because the relatively constant forecasts are lagging well behind the observations.

Under fairly unrealistic assumptions it is possible to develop an estimate of the standard deviation of the tracking signal that could be used to set control limits statistically. However, in many applications, limits for the tracking signal as with limits for the data filter, are adjusted based on experience.

TABLE 9.6

t Period	d_t Actual	F_t Forecast	e_t Error	SE_t	$SMAD_t$	TS_t
1	101	100	1	0.15	1.85	0.08
2	104	100.1	3.9	0.71	2.16	0.33
3	98	100.5	−2.5	0.23	2.21	0.10
4	108	100.2	7.8	1.37	3.05	0.45
5	116	101	15	3.41	4.84	0.70
6	124	102.5	22.5	6.27	7.50	0.84

When the tracking signal goes out of control, we should determine the cause. Finding the reason for the out-of-control signal involves many of the same procedures that are used in identifying an appropriate model. For example, we might change the form of the time series model to include or remove trend or seasonality, or we might change the values of the smoothing constants. In any case, we would also reset the tracking signal to 0 to avoid a false out-of-control signal in the future.

SUMMARY

Forecasts provide useful inputs for planning activities in the operations, marketing, and financial functions of a firm. Forecasting models are different from other models used to aid in decision making because the forecasts provide useful inputs for other models rather than influencing decisions directly.

There are three general classes of forecasting techniques: qualitative, causal, and time series. This chapter concentrates on the techniques of time series analysis, because for a large number of situations the methods are simple to implement and have sufficient accuracy. All time series techniques are based on the assumption that existing data patterns will continue into the future. This assumption is more likely to be correct over the short term than it is over the long term, so that time series methods provide reasonably accurate short-term forecasts but may do poorly further into the future.

For constant data patterns including only random fluctuations, a moving average forecast method is attractive. It provides the capability of smoothing, that is, canceling out random fluctuations, while still maintaining some response to changes. However, a more attractive method is simple exponential smoothing. It includes all of the attractive features of moving averages, but also provides the appealing feature of placing greater emphasis on more recent data. In addition, simple exponential smoothing has small computational requirements, has low data storage needs, and represents a sensible way of updating forecasts as new observations become available. This method takes the approach of partitioning the available information into an old part and a new part. As a result, the method includes learning in its approach: whenever we receive a new piece of information, we "learn" from it by taking our old information and adding to it a fraction of the error. Our choice of the smoothing constant indicates how much we want our new forecast to be influenced by the size of the error.

It is relatively easy to expand simple exponential smoothing to deal with more complicated models. Specifically, Holt's method incorporates a linear trend in the data, while Winters' method can deal with both linear trend and multiplicative seasonality. Both of these techniques rely on the basic approach of simple exponential smoothing expressed in the formula

$$\text{new forecast} = \binom{\text{smoothing}}{\text{constant}}\binom{\text{actual}}{\text{observation}} + \left(1 - \binom{\text{smoothing}}{\text{constant}}\right)\binom{\text{old}}{\text{forecast}}$$

The quality of a forecast can be evaluated using two categories: bias and precision. Bias refers to whether forecasts are consistently higher or lower than actual observations. Fortunately, most forecasting techniques are unbiased. Even if forecasts are unbiased, they may still be imprecise. Precision is a measure of variability in the forecast error. Bias represents a systematic error for which compensation can be made, whereas lack of precision indicates erratic, harder to repair errors. There are several appropriate measures for each of these categories.

Monitoring of forecasts uses two control tests that are designed to detect changes in the underlying data-generating process. The data filter test helps to detect unusual occurrences, such as clerical errors or sudden large changes in the actual data pattern. The tracking signal test helps identify a basic change in the data pattern or a change in the coefficients of the forecasting equation.

The forecasting techniques and forecast-monitoring approaches discussed in this chapter are only part of a larger forecasting system, which includes forecast generation, forecast monitoring, and management judgment. It is important to recognize that quantitative forecasts may be modified using management judgment to produce a modified forecast or prediction that is then used for planning purposes.

EXERCISES

SIMPLE TECHNIQUES AND EXPONENTIAL SMOOTHING

1 The recent demand history for a product is shown below:

Month	September	October	November	December	January	February
Demand	80	76	86	81	82	?

a What is the February forecast, using a 3-month moving average?

b Suppose instead that a procedure for simple exponential smoothing is begun in January. Assume the forecast for January was 80.8. Then, after the demand of 82 is observed in January, what is the forecast for February if the procedure employs $\alpha = 0.1$?

c Procedures 1 and 2, described below, are alternatives to the exponential smoothing procedure of (b), to be considered for use in February and the months to follow. For each alternative, give one disadvantage the procedure exhibits in comparison with exponential smoothing.

Procedure 1: Compute the forecast for month $(t + 1)$ from $0.1d_t + 0.9d_{t-1}$, where d_t denotes demand in month t.

Procedure 2: Compute the forecast for month $(t + 1)$ from $0.1d_t + 0.9\bar{d}_t$, where d_t denotes demand in month t and $\bar{d}_t$ denotes average demand in all months prior to t.

2 Consider the following demand observations

t	1	2	3	4	5
d_t	12	14	13	16	18

a Use simple exponential smoothing with $L_0 = 10$ and $\alpha = 0.2$ to compute F_t values. What is F_{5+1}?

b Repeat (a) for $\alpha = 0.3$ and $\alpha = 0.5$. What is F_{5+1} in each case?

c On the basis of *MAD* (mean absolute deviation), which smoothing constant (0.2, 0.3, or 0.5) is most accurate?

3 Two employees of a firm have been having a forecasting contest for the past 12 months. Each has been using no-trend exponential smoothing with $\alpha = 0.2$, but George has been calculating his forecast monthly, whereas Mary updates weekly. Three months ago there was a substantial drop in demand. Prior to that time demand had been fluctuating around an average of 200 per week, but now it seems to be close to 100. Who is more likely to have an accurate forecast, given the recent drop? Why?

4 The International Paper Company uses simple exponential smoothing to forecast demand for three-hole punched paper. They feel that demand for this product is constant and that no trend in demand exists. However, they think that a jump (a permanent one-time increase) has occurred in demand. After the jump they believe that demand, once again, will be constant. At the end of February, the forecasted demand for March was 150 units.

a If the jump took place *after* March, which of the following values of α is more appropriate for their forecasting model, $\alpha = 0.10$ or $\alpha = 0.30$? Why?

b It is now the end of April. The actual demands were 300 in March and 330 in April. Compute forecasts for May and June using $\alpha = 0.2$.

c They are using these forecasts as a basis for deciding on production quantities of three-hole punched paper. What difficulties (if any) do you foresee in using simple exponential smoothing in this situation?

5 "Heads will roll," shouted John Willard as he stormed out of the meeting with the Operations Research group. This terminated a meeting that had been called quickly when it was discovered that a data recording error had fouled up some forecasts made by the recently installed single-equation exponential smoothing model. Three months ago a clerk had incorrectly entered the June demand (d_6) as 1500 units when it should have been 150 units.

"Our old forecast method (next month = last month) would have noticed this error and we would have corrected it immediately," John shouted. "The problem with this crazy exponential method with its small weighting value ($\alpha = 0.2$) is that the influence of the error is so small that we might never have discovered it. And you claim that there is no way to correct it now because all you have is the current average, A_9, produced *after* including the September demand. Well, you'd better correct it, or heads will roll!"

Assuming that all you have is the above data, show how to correct the current average A_9.

THE HOLT AND WINTERS METHODS

6 For the demand observations in Exercise 1, use Holt's method with $\alpha = 0.3$ and $\beta = 0.3$ to answer the following. Use $T_0 = 0$, and $L_0 = 80$.

a What is F_{5+1}?

b What is F_{5+1} from the best constant model in Exercise 1?

c Calculate *MAD* (mean absolute deviation) for the F_{t+1} values produced by Holt's method.

7 For 2 years Risky Parts Co. has been using Winters' exponential smoothing model, with trend and seasonal factors. They are using smoothing constants of $\alpha = 0.05$, $\beta = 0.5$, and $\gamma = 0.0$. They update the permanent and trend components monthly but do *not* update seasonal factors.

a It is now May 1, and the permanent and trend components have been updated after receiving April's demand. Use this information as shown below to forecast demand for May, for June, for July, and for August:

$L_{apr} = 178.3$

$T_{apr} = 1.2$

seasonal factors: (S_t terms)

0.90 (April)   0.95 (May)   1.05 (June)

0.85 (July)   1.02 (August)

b It is now May 31, and May's demand was 205. Use this new information to forecast for June, July, and August.

c Why are the forecasts in (b) different from those in (a)?

8 Review Exercise 4. International Paper has now decided that a trend in demand *does* exist and that the nonseasonal version of the Winters model should be used.

a They have also decided that the exponentially smoothed base level at the end of February was 150, the estimate of the trend at the end of February was 10 units per month, and the β should be 0.4. They still want to use α of 0.2. What is the estimate of the trend after the demand for March is received?

b Based on (a), what are the forecasts for May and June as of the end of March?

9 The accompanying table is an excerpt from the records of a company that has been using exponential smoothing for a long time. The data have been deseasonalized, so that seasonal factors can be ignored.

t	Deseasonalized demand	L_t ($\alpha = 0.4$)	T_t ($\beta = 0.1$)	$SMAD_t$ ($\delta = 0.2$)
108	555.3	563.8	8.1	11.3
109	558.3	566.5	7.6	11.8
110	571.7	573.1	7.5	9.9

In all cases L, T, and $SMAD$ were determined after the demand for the appropriate month became known. For example, L, T, and $SMAD$ for $t = 108$ were determined including the actual demand of 555.3.

a At the end of month 109, what was the forecast for month 110?

b At the end of month 109, what was the forecast for month 112?

c At the end of month 110, what was the forecast for month 112?

d Explain why the answer to part (c) is lower than the answer to part (b). (What happened in month 110 that would suggest that the forecast should be revised downward?)

e It is now the end of month 111. The deseasonalized demand in month 111 was 567.9. What is the forecast for month 112. (This will require you to update your values of L and T.)

f Put a 95% confidence interval around your answer to (e).

10 Two products, frosting mix and cake mix, share the same seasonal pattern but have different trends. We are now at the beginning of September, and the exponential smoothing calculations have been carried out to include August sales, except for the last few steps.

a Given the following information, construct forecasts for the next 3 months.

Month t	Seasonal Factors	Cake Mix Intercept L_t	Cake Mix Trend T_t	Frosting Mix Intercept L_t	Frosting Mix Trend T_t
August	1.0	90,000	0	51,000	1,000
September	1.1				
October	1.2				
November	1.4				

b Time passes. It is now October 1, and September sales were 94,000 cases of cake mix and 58,000 cases of frosting mix. Compute new forecasts for October and November. Use $\alpha = 0.1$ for both products, but use $\beta = 0$ for cake and $\beta = 0.2$ for frosting. Do not update seasonal factors.

11 The Southern Barnesville Distribution Company purchases small gift items in bulk, packages them, and sells then to retail stores. At the end of December 1981 (after including the December demand) the following information was provided by their forecasting system:

(1) $L_{\text{dec}} = 65.0$ and $T_{\text{dec}} = 2.0$.

(2) December has a seasonal factor of 1.2, and January has a seasonal factor of 0.8.

(3) There is no seasonality in other months.

(4) $\alpha = 0.2$, $\beta = 0.1$, and $\gamma = 0.0$.

a What was their forecast (as of the end of December) for January? For February? For March?

b If January demand actually was 80 units, what forecast do they make (as of the end of January) for February? For March? For April?

12 Review Exercise 11. Starting on February 1 the company runs a nonrecurring promotion campaign (with a price reduction) and plans on continuing the promotion during February and March. They believe that the promotion will increase sales by 10 units during February and by 10 units during March. They also believe that the promotion will have *no effect* on other months. They are going to assume this +10 figure in making their forecasts.

Now assume (after including the January demand) that the following information is provided by the forecasting system:

(1) $L_{\text{jan}} = 80.0$ and $T_{\text{jan}} = 2.0$.

(2) December has a seasonal factor of 1.2 and January has a seasonal factor of 0.8.

(3) There is no seasonality in other months.

(4) $\alpha = 0.2$, $\beta = 0.1$, and $\gamma = 0.0$.

a If February demand actually was 95 units, what forecast should they make (as of the end of February) for March? For April?

b Describe briefly what other effect (than that which the firm assumes) the promotion might have.

13 Timberhill Power Tool Co. has experienced irregular demand for one of its most popular models of chain saws. They use single-equation exponential smoothing with $\alpha = 0.5$. At the end of February, after including February's demand, their forecast for demand in March was 200 units. Later on, they found that the actual March demand was 300 units, and that the actual April demand was 350 units.

a After incorporating April's demand, what is the forecast for May?

b After incorporating April's demand, what is the forecast for June?

14 Review Exercise 13. One of the power drills at Timberhill has had a growing demand pattern. At the end of February (after including the February demand) the following information was provided by their forecasting system:

(1) $L_{feb} = 290.0$, $T_{feb} = 10.0$, and $SMAD_{feb} = 50.0$

(2) The seasonal factors for other months are as follows:

Month	Factor
March	0.7
April	0.9
May	1.2
June	1.5

(3) $\alpha = 0.2$, $\beta = 0.0$, and $\gamma = 0.4$.

(4) $SMAD_t$ is calculated using $\delta = 0.2$.

a As of the end of February, what were their forecasts for March, April, May, and June?

b If March demand actually was 150 units, what are their forecasts (as of the end of March) for April, May, and June? What is $SMAD$ as of the end of March?

c What is a 95% confidence interval for the April forecast calculated in (b)?

15 Review Exercise 14. Starting on May 1 Timberhill runs a 10-day, nonrecurring promotion campaign. They believe that the promotion will have no effect in other months. Now assume (after including the April demand) that their forecasting system provides the following information:

(1) $L_{apr} = 325.0$, $T_{apr} = 15.0$, and $SMAD_{apr} = 60.0$.

(2) The seasonal factors for other months are as follows:

Month	Factor
May	1.2
June	1.5
July	1.3

(3) $\alpha = 0.2$, $\beta = 0.0$, and $\gamma = 0.4$.

(4) $SMAD_t$ is calculated using $\delta = 0.2$.

a If May demand actually was 650 units, what forecast do they make (as of the end of May) for June and July?

b What is a 95% confidence interval for each of the forecasts in (a)?

c Describe briefly what other effect (than that which the firm assumes) the promotion might have.

16 Blanchard Importing and Distributing Co. is forecasting demand for quarts of 80-proof vodka. They use single-equation exponential smoothing with $\alpha = 0.2$. At the end of February, after including February's demand, their forecast for demand in March was 300 units. Later on, they find that the actual March demand was 400 units, that the actual April demand was 500 units, and that the actual May demand is 600 units.

a After incorporating May's demand, what is the forecast for June?

b After incorporating May's demand, what is the forecast for July?

17 Review Exercise 16. At Blanchard, demand for quarts of gin has a different pattern. At the end of February 1982 (after including the February demand) the following information was provided by their forecasting system:

(1) $L_{feb} = 400$, $T_{feb} = 25.0$, and $SMAD_{feb} = 40.0$.

(2) The seasonal factors for other months are as follows:

Month	Factor
March	0.4
April	0.3
May	1.5
June	1.8

(3) $\alpha = 0.3$, $\beta = 0.1$, and $\gamma = 0.5$.

(4) $SMAD_t$ is calculated using $\delta = 0.4$.

a As of the end of February, what are their forecasts for March, April, May, and June?

b If March demand actually is 170 units, what is their forecast (as of the end of March) for April, May, and June?

c What is $SMAD$ as of the end of March?

d What is a 90% confidence interval for the April forecast calculated in (b)?

18 Review Exercise 17. Starting on September 1 Blanchard runs a 10-day, nonrecurring promotion campaign for quarts of scotch whiskey. They believe that the promotion will have an additive effect in September and that it will have no effect in other months.

Assume (after including the August demand) that their forecasting system provides the following information for quarts of scotch:

(1) $L_{aug} = 300.0$, $T_{aug} = 20.0$, and $SMAD_{aug} = 50.0$.

(2) The seasonal factors for other months are as follows:

Month	Factor
September	1.3
October	1.4
November	1.3

(3) $\alpha = 0.3$, $\beta = 0.1$, and $\gamma = 0.5$.

(4) $SMAD_t$ is calculated using $\delta = 0.4$.

a If September demand actually was 850 units, what forecast do they make (as of the end of September) for October and November? Why?

b Based on the success of September's promotion, at the end of September Blanchard decided to run the *same* promotion for quarts of scotch in November. What forecast do they make *now* (as of the end of September) for October and November? Why?

Chapter 10
INVENTORY MODELS

Hogan Office Products Company

The Hogan Office Products Company stocks a wide variety of office supplies for businesses in a large metropolitan area. One of its most popular items is a large fireproof filing cabinet, sales of which have been running at the rate of about 2000 cabinets per year. The firm orders these cabinets from a manufacturer who charges $100 per cabinet. The accountant at Hogan has estimated that each order from the manufacturer incurs a fixed cost of $32, reflecting clerical work and delivery expenses. She further estimates that holding costs for this type of item are about 20% per year. In light of these figures, the accountant believes that there should be a change in the current ordering policy of ordering 40 cabinets at the start of each week.

An **inventory** is an idle resource or a quantity of stock that is held in order to meet some future need. For example, the Hogan Company holds inventories of filing cabinets so that it can quickly and conveniently satisfy customer orders as they occur. The use of inventories is widespread and occurs for several reasons. In this chapter we shall be concerned with the basic modeling approaches for analyzing inventories, and we concentrate on two of the most important reasons for holding inventory, economy and uncertainty.

Considerations of **economy** encourage firms to use inventories to reduce costs. For example, a firm may purchase goods in bulk (thus creating a large inventory) to take advantage of vendor quantity discounts. In addition, it may produce items in batches (again creating an inventory) to minimize total costs of production. Also, the firm may desire inventories of finished goods so that it can ship large quantities and benefit from economies of scale in transportation.

Inventories also protect a firm against **uncertainty.** Typical unforeseen events include changes in manufacturing yields, equipment breakdowns, transportation delays, and errors in demand forecasts. Inventories provide some protection against the consequences of such events.

There are many other reasons for holding inventory. For example, inventories allow a firm to reduce the time required to meet customer demand. Also, between-stage inventories make it possible to develop separate operating policies for each stage in the production-distribution process. Such inventories eliminate the need to precisely match the supply rate and demand rate in the short run. Although these reasons for holding inventory are important, they are similar in nature to economy and uncertainty. Thus, we will not analyze them here.

It might seem that more inventory is always better than less inventory. However, excessive inventory can be harmful because it uses too much of a firm's assets and can limit such other activities as research and development, equipment replacement, or capacity expansion. As a result, the general problem of managing inventory is to maintain those stocks that provide suitable flexibility for production and distribution without tying up an excessive amount of a firm's assets.

The control of inventories has become a pervasive managerial problem for many firms. Perhaps because inventory *problems* are so prevalent, the development of inventory *models* has received considerable attention. The main purpose of an inventory model is to capture the important trade-offs affected by inventory-related decisions. In this chapter we do not deal in depth with the nature of inventory problems. Instead we emphasize the elements of inventory models and their ability to reflect the features of real inventory systems.

First, we shall examine models that reflect the economic incentives that can lead a firm to create and replenish inventory in batches. This rationale leads to what is called **lot-size stock,** because selection of a lot size for replenishment batches is made primarily to exploit the relevant cost structure. We shall also examine the rationale for **safety stock,** in which a firm builds a reserve into its inventory holdings because of uncertainty about its operating environment.

THE BASIC LOT-SIZE MODEL

Most inventory models are intended to answer two main questions: (1) **When** should inventory be acquired? and (2) **How much** inventory should be acquired? In dealing with these questions we begin with a model that requires a number of simplifying assumptions. Even though the assumptions may appear unrealistic, the basic model is important for both practical and conceptual reasons.

On the practical side, the simple model describes one of the central cost trade-offs in inventory management. It also provides a coarse guide for lot-size decisions even when the assumptions are not met. On the conceptual side, the simple model establishes a framework for model building and analysis, making it possible to enrich the model systematically with more realistic assumptions. Below is a list of the assumptions in the basic model.

Assumption 1
The analysis covers a single product; other products are independent.

Assumption 2
Demand for the product is known with certainty.

Assumption 3
Demand occurs at a constant rate.

Assumption 4
All demand is met on time.

Assumption 5
A replenishment batch is delivered to storage all at one time.

Assumption 6
Replenishment orders are filled instantaneously.

Assumption 7
Each replenishment incurs a fixed cost and also a variable cost based on a constant unit price.

Assumption 8
Inventory charges are based on the average stock level.

It may be helpful to think about the cases these assumptions exclude:

Assumption 1
Situations in which multiple products compete for common resources (such as storage space or replenishment capacity) or in which there are cost incentives to order several products from the same supplier.

Assumption 2
Situations in which demand is uncertain.

Assumption 3
Situations in which demand fluctuates in a predictable fashion (e.g., because of trend or seasonal effects).

Assumption 4
Backordering (i.e., choosing to meet demand late) as well as lost sales.

Assumption 5
The possibility of splitting the lot into portions that are delivered over an interval of time. It also excludes situations in which replenishment is provided by a production system from which new items "trickle" into inventory at a finite rate of replenishment.

Assumption 6
Replenishment lead time (i.e., a delay between the placing of an order and its delivery).

Assumption 7

Quantity discounts in which a large purchase quantity will lead to a reduced unit price.

Assumption 8

Situations in which inventory charges are based on the maximum level of stock.

Later on, we shall relax some of the assumptions, but we begin with the simple model based on Assumptions 1–8 in order to emphasize fundamental properties. Under these assumptions, a graph of inventory level versus time takes the form shown in Figure 10.1, where q denotes the constant size of each replenishment lot. Although we assume that each replenishment lot is the same size, it is possible to show that varying the lot size cannot reduce costs. In this "sawtooth" pattern, the inventory level jumps at each replenishment. Then, because of the assumption of constant demand, the inventory level declines at a constant rate until the next replenishment. Because delivery is instantaneous, there is no reason to place a replenishment order until inventory drops to 0. Consequently, the inventory level in the figure fluctuates repeatedly from a peak of q items down to 0.

In the simplified scenario of the basic model we consider ordering costs and holding costs. **Ordering costs** are the costs associated with the purchase of a replenishment lot, including the purchase cost of the product. For a lot containing q items we denote the ordering cost as

$$f + vq \tag{10.1}$$

In this form we use f to denote the fixed cost of ordering, and we use v to denote the variable cost per item. Thus, the ordering cost has a fixed component and a linear variable component. The fixed component includes those replenishment

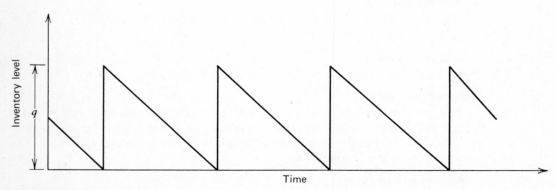

FIGURE 10.1

costs that do not vary with the size of the lot. Typically, this component could include the cost of paperwork or record keeping, communication costs, the fixed portion of freight charges, and inspection costs. The variable component includes those costs that are proportional to the size of the lot, such as purchase costs, transportation fees, and handling costs.

Let d represent the demand rate expressed on an annual basis (i.e., in terms of items per year). Then the number of replenishments required in a year will be d/q. Because the ordering cost is incurred with each replenishment order, we obtain

$$\text{annual ordering cost} = (f + vq)\left(\frac{d}{q}\right) = \frac{fd}{q} + dv \qquad (10.2)$$

Note that the first part of this expression varies inversely with q. That is, the larger the size of each replenishment lot, the smaller the annual total of fixed replenishment costs, because there will be fewer replenishments per year. Also note that we could express the demand rate in terms of items per period, where a period could be a week, or a month, or a quarter. In this case equation (10.2) represents the ordering cost per period rather than per year.

Holding costs include all costs associated with maintaining an item in inventory. In approximate terms, holding costs are proportional to the number of items held and to the length of time they are held. If y units of an item are held in inventory for an interval of t years, then we calculate the total holding cost as

$$hyt \qquad (10.3)$$

In this form we use h to denote the annual cost of holding one unit. The major component of h is the opportunity cost of tying up capital in inventory instead of investing it elsewhere or reducing the amount of the firm's loans. Other components include taxes, insurance, handling, storage, shrinkage, obsolescence, and deterioration. In each case, notice that these costs vary directly with the size of the inventory: The more items held in stock, the greater the holding cost.

Sometimes the annual holding cost is expressed as a percentage of the variable cost per item. In this form we write

$$h = \alpha v$$

where α is the appropriate fraction. For example, at the Hogan Office Products Company, the holding cost is 20%. This means that an item worth $v = \$100$ will have an annual holding cost of \$20, while an item worth $v = \$50$ will have an annual holding cost of \$10.

In determining the total holding cost for a year, notice that the inventory level during the year is not constant. However, the average stock level in Figure 10.1 is $q/2$, since the inventory fluctuates uniformly between 0 and q. Under

Assumption 8 the total holding cost in a year is equivalent to the cost that would be incurred if the inventory level were constant at $q/2$. Therefore, we obtain

$$\text{annual holding cost} = \frac{hq}{2} \qquad (10.4)$$

Note that this expression varies directly with q. The larger the size of each replenishment lot, the larger the average inventory, and the greater the annual total of holding costs.

In general, the dimensions of the cost parameter h could be dollars per item per period. If h is expressed in dollars per item per period, then equation (10.4) represents the holding cost per period rather than per year. The important point is that the dimensions of parameters d and h must be consistent, since they both denote rates per unit of time.

Combining the two types of costs from equations (10.2) and (10.4), we obtain

$$\text{total annual cost} = \text{annual ordering cost} + \text{annual holding cost}$$

$$= \frac{fd}{q} + dv + \frac{hq}{2} \qquad (10.5)$$

The expression in equation (10.5) serves as a criterion for the choice of a lot size. Note, however, that the middle term does not depend on the decision to be made. This term, dv, represents the total annual cost of meeting demand. It is independent of the lot size quantity q because the unit price v is constant. As a result, if we focus only on the costs that depend on the lot size, the objective function becomes

$$C(q) = \frac{fd}{q} + \frac{hq}{2} \qquad (10.6)$$

where $C(q)$ represents the total annual cost that depends on the decision variable q.

When we represent the function $C(q)$ graphically, as in Figure 10.2, the ordering component (fd/q) is the portion that varies inversely with q, while the holding component $(hq/2)$ is the portion that varies directly with q. The sum of these two components is the U-shaped curve that corresponds to $C(q)$. The minimum cost occurs for a lot size equal to q^*, where it is possible to show that

$$q^* = \sqrt{\frac{2fd}{h}} \qquad (10.7)$$

This quantity is frequently called the **economic order quantity,** or **EOQ.** It prescribes the optimal choice of a replenishment lot size to balance annual ordering costs (which decrease as q increases) and annual holding costs (which increase

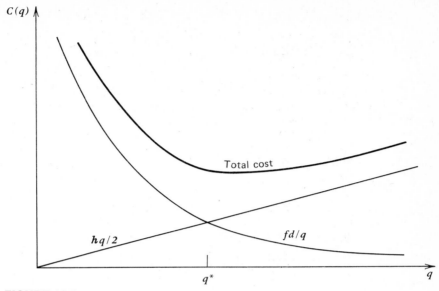

C(q)

Total cost

hq/2

fd/q

q*

q

FIGURE 10.2

as q increases). We can derive a formula for the optimal value of the total annual cost by substituting equation (10.7) into equation (10.6) to obtain

$$
\begin{aligned}
C(q^*) &= \frac{fd}{q^*} + \frac{hq^*}{2} \\
&= \sqrt{\frac{fdh}{2}} + \sqrt{\frac{fdh}{2}} \\
&= \sqrt{2fdh}
\end{aligned}
$$
(10.8)

From equation (10.8) we see that at the optimal order quantity q^* the ordering component (fd/q^*) is *exactly* equal to the holding component $(hq^*/2)$. This result has great benefit as a diagnostic tool for evaluating an inventory system that meets the assumptions of our simple model. Specifically, the system is not operating in an optimal fashion unless the annual ordering costs are equal to annual holding costs.

In the setting of the Hogan Office Products Company, the given parameters are

$f = 32$ per order

$h = 0.20(100) = 20$ per cabinet per year

$d = 2000$ cabinets per year

From the formula in equation (10.7) the optimal order quantity is

$$q^* = \sqrt{\frac{2(32)(2000)}{20}} = 80 \text{ cabinets}$$

Therefore, the optimal policy is to order 80 cabinets rather than 40. The value of the objective function in this case can be found either by substitution of q^* in equation (10.6):

$$C(q^*) = \frac{32(2000)}{80} + \frac{20(80)}{2}$$

$$= 800 + 800$$

$$= 1600 \text{ per year}$$

or, directly from equation (10.8):

$$C(q^*) = \sqrt{2(32)(2000)(20)} = 1600 \text{ per year}$$

In examining these results, we see that for the economic order quantity $q^* = 80$ the annual ordering cost (800) equals the annual holding cost (800). Also, we find that the total annual cost of the system is actually $201,600. Of this total, 200,000 comes from the cost of meeting demand ($100 per item × 2000 items per year) and does not depend on the choice of the lot size. However, the other 1600 does depend on our decision.

For the current policy of ordering 40 cabinets we find from equation (10.6) that

$$C(q) = \frac{32(2000)}{40} + \frac{20(40)}{2}$$

$$= 1600 + 400$$

$$= 2000 \text{ per year}$$

By comparison, we see that the current policy costs $400 more per year than the optimal policy.

Finally, we can see how the simple model answers both of the important questions for an inventory system. First of all, our answer to the "how much" question is to order $q^* = 80$. In addition, we find that the answer to the "when" question is to order

$$\frac{d}{q^*} = \frac{2000}{80}$$

$$= 25 \text{ times per year}$$

This means placing orders approximately once every 2 weeks.

SENSITIVITY ANALYSIS

Sensitivity analysis in the basic inventory model is important because the model assumptions are fairly restrictive. By examining alternatives to the original assumptions, we can investigate questions of structural validity in the basic model. In later sections we describe some of the more interesting alternatives. Here we deal with issues of parametric validity. This type of sensitivity analysis is important because in actual practice it is often difficult to obtain precise values for the parameters of the model. For example, the model assumes that the demand rate is known in advance, but in practice it may be necessary to work with demand estimates that are in error. In addition, fixed costs and holding costs are usually very difficult to measure accurately, and the analysis may have to rely on approximate figures.

It is relatively simple to perform sensitivity analyses in the basic inventory model because there is only one decision variable, the order quantity q. An error in the assumed value of a parameter will have an impact on the choice of q and in turn will have an impact on the total cost $C(q)$. The first part of this impact—the effect on q—is easy to trace because we obtain q from the formula in equation (10.7). For example, if the fixed cost of $32 per order estimated by Hogan's accountant is in error, and the true figure should be $80, then the true optimal decision is

$$q^* = \sqrt{\frac{20(80)(2000)}{20}} \cong 126 \text{ cabinets}$$

rather than 80 as originally calculated. Thus, with the aid of the formula for an optimal order quantity, we can trace the impact of a change in a parameter on the decision variable.

The second part of the analysis is to determine the effect on costs. Suppose that there is a true set of model parameters (whose values might be difficult to obtain precisely) and that this set yields an optimal decision q^* and optimal costs $C(q^*)$. Now suppose that we use a value of q that is different from q^*. One way to assess the impact on total cost is to use a relative measure E, equal to the ratio of actual costs to optimal costs:

$$E = \frac{C(q)}{C(q^*)}$$

$$= \frac{fd/q + hq/2}{C(q^*)}$$

$$= \frac{fd/q}{C(q^*)} + \frac{hq/2}{C(q^*)} \tag{10.9}$$

In the denominator of this expression we have

$$C(q^*) = \frac{fd}{q^*} + \frac{hq^*}{2}$$

In deriving equation (10.8) we saw that q^* equates the ordering component with the holding component of annual cost, so that $fd/q^* = hq^*/2$. Therefore, we can write $C(q^*)$ either as $2fd/q^*$ or as hq^*. Using this result, we can rewrite equation (10.9):

$$E = \frac{fd/q}{2fd/q^*} + \frac{hq/2}{hq^*}$$

$$= \frac{1}{2}\left(\frac{q^*}{q} + \frac{q}{q^*}\right) \tag{10.10}$$

For convenience, let $x = q/q^*$, the ratio of the actual lot size to the optimal lot size. Then we can think of the ratio E as a function of x and write

$$E(x) = \frac{1}{2}\left(\frac{1}{x} + x\right) \tag{10.11}$$

In summary, equation (10.11) describes the impact on total cost of using a lot size different from the optimal lot size.

In the Hogan example, an error in the data induced the firm to use a lot size of $q = 80$ instead of the "true" optimal value of $q^* = 126$. Therefore, $x = q/q^* = 0.635$, and the impact on total cost is

$$E(x) = \frac{1}{2}\left(\frac{1}{0.635} + 0.635\right) = 1.10$$

In other words, the use of incorrect data results in annual costs that are 10% higher than the optimal annual cost that would be achieved if the analysis used the correct parameter.

Some representative values of the function $E(x)$ are given in the table below.

x	0.50	1.00	1.05	1.10	1.20	1.50	2.00
$E(x)$	1.25	1.00	1.001	1.005	1.017	1.083	1.25

These figures indicate that total cost is very insensitive to small errors in the choice of a lot size. For instance, the table shows that when a lot size 20% larger than optimum is employed (i.e., $x = 1.2$), total costs will be only 1.7% above optimum.

Equation (10.11) gives the relative increase in total cost due to a specified error in the choice of lot size. In the spirit of a range of validity, we might ask: For a specified maximum increase in total cost, what error range in the choice of a lot size is permissible? Let β denote the maximum permissible value of $E(x)$. Then we require

$$\beta \leq \frac{1}{2}\left(\frac{1}{x} + x\right) \tag{10.12}$$

The range of x values that satisfy this relationship is called an **economic range,** as illustrated graphically in Figure 10.3. By treating equation (10.12) as an equality and solving for x, we can derive a formula for the endpoints of the economic range. The result is

$$x = \beta \pm \sqrt{\beta^2 - 1} \tag{10.13}$$

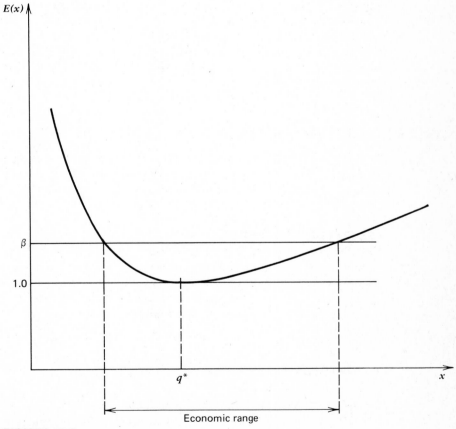

FIGURE 10.3

For example, for the Hogan Company, suppose that the optimal lot size is found to be $q^* = 126$. The limits on a 5% economic range ($\beta = 1.05$) are given by

$$x = 1.05 \pm \sqrt{(1.05)^2 - 1}$$
$$= 1.05 \pm 0.1025$$
$$= 0.9125 \text{ and } 1.1525$$

Since $x = q/q^*$, we have $q = xq^*$. Thus, in this case we find

$$q = 0.9125(126) \quad \text{and } q = 1.1525(126)$$
$$q \cong 115 \quad \text{and } q \cong 145$$

In other words, when the optimal lot size is $q^* = 126$ we can permit the actual lot size to fall between 115 and 145 and still experience no more than a 5% increase in total cost. A similar analysis shows that we could permit q to be as small as 63 (one-half of q^*) or as large as 252 (twice q^*) and have the increase in total cost be no more than 25%.

Thus, with sensitivity analysis we have demonstrated the **robustness** of the economic order quantity inventory model: Total cost is extremely insensitive to small errors in the choice of a lot size. This characteristic of the model gives it great practical value.

MODIFIED ASSUMPTIONS IN THE BASIC LOT-SIZE MODEL

In this section we investigate common changes in the assumptions of the basic lot-size model. This exercise will demonstrate that it is possible to enrich the model with much more realistic assumptions.

INVENTORY CHARGES

Under Assumption 8 of the basic model, we base holding costs on the average inventory level. Suppose, in addition, that inventory charges at the warehouse are based on the maximum inventory level that will ever be in stock. Then we can let h denote those holding costs that vary with the average inventory level, and we can let w denote those that vary with the maximum level. In this situation we obtain

$$\text{annual holding costs} = wq + \frac{hq}{2} = \frac{(2w + h)q}{2} \tag{10.14}$$

By virtue of the change in Assumption 8, the expression $(2w + h)$ now plays the role of h in the basic model. Not surprisingly, this modification directly affects annual cost:

$$C(q) = \frac{fd}{q} + \frac{(2w + h)q}{2} \tag{10.15}$$

and also the *EOQ:*

$$q^* = \sqrt{\frac{2fd}{(2w + h)}} \tag{10.16}$$

In the Hogan example, suppose that in addition to the 20% holding cost, there is a $5 per cabinet per year warehousing charge on space that must be rented for storage of filing cabinets. Because the space needed corresponds to the maximum inventory level, the optimal lot size becomes

$$q^* = \sqrt{\frac{2(32)(2000)}{[(2)(5) + 20]}} \cong 65 \text{ cabinets}$$

Therefore the optimal policy would be to rent space for 65 cabinets in the warehouse.

Notice that this general formula gives us the capability to deal either with charges on average inventory or with charges on maximum inventory or with charges on both. For example, if there is no charge on maximum inventory, then equation (10.16) reduces to equation (10.7). Also, if there is no charge on average inventory, then equation (10.16) reduces to $q^* = \sqrt{fd/w}$.

LEAD TIMES

Under Assumption 6 of the basic model, replenishment occurs instantaneously whenever a replenishment order is placed. Suppose instead that there is a known lead time of t periods—that is, the quantity arrives t periods after the order is placed. Then we can implement an optimal policy by anticipating when the inventory level will drop to 0 and placing the order t periods in advance. With this modification the replenishment order still arrives when inventory reaches 0. As a result, there is no need to modify the optimal order quantity. This timing is shown in Figure 10.4.

Note that there are two ways of interpreting the replenishment timing:

1. Order t periods before inventory drops to 0.
2. Order when inventory level drops to td.

In either case the information still answers the question of "when" to replenish inventory. In the second interpretation, however, the ordering of a replenishment lot is determined by inventory status instead of by timing. The inventory

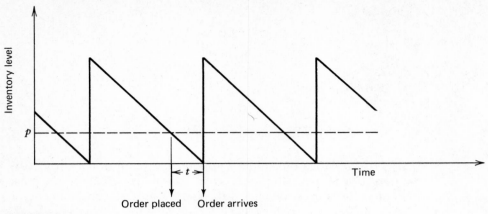

FIGURE 10.4

level at which to order is called the **order point** or **trigger level.** If p denotes the order point, then its formula is simply

$$p = td \tag{10.17}$$

In this situation the operating policy takes the form: When inventory level reaches p, order a replenishment lot of size q. This so-called **order-point/order-quantity** policy arises from the modification of Assumption 6 to allow for replenishment lead times.

   In the Hogan example, suppose that the manufacturer's lead time is 1 week. Because the demand rate is 40 cabinets per week, the order point should be

$$p = td = 1(40) = 40$$

Therefore, the operating policy for the filing cabinets will be: When inventory level reaches 40, order a replenishment lot of size 80.

   This approach is valid only when the lead time is less than or equal to the time between successive replenishment orders. For longer lead times it is necessary to provide a different analysis.

   For example, consider the situation for Hogan Office Products Company when $q^* = 80$ (implying a 2-week period between orders) and $t = 5$ (a 5-week lead time). Here we must recognize that the "effective" lead time is still 1 week, since a quantity of 80 units will arrive 1 week after placement of a replenishment order. The only difference is that when 80 units arrive, the order was placed 5 weeks previously. During that 5-week period, however, Hogan will have placed two more orders. Figure 10.5 describes this timing.

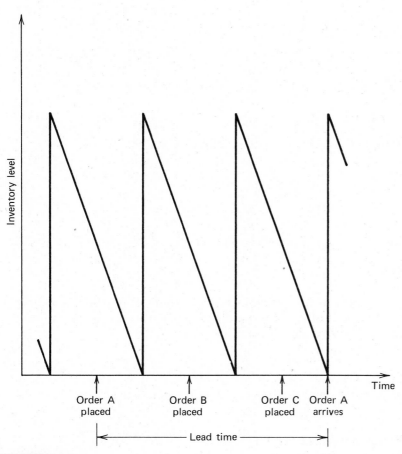

FIGURE 10.5

Fortunately, it is easy to deal with this problem. From Figure 10.5, it is clear that we could define the effective lead time, t_{eff}, as follows:

t_{eff} = time between placement of an order and the next arrival of an order

Stated in symbols:

$$t_{eff} = t - k\left(\frac{q}{d}\right)$$

where q/d represents the time between placement of orders and k is the largest integer less than or equal to td/q.

With this definition we can write equation (10.17) as follows:

$$p = t_{eff}d \tag{10.18}$$

Applying this approach to the Hogan example, we see that

$$\frac{q}{d} = \frac{80}{40}$$

$$= 2 \text{ weeks}$$

Also, because the lead time is 5 weeks, we have $td/q = 2.5$ and $k = 2$, so that

$$t_{eff} = 5 - 2(2) = 1 \text{ week}$$

Again, Figure 10.5 demonstrates graphically that there is, in fact, a period of 1 week between placement of an order and the next arrival of an order. In this case the order point is given by equation (10.18):

$$p = 1(40) = 40$$

which is the same order point as the one that corresponds to a 1-week lead time.

FINITE REPLENISHMENT RATE

Under Assumption 5 we model the behavior of a *pure* inventory system—that is, a system that obtains its replenishment from an external supply source. In contrast, many integrated manufacturers replenish inventory from an internal production source. In the *integrated* system, an order for a replenishment lot will trigger a production run in the manufacturing facility. The items produced in this production run arrive at the inventory system individually, without waiting for the entire production run to be complete. In this case the level of inventory does not go up instantaneously. Instead, it rises gradually during the production run and reaches a peak as the last item in the replenishment lot is finished.

Let r denote the production rate in the integrated system. We will assume that $r > d$, otherwise the production facility would never be able to keep up with demand. During the production run replenishment items flow into inventory at the rate r, but at the same time stock is being depleted by demand at the rate d. Therefore, the net rate at which inventory level rises is $(r - d)$. Because the production run lasts for q/r periods, the peak inventory level is equal to

$$\frac{(r - d)q}{r} = q \left(1 - \frac{d}{r} \right) = q(1 - \rho) \tag{10.19}$$

where $\rho = d/r$. The graph of inventory level behavior is shown in Figure 10.6. After the production run has ended, however, a finite amount of time remains until another run can begin. Thus, the peak inventory level must be sufficient to meet demand during the "idle" portion of the cycle. Of course, during this idle period the manufacturing facility might well be used to produce another item. The difference between this pattern and the one in Figure 10.1 reflects the fact that we have modified Assumption 5 to allow for a finite replenishment rate.

In the integrated system the **ordering cost** for a replenishment batch of q items is still expressed as $f + vq$. Here the fixed cost f includes costs incurred in conjunction with setting up the facility for the production run, in addition to the record keeping and inspection costs that might still be as relevant in the integrated situation as they were in the pure inventory system. For example, the fixed costs might include labor costs associated with machine changeovers, scrap costs associated with "learning" effects, and the opportunity cost of nonproductive setup time if the facility would otherwise be engaged in a different kind of

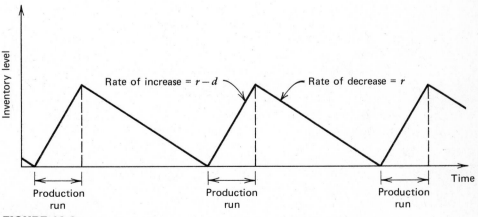

FIGURE 10.6

production. As before, the variable cost vq includes costs that are proportional to the size of the lot, such as variable labor, material, and overhead components of production cost. Therefore, the form of the annual ordering cost would remain unchanged from equation (10.2).

Holding costs reflect the same factors in the integrated system as in the pure inventory system. The only difference from the original analysis in calculating the annual holding cost is that the average inventory level is now $(1 - \rho)q/2$. Thus, when we restrict attention to the costs that depend on the lot size, the objective function becomes

$$C(q) = \frac{fd}{q} + \frac{h(1 - \rho)q}{2} \tag{10.20}$$

Comparing the structure of this function to the one in equation (10.6), we find that the only difference is that the role of the unit holding cost h in equation (10.6) is now played by $h(1 - \rho)$. Because the mathematical structure of the objective function is otherwise the same, the optimal lot size is given by

$$q^* = \sqrt{\frac{2fd}{h(1 - \rho)}} \tag{10.21}$$

and an expression for the optimal value of the objective function is

$$C(q^*) = \sqrt{2fdh(1 - \rho)} \tag{10.22}$$

As an aside, notice that $\rho = 0$ corresponds to an infinite replenishment rate. For such a case the results of equations (10.21) and (10.22) reduce to those of equations (10.7) and (10.8) for the basic model.

As an example, suppose the Hogan Office Products Company has access to some manufacturing equipment with which it could produce its own cabinets at a rate of 200 per week. As a result, $\rho = d/r = 40/200 = 0.2$. Also, suppose that in this production environment the fixed cost of setting up for a production run amounts to \$120, while the variable cost of producing a cabinet is only \$60. Because the holding cost rate of 20% presumably still applies, we can calculate the optimal replenishment quantity from equation (10.21) as follows:

$$q^* = \sqrt{\frac{2(120)(2000)}{(0.2)(60)(1 - 0.2)}} \cong 224 \text{ cabinets}$$

The peak inventory level is $q(1 - \rho) = 224(0.8) \cong 179$ cabinets, and from equation (10.20) the optimal total cost is

$$C(q^*) = \frac{120(2000)}{224} + \frac{(0.2)(60)(1 - 0.2)(224)}{2}$$

$$= 1071 + 1075$$

$$= 2146$$

We could produce the same result from equation (10.22) by calculating

$$C(q^*) = \sqrt{2(120)(2000)(0.2)(60)(1 - 0.2)}$$

$$= 2146$$

Once more we find that, for the optimal lot size in equation (10.20), annual ordering costs essentially equal annual holding costs. (Here they are not exactly equal only because we rounded the lot size to the integer 224.)

QUANTITY DISCOUNTS

Under Assumption 7 of the basic model, a replenishment order of size q incurs a purchase cost with a fixed component and a variable component in the form vq. Further, we have assumed that v, the variable cost per unit, is constant. In some situations, however, vendors offer a price break for large orders. The form of the price break is frequently a discount on the unit cost, offered for a sufficiently large lot size. The existence of such a discount violates the assumption of a constant variable cost per unit, and the investigation of optimal lot sizes when quantity discounts exist is a topic that might well arise in assessing the structural validity of the basic model.

Suppose that a vendor offers two unit costs, depending on the purchase quantity, in the form of the following schedule:

for $q < B$ the unit price is v_1

for $q \geq B$ the unit price is v_2

where B is called the **break point** and we assume that $v_1 > v_2$. This situation creates an additional trade-off to be considered in selecting a lot size. In the basic model, the optimal order quantity finds the best trade-off between fixed and holding components of total inventory cost. With the possibility of a quantity discount, however, it might be desirable to choose an order quantity that does not minimize total inventory cost in order to take advantage of lower unit prices. In the basic model we ignored the variable purchase cost (dv) because the variable cost per year was constant in equation (10.5). However, we must consider this component of annual cost when quantity discounts exist.

If there were no discount and the applicable unit price were v_1, the objective function would be written in the form of equation (10.5):

$$C_1(q) = \frac{fd}{q} + \frac{h_1 q}{2} + dv_1 \tag{10.23}$$

where the subscript denotes parameters that actually depend on the lot size. (Here we assume that the unit holding cost is expressed as a percentage of the unit price, so that $h_1 = \alpha v_1$.) The subscript 1 simply denotes the first range in the price break schedule. In this spirit we can write the optimal lot size when v_1 applies as $q_1^* = \sqrt{2fd/h_1}$.

On the other hand, if the applicable unit price were v_2, the objective function would be

$$C_2(q) = \frac{fd}{q} + \frac{h_2 q}{2} + dv_2 \tag{10.24}$$

where $h_2 = \alpha v_2$ and the subscript refers to the second range in the price break schedule. For this case the optimal lot size would be $q_2^* = \sqrt{2fd/h_2}$.

Because $v_2 < v_1$ and $h_2 < h_1$, it follows from equation (10.24) that $C_2(q) < C_1(q)$ for any given value of q. In graphical terms, the cost curve $C_2(q)$ lies below the curve $C_1(q)$. Therefore, the minimum-cost point on the curve $C_2(q)$ is certain to be better (lower in cost) than the minimum-cost point on the curve $C_1(q)$. Therefore, q_2^* is the optimal lot size, provided that we can order the quantity q_2^* at the unit price v_2.

Lot sizes $q \geq B$ are said to be **admissible** for the unit price v_2 under the terms of the price-break schedule. Similarly, lot sizes $q < B$ are admissible for v_1, but they are not admissible for v_2. Therefore, the relevant objective function is actually a combination of $C_1(q)$, over the q values admissible for v_1, and $C_2(q)$, over the q values admissible for v_2. The graphical structure of the relevant objective function is illustrated in Figure 10.7. It should be obvious that if q_2^* is admissible for v_2 then q_2^* is the optimal lot size.

Suppose, however, that q_2^* is not admissible for v_2, because q_2^* is too small to obtain the unit price v_2. In this situation the analysis must recognize the inherent trade-off explicitly. A look at Figure 10.7 reveals that when q_2^* is not admissible for v_2 the relevant portion of $C_2(q)$ will always be an increasing function. In this case the minimum-cost lot size admissible for v_2 will be the smallest lot size admissible for v_2, or simply the break point quantity B. The associated cost is obtained from equation (10.24):

$$C_2^* = C_2(B) = \frac{fd}{B} + \frac{h_2 B}{2} + dv_2 \tag{10.25}$$

where C_2^* denotes the minimum cost on the relevant portion of $C_2(q)$. Meanwhile, the minimum-cost lot size for v_1 will be q_1^*, and from equation (10.23) we have

$$C_1^* = C_1(q_1^*) = \frac{fd}{q_1^*} + \frac{h_1 q_1^*}{2} + dv_1 \tag{10.26}$$

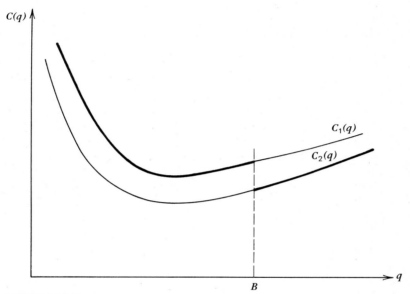

FIGURE 10.7

where C_1^* denotes the minimum cost on the relevant portion of $C_1(q)$. In general, there is no way to know whether C_1^* or C_2^* is lower except by direct calculation and comparison.

In the Hogan example suppose that the appropriate parameters are $f = 32$ and $d = 2000$ per year, and that the holding cost is 20% per year. We found earlier that in this case the optimal lot size is 80 cabinets. Suppose now that the manufacturer of the filing cabinets offers the following price break schedule:

unit price $v_1 = \$100$ for $q < 250$

unit price $v_2 = \$98$ ·for $q \geq 250$

We first compute q_2^* to see whether it is admissible for v_2:

$$q_2^* = \sqrt{\frac{2(32)(2000)}{(0.2)(98)}} \cong 81$$

Here we see that $q_2^* = 81$ is inadmissible because the unit price of $98 applies only when replenishment orders are for 250 items or more. Therefore, the minimum cost on the relevant portion of $C_2(q)$ occurs for the lot size $q = B = 250$, for which

$$C_2^* = \frac{32(2000)}{250} + \frac{(0.2)(98)(250)}{2} + 2000(98) = 198,706$$

On the relevant portion of $C_1(q)$ the minimum cost is achieved for the lot size $q_1^* = 80$, for which

$$C_1^* = \frac{32(2000)}{80} + \frac{(0.2)(100)(80)}{2} + 2000(100) = 201,600$$

Therefore, the optimal lot size in this situation is 250 cabinets, and the annual total cost is $198,706. In this situation the savings due to the price break more than offset the increase in total fixed and holding costs at the price-break quantity.

When there is more than one price break, similar reasoning applies. In general, we can have n distinct unit prices and $(n - 1)$ break points, as follows:

for $q < B_1$	unit price $= v_1$
for $B_1 \leq q < B_2$	unit price $= v_2$
.	.
.	.
.	.
for $B_{n-2} \leq q < B_{n-1}$	unit price $= v_{n-1}$
for $q \geq B_{n-1}$	unit price $= v_n$

ALGORITHM 10.1
Determining an Optimal Lot Size When Price Breaks Exist

1. Let $k = n$ and $B_k = \infty$.
2. Calculate $q_k^* = \sqrt{2fd/h_k}$.
3. If q_k^* is admissible for v_k (that is, $B_{k-1} \leq q_k < B_k$), then go to Step 6.
4. B_{k-1} is the best admissible order quantity for v_k. Calculate $C_k^* = fd/B_{k-1} + h_k B_{k-1}/2 + dv_k$.
5. Reduce k by 1 and go to Step 2.
6. Because q_k^* is admissible for v_k, calculate $C_k^* = fd/q_k^* + h_k q_k^*/2 + dv_k$.
7. Compare C_k^* with all C_j^* that have previously been calculated (for $j > k$). The lowest C_j^* and its corresponding order quantity are optimal.

With this set of price breaks, Algorithm 10.1 determines an optimal lot size. The algorithm does not necessarily consider admissible lot sizes for every unit price. Instead, it stops when it encounters an admissible q_k^* and makes the final comparisons at Steps 6 and 7. Curtailing the search in this way does not overlook any order quantities that could be optimal.

As an example, suppose that the manufacturer of the filing cabinets offers a revised price-break schedule:

unit price $v_1 = \$100$ for $q < 50$

unit price $v_2 = \$99$ for $50 \le q < 250$

unit price $v_3 = \$98$ for $q \ge 250$

The solution procedure begins with $k = 3$.

Step 2 $q_3^* = \sqrt{2(32)(2000)/0.2(98)} \cong 81$ (inadmissible)

Step 4 Because q_3^* is inadmissible, we use $B_3 = 250$.

$$C_3^* = 32(2000)/250 + 0.2(98)(250)/2 + 2000(98)$$
$$= 198,706$$

At Step 5 we reduce k to 2.

Step 2 $q_2^* = \sqrt{2(32)(2000)/0.2(99)} = 80$ (admissible)

Step 6 $C_2^* = 32(2000)/80 + 0.2(99)(80)/2 + 2000(99)$
$$= 199,592$$

Step 7 Compare C_2^* with C_3^*

The optimal order quantity is 250.

In this example there is no need to consider $k = 1$ because q_2^* is admissible.

In this section we have considered several ways of extending the basic lot-size model by replacing its simple assumptions with more realistic conditions. The *EOQ* of equation (10.7) anchored each of these investigations of structural validity. In the next section we consider an extension that changes the nature of economic order quantities and also the analysis by which they are determined.

THE DYNAMIC LOT-SIZE MODEL

The structural validity of the basic lot-size model is certainly open to question when demand follows a trend or seasonal pattern or delivery contracts provide for nonconstant demands. Therefore, it is quite useful to extend the basic model beyond Assumption 3 when the demand rate is not assumed to be constant. In this section we examine the implications of this modification for model formulation and analysis, while preserving the other assumptions of the basic lot-size model. Thus, we deal with a pure inventory system for a single product in which demand is known in advance and there is no uncertainty. We seek a replenishment schedule that will minimize the sum of ordering and holding costs given that all demand must be met on time.

In order to describe demand behavior, assume that we are looking for a replenishment schedule for the next N periods, numbered $t = 1, 2, \ldots, N$. Let d_t denote demand in period t. Such an approach involves a discrete-time view of demand, in contrast to the continuous-time view that characterizes the basic lot-size model. However, we shall find it convenient to assume that there is at most one replenishment order placed in any period, but within this restriction the designation of a "period" is arbitrary. A period could be equal to a day, a week, or a month.

The discrete-time structure allows us to treat holding costs in a special way. For instance, consider Figure 10.8, which depicts two replenishment schedules for a hypothetical two-period problem. Plan A calls for only one replenishment order, at the start of period 1. This order must meet demand for both periods. Plan B calls for one replenishment order each period, with no inventory carried from period 1 into period 2. Figure 10.8 shows that certain triangular portions of the inventory graph are common to both plans. For ease of identification these common areas are shaded. The average inventory level in these shaded

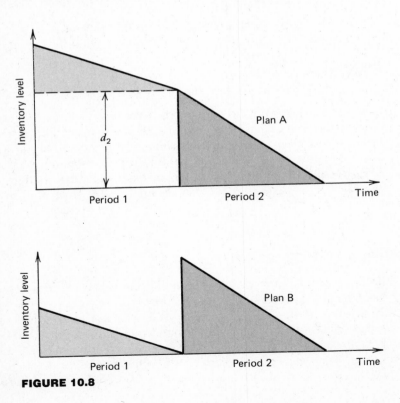

FIGURE 10.8

portions of the graph is the same under either plan, and therefore it cannot be affected by the ordering policy. In fact, only the inventory carried over to period 2 from period 1 distinguishes the total holding cost of Plan A from the total holding cost of Plan B. Under Plan A this quantity is d_2, held throughout period 1, and under Plan B this quantity is 0.

In general, we shall ignore the portions of the inventory graph that are common to all plans, since these components of total cost are not affected by ordering decisions. The implication of this approach is that we assess holding costs *only* upon inventory held throughout a period. Under this cost convention, holding cost is assessed only on the inventory remaining at the end of a period. Let i_t denote the inventory level at the end of period t. Then the holding cost for period t will be hi_t, where h denotes the holding cost in dollars per item per period. Thus, we have

$$\text{total holding cost} = \sum_{t=1}^{N} hi_t \tag{10.27}$$

As in the basic lot-size model, assume that the form of the ordering cost is

$$f + vq_t$$

where q_t is the order quantity in period t. Let $\delta(q)$ denote an indicator function to show whether an order is placed. In other words, $\delta(q) = 1$ if $q > 0$ (to show that an order is placed) and $\delta(q) = 0$ if $q = 0$ (to show that no order is placed). With this notation we can write the total cost for the N periods as follows:

$$\sum_{t=1}^{N} [f\delta(q_t) + vq_t + hi_t] \tag{10.28}$$

where

$$i_t = \sum_{k=1}^{t} q_k - \sum_{k=1}^{t} d_k \qquad (t = 1, 2, \ldots, N) \tag{10.29}$$

By assumption, all demand is met on time, so that $i_t \geq 0$. Furthermore, we are assuming that there is no initial inventory and that there is no need for final inventory. Thus, $i_0 = i_N = 0$. Because of this assumption, we are able to write the expression for i_t in equation (10.29) as the difference between cumulative purchases and cumulative demand.

The middle terms of equation (10.28) sum to a constant, since

$$\sum_{t=1}^{N} vq_t = v \sum_{t=1}^{N} d_t$$

Therefore, as in the basic model, we can ignore the linear portion of the ordering cost when we search for an optimal solution. The task is then as follows:

minimize

$$\sum_{t=1}^{N} [f\delta(q_t) + hi_t] \tag{10.30}$$

subject to

$$i_t = \sum_{k=1}^{t} q_k - \sum_{k=1}^{t} d_k \geq 0 \qquad (t = 1, 2, \ldots, N)$$

The search for an optimal plan is aided by two properties that limit the number of plans that must be compared. These properties are discussed below.

DOMINANT PLANS

Suppose we propose a plan with a period t $(1 < t \leq N)$ in which there is a replenishment order $(q_t > 0)$ and also in which there is inventory carried over from the previous period $(i_{t-1} > 0)$. Figure 10.9 shows a partial graph of inventory behavior for this plan, along with an alternate plan. Under the alternative, the quantity i_{t-1} is not acquired before period t but instead is added to the proposed replenishment order in period t. Otherwise, the plans are identical. Therefore, under the alternate plan:

1. Inventories in period $t - 1$ are lower than in the proposed plan, and as a result, holding costs in period $t - 1$ are lower.
2. Because both plans call for a replenishment in period t, fixed costs in period t are the same.
3. Costs prior to period $t - 1$ are at least as low as those in the proposed plan (and possibly better, if there is a savings in earlier holding or fixed costs).

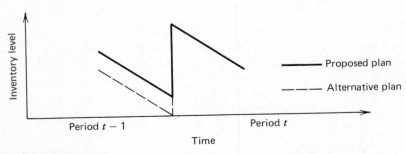

FIGURE 10.9

The alternate plan is a strict improvement on the proposed plan, because it satisfies demand at lower total cost. We conclude that in searching for an optimal plan we can ignore plans such as the proposed plan. To put it more formally:

Property 1
There exists an optimal plan in which $i_{t-1}q_t = 0$. In other words, in each period either the incoming inventory or the replenishment quantity is 0.

In searching for an optimal plan we can limit attention to plans with the property $i_{t-1}q_t = 0$. Such plans are called **dominant** plans, because (in light of Property 1) they dominate other kinds of plans in the sense of achieving lower costs. As a consequence, it is never desirable to have a period's beginning inventory represent only a fraction of the period's demand. This means that an optimal plan will have the characteristic that production in a period must satisfy demand for that period *or* for that period and the next period *or* for that period and the next two periods, and so on. The task remains to search among the dominant plans for an optimum. An efficient computational scheme for performing this search is the result of a second property.

RECURSIVE CALCULATIONS
Assume we are solving an N-period problem, and suppose we were told that inventory should be 0 at the end of period t, for some value of $t < N$. This information allows us to split the N-period problem into two portions: one portion covering periods 1 through t with no final inventory, and the other portion covering periods $t + 1$ through N in some fashion. It should be obvious that the first portion is simply a shortened (t-period) version of the N-period problem. Moreover, if we had access to the optimal solution for this t-period problem, we could insert that solution in the N-period analysis and then concentrate only on finding the optimal plan for the portion covering periods $t + 1$ through N. Formally,

Property 2
Given that $i_t = 0$ in the optimal solution to an N-period problem ($1 \leq t < N$), then in determining an optimal N-period plan it suffices to use the optimal plan for the subproblem consisting of periods 1 through t.

The difficulty with this result is that we cannot expect to be "told" that $i_t = 0$. Nevertheless, we can at least exploit the fact that *given* $i_t = 0$ we know how to split the N-period problem into two subproblems. This insight is the basis for the solution algorithm described below.

An optimal plan for the N-period problem has the property that the final replenishment order must be delivered *somewhere* between periods 1 and N. Of course, if the final replacement occurs in the first period, then there is just one order for the entire planning period, and there is no need to decompose the problem into subproblems. Instead, suppose that the final replenishment occurs in period $t > 1$. Then $q_t > 0$, and by Property 1 we need to consider only plans in which $i_{t-1} = 0$. However, given $i_{t-1} = 0$, we know from Property 2 that the structure of the optimal plan will be: *first,* the optimal plan covering periods 1 through $t - 1$, *then* the final replenishment order. The task remaining is to check all the possibilities for the timing of the final order. Furthermore, this same procedure can be applied to the solution of the shorter subproblems, at earlier stages. From these observations we construct the solution procedure shown as Algorithm 10.2.

ALGORITHM 10.2
Determining Optimal Quantities for the Dynamic Lot-Size Model

1. (Initialization)

   Let $t = 1$, $C(1,1) = f$, $C_1^* = f$, $P_1^* = 1$.

2. (Time increment)

   Increment t by 1.

3. (Calculate the minimum cost for the t-period problem given that the final replenishment occurs in period k.)

   For $1 \leq k \leq t - 1$, let $C(k, t) = C(k, t - 1) + h(t - k)d_k$.

   For $k = t$, let $C(t, t) = C_{t-1}^* + f$.

4. (Find the minimum cost for the t-period problem, and the corresponding plan.)

   let $C_t^* = \min\{C(k, t)\}$ for $1 \leq k \leq t$

   let $P_t^* =$ the k-value for which the minimum occurs.

5. (End of problem)

   If $t = N$, stop. C_N^* is the optimal cost.

   Otherwise, return to Step 2.

To follow the algorithm, some additional notation is helpful:

$C(k, t) =$ minimum cost for the t-period problem, given that the final replenishment occurs in period k

$C_t^* =$ minimum cost for the t-period problem

$P_t^* =$ the period in which the last replenishment occurs, for the minimum-cost solution to the t-period problem

The critical portion of the algorithm is Step 3, where we calculate values of $C(k, t)$. For $1 \leq k \leq t - 1$, $C(k, t)$ can be calculated from $C(k, t - 1)$, the minimum cost for the $(t - 1)$-period problem when the last order also occurs in period k. The only modification needed is to reflect the additional holding cost for the items that are delivered in period k to satisfy demand during period t. These items are held $(t - k)$ periods, and the corresponding holding cost is $h(t - k)d_t$. Therefore

$$C(k, t) = C(k, t - 1) + h(t - k)d_t$$

For $k = t$, however, the reasoning is different. Given that a replenishment occurs in period t, this means i_{t-1} will be 0. The t-period problem (and its cost) can be split into two portions, using the rationale of Properties 1 and 2. The first portion costs C_{t-1}^*, which is the minimum cost of reaching the end of period $(t - 1)$ with no inventory, while the second portion costs f, the fixed cost associated with obtaining a replenishment in period t. Therefore,

$$C(t, t) = C_{t-1}^* + f$$

To illustrate the calculations, consider a four-period problem in which the demands are 70, 90, 110, and 130; and suppose that $h = 1$ and $f = 250$. In Table 10.1 we display a convenient format for summarizing the calculations of Algorithm 10.2. The table contains four columns, one for each period, and the given demand pattern appears along the top. The body of the table will contain the $C(k, t)$ values as we calculate them, and the optimal solution to subproblems will be summarized in the bottom two rows.

The Initialization step of Algorithm 10.2 is reflected in Table 10.1. The only way to meet demand in period 1 is to schedule a replenishment in period 1, incurring the fixed cost of 250. Therefore, the minimum cost for the 1-period problem, given that the final replenishment occurs in period 1, must be 250. We have entered this figure in Table 10.1 as $C(1, 1)$. Furthermore, since there was only one alternative to consider, we have that C_1^*, the minimum cost for the 1-period problem, must also equal 250. In addition, the last replenishment in this schedule occurs at $P_1^* = 1$. The values of C_1^* and P_1^* are shown in Table 10.1 at the bottom of the column for $t = 1$.

TABLE 10.1

| | t | 1 | 2 | 3 | 4 |
	d_t	70	90	110	130
	$k = 1$	250			
$C(k, t)$	$k = 2$				
	$k = 3$				
	$k = 4$				
	C_t^*	250			
	P_t^*	1			

At Step 2 we increment t and consider the ways of meeting demand in period 2. There are two ways, according to whether the final replenishment occurs in period 1 or period 2, and their two costs are denoted $C(1, 2)$ and $C(2, 2)$, respectively. If the final replenishment occurs in period 1, we have $k = 1$ and $t = 2$. Here we order 160 units in period 1. Of these 160 units, 70 will meet demand in period 1, while the remaining 90 will be held to meet demand in period 2. Step 3 of the algorithm yields

$$C(1, 2) = C(1, 1) + h(2 - 1)d_2 = C(1, 1) + 1(1)(90)$$

where we previously calculated $C(1, 1)$ to be 250. Thus,

$$C(1, 2) = 250 + 90 = 340$$

In the other case ($k = 2$) the final replenishment occurs in period 2. The cost of this alternative will be the minimum cost of getting to the end of period 1, with no final inventory, plus the cost of replenishment in period 2 to meet demand in period 2. Stated in symbols, Step 3 yields

$$C(2, 2) = C_1^* + f = 250 + 250 = 500$$

At Step 4 we choose the lower of these two costs to be the minimum cost for the 2-period problem:

$$C_2^* = \min\{C(1, 2), C(2, 2)\} = \min\{340, 500\} = 340$$

Finally, since the minimum occurred for $k = 1$, we have $P_2^* = 1$. Table 10.2 displays these calculations in the column for $t = 2$. These results mean that the least expensive way of solving the 2-period problem is to place one order (for 160 units) in period 1 and to carry 90 units into period 2.

TABLE 10.2

	t	1	2	3	4
	d_t	70	90	110	130
	$k = 1$	250	340		
$C(k, t)$	$k = 2$		500		
	$k = 3$				
	$k = 4$				
	C_t^*	250	340		
	P_t^*	1	1		

Returning to Step 2, we increment t and consider the ways of meeting demand in period 3. Now there are three alternatives, according to whether the last replenishment occurs in period 1, 2, or 3. If it occurs in period 1, the schedule matches the one underlying $C(1, 2)$ with the addition of 110 units to the replenishment in period 1. These units are held two periods, giving rise to the cost indicated in Step 3:

$$C(1, 3) = C(1, 2) + h(3 - 1)d_3 = C(1, 2) + 1(2)(110)$$
$$= 340 \quad + \quad 220 \quad = 560$$

Similarly, if the last replenishment occurs in period 2, we obtain

$$C(2, 3) = C(2, 2) + h(3 - 2)d_3 = C(2, 2) + 1(1)(110)$$
$$= 500 \quad + \quad 110 \quad = 610$$

Third, if the last replenishment occurs in period 3, then we must reach the end of period 2 with no final inventory. The minimum cost of doing so is 340, as we found when we filled out Table 10.2. Therefore, using the formula of Step 3, we obtain

$$C(3, 3) = C_2^* + f = 340 + 250 = 590$$

Then at Step 4 we identify the minimum of the three costs:

$$C_3^* = \min\{C(1, 3), C(2, 3), C(3, 3)\}$$
$$= \min\{560, 610, 590\}$$
$$= 560$$

Thus, the best schedule for the three-period problem has a single replenishment occurring in period 1. Table 10.3 summarizes these calculations.

TABLE 10.3

		1	2	3	4
	t	1	2	3	4
	d_t	70	90	110	130
	$k = 1$	250	340	560	
	$k = 2$		500	610	
$C(k, t)$	$k = 3$			590	
	$k = 4$				
	C_t^*	250	340	560	
	P_t^*	1	1	1	

Finally, we complete the calculations of $C(k, t)$ values by returning to Step 2 and incrementing t. This time there are four alternatives:

$$C(1, 4) = C(1, 3) + 1(3)(130) = 560 + 390 = 950$$
$$C(2, 3) = C(2, 3) + 1(2)(130) = 610 + 260 = 870$$
$$C(3, 3) = C(3, 3) + 1(1)(130) = 590 + 130 = 720$$
$$C(4, 4) = C_3^* + f = 560 + 250 = 810$$

At Step 4 we find

$$C_4^* = \min\{C(1, 4), C(2, 4), C(3, 4), C(4, 4)\} = 720$$

with $P_4^* = 3$. These calculations are shown in Table 10.4

Having completed the calculations, Step 5 indicates that the optimal cost is $C_4^* = 720$. From Table 10.4 we can tell that the final replenishment occurs in period $P_4^* = 3$. That means $q_3 = 240$ (equal to demand from period 3 to the end of the problem) and also $i_2 = 0$. To construct the remainder of the optimal plan, recall from Property 2 that since $i_2 = 0$ we can consider periods 1 and 2 as a separate two-period subproblem. Earlier in the calculations we found that $P_2^* = 1$, which means that the final replenishment in this two-period subproblem occurs in period 1. Therefore, $q_1 = 160$ (equal to demand from period 1 to the end of the subproblem). In summary, the optimal plan is

t	1	2	3	4
q_t	160	0	240	0

In general, we reconstruct the optimal plan from the calculations by identifying P_N^*. This implies that for $t = P_N^*$ the optimal plan will have $q_t > 0$ and $i_{t-1} = 0$.

TABLE 10.4

t	1	2	3	4
d_t	70	90	110	130
$k = 1$	250	340	560	950
$k = 2$		500	610	870
$k = 3$			590	720
$k = 4$				810
C_t^*	250	340	560	720
P_t^*	1	1	1	3

From Property 2, we can treat periods 1 through $(t - 1)$ as a separate subproblem, and we can reconstruct its optimal plan in a similar fashion. We can repeat this procedure until we determine the size of the order in period 1.

Finally, there are two simple ways to extend the model. First, suppose there is an initial inventory ($i_0 > 0$). In this case we schedule this inventory to meet demand at the beginning of the problem. Once this inventory is allocated, we are left with revised or *net* demands, and no initial inventory; and we can use Algorithm 10.2. In our example, suppose $i_0 = 75$. Then our net demands become

t	1	2	3	4
d_t	0	15	110	130

Algorithm 10.2, applied to this problem, will produce an optimal policy.

Second, suppose that there is a requirement for final inventory ($i_N > 0$). In this case we simply add this requirement to the last demand, d_N, and proceed by applying Algorithm 10.2 to the revised problem. In our example, suppose $i_4 = 22$. Then we set $d_4 = 152$ and proceed with the algorithm.

MODELS WITH UNCERTAIN DEMAND

Under Assumptions 2 and 4 of the basic lot-size model all demand is met on time, and demand is known with certainty. An alternative scenario, more suitable for some inventory analyses, is to treat demand as uncertain and also to allow for lost sales or backorders. In this context we may view the demand parameter d as the mean demand rate, which might be a good long-term estimate but which is subject to forecast errors in the short term.

Consider an inventory system operating under an order-point/order-quantity control procedure in which lead time is constant: When the inventory level drops to the order point p, an order is placed for a replenishment lot of size q. Figure 10.10 describes the behavior of this system.

During the lead time, while the system is awaiting the delivery of replenishment stock, there is only the quantity of p items available to meet demand. Suppose that demand during the lead time is denoted D and is treated as a random variable. Let μ denote $E[D]$, the mean or expected value of this distribution.

The link between this probabilistic scenario and the analysis of the basic lot-size model (with lead times) is the fact that $p = \mu$. Because d represents the mean demand rate, $p = td$ represents the mean demand during the lead time interval t. In other words, the analysis of the basic model provides for only enough stock to satisfy expected demand during the lead time. In order to satisfy a greater portion of demand, an additional stock must be available when a replenishment

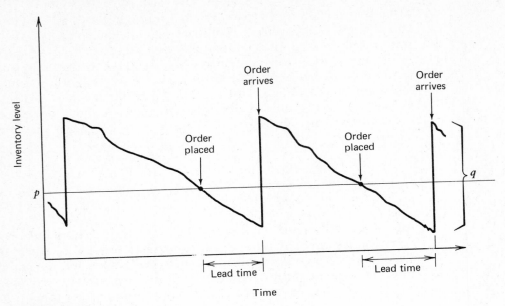

FIGURE 10.10

order is placed. This additional stock, called **safety stock,** provides a reserve in case lead time demand exceeds its expected value.

In order to describe the effects of safety stock in quantitative terms, we must know the probability distribution for lead time demand. Let $F(x) = P(D \leq x)$ denote the cumulative distribution function for this probability model. Then $F(x)$ represents the probability that lead time demand will be less than or equal to x. Equivalently, $F(x)$ is the probability that an order point equal to x is sufficient to satisfy all demand during the lead time.

In the Hogan example, suppose that lead time demand is modeled by a normal distribution with mean $\mu = 40$ and standard deviation $\sigma = 5$. If there is no safety stock, then the order point is $p = \mu = 40$ and the probability of meeting lead-time demand is given by

$$P(D \leq 40) = F(40) = 0.50$$

If there is a safety stock of 5 items, then the order point is equal to mean demand plus this reserve quantity, or $p = 40 + 5 = 45$. The probability of meeting lead-time demand is given in this case by

$$P(D \leq 45) = F(45) = 0.8413$$

If we increase the safety stock to 10 items, then the order point is $p = 50$ and the probability of meeting lead-time demand increases to

$$P(D \leq 50) = F(50) = 0.9772$$

These probabilities are sketched in Figure 10.11

The probability that the available inventory at the order point will be sufficient to meet lead time demand is usually called the **service level.** Using the notation introduced above, we have

$$\text{service level} = P(D \leq p) = F(p) \qquad (10.31)$$

Now suppose that some safety stock is held in inventory. Because demand during the lead time is random, there will be some lead times during which none of the safety stock is needed, and there will be other lead times during which some or all of the safety stock is consumed. If demand happens to be less than the mean, then the inventory level when the replenishment order arrives will be higher than the safety stock quantity; but if the demand happens to be more than the mean, then the inventory level when the order arrives will be lower than the safety stock quantity. On average, this inventory level at the end of the lead time will be approximately equal to the safety stock level provided that lost sales are infrequent.

This observation suggests that a graph of average inventory behavior (with the randomness suppressed) will resemble Figure 10.12. Therefore, when we examine the long-run behavior of the system, we find that the safety stock is a quantity held in stock entirely in addition to the average stock that appears in the basic model. For each item of safety stock, on average the firm can expect to incur a cost equal to the holding cost for that item. In other words, we have

$$C(s) = hs \qquad (10.32)$$

where s represents the safety stock level and $C(s)$ represents the total annual cost of holding safety stock. Coupling this annual cost with $C(q)$, the annual cost associated with the lot-size quantity, we find

$$C(q, s) = C(q) + C(s) \qquad (10.33)$$

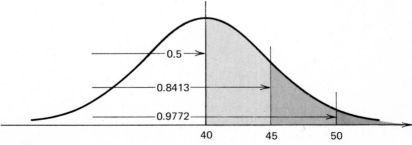

FIGURE 10.11

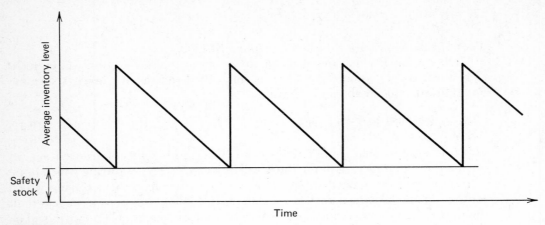

FIGURE 10.12

where $C(q, s)$ represents the total annual cost of the order-point/order-quantity system. For example, in the basic lot-size model, we have

$$C(q, s) = \frac{fd}{q} + \frac{hq}{2} + hs \qquad (10.34)$$

The cost behavior of safety stock gives rise to a trade-off inherent in the decision to employ safety stock: higher service levels require higher holding costs. The table below delineates this trade-off for the Hogan example, under the assumption that demand during the lead time follows a normal distribution with mean $\mu = 40$ and standard deviation $\sigma = 5$.

Order Point p	Safety Stock s	Annual Cost of Safety Stock $C(s)$	Service Level $F(p)$
40	0	$ 0	0.50
44	4	80	0.79
48	8	160	0.95
52	12	240	0.99
56	16	320	0.999

The right-hand pair of columns shows the trade-off between the cost of safety stock and the service level provided. The economics of this trade-off become more clear if we note that low service levels have a large number of lost sales or back orders (and, thus, large stockout penalties), while high service levels have small stockout penalties. Figure 10.13 depicts these costs and shows that concep-

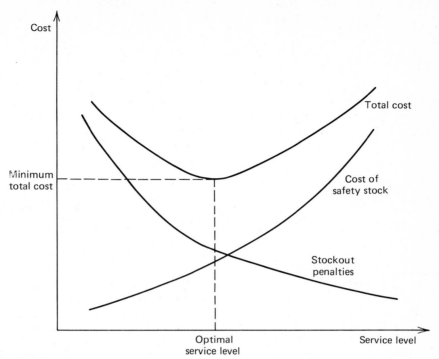

FIGURE 10.13

tually there will be a service level and its associated safety stock for which total costs are minimized.

A different approach is to interpret the service level as the long-run proportion of demand that is satisfied under a particular safety stock policy. This interpretation is different from ours for two reasons. First, our service level analysis applies only to the lead time interval, not to the entire replenishment cycle. In the Hogan example the lead time is 1 week, but when $q^* = 80$ the replenishment cycle is 2 weeks in length. Second, our service level actually measures the long-run proportion of lead time occurrences in which demand is met, rather than the long-run proportion of demand that is met. However, we can measure this latter proportion with appropriate calculations.

To demonstrate this second approach, consider a situation in which lost sales can occur. We define $p_k = P(D = k)$ as the (discrete) probability distribution function for demand during the lead time, and S as the number of lost sales during a particular lead time. Because lost sales occur only when actual demand D exceeds the order point p, we have

$$S = \max\{0, D - p\} \tag{10.35}$$

The expected value of lost sales per cycle is

$$E[S] = E[\max\{0, D - p\}] = \sum_{k=p+1}^{\infty} (k - p)P_k \tag{10.36}$$

On the average, the total demand in a replenishment cycle consists of demand that is met (q), plus demand that is lost ($E[S]$). Thus, the overall proportion of demand met from stock is

$$\frac{q}{(q + E[S])} \tag{10.37}$$

For the special case in which a normal probability model is used, the appropriate formula for lost sales per replenishment cycle becomes

$$E[S] = \sigma N(z) \tag{10.38}$$

where $z = (p - \mu)/\sigma$, and $N(z)$ is the unit normal loss function tabulated in the appendix. It is possible to develop a similar form of analysis to deal with situations in which backorders occur instead of lost sales. In such situations a replacement for equation (10.37) gives the proportion of demand met from stock:

$$\frac{(q - E[S])}{q} \tag{10.39}$$

With the use of equation (10.37) and the recognition that the annual number of lost sales is $E[S]d/q$ we can develop Table 10.5 for the situation facing Hogan Office Products Company when they use $q* = 80$.

TABLE 10.5

Order Point	Safety Stock	z	$N(z)$	$E[S]$ Lost Sales per Cycle	$E[S]d/q$ Annual Number of Lost Sales
40	0	0.0	0.3989	1.9945	49.862
44	4	0.8	0.1202	0.6010	15.025
48	8	1.6	0.0232	0.1160	2.900
50	10	2.0	0.00849	0.0424	1.060
51	11	2.2	0.00489	0.0244	0.610
52	12	2.4	0.00272	0.0136	0.340
53	13	2.6	0.00146	0.0073	0.182
54	14	2.8	0.000761	0.0038	0.095

TABLE 10.6

Order Point	Safety Stock	Annual Cost of Safety Stock	Annual Lost Sales	Annual Cost of Lost Sales	Annual Total Cost
40	0	$ 0	49.862	$2492	$2493
44	4	80	15.025	751	831
48	8	160	2.900	145	305
50	10	200	1.060	53	253
51	11	220	0.610	30	250
52	12	240	0.340	17	257
53	13	260	0.182	9	269
54	14	280	0.095	5	285

Suppose that Hogan loses $50 in profit contribution for each lost sale. Using the annual holding cost of $20 per unit we can determine the total economic consequences of holding safety stock and of incurring lost sales, as shown in Table 10.6. From the table we see that the annual costs of safety stock and of lost sales are minimized when we have an order point of 51 cabinets.

Notice that the annual number of lost sales depends on the lot size q. This means that the required amount of safety stock also depends on q. To illustrate this point, suppose that Hogan uses an order quantity of 200 instead of the optimal quantity of 80. Then the lost sales analysis is given by Table 10.7.

If we use $50 per unit for lost profit and $20 per unit for holding cost, then we obtain the total costs shown in Table 10.8. In this new table we see that total

TABLE 10.7

Order Point	Safety Stock	z	N(z)	E[S] Lost Sales per Cycle	E[S]d/q Annual Number of Lost Sales
40	0	0	0.3989	1.9945	19.94
44	4	0.8	0.1202	0.6010	6.01
45	5	1.0	0.0833	0.4165	4.17
46	6	1.2	0.0561	0.2805	2.80
47	7	1.4	0.0367	0.1835	1.84
48	8	1.6	0.0232	0.1160	1.16
49	9	1.8	0.0143	0.0715	0.72
50	10	2.0	0.00849	0.0424	0.42
54	14	2.8	0.000761	0.0038	0.04

TABLE 10.8

Order Point	Safety Stock	Annual Cost of Safety Stock	Annual Lost Sales	Annual Cost of Lost Sales	Annual Total Cost
40	0	$ 0	19.94	$997	$998
44	4	80	6.01	301	381
45	5	100	4.17	209	309
46	6	120	2.80	140	260
47	7	140	1.84	92	232
48	8	160	1.16	58	218
49	9	180	0.72	36	216
50	10	200	0.42	21	221
54	14	280	0.04	2	282

annual costs are minimized by an order point of 49 cabinets. This change from 51 to 49 occurs because we have changed the annual number of cycles from 25 to 10.

Notice that the change in order quantity from 80 to 200 gave fewer annual ordering cycles. A comparison of Tables 10.6 and 10.8 reveals that this change reduced the annual cost of safety stock and lost sales from 250 to 216. However, if we consider the lot-size costs, we find that the lot size of 200 incurs an annual cost of $2320, whereas the optimal lot size of 80 incurs an annual cost of $1600. As a result, the *total* system cost (lot size, safety stock, and lost sales) would be lowest for the original system, as summarized in Table 10.9.

TABLE 10.9

Order Quantity	Lot Size Cost	Safety Stock Cost	Lost Sales Cost	Total Cost
40	$1600	$220	$30	$1850
200	2320	180	36	2536

SUMMARY

The basic inventory model is relatively simple in the sense that it contains one decision variable (the lot size) and examines one trade-off. In the basic model this trade-off involves fixed ordering costs and inventory holding costs, and the objective function examines total variable cost for a designated period of time such as a year. Optimization of the basic model yields a square-root formula for the optimal lot size, often called the *EOQ* formula. Parametric analysis of the basic model reveals that the total variable cost is relatively insensitive to small departures from the optimal lot size.

The basic model rests on a number of simplifying assumptions. A critical look at the validity of these assumptions shows that modifications are necessary if the model is to faithfully represent several characteristics of inventory problems found in practice. For example, when the assumption of a constant variable purchase cost is modified to permit quantity discounts, the method for determining an optimal lot size becomes more complicated: Nothing as simple as the *EOQ* formula will suffice. Also, when the assumption of constant demand is modified to allow for fluctuations, the style of analysis changes substantially: The dynamic lot-size model uses a discrete-time structure and relies on an optimization approach suitable for multiperiod formulations. Finally, when the assumption of deterministic demand is modified to allow for uncertainty and for lost sales, another trade-off arises. This trade-off involves the balance between the holding cost of safety stock and the opportunity cost of lost sales.

These variations on the basic model arise from considerations of structural validity, which involve the relation between the conclusions of model analysis and the assumptions that account for the model's structure. Because a number of assumptions account for the structure of the basic inventory model, there are many instances in which we should question these assumptions and consider alternative assumptions. Much of this chapter has been devoted to exploring the implications of such alternatives in the structure and analysis of inventory models.

EXERCISES

BASIC LOT-SIZE MODEL

1 Ettenger Electronics Company manufactures printed circuits and other electronic components. In the final production stage, the printed circuits are each mounted on a heavy cardboard panel that is purchased from a supplier of paper products. The printed circuits are produced to meet customer demand, which occurs at a relatively uniform rate of 6000 per year. The purchasing department at Ettenger has determined that the fixed replenishment cost is $40 and holding costs are 20% per year. The supplier charges $2.50 for each panel. Determine the optimal order quantity.

2 A supplier of custom-made metal fixtures quotes the cost of q units as $250 + 20q$ dollars. The purchaser of these fixtures requires 2400 units per year and uses them at a uniform rate. In addition, the purchaser's direct costs for filling out order forms, receiving, inspection, and so on amount to $50 per shipment. The inventory carrying charge is 20% per year. What is the optimal order quantity for the purchaser?

3 A popular item stocked by Greenwald's Department Store has an anticipated demand of 600 units for next year. The cost to purchase these units from a local supplier is $20 per unit and $12 to prepare the purchase order. The annual carrying cost is $4 per unit. If Greenwald's is currently ordering 100 units at a time, how much can be saved by changing to the optimal order quantity?

4 The accounting department at Meminger College uses an average of 5000 printed invoice tablets per year. These tablets are obtained from a local printing company that normally sells them at a price of $4.60 per tablet. The accounting department at Meminger has determined that the fixed ordering cost is $10 each time an order is placed and has estimated inventory charges at 20% per year. What is an optimal order quantity for the tablets?

5 The Major Airline Company is seeking to develop an economically rational way to determine the frequency with which it should offer its training program for new flight attendants. The company requires a staff of about 1000 flight attendants to maintain the desired level of service in its fleet of airplanes. The attendants have a propensity to quit at a phenomenal rate—their average job tenure being about 2 years (104 weeks). Thus, annual demand is for 500 people.

Reasonable salaries are offered to new attendants and, in addition, they are given an extensive training course for new attendants at Major Airline's home base. The training course for new attendants takes 6 weeks, after which there is a further week of vacation and travel time before the attendant enters the pool from which new attendants are drawn for their initial assignment to an air crew. While the attendants are in this pool, they continue to draw their salaries although, from the point of view of the company, they are "unemployed" until they join their air crew. In spite of this cost, Major Airline prefers to maintain this approach (rather than to train attendants after vacancies occur) in order to be reasonably sure of having a continually available staff of trained attendants. Although there is some randomness about the rate at which attendants are withdrawn from the pool and actively "employed," in general it may be said that they are required for air-crew replacements at a fairly steady rate the year round. Recruitment of new trainees does not appear to be a serious problem—that is, trainees can be hired when needed—and they do not draw any salary until the date they report, as scheduled, to the training school. The trainees are paid continually after they report. An insignificant number of trainees drop out or fail during the training period.

The training cost is rather expensive. This cost consists almost exclusively of the salaries of the people employed to train them, known as a "training team." A training team consists of 10 highly trained instructors and their 10 supporting personnel. Such a training team is paid by the training school *only* for those periods that it is actively engaged in a training program. Its effectiveness seems to be almost independent of the size of the class or whether other classes are simultaneously in progress.

a Using the general information presented above and numerical data selected (with discrimination) from the data table below, compute the size of an "economic lot" of flight attendant trainees. What would be the total cost of this optimal policy considering that the lot size must be an integer? (There is no need to include dv in your total cost calculation.)

b What would be the time interval in weeks between the beginning of each new class?

c Modify the optimal solution in part (a) for scheduling efficiency to provide a new class starting every 6 weeks. What would be the class size under the revised plan? (An integer.) How much would the revised solution cost?

Data Table

Average airplane capacity: 100 passengers
Average airplane speed: 500 miles per hour
Average airplane cost: $10,000,000
Average air-crew size: 6
Average pilot's salary: $5200 per month
Average new attendant's salary: $1000 per month
Average training instructor's salary: $440 per week
Average training support personnel salary: $160 per person per week

---

6 A distributor of a product sells 100,000 units annually, costing $0.10 each. Because of the limited shelf life of the item, they are air-freighted to the distributor at his expense ($48 per order regardless of the size of the order). It costs the distributor directly $10 annually to store 1000 units of the product; in addition, the cost of capital is estimated at 14% per year.

a Find the economic order quantity and the total annual inventory and ordering cost.

b If you use the economic order quantity, what is the time between orders (in months)?

c How would you revise your answer to (a) if the maximum shelf life of the product was 2 months ($\frac{1}{6}$ year)? In other words, how much should you order and what is the annual inventory and ordering cost? What is the difference in cost between this solution and your solution to (a)?

SENSITIVITY ANALYSIS

7 Review Exercise 1. Find a 5% economic range for order quantities.

8 Review Exercise 3. Use the formula for $E(x)$ to verify the cost savings for Greenwald's Department Store.

9 Suppose that the demand parameter in *EOQ* analysis is obtained from forecast data, while the cost parameters are measured accurately. Suppose, in addition, that the maximum possible error in the demand forecast is known to be e. That is, if the true (but unknown) demand rate is d, then the forecast will lie between $(1 - e)d$ and $(1 + e)d$. We wish to determine what this forecast error implies in terms of variable cost.

a To formulate this question in a special case, consider an *EOQ* analysis with a single product for which the relevant parameters are $d = 2000$ units per year, $f = 25$ per order, and $h = 1$ per unit per year. Suppose the maximum possible forecast error is 10%. That is, $e = 0.10$ and the forecast of d lies between 1800 and 2200. The lot size will be calculated from the formula using the forecast. What is the largest possible total variable cost that can occur? What is the ratio of this cost to the optimal variable cost?

b Derive a general formula for the relative error in the total variable cost as a function of the error e in the forecast.

10 An inventory control system uses the basic *EOQ* model to determine replenishment quantities; however, its cost estimates are sometimes in error. We wish to determine what consequences such an estimation error will have on total variable cost.

a For example, suppose the system parameters are $d = 2000$ units per year, $f = 20$ per order and $h = 1$ per unit per year. Although the true fixed cost of ordering is $f = 20$, the cost estimation system is unreliable and may make an error of as much as 20% in estimating the true value of f. What is the largest possible total variable cost that can occur if an error is made? What is the ratio of this amount to the optimal variable cost (which would result if no estimation error were made)?

b In general, suppose that f is erroneously estimated as zf, where $z \neq 1$. Let $C(z)$ denote the actual value of total variable cost that results when the error is made. Let C^* denote the optimal value of total variable cost (which would have resulted if no estimation error were made.) Find an expression for the ratio $C(z)/C^*$.

11 a Demand for widgets occurs at an absolutely constant rate of $d = 10,000$ units per year; $h = 5$ per unit per year and $f = 9.25$ per order. Evaluate the cost of the current policy of ordering batches of 1000 units, and compare it to the optimal policy.

b How important is it to follow the optimal policy precisely? For example, what happens to the costs that depend on the lot size if q is 50% above optimal in question (a)? What if it is 50% below optimal? Also, what is the cost of rounding the optimal *EOQ* to the nearest 100 units? How do all of these costs compare to the cost of the current policy of $q = 1000$?

DYNAMIC LOT-SIZE MODEL

12 The Coleman Appliance Company produces washing machines for a variety of retailers, but 60% of its output is sold to a single retail chain. Because this chain accounts for such a large proportion of the demand at Coleman, it has become management policy to schedule the production lines so that all orders from the chain are filled on time. On their part, the retail chain provides reliable demand data for 6 months in order to help Coleman develop its plans. For the coming 6 months the retail chain's requirements are as follows:

Month	1	2	3	4	5	6
Demand	150	200	200	100	100	150

Coleman's plant manager permits at most one production run per month on this style of washing machine, because each run entails a lengthy setup of the facility, costing $600. Plant capacity is more than adequate to handle production runs up to 1000 washers in a month. In addition, there is ample warehouse space available if storage is needed, and Coleman's accounting department estimates the holding cost on washers to be $2 per month. Determine an optimal production plan for the 6-month period and the variable cost involved.

13 Ettenger Electronics Company is under contract to supply NASA with the following quantities of a minicomputer component over the next 12 months:

(25, 50, 100, 175, 200, 200, 175, 150, 100, 75, 200, 150)

The components are produced in lots, and each component costs $300 in variable production costs. The setup cost for each production run is $1200, and no more than one run can be scheduled for a given month. Holding costs are assessed at 20% per year. Determine an optimal production plan for the year.

14 The theory underlying the Dynamic Lot-Size Model provides an important simplification in Step 3 of the calculations. The computation of C_t^* can be written

$$C_t^* = \min\{C(k, t)\} \text{ for } \gamma \le k \le t$$

where $\gamma = P_{t-1}^*$. In other words, the calculation of the minimum requires only the comparison of the costs $C(k, t)$ for $k = P_{t-1}^*$ through $k = t$.

a Using the formulas for $C(k, t)$, show why this simplification holds.

b Identify which calculations of $C(k, t)$ can be omitted in Exercises 12 and 13 by invoking this result.

FINITE PRODUCTION RATE

15 Determine the number of production runs for an item if $d = 15,000$ units per year, $r = 100$ units per working day, $f = 25$, and $h = 5$ per unit per year. There are 250 working days per year. What are the effects on cost of modifying the optimal answer by rounding to include realistic considerations, such as having an integer number of days between the start of production runs?

16 The cooler in a cottage cheese manufacturing plant can hold 600 cases of cottage cheese. The average daily demand is 120 cases, the daily production rate is 960 cases, and the production setup cost is $100. The annual carrying cost is $12 per case. (Assume 250 days per year.)

a What is the economic production quantity?

b What is the sum of annual holding and setup costs?

c How many cases of cottage cheese can be produced in a run, given that the maximum inventory cannot exceed the capacity of the cooler? What is the difference in cost between this policy and the cost of the unconstrained policy?

17 The production people at Poober & Cork, Ltd. were in the process of determining the optimal number of P-2215 units to manufacture on each production run.

The P-2215 unit had been test-marketed over the past year, and the sales people were confident that there would be a steady demand for the P-2215 at the rate of about 500 units per week. (Assume a 5-day week and a 50-week year.) The units sold in the test market had been produced in three production runs. The first of these runs, of $2\frac{1}{2}$ days duration, had produced 500 P-2215 units at a recorded cost of $27,000. The second, more extensive run had taken 4 weeks and produced 4000 units at a cost of $195,000. The third run, even larger, had produced 7500 units in $7\frac{1}{2}$ weeks at a cost of $363,000.

In order to reckon up these costs in a form applicable to the computation of an economic lot size, the Poober & Cork personnel felt that the fixed element of cost incurred in the three previous production runs could be used to represent the cost of setting up a production run and the variable element would represent the cost of materials and the actual cost of the transformation operations.

In examining the possibility of keeping an inventory of complete P-2215 units, the Poober & Cork people recognized that it would not necessarily be particularly cheap nor especially simple to control. Annual inventory carrying costs were estimated at 25% of their value in terms of variable cost to manufacture. The control problem would result from the fact that they planned to produce the P-2215 unit in the same way, using the same personnel and equipment, as they had in the three prior runs. Under these circumstances, given a steady demand for the product, P-2215 units would often be flowing into inventory (from the plant) and out of inventory (to the customers) at the same time.

Using the information and assumptions given above, compute the economic run size for Poober & Cork.

QUANTITY DISCOUNTS

18 In the Hogan example, suppose that the same discount is offered on the purchase cost of filing cabinets but the price break occurs at a quantity Q larger than 250. How large does Q have to be in order for $q_1^* = 80$ to be the optimal lot size?

19 Suppose two price breaks are offered, in a schedule that takes the following form:

for $q < B_1$	unit cost is v_1
for $B_1 \leq q < B_2$	unit cost is v_2 $(v_2 < v_1)$
for $B_2 \leq q$	unit cost is v_3 $(v_3 < v_2)$

Now the relevant objective function can be viewed as a combination of $C_1(q)$, $C_2(q)$, and $C_3(q)$. Draw a graph of these three functions, and for each of the cases below select break points B_1 and B_2 so that the designated lot size is optimal.

a q_3^*

b B_2

c q_2^*

d B_1

e q_1^*

20 Tada Graphics is a printing business that has been in operation over 25 years. It staffs about 35 to 40 printers, operators, and stock crew on an average 8-hour shift, with three shifts daily. Administrative staff is about 45 to 55 employees, not including salespersons. Tada Graphics has a plant in Los Angeles, the main distributing center, and three subsidiary companies, located in San Diego, Hawaii, and Oklahoma. Customer service throughout this area involves about 30 regular major customers and about 7000 other regular customers throughout the year.

Tada Graphics prints paper and forms in different sizes, colors, multisheets, qualities, and quantities. The warehouse space is approximately 25,000 square feet, and it has about a 6- to 8-week inventory supply of bulk-quantity rolled paper. This paper is stored in bins segregated by the quality of paper, then by the size, and then by color. The company carries approximately 142 stock items.

Most of the ordering is done by a computer program based on statistical data that Tada Graphics has gathered. As an example, the company has received an order for 850 pounds of No. 15 white 9-inch paper to be printed. This is a *regular* monthly order that must be filled and represents the total of this type of paper to be used monthly. The cost of ordering this paper is put at $10, and it can be selected from one of two different sources. One choice is the mill, and the other choice is the Los Angeles distributor. Carrying costs have been figured at 12% per year. Determine the amount to order and which supplier to order it from, how often to order, and the annual total cost.

Supplier	Quantity	Price
Los Angeles	Any	$33.00/100 pounds
Mill	$\geq 2,500$	$32.50/100 pounds
Mill	$\geq 5,000$	$32.00/100 pounds
Mill	$\geq 10,000$	$31.50/100 pounds

21 Middlearth is a candle-making firm that was established in 1970 when two individuals began making candles for swap meets. This small venture has now grown into a corporation with annual sales of a quarter of a million dollars, shipping to 300 cities across the nation. Middlearth produces 23 different types of candles and 19 types of planters. The production of candles and planters involve completely different entities within the corporation as they involve different processes and personnel. Attention is concentrated on the production of candles that are wood or ceramic filled with wax. They fall into five basic groups: cirio wood, manzanita, gourd, ceramic, and turned wood. The ceramic candles have been the poorest sellers, and at present Middlearth has an excess inventory.

The rapid growth rate accompanied by increased demand (which far exceeds production) has caused many production and cost problems for the corporation. As a result, there is an opportunity cost associated with capital of 40% per year. Middlearth also has a problem of determining the amount and time to order its supplies. An example of this is the policy concerning shipping boxes. The average demand for shipping boxes is 1436 per month, and the policy has been to order the largest lot size available on the grounds that it is the cheapest and order filling would not take place as quickly as for the smaller lots. The cost of ordering has been determined at $6.66 every time an order is placed, regardless of size. The price break is as follows:

$Q \geq$ 500 boxes at $0.55/box

$Q \geq$ 1000 boxes at $0.50/box

$Q \geq$ 2500 boxes at $0.38/box

a Determine which lot size gives the cheapest total annual cost, how often the lot should be ordered, and the total annual cost.

b If the opportunity cost of capital were 10% per year instead of 40% per year, would your lot-size decision change? Why?

SAFETY STOCK ANALYSIS

22 Review Exercise 1. Suppose that a further study indicates that lead-time demand during the 2-week lead time follows a normal distribution with mean $\mu = 240$ and standard deviation $\sigma = 40$.

a Determine how large a safety stock (of cardboard panels) will be needed in order to achieve each of the following service levels:

(1) 90%

(2) 95%

(3) 98%

b Suppose that the firm assesses the opportunity cost of lost sales (when a stockout occurs in the panel inventory) at $10 per unit. Find the safety stock level that provides an optimal trade-off between holding costs and opportunity costs.

23 Review Exercise 3. Suppose that lead time is always 1 week and that weekly demand follows a Poisson distribution with a mean of 12.

a Assume the safety stock level is set at 6. Calculate the service level and the expected number of lost sales per year.

b Repeat (a) for a safety stock level of 8.

c Repeat (a) for a safety stock level of 10.

24 A firm is operating an inventory system for a flammable chemical agent. Its weekly carrying costs, mainly due to insurance premiums and material handling expenses, are calculated to be $0.10 per cubic foot. Each replenishment order requires the supplier to perform a setup operation for which it charges the firm $400. Delivery lead times from the supplier are fixed at 1 week. Sales data have indicated that demand in any given week can be assumed to be normally distributed with mean 300 cubic feet and standard deviation 100 cubic feet. The operating policy is determined by *EOQ* analysis using mean demand data, and a safety stock is maintained so as to limit the probability of a stockout to no more than 0.05 in any order cycle. For this system, determine

a The optimal lot size and the optimal order point.

b The extra weekly cost (i.e., above the *EOQ* policy) due to carrying safety stock.

c The total weekly variable cost associated with the optimal policy and the 95% service level.

25 Review Exercise 24. Suppose that the opportunity cost per unit is $6 on lost sales. What safety stock quantity will provide an optimal balance of annual holding costs and annual opportunity costs?

26 Review the trade-off models in Chapter 8. The trade-off between holding costs and opportunity costs may be viewed as an application of the shortage/surplus trade-off model, where the single decision variable is the safety stock level.

a Let s denote the unit opportunity cost for lost sales, and assume that a continuous probability model applies. Use the results in Chapter 8 to show that the optimal order point is given by

$$F(p) = \frac{sd}{sd + hq}$$

b Apply the formula in (a) to the Hogan Office Products Company example in this section and verify that 51 cabinets is an optimal order point.

27 International Paper Company has hired you as an inventory consultant. They have used a sophisticated computer method to forecast weekly demand for three-hole punched paper; the forecast indicates an average demand of 300 reams of paper per week, 52 weeks a year, and the standard deviation of the weekly forecast is 20 reams. The paper is purchased from an outside vendor with a lead time of exactly 2 weeks. They have found that during the 2-week lead time the standard deviation of the forecast is exactly 32 reams. Using an *EOQ* model, International Paper has chosen to place orders twice a year.

a What should the order point be in order to achieve an average of one stockout in 10 years, assuming that the normal probability distribution applies?

b How much safety stock is included in the answer to part (a)?

c How much reduction would there be in safety stock if the lead time were reduced from 2 weeks to 1 week?

d Suppose that *instead* of reducing the lead time you improved the forecast accuracy. How much reduction would there be in safety stock if the standard deviation of the forecast were cut from 32 to 16 for the 2-week lead time?

e Suppose that *instead* of doing either of the above you were to change the policy about stockouts. What would the reduction be in the average inventory level if International Paper were to keep the lead time at 2 weeks and were to permit an average of one stockout every 5 years instead of the current policy of one stockout every 10 years?

f What significance do the answers to (c), (d), and (e) have for the manager? In particular, if the changes above were equally costly, what change or changes would be preferable?

28 The inventory control manager for Davidson Electronics has identified the following information about one of the firm's repair parts:

lead time   = 9 weeks

weekly demand = 25 units

Furthermore, the manager has found that the following relationship actually exists between mean demand during the lead time and the standard deviation of demand forecast errors during the lead time:

$$\begin{matrix} \text{standard deviation} \\ \text{of demand forecast} \\ \text{errors} \end{matrix} = \sqrt{\begin{matrix}\text{lead time} \\ \text{in} \\ \text{weeks}\end{matrix} \times \begin{matrix}\text{weekly} \\ \text{demand}\end{matrix}}$$

Davidson Electronics has the problem of choosing between two safety stock policies:

Policy A (Currently Used)
Set safety stock equal to 1 week's demand for the item.

Policy B (Proposed)
Set safety stock to achieve a 95% chance of no stockout
    during the lead time.

a What is the difference in the amount of safety stock required by the two policies under the current conditions?

b Demand for the repair part is growing. "In particular," said one consultant, "demand is expected to achieve a level of 100 units per week next year." Assume that no other relationships change; what is the difference in the amount of safety stock required by the two policies when this growth occurs?

c What are the implications of your answers to (a) and (b) for an inventory system?

29 Consider an item controlled under an order-point/order-quantity system. The basic information is as follows:

d = 40,000 units per year

f = 15 per order

v = 1.60 per unit

h = 0.40 per unit per year

Desired service level = 95% chance of no stockout in the lead time

Cost of lost sale = $1 per unit

Two forecasting systems could be used to forecast demand for the item, with the following characteristics:

System	Annual Operating Cost	Standard Deviation of Lead-Time Demand
A	$200	1000
B	35	2300

For both systems the forecast errors are normally distributed with a mean of 0 and the specified value of the standard deviation.

Assuming that the firm is interested in minimizing total annual costs, including system operation cost, which forecasting system should be used? Why?

Chapter 11

QUEUEING MODELS

The Ovington Bank and Trust Company

The main branch of the Ovington Bank and Trust Company is located along a main road not far from a large industrial park. The branch operates a drive-in window that is extremely busy during the hours of 4–7 P.M., when employees from the industrial park leave work. During this period, customers arrive at the rate of about 50 per hour. Existing studies indicate that servicing a drive-in customer requires an average of 1 minute. The branch manager is concerned that the new drive-in teller frequently sits idle, yet at other times there are long lines of waiting drive-in customers. Lately, the branch manager has been wondering whether these contradictory observations imply some problem in the system's design.

Queues are waiting lines that form when demand for service exceeds the capacity to provide service in the short run, and they symbolize congestion. The study of queues helps us to understand the behavior of systems that provide service, particularly systems in which the probabilistic nature of demands and services creates a fluctuating load on the system.

Queues are common in our everyday lives. We are quite familiar with waiting lines that form at grocery check-out counters, traffic lights, ticket windows, and gas stations. However, waiting lines do not always consist of people. We can also think of automobiles waiting for repair, ships waiting for an unloading dock, and computer programs awaiting execution.

Queueing models provide some help in understanding the causes of congestion in such systems and also in evaluating possible responses. Thus, there are two themes in the application of queueing theory: description and optimization. Description involves mathematical analysis of queue behavior and investigation of the effect of certain parameters on various performance measures. Optimization involves the search for economically desirable design parameters. In the latter case this search for an optimal design involves a comparison of queue behaviors. As a result, the descriptive approach is a vital component of the optimization approach.

In evaluating the performance of a service system we consider two main factors: responsiveness to customer demands and utilization of service capability. For instance, in assessing **responsiveness** we might measure the average customer waiting time or the probability that a customer will have to wait at all. On the other hand, in assessing **utilization** we might measure the proportion of time the service facility is idle or the proportion of time it is fully loaded. In principle, we would like to measure both the monetary cost of waiting and the cost of providing service. Then, with this information we could seek the design that achieves minimum total cost. Unfortunately, measurements of this sort are not always practical or possible. Instead, we often find it more realistic to seek a balance of responsiveness and utilization, without attempting to measure their costs on a common scale.

For example, the branch manager at Ovington Bank and Trust appears to be most interested in the queue length as a measure of responsiveness and in the amount of idle time as a measure of utilization. A queueing model provides some understanding of what to expect at the drive-in window for these two dimensions of performance.

Figure 11.1 depicts the primary elements in a queueing system. Demands for service are initiated by members of an identifiable **source population.** These demands occur randomly and arrive over time at the **service facility.** If capacity is adequate in the short run, the demands are serviced immediately upon their arrival; otherwise there is a delay and a queue forms. In generic terms, we describe the arrivals as **customers** waiting to be processed by one or more **servers.**

To build a model for analyzing a queueing system we need to specify the process by which customers arrive and the process by which they are served. In

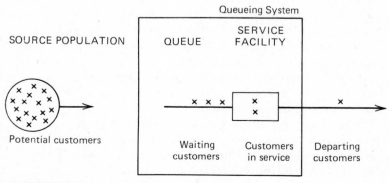

FIGURE 11.1

specifying the arrival process, we first identify the source population by its size, finite or infinite. Typically, we assume that the source population is infinite except when it is quite small (e.g., less than 20). We then characterize the statistical properties of customer arrivals by describing the probability distribution for the time between arrivals. One important type of arrival process is the case of "random" arrivals, which we examine later in some detail.

In specifying the service process, we first identify the size of the service facility in terms of the number of servers or service channels. Then we characterize the statistical properties of services by describing the probability distribution for service time. One very useful special case for the service time distribution is the exponential model, which we also examine in a later section.

Another aspect of system operation is the **queue discipline,** which is the procedure governing the selection of a customer from the queue when a server becomes free. A common approach is to serve customers in the order they arrive, a selection procedure known as First Come, First Served (or FCFS). Queues with systematic types of other selection procedures are referred to as **priority queues.**

As reflected in Figure 11.1, the arrival process, service process, and queue discipline are the primary elements in a queueing system. We can accommodate a number of additional factors in queueing analysis, but in this chapter we shall concentrate only on the more simple models.

BASIC CONCEPTS FOR QUEUEING ANALYSIS

We use the number of customers in the system to define the system's status at any point in time. Specifically, the number of customers in the system is equal to the number in service plus the number waiting in the queue. This quantity also tells us how many servers are idle. We define N_t as the number of customers in the system at time t. Figure 11.2 shows an example of how N_t might behave in a single-server system. Notice that N_t changes up or down in steps of 1. Here we are assuming that two or more customers never arrive at precisely the same time. Furthermore, at each arrival N_t increases, and at each service completion N_t decreases.

Figure 11.2 also shows interarrival times, service times, and waiting times. In particular, we define

T_k = interarrival time for the kth customer; the time between the arrival of customer $(k - 1)$ and customer k

S_k = service time for the kth customer, measured from the time service is initiated for customer k to the time it is completed

W_k = waiting time for the kth customer, including the time spent waiting for service to begin and the time spent being served

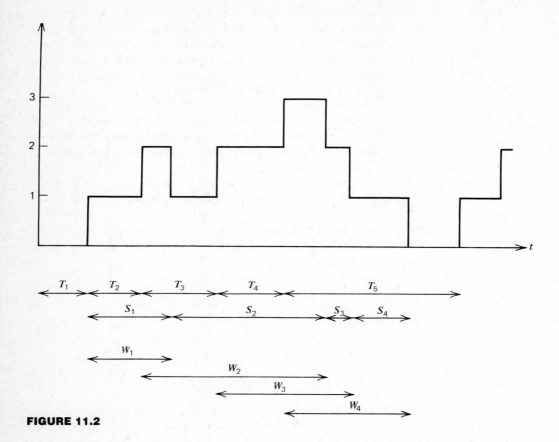

FIGURE 11.2

If the interarrival times T_k or the service times S_k are random, then N_t will be a random variable. As a result, we would describe N_t with a probability distribution,

$$P_n(t) = P(N_t = n), \; n = 0, 1, 2, \ldots$$

where, in principle, we could specify the $P_n(t)$ values for every point in time.

We should expect that early in the evolution of the queueing system this probability distribution would depend heavily on the initial number of customers in the system (N_0) and on how long the system has been in operation (t). Later on, however, we would expect the system to reach a stage in which its behavior is not dependent on the initial state or on how long the system has been in operation. For instance, suppose that service is initiated when there are several customers waiting. This means that early in the process it is unlikely that the server will be idle, although eventually the proportion of server idle time will reach a stable level.

Figure 11.3 shows how the probability distribution of N_t might develop over time. We say that such a system passes through a **transient** phase of operation (during which its status depends heavily on initial conditions) and approaches a **steady-state** phase (during which its status is independent of initial conditions). The important point is that during the transient phase the probability distribution $P_n(t)$ depends on t, while in the steady-state phase it does not. As a result, when we focus on steady-state performance we can ignore the time component. Then we can define N as the number of customers in the system at steady state, and P_n as the probability that there are n customers in the system. Stated in symbols $P_n = P(N = n)$.

For the practical systems we might want to analyze, the steady-state assumption will often be a realistic simplification of actual behavior. Most of the empha-

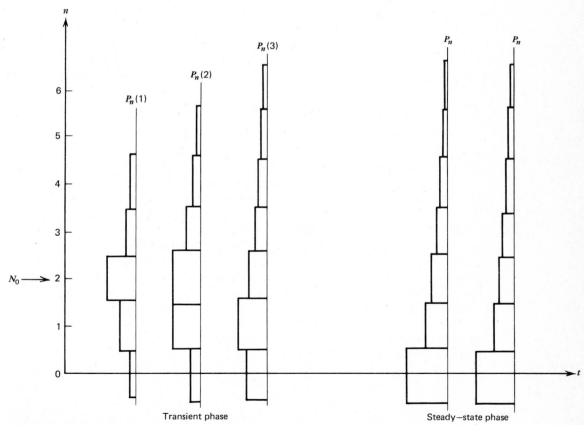

FIGURE 11.3

sis in the practical analysis and design of queueing systems is on steady-state performance, and that will be our focus in the remainder of this chapter. In addition to the number of customers, some other important steady-state performance measures are the following:

L = mean number of customers in the system

L_q = mean number of customers waiting (in the queue) for service to begin

W = mean customer waiting time, including service time

W_q = mean customer queueing time, until service begins

The value L is the mean of the probability distribution for N:

$$L = \sum_{n=0}^{\infty} nP_n \tag{11.1}$$

In addition, the quantities L and W are related by a very fundamental result:

$$L = \lambda W \tag{11.2}$$

where λ denotes the mean arrival rate. In words, λ represents the mean number of arrivals per unit of time. Equivalently, $1/\lambda$ is the mean time between arrivals. Therefore, the random variables T_k, illustrated in Figure 11.2, have a mean value of $1/\lambda$.

To understand why formula (11.2) holds, suppose we focus on a particular customer. On average, the time that elapses between the customer's arrival and departure is W. At the moment of departure, suppose the customer looks back and counts how many customers remain in the system. On average, this will be the mean number of customers in the system, L. However, this number will also be the mean number of arrivals that occurred while our customer was in the system, or λW, because the mean arrival rate is λ customers per unit time during the interval W. Therefore, L and λW should be equivalent.

The equation $L = \lambda W$ is a relationship among average values, and as such it applies to a broad class of queueing systems without regard for the detailed characteristics of the arrival process or the service configuration. Suitably interpreted, the result holds for all the cases treated in this chapter.

The reasoning used to justify equation (11.2) also applies to the relation between the mean queueing time and the mean number of customers in the queue, yielding a companion formula

$$L_q = \lambda W_q \tag{11.3}$$

A third queueing formula provides the link between equations (11.2) and (11.3). Notice that a customer's waiting time consists of queueing time plus service time. Therefore, the mean waiting time must be equal to the mean queueing time plus the mean service time:

$$W = W_q + \text{mean service time}$$

The usual convention in queueing analysis is to let μ denote the mean service rate for an individual server. Thus, the mean service time is $1/\mu$. In other words, μ represents the mean number of customers that a server can serve per unit of time. Equivalently, $1/\mu$ is the mean length of a customer's service interval. Therefore, the random variables S_k, illustrated in Figure 11.2, have a mean value of $1/\mu$. Our equation can be written

$$W = W_q + \frac{1}{\mu} \tag{11.4}$$

We can use equations (11.2) to (11.4) to calculate summary performance measures for all the queueing systems in this chapter.

THE ROLE OF THE POISSON AND EXPONENTIAL DISTRIBUTIONS

The fundamental models for queueing analysis deal with demand processes that involve random arrival of customers. The concept of random arrivals has a very specific meaning for queueing models: It prescribes the arrival of customers as occurring one at a time and at a constant average rate. This concept excludes the possibility that two or more customers will arrive precisely together. It also excludes the possibility that the average rate at which customers arrive will fluctuate systematically. For example, suppose we wanted to model the arrival process at the Ovington Bank's drive-in window over an entire day. In the course of a full day the customer arrival rate would fluctuate systematically from low levels at midmorning, when employees in the industrial park are at work, to high levels in the late afternoon, when the park's employees leave work. Thus, our definition of random arrivals would not apply unless we focus only on shorter periods, such as the afternoon rush hour, when the average arrival rate is constant.

There are two other important features of random arrivals. First, the arrivals are independent of each other and independent of the state of the system. In other words, the time until the next arrival does not depend on when the previous arrival occurred or on how many arrivals have occurred. This feature is sometimes called the **memoryless** property, in the sense that the future of the demand process does not depend on its past history. Second, the probability of an arrival during a specified time interval depends only on the length of that interval. In other words, the probability that an arrival will occur during a specific interval does not depend on how long the arrival process has existed. This feature, called the **stationarity** property, reflects the fact that equal size intervals are associated with equal probabilities, whenever they occur.

To explore the implications of random arrivals, consider the process in which customers arrive at the Ovington Bank's drive-in window. Suppose that on the average these arrivals occur at the rate of one every 5 minutes; and let us assume that arrivals occur one at a time, at a constant average rate. Here, these assumptions mean that the arrivals are independent of each other, so that the existence of a line at the window has no influence on the occurrence of additional arrivals. Because arrivals occur at the mean rate of one every 5 minutes, on average there are 12 arrivals in an hour, but in any particular hour the actual number of arrivals is random. We seek a probabilistic description of that random number.

Suppose we divide the 1-hour interval into 60 one-minute segments, and let us ignore the possibility of more than one arrival occurring in any 1-minute segment. Given the mean arrival rate of one every 5 minutes, the probability of an arrival in a 1-minute segment is $\frac{1}{5}$. Because we assume that the segments are independent, we can view the set of 60 segments as representing 60 independent trials in which the probability of success (an arrival) in each trial equals $\frac{1}{5}$. Then we can use a binomial model to describe the number of arrivals. For the binomial model, the probability of k successes in n trials takes the form

$$P(k) = \binom{n}{k} p^k (1 - p)^{n-k}$$

In addition, the number of successes has a mean of np and a variance of $np(1 - p)$. For example, when $n = 60$ and $k = 5$ the probability of five arrivals is

$$P(5) = \binom{60}{5}\left(\frac{1}{5}\right)^5\left(\frac{4}{5}\right)^{55} = 0.0087$$

Furthermore, the mean and variance of this particular binomial distribution are

$$\text{mean} = 60\left(\frac{1}{5}\right) = 12 \qquad \text{variance} = 60\left(\frac{1}{5}\right)\left(\frac{4}{5}\right) = 9.6$$

It may seem unrealistic to assume that we could ignore the possibility of more than one arrival in a 1-minute segment. Such an assumption would be less severe, however, if we were to divide the hour into 120 thirty-second segments and assume that no more than one arrival can occur in any of these segments. Now our binomial model consists of 120 independent trials, each with a success probability equal to $\frac{1}{10}$. (With a mean arrival rate of one every 5 minutes, the probability of an arrival in a 30-second segment is $\frac{1}{10}$.) We have

$$P(k \text{ arrivals in an hour}) = \binom{120}{k}\left(\frac{1}{10}\right)^{k}\left(\frac{9}{10}\right)^{120-k}$$

Here, when $k = 5$ we find that $P(5) = 0.0104$. Also, the summary parameters of the distribution are

$$\text{mean} = 120\left(\frac{1}{10}\right) = 12 \qquad \text{variance} = 120\left(\frac{1}{10}\right)\left(\frac{9}{10}\right) = 10.8$$

Again, we might find it unrealistic to ignore the possibility of more than one arrival in a 30-second segment, and we might want to choose an even smaller segment. For a 10-second segment we obtain

$$P(5) = 0.0120 \qquad \text{mean} = 12 \qquad \text{variance} = 11.6$$

In this way, we can choose the segment length to be as small as we please. The smaller our choice, the less severe is the assumption that we can ignore the possibility of more than two arrivals in a segment. The assumption becomes perfectly tolerable only as the segment size approaches 0 and the number of trials in our binomial model becomes infinite.

In this limiting case the binomial model approaches a Poisson model. The general form of the Poisson model for random arrivals is the following:

$$P(k \text{ arrivals}) = \frac{(\lambda t)^{k}e^{-\lambda t}}{k!} \qquad k = 0, 1, 2, \ldots$$

where λ represents the mean arrival rate and t represents the length of the interval being studied. For this distribution the mean and the variance are both equal to λt. Looking back, we see that each of the binomial models had a mean of 12 and a variance that approached 12 as the segment size grew smaller. The values of $P(5)$ also approached the Poisson value, which is 0.0127 as we can verify in the Poisson probability table that appears in the Appendix.

The main point here is that the assumption of random arrivals has a very specific meaning; an equivalent form is the assumption that the number of arrivals during a fixed time interval follows a Poisson probability model. Therefore, a random arrival process is often called a **Poisson arrival process.** The significance of the Poisson model is twofold. First, the Poisson model is analytically convenient, and with this assumption we can study queues extensively with the use of very basic methods. For this reason many queueing studies begin with the presumption of Poisson arrivals, simply to get some understanding of the essential system relationships. Second, the Poisson model has considerable empirical validity. Several investigations of actual queueing systems have discovered that the Poisson model closely approximates the observed arrival process. Empirical studies of this sort commonly count the number of arrivals in a fixed time interval. Several observations of this interval lead to a frequency distribution for the number of arrivals. Then, using standard statistical tests for distribution fitting, it is possible to test the Poisson distribution as a representation of the empirical frequencies.

A further aspect of random arrivals involves the relationship between the Poisson and exponential distributions. Consider a Poisson arrival process and a particular interval of length t. We have

$$P(k \text{ arrivals}) = \frac{(\lambda t)^k e^{-\lambda t}}{k!}$$

$$P(\text{no arrivals}) = e^{-\lambda t}$$

Suppose we start observing the arrival process at time 0, and let T denote the (random) time until the next arrival. Then

$$P(T > t) = P(\text{no arrivals until time } t) = e^{-\lambda t}$$

$$P(T \leq t) = 1 - P(T > t) = 1 - e^{-\lambda t}$$

This is a statement about the cumulative distribution function of the random variable T, and we recognize the form as that of an exponential distribution with a mean of $1/\lambda$. In other words, the assumption of Poisson arrivals is equivalent to the assumption that the time between arrivals follows an exponential distribution. In our example above, where the mean arrival rate is $\lambda = 12$ per hour, the interarrival times follow an exponential distribution with a mean of $\frac{1}{12}$ hour or 5 minutes.

Finally, the queueing model requires a description of the service process in probabilistic terms. The service time for a customer is a random variable (denoted S) described by the probability distribution for service times. In the elementary models we assume that this is also an exponential distribution, with the mean service rate denoted by μ. In other words, the cumulative distribution function for the random variable S is given by

$$P(S \leq x) = 1 - e^{-\mu x}$$

The mean and the standard deviation of this distribution are both equal to $1/\mu$. Here again the exponential distribution plays an important role. From the discussion above regarding arrivals, it follows that this assumption means that while a server is busy, service completions will occur at random, one at a time, at the constant rate μ. The assumption of exponential service times is theoretically convenient in that we can use elementary methods to analyze queues with Poisson arrivals and exponential service times. Moreover, the exponential model has proven to be a very useful model in practical applications because it approximates many empirical service time distributions. As in the case of Poisson arrivals, we can test the exponential model for service times by taking a sample of service-time observations, constructing a frequency distribution of observed times, and performing standard statistical tests for goodness of fit with the exponential probability distribution.

THE SIMPLE QUEUE

The single-server queue with Poisson arrivals (from an infinitely large source population) and exponential service times is the most elementary model of queueing analysis. We refer to this case as the **simple queue.** To examine its behavior we introduce an approach involving **transition diagrams.** We can also apply this approach to the study of steady-state performance in other queues with random arrivals and exponential service times. In this section we investigate the special form of the analysis for the case of the simple queue, and in the next section we apply the general form of the analysis to a variety of queueing models.

For steady-state analysis we focus on N, the number of customers in the system, and we seek the probability distribution P_n that describes the state of the system in terms of the behavior of N. An important factor is that the state variable N changes up or down in steps of 1 as arrivals and departures occur in the system. These steps are called **transitions,** and we represent them in a diagram such as the one in Figure 11.4. The numbered nodes in the diagram represent the possible system states, $n = 0, 1, 2, 3, \ldots$; and the arrows represent possible transitions. Thus, there is an arrow from each state n to the adjacent state $n + 1$, to represent an arrival transition, and an arrow from state n to state $n - 1$ (except when $n = 0$), to represent a departure transition. Each arrow is labeled by the rate at which the corresponding transition occurs. In the simple queue this means that all arrival transitions occur at the rate λ, while all service transitions occur at the rate μ.

The transition diagram describes the rate at which the system enters and leaves the various states. For example, the rate at which the system enters state $N = 0$ is equal to the transition rate from $N = 1$ to $N = 0$, multiplied by the probability that the system is in state $N = 1$, or μP_1. We know that μ is the overall mean service rate. Because P_1 is the long-run proportion of time the system is in state $N = 1$, we can interpret μP_1 as the mean rate at which the system moves from $N = 1$ to $N = 0$ by means of a service completion. Similarly, we can interpret μP_2 as the mean rate at which the system enters state $N = 1$ by means of a service completion. In addition, λP_0 is the mean rate at which the system enters state $N = 1$ by means of an arrival. Combining these two rates, we conclude that the overall rate at which the system enters state $N = 1$ is equal to $\lambda P_0 + \mu P_2$, since there are two transitions involving entry to $N = 1$. Similarly, the overall rate at which the system leaves $N = 1$ is equal to $\mu P_1 + \lambda P_1$. The lists in Figure 11.4 summarize the entering and leaving rates for the simple queue.

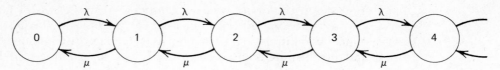

State	Entry Rate	Leaving Rate
0	μP_1	λP_0
1	$\lambda P_0 + \mu P_2$	$\lambda P_1 + \mu P_1$
2	$\lambda P_1 + \mu P_3$	$\lambda P_2 + \mu P_2$
3	$\lambda P_2 + \mu P_4$	$\lambda P_3 + \mu P_3$
4	$\lambda P_3 + \mu P_5$	$\lambda P_4 + \mu P_4$
.	.	.
.	.	.
.	.	.
n	$\lambda P_{n-1} + \mu P_{n+1}$	$\lambda P_n + \mu P_n$
.	.	.
.	.	.
.	.	.

FIGURE 11.4

We can think of the transition diagram as modeling the flow of the system among states. In the steady state this flow involves transitions into and out of all the states, with entering rates and leaving rates that might vary according to state. However, there is as much of a tendency to leave any state as to enter it. In formal terms, steady-state flow is governed by a **conservation** law, which states that for each state the entry rate must be equal to the leaving rate. To see why this law should hold, think of the states in Figure 11.4 as containers and the arrows as pipes connecting the containers, through which water flows. The total amount of water in the system represents the total probability that the system will be in one of its states. If the rate of flow into a container were to exceed the rate of outflow, there would be a net accumulation of water in that container; and as time passed, all the water would eventually end up there. In the queueing system there is an analogous interpretation. If the entry rate for state n were to exceed the leaving rate for state n, then the system would eventually be certain to reach state n and remain there. However, this behavior does not occur, because randomness in arrivals and services guarantees that the system cannot remain in any particular state. Therefore, the conservation law must hold.

The conservation law prescribes equality between the entering and leaving rates listed in Figure 11.4, yielding a set of equations:

$$\mu P_1 = \lambda P_0$$
$$\lambda P_{n-1} + \mu P_{n+1} = (\lambda + \mu)P_n \qquad n \geq 1$$

(11.5)

We interpret these as a system of equations in the unknown state probabilities $P_0, P_1, P_2, \ldots$. There is an infinite number of equations, but we can solve them easily if we take them one at a time. We begin with the equation for $n = 0$ and solve for P_1 in terms of P_0:

$$P_1 = \frac{\lambda}{\mu} P_0$$

Next, we take the equation for $n = 1$ and solve for P_2, substituting the above expression for P_1:

$$P_2 = \frac{\lambda + \mu}{\mu} P_1 - \frac{\lambda}{\mu} P_0 = \left(\frac{\lambda + \mu}{\mu}\right) \frac{\lambda}{\mu} P_0 - \frac{\lambda}{\mu} P_0 = \left(\frac{\lambda}{\mu}\right)^2 P_0$$

Similarly, the equation for $n = 2$ yields

$$P_3 = \left(\frac{\lambda}{\mu}\right)^3 P_0$$

At this point we can begin to see a pattern emerging, and we can guess that the general form of the solution is

$$P_n = \left(\frac{\lambda}{\mu}\right)^n P_0 \tag{11.6}$$

To confirm that this is in fact the solution, we substitute this relation in equations (11.5) for state n:

$$\lambda \left(\frac{\lambda}{\mu}\right)^{n-1} P_0 + \mu \left(\frac{\lambda}{\mu}\right)^{n+1} P_0 = (\lambda + \mu) \left(\frac{\lambda}{\mu}\right)^n P_0$$

Dividing through by $(\lambda/\mu)^{n-1} P_0$, we obtain

$$\lambda + \mu \left(\frac{\lambda}{\mu}\right)^2 = (\lambda + \mu) \left(\frac{\lambda}{\mu}\right)$$

$$\lambda + \frac{\lambda^2}{\mu} = \frac{\lambda^2}{\mu} + \lambda$$

Because this equation obviously holds, the formula in equation (11.6) must indeed provide the solution to the system of equations in (11.5), at least in terms of P_0.

To specify the steady-state distribution completely we need to know P_0, but we can utilize the fact that the probabilities in a distribution must add to 1.

Therefore,

$$\sum_{n=0}^{\infty} P_n = 1$$

or

$$\sum_{n=0}^{\infty} \left(\frac{\lambda}{\mu}\right)^n P_0 = \left[1 + \frac{\lambda}{\mu} + \left(\frac{\lambda}{\mu}\right)^2 + \left(\frac{\lambda}{\mu}\right)^3 + \cdots\right] P_0 = 1$$

Using the formula for the sum of a geometric series, this relationship becomes

$$P_0 = \left[1 + \left(\frac{\lambda}{\mu}\right) + \left(\frac{\lambda}{\mu}\right)^2 + \left(\frac{\lambda}{\mu}\right)^3 + \cdots\right]^{-1} = \left[\frac{1}{1 - \lambda/\mu}\right]^{-1} = 1 - \frac{\lambda}{\mu}$$

The formula for an infinite geometric series holds only as long as $\lambda/\mu < 1$; otherwise the series diverges. We interpret this result as follows: The steady-state distribution of N does not exist unless $\lambda/\mu < 1$. In this case, from equation (11.6) we have

$$P_n = \left(\frac{\lambda}{\mu}\right)^n \left(1 - \frac{\lambda}{\mu}\right) \qquad n = 0, 1, 2, \ldots$$

or

$$P_n = \rho^n (1 - \rho) \qquad n = 0, 1, 2, \ldots \tag{11.7}$$

where $\rho = \lambda/\mu < 1$ is called the **traffic intensity.**

The traffic intensity for the simple queue is the ratio of the mean arrival rate to the mean service rate. Clearly, if the traffic intensity is greater than 1, then on the average, arrivals occur faster than they can be serviced. Intuitively we should expect that in such a case the number of customers in the system would ultimately become infinite and that no steady-state distribution would exist. We say the system **saturates.**

The algebra that leads to equation (11.7) indicates that saturation also occurs when the mean arrival rate just equals the mean service rate. Only when the mean service rate exceeds the mean arrival rate will the simple queue reach stable, long-run behavior; and we can describe this behavior by the model in equation (11.7), a geometric distribution for the random variable N. Once we have specified the distribution of the number of customers in the system, we can calculate several measures of system performance. In the discussion to follow we assume that the system does not saturate.

We can interpret the long-run probability that there are no customers in the system as the proportion of time that the server is idle. From equation (11.7) this probability is

$$P_0 = 1 - \rho$$

Conversely, the server is busy with probability ρ.

We can calculate the expected number of customers in the system as the expected value of the N distribution:

$$L = E[N] = \sum_{n=0}^{\infty} nP_n = \sum_{n=1}^{\infty} n(1 - \rho)\rho^n = (1 - \rho) \sum_{n=1}^{\infty} n\rho^n$$

$$= (1 - \rho) \frac{\rho}{(1 - \rho)^2} = \frac{\rho}{1 - \rho} = \frac{\lambda}{\mu - \lambda}$$

The number of customers waiting in the queue is $N - 1$ when $N \geq 1$ and 0 otherwise. Thus, the expected queue length is

$$L_q = \sum_{n=1}^{\infty} (n - 1)P_n = \sum_{n=1}^{\infty} nP_n - \sum_{n=1}^{\infty} P_n = L - (1 - P_0)$$

$$= \frac{\rho}{1 - \rho} - \rho = \frac{\rho^2}{1 - \rho} = \frac{\lambda^2}{\mu(\mu - \lambda)}$$

For a customer who arrives when there are N customers already in the system, the total waiting time will be equivalent to $N + 1$ service times. Thus, we reason that the expected waiting time for an arriving customer should be $E[N + 1]$ multiplied by the mean service time of $1/\mu$, or

$$W = \frac{1}{\mu} E[N + 1] = \frac{1}{\mu} (E[N] + 1) = \frac{1}{\mu} (L + 1) = \frac{1}{\mu} \left(\frac{1}{1 - \rho} \right) = \frac{1}{\mu(1 - \rho)} = \frac{1}{\mu - \lambda}$$

Similarly, we can think of the waiting time prior to the initiation of service as being equivalent to N service times. Therefore, the expected queueing time should be $E[N]$ multiplied by $1/\mu$ or

$$W_q = \frac{1}{\mu} E[N] = \frac{1}{\mu} L = \frac{\lambda}{\mu(\mu - \lambda)}$$

We have outlined how to deduce the quantities L, L_q, W, and W_q from the probability distribution for N. In more complicated queueing systems, however, such derivations often turn out to be quite difficult or impossible. In most cases a more convenient strategy is to develop a formula for one of the four quantities and then rely on the queueing formulas (11.2) to (11.4) to produce the others.

In the Ovington Bank and Trust example let us assume that statistical analysis confirms that the arrival process is Poisson with a stable arrival rate of $\lambda = 50$ customers per hour in the period from 4–7 P.M., and that the distribution of service times is exponential with a service rate of $\mu = 60$ customers per hour. In the relevant formulas we use $\rho = \lambda/\mu = 0.833$, and we find

$$P_0 = 1 - \rho = 0.167 \qquad L = \frac{\rho}{1 - \rho} = 5 \text{ customers}$$

Thus, the branch manager should expect to find the drive-in teller idle about 17% of the time, although the average number of cars in line should be 5, counting the customer being served. In fact, from equation (11.7), the probability that there will be more than five customers in the system is 0.33. Direct substitution in the queueing formulas (11.2) to (11.4) yields

$$W = \frac{L}{\lambda} = 0.1 \text{ hour (6 minutes)}$$

$$W_q = W - \frac{1}{\mu} = 0.083 \text{ hour (5 minutes)}$$

$$L_q = \lambda W_q = 4.17 \text{ customers}$$

At first glance, it may seem strange that L and L_q do not differ by exactly 1. However, it is important to remember that the number of customers in the system and the number in queue do not always differ by 1; they are both 0 when the system is idle. The two numbers differ by 1 only when the system is busy, or 0.83 of the time in our example. Therefore, it is logical to find that the difference between L and L_q is 0.83.

VARIATIONS OF THE BASIC MODEL

We can generalize the techniques used in deriving the properties of the simple queue to deal with such features as servers operating in parallel, limited waiting space for customers, and small source populations. To achieve this generality, we must allow the arrival and service rates to be state dependent. In other words, the arrival and service rates depend on the value of N. Specifically, our notation will be

λ_n = arrival rate to the system when $N = n$

μ_n = system service rate when $N = n$

With this perspective we can model queueing systems in which the demand intensity or service capacity may vary according to the number of customers in the system. We maintain the assumption of Poisson arrivals and exponential services. Under this assumption we allow for arrivals that occur one at a time and at an average rate that remains constant while the system remains in a given state. When the state of the system changes, arrivals continue to occur at random, one at a time, but at a *different* average rate that persists while the system remains in the new state. Similarly, we can model queueing systems in which the service rate is different according to the number of customers in the system.

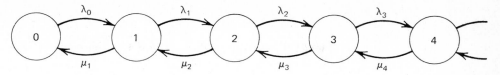

State	Entry Rate	Leaving Rate
0	$\mu_1 P_1$	$\lambda_0 P_0$
1	$\lambda_0 P_0 + \mu_2 P_2$	$\lambda_1 P_1 + \mu_1 P_1$
2	$\lambda_1 P_1 + \mu_3 P_3$	$\lambda_2 P_2 + \mu_2 P_2$
3	$\lambda_2 P_2 + \mu_4 P_4$	$\lambda_3 P_3 + \mu_3 P_3$
4	$\lambda_3 P_3 + \mu_5 P_5$	$\lambda_4 P_4 + \mu_4 P_4$
.	.	.
.	.	.
.	.	.
n	$\lambda_{n-1} P_{n-1} + \mu_{n+1} P_{n+1}$	$\lambda_n P_n + \mu_n P_n$

FIGURE 11.5

Figure 11.5 shows the general form of the flow diagram for state-dependent arrival and service rates. Note, for example, that in this case we write the entry rate for state $n = 2$ as $\lambda_1 P_1 + \mu_3 P_3$ and the leaving rate for state $n = 2$ as $(\lambda_2 + \mu_2) P_2$. Following the logic of the analysis for the simple queue, we can employ the conservation law governing flow rates to derive a system of steady-state equations for the general diagram. The unknowns in this system of equations are again the state probabilities P_n, and it is possible to show that the solution of this system is

$$P_n = \frac{\lambda_0 \lambda_1 \cdots \lambda_{n-1}}{\mu_1 \mu_2 \cdots \mu_n} P_0 \tag{11.8}$$

where P_0 is defined by the requirement that all the state probabilities must sum to one:

$$\sum_{n=0}^{\infty} P_n = 1 \tag{11.9}$$

Looking back, we can see that the simple queue is the special case of equation (11.8) in which $\lambda_n = \lambda$ and $\mu_n = \mu$. In addition, the flexibility of state-dependent rates allows us to analyze several variations of the basic model, including the cases shown in Figure 11.6.

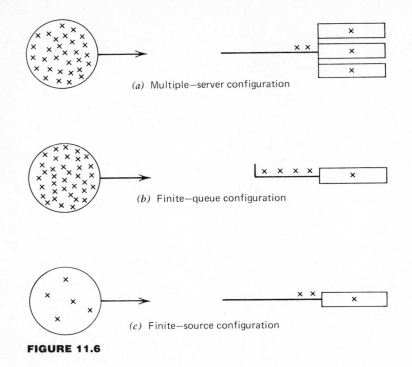

(a) Multiple—server configuration

(b) Finite—queue configuration

(c) Finite—source configuration

FIGURE 11.6

MULTIPLE SERVERS

As an introduction to the analysis of queueing systems with state-dependent rates, consider a system with Poisson arrivals from an infinite source population and with exponential service times. Suppose now that there are s identical servers operating in parallel. In this model the arrival process is the same as in the simple queue, but the service process is different. When $N < s$ there are N services occurring simultaneously, so that the system's service rate is $N\mu$; and when $N \geq s$ there are s services occurring simultaneously, so that the system's service rate is $s\mu$. Stated in terms of state-dependent service rates this means

$$\lambda_n = \lambda$$

and

$$\mu_n = n\mu \qquad (n < s)$$
$$\mu_n = s\mu \qquad (n \geq s)$$

With this specification, equation (11.8) for state probabilities yields

$$P_n = \frac{\lambda^n}{n! \mu^n} P_0 \qquad \text{for } 1 \leq n < s$$

$$P_n = \frac{\lambda^n}{s! s^{n-s} \mu^n} P_0 \qquad \text{for } n \geq s$$

We determine the value of P_0 from equation (11.9), yielding

$$P_0 = \left[\sum_{n=0}^{s-1} \left(\frac{\lambda^n}{n! \mu^n} \right) + \sum_{n=s}^{\infty} \left(\frac{\lambda^n}{s! s^{n-s} \mu^n} \right) \right]^{-1}$$

$$= \left[\sum_{n=0}^{s-1} \left(\frac{\lambda^n}{n! \mu^n} \right) + \frac{\lambda^s}{s! \mu^s} \left(\frac{s\mu}{s\mu - \lambda} \right) \right]^{-1} \qquad (11.10)$$

We can calculate this value for $\lambda < s\mu$. For $\lambda \geq s\mu$ the aggregate capacity of the system to provide service does not exceed the arrival rate, and such a system will saturate. Furthermore, we can show that for the multiple-server model:

$$L_q = \frac{P_0 \lambda^s}{s! \mu^s} \left[\frac{\lambda s \mu}{(s\mu - \lambda)^2} \right] \qquad (11.11)$$

From this value it is possible to compute the summary values of W_q, W, and L from formulas (11.2) to (11.4).

In the example of Ovington Bank and Trust, suppose that the bank were to add a second drive-in lane served by a second teller. The appropriate model for analysis would then be the multiple-server model with $s = 2$. We use equation (11.10) to calculate $P_0 = 0.4118$, and we use equation (11.11) to calculate $L_q = 0.1756$ customers. Then

$$W_q = \frac{L_q}{\lambda} = 0.0035 \text{ hour } (0.2 \text{ minute})$$

$$W = W_q + \frac{1}{\mu} = 0.0202 \text{ hour } (1.2 \text{ minutes})$$

$$L = \lambda W = 1.01 \text{ customers}$$

Therefore, the addition of a second drive-in lane at the bank raises the probability of an idle system from 0.17 to 0.41 but reduces the mean number of customers in the system from 5 to 1.01. Also, the probability of more than five customers in the system drops from 0.33 to 0.008.

From the example it is clear that calculation of P_0 according to equation (11.10) is extremely cumbersome. Fortunately, it is possible to simplify this task. Note that P_0 depends only on two parameters, s (the number of servers) and λ/μ (the traffic intensity when $s = 1$). As a result, we can envision a table that lists the value of P_0 for various combinations of s and λ/μ. The appendix contains one such table.

To illustrate use of the table, let us return to the Ovington Bank and Trust problem. From the information given, we can calculate

$$\frac{\lambda}{\mu} = \frac{50}{60}$$

$$= 0.833$$

This value does not appear in the P_0 table, which has values of λ/μ in steps of 0.05. For convenience, the following is an excerpt from the P_0 table:

λ/μ	$s = 1$	$s = 2$	$s = 3$	$s = 4$
0.80	0.2000	0.4286	0.4472	0.4491
0.85	0.1500	0.4035	0.4248	0.4271

For $s = 2$ we see that $P_0 = 0.4286$ when $\lambda/\mu = 0.80$ and that $P_0 = 0.4035$ when $\lambda/\mu = 0.85$. Interpolating between these values, we arrive at $P_0 = 0.4119$, which is extremely close to 0.4118, the value we calculated using equation (11.10). To continue with the example, through interpolation we find that $P_0 = 0.4323$ for $s = 3$ and 0.4344 for $s = 4$. Substituting these values into equation (11.11), and using equations (11.2) to (11.4), we arrive at the following results:

	$s = 1$	$s = 2$	$s = 3$	$s = 4$
P_0	0.1667	0.4119	0.4323	0.4344
L_q	4.17	0.1756	0.0222	0.0029
W_q	0.083	0.0035	0.0004	0.0001
W	0.1	0.0202	0.0171	0.0167
L	5	1.01	0.8556	0.8362

Besides illustrating the use of the table, this example demonstrates the phenomenon of diminishing returns in queueing. Specifically, as we increase the number of servers in the system, each additional server yields a much smaller reduction than any of its predecessors.

FINITE QUEUE

Suppose there is limited space for waiting customers in a single-server queue. For example, at a gas pump there may be limited waiting space for cars, or at a work station on a production line there may be limited waiting space for subassemblies. Let m denote the maximum possible number of customers in the system. Then there are Poisson arrivals except for the fact that there is no possibility of an arrival when $N = m$. In terms of state-dependent arrival and service rates we have

$$\lambda_n = \lambda \qquad (0 \le n < m)$$
$$\lambda_n = 0 \qquad \text{otherwise}$$

$$\mu_n = \mu \qquad (1 \le n \le m)$$
$$\mu_n = 0 \qquad \text{otherwise}$$

Substituting these rates into equations (11.8) and (11.9) we obtain

$$P_n = \left(\frac{\lambda}{\mu}\right)^n \left[\frac{1 - \lambda/\mu}{1 - (\lambda/\mu)^{m+1}}\right] \qquad (0 \le n \le m)$$

These steady-state probabilities are the basis for the calculation of summary performance measures. The mean number of customers in the system must be calculated directly from the definition

$$L = \sum_{n=0}^{m} n P_n$$

In order to exploit the queueing formulas (11.2) to (11.4), we must be careful to notice that the arrival rate depends on the system's state. In this case we define the mean arrival rate $\bar{\lambda}$ to be the mean value of the state-dependent arrival rates:

$$\bar{\lambda} = \sum_{n=0}^{\infty} \lambda_n P_n = \sum_{n=0}^{m-1} \lambda P_n = \lambda(1 - P_m)$$

We can then use the quantity $\bar{\lambda}$ in place of λ in formulas (11.2) to (11.4).

FINITE SOURCE

When there are only a relatively small number of potential customers in the source population, the arrival rate is strongly dependent on how many members of the population are already in the queue. As a result, our previous assumption of a very large source population is no longer valid. The classic example of this situation is the **machine interference problem,** in which m machines operate in a production shop but break down from time to time and need repair. The repairman provides service, and the queue consists of broken-down machines awaiting repair service. The machines break down at random, one at a time, at a constant rate for each machine. We assume that the repair times follow an exponential distribution with a mean repair rate of μ.

We can view the machine interference model as a simple queue with a finite source population. By assuming that the breakdown processes of the various machines are independent, we multiply λ by the number of machines operating to get the total breakdown rate. Viewed from the perspective of the queue, this means that the arrivals will be Poisson arrivals with a rate equal to λ multiplied by the number of machines not in the queueing system. In terms of state-dependent rates we have

$$\lambda_n = (m - n)\lambda \qquad (0 \le n \le m)$$
$$\lambda_n = 0 \qquad \text{otherwise}$$

$$\mu_n = \mu \qquad (1 \le n \le m)$$
$$\mu_n = 0 \qquad \text{otherwise}$$

Substituting these rates into equations (11.8) and (11.9) we obtain

$$P_n = m(m - 1) \cdot \cdot \cdot (m - n + 1) \frac{\lambda^n}{\mu^n} P_0 \qquad (1 \le n \le m) \tag{11.12}$$

$$P_0 = \left[1 + \sum_{n=1}^{m} m(m - 1) \cdot \cdot \cdot (m - n + 1) \frac{\lambda^n}{\mu^n} \right]^{-1} \tag{11.13}$$

As a numerical example, suppose that $m = 5$, $\lambda = 3$ breakdowns per week and $\mu = 5$ repairs per week. From equation (11.12)

$$P_1 = 5(0.6)P_0$$
$$P_2 = 20(0.6)^2 P_0$$
$$P_3 = 60(0.6)^3 P_0$$
$$P_4 = 120(0.6)^4 P_0$$
$$P_5 = 120(0.6)^5 P_0$$

Then from equation (11.13)

$$P_0 = [1 + 5(0.6) + 20(0.6)^2 + 60(0.6)^3 + 120(0.6)^4 + 120(0.6)^5]^{-1} = 0.02$$

The steady-state probabilities are therefore

n	0	1	2	3	4	5
P_n	0.02	0.06	0.15	0.26	0.32	0.19

and the mean of this distribution is $L = 3.37$. Thus, a system with these parameters would have, on the average, less than two of its five machines in operation; and the repairman would be busy 98% of the time.

Two fundamental strategies exist for improving performance in the machine interference problem: One is to add more repairmen, and the other is to use spare machines. From equations (11.8) and (11.9) we can derive summary performance measures for systems in which these strategies are employed, provided that we use the correct specifications of λ_n and μ_n. Also notice that in the finite-source model, as in the finite-queue model, the arrival rate depends on the system's state. In the finite-source case the mean arrival rate is

$$\bar{\lambda} = \sum_{n=0}^{\infty} \lambda_n P_n = \sum_{n=0}^{m} (m - n)\lambda P_n = m\lambda \sum_{n=0}^{m} P_n - \lambda \sum_{n=0}^{m} nP_n$$

In this formula, ΣP_n is equal to 1 because P_n is a probability distribution, and ΣnP_n is equal to L by definition. Thus

$$\bar{\lambda} = m\lambda(1) - \lambda(L) = \lambda(m - L)$$

In our example, $\lambda = 3$, $m = 5$ and $L = 3.37$, so that $\bar{\lambda} = 4.89$ breakdowns per week. We use this quantity in place of λ when making calculations in the queueing formulas (11.2) to (11.4).

DESIGN CONSIDERATIONS IN QUEUES

We noted earlier that there are two ways in which we can use queueing models. In queue **analysis** we quantify the performance of a particular system, while in queue **design** we select a system configuration on the basis of comparisons among alternative systems. To address questions of queue design, it is necessary to examine the inherent performance trade-offs in an economic context. In this respect, queueing analysis resembles many other kinds of analysis in that it deals with design choices under conflicting objectives.

Perhaps the most fundamental economic choice in queueing systems involves service capacity. Typically, demands on a service facility are exogenous—that is, they are not directly controlled by activities at the facility—whereas the service process is a matter for choice in a system design. Conceptually, this means that the basic trade-off involves waiting costs and service costs. As we invest more resources in service capacity, customers spend less time waiting, and waiting costs decline. On the other hand, the cost of providing service rises with increasing capacity, giving rise to the two cost curves depicted in Figure 11.7.

A systems view recognizes both cost components and seeks the optimal capacity level that minimizes the combined sum of waiting costs and service costs. The decision variable that represents capacity might reflect speed of service, where a fast server costs more to employ than a slower server. More commonly, service speeds are fixed and the decision variable is simply the number of parallel channels to use.

Of course, this approach presumes that we can quantify customer waiting costs. For example, if customers are production facilities awaiting repair, then waiting costs might represent profits that are lost while the facilities are down. If customers are couriers awaiting assignment by a dispatcher, then waiting costs might represent the salaries paid the couriers while they are idle.

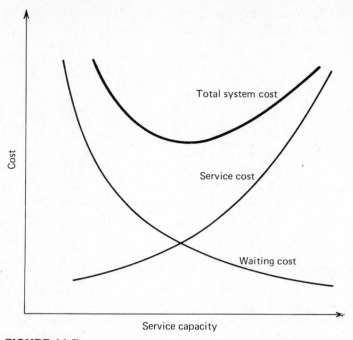

FIGURE 11.7

When we can quantify waiting costs we are able to directly examine the trade-off represented in Figure 11.7. Let c_w represent the cost per unit of time incurred by each customer in the system, and let c_s represent the cost per unit of time for supplying service in one channel. Then the expected waiting cost incurred by an arriving customer is c_wW. The waiting cost (WC) per unit time is simply this cost per customer multiplied by the rate at which customers arrive or

$$WC = \lambda c_w W$$

Because $L = \lambda W$, we also have

$$WC = c_w L$$

Meanwhile the service cost (SC) per unit time is the cost per channel multiplied by the number of channels or

$$SC = c_s s$$

Therefore, the total cost (TC) per unit time can be written as

$$TC = WC + SC = c_w L + c_s s$$

When the decision variable is represented by speed of service, we can expect that c_s will be a function of the average service rate μ, and the objective will be to minimize TC as a function of μ. On the other hand, if the decision variable is the number of channels, we can expect that c_s will usually be a constant, and the objective will be to minimize TC as a function of s. In such cases, we determine the optimal value of the decision variable by searching over its possible values in order to find the best choice.

As an example, consider the problem facing the manager of Ovington Bank and Trust. The addition of a second drive-in lane at the bank would reduce the average number of customers in the system from 5 to 1.01. A third lane would reduce the number to 0.86, and a fourth lane would reduce it to 0.84. Let us assume that the teller is paid $5 per hour ($c_s$) and that the manager believes that the value of a customer's time is $10 per hour ($c_w$). As a result, the total cost per hour is

$$TC = 10L + 5s$$

Given our knowledge of L as a function of s, we can calculate

$$TC_1 = 10(5) + 5(1) = 55.00$$
$$TC_2 = 10(1.01) + 5(2) = 20.10$$
$$TC_3 = 10(0.86) + 5(3) = 23.60$$
$$TC_4 = 10(0.84) + 5(4) = 28.40$$

In other words, the system total cost would be minimized by adding the second lane.

In many situations it is relatively easy to estimate the value of c_s, but it is difficult to estimate c_w. For instance, the manager at Ovington Bank and Trust knows the teller's wage rate but has to estimate the average waiting cost for a customer. Even if the manager did not know a specific value of c_w, some analysis would be possible by formulating the total cost as a function of c_w. Specifically, we have

$$TC_1 = 5c_w + 5$$
$$TC_2 = 1.01c_w + 10$$
$$TC_3 = 0.86c_w + 15$$
$$TC_4 = 0.84c_w + 20$$

Solving any two adjacent equations simultaneously gives a break-even value of c_w, the value at which the total costs are equal. In order to find the break-even value of c_w for TC_1 and TC_2, we simply equate TC_1 with TC_2 and solve for c_w:

$$5c_w + 5 = 1.01c_w + 10$$
$$c_w = 1.25$$

Similarly, for TC_2 and TC_3 the break-even value of c_w is \$33.33, and for TC_3 and TC_4 it is \$250. If the manager believes that the cost of waiting is less than \$1.25 per hour, then the single-lane facility would be the least expensive; if it is between \$1.25 and \$33.33 per hour, then the two-lane facility would be the least expensive, and so on for the three- and four-lane facilities. In this example, a precise value for c_w may not be necessary in order to find the optimal number of servers; the manager can estimate the cost very roughly and still be confident of having the optimal system design.

Another issue in system design involves the **pooling** of servers. In recent years many banks have established a single line for all customers waiting for the services of a teller, rather than permitting separate lines in front of each teller's window. Analogously, a typing pool treats incoming work as if it were in a single queue, as compared to a system that assigns typists to perform only work from designated sources.

The principle involved in pooling is that idle capacity is not permitted while customers wait, and we can illustrate this concept with simple examples. Suppose we assign one typist to office A and another typist to office B. Assume that we can model the arrival of typing jobs as a simple queue with $\lambda = 1$ job per hour and $\mu = 1.25$ jobs per hour. If the work flows are separate, the typists function as two independent single-server systems. For either typist the average time a job is in the system can be calculated as follows:

$$W = \frac{1}{\mu - \lambda} = \frac{1}{1.25 - 1} = 4 \text{ hours}$$

On the other hand, if we pool capacity, the typists function as a single two-server system. Then the average time in the system is calculated in the following steps:

From equation (11.10), $P_0 = \left[1 + \frac{2}{1.25} + \frac{(2)^2}{2(1.25)^2} \left(\frac{2.5}{2.5 - 2} \right) \right]^{-1} = 0.111$

From equation (11.11), $L_q = (0.111) \frac{(2)^2}{2(1.25)^2} \left[\frac{(2)(2)(1.25)}{(2.5 - 2)^2} \right] = 2.84$

From equation (11.3), $W_q = \frac{L_q}{\lambda} = \frac{2.84}{2} = 1.42$

From equation (11.4), $W = W_q + \frac{1}{\mu} = 1.42 + 0.8 = 2.22 \text{ hours}$

This reduction in waiting time is accomplished without changing the productivity standard for individuals in the system but by redesigning the configuration of the service activity.

In finite queues an added dimension of system capacity involves the maximum allowable queue length. As this maximum level increases, the probability of overflow decreases. In economic terms, overflows (i.e., arriving customers

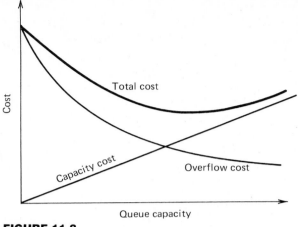

FIGURE 11.8

turned away for lack of waiting space) symbolize opportunity costs, giving rise to the cost trade-off described in Figure 11.8.

In some systems, particularly in service agencies, the focus is on service level more often than on waiting costs, and we measure the benefits of increased capacity in terms of better service. For example, a police department's choice of the number of patrols may be linked to the probability that an emergency call can be answered immediately. In this case we would specify a minimum desired level of service and the problem would be to determine the (cheapest) capacity level at which we could achieve this level. Such an approach is embodied in Figure 11.9.

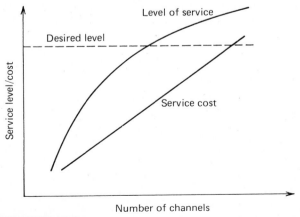

FIGURE 11.9

SENSITIVITY ANALYSIS

Because many measures of queueing performance are expressed in terms of formulas, it is possible to examine directly the sensitivity of these measures to parametric assumptions. For example, in the case of the Ovington Bank and Trust drive-in window, we saw earlier that the mean waiting time was calculated to be 0.1 hour (6 minutes). The branch manager might be concerned about how this figure will change as the branch becomes more popular and the arrival rate of customers increases. Specifically, we might want to know how much growth in demand would be required to make the waiting time exceed 10 minutes. Because the formula for mean waiting time is

$$W = \frac{1}{\mu - \lambda} = \frac{1}{60 - \lambda},$$

we can solve for values of λ for which the mean waiting time is less than or equal to 10 minutes ($\frac{1}{6}$ hour) by solving

$$\frac{1}{60 - \lambda} \leq \frac{1}{6}$$

$$60 - \lambda \geq 6$$

$$\lambda \leq 54$$

Therefore, as long as the average arrival rate (which reflects the popularity of the branch) rises from its current rate of 50 customers per hour to no more than 54 customers per hour, the mean waiting time will not exceed 10 minutes.

In multiple-server models, however, the formulas are more complicated than for the simple queue, and the computational demands of parametric analysis are correspondingly more difficult. For example, suppose that there are two drive-in lanes at the Ovington Bank's drive-in window. Then to find the values of λ for which $W \leq 10$ minutes, we must return to the P_0 tables and equation (11.11) and perform the detailed calculations summarized below.

λ	P_0	L_q	W
50	0.412	0.175	0.020
100	0.091	3.788	0.054
110	0.043	9.645	0.104
112	0.034	12.616	0.129 (8 minutes)
114	0.026	17.587	0.171 (10.3 minutes)

Apparently, in the two-server system the mean waiting time will not exceed 10 minutes as long as $\lambda < 114$ (approximately).

Perhaps the most significant feature of the analytic results for the simple queue is the prevalence of the factor $1/(\mu - \lambda)$. The measures L, L_q, W, and W_q

are all related to the reciprocal of $(\mu - \lambda)$, or, essentially, to the reciprocal of $(1 - \rho)$, thus leading to very pronounced nonlinear behavior. For example, Figure 11.10 shows a graph of the mean number in the system, L, as a function of ρ. We see that L is relatively insensitive to small changes in ρ when ρ is small (e.g., $\rho = 0.5$), but the L curve rises quite sharply as ρ approaches 1.

If we wish to investigate questions of structural validity, we must deal with queues in which the assumptions of Poisson arrivals and exponential service

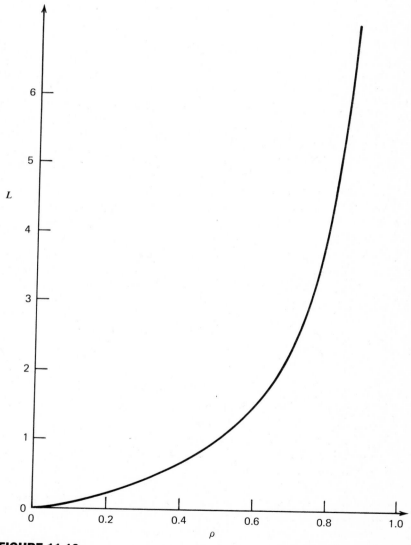

FIGURE 11.10

times do not hold. For the most part, the analysis of such queueing models is beyond the scope of this text. However, one result is of particular interest. Consider a single-server queue with Poisson arrivals, but suppose that the form of the service-time distribution is left arbitrary. As before, let μ denote the mean service rate, so that the mean of the service-time distribution is $1/\mu$. In addition, let σ^2 denote the variance of the service-time distribution. Then it is possible to show that the mean number of customers in the queue is given by

$$L_q = \frac{\rho^2 + \lambda^2 \sigma^2}{2(1 - \rho)} \tag{11.14}$$

This formula is more general than the formula presented earlier for the simple queue because it requires no restrictive assumption about the form of the service time distribution. Even though the overall mean service rate is μ, this general model does *not* require that the service rate be a constant while the system is in a particular state. The simple queue is the special case in which service times follow an exponential distribution and, as a consequence, the variance of the service time distribution is equal to the square of the mean, or $\sigma^2 = 1/\mu^2$. Substituting this relationship into equation (11.14) yields

$$L_q = \frac{\rho^2 + \rho^2}{2(1 - \rho)} = \frac{\rho^2}{(1 - \rho)}. \tag{11.15}$$

When we substitute $\rho = \lambda/\mu$ in this equation we obtain the result previously established for the simple queue. For the sake of comparison, we can consider the case in which the service time is a constant. Because in this case $\sigma^2 = 0$, equation (11.14) reduces to

$$L_q = \frac{\rho^2}{2(1 - \rho)} \tag{11.16}$$

In other words, when the service time is constant the mean number of customers in the queue is one-half of what it would be when the service time has an identical mean but follows an exponential distribution.

In most applications the assumptions of constant service times and of exponential service times represent two extremes on the spectrum of service-time assumptions. The corresponding range of L values obtained from equations (11.15) and (11.16) begins to provide some information relating to structural validity. As with the other queueing models introduced earlier, we can obtain additional performance measures for the single-server system with arbitrary service times from the queueing formulas (11.2) to (11.4).

SUMMARY

Queueing models offer a means of studying systems that provide service, and they are particularly useful in their ability to relate system performance to the probabilistic nature of the demand and service processes. With the aid of a queueing model it is possible to describe the behavior of congestion in a service system and to predict system performance under various operating conditions.

A significant feature of queueing models is their ability to capture the inherent dynamic and probabilistic behavior of service systems. We characterize the system's behavior with probability distributions that describe the state of the system, although it is often more convenient to rely on summary measures of performance, such as mean waiting time or mean queue length. In this chapter we classified the dynamic behavior of service systems into transient and steady-state phases, and we focused on the properties of steady-state performance. The steady-state description applies in the long run, when a system has an opportunity to reach dynamic equilibrium.

The analysis of queueing models demonstrates the kind of information needed to carry out a queueing study. The most important information is a description of the probabilistic nature of arrivals and services. The elementary models rely on an assumption of random arrivals, an assumption that should be verified in order to use the models convincingly. The elementary models also rely on the assumption of exponential service time distributions and on service configurations that we can represent in the state transition diagrams. However, we saw that we can relax this particular assumption, at least for a single-server system, and still compute the important measures of performance. Queueing analysis leads to formulas for probabilities and summary measures, and these formulas reflect the prominent role of the parameters λ and μ, which describe the average demand intensity and the capacity of a service channel, respectively.

With the formulas we have compiled, it is possible to proceed from a descriptive approach to a normative approach and to investigate trade-offs in system design. Decision making aimed at optimization in queueing models often requires only straightforward methods for listing alternatives, computing and comparing performance measures, and searching systematically for the best alternative.

EXERCISES

THE POISSON AND EXPONENTIAL DISTRIBUTIONS

1 Records at the Meade County Hospital show the daily number of admissions on the maternity ward during the night shift (10 P.M.–6 A.M.). A random sample of 40 days from the records of the past 3 years shows the following admission counts.

7	5	8	2	5
5	6	6	6	5
7	6	3	7	10
5	3	5	4	5
4	4	7	3	8
1	3	5	6	6
4	7	6	5	8
6	6	6	4	5

a What is the mean arrival rate (in maternity admissions per hour) during the night shift at the maternity ward?

b Determine whether these data fit a Poisson distribution.

2 A study of repair times at Metropolis City Bus Garage has been underway for some time. A random sample of repair tickets provided the following repair times, in hours, on unscheduled maintenance jobs. (Because of the way that the tickets are filled out, times are recorded to the nearest one-tenth of an hour.)

0.1	6.6	1.7	0.7	0.4
1.0	3.2	2.1	0.7	1.4
3.3	0.1	9.3	1.1	2.6
1.1	4.4	2.6	0.9	0.8
1.2	1.5	1.9	2.8	0.6
3.3	2.2	0.3	1.0	0.1
4.6	2.7	0.9	3.0	4.9
1.1	6.3	1.0	2.5	5.5

a Estimate the mean repair time.

b Estimate the variance of the repair-time distribution.

c If repair times follow an exponential distribution, what relationship would you expect between the estimates in parts (a) and (b)?

d Determine whether the sample data fit an exponential distribution.

3 The duration of a long-distance phone call in a particular locality is known to follow an exponential distribution with a mean of 3 minutes.

a What is the probability that a long-distance call will last more than 5 minutes?

b Given that a particular long-distance call has already lasted 10 minutes, what is the probability that it will last more than a total of 15 minutes?

c What proportion of long-distance calls takes less than 3 minutes?

THE SIMPLE QUEUE

4 Jobs arrive at a particular work center according to a Poisson input process at a mean rate of two per day, and the operation time has an exponential distribution with a mean of $\frac{1}{4}$ day. Enough in-process storage space is provided at the work center to accommodate three jobs in addition to the one being processed. When this space is full, it is necessary to use an inconvenient area for the overflow. What proportion of time will the overflow area be in use?

5 Customer arrivals at Buddy's Bi-Lo self-service gas station occur in a Poisson process at an average of one every 5 minutes during the day. Buddy has only a single pump to serve all customers, so that the system operates as a single-channel queue. The time required for a customer to pull up, pump gas, pay, and leave is a random variable that conforms approximately to an exponential probability distribution with a mean of 4 minutes. Assuming there is room for any number of waiting customers at Buddy's and that steady-state analysis is appropriate,

a What is the mean number of customers in the system?

b What is the probability that more than three cars are waiting in the queue for the pump to become free?

c What is the probability that there are no cars at Buddy's at a given moment during the day?

6 At the Bishopric Beverage and Bottling Company there are several automatic bottling lines that fill bottles with a variety of soft drinks. A production run on any of the lines requires a careful setup to set the lot size, to adjust the equipment to the specifications of the particular bottle size and shape, and to assure that the proper liquids are poured in. Once the setup is done, the production run proceeds automatically without the need for supervision. At the completion of the run a signal is given to show that the line is ready for the next setup.

The company uses a single "setup man" to perform all the setups. He moves from line to line responding to ready signals as they occur. The length of time required to perform a particular setup varies considerably according to how different the next lot is from the one before it. As a consequence, setup times tend to conform to an exponential distribution with a mean of 30 minutes. In addition, there is considerable variability in lot sizes, and so the occurrence of ready signals is essentially random with a mean rate of 1.5 per hour.

a What proportion of the time is the setup man busy?

b What proportion of the time are there more than two lines out of production (inactive)?

c What is the average number of inactive lines?

d For how long, on the average, is a line inactive, between its ready signal and the actual start of its next production run?

7 Marshall Manufacturing Company is in operation around the clock, and there is continual demand at its central stockroom. The employees requiring service at the stockroom are called couriers. There are a large number of couriers in the work force, and they are responsible for supplying materials, tooling, and equipment to workers on several production lines. The company is planning to analyze the queueing system at the stockroom.

Couriers arrive randomly at the stockroom at the rate of nine per hour. At present there is one stockroom attendant working each shift, filling the couriers' requests. The time required to fill requests tends to follow an exponential distribution with a mean of 6 minutes.

Use the simple queue as a model to analyze this system, and answer the following questions.

a What proportion of the time is the attendant idle?

b What is the probability that there are no couriers waiting to submit requests to the attendant?

c What is the average number of couriers in the system?

d What is a courier's average waiting time at the stockroom?

PARALLEL SERVERS

8 Admissions to the maternity ward at Meade County Hospital occur randomly at an average of six per day. The typical maternity patient spends much more time in a labor room than in the delivery room or the prep room. Concern about limited facilities on the ward is focused on the availability of only four labor rooms.

The time spent in labor is a random variable with a mean of 10 hours. Experience suggests that an exponential distribution is a reasonable model for labor times. Using this assumption, calculate the probability that there will be more than four patients in labor at any one time.

9 Review Exercise 5. Suppose that Buddy had three pumps, one at each of three service islands, instead of just one pump. For that configuration calculate

a The mean number of customers in the system.

b The probability that more than four cars are waiting in the queue for a pump to become free.

c The probability that there are no cars at Buddy's at a given moment during the day.

10 Review Exercise 6. Suppose that Bishopric were to employ two setup men to work simultaneously. Assume that only one man is needed to perform a particular setup and that the setup time distribution is exponential with mean 30 minutes for either setup man. Calculate

a The proportion of time both setup men are busy.

b The proportion of time both setup men are idle.

c The proportion of time there are more than two lines not producing.

d The average number of lines not producing.

e The average nonproductive time for a bottling line.

f The utilization of the setup men's capacity.

11 Review Exercise 7. Suppose that the Marshall Company is thinking about hiring a second stockroom attendant on all shifts. Assume that the two-server model applies.

a What proportion of the time are both attendants idle?

b What proportion of the time are both attendants busy?

c What is the utilization of attendant capacity?

d What is the probability that there are no couriers waiting to submit a request?

e What is the average number of couriers in the system?

12 Review Exercises 5 and 9. In reality, Buddy's Bi-Lo gas station is situated on a relatively small lot and has limited space for cars. If Buddy continues to operate with a one-pump facility, he will have room for seven waiting cars, other than the one at the pump; if he changes to a three-pump facility, he will have room for only three waiting cars, other than those at the pumps.

a For the one-pump configuration find the steady-state distribution for the number of cars in the system and compute the rate at which potential customers are lost due to lack of waiting space.

b Calculate the mean number of customers in the one-pump system.

c For the three-pump configuration find the steady-state distribution for the number of cars in the system and compute the rate at which potential customers are lost due to lack of waiting space.

d Calculate the mean number of customers in the three-pump system.

13 The city of Metropolis is contemplating a redesign of its Transportation Maintenance Facility. At present the facility consists of two servicemen, one exclusively for bus repairs and one for trolley repairs. One alternative to this design is to leave the repairmen undesignated, so that they could each work on either buses or trolleys, as the work arrives. A second alternative is to permit the servicemen to work together as a two-man crew on every task.

Bus repair jobs arrive at the facility randomly at an average rate of 12 per week, while trolley repair jobs arrive randomly at an average rate of six per week. In the present system, the time required for one serviceman (working alone) to complete a repair job follows an exponential distribution, and the average service rate is 15 jobs per week on either type of job. However, if the servicemen work as a two-man crew, the service rate will be 24 jobs per week since some jobs are not well-suited to a two-man repair crew.

Compare the three possible designs in order to determine which performs most efficiently:

a The present system, with designated service.

b The combined system, with parallel service and no designations.

c The crew system, with the adjusted service rate.

MACHINE INTERFERENCE MODEL

14 A clinic operates four X-ray machines and has room to utilize all four at once if they are in working condition. These machines break down from time to time, in a manner that can be modeled as a Poisson process with mean rate $\lambda = 2$ per week for each machine. In order to service these machines, the clinic employs two maintenance men. Repairing an X-ray machine is a one-man task for either of these maintenance men, who have in the past taken an average of 0.4 week to repair a machine. Furthermore, a study of the repair process indicates that repair times appear to follow an exponential distribution. What is the effective capacity of the X-ray facility?

15 Consider the machine interference example problem in this chapter. Suppose that two repairmen are used instead of one. Assume that only one repairman can work on a machine at a time.

a Draw a transition diagram for this case and label it with the specific values of λ_n and μ_n that apply.

b Find the steady-state distribution of the number of machines out of operation.

c What is the mean number of machines in operation?

d What proportion of the time are both repairmen idle?

e What proportion of the time are both repairmen busy?

16 Consider the machine interference example problem in this chapter. Suppose that an additional machine is purchased, so that there would be one spare. In other words, the spare could only be used when at least one machine is out of operation, and at most five machines would be in operation at any time.

a Draw a transition diagram for this case and label it with the specific values of λ_n and μ_n that apply.

b Find the steady-state distribution of the number of machines in need of repair.

c What is the mean number of machines in operation?

d What proportion of time is the repairman busy?

ECONOMIC TRADE-OFFS

17 The Weinert Company advertises for a machinist who will be able to recondition and reassemble a highly specialized part. Two candidates apply. The first wants $100 per day and claims to be able to recondition and reassemble three parts per day. The second wants $150 per day but claims to be able to recondition and reassemble four parts per day. Service times tend to be exponentially distributed for both machinists. Arrival of failed parts (from the company's own equipment) is random, averaging two per day.

If the company estimates that the time during which the failed part is being worked on (or is awaiting repair) costs $50 per day in lost profits, which machinist should be hired?

18 An executive in a newly created position is thinking about how to establish his typing staff. His budget is sufficient to hire two "level A" typists or three "level B" typists. He knows that, on the average, level B typists have productivity of $\frac{2}{3}$ those of level A typists and are paid approximately $\frac{2}{3}$ the salary of level A typists. Thus, the average productivity per salary dollar would seem to be equivalent for either choice.

Develop a queueing model to determine whether two such systems can be expected to provide equivalent service, as measured by the average backlogs of work in the typing system.

19 Review Exercises 6 and 10. At the Bishopric Bottling Company a decision must be reached on the question of how many setup men to hire. The plant operates on an 8-hour day, and setup men are paid $8 per hour, including fringe benefits. The opportunity cost to the company of an idle line is $15 per hour in lost profits. Should a second setup man be hired?

20 Review Exercises 7 and 11. At the Marshall Company suppose that the average wage rate for a courier is $8 per hour, while the average for an attendant is $6 per hour. The Marshall Company wishes to hire enough attendants to optimize the total costs in the stockroom system. Their criterion is the sum of salary costs paid to attendants plus the salary costs paid to couriers while they are idle. How many attendants should be hired?

21 Trucks are unloaded at a warehouse by an unloading crew. A crew of any size unloads a truck at a rate that is proportional to the number of men on the crew. For any size crew, however, the unloading time is exponentially distributed.

The trucks arrive at the warehouse randomly (i.e., in a Poisson process) at a mean rate of λ per hour. The distribution company, which employs both drivers and crew, estimates that the idle cost for its trucks is $\$C_1$ per hour. On the other hand, the company also pays the crew, and for a crew that can unload at a mean rate of μ, the labor cost is figured at $\$\mu C_2$ per hour.

a Find an expression for the optimal mean unloading rate (based on which the company can decide how large its crew should be for minimum cost operation).

b Suppose one man can unload a truck in 2 hours. What is the optimal crew size when $\lambda = 2$, $C_1 = 12$, and $C_2 = 6$?

SENSITIVITY ANALYSIS

22 Review Exercise 17. Suppose that an important consideration in the selection of a machinist is the prospect of an increase in the arrival rate (λ) of failed parts. For each machinist find the values of λ for which total system cost per day will be less than $\$250$.

23 Review Exercise 6. Think of the mean setup time as a function of the amount of experience the setup man has.

a For what values of the mean setup time will the setup man be busy less than 90% of the time?

b For what values of the mean setup time will the average inactive time for bottling lines exceed 3 hours?

c Draw a graph of the average inactive time, sketched as a function of the mean setup time.

d Suppose that a better model for the distribution of setup times is a normal distribution with a mean of 30 minutes and a standard deviation of 10 minutes. What is the average nonproductive time for a bottling line?

e How small could the answer to (d) become if the setup time distribution had the same mean but a smaller standard deviation?

24 Gordon's Body Shop is a one-man auto repair business. At present, the proprietor, Mr. Gordon, operates out of a small garage and charges relatively low prices, earning an average profit of $\$30$ per job. He is thinking, however, about a new service policy, which he hopes will generate additional business. Because car owners are normally concerned about repair delays, Mr. Gordon plans to deduct $\$2$ from the price of the job for every hour that a car is in the shop until its work is completed. Mr. Gordon also figures that he can raise the average price of a repair job by $\$10$, but because he averages only one job per hour, he figures that he will come out ahead. Currently, repair jobs arrive randomly at Gordon's at an average rate of 30 per week. (A "week" is 40 hours at the shop, since Mr. Gordon is scrupulously devoted to several hobbies and refuses to work overtime.) The wide variety of repair problems that come to the shop lends itself to the use of an exponential distribution as a model for the distribution of repair times.

a Suppose that the planned increase in price and the delay-time rebate tend to offet each other, so that the volume of business remains unchanged. How will Mr. Gordon's profits be affected?

b Suppose instead that the delay-time rebate works and the volume rises to an average of 36 jobs per week. What impact will this change have on Mr. Gordon's profits?

c Assume the conditions in (b) hold and that Mr. Gordon decides to maintain his new policy. How much should Mr. Gordon be willing to pay (as a weekly wage) to hire a second full-time repairman?

25 A paint manufacturing facility operates as a simple queue but with sequence-dependent setup (cleaning) times. Orders arrive randomly at an average rate of five per hour, with each order corresponding to one color of paint. Production times (reflecting order sizes) have an exponential distribution with a mean of 3 minutes. The setup times (in minutes) between various production runs are given by the following matrix:

From	To 1	2	3	4
1	0	5	7	12
2	4	0	6	10
3	8	6	0	8
4	15	10	5	0

The orders are processed in the same sequence in which they arrive.

a What is the average queueing time for the orders?

b What would it be if there were no setups?

Chapter 12
SIMULATION

Layton Electronics Company

Sales of its home video system have been so successful that the Layton Electronics Company must decide how much new production capacity to add and when to add it. Until now, this product has been made at Layton's new products center, but it is now necessary to build a separate production facility to accommodate the growth in sales.

In the coming year, the market segment in which Layton competes is expected to account for 100,000 units of sales, with Layton's share estimated at 18%. However, because of its reputation for dependable quality and efficient service, Layton expects its proportion to improve by 10% per year. In addition, most predictions indicate that the market's annual growth rate will remain around 16% before leveling off after 4 years. Economic analysts at Layton also predict that with this growth surge will come an end to the high profit margins now being realized, and they have developed specific forecasts that show margins shrinking rapidly.

An industrial engineering study team has developed a design for a new manufacturing plant, with provisions for adding expansion wings later on, if that becomes desirable. Unfortunately, capacity increments of this sort are not very efficient. Accounting studies at Layton indicate that for every thousand units of annual capacity built into the initial plant, there will be annual fixed costs of $40,000. However, this cost will double for capacity units built through subsequent extensions of the initial plant. In addition, Layton estimates that general and administrative fixed costs will be $1 million, regardless of plant size.

Profits from recent sales of the video systems have contributed to Layton's short-term portfolio, currently valued at $400,000 and earning about 12% per year before taxes. Although this fund provides Layton with the financial resources to expand, the financial vice-president is concerned about the impact expansion will have on the fund. With the help of some staff members, the vice-president has assembled a summary table describing the relevant marketing and financial data. The next task is to examine the implications for alternative expansion strategies.

Factor	This Year's Value	Future Behavior
Portfolio	$400,000	12% pretax return (tax rate = 0.48)
Variable cost	$ 325	6% annual increase
Gross margin	$ 175	20% annual decrease
Market size	100,000	16% annual increase
Market share	0.18	10% annual increase

Simulation is a modeling tool that can be especially helpful to managers of complex systems. As we begin to study the simulation approach, we should keep in mind that simulation is fundamentally a modeling technique, and that it provides benefits similar to those provided by other modeling techniques. Most importantly, simulation can help a manager discern important cause-and-effect relationships by representing the essential elements, structures, and parameters of the system to be managed. Such a representation helps the decision maker to *understand* existing problems and to *analyze* possible ways of improving system performance.

In general, we think of a simulation model as distinct from an analytic model because it deals explicitly with individual system elements and with the specific events in which those elements undergo change. By tracing the detailed effects of these changes, a simulation model uses a "bottom-up" approach to describe the performance of an entire system. In contrast, analytic models often have a "top-down" orientation because they deal directly with the aggregate performance of the entire system, without the need to explicitly treat detailed changes.

Compared to analytic techniques in model building, simulation provides some distinctive advantages due to its flexibility. A simulation model can accommodate a great deal of complexity and still provide useful information when analytic techniques may be inadequate or infeasible. In addition, it is often possible to build simulation models with a modular structure. As a result, it is a simple matter to make fundamental changes in one portion of the model without affecting other portions. With an analytic approach, however, such changes may make it necessary to restart the model-building process.

We often think of simulation as an experimental approach because it shares many of the advantages of a laboratory experiment. Compared to a full-scale field test, for example, simulation is very convenient and inexpensive. It allows for alterations and adjustments of parameters and conditions, and it creates a controlled environment in which tests can be repeated for greater precision or greater persuasiveness in analyzing the results.

In principle, the computer is not essential to simulation. Nevertheless, the computational requirements of applying simulation in complex situations can be so severe that only a computer-based methodology is practical. As we look at the simulation approach in more detail, we shall illustrate its basic concepts with simple examples that allow for "pencil-and-paper" simulations. Our emphasis, however, will be on those aspects of the approach that lend themselves readily to computer implementation.

In the situation facing Layton Electronics, a deterministic simulation model can help management analyze the firm's prospects. The model describes the company in terms of a number of related variables and traces the values of these variables as they change with time. In order to look specifically at the model, we can classify the variables (somewhat arbitrarily) as belonging to the production, marketing, or financial sectors of the firm.

In the production sector we create variables to represent capacity, output level, and costs. For example, we write

$$CAP = PLNT \tag{12.1}$$

as an equation to express the fact that initially capacity is equal to the plant size. Later on, of course, we can increase capacity by extending the plant. Next, the production level will be equal to demand, if capacity is adequate; otherwise, production will be at capacity, and some demand will go unmet. To express this relationship we write

$$PRODN = \min(DMD, CAP) \tag{12.2}$$

Now, with the production level determined, we can compute variable manufacturing cost as the product of unit cost and the production level:

$$VCOST = UCOST * PRODN \tag{12.3}$$

Next, for Layton the annual facilities cost will be $40 for each unit of initial plant capacity, plus $80 for each unit of extended capacity. Thus,

$$FCOST = 40 * PLNT + 80 * (CAP - PLNT) \tag{12.4}$$

Finally, total annual cost includes the variable manufacturing cost as well as the facilities cost and the general and administrative costs. Here we write

$$TCOST = VCOST + FCOST + 1{,}000{,}000 \qquad (12.5)$$

Thus, five equations represent the major relationships in the production sector of the firm's description.

In the marketing sector, we develop relationships that specify sales and price. For example, Layton's potential demand is the product of its potential market share and the market size, or

$$DMD = SHR * MKT \qquad (12.6)$$

However, as we noted earlier, we may not meet demand entirely if capacity is too tight. Therefore, we represent actual sales as

$$SALES = \min(DMD, PRODN) \qquad (12.7)$$

Just as we recognize the distinction between potential demand and actual sales, we should also make a distinction between potential market share, which we utilized above, and actual market share, which we can now represent as

$$ASHR = SALES/MKT \qquad (12.8)$$

Finally, we express the definition of selling price in terms of unit cost and gross margin:

$$PRICE = UCOST + MGN \qquad (12.9)$$

Thus, we have developed four equations to comprise the marketing sector of the firm's description.

In the area of finance, we begin with a calculation of revenue from sales:

$$REV = PRICE * SALES \qquad (12.10)$$

Next we compute the firm's gross income from two components: the pretax operating profit (revenue minus total annual cost) and the investment income yielded by the short-term portfolio. We write

$$INC = REV - TCOST + 0.12 * PORT \qquad (12.11)$$

Because the effective tax rate is 48%, we express tax payments as

$$TAX = 0.48 * INC \qquad (12.12)$$

For net (after-tax) income we then write

$$NET = INC - TAX \tag{12.13}$$

Thus, four more equations represent the financial sector of our description.

In addition to the descriptive equations already introduced, our model requires a module that reflects how certain elements change over time. For example, in the production sector, unit costs increase at a 6% annual rate, so we add subscripts to show the relationship between unit costs in year t and unit costs in year $t + 1$:

$$UCOST_{t+1} = 1.06 * UCOST_t \tag{12.14}$$

Another consideration in the production sector is the change in capacity. Total capacity in year $t + 1$ will be equal to the level in the previous year, augmented by any new extension. We write

$$CAP_{t+1} = CAP_t + EXT_{t+1} \tag{12.15}$$

In the marketing sector, we represent the 16% anticipated growth in market size as

$$MKT_{t+1} = 1.16 * MKT_t \tag{12.16}$$

We express the shrinkage behavior of product margins in analogous fashion:

$$MGN_{t+1} = 0.8 * MGN_t \tag{12.17}$$

In order to deal with the anticipated 10% annual increase in Layton's proportion of the market, we recall the distinction between potential share and actual share. We reason that the 10% factor will likely apply to the relation between current actual share and future potential share, and we write

$$SHR_{t+1} = 1.1 * ASHR_t \tag{12.18}$$

In the financial sector we represent the fact that Layton's short-term portfolio will increase each year by the amount of net income, which includes the 12% annual return on the existing portfolio. Thus, we write

$$PORT_{t+1} = PORT_t + NET_t \tag{12.19}$$

In summary, we have written 19 equations to define the major variables describing the firm and to trace the anticipated changes in those variables. This collection of 19 equations constitutes our simulation model.

We activate this model by specifying a set of initial conditions. Most of the initial conditions are already known:

MKT = 100,000

SHR = 0.18

UCOST = 325

MGN = 175

PORT = 400,000

We treat another initial condition, the plant size, as a decision variable. Suppose we choose an initial plant size of 20,000 units:

PLNT = 20,000

Then we can use the first 13 equations (in an appropriate order) to determine numerical values for all model variables. Table 12.1 contains this set of calculations leading us to a figure of \$726,960 for net income in the current year.

The next phase of calculations determines new values for the variables that were set by the initial conditions. Table 12.2 outlines the calculations for the second year:

$UCOST_2 = 344.50$

$MKT_2 = 116,000$

$MGN_2 = 140$

$SHR_2 = 0.198$

$PORT_2 = 1,126,960$

Last, we must choose the size of any planned extension to the plant. For example, let us plan an extension of 2000 units. Then, equation 15 for Table 12.2 shows that we obtain

$CAP_2 = 22,000$

We are now in a position to repeat the calculations in equations (12.2) to (12.13) in order to determine operating levels and cash flows for the second year. Following the logic of the calculations in Table 12.1, we find that the net income in the second year is \$652,722, increasing the value of the portfolio to \$1,779,682.

If we continue adding 2000 units of capacity each year and pursue the calculations, we can compute the values of several quantities after 4 years, such as

Market size: 156,090.

Layton share: 0.17.

Operating profit: \$49,600.

Portfolio size: \$2,348,300.

TABLE 12.1

Number	Equation	Calculation
1	CAP = PLNT	CAP = 20,000
6	DMD = SHR * MKT	DMD = 0.18(100,000) = 18,000
2	PRODN = min(DMD, CAP)	PRODN = min(18,000;20,000) = 18,000
3	VCOST = UCOST * PRODN	VCOST = 325(18,000) = 5,850,000
4	FCOST = 40 * PLNT + 80 (CAP − PLNT)	FCOST = 40(20,000) + 80(0) = 800,000
5	TCOST = VCOST + FCOST + 1,000,000	TCOST = 5,850,000 + 800,000 + 1,000,000 = 7,650,000
7	SALES = min(DMD, PRODN)	SALES = min(18,000;18,000) = 18,000
8	ASHR = SALES/MKT	ASHR = 18,000/100,000 = 0.18
9	PRICE = UCOST + MGN	PRICE = 325 + 175 = 500
10	REV = PRICE * SALES	REV = 500(18,000) = 9,000,000
11	INC = REV − TCOST + 0.12 * PORT	INC = 9,000,000 − 7,650,000 + 0.12(400,000) = 1,398,000
12	TAX = 0.48 * INC	TAX = 0.48(1,398,000) = 671,040
13	NET = INC − TAX	NET = 1,398,000 − 671,040 = 726,960

In these figures we can see that this particular capacity strategy leads to a portfolio worth over \$2 million, as well as pretax profits from operations of about \$50,000 in the fourth year. However, the choice of capacity increments restricts Layton's share to the point where its fourth-year sales represent only about 17% of the total market.

This simple experiment illustrates some of the important features of the simulation approach. First, we focused on detailed relationships among the model elements rather than on aggregate relationships. We made no direct attempt to write the fourth-year portfolio value as a function of the parameters, decision variables, and initial conditions. Instead, we produced the value by tracing, on a year-by-year basis, the detailed changes in the production, marketing, and financial sectors.

TABLE 12.2

Number	Equation	Calculation
14	$UCOST_{t+1} = 1.06 \, UCOST_t$	$UCOST_2 = 1.06(325) = 344.50$
16	$MKT_{t+1} = 1.16 * MKT_t$	$MKT_2 = 1.16(100,000) = 116,000$
17	$MGN_{t+1} = 1.8 * MGN_t$	$MGN_2 = 0.8(175) = 140$
18	$SHR_{t+1} = 1.1 * ASHR_t$	$SHR_2 = 1.1(0.18) = 0.198$
19	$PORT_{t+1} = PORT_t + NET_t$	$PORT_2 = 400,000 + 726,960 = 1,126,960$
15	$CAP_{t+1} = CAP_t + EXT_t$	$CAP_2 = 20,000 + 2,000 = 22,000$

Second, our approach in building the simulation model was descriptive, because we simply calculated the implications of a particular capacity plan. Our model does not identify an optimal plan, nor does it even contain a systematic way of locating improvements in the specific plan we studied. We would have to find improvements either by trial and error or by employing some insights gained from an examination of the model's results.

In our example, one insight came from noticing that the capacity plan restricted Layton's market share. If we were to increase the initial plant size from 20,000 in steps of 4000, we would discover the following results:

Plant Size	Market Share (%)	Final Portfolio
20,000	16.7	$2.35 million
24,000	19.2	2.50
28,000	21.8	2.40
32,000	23.9	2.19

Thus, as we increase the plant size we obtain a larger share of the market. The portfolio value also grows, but only to a peak of about $2.5 million. Of course, if we wanted to find a plan that maximizes portfolio value, we would have to undertake a more extensive search, using insights about the choice of capacity increments as well as the initial plant size.

Another feature is that our model can deal with several performance measures at once. Whereas most optimization approaches utilize a single criterion, the simulation approach makes it possible to examine several performance measures. In the Layton case, for example, we can easily imagine that the firm would be concerned about both its market share and its operating profit in the fourth year, as well as the value of its portfolio. To some extent, these measures are conflicting; and a simulation model provides a means of exploring the trade-offs among them.

Once we find a desirable plan we can investigate the effects of changing certain of the parameters. By altering one of the parameters and repeating the model's calculations, we can determine whether any of the performance measures is very sensitive to a change in a particular parameter. This type of exploration is sometimes called "what if" analysis.

In the Layton example we might wonder about the results if the market growth rate is lower or higher than 16%. To answer that question we would select a new value for the market growth rate and repeat the calculations. For instance, suppose we set the initial plant size at 24,000 units. Then, if we change the market growth rate from 16% down to 10% or up to 22%, we find the following:

Market Growth Rate (%)	Final Portfolio
10	$2.30 million
16	2.50 million
22	2.60 million

In this comparison we change the market growth rate by ±6% and find the impact on the final portfolio value. The results suggest a certain "upside risk," in the sense that the portfolio value does not increase with the larger growth rate by as much as it decreases with the lower growth rate. This insight might lead us toward a different choice of a capacity plan.

Our simulation model contains very straightforward arithmetic, although the computations are fairly tedious to carry out by hand. Thus, the model is well-suited to implementation on a computer. In fact, we stated the model's equations in a way that anticipated their conversion to computer code. In Figure 12.1 we

```
100 PRINT
110 PRINT "  Layton Electronics Model  "
120 PRINT
130 PRINT "Year", "Sales", "Capacity", "Op. Prof.", "Income"
140 '                    Read model parameters
150 READ MKT, SHR, UCOST, MGN, PORT
160 REAL PLNT
170 LET CAP = PLNT
180 '                    Initialize time
190 LET T = 1
200 '          Main loop (time loop) begins here
210 '                  Marketing/Production module
220 LET DMD = SHR * MKT
230 LET PRODN=DMD
240 IF CAP<DMD THEN LET PRODN=CAP
250 LET VCOST=UCOST*PRODN
260 LET FCOST=40*PLNT+80*(CAP-PLNT)
270 LET TCOST=VCOST+FCOST+1000000
280 LET SALES=DMD
290 IF PRODN<DMD THEN LET SALES=PRODN
300 LET ASHR=SALES/MKT
310 LET PRICE=UCOST+MGN
320 '                    Financial Module
330 LET REV=PRICE*SALES
340 LET INC=REV-TCOST+.12*PORT
350 LET TAX=.48*INC
360 LET NET=INC-TAX
```

FIGURE 12.1

```
370 LET PORT=PORT+NET
380 '                    Report
390 PRINT T,SALES,CAP,(REV-TCOST)/1000,NET/1000
400 IF T=4 THEN 500
410 '              Dynamic relations (end of time loop)
420 LET UCOST=1.06*UCOST
430 READ EXT
440 LET CAP=CAP+EXT
450 LET MKT=1.16*MKT
460 LET MGN=.8*MGN
470 LET SHR=1.1*ASHR
480 LET T=T+1
490 GOTO 200
500 PRINT
510 PRINT "FINAL VALUES"
520 PRINT "MARKET",MKT
530 PRINT "SHARE",ASHR
540 PRINT "PORTFOLIO(000)",PORT/1000
550 PRINT
560 '                    Parameters
570 DATA 100000,.18,325,175,400000
580 '                    Initial plant
590 DATA 20000
600 '                    Capacity parameters
610 DATA 2000,2000,2000
620 END
```

FIGURE 12.1 (Continued)

show a computer program for the Layton model. In this form the initial conditions are described in statement 570. Then, the decisions for initial plant size and for subsequent capacity increments are represented in statements 590 and 610. The program reads the initial conditions that activate the model; then, using the decision quantities, it performs the calculations we described in equations (12.1) to (12.19). For each year the program reports sales, capacity, pretax operating profit, and net income. Then it reports final values of market size, market share, and portfolio value.

In the first run shown in Figure 12.2, the program reproduces the base case results, but considerably faster than we could obtain the figures with hand calculations. In the subsequent runs of Figure 12.2 we reproduce the comparison of initial plant sizes. In this comparison we simply need to modify the information in statement 590 and rerun the program. Each time the program quickly and accurately performs the computations.

In practice, the term "simulation" often carries with it the connotation of a computer model, although, as we have seen, it is possible to develop a simulation model without the computer. However, the distinction may not be very important. We can think of the Layton model as taking either the form of 19 equations or the form of a computer program. From either viewpoint the model has a tangible form in which we can see detailed relationships and a descriptive orientation. These features distinguish the simulation approach.

Flexibility is another important characteristic of our model. As we saw earlier, our set of equations (or, equivalently, our computer program) is organized into modules that could lend themselves to more detailed enhancements. For example, we could enhance the marketing module by showing explicitly how sales are affected by advertising and promotion. Similarly, we could enrich the

```
RUN

   Layton Electronics Model

Year     Sales             Capacity      Op. Prof.     Income
 1        18000             20000          1350          726.96
 2        22000             22000          1119.999      652.7218
 3        24000             24000           568          406.4122
 4        26000             26000            49.6        162.2043

FINAL VALUES
MARKET           156089.6
SHARE              0.166571
PORTFOLIO(000)                      2348.298


Ok
590 DATA 24000
RUN

   Layton Electronics Model

Year     Sales             Capacity      Op. Prof.     Income
 1        18000             24000          1190          643.76
 2        22968             26000          1095.52       634.801
 3        28000             28000           856          549.8622
 4        30000             30000           248          268.0136

FINAL VALUES
MARKET           156089.6
SHARE              0.1921973
PORTFOLIO(000)                      2496.437


Ok
590 DATA 28000
RUN
```

FIGURE 12.2

```
     Layton Electronics Model

Year      Sales               Capacity      Op. Prof.      Income
  1        18000               28000         1030           560.56
  2        22968               30000         935.52         546.4094
  3        29307.17            32000         842.403        532.0845
  4        34000               34000         446.4          359.365


FINAL VALUES
MARKET              156089.6
SHARE                 0.2178236
PORTFOLIO(000)                             2398.419


OK
590 DATA 32000
RUN

     Layton Electronics Model

Year      Sales               Capacity      Op. Prof.      Income
  1        18000               32000         870            477.36
  2        22968               34000         775.52         458.0177
  3        29307.17            36000         682.403        438.1771
  4        37395.95            38000         590.678         417.8224


FINAL VALUES
MARKET              156089.6
SHARE                 0.23958
PORTFOLIO(000)                             2191.377
```

FIGURE 12.2 (Continued)

representation of production factors and financial factors by including considerations of quality control, inventory, dividend policy, and working capital. We
could even add new modules to represent such functions as distribution, research and development, or purchasing. Enhancements such as these would
require more complexity in the form of additional variables, parameters, and
equations for our model, but the added complexity could make the model more
realistic. With the existing model structure we could make one of these refinements in one module while leaving the other modules essentially intact. This
type of flexibility permits refinements on a modular basis in order to achieve
greater depth and breadth.

Finally, we should emphasize that the Layton simulation is deterministic
because the model has no random elements. As a result, if we were to repeat the
simulation, we would obtain identical outcomes. In the next section, however, we

examine how to build a simulation model to incorporate random elements. This capability permits the use of simulation techniques in studies that reach beyond the realm of certainty, thus extending the potential of simulation as a modeling approach.

SIMULATING RANDOM BEHAVIOR

In the problem facing Layton Electronics Company, several of the parameters used in the analysis are actually uncertain. If the degree of uncertainty is relatively small, then it might be reasonable to treat all the parameters as if they were perfectly known and to proceed with deterministic analysis. On the other hand, if the degree of uncertainty is quite high, then we might want to reflect this fact in our model so that it can provide information on the likelihoods of different outcomes. In this section we examine how to incorporate uncertainty in our simulation model.

For the purposes of illustration, let us suppose that the two major sources of uncertainty in Layton's case are the growth rates for market size and for market share. In our deterministic model we assumed growth rates of 16% and 10%, respectively. At these rates we can confirm that Layton's sales could climb to as much as 37,396 units in the fourth year under an aggressive capacity strategy that provides for meeting all demand. Suppose now that analysts at Layton have developed a probability model for each of these growth rates. For example, assume that the model for market size is the following:

Market-size growth rate (%)	10	16	20
Probability	0.2	0.5	0.3

This means that the market's annual growth rate over the 4-year period could be as low as 10% and as high as 20%. For example, there is a probability of 0.2 that the growth rate will be 10% (giving a total market of 133,100 in the fourth year). There is also a probability of 0.3 that the growth rate will be 20% (for a total market of 172,800); and a probability of 0.5 that the growth rate will be 16% (for a market of 156,090).

Suppose that the following distribution represents the market-share growth rate.

Market-share growth rate (%)	6	8	10	16
Probability	0.1	0.4	0.3	0.2

This means that Layton's proportion of the total market will grow at an annual rate that could be as low as 6% (with probability 0.1) and as high as 16% (with probability 0.2).

With this probabilistic view of the two market phenomena, we are uncertain about Layton's potential demand in the fourth year. In order to simulate the probabilistic behavior of demand over the 4-year period, we need a device capable of producing the random outcomes prescribed by the given probability distributions. For example, the device must produce a market-size growth rate of 10% with probability 0.2, a rate of 16% with probability 0.5, and a rate of 20% with probability 0.3.

For this purpose we can use a device based on sampling from a table of random numbers, such as the one in the Appendix. In a random-number table, any two-digit sample we select randomly is equally likely to be one of the hundred numbers from 00 to 99. Next, we need to match each random number with an outcome of the process we are simulating. This matching must be accomplished in such a way that the simulated outcomes have the correct probability of occurring.

When we simulate the growth rate of market size, one convenient scheme is to assign the numbers 00 to 19 (the first 20 equally likely outcomes) to the outcome "10% growth rate" and so on. Then, if the actual random number drawn from the table falls in the range 00–19, we set the growth rate at 10%. Similarly, if the random number lies in the range 20–69, we set the rate at 16%; and if the random number lies in the range 70–99, we set the growth rate at 20%. In this way, the number drawn from the table determines the market-size growth rate in accordance with the given distribution of probabilities.

With an analogous device, we can simulate the market-share growth rate, using the following rule for associating growth rates with random numbers:

Range of Numbers	Growth Rate (%)
00–09	6
10–49	8
50–79	10
80–99	16

Once we have set the two growth rates using the random-number device, we can proceed with the simulation just as we did in the deterministic case. The important point is that this approach requires both a random-number generator and a way of matching the outcomes of the random-number generator with the outcomes of the process being simulated.

For the time being, let us focus on the demand portion of the model, assuming that Layton has enough capacity to meet demand. We shall use a portion of the random-number table, reproduced as Table 12.3. Suppose we begin reading random numbers from the first two columns of Table 12.3 in order to determine the two growth rates. The first two numbers drawn are 43 and 75. Using the

TABLE 12.3

43	75	29	72	11	04	50	75	98	41	14
05	41	99	19	09	49	52	87	48	78	34
61	44	16	54	82	69	31	13	29	68	00
24	83	67	09	91	39	24	38	65	25	12
81	33	14	15	73	27	43	21	56	34	43
93	42	93	94	45	72	73	99	77	59	13
96	34	17	47	79	08	77	81	74	34	35
03	09	70	97	53	31	91	52	74	71	18
99	39	14	43	89	65	25	71	73	56	66
44	74	87	57	08	07	67	73	46	54	28

decision rules we specified above, the number 43 allows us to set the market-size growth rate at 16%, while the number 75 lets us set the market-share growth rate at 10%. These two growth rates imply a market size in the fourth year equal to 156,090 with Layton's proportion being just under 0.24. Therefore, Layton's fourth year sales will be 37,396.

Imagine a population of all possible demand levels that could occur under the assumed probability distributions. Our calculation, which represents a single *realization* of the simulated demand process, is just a sample from that demand population. In order to get more information about this population, we can repeat the simulation. Thus, for a second trial we would use the next row of numbers from the first two columns of Table 12.3. These numbers determine two rates in accordance with the given distributions, and we thus produce a new realization. Table 12.4 summarizes a sequence of ten such trials, where we draw

TABLE 12.4

Trial	Random Number	Market Growth Rate (%)	Random Number	Market-Share Growth Rate (%)	Sales
1	43	16	75	10	37,396
2	5	10	41	8	30,180
3	61	16	44	8	35,393
4	24	16	83	16	43,855
5	81	20	33	8	39,182
6	93	20	42	8	39,182
7	96	20	34	8	39,182
8	3	10	9	6	28,534
9	99	20	39	8	39,182
10	44	16	74	10	37,396
					369,482

the random numbers from the first two columns of successive rows in the random number table.

A manager at Layton might want to know the sales level in the fourth year. Because growth rates are uncertain, however, the sales level itself is uncertain. Under these circumstances, the manager could only hope to get a description of the sales level in probabilistic terms. Repeated simulations, such as those in Table 12.4, provide information about the probability distribution for sales. In particular, we can think of the 10 realizations of sales shown in the table as 10 independent samples from the population of sales values. By applying the principles of classical statistics we can use these sample observations to make inferences about the population from which they come.

For example, let x_i denote the value of sales produced on the ith realization in the simulation experiment. The sample average ($\bar{x}$) is

$$\bar{x} = \frac{1}{10} \sum_{i=1}^{10} x_i = 36{,}948.2$$

The sample average provides an estimate of the population mean; therefore, on the basis of the simulation outcomes we estimate the mean of the sales distribution to be 36,948. Also, the sample variance (s^2) is

$$s^2 = \frac{1}{10 - 1} \sum_{i=1}^{10} (x_i - \bar{x})^2 = 20{,}787{,}800$$

In this form the sample variance is an unbiased estimate of the population variance; therefore, we estimate the variance of the sales distribution to be 2.08×10^7 and the standard deviation s to be 4559. We can use these estimates of the population mean and standard deviation to construct confidence intervals for the population mean.

We can construct a 90% confidence interval for the mean with the formula

$$\bar{x} \pm t_{0.05} s_{\bar{x}}$$

Here, $s_{\bar{x}}$ is the estimated value of the standard error for a sample average. For a sample of size n, this quantity is $s/\sqrt{n}$. Also, $t_{0.05}$ denotes the value from a t distribution for which the right-hand tail probability is 0.05. This means that 90% of the area under the t distribution lies between $-t_{0.05}$ and $+t_{0.05}$. In the confidence interval formula the value of $t_{0.05}$ is associated with $(n - 1)$ degrees of freedom for a sample size of n. Thus, in our example the 90% confidence interval for the mean of the sales distribution is

$$\bar{x} \pm t_{0.05} \frac{s}{\sqrt{n}} = 36{,}948 \pm \frac{(1.833)4559}{\sqrt{10}}$$

$$= 36{,}948 \pm 2{,}643$$

$$\text{or } 34{,}305 \text{ to } 39{,}591$$

Also, the manager at Layton might be interested in the probability that sales will exceed 36,000 in the fourth year. Although we cannot deduce this value without knowledge of the population distribution, we can estimate it from the proportion of times (denoted by $\hat{p}$) that sales exceed 36,000 in the sample. From Table 12.4 we can see that sales are greater than 36,000 seven times, so that $\hat{p} = 0.7$. Then we can approximate a 90% confidence interval for the true proportion by the formula

$$\hat{p} \pm z_{0.05} \sqrt{\frac{\hat{p}(1 - \hat{p})}{n}}$$

where $z_{0.05}$ is the value from a normal distribution for which the right-hand tail probability is 0.05. In our example the 90% confidence interval for the true proportion is

$$\hat{p} \pm z_{0.05} \sqrt{\frac{\hat{p}(1 - \hat{p})}{n}} = 0.7 \pm 1.645 \sqrt{\frac{0.7(0.3)}{10}}$$

$$= 0.7 \pm 0.24$$

$$\text{or } 0.46 \text{ to } 0.94$$

Thus, we are 90% confident that the true proportion lies between 0.46 and 0.94.

Presumably, the decision makers at Layton would like to work with more precise estimates than these; that is, they would like smaller confidence intervals. To tighten the tolerances they would require a larger sample. In fact, for a given precision we can use standard statistical techniques to estimate how large a sample size would be required.

As an example, suppose that the managers at Layton want the width of the 90% confidence interval for the mean of the sales distribution to be at most ± 100. In other words, they want the 90% confidence interval to be $\bar{x} \pm 100$. To achieve this precision, we set

$$t_{0.05} \frac{s}{\sqrt{n}} = 100$$

Anticipating that we shall need a large sample, we substitute $z_{0.05}$ for $t_{0.05}$. Rearranging, we get

$$\sqrt{n} = \frac{z_{0.05}s}{100}$$

or

$$n = \left(\frac{z_{0.05}s}{100}\right)^2$$

Thus, we find

$$n = \left[\frac{(1.645)(4559)}{100}\right]^2$$

$$= 5624.3$$

In other words, to achieve the desired precision of ± 100 (instead of the current precision of ± 2643), we need a sample size of 5625 instead of the current sample size of 10.

This example illustrates how we can use simulation as a sampling mechanism to analyze probabilistic outcomes. In this case we analyzed the fourth-year sales volume at the Layton company. Reviewing the information produced by our original simulation in Figure 12.2, we should realize that Layton's management would be interested in the analysis of operating profit and portfolio level, as well as sales volume. We could easily produce such an analysis, because we can translate sales volumes into profits and portfolio increments. Thus, we could use a similar approach to describing operating profits and portfolio levels in probabilistic terms.

Computer-based sampling procedures such as this one are often called **Monte Carlo methods**, reminding us of the repeated sampling "experiments" performed in the casino at Monte Carlo. This class of simulation models has what we might call a **static** emphasis—an emphasis on the state of a system at a single point in time, such as Layton's sales volume in the fourth year. By contrast, another class of simulation models has a **dynamic** emphasis—an emphasis on the evolving development of a system over time. We shall deal with some examples of this latter type later in the chapter.

We carried out the example simulation by hand with the aid of a table of random numbers. However, an actual computer implementation does not use such tables. Instead, computers can generate an equivalent set of numbers by means of a **random-number generator.** A random-number generator is essentially a program that can generate a number U that behaves as if it is evenly distributed between 0 and 1. Most programming languages contain such random-number generators. Thus, to represent the market-size growth rate in our example, we would ask the program to generate a value for U. We would then employ the following rule:

If $0.0 \leq U < 0.2$, set growth rate to 10%.
If $0.2 \leq U < 0.7$, set growth rate to 16%.
If $0.7 \leq U < 1.0$, set growth rate to 20%.

Random-number generators typically have the capability to repeat a sequence of U values. This capability is particularly important when we want to compare simulation outcomes for alternative actions. After recording a sample of simulation results for one action, we can retrieve the same random numbers to sample the results under a different action. This approach allows us to isolate the effects of different actions on system outcomes. When we use a different sequence of U values for the second set of results, performance differences may simply reflect differences in the random numbers; however, when we use the *same* sequence, performance differences are due only to the differences between actions. In either case, the significance of performance differences is still a matter of statistical evaluation, but the use of repeatable sequences allows us to exploit the power of "paired-comparison" statistical methods in the evaluation.

Once we isolate the effects of different actions on system outcomes, we can begin to search for desirable policies. Just as we can search for "very good" policies with the deterministic version of the Layton model, so can we also search with the probabilistic model, with the understanding that we are looking for a policy that is "better" than another in a statistical sense.

GENERATING SAMPLES FROM GIVEN DISTRIBUTIONS

The example in the previous section required the simulation of only a very simple probability distribution. However, we can generalize the concepts to virtually all discrete and continuous distributions. In the discussion that follows we examine these techniques as they would be implemented on a computer, that is, based on the capabilities of a random-number generator that provides a sequence of numbers U that are evenly distributed between 0 and 1 (i.e., U is a sample from the probability distribution function shown in Figure 12.3.) We could implement the same techniques by hand simply by using a table of random numbers in place of a random-number generator.

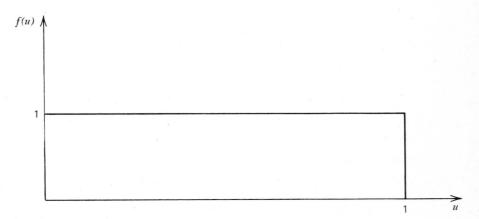

FIGURE 12.3

Consider the discrete random variable X with the following distribution:

Outcome	x	1	2	3	4	5
Probability	P_x	0.10	0.25	0.35	0.20	0.10

Suppose that we partition the distribution of U into five regions as shown in Figure 12.4. These regions correspond to the possible values of the random variable X, and the region sizes reflect the values of the probability mass function P_x. A simple decision rule, corresponding to this partition, yields values of X with the desired probabilities:

If $0.0 \leq U < 0.10$, set $X = 1$.
If $0.10 \leq U < 0.35$, set $X = 2$.
If $0.35 \leq U < 0.70$, set $X = 3$.
If $0.70 \leq U < 0.90$, set $X = 4$.
If $0.90 \leq U \leq 1.00$, set $X = 5$.

For another view of this process examine Figure 12.5, which shows the cumulative distribution function $F(x)$ for the random variable X. The cumulative distribution function (cdf) is defined by

$$F(x) = P(X \leq x)$$

The cdf $F(x)$ evaluated at x gives the probability that the random variable will be less than or equal to x. Think of the process of generating U as selecting a point along the vertical axis in Figure 12.5. From this point, move to the right on the graph until the function $F(x)$ first equals or exceeds this height. The x value at

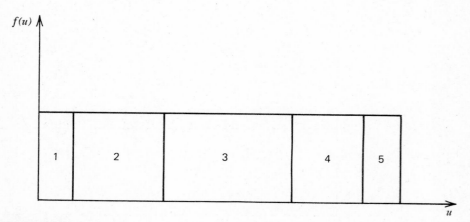

FIGURE 12.4

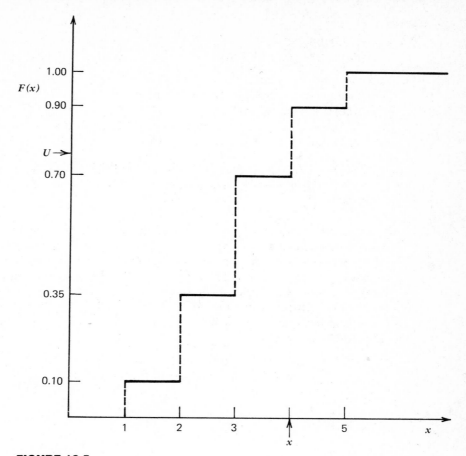

FIGURE 12.5

which $F(x)$ first becomes large enough is the desired value of X, the random variable. In principle, we can use this method for generating samples from *any* discrete probability distribution. The steps are

1. Obtain the random number U.
2. Find the smallest x for which $F(x) \geq U$.

As long as the U values are uniformly distributed between 0 and 1, the x values will behave as samples from the given probability distribution.

As an illustration, suppose we want to generate a sequence of values that simulates outcomes from a Poisson distribution with mean 3. The Poisson distribution is described in the following table, which is excerpted from the larger table in the appendix:

x	0	1	2	3	4	5	6	7
P_x	0.0498	0.1493	0.2241	0.2240	0.1681	0.1008	0.0504	0.0216
$F(x)$	0.0498	0.1991	0.4232	0.6472	0.8153	0.9161	0.9665	0.9881

Now suppose we obtain the U values from Table 12.3, where we combine the first and second columns to form four-digit numbers between 0 and 1. For example, the sequence of U values is 0.4375 (row 1), 0.0541 (row 2), 0.6144 (row 3), and so on. For each U value we find the sample outcome from the Poisson table by locating the first x value for which $F(x) \geq U$:

U value	0.4375	0.0541	0.6144	0.2483	0.8133	0.9342
x value	3	1	3	2	4	6

We can use an analogous technique for dealing with continuous probability distributions. In the continuous case the cumulative distribution function is always a smooth curve rather than a step function. Once again, however, we can interpret the process of generating a value of U as selecting a point along the vertical axis on the graph of the function $F(x)$. From this point, we move to the right on the graph to the intersection with $F(x)$. The x value at which this intersection occurs identifies the desired value of x. (See Figure 12.6.) The general steps in the method are

　*1. Obtain the random number U.

　2. Determine the x value for which $F(x) = U$.

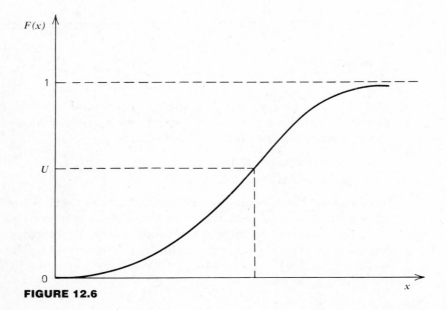

FIGURE 12.6

To illustrate the continuous case, suppose that we want to generate a sequence of values that simulates outcomes from an exponential distribution with mean 4. For this particular distribution the cumulative distribution function is

$$F(x) = 1 - e^{-0.25x}$$

In Step 2 of the procedure given above, we need to set $U = F(x)$ and solve for x. Thus,

$$U = 1 - e^{-0.25x}$$
$$e^{-0.25x} = 1 - U$$
$$-0.25x = \ln(1 - U)$$
$$x = -4 \ln (1 - U) \tag{12.20}$$

We find that we can express the transformation directly, by means of equation (12.20). In fact, we can simplify this relation slightly by recognizing the fact that if values of U are evenly distributed between 0 and 1, then so are the values of $(1 - U)$. Therefore, we can write an equivalent transformation as

$$x = -4 \ln U \tag{12.21}$$

Now suppose we obtain U values from Table 12.3, column 3. The transformation equation (12.21) yields the x values shown below.

U value	0.29	0.99	0.16	0.67	0.14	0.93	0.17
x value	4.95	0.040	7.33	1.60	7.86	0.290	7.09

In the case of the Poisson distribution we used four-digit random numbers because our Poisson table contained probabilities that were accurate to four places. When we illustrated sampling from an exponential distribution, however, we reverted to two-digit random numbers. Using two-digit random numbers yields samples with limited precision, because the procedure generates only 100 distinct possible outcomes. If we want additional precision, we can use random numbers with four digits, five digits, or even more. For most practical purposes, however, four-digit random numbers are more than adequate.

As the foregoing discussion indicates, we can generate samples from a given probability distribution in a similar way for both discrete cases and continuous cases. This approach is called the **inverse transformation method** because it prescribes how to transform a U value to an x value via the inverse of the cumulative distribution function. The method is a simple and flexible technique for generating random samples from specified distributions. Other techniques also exist and may be more convenient to use in certain circumstances. We illustrate this point with the example of the normal distribution.

Suppose we are constructing a computer simulation in which we want to generate random samples from a normal distribution with mean μ and standard deviation σ. First, note that we only need to generate x values that simulate outcomes from a standard normal distribution (that is, a normal distribution with $\mu = 0$ and $\sigma = 1$). Then, for each x value, we can set $y = \mu + \sigma x$ to obtain y values that behave as samples from our desired population. Next, in order to apply the inverse transformation method, we would need to specify the function $F(x)$, representing the cumulative distribution function for the standard normal distribution. Unfortunately, we cannot write this function in a way that allows us to solve for the value of x corresponding to a given value of $F(x)$. To deal with this problem we could employ a normal table, which gives the values of $F(x)$ at specified points and which permits interpolation to approximate the relationship between x and $F(x)$. Usually, we would want to have access to this function at x values from 0 to 3, in steps of 0.01. Using a tabular approach, we would have to provide our computer program with the 301 values that comprise the normal table.

For convenience in programming, however, we can use an alternative technique. Let U_1 and U_2 represent two successive values provided by our computerized random-number generator. Let

$$x = (-2 \ln U_1)^{\frac{1}{2}} \cos(2\pi U_2) \tag{12.22}$$

Using advanced methods of probability analysis it is possible to show that the x values calculated in equation (12.22) behave as if they are samples from a standard normal distribution. Moreover, since the natural logarithm and cosine functions in equation (12.22) are standard functions in most computer languages, the single computer statement corresponding to equation (12.22) will yield standard normal samples from pairs of random numbers.

Finally, let us illustrate how to construct a simulation experiment involving both a continuous random variable and a discrete random variable. Consider an inspection station on an assembly line for an electronic component. The inspection station includes a rework facility for repairing defective items. Each time a defective component is discovered, it is sent to the rework facility. Assume that the goal of building a simulation model is to investigate the workload at the facility.

Suppose we know that the number of defectives in a production run of 100 components follows a Poisson distribution with a mean of 3. Furthermore, suppose that the time required to perform a given repair job is also random and follows an exponential distribution with a mean of 4 hours. Clearly, the amount of repair work associated with any batch of 100 components will be random, and we can employ simulation to estimate the mean and variance of the workload per batch.

Figure 12.7 shows a flow chart for the simulation. For each batch in the simulation (where i is the batch index) we need to draw a random sample (de-

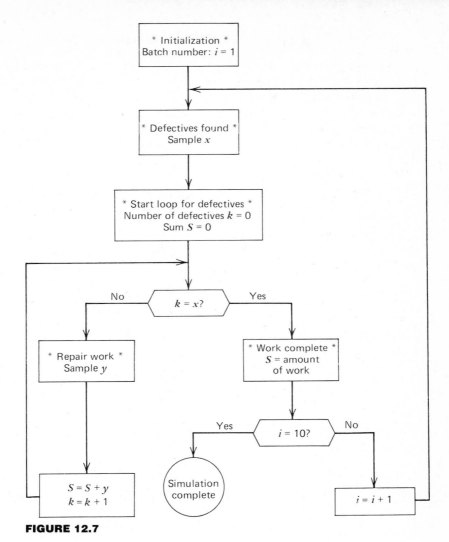

FIGURE 12.7

noted x in the figure) from the Poisson distribution to represent the number of defectives. For each defective (where k is the index for defectives) we need to draw a random sample (denoted y) from the exponential distribution to represent the amount of repair work. The total required repair work in the batch is then just the sum of these times. For the Poisson samples, the random numbers are four-digit decimal fractions (in our case formed from columns 5 and 6 of Table 12.3); and we determine the sample value by reference to the table of cumulative Poisson probabilities introduced earlier. For the exponential samples, the random numbers are two-digit decimal fractions (here from columns 7 to 9 of Table 12.3); and we use equation (12.21) to compute the sample value. The data in Table 12.5 represent the results of simulating 10 production runs. This sample yields an estimated mean of 7.84 hours of repair work per batch, with an estimated standard deviation equal to 5.56.

In summary, we have seen how to represent a variety of probability models in the simulation process. For computer implementation, we require only that the computer have the capability to provide a sequence of random numbers evenly distributed between 0 and 1. Then we can transform this sequence to

TABLE 12.5

Batch Number	Random Number	Defectives	Random Number	Repair Work	Total Work for Batch
1	0.1104	1	0.50	2.77	2.77
2	0.0949	1	0.52	2.62	2.62
3	0.8269	5	0.31	4.68	
			0.24	5.71	
			0.43	3.38	
			0.73	1.26	
			0.77	1.05	16.08
4	0.9139	5	0.91	0.38	
			0.25	5.55	
			0.67	1.60	
			0.75	1.15	
			0.87	0.56	9.24
5	0.7327	4	0.13	8.16	
			0.38	3.87	
			0.21	6.24	
			0.99	0.04	18.31
6	0.4572	2	0.81	0.70	
			0.52	2.62	3.32
7	0.7908	4	0.71	1.37	
			0.73	1.26	
			0.98	0.08	
			0.48	2.93	5.64
8	0.5331	3	0.29	4.95	
			0.65	1.72	
			0.56	2.32	8.99
9	0.8965	5	0.77	1.05	
			0.74	1.20	
			0.74	1.20	
			0.73	1.26	
			0.46	3.11	7.82
10	0.0807	1	0.41	3.57	3.57
				Total	78.36

simulate outcomes from any specified probability distribution. This capability gives simulation models the flexibility to represent a variety of probabilistic phenomena.

SIMULATION EXAMPLES AND DETAILS

Earlier we drew a distinction between static and dynamic emphases in simulation models. A model with a static emphasis will focus on the status of a particular system at a single point in time. The status indicator might be the year-end value of a firm's portfolio or the amount of repair work in a production lot, as in the examples treated earlier. On the other hand, a model with a dynamic emphasis considers the changes in a particular status measure as it evolves over time. In this section we use two examples to illustrate some of the features of models having a dynamic emphasis. The first example examines the simulation of a simple queue and the second describes the simulation of an inventory system.

SIMULATING THE SIMPLE QUEUE

Because a queue is a waiting line of customers, a simulation of a queue naturally tracks the level of congestion in the queueing system. We might measure this congestion by the proportion of time the system is busy, by the average waiting time for a customer, or by the average number of customers in the system. In any event, these measures of congestion do not represent the status of the system at a specified point in time. Instead, they represent summary measures of queue behavior during a specific time interval.

In organizing a queueing simulation, we describe the **status** of a queueing system by the number of customers in the system. Then, we can trace the evolution of the queueing process simply by keeping track of the number of customers in the system. Furthermore, we know that the number of customers will change only with the occurrence of certain **events**, specifically, arrivals to the system and completions of service.

In general, when we simulate the dynamic behavior of a complex system, we keep track of a set of variables that describe the system's status. Certain events change these **state variables** in definite ways. Thus, our simulation must have the ability both to recognize the occurrence of state-change events over time and to trace the changes induced by those events.

For a queueing system with a single server, we begin with the following notation:

N = number of customers in the system (state variable).

A = time of next arrival (event).

C = time of next service completion (event).

T = time of event being simulated.

The two random variables in the queueing process are the service times and the lengths of the intervals between successive customer arrivals. Each time the simulation requires information about an interval between arrivals it will generate a sample value (called x_1) from the interarrival time distribution; and when it requires information about a service time it will generate a sample value (called x_2) from the service-time distribution. For a given specification of the interarrival-time distribution and the service-time distribution, the procedure for generating samples for x_1 and x_2 is the procedure described in the previous section. Thus, for example, if the interarrival times follow an exponential distribution with a mean of 4 minutes, the sampling procedure obtains a number U from the random-number generator and utilizes the transformation in equation (12.21) to generate an appropriate sample each time x_1 is needed. We illustrate the specific steps in the simulation by following the flow chart in Figure 12.8.

Initialization. To start the simulation, we set $N = 0$ and $T = 0$. We also set C equal to a large number, since there is no need to plan for the next service completion when the system is idle. The initial event will be the first arrival, and we assign its occurrence time A by generating a value for x_1 and setting $A = x_1$.

Finding the Next Event. The next event to be simulated can be determined by comparing A and C. If $A \le C$, the next event is an arrival; otherwise, it is a service completion.

Arrival Event. At the occurrence of an arrival we update the time of the simulation by setting $T = A$, and we recognize the change in the state of the system by adding one to N. We plan the next arrival event by generating a value of x_1 and replacing A by $(T + x_1)$. If $N = 1$, the new arrival begins service immediately, and we plan the next service completion event by generating a value for x_2 and replacing C by $(T + x_2)$.

Completion Event. At the occurrence of a service completion we update the time of the simulation by setting $T = C$, and we recognize the change in the state of the system by subtracting one from N. We plan the next completion (unless the current event leaves the system idle) by generating a value for x_2 and replacing C by $(T + x_2)$. If the system is idle, we set C equal to a large number.

Time Check. After recording the changes surrounding an event, we make a check to see whether the planned time limit for the simulation run has been reached. If so, the simulation terminates; otherwise, we find the next event and process its changes.

When we carry out a simulation experiment on a computer, we perform the record-keeping tasks with a computer program. In general, this means the program must

1. Obtain random samples from prescribed distributions.
2. Keep track of the state of the system.

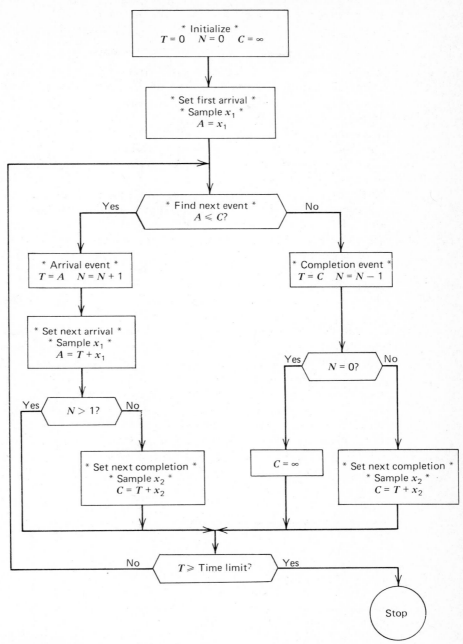

FIGURE 12.8

3. Trace changes of state that occur at events.

4. Collect data in an appropriate form for later summary.

In the queueing simulation modeled in Figure 12.8, we need random samples whenever we want to determine the timing of the next event. At each arrival event we obtain a sample from the distribution of interarrival times to set the time of the next arrival. Similarly, at each service completion event (when the system is nonempty) and at each arrival to an empty system we obtain a sample from the distribution of service times to set the time of the next completion.

The state of the queueing system is simply the number of customers in the system, N. The events are of only two types: an arrival event, which increases N, and a service completion event, which decreases N. To keep track of the occurrence of events over time the program utilizes a **next-event calendar**. This calendar is a list of future events for which the time has been set: in this case, the time of the next arrival, A, and the time of the next completion, C. The program logic identifies the next event by finding the minimum of A and C, and then the program follows the state-change rule for that event. The simulation thus proceeds from event to event, each time performing the necessary record-keeping tasks. Table 12.6 displays a record of the events in a 1-hour simulation of a queue with arrival rate of 24 per hour and service rate of 30 per hour. (The event times are shown in minutes.)

Finally, there is a need to collect data as the simulation progresses. In the case of a queueing model the primary objective of data collection is to estimate the probability distribution of the state variable N. We keep track of the proportion of time in the simulation that N takes on the values 0, 1, 2, . . . , and so on. At each arrival and at each completion the value of N changes, and the program records the amount of time the system has remained at a particular value of N. After the simulation is completed, we divide the total amount of time accumulated at each N value by the length of the simulation to compute the proportion of time for each N value. These proportions comprise the sample probability

TABLE 12.6

```
RUN
GIVE ARRIVAL RATE? 0.4
SERVICE RATE? 0.5
TIME LIMIT? 60
ARRIVAL    AT TIME  0.838        NO. IN SYSTEM= 1
ARRIVAL    AT TIME  1.791        NO. IN SYSTEM= 2
ARRIVAL    AT TIME  1.793        NO. IN SYSTEM= 3
COMPLETION AT TIME  2.297        NO. IN SYSTEM= 2
ARRIVAL    AT TIME  2.883        NO. IN SYSTEM= 3
ARRIVAL    AT TIME  5.374        NO. IN SYSTEM= 4
COMPLETION AT TIME  6.343        NO. IN SYSTEM= 3
```

TABLE 12.6 (Continued)

ARRIVAL AT TIME 6.705	NO. IN SYSTEM= 4
ARRIVAL AT TIME 6.873	NO. IN SYSTEM= 5
COMPLETION AT TIME 10.354	NO. IN SYSTEM= 4
ARRIVAL AT TIME 10.664	NO. IN SYSTEM= 5
COMPLETION AT TIME 12.701	NO. IN SYSTEM= 4
COMPLETION AT TIME 12.923	NO. IN SYSTEM= 3
COMPLETION AT TIME 13.995	NO. IN SYSTEM= 2
ARRIVAL AT TIME 14.307	NO. IN SYSTEM= 3
COMPLETION AT TIME 15.540	NO. IN SYSTEM= 2
COMPLETION AT TIME 15.922	NO. IN SYSTEM= 1
COMPLETION AT TIME 23.169	NO. IN SYSTEM= 0
ARRIVAL AT TIME 28.315	NO. IN SYSTEM= 1
COMPLETION AT TIME 29.675	NO. IN SYSTEM= 0
ARRIVAL AT TIME 30.770	NO. IN SYSTEM= 1
ARRIVAL AT TIME 32.266	NO. IN SYSTEM= 2
ARRIVAL AT TIME 34.810	NO. IN SYSTEM= 3
COMPLETION AT TIME 35.112	NO. IN SYSTEM= 2
ARRIVAL AT TIME 35.303	NO. IN SYSTEM= 3
COMPLETION AT TIME 35.383	NO. IN SYSTEM= 2
COMPLETION AT TIME 36.065	NO. IN SYSTEM= 1
ARRIVAL AT TIME 37.508	NO. IN SYSTEM= 2
ARRIVAL AT TIME 38.784	NO. IN SYSTEM= 3
ARRIVAL AT TIME 40.628	NO. IN SYSTEM= 4
ARRIVAL AT TIME 41.290	NO. IN SYSTEM= 5
ARRIVAL AT TIME 47.135	NO. IN SYSTEM= 6
ARRIVAL AT TIME 48.654	NO. IN SYSTEM= 7
ARRIVAL AT TIME 48.974	NO. IN SYSTEM= 8
ARRIVAL AT TIME 49.459	NO. IN SYSTEM= 9
COMPLETION AT TIME 50.428	NO. IN SYSTEM= 8
COMPLETION AT TIME 51.705	NO. IN SYSTEM= 7
ARRIVAL AT TIME 53.755	NO. IN SYSTEM= 8
COMPLETION AT TIME 55.175	NO. IN SYSTEM= 7
COMPLETION AT TIME 57.471	NO. IN SYSTEM= 6
ARRIVAL AT TIME 57.841	NO. IN SYSTEM= 7
ARRIVAL AT TIME 58.042	NO. IN SYSTEM= 8
COMPLETION AT TIME 59.464	NO. IN SYSTEM= 7
COMPLETION AT TIME 60.568	NO. IN SYSTEM= 6

SIMULATION RESULTS AT TIME 60.56838

MEAN NUMBER IN SYSTEM= 3.515693

P(N) DISTRIBUTION FROM N=0 TO 9

0.117 0.206 0.099 0.130 0.038 0.188 0.031 0.099 0.076 0.016

distribution compiled from the simulation. The simulation summarized in Table 12.6 produced a sample probability distribution that is shown (along with its mean) at the bottom of the table. From the same probability distribution it is possible to obtain estimates of mean waiting time, utilization, and cost performance in the queueing system.

The queueing simulation illustrates one means of moving a simulation model through time. In this case the movement is event by event. Future events are kept on a calendar, and the simulation always proceeds to the next event. For each event, the simulation updates the state of the system, the event calendar, and appropriate summary data, and continues in this fashion until its time limit is reached. This approach is called an **event-driven simulation.**

SIMULATING A SINGLE-ITEM INVENTORY SYSTEM

Assume that the local distributor for a computer manufacturer maintains a small inventory of terminals with which it can fill customer orders. The industry has become quite competitive, and the distributor has found that customers will take their business elsewhere if there is no stock available to meet their demands. On the other hand, the manufacturing plant can provide only a 3-week response time on replenishment orders. Furthermore, the manufacturing plant does not permit distributors to have more than one outstanding replenishment order at any time. The distributor would like to operate with as small an inventory as possible, consistent with meeting 90% of customer demand. Let us examine how a simulation model can help the distributor evaluate the following inventory control policy:

1. At the end of each week, count the number of terminals, N, that are in stock or already on order. We call N the **inventory position**.
2. If $N < 20$, place an order for a replenishment quantity of $(50 - N)$ from the manufacturer.

The primary state variable in this simulation is the distributor's stock level. However, it is convenient to define a number of additional variables that provide status or timing information. Let

I = distributor's stock level

Q = size of replenishment order outstanding

T = week of simulation

R = time of latest replenishment order

D = customer demand in a week

The random variables in the system are the successive weekly demands, D. Each week the simulation draws a sample value d from the demand distribution using the techniques described earlier. The simulation follows the flow chart in Figure 12.9.

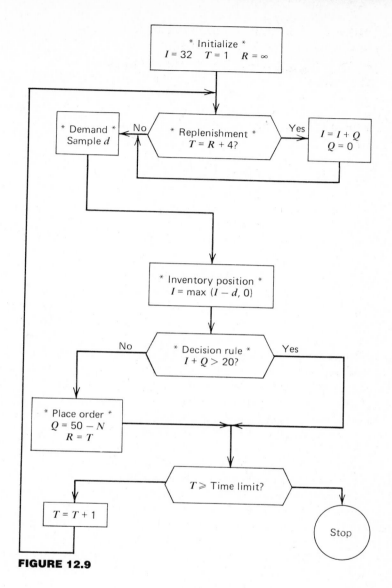

FIGURE 12.9

Initialization. First we specify the inventory level at the start of week 1. (In Figure 12.9, the initial level is set arbitrarily at 32.) We then set $T = 1$ and R at an arbitrary large value.

Replenishment. At the beginning of each week, we determine whether a replenishment order arrived at the very end of the preceding week. Because there is a 3-week lead time, the condition $T = R + 4$ indicates that a delivery occurred. If an order was delivered, we update the inventory level to reflect the new items in stock.

Inventory Position. We simulate demand d for the week, and we reduce the inventory position N at the week's end to $I - d$. If this quantity is negative, the actual stock level remains at 0 and the number of lost sales is $d - I$. Otherwise, $I - d$ represents the stock level on hand. This stock will be increased by a replenishment quantity if an order is due to be delivered.

Decision Rule. In order to implement the inventory control policy, we compare $N = I + Q$ to 20. If $N < 20$, we place an order of $Q = 50 - N$, and we set the replenishment time $R = T$; otherwise, we simply proceed.

Time Check. After recording the week's transactions, we check to see whether the planned time limit has been reached. If so, we terminate the simulation; otherwise, we increment T by one and proceed to the following week.

As in the queueing simulation of the previous section, the inventory simulation program must obtain random samples from a prescribed distribution, keep track of the state of the system, trace state changes that occur at events, and collect data. In this instance, we draw random samples whenever the program requires a number for demand in a given week. Notice that we do not represent individual customer demands explicitly in the model, for we need to know only demand during the course of a week in order to keep track of the inventory position. The inventory position is the relevant state variable, and the simulation model traces the effects of two kinds of events: replenishment and demand. The delivery of a replenishment order increases inventory position by an amount equal to the size of the order quantity, while demand reduces inventory position.

Table 12.7 shows a 30-week simulation of the inventory system assuming that weekly demands follow a Poisson distribution with mean 8. The simulation program reports summary data for each week: the total demand, the stock level at the end of the week (excluding any replenishment order that might be arriving), and the number of sales lost. One way to measure the approximate average stock level during the week is to average the beginning inventory level and the ending inventory level each week. These weekly figures are averaged over the course of the simulation to produce a summary average inventory level of 15.9 units. In addition, by subtracting the lost sales from total demand we compute the percentage of customer demand that is filled. The figure of 86.3% is a bit short of the distributor's goal, although the sample of only 30 weeks may be too small to conclude that less than 90% will be met. However, if longer simulation runs bear out this conclusion, the distributor might well want to use the simulation program to evaluate whether some other decision rule will meet the 90% performance goal.

Although the model of Figure 12.9 simulates demand and inventory behav-

TABLE 12.7

```
WK 1   DEMAND= 10  INVENTORY= 22 LOST= 0
WK 2   DEMAND= 5   INVENTORY= 17 LOST= 0
WK 3   DEMAND= 5   INVENTORY= 12 LOST= 0
WK 4   DEMAND= 5   INVENTORY= 7  LOST= 0
WK 5   DEMAND= 9   INVENTORY= 0  LOST= 2
WK 6   DEMAND= 8   INVENTORY= 25 LOST= 0
WK 7   DEMAND= 2   INVENTORY= 23 LOST= 0
WK 8   DEMAND= 6   INVENTORY= 17 LOST= 0
WK 9   DEMAND= 13  INVENTORY= 4  LOST= 0
WK 10  DEMAND= 5   INVENTORY= 0  LOST= 1
WK 11  DEMAND= 3   INVENTORY= 0  LOST= 3
WK 12  DEMAND= 5   INVENTORY= 28 LOST= 0
WK 13  DEMAND= 5   INVENTORY= 23 LOST= 0
WK 14  DEMAND= 5   INVENTORY= 18 LOST= 0
WK 15  DEMAND= 1   INVENTORY= 17 LOST= 0
WK 16  DEMAND= 6   INVENTORY= 11 LOST= 0
WK 17  DEMAND= 11  INVENTORY= 0  LOST= 0
WK 18  DEMAND= 11  INVENTORY= 21 LOST= 0
WK 19  DEMAND= 5   INVENTORY= 16 LOST= 0
WK 20  DEMAND= 7   INVENTORY= 9  LOST= 0
WK 21  DEMAND= 8   INVENTORY= 1  LOST= 0
WK 22  DEMAND= 11  INVENTORY= 0  LOST= 10
WK 23  DEMAND= 8   INVENTORY= 26 LOST= 0
WK 24  DEMAND= 10  INVENTORY= 16 LOST= 0
WK 25  DEMAND= 12  INVENTORY= 4  LOST= 0
WK 26  DEMAND= 6   INVENTORY= 0  LOST= 2
WK 27  DEMAND= 11  INVENTORY= 0  LOST= 11
WK 28  DEMAND= 6   INVENTORY= 28 LOST= 0
WK 29  DEMAND= 3   INVENTORY= 25 LOST= 0
WK 30  DEMAND= 9   INVENTORY= 16 LOST= 0

SIMULATION RESULTS
- - - - - - - - - - - - - - - - - - -

AVG, INVENTORY LEVEL 15.9
PERCENT DEMAND MET 0.8625592
```

ior 1 week at a time, rather than in complete detail by individual customers, the simulation is still able to keep track of how much demand is met and how much is lost. In this type of simulation, then, it is possible to increment time regularly and uniformly, without the need for an event calendar such as the one used in the queueing simulation discussed previously. In contrast to an event-driven structure, this alternative approach is called a **time-driven simulation.**

MAKING SIMULATION WORK

Our discussion has emphasized the fact that simulation models are simple and mathematically straightforward. In fact, to informed users, a simulation model is virtually transparent because it represents directly those features of a real system that are interesting to study. These characteristics of simulation are usually its strengths, but they also create the risk that users may place too much faith in the results of a simulation study. As with any model, we believe that the best way to deal with problems of misuse of the model is to describe both the strengths and weaknesses of the model and to discuss the process of implementation. As a result, in this section we outline the steps involved in an effective simulation project and some of the technical problems such a project may encounter.

Perhaps the most fundamental task of a simulation project is a managerial one: identifying an appropriate problem to study. The project must be motivated by the need to make an important decision. A common mistake is to treat the creation of a simulation model as the project's major goal. On its own, however, a simulation model has little intrinsic value; its value comes from its potential role in helping to enhance the performance of a system, to improve the effectiveness of a decision, or to confirm the value of a policy. Thus, the key managerial task is to clarify the project's objectives by defining the problem to be solved. Once this task is accomplished, the simulation model becomes valuable as a decision aid.

A related managerial task is to determine the level of complexity at which the problem will be addressed. In practical terms, managers must allocate the resources to spend on the simulation project, for greater detail will obviously require greater resources. By determining the level of detail we determine the cost of a simulation project. In this context part of the art of management is the ability to assess the likely benefits from a simulation project. With this assessment we can choose a level of detail so that the benefits of the simulation study are greater than its costs. There is also a risk that too much detail in the model will be counterproductive. A model-building proverb states that a manager prefers a simpler model that is understandable to a more sophisticated model that is confusing.

The main steps in a simulation study are more or less standard, although it is difficult to give a comprehensive list that applies to every situation. Usually we would expect to find the following major stages in the project: studying the problem, developing and validating the model, experimenting with the model, and finally, drawing conclusions for decision making.

The first technical step is to study the system being simulated. The goal of such a study is to establish a good description of the elements, relationships, and processes we wish to capture in the simulation model. We may employ casual observation or careful record keeping in this effort. For example, in the rework study of Figure 12.7 we would need to keep detailed records showing numbers of defectives and repair times per unit in order to develop the probability models used in the simulation. Sometimes we might also require extensive interviews with people knowledgeable about the system.

The next technical step is to develop the simulation model, typically by designing and debugging a simulation program. Although we have referred to computer programming in very general terms, there exist several special-purpose programming languages that are designed to streamline this programming task. To support corporate planning models, such as the Layton Electronics simulation, there are a number of management-oriented languages often called "financial planning" or "corporate modeling" languages. Some of the better-known language names are IFPS, EMPIRE, and SIMPLAN. To support simulations with a dynamic emphasis, such as the queueing model of Figure 12.8, there are a number of languages that explicitly provide for describing elements and events, for keeping track of simulated time, and for gathering relevant statistics. Some of the more popular languages in this vein are GPSS, SIMSCRIPT, and GASP.

Once we have a program that runs, we must **validate** the model. Validation is the process of demonstrating that the model faithfully reflects the actual elements and relationships it was intended to represent. Because validation is essentially a process of persuading the user that the model functions as intended, there are no hard and fast rules for validation. However, we can repeat some well-established suggestions.

When we build a simulation model to represent an existing system, an important step in validation is to demonstrate that the model can replicate historical behavior. Specifically, when we use last year's parameters and last year's conditions to activate the model, we should expect the model to replicate last year's performance. To help validate the Layton Electronics model, for example, we might run the simulation with the price and cost data of previous years, along with the market growth rates of previous years, to show that the model yields the financial performance that actually occurred. The ability to replicate historical patterns might help substantiate the validity of the model, but we must keep in mind that historical validity does not guarantee predictive validity. Although the model replicates previously observed performance, that does not mean it will be as successful at predicting performance under new sets of conditions.

An additional step in validating the model is to demonstrate that it yields logical results in extreme cases. In the inventory model of Figure 12.9, for example, when we change the reordering rule so that a replenishment is triggered at a level of 250 instead of 25, we should find that no demand is lost. Alternatively, in the queueing example of Figure 12.8 we would expect that the mean number in the system grows when the ratio of arrival rate to service rate increases and falls when the ratio decreases.

Another possibility for validating the model is to find a simple special case for which analytical results exist and to show that the model output is consistent with theoretical behavior. In the rework study, for example, we might replace the repair-time distribution by a constant time of 4 minutes per defective. Then, except for scaling, we should find that the repair time per batch follows a Poisson distribution, matching the distribution of the number of defectives per batch.

The main investigation step in the project is to experiment with the model. We consciously use the term "experiment" to suggest the work done by a scientist in a laboratory. In such a context, an experimental approach involves the testing of a particular hypothesis about the relationship between certain independent variables and certain dependent variables. In order to carry out the test we, as scientists, would design an experiment in which we could alter the independent variables while holding other variables and parameters constant. In a decision-making context we can think of the hypothesis as a statement about the consequences of a particular action (such as expanding capacity, altering priority rules, or introducing a new product) upon specific performance measures (such as market share, level of congestion, or company profits). Thus, we can think of a simulation model as playing the role of a "subject" being used to test the hypothesis. Under carefully controlled conditions we expose the simulation model to certain inputs, and we collect data on the model's outputs. By analyzing the data we can draw conclusions about the possible consequences of the decision under consideration.

Thus, the experimental step in the simulation project utilizes the model in exploring alternative decisions, policies, or designs. As our analogy with a laboratory suggests, this process should be organized into a logical sequence of related experiments. Moreover, when the model contains probabilistic components, statistical analysis of the experimental results is vital. Finally, when conclusions are drawn based on the statistical analysis, there is often good reason to perform additional experiments, in order to test the sensitivity of those conclusions to the model's parameters and structural assumptions. With simulation models, we carry out sensitivity analysis by changing parameters or assumptions and then rerunning the model.

When we introduced Monte Carlo sampling earlier in this chapter, we showed how to use some basic statistical concepts to analyze simulation outcomes. Although the example of estimating Layton's market share demonstrated the use of simple statistical aids helpful in interpreting simulation results, we must also point out that in more complicated models the statistical analysis can be quite difficult. In what follows we discuss some common areas of difficulty that exemplify tactical problems in performing simulation experiments.

Simulation models with a dynamic emphasis usually exhibit **transient** effects. The specific initial conditions used to activate the model may produce an early "warm-up" period that is not representative of longer-run performance. If we are interested in measuring performance under the stable conditions of long-run behavior, we want to exclude from our data gathering those measurements taken during this initial transient period. In the queueing model, for example, the number of customers waiting in queue early in the simulation will tend to be small because we started the simulation with no customers present. This will be the case even when the long-run average length of the waiting line is quite large. The problem is to detect when the transient period has ended.

A related problem in dynamic simulation with probabilistic components involves the accuracy of parameter estimation. Assuming we can identify the onset of long-run behavior, we would like to take several recordings of the relevant performance measure in order to estimate it precisely. This process is analogous to taking a large sample size in order to obtain tight confidence intervals. In classical sampling theory the observations are independent, and it is easy to analyze the relationship between sample size and precision of the confidence interval. In a dynamic simulation, however, repeated observations of the same performance measure are not independent. Again referring to the queueing model for illustration, suppose we record the waiting time in the system for each customer. In particular, suppose that the existence of a very long waiting line at some stage causes one customer's waiting time to be quite large. The next customer is also likely to encounter a relatively long waiting time because that customer's arrival is likely to have occurred during a period of congestion. Thus, a sample of the waiting times encountered by successive customers will consist of dependent observations. The problem is to determine correct confidence intervals based on these dependent observations.

Even when we can find formulas for confidence intervals that apply in the simulation context, we often discover that relatively long simulation runs yield fairly imprecise estimates. This is also the case if relatively rare events have a substantial impact on the performance measure we are emphasizing. For a given run length, the problem is to modify the sampling devices within the simulation in a way that tightens confidence intervals without introducing bias into the estimates. The name for this type of modification is **variance reduction.**

Our main point is that, as an experimental approach, simulation creates its own special problems of statistical analysis. There are advanced statistical techniques to deal with transient effects, estimation accuracy, and variance reduction. Although recent research has developed ways to deal with such tactical problems, these techniques are beyond the scope of this text.

SUMMARY

Simulation is a modeling technique, and it shares a number of characteristics with other kinds of modeling techniques. Most important, simulation helps decision makers understand and analyze the relation between their own actions and the performance of the system for which they are responsible. The construction of a simulation model requires a specific representation of the elements, relationships, parameters, and variables that describe the phenomena under study. A simulation model also requires a specific representation of the procedures and events by which the system's status undergoes change. These requirements force the model builder to be explicit in describing the components of the system to be managed.

Simulation is primarily a descriptive approach in modeling, rather than a normative approach. Its aim is to provide some insight into the aggregate relationships in complex systems based on an understanding of the detailed relationships that exist. Some of the examples and exercises in this chapter suggest how to use simulation to compare decision alternatives: this is the first step in a normative approach. A more ambitious use of simulation (as with other modeling techniques) is to seek improvements in system performance and, ultimately, to determine optimal decisions.

Simulation is distinctive as a modeling technique in several respects, most of which relate to its flexibility. First, we can use a simulation model to represent both deterministic phenomena and probabilistic phenomena. In the latter case we can model probabilistic behavior with the use of Monte Carlo sampling, and we can apply the concepts to both continuous and discrete probability structures. Second, we can utilize simulation models not only in problems where there are primarily static emphases but also in those where there are dynamic emphases. Third, because a simulation model is usually modular in design, we can refine or alter portions of the model without affecting the rest of the model. This feature is important in the adaptation of simulation techniques to the computer. Finally, a simulation model is virtually free from the demands of specific mathematical forms. In using some other analytic models we depend critically on such mathematical restrictions as linear cost functions or normal probability laws, but with a simulation model we need not be wedded to such conditions.

The advantages of all this flexibility come with a price, and we have previously alluded to some of the disadvantages. To the extent that simulation results are akin to experimental results, their interpretation requires statistical reasoning. Sometimes the strongest conclusion that can be reached from a simulation study of a particular hypothesis is that the hypothesis cannot be rejected on the basis of the simulation data. Also, as in most experimental settings, the conclusions drawn from simulation results are usually very specific. If a number of conditions are prescribed in order to carry out an experiment, the conclusions apply only under those conditions. Drawing generalizations based on simulation results can be quite difficult, and thorough sensitivity analyses can be very costly. In addition, there are a number of managerial and technical tasks that must be carried out effectively in order for a simulation project to succeed. Last, the descriptive nature of simulation results may also be a drawback. The decision maker who seeks normative conclusions from a modeling approach may be frustrated with simulation's inability to guarantee optimal solutions to complex problems. Nevertheless, in highly complicated situations simulation may provide the only practical way to study changes by means of a model.

EXERCISES

LAYTON ELECTRONICS MODEL

1 A capacity plan for Layton Electronics Company consists of an initial plant size and three subsequent capacity increments. For each of the following criteria, find a capacity plan that achieves a maximum level.

a Market share in the fourth year.

b Operating profit in the fourth year.

c Portfolio value at the end of the fourth year.

2 Incorporate into the Layton program the probability distributions for market-size growth and for market-share growth. Thus, construct a program that will yield a single realization of the 4-year future in Layton's marketing, production, and finance sectors. For each of the plans determined in Exercise 1, run the model 20 times (for 20 different random number sequences) and estimate the mean values of

a Market share in the fourth year.

b Operating profit in the fourth year.

c Portfolio value at the end of the fourth year.

3 Construct a 90% confidence interval for each of the estimates in Exercise 2.

MONTE CARLO SIMULATION

4 A potato farmer is evaluating the profit potential for this year's crop. Based on previous experience, along with some idea of economic and meteorological trends, he has come up with the following probability distributions for some of the key factors.

Price ($/hundredweight)	3	4	5
Probability	0.25	0.40	0.35

Yield (hundredweight/acre)	200	225	250
Probability	0.3	0.4	0.3

Cost ($/acre)	750	1000
Probability	0.75	0.25

The farmer's profit is (price × yield) − cost, but this quantity is a random variable. Simulate 20 profit outcomes by hand and answer the following questions.

a What is the estimated mean profit based on the simulation data?

b What is the estimated probability that profit will be positive?

c What is the estimated probability that profit will be greater than $50 per acre?

d Construct 90% confidence intervals for the estimates in (a), (b), and (c).

e What is the true mean profit?

5 Repeat Exercise 4 using a computer program, with a sample size of 200.

6 A small construction project consists of six activities. These activities are related by technological restrictions that require that no activity can be started until all of its predecessor activities are complete. Furthermore, the duration of each activity is uncertain, and the project manager has provided an estimate of each activity's duration under optimistic, normal, and pessimistic conditions. The activity durations are also independent (which means that a given activity requires its optimistic, normal, or pessimistic time independently of what any other activity requires.) The table below describes the project.

Activity	Predecessors	Optimistic Duration	Normal Duration	Pessimistic Duration
A	None	5	7	9
B	None	2	9	10
C	A,B	5	13	15
D	A,B	13	15	23
E	C,D	4	6	14
F	C,D	4	5	6

a If each activity can be carried out at its normal duration, how long will the project take?

b For each activity assume the optimistic, normal, and pessimistic durations are equally likely. Simulate 20 trials by hand to estimate the mean project duration.

c For each activity assume the normal duration is three times as likely as either the optimistic or pessimistic durations. Simulate 20 trials to estimate the mean project duration.

d Find a 90% confidence interval for the estimated mean in (c).

e Under the conditions in (c) what is the estimated probability that the project takes longer than the deterministic time calculated in (a)?

7 Repeat Exercise 6 using a computer program with a sample size of 200.

8 In an inventory control system, the interval between the time a replenishment order is placed and the time the order is delivered is called the lead time. In determining an inventory control policy, an important part of the analysis is describing the behavior of demand during the lead time.

A retail store sells automatic dishwashers in a suburban market. Demand in a given week follows a Poisson probability distribution, and the average demand rate is eight units per week. In addition, the regional distributor of the dishwashers is somewhat unreliable in delivering replenishment units when the retail store places orders. In fact, experience indicates that the probability distribution for the lead time (in weeks) is the following:

Weeks	1	2	3	4
Probability	0.4	0.3	0.2	0.1

a Using a table of random numbers, simulate 10 lead times, each time recording the total number of units demanded during the lead time.

b Estimate the mean demand during the lead time.

c Estimate the standard deviation of demand during the lead time.

d Estimate the stock level necessary to meet all demand during the lead time with a probability of 0.9.

e Construct a 95% confidence interval for the estimate in (b).

9 Repeat Exercise 8 using a computer program, with a sample size of 100.

DYNAMIC SIMULATION

10 Using the simulation logic in Figure 12.8, simulate by hand the behavior of a single channel queue under the following conditions:

Poisson arrivals with a mean arrival rate of 50 per hour.

Normal service times with $\mu = 1$ minute and $\sigma = 0.25$ minute

Time limit = 0.5 hours.

From the sample distribution of N (the number of customers in the system) estimate

a The probability that the system is idle.

b The mean number of customers in the system.

11 Repeat Exercise 10 using a computer program, with a time limit of 50 hours.

12 At the Bishopric Beverage and Bottling Company there are several automatic bottling lines that fill bottles with a variety of soft drinks. A production run on any of the lines requires a careful setup to set the lot size, to adjust the equipment to specifications of the particular bottle size and shape, and to assure that the proper liquids are poured in. Once the setup is done, the production run proceeds automatically without the need for supervision. At the completion of the run a signal is given to show that the line is ready for the next setup.

The company uses a single "setup man" to perform all the setups. He moves from line to line responding to ready signals as they occur. The length of time required to perform a particular setup varies considerably according to how different the next lot is from the one before it. As a consequence, setup times tend to conform to an exponential distribution with a mean of 30 minutes. In addition, there is considerable variability in lot sizes, and so the occurrence of ready signals is essentially random with a mean rate of 1.5 per hour.

The work of the setup man can be modeled as a queueing system in which idle machines wait "in line" for setup service. Use a queueing simulation program to analyze the behavior of this system, based on a 200-hour simulation run. Answer the following questions based on the simulation output.

a What proportion of time is the setup man idle?

b What is the probability that all bottling lines are either active or in the process of being set up?

c What is the average number of inactive bottling lines?

13 Change the model in Exercise 12 so that setup times follow a normal distribution with mean $\mu = 30$ minutes and standard deviation $\sigma = 10$ minutes. Repeat the experiment of Exercise 3 and answer the same questions based on the output from the revised simulation.

14 A company has been having a maintenance problem with a certain complex piece of equipment. This equipment contains four identical vacuum tubes that have been the cause of the trouble. The problem is that the tubes fail fairly frequently, thereby forcing the equipment to be shut down while making a replacement. The current practice is to replace tubes only when they fail. However, a proposal has been made to replace all four tubes whenever any of them fails, to reduce the frequency with which the equipment must be shut down. The objective is to compare these two alternatives on a cost basis.

The pertinent data are the following. For each tube, the operating time until failure has approximately a uniform distribution from 120 to 200 hours. The equipment must be shut down for 1 hour to replace one tube or for 2 hours to replace all four tubes. The total cost associated with shutting down the equipment and replacing tubes is $75 per hour plus $50 for each new tube.

a Simulate by hand the current policy over 1000 operating hours, assuming that four new tubes are in the equipment initially. Estimate the average maintenance cost per hour.

b Simulate by hand the proposed policy over 1000 operating hours, assuming the same initial status as in (a). Estimate the average maintenance cost per hour.

15 Repeat Exercise 14 using a computer program, with a time limit of 100,000 hours.

16 A portion of a production line contains two stations, Assembly and Test, each assigned to a single operator. Under the existing design, components are first assembled, then tested, as shown in the diagram below. A large inventory provides a stock of components sufficient to keep both stations busy all day.

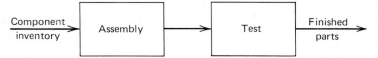

Sampling studies indicate that the time required for the assembly operation follows an exponential probability law with a mean of 4 minutes; in addition, the time required for the test operation is independent of the assembly time and also follows an exponential distribution with a mean of 4 minutes. Although the line appears "balanced" on the basis of mean operation times, a problem arises due to lack of storage space between the two operators. The assembly operator must hold onto the item just completed until the test operator is free to start testing it. If the test operator is busy, the assembly operator cannot start on the next item and will remain idle until the bottle-neck clears.

a Simulate by hand 1 hour's operation of this system to estimate (1) the proportion of time the Assembly operator is busy, (2) the proportion of time the Test operator is busy, (3) the output rate per hour. Start the simulation with the Test operator idle and the Assembly operator just beginning an operation.

b Suppose that storage space for one assembled unit is created between the two stations. (This means that the Assembly operator can put an assembled unit into this space and begin work on the next item, provided that the space is free). Simulate 1 hour's operation under this design and estimate the modified values of the three quantities given in (a).

17 Repeat Exercise 16 using a computer program, with a time limit of 100 hours.

18 Customer arrivals at Buddy's Bi-Lo self-service gas station exhibit exponential interarrival times with an average of one arrival every 5 minutes during the day. Buddy has only a single pump to serve all customers, so that the system operates as a single channel queue. The time required for a customer to pull up, pump gas, pay, and leave is a random variable that conforms approximately to a uniform distribution with a range from 1 minute to 7 minutes. Assuming there is room for any number of waiting customers, it is desired to estimate

a The mean number of customers in the system.

b The probability that more than three customers are waiting for a pump to become free.

Simulate by hand 1 hour of operation at Buddy's, and estimate the quantities described in (a) and (b).

19 Review Exercise 18. Suppose that there are two pumps at Buddy's instead of just one.

a Draw a flow chart for a simulation of queue behavior at Buddy's.

b Simulate 1 hour of operation at Buddy's, and estimate the mean number of customers in the system.

20 Waldman's Sporting Goods Store maintains a checking account at a local bank. Each day the store's receipts are deposited in the account, and each day certain withdrawals are taken out of the account to pay the store's operating expenses. The amount of deposits and the amount of withdrawals on a given day are independent of each other. Data obtained from the bank indicate that the following probability distributions describe the random behavior of deposits and withdrawals.

Deposits (in hundreds of dollars)

x	1	2	3	5	8	10
P_x	0.05	0.15	0.20	0.30	0.20	0.10

Withdrawals (in hundreds of dollars)

x	1	2	3	5	6	8
P_x	0.10	0.10	0.35	0.25	0.15	0.05

The checking-account funds earn no interest, but under an agreement with Waldman's the bank operates with the following scheme:

When the daily account balance reaches or exceeds $1,200, transfer all but $100 to an interest-bearing account.

When the daily account balance becomes negative, cover the deficit with a temporary loan of bank funds.

At present, the interest-bearing account earns interest at an annual rate of 5%, while the bank's deficit-coverage loans are made at an interest rate of 10%.

Simulate a month (20 days) of deposits and withdrawals at Waldman's account to estimate the net interest income under the bank scheme.

21 A small car-rental agency leases a fleet of cars from a major auto manufacturer and rents cars to local customers at competitive prices. The agency is currently studying how large a fleet it should use. Historical data suggest the following probability distributions for customer behavior.

Customers per day	0	1	2	
Probability	0.4	0.3	0.3	
Length of contract (days)	1	2	3	7
Probability	0.3	0.2	0.1	0.4

The agency is open for business 7 days a week. The lease cost for each car in its fleet is $10 per day. The net profit on rental contracts (exclusive of the lease cost) averages about $16 per day.

Suppose the agency decides to keep a fleet of four cars. Simulate 2 weeks of rental business in order to estimate

a The average weekly profit from rental operations.

b The probability that a potential customer would find no cars available.

22 Draw a flow chart for the simulation of a queueing system that operates with three parallel servers.

23 Describe how to alter the inventory simulation in Figure 12.9 for a situation in which replenishment lead times are random.

CASES

SCOTT PAPER COMPANY

Scott Paper Company, founded in 1879, has extensive manufacturing and distribution installations in the U.S. and abroad; in addition, the company owns nearly 3 million acres of timberland. Sales in 1969 were $731 million (up from $514 million five years earlier) with net income of $60 million. The greatest percentage of the sales volume comes from the Packaged Products Division (PPD); the balance of the company's business comes from the other Divisions, chiefly from the S. D. Warren Division; the Plastic Coating Corporation, a subsidiary; the Foam and Container Division; and the International Division.

The Packaged Products Division (PPD) of Scott Paper Company manufactures and markets a variety of consumer and industrial paper products, including paper towels, napkins, facial and toilet tissue, and waxed paper. Wood pulp, the principal raw material used in making the paper products, comes from another division of Scott or from open market purchases and is processed at PPD paper mills. This processing, illustrated in Figures 1 and 2, begins at the huge paper making machines. Output from these machines (rolls of about seven feet long and five feet in diameter called "parent rolls") goes to rewinders and decorators where, depending on the particular product being made, the paper is printed, embossed, etc. The paper is cut to size, wrapped, and packed in cases in the finishing operation and then moved to the mill's distribution center and placed in finished products inventory. From the inventory, some product is shipped to other distribution centers (not all Scott products are made at each mill); these shipments are called "stock transfers." The rest of the product is shipped in van or carload lots directly to customers. If the lot contains a single product type, it is a "solid" shipment. If not, a "mixed" shipment.

Paper-making is a capital-intensive industry due to the high cost ($12–$15 million) of paper machines. One of the major pre-occupations of the PPD management, therefore, is the efficient scheduling of work on the different machines at different mills to fulfill the forecast production requirements. These machines are not uniform. On the contrary, each machine (Scott has 40 paper machines, 30 rewinders and rewinder-decorators, and 75 finishing machines) has different production rates for different kinds of paper and products. The production required is broken down by sales area, each served by a particular distribution center. The Scheduling Department of PPD then divides the work among the various mills trading off production economies (due to efficient machine/brand combinations) against transportation costs of shipping the output to distant distribution centers and taking into account the variable production rates on different machines. There are seven mills with associated distribution centers, and three distribution centers that are warehouses only (see Figure 3).

Source: Copyright © 1970 by the President and Fellows of Harvard College. This case was prepared by Judith Selvidge (DBA) under the direction of Richard F. Meyer as a basis for class discussion rather than to illustrate effective or ineffective handling of an administrative situation. Reprinted by permission of the Harvard Business School.

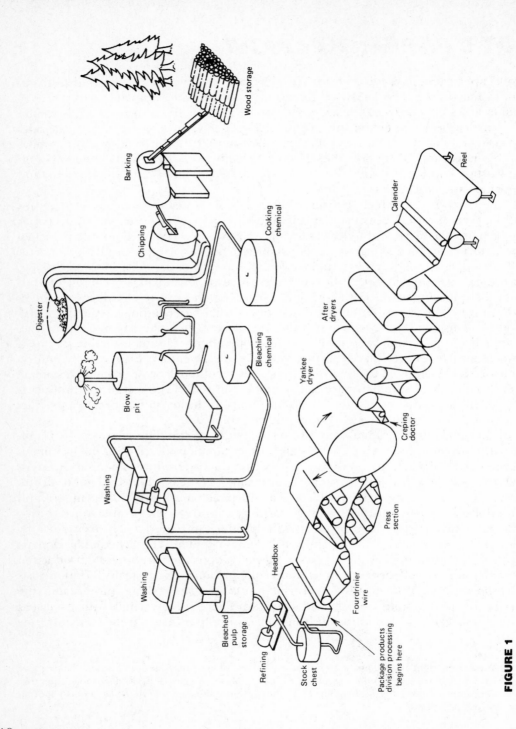

Wood storage

Barking

Chipping

Cooking chemical

Digester

Blow pit

Bleaching chemical

Washing

Washing

Bleached pulp storage

Refining

Stock chest

Headbox

Package products division processing begins here

Fourdrinier wire

Press section

Creping doctor

Yankee dryer

After dryers

Calender

Reel

FIGURE 1

540

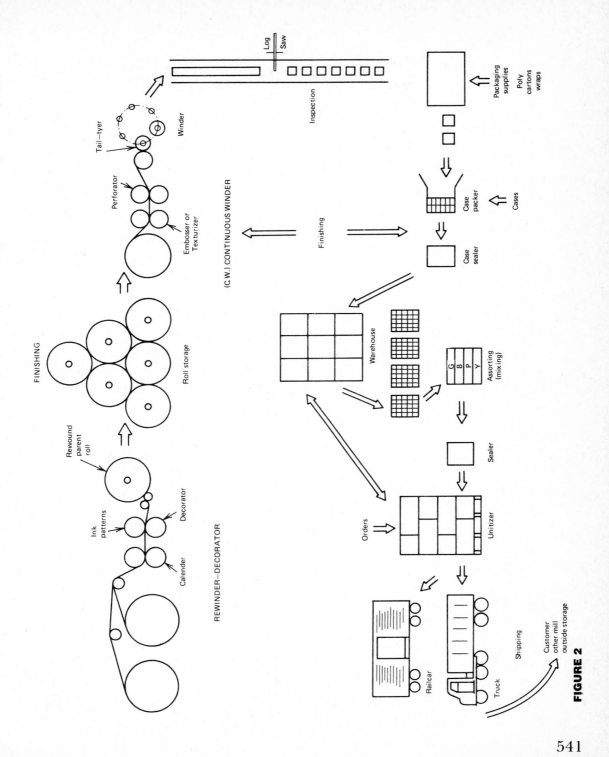

FIGURE 2

541

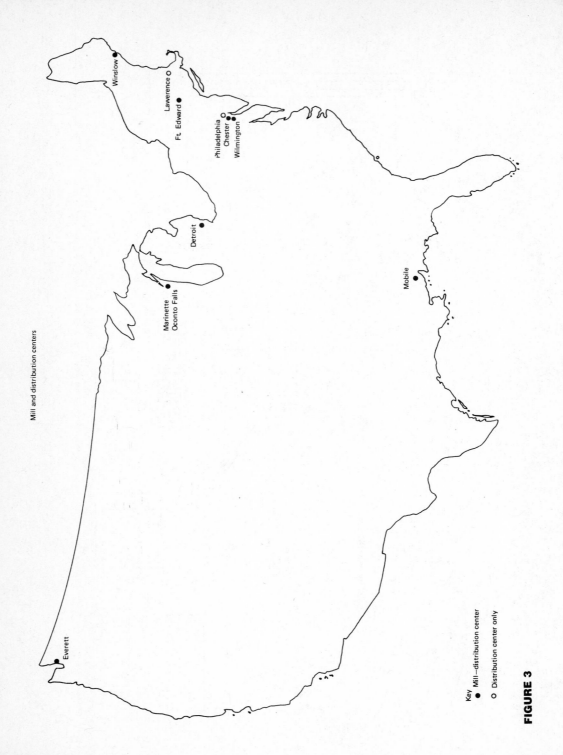

Mill and distribution centers

Winslow

Lawerence ○

Ft. Edward ●

Philadelphia
Chester ○ ●
Wilmington ●

Detroit ●

Marinette
Oconto Falls ●

Mobile ●

Everett ●

Key
● Mill—distribution center
○ Distribution center only

FIGURE 3

In the middle 1950's Scott was a pioneer in the use of computers to aid in solving this scheduling-distribution problem. The corporate Operations Research group designed, built, and patented a special analog computer in which the different paper machine-rewinder-decorator-finisher-distribution center-sales area combinations were represented by electrical circuits. By sending a current (corresponding to total annual production) through the system of circuits and then measuring the output current at the end of every branch, a series of numbers was obtained each of which could be translated into *annual* tons of paper products produced on that particular machine combination and delivered to a customer via the specified distribution center. By applying voltages (representing production rates) at the nodes of the circuits (representing the paper machines) the ranges of permissible production rates could be explored by the model. The OR group had the responsibility for running the computer and for recording and interpreting the computer solution. The resulting recommendations were sent to the Scheduling Department in PPD where monthly schedules for each mill were drawn up by hand. In addition to determining the monthly targets or quotas for each mill—these quotas are subject to negotiation between the Scheduling Department and the mills—the Scheduling Department controls or reschedules the assignments during the month as necessary to account for machine breakdowns, changes in level of demand for a product, etc. This rescheduling accounts for about 60% of the work of the department.

During the 1960's Scott's business increased significantly. This increase in sales volume, number of mills, and particularly the proliferation of products placed a strain on the capacity of the analog computer and on the ability of the Scheduling Department to convert annual production amounts into monthly output by brands. Management suspected that greater automation of scheduling would increase the PPD contribution to profits with the existing machines, postpone the need for investment in new paper machines, and eliminate the vulnerability of the company under the current system where essentially only one man was experienced enough to perform hand scheduling.

In 1967 the idea of using linear programming (LP) techniques and a large digital computer to deal with the scheduling problem was considered. The proponents of this approach thought that optimization methods applied to the allocation of machine time could automatically provide the best production schedule for each month. The corporate OR group prepared a detailed technical proposal explaining how they would develop such an LP solution; higher management, however, eventually decided to set up a separate team of three men, one from the OR group and two from PPD, to carry out this LP task. The team was temporarily assigned to the Management Information Services (MIS) group in PPD.

Chuck MacFarlan, the OR representative on the team, was an electrical engineer who had played a major role in the development of the company's analog computer. His experience, typical of the OR group which had been a part of the Research Division, came mainly from one-time studies of problems referred to the group from all over the company. These studies ranged from designing a "woodlands model" of tree growth to participating in new mill location decisions. As work on this new project began, Mr. MacFarlan took on the job of learning about LP and about the general-purpose computer program developed by IBM for solving LP problems.

The second team member came from the PPD accounting department and was given primary responsibility for the many decisions about how to calculate and assign variable manufacturing costs for the new computer model. He also began to define the division's goals in terms of different objective functions for the LP. After a few months of association with the project, however, he was promoted and left the project. An analyst/programmer with EDP experience was the third member of the team. He was to bring to the project a familiarity with the "systems" side of setting up operational problems for solution on a digital computer.

An initial contact was made with the prospective users of the computer model, the Scheduling Department. They were asked to list all the information required or desirable in the monthly schedules which the computer would prepare. However, the precise scope of the model—in terms of the restrictions, assumptions, and objectives—was not determined in advance of the programming.

During the next 12 months Mr. MacFarlan, with the help of a student working part time for Scott Paper, developed and programmed the model, which came to be called the Monthly Production Scheduling (MPS) system. Mr. MacFarlan's detailed knowledge of the production process enabled him to work independently, while the systems analyst coordinated the preparation of data input to the program.

MPS generates monthly production and distribution plans for each mill to satisfy estimated sales demand and inventory requirements. Potential manufacturing savings (due to selection of efficient machine/brand combinations) are traded off against stock transfer costs. The LP matrix consists of 463 rows and 2871 columns broken down as follows:

Constraints	No. of Rows
Demand (sales forecasts) by distribution center and brand (in 0000 cases)	230
Machine capacities (paper machine, decorator, finisher, rewinder) (in days)	140
Mill totals by product (average monthly production for each product at each mill—not all products are produced at every mill) (in 0000 cases)	93

Activities	No. of Columns
Production rate (of brand A on machines B, C, & D at Mill E) (in days/0000 cases)	155
Stock transfers (23 brands among 10 distribution centers) (0000 cases)	2070
Beginning and ending inventories (at each distribution center) (0000 cases)	460
Slack variables (production for promotional purposes) (0000 cases)	186

The MPS considers the coming six-month period. Initially a computer solution is calculated for the six-month interval, viewed as a single period. (This requires from 15–27 hours of machine time on an IBM 360/40.) Then using this optimal solution as a starting point the matrix solution processor is rerun for each month separately (given the monthly sales forecast) to generate the monthly production schedules. These subsequent runs take about one hour of computing time each.

The model covers only a limited part of the PPD activities. It starts at the pulp end of the business with an incomplete description of pulp availability: although the *cost* of pulp is included in the formulation, there is no limit on the available supply. At the other end of the business, the distribution of products is taken only as far as stock transfers to distribution centers rather than on through to the customer.

By the middle of 1968 the Scheduling Department had been given the first examples of MPS output; Mr. MacFarlan had begun work on other projects including potential extensions of MPS; and the systems analyst was preparing to leave the MIS group, having been promoted to a job in his field of specialization, transportation.

At this point another programmer, Jack Lazlow, was assigned to the MPS project to handle the final details of getting the program into everyday use. He had been peripherally connected with earlier work on MPS, having written programs to generate sales forecasts which formed part of the input to the MPS system. As he began his new assignment, Mr. Lazlow was surprised to learn that a great deal of work remained to be done in explaining the new system and its output to the Scheduling Department. The head of the Scheduling Department, referring to the samples of MPS output, pointed out that many of the machine assignments in the computer solution did not seem to make any sense. He wanted an explanation of how these "funny" numbers were obtained. Mr. Lazlow realized that he himself did not understand the program well enough to describe how the machine assignments were computed, and so he began to learn about LP in general and in particular about the way this scheduling problem had been formulated. His efforts were hampered by the nearly total lack of documentation of the work done so far. Most helpful to him during this period was Manny Spenser, the part-time programmer who had assisted Mr. MacFarlan during the writing of the MPS system. Mr. MacFarlan was caught up in other things at this time and, although he was the person who most thoroughly understood the LP theory and its implementation in the MPS program, he quickly lost patience when trying to explain it to others, especially the users.

Concurrently with Mr. Lazlow's effort, the head of the Scheduling Department and his new assistant were making a lot of hand calculations in an attempt to try to figure out or disprove the assignments of the MPS output. As the two parties to the project at this stage, the users and the MIS programmers, increased their understanding of the system they met frequently and engaged in fairly heated discussions— mainly about *details* of the system, but also touching upon basic questions—of what the system did and what it was supposed to do. The Scheduling Department, far from considering MPS an improvement on the old system, was generally critical of the results. They noticed several errors in the model formulation ranging from steps left out in the production process (the capacity of the rewinders had not been included as a constraint) to nonlinearity in the constraint equations. Apart from the purely technical mistakes the Scheduling Department also found the output format to be difficult to use: the solution was given in LP terminology—"activities," "shadow prices," etc.— buried in a lot of irrelevant material. Furthermore, they were uncomfortable with the LP *method* in which the details of the calculation took place inside the system with only the final solution being available for scrutiny. The schedulers were used to seeing how a particular schedule developed, allowing them to check the "reasonableness" of the answer. One source of considerable misunderstanding between the users and the programmers was the precise form of objective function specified in the LP. Originally a minimum-cost formulation had been tried, but before long this was changed to a maximum-contribution-to-profit formulation, allowing excess capacity to be applied toward the production of high-profit items for promotional purposes. The users grasped in a general way the "objective" of the LP system but a great deal of discussion and analysis of results took place before they were made aware of the importance of the exact formulation and, particularly, the provision for filling the excess capacity.

As the months passed Mr. Lazlow was disturbed to realize that as their understanding of the MPS system grew, the users seemed to put more emphasis on showing what was wrong with the program than on finding ways of making it work. Although the computer solution was produced for each month, the Scheduling Department apparently did not base its decisions on the MPS figures.

HOLLINGSWORTH PAPER COMPANY

The Hollingsworth Paper Company is an integrated manufacturer of paper products for markets throughout the United States. Its Container Division produces corrugated cardboard boxes at four plants and sells through six regional distribution centers (DC's). Last year's sales of nearly 60,000 tons accounted for revenues of almost $30 million. A regional breakdown of sales is given in Exhibit 1.

EXHIBIT 1 Last Year's Sales by Geographic Region

Northeast sales (Boston DC)	2,600 T	4%
Northeast sales (Philadelphia DC)	9,700 T	17%
Southeast sales (Atlanta DC)	15,500 T	26%
Midwest sales (Chicago DC)	10,100 T	17%
Southwest sales (Houston DC)	13,400 T	23%
Far West sales (San Francisco DC)	7,500 T	13%
	58,800 T	100%

Cardboard containers are designed to meet a variety of customer needs. This variety reflects such features as size, shape, thickness, and type of closure. However, the technology is fairly simple, and competitors have the capability to manufacture the same products. To maintain its 10% share of the market, Hollingsworth emphasizes its quick and reliable delivery service. The firm has established its DC's to stock most of its standard items close to the major demand locations, but even specialty orders are processed through the DC's just to simplify paperwork.

Because there are several firms in the industry, and because few proprietary advantages exist, the market for cardboard boxes is quite competitive. The prices offered the customer are virtually the same no matter where the product is made or what its delivery route. This means that the manufacturer absorbs its own freight costs. With price competition as strong as it is, Hollingsworth's freight costs are a critical part of the profit picture.

PRODUCTION AND DISTRIBUTION FACILITIES

At present Hollingsworth has four plants with one-shift capacities in the range of 12,000 to 16,000 tons per year. At two of the four plants last year's production fell below one-shift capacity, while in the other two plants a substantial amount of second-shift output was necessary. This pattern reflected the concentration of sales in the Midwest and South. Details are given in Exhibit 2.

The plant located in Nashua, New Hampshire, is Hollingsworth's oldest facility. Its layout and equipment are somewhat outmoded; consequently, its productivity is relatively low. The Portland, Oregon, plant is the company's newest site, with a work force roughly one-half the size of Nashua's. Labor rates are cheapest at Asheville, North Carolina, and most expensive at St. Louis, Missouri. Variations in the process and wage rates, together with different utilizations, result in somewhat different costs at each location. An accounting summary of last year's operations revealed that costs per ton varied from a low of $397.70 at Portland to a high of $447.30 at Nashua. Exhibits 3 to 5 provide some additional details on these figures.

EXHIBIT 2 Plant Capacities and Production

Plant	One-Shift Capacity	Production	Percent Utilization of One-Shift Capacity
Nashua, NH	14,000 T	12,300 T	88%
Asheville, NC	12,000 T	15,500 T	129%
St. Louis, MO	16,000 T	23,500 T	147%
Portland, OR	12,000 T	7,500 T	63%
Total	54,000 T	58,800 T	109%

EXHIBIT 3 Total Costs (per ton)

	Variable Costs	Allocated Fixed Costs	Total Costs
Nashua	$439.80	$ 8.50	$448.30
Asheville	406.60	10.30	416.90
St. Louis	400.40	8.10	408.50
Portland	379.70	18.00	397.70

EXHIBIT 4 Plant Variable Costs (per ton)

	Materials	Labor	Supervision	Other Overhead	Fringe* Benefits	Total
Nashua						
1st Shift	$299.20	$104.00	$19.60	$3.40	$13.60	$439.80
2nd Shift	299.20	110.80	20.80	3.40	14.48	448.68
Asheville						
1st Shift	305.20	76.00	13.00	1.20	9.80	405.20
2nd Shift	305.20	81.00	13.60	1.20	10.40	411.40
St. Louis						
1st Shift	301.20	74.60	12.40	.90	9.60	398.70
2nd Shift	301.20	78.80	13.10	.90	10.10	404.10
Portland						
1st Shift	299.20	61.40	10.10	1.10	7.86	379.60
2nd Shift	299.20	65.00	10.70	1.10	8.32	384.32

* 11% of labor and supervision.

EXHIBIT 5 Plant and Fixed Costs

	Supervision	Fringe* Benefits	Other Overhead	Depreciation	Total
Nashua					
1st Shift	$60,000	$6,600	$8,000	$30,000	$104,600
2nd Shift	30,000	3,300	2,000	—	35,300
Asheville					
1st Shift	60,000	6,600	8,000	50,000	124,600
2nd Shift	30,000	3,300	2,000	—	35,300
St. Louis					
1st Shift	60,000	6,600	8,000	80,000	154,600
2nd Shift	30,000	3,300	2,000	—	35,300
Portland					
1st Shift	60,000	6,600	8,000	60,000	134,600
2nd Shift	30,000	3,300	2,000	—	35,300

* 11% of labor and supervision.

PATTERNS OF DISTRIBUTION

Facing the competitive market with tight margins, Hollingsworth has paid particular attention to its freight costs. For a number of years, its policy has been to supply each DC from the nearest plant, thus minimizing the freight component of cost. Last year's freight rates are reproduced in Exhibit 6. Under this company policy, the Nashua plant supplies the Boston and Philadelphia DC's, Asheville supplies the Atlanta DC, St. Louis supplies the Chicago and Houston DC's, and Portland supplies the San Francisco DC. This pattern results in very different profits in the various regions, ranging from around $40 per ton in Chicago to a slight loss in Philadelphia. The DC managers, whose annual bonus partly reflects the profits made in their region, have complained about this system for years. Exhibit 7 summarizes last year's records.

EXPANSION PROPOSALS

Over the years Hollingsworth has made investments to improve its productive capacity in several places. As sales in the Midwest grew, the St. Louis plant was expanded. New equipment was installed in Asheville to keep pace with sales growth in the South. Based on these experiences, the engineering staff was eventually able to design the new Portland plant, which reduced the cost of meeting demand in the West. Few improvements, however, have been implemented at Nashua. The two-story layout hampers innovation, and the engineers have expressed some concern about whether the old building is strong enough to support some of the heavier pieces of machinery now used elsewhere.

As a continuation of these investment initiatives, the Facilities Planning Committee at Hollingsworth has produced two large-scale expansion plans to help meet predicted sales growth over the next eight to ten years. One proposal involves a large addition to the St. Louis plant, while the second proposal involves construction of a new plant in Houston.

The St. Louis proposal calls for an expansion of the existing plant sufficient to raise its annual one-shift capacity to 28,000 tons. The cost for the building for this

EXHIBIT 6 Last Year's Transportation Rates per Ton

From:	Boston	Philadelphia	Atlanta	Chicago	Houston	San Francisco
Nashua	$ 16.00	$ 20.00	$ 64.00	$56.00	$72.00	$104.00
Asheville	52.00	48.00	20.00	56.00	56.00	88.00
St. Louis	56.00	52.00	56.00	20.00	32.00	72.00
Portland	112.00	112.00	104.00	64.00	68.00	36.00
Houston	64.00	60.00	48.00	30.00	0.00	76.00

EXHIBIT 7 Last Year's Profits per Ton

	Selling Price	Cost of Goods Sold	Warehousing, Selling and Administrative Expenses	Freight Absorbed	Net Profit Before Taxes
Boston	$500.00	$448.30	$32.00	$16.00	$ 3.70
Philadelphia	500.00	448.30	32.00	20.00	(0.30)
Atlanta	500.00	416.90	29.00	20.00	34.10
Chicago	500.00	408.50	31.00	20.00	40.50
Houston	500.00	408.50	30.00	32.00	29.50
San Francisco	500.00	397.70	32.00	36.00	34.30

* Includes a 4% sales commission.

expansion has been estimated at $1.6 million, and there is adequate land at the St. Louis site. The equipment investment is estimated to be $1.5 million. The plant expansion would afford Hollingsworth an opportunity to use the latest machinery available.

The Houston proposal calls for building a new plant with annual one-shift capacity of 12,000 tons. Although Hollingsworth already has a DC located in Houston, there would be a need to purchase land for the new plant. The cost of land is estimated at $500,000. The plant itself would cost about $2 million, while the investment in equipment is estimated at $1.5 million, since the technology would be much the same as in the St. Louis expansion. Additional estimates for the two proposals are shown in Exhibit 8.

As mentioned earlier, the Facilities Planning Committee anticipates that some kind of expansion will be needed to meet the needs of the market during the next 8–10 years. Over that period, the costs of labor, materials, and freight are likely to increase at slightly different rates, but the company controller has commented that the firm's cost structure is not likely to change drastically.

EXHIBIT 8 Anticipated Costs for New Facilities

	Houston	St. Louis
Variable costs per ton:		
Direct materials	$302.40	$301.20
Direct labor	57.00	60.40
Supervision	9.00	10.00
Other overhead*	1.00	1.00
Fixed operating costs per year:		
Supervision	$60,000	$40,000
Other overhead*	8,000	8,000

* Includes supplies, heat, light, power, insurance.

RED BRAND CANNERS (A)

On Monday, September 13, Mr. Mitchell Gordon, Vice-President of Operations, asked the Controller, the Sales Manager, and the Production Manager to meet with him to discuss the amount of tomato products to pack that season. The tomato crop, which had been purchased at planting, was beginning to arrive at the cannery, and packing operations would have to be started by the following Monday. Red Brand Canners was a medium-sized company which canned and distributed a variety of fruit and vegetable products under private brands in the western states.

Mr. William Cooper, the Controller, and Mr. Charles Myers, the Sales Manager, were the first to arrive in Mr. Gordon's office. Dan Tucker, the Production Manager, came in a few minutes later and said that he had picked up Produce Inspection's latest estimate of the quality of the incoming tomatoes. According to their report, about 20% of the crop was Grade "A" quality and the remaining portion of the 3,000,000-pound crop was Grade "B."

Gordon asked Myers about the demand for tomato products for the coming year. Myers replied that they could sell all of the whole canned tomatoes they could produce. The expected demand for tomato juice and tomato paste, on the other hand, was limited. The Sales Manager then passed around the latest demand forecast, which is shown in Exhibit 1. He reminded the group that the selling prices had been set in light of the long-term marketing strategy of the company, and potential sales had been forecasted at these prices.

Bill Cooper, after looking at Myers' estimates of demand, said that it looked like the company "should do quite well (on the tomato crop) this year." With the new accounting system that had been set up, he had been able to compute the contribution for each product, and according to his analysis the incremental profit on the whole tomatoes was greater than for any other tomato product. In May, after Red Brand had signed contracts agreeing to purchase the grower's production at an average delivered price of 6 cents per pound, Cooper had computed the tomato products' contributions (see Exhibit 2).

Dan Tucker brought to Cooper's attention that, although there was ample production capacity, it was impossible to produce all whole tomatoes as too small a portion of the tomato crop was "A" quality. Red Brand used a numerical scale to record the quality of both raw produce and prepared products. This scale ran from zero to ten, the higher number representing better quality. Rating tomatoes according to this scale, "A" tomatoes averaged nine points per pound and "B" tomatoes averaged five points per pound. Tucker noted that the minimum average input quality for canned whole tomatoes was eight and for juice it was six points per pound. Paste could be made entirely from "B" grade tomatoes. This meant that whole tomato production was limited to 800,000 pounds.

Source: Reprinted from *Stanford Business Cases 1965* with permission of the publishers, Stanford Graduate School of Business, © 1965 by the Board of Trustees of the Leland Stanford Jr. University.

EXHIBIT 1 Demand Forecasts

Product	Selling Price per Case	Demand Forecast (Cases)
24—2½ whole tomatoes	$4.00	800,000
24—2½ choice peach halves	5.40	10,000
24—2½ peach nectar	4.60	5,000
24—2½ tomato juice	4.50	50,000
24—2½ cooking apples	4.90	15,000
24—2½ tomato paste	3.80	80,000

Gordon stated that this was not a real limitation. He had been recently solicited to purchase 80,000 pounds of Grade "A" tomatoes at 8½ cents per pound and at that time had turned down the offer. He felt, however, that the tomatoes were still available.

Myers, who had been doing some calculations, said that although he agreed that the company "should do quite well this year," it would not be by canning whole

EXHIBIT 2 Product Item Profitability

Product	24—2½ Whole Tomatoes	24—2½ Choice Peach Halves	24—2½ Peach Nectar	24—2½ Tomato Juice	24—2½ Cooking Apples	24—2½ Tomato Paste
Selling Price	$4.00	$5.40	$4.60	$4.50	$4.90	$3.80
Variable costs:						
Direct labor	1.18	1.40	1.27	1.32	.70	.54
Variable OHD	.24	.32	.23	.36	.22	.26
Variable selling	.40	.30	.40	.85	.28	.38
Packaging material	.70	.56	.60	.65	.70	.77
Fruit[1]	1.08	1.80	1.70	1.20	.90	1.50
Total variable costs	3.60	4.38	4.20	4.38	2.80	3.45
Contribution	.40	1.02	.40	.12	1.10	.35
Less allocated OHD	.28	.70	.52	.21	.75	.23
Net profit	.12	.32	(.12)	(.09)	.35	.12

[1] Product usage is as given below

Product	Pounds per case
Whole tomatoes	18
Peach halves	18
Peach nectar	17
Tomato juice	20
Cooking apples	27
Tomato paste	25

EXHIBIT 3 Marginal Analysis of Tomato Products

Z = Cost per pound of A tomatoes in cents
Y = Cost per pound of B tomatoes in cents

(1) $(600{,}000 \text{ lbs.} \times Z) + (2{,}400{,}000 \text{ lbs.} \times Y) = (3{,}000{,}000 \text{ lbs.} \times 6)$

(2) $\dfrac{Z}{9} = \dfrac{Y}{5}$

Z = 9.32 cents per pound
Y = 5.18 cents per pound

Product	Canned Whole Tomatoes	Tomato Juice	Tomato Paste
Selling price	$4.00	$4.50	$3.80
Variable cost			
(excluding tomato costs)	2.52	3.18	1.95
	$1.48	$1.32	$1.85
Tomato cost	1.49	1.24	1.30
Marginal profit	($ .01)	$ .08	$ .55

tomatoes. It seemed to him that the tomato cost should be allocated on the basis of quality and quantity rather than by quantity only as Cooper had done. Therefore, he had recomputed the marginal profit on this basis (see Exhibit 3), and from his results, Red Brand should use 2,000,000 pounds of the "B" tomatoes for paste, and the remaining 400,000 pounds of "B" tomatoes and all of the "A" tomatoes for juice. If the demand expectations were realized, a contribution of $48,000 would be made on this year's tomato crop.

RED BRAND CANNERS (B)

The meeting in Mitchell Gordon's office dragged on without a resolution. Finally, Mr. Gordon brought the meeting to an end so that he could attend the dinner meeting of the local chapter of The Institute of Management Sciences. He asked Bill Cooper, Charles Myers, and Dan Tucker to think about the alternatives for another day or two.

Mr. Gordon had promised a friend that he would come to the dinner meeting, but he was not looking forward to it. He hated to leave the production plans unresolved, and the topic on the evening's agenda sounded rather technical. However, the speaker turned out to be a lively professor from a midwestern business school, and his exposition of linear programming captured Mr. Gordon's attention. After a while, Mr. Gordon's notes contained the table shown in Exhibit 1. He was convinced that a

EXHIBIT 1

Variable:	WH	JU	PA			
1) max	1.48	1.32	1.85			
2)	1	0	0	≤	800	W market
3)	0	1	0	≤	50	J market
4)	0	0	1	≤	80	P market
5)	18	20	25	≤	3000	Pounds fruit
6)	13.5	5	0	≤	600	Quality

linear programming model could shed some light on the matter that had been discussed in his office that afternoon.

The speaker demonstrated some linear programming software that could be run on a personal computer, and Mr. Gordon could not resist buying one of the speaker's diskettes and getting some basic instructions.

The next morning, Mr. Gordon arrived at work early and went right to work at his personal computer. The information in his model (Exhibit 1) produced the results shown in Exhibit 2.

When he showed these results to Mr. Cooper, the controller was not impressed. Cooper pointed out that the fruit cost had been ignored. Since the tomato cost was different for each type of product, its $0.06 per pound cost ought to be subtracted from each of the contribution figures. Mr. Gordon argued that it shouldn't matter because the tomatoes were a fixed cost, but Cooper wanted to see the figures. When Mr. Gordon went back and revised his original model, he was surprised to see the new

EXHIBIT 2

```
          OBJECTIVE FUNCTION VALUE

   1)        225.35560

VARIABLE          VALUE         REDUCED COST
   WH          38.888890          .000000
   JU          15.000000          .000000
   PA          80.000000          .000000

   ROW      SLACK OR SURPLUS      DUAL PRICES
   2)          761.111100          .000000
   3)           35.000000          .000000
   4)             .000000          .402778
   5)             .000000          .057889
   6)             .000000          .032444
```

results. (See Exhibits 3 and 4.) The revised figures disturbed him, and he didn't like the prospect of losing this debate to Cooper.

He also had to address the question of those additional 80,000 pounds of fruit. He contacted last evening's speaker and was told that, on the basis of the first model's solution, the extra tomatoes looked like a good buy, even at $0.09 per pound. Just to convince himself, Mr. Gordon sat down at his personal computer and extended his original model to include an option to purchase extra tomatoes (Exhibit 5). The response (Exhibit 6) seemed to indicate that the purchase should be made, just like he had been told. However, when he tried to account for the $0.06 fruit cost (Exhibit 7) the purchase looked undesirable (Exhibit 8). At this point he felt pretty confused and ready to give up.

EXHIBIT 3

Variable:	WH	JU	PA			
1) max	0.40	0.12	0.35			
2)	1	0	0	≤	800	W market
3)	0	1	0	≤	50	J market
4)	0	0	1	≤	80	P market
5)	18	20	25	≤	3000	Pounds fruit
6)	13.5	5	0	≤	600	Quality

EXHIBIT 4

```
              OBJECTIVE FUNCTION VALUE

   1)           45.7777800

VARIABLE          VALUE              REDUCED COST
   WH           44.444440              .000000
   JU             .000000              .028148
   PA           80.000000              .000000

   ROW        SLACK OR SURPLUS        DUAL PRICES
   2)           755.555500              .000000
   3)            50.000000              .000000
   4)              .000000              .350000
   5)           200.000000              .000000
   6)              .000000              .029630
```

EXHIBIT 5

Variable:	WH	JU	PA	ABUY			
1) max	1.48	1.32	1.85	−0.085			
2)	1	0	0	0	≤	800	W market
3)	0	1	0	0	≤	50	J market
4)	0	0	1	0	≤	80	P market
5)	18	20	25	−1	≤	3000	Pounds fruit
6)	13.5	5	0	−1	≤	600	Quality
7)	0	0	0	1	≤	80	Extra A's

EXHIBIT 6

```
          OBJECTIVE FUNCTION VALUE

  1)         225.782200

VARIABLE           VALUE            REDUCED COST
   WH          45.555560              .000000
   JU          13.000000              .000000
   PA          80.000000              .000000
 ABUY          80.000000              .000000

   ROW      SLACK OR SURPLUS        DUAL PRICES
   2)          754.444500             .000000
   3)           37.000000             .000000
   4)             .000000             .402778
   5)             .000000             .057889
   6)             .000000             .032444
   7)             .000000             .005333
```

EXHIBIT 7

Variable:	WH	JU	PA	ABUY			
1) max	0.40	0.12	0.35	−0.085			
2)	1	0	0	0	≤	800	W market
3)	0	1	0	0	≤	50	J market
4)	0	0	1	0	≤	80	P market
5)	18	20	25	−1	≤	3000	Pounds fruit
6)	13.5	5	0	−1	≤	600	Quality
7)	0	0	0	1	≤	80	Extra A's

EXHIBIT 8

```
            OBJECTIVE FUNCTION VALUE

  1)          45.7777800

VARIABLE          VALUE          REDUCED COST
    WH          44.444440          .000000
    JU            .000000          .028148
    PA          80.000000          .000000
  ABUY            .000000          .055370

   ROW       SLACK OR SURPLUS     DUAL PRICES
    2)          755.555500          .000000
    3)           50.000000          .000000
    4)             .000000          .350000
    5)          200.000000          .000000
    6)             .000000          .029630
    7)           80.000000          .000000
```

RUBICON RUBBER COMPANY

On Friday, February 13, 1970 Mr. George Nelson, Manager of the Tire Division of Rubicon Rubber Company, was boarding a plane enroute to a New York meeting with representatives of Eastern Auto Stores to negotiate a final contract for the delivery of automobile snow tires. A preliminary version of the contract called for the delivery of 15,000 medium-grade nylon-cord tires and 11,000 high-grade fiberglass-cord tires over the three-month summer delivery period. Prices had tentatively been set at $7.00 for the nylon tires and at $9.00 for the fiberglass.

Mr. Nelson had approximately two hours of time during the flight in which to review his notes and to examine the analysis prepared for him by Jim Leader, a new member of the staff and a recent MBA. Mr. Nelson felt that there were a number of things which he had to resolve before he felt secure in finalizing the contract, so he was anxious to get to work quickly to avoid the possibility of a conversation with the fellow in the next seat.

Source: Copyright © 1971 by the President and Fellows of Harvard College. This case was prepared by Paul Roberts under the direction of John W. Pratt as a basis for class discussion rather than to illustrate effective or ineffective handling of an administrative situation. Reprinted by permission of the Harvard Business School.

BACKGROUND

Rubicon Rubber Company is a small company located in Independence, Ohio. It manufactures a variety of rubber products including tires for fork lift trucks and small tractors. Founded in 1950 the company had grown rapidly in its early years and more slowly recently. Sales last year were three million dollars. Future growth for the company appeared to be closely linked to the development and sale of specialty tractors and fork lift trucks by the manufacturers of this equipment in western Ohio. Although most of Rubicon sales are tires for the small tractor industry and rubber specialty products, Rubicon has for the past two years taken contracts to manufacture small runs of regular automobile snow tires for Eastern Auto Stores, one of the larger distributors of auto replacement tires. These small contracts supplemented the larger ones placed with the major tire manufacturers elsewhere in Ohio. Those produced under the contracts bore the Eastern trademark and were to Eastern's specifications.

Rubicon has found it advantageous to take these short lead-time contracts to utilize surplus capacity. (Expansion of plant and facilities in 1967 had left Rubicon with excess capacity that was expected to be fully utilized in time.) Normal production planning allows tire machine utilization to be determined relatively accurately eight months in advance.

The contract with Eastern calls for a staged delivery schedule of the two types of snow tires over the three summer months as indicated in Exhibit 1. The major problem in planning the production of these tires is the availability of sufficient tire machine capacity to ensure that the contract can be satisfied. Only two types of machines could potentially be used in molding tires of the sort covered by the contract, the Wheeling and Regal machines. Virtually no time is available on either type machine until the first of June. After that time unused capacity is available spasmodically between other contracts. A table of anticipated machine availability as prepared by Joe Tabler, the production supervisor, is shown in Exhibit 2.

The two types of molding machines are similar except for their speeds. That the Wheeling machine is somewhat faster for both types of tires than the older Regal machine is shown by the production figures of Exhibit 3. This has tended to complicate production planning in previous years.

There is also a difference in productivity between nylon and fiberglass. This is due primarily to mold fastenings. The molds for the nylon tires are somewhat more

EXHIBIT 1 Delivery Schedule

Date	Nylon	Fiberglass
June 30	4,000	1,000
July 31	8,000	5,000
August 31	3,000	5,000
Total	15,000	11,000

EXHIBIT 2 Molding Machine Production Hours Available

	Wheeling Machine	Regal Machine
June	700	1,500
July	300	400
August	1,000	300

EXHIBIT 3 Production
Capacity in Hours/Tire by Type
Machine for Each Tire

	Nylon	*Fiberglass*
Wheeling machine	.15	.12
Regal machine	.16	.14

difficult to work with than those used for fiberglass tires. Since Eastern provides the molds there is no easily made modification to basic equipment that is feasible in the short run. A machine shop modification could be made to improve efficiency, but it has never seemed practical in view of the short-time duration of the contract.

Costs (shown in Exhibit 4) have been prepared by the accounting department for use in production planning. The difference in costs between the two machines shown in Exhibit 4 was due primarily to a difference in initial equipment purchase price. Material costs for the nylon tire were estimated to be $3.10 and for the fiberglass tire $3.90. Finishing, packaging, and shipping were not expected to exceed 23 cents per tire. Costs were based on actual costs last year adjusted for price increases.

Warehouse space was not expected to be available within the company, since inventory would be at a seasonal high and the company would be receiving materials for fall production of new tractor tires. However, tires could be stored at a local warehouse at a cost of approximately 10 cents per tire per month. There was a storage area adjacent to the production shop where up to one month's production could be kept until delivered to the warehouse or to Eastern. Monthly storage costs at the warehouse were assessed on the tires as they were placed into storage and space had to be reserved ahead of time. Shipping was scheduled three days prior to the end of the month for delivery the last day of the month.

THE DECISION PROBLEM

As Mr. Nelson sat down he pulled the Eastern Auto file from his briefcase and thought back over the short meeting with Jim Leader that he had managed to squeeze in before rushing to the airport. He had assigned the job of planning the production schedule to Jim even though he was new with the company, because Jim was bright and appeared to be an independent thinker. Since time was short Mr. Nelson remembered the misgivings he had experienced when he found that Jim had formulated the problem as a linear program. Now he was forced to think back to his own exposure to this subject in his attempt to understand what Jim had done. At the same time he remembered that he had often thought the problem "looked like" a programming

EXHIBIT 4 Production Planning
Costs by Machine Type

Wheeling Machine

Initial cost: $50,000
Depreciation method: Straight line
Life: 5 years

Machine amortization	$ 4.17/hr
Operating labor	3.75/hr
Supervision	0.25/hr
Overhead	2.00/hr
Total	$10.07/hr

Regal Machine

Initial cost: $45,000
Depreciation method: Straight line
Life: 5 years

Machine amortization	$ 3.75/hr
Operating labor	3.75/hr
Supervision	0.25/hr
Overhead	2.00/hr
Total	$ 9.75/hr

---

problem but there never seemed to be time to work out the details. Jim had prepared a short memo attached to the computer output which Mr. Nelson planned to study (see Exhibit 5).

He also thought back to the meeting with Tabler. Tabler had mentioned when he produced his equipment schedule that an additional Wheeling tire machine was due to arrive the last of August. For a $200 fee it could be expedited to arrive a month earlier. Tabler had estimated that early arrival would make available 172 additional hours of Wheeling machine time in August.

Normally, vacations were scheduled during the three summer months with approximately one-third of the staff gone during each month. Mr. Nelson felt he would be able to put together the required manpower, though it would almost inevitably involve delaying some vacations until Christmas and hiring a few temporary men. Providing supervisory staff would present similar problems.

About one-half of overhead costs was equipment depreciation and the other half was due to office expense. Overhead was allocated on the basis of direct labor and amounted to 50% of labor and supervision. The company had not computerized its clerical operations, so the presence of the Eastern contract would call for considerable office work.

As he prepared to go over the material, Mr. Nelson ticked off in his mind a few of the things that he would like to have at the conclusion of his analysis, whether or not he found Jim's L.P. approach satisfactory.

1. A summary of costs and revenues that he could show his boss John Toms, President of Rubicon, when he returned from the meeting with Eastern.
2. Materials for drafting a memo to Joe Tabler, telling him which machines to schedule for what, when, and whether to expedite the new machine.
3. A schedule of warehouse needs so that he could reserve space at the Bekson Warehousing Company.
4. A tentative schedule for the maintenance department indicating when the yearly maintenance check on the various machines could be performed.

One final worry he hoped to resolve before going into the meeting involved what his strategy should be if Eastern asked for more fiberglass tires. The Eastern representative to whom he had talked on the telephone the previous day had suggested that Eastern just might want more since sales had been very good the previous year. As he turned to the task of analysis, he noted the weather outside and thought to himself that if there were time due to delays in landing at the Kennedy Airport he would like to explain to himself what was going on with those dual variables, but the other matters seemed more important at the moment.

EXHIBIT 5

Memorandum

TO: George Nelson
FROM: Jim Leader
SUBJECT: Scheduling for Eastern Auto Tire Contract

I have formulated the equipment and scheduling problem for this contract as a linear programming problem. I could see that there was not time to do what you wanted without taking this approach and also I believe the answers to be better than I could do by hand.

The problem is one of minimizing the cost of producing and storing tires. (See the L. P. Tableau of Attachment 1).

From the Tableau you can see that there are two kinds of choice variables:

1. The number of each type tire to be scheduled on the Wheeling machine and the number on the Regal machine in each month.

I have designated these as follows:

W_n = Number of nylon tires to be produced on the Wheeling machine.
W_g = Number of fiberglass tires to be produced on the Wheeling machine.
R_n = Number of nylon tires to be produced on the Regal machine.
R_g = Number of fiberglass tires to be produced on the Regal machine.

EXHIBIT 5 (Continued)

2. The number of each type placed to be in inventory at the end of the month.

For the inventory variables:

I_n = Number of nylon tires to be carried into inventory at the end of each month.

I_g = Number of fiberglass tires to be carried into inventory at the end of each month.

Note that I have used the subscripts n = nylon and g = fiberglass. I have also used superscripts above the numbers to indicate the month since most of the variables are defined in all three time periods; 1 = June, 2 = July, and 3 = August.

Thus, the variable W_g^3 stands for the number of fiberglass tires to be produced in August on the Wheeling machine. (Please note that these superscripts are a symbolic way of distinguishing between the months; W_g^3 does *not* mean raise W_g to the third power.)

The constraints are of two types:

1. The constraints on the available machine time in each month, and
2. Demand or delivery constraints in each month.

To determine the machine availability constraint in each month, I took the number of nylon tires made on Wheeling equipment times the hours per nylon tire plus the number of fiberglass tires made on Wheeling equipment times the hours per fiberglass tire. This gives the total number of Wheeling machine hours for the month which must be less than the Wheeling hours available in that month. For July:

$$.15 \, W_n^2 + .12 \, W_g^2 \leq 300 = \text{availability of Wheeling hours in July.}$$

The demand constraints stipulate that the tires produced in a month plus the tires in inventory from the last month less the amount returned to inventory at the end of this month must equal the amount demanded in that month. Thus, for July the nylon tire equation is:

$$W_n^2 + R_n^2 + I_n^1 - I_n^2 = 8,000 = \text{the demand for nylon tires in July.}$$

The program seeks to minimize the total cost* of operating the tire machines and storing inventory over the entire three-month period. The computer output for the problem is shown in Attachment 2. For your convenience, I have also indicated the principal results from the computer output on the Tableau itself.

---

* The costs of operating the tire machines are taken to be the sum of operating cost and supervision plus half the overhead charge.

ATTACHMENT 1 The Linear Programming Tableau*

	JUNE — Nylon W_n^1	Nylon R_n^1	Glass W_g^1	Glass R_g^1	Inventory I_n^1	Inventory I_g^1	JULY — Nylon W_n^2	Nylon R_n^2	Glass W_g^2	Glass R_g^2	Inventory I_n^2	Inventory I_g^2	AUGUST — Nylon W_n^3	Nylon R_n^3	Glass W_g^3	Glass R_g^3		RHS	Dual Variables
MACHINE — June — Wheeling	.15		.12														≤	700	.333
June — Regal		.16		.14													≤	1500	1.166
TIME — July — Wheeling							.15		.12								≤	300	.625
July — Regal								.16		.14							≤	400	.333
CONSTRAINTS — Aug. — Wheeling													.15		.12		≤	1000	.8
Aug. — Regal														.16		.14	≤	300	.64
DEMAND — June — Nylon	1	1			−1												=	4000	.8
June — Glass			1	1		−1											=	1000	.64
July — Nylon					1		1	1			−1						=	8000	.9
July — Glass						1			1	1		−1					=	5000	.74
CONSTRAINTS — Aug. — Nylon											1		1	1			=	3000	.8
Aug. — Glass												1			1	1	=	5000	.64
OBJECTIVE	.75	.80	.60	.70	.10	.10	.75	.80	.60	.70	.10	.10	.75	.80	.60	.70		Minimum	
OPTIMAL SOLUTION	1866.6	7633.3	3500.00		5499.9	2500.0	2500.7		2499.9				2666.6	333.3	5000.0			Opt. Value of Objective $19173.33	

* All blanks are zeros.

ATTACHMENT 2

LP OPTIMUM FOUND AT STEP   18

OBJECTIVE FUNCTION VALUE

1)   19173.3300

VARIABLE	VALUE	REDUCED COST
W1N	1866.666000	.000000
R1N	7633.333000	.000000
W1G	3500.000000	.000000
R1G	.000000	.060000
I1N	5500.000000	.000000
I1G	2500.000000	.000000
W2N	.000000	.025000
R2N	2500.000000	.000000
W2G	2500.000000	.000000
R2G	.000000	.047500
I2N	.000000	.200000
I2G	.000000	.200000
W3N	2666.667000	.000000
R3N	333.333500	.000000
W3G	5000.000000	.000000
R3G	.000000	.060000

ROW	SLACK OR SURPLUS	DUAL PRICES
2)	.000000	.333333
3)	278.666600	.000000
4)	.000000	1.166667
5)	.000000	.625000
6)	.000000	.333333
7)	246.666600	.000000
8)	.000000	-.800000
9)	.000000	-.640000
10)	.000000	-.900000
11)	.000000	-.740000
12)	.000000	-.800000
13)	.000000	-.640000

NO. ITERATIONS=   18

ATTACHMENT 2 *(Continued)*

RANGES IN WHICH THE BASIS IS UNCHANGED

OBJ COEFFICIENT RANGES

VARIABLE	CURRENT COEF	ALLOWABLE INCREASE	ALLOWABLE DECREASE
W1N	.750000	.025000	.059375
R1N	.800000	.075000	.050000
W1G	.600000	.047500	.020000
R1G	.700000	INFINITY	.060000
I1N	.100000	.025000	.054286
I1G	.100000	.047500	.020000
W2N	.750000	INFINITY	.025000
R2N	.800000	.054286	INFINITY
W2G	.600000	.020000	INFINITY
R2G	.700000	INFINITY	.047500
I2N	.100000	INFINITY	.200000
I2G	.100000	INFINITY	.200000
W3N	.750000	.050000	.075000
R3N	.800000	.075000	.050000
W3G	.600000	.060000	INFINITY
R3G	.700000	INFINITY	.060000

RIGHTHAND SIDE RANGES

ROW	CURRENT RHS	ALLOWABLE INCREASE	ALLOWABLE DECREASE
2	700.000000	1145.000000	261.250000
3	1500.000000	INFINITY	278.666600
4	300.000000	300.000000	261.250000
5	400.000000	880.000000	278.666600
6	1000.000000	50.000030	231.250000
7	300.000000	INFINITY	246.666600
8	4000.000000	1741.667000	7633.333000
9	1000.000000	2177.083000	3500.000000
10	8000.000000	1741.667000	5500.000000
11	5000.000000	2177.083000	2500.000000
12	3000.000000	1541.667000	333.333500
13	5000.000000	1927.083000	416.666900

CITY OF CENTERVILLE

Early in May Bruce Forsyth of Ripley Bros., Inc., noticed an announcement in the *Daily Bond Buyer* that Centerville was once again going to the public market to raise $20,000,000 through an issue of serial public improvement bonds. As was the case with past Centerville issues, the choice of underwriter was to be made on the basis of sealed competitive bids for the entire issue, the bids to be opened on Thursday, June 11, 1978. The bonds would go to the bidder with the coupon schedule representing the lowest net interest (NIC) to Centerville. (The appendix describes NIC.) Ripley Bros., as a matter of course, considered all municipal issues of one million dollars or more in order to decide to either form a bidding syndicate or to join a syndicate headed by another firm. Consequently, Bruce wrote immediately to Centerville requesting a copy of the invitation to bid.

Bruce spent most of that morning reacquainting himself with the various municipal issues on which his firm had bid in recent years. He found bids on several Centerville issues over the years. On the majority of these occasions, Ripley Bros. had been a major bracket participant in a syndicate headed by the Southern Oregon Trust Company. Bruce was not in the least surprised, therefore, when later that week he received a letter from Southern Oregon, again inviting Ripley Bros. to be a major bracket participant in a syndicate formed to bid on this latest Centerville issue.

A preliminary pricing meeting was scheduled for Tuesday, June 2 at Southern Oregon's headquarters. Each member of the syndicate, in formulating pricing ideas to be discussed at this meeting, was expected to have analyzed specific characteristics of the Centerville issue and more general information related to current status of the bond market.

After he received Southern Oregon's invitation, Bruce began to consider current trends in bond prices, yields, and market receptivity to new issues. Two of the most important barometers of the status of the bond market were the size of the current floating supply of municipal bonds available in the secondary market and the visible supply of new municipal issues coming to the market within the next thirty days. Bruce found, however, that neither factor (alone or when considered together) indicated an unusual situation which required any special pricing considerations.

In addition to the aggregate supply of bonds, Bruce also reviewed the current reoffering yields on bonds of various maturities already on the market. In conjunction with a bond buyer index of the average 20-year maturity yields for a selected group of securities, he developed what he thought the yield curve for the Centerville issue should be.

On the afternoon of June 2, Bruce arrived at Southern Oregon's headquarters for the general syndicate pricing meeting. After some discussion, it became apparent that

Source: Copyright © 1978 by the President and Fellows of Harvard College. This case was prepared by Roy D. Shapiro as a basis for class discussion rather than to illustrate effective or ineffective handling of an administrative situation. Reprinted by permission of the Harvard Business School.

TABLE 1

Year	Reoffering Yield
1	3.10%
2	3.35
3	3.55
4	3.75
5	3.95
6	4.10
7	4.20
8	4.30
9	4.35
10	4.45
11	4.55
12	4.65
13	4.75
14	4.85
15	4.90
16	4.95
17	5.00
18	5.00
19	5.05
20	5.05

there was some divergence of opinion between various underwriters as to both what the proposed yield and the appropriate spread[1] should be.

Early in the meeting it was announced by Jerry Lerman of Southern Oregon that another major syndicate had been formed by the Valley Bank and Trust Company to bid on the Centerville issue. The underwriters agreed that this information necessitated contemplation of a more aggressive bid (i.e., lower NIC) than many of them had considered in their initial pricing analysis.

Discussions continued for the rest of the afternoon and finally the group agreed on the reoffering schedule outlined above in Table 1 and a gross underwriters' spread of $15 per $1,000 bond.

With the reoffering schedule agreed upon, all that remained to be done at the pricing meeting was to establish a coupon schedule to yield the lowest possible net interest cost to Centerville. Appropriate to this discussion, Jerry Lerman announced the restrictions that Centerville had communicated to him with regard to coupons, bid premiums and discounts. First it had been decided that due to the difficulty of placing them in the market, they would accept no discounted bonds.[2] Second, there was to be

---

[1] Underwriters' profit.

[2] Bonds which had coupon rates lower than the reoffering yields at which they were planned to sell.

an upper limit on the premium for which any bond could sell. This limit was set at 8.5% above par.[3] Furthermore, the gross receipts to Centerville after underwriters' profit was to be at least the par value of the issue. These constraints together with the proposed spread of $15 per $1,000 bond provided the context in which the syndicate could develop a bid with the lowest net interest cost to Centerville.

APPENDIX

Municipal bonds are generally sold on a serial basis. That is, a $20-million, 20-year issue normally consists of 20 separate groups of $1 million in bonds. Each group has its own coupon (interest) rate and its own maturity. The municipality pays interest semi-annually at half the coupon rate until the bond matures, at which time the par value of the bond is repaid to the investor.

Under the net interest cost (NIC) method a municipality minimizes the net interest it will pay. Net interest cost is defined as the total of interest payments less an adjustment for proceeds at the time of issue. This adjustment is equal to the gross proceeds from the issue less par value and the underwriters' spread (profit).

Exhibits 1 and 2 show net interest cost calculations for a previous Centerville issue of $38 million over a 20-year period, on which the underwriters took $13 per $1000 bond. As Exhibit 2 suggests, there are many possible coupon schedules given a reoffering yield schedule and an underwriters' spread. Centerville's policy has been to select the coupon schedule with the lowest NIC (Column D in Exhibit 2). As is evident from these examples, the time value of money is not considered in the NIC calculations.

[3] E.g., no $100 face value bond could have a coupon such that the bond would sell for more than $108.50.

EXHIBIT 1 Production and Net Interest Cost

(1) Years To Maturity	(2) Number Of Bonds	(3) Reoffering Yield	(4) Coupon	(5) Price Of Bond	(6) Production (5) × (2)	(7) Bond Years	(8) Interest Payments
1 (1971)	1,900	5.40%	6¾%	101.30%	$ 1,924,700	1900	$ 128,250
2	1,900	5.50	6¾	102.34	1,944,460	3800	256,500
3	1,900	5.60	6¾	103.14	1,959,660	5700	384,750
4	1,900	5.65	6¾	103.89	1,973,910	7600	513,000
5 (1975)	1,900	5.70	6¾	104.51	1,985,690	9500	641,250
6	1,900	5.80	6¾	104.76	1,990,440	11400	769,500
7	1,900	5.85	6¾	105.11	1,997,090	13300	897,750
8	1,900	5.90	6¾	105.36	2,001,840	15200	1,026,000
9	1,900	5.95	6¾	105.51	2,004,690	17100	1,154,250
10 (1980)	1,900	6.00	6¾	105.58	2,006,020	19000	1,282,500
11	1,900	6.00	6¾	105.98	2,013,620	20900	1,410,750
12	1,900	6.05	6¾	105.91	2,012,290	22800	1,539,000
13	1,900	6.10	6¾	105.78	2,009,820	24700	1,667,250
14	1,900	6.15	6¾	105.58	2,006,020	26600	1,795,500
15 (1985)	1,900	6.20	6¾	105.32	2,001,080	28500	1,923,750
16	1,900	6.25	6¾	105.01	1,995,190	30400	2,052,000
17	1,900	6.30	6¾	104.65	1,988,350	32300	2,180,250
18	1,900	6.30	6¾	104.80	1,991,200	34200	2,308,500
19	1,900	6.70	4	71.22	1,353,180	36100	1,444,000
20 (1990)	1,900	6.70	4	70.49	1,339,310	38000	1,520,000
	38,000				$38,498,560	399000	$24,894,750

Gross Production	$38,498,560		Gross Interest Cost	$24,894,750
Par Value	38,000,000		Adjustment	4,560
Premium	498,560		Net Interest Cost	$24,890,190
Spread ($13 × 38,000)	494,000		Bond years	399,000
Adjustment	4,560		NIC/Bond yr.	$62.38
			NIC rate	6.238%

EXHIBIT 2

(1) Year To Maturity	(2) Number Of Bonds	(3) Reoffering Yields	(4) Bond Years	Alternative Coupon Selections			
				A Coupon	B Coupon	C Coupon	D Coupon
1 (1971)	1900	5.40%	1900	6¾%	6¾%	6½%	7%
2	1900	5.50	3800	6¾	6¾	6½	7
3	1900	5.60	5700	6¾	6¾	6½	7
4	1900	5.65	7600	6¾	6¾	6½	7
5 (1975)	1900	5.70	9500	6¾	6¾	6½	7
6	1900	5.80	11400	6¾	6¾	6½	7
7	1900	5.85	13300	6¾	6¾	6½	7
8	1900	5.90	15200	6¾	6¾	6½	7
9	1900	5.95	17100	6¾	6¾	6½	7
10 (1980)	1900	6.00	19000	6¾	6¾	6½	7
11	1900	6.00	20900	6¾	6¾	6½	7
12	1900	6.05	22800	6¾	6¾	6½	7
13	1900	6.10	24700	6¾	6¾	6½	7
14	1900	6.15	26600	6¾	6¾	6½	7
15 (1985)	1900	6.20	28500	6¾	6¾	6½	7
16	1900	6.25	30400	6¾	6¾	6½	7
17	1900	6.30	32300	6¾	6¾	6½	7
18	1900	6.30	34200	6¾	5	6½	7
19	1900	6.70	36100	4	5	5½	2¾
20 (1990)	1900	6.70	38000	4	5	5½	2¾

Gross Production (000)				38,499	38,555	38,544	38,556
Net Interest Cost (000)				24,890	24,976	25,144	24,719
Net Interest Cost Rate				6.238%	6.275%	6.314%	6.210%
Bond with Maximum Premium							
(a) Maturity (year)				1981	1981	1981	1982
(b) Value (% Face Value of Bond)				105.98%	105.98%	103.98%	108.02%
Bond with Maximum Discount							
(a) Maturity (year)				1990	1990	1990	1990
(b) Value (% Face Value of Bond)				70.49%	81.42%	86.88%	56.83%

HUNT-WESSON FOODS, INC.*

In late 1971, Mr. Steven Niino, Manager of Operations Research at Hunt-Wesson Foods, Inc., met with Professor Arthur Geoffrion, a consultant from the Graduate School of Management of UCLA, to initiate a comprehensive distribution planning project. In the previous few years, the company had faced pressing distribution-center expansion and relocation problems, and rather than make a series of smaller regional decisions, management had made a commitment to a computer-based model which would rebalance the company's entire distribution system. This involved the potential relocation of distribution centers, reassignment of customers to the centers, and the determination of how products would flow through the system.

The end result of this study was a large-scale mixed integer programming model which has served throughout the 1970's as the major tool for Hunt-Wesson's warehouse location and distribution planning decisions. The cost savings attributable to this model have been estimated to be greater than $1,000,000 annually.

HISTORY OF HUNT-WESSON FOODS, INC.

Hunt-Wesson Foods, Inc. is a subsidiary of Hunt Foods and Industries, Inc., formed by a merger between Hunt Foods and Industries, Inc. and Wesson Oil and Snowdrift Co., Inc. on June 30, 1960. Wesson's nationally branded food products such as Wesson vegetable oil and Snowdrift, a premium quality solid shortening, provided Hunt Foods and Industries, Inc. with additional well-known products to complement the Hunt brand name and add balance and diversification. In addition, Wesson's direct sales organization, with distribution to institutions, industrial customers, and retail outlets, provided economies of scale as well as very promising areas for increasing Hunt's marketing efforts.

Hunt Foods and Industries, Inc. began as Hunt Brothers Fruit Packing Company, a small regional food processor formed in 1890. By 1943, the firm had grown to approximately $10 million in sales, and the company began a series of acquisitions and mergers with the express purpose of promoting additional brand recognition for their products. Between 1943 and 1956, Hunt purchased or merged with several

---

* Much of the information contained herein was obtained from the several excellent articles written by Professor Arthur Geoffrion, "Multicommodity System Design by Benders Decomposition" written with G. W. Graves, *Management Science,* January 1974; "A Guide to Computer-Assisted Methods for Distribution Systems Planning," *Sloan Management Review,* Winter 1975; and "Better Distribution Planning with Computer Models," *Harvard Business Review,* July-August 1976. Special thanks are due to Mr. Robert Lowery and other members of Hunt-Wesson management for their cooperation and willingness to provide additional information for this case.

Source: Copyright © 1978 by the President and Fellows of Harvard College. This case was prepared by Roy D. Shapiro as a basis for class discussion rather than to illustrate effective or ineffective handling of an administrative situation. Reprinted by permission of the Harvard Business School.

other food producers/processors and in 1955 acquired Glass Containers, Inc. to produce containers for Hunt's products. In 1956 Hunt Foods, Inc. (the name was changed in 1945) acquired the Ohio Match Company, and in 1957 the name was changed to Hunt Foods and Industries, Inc. By 1960, Hunt had sales of $164 million and net income of $3 million and was engaged directly or through its subsidiaries in processing, manufacturing, packaging, and selling tomato products, specialty fruits and vegetables, cans, glasses, and can-making machinery, and in manufacturing and leasing peach-pitters.

Wesson Oil and Snowdrift Co., Inc. was the product of a 1925 merger of three companies, the largest of which was the Southern Cotton Oil Company. Between 1925 and 1960 the company rapidly expanded both through internal growth and by merger and acquisition. By 1959 Wesson had sales of $147 million and a net income of $6.1 million, fully owned seven subsidiaries, and had a controlling interest in three others. Wesson and its subsidiaries manufactured and packaged a wide variety of food products, including vegetable oil, shortening, margarine, mayonnaise, salad dressing, seafood, and vegetables.

After the merger the firm grew rapidly, and in 1968 Hunt Foods and Industries, Inc. merged with Canada Dry Corporation and McCall Corporation to form Norton-Simon, Inc. Since 1968 Hunt-Wesson has continued to grow both internally and through acquisitions (in 1970, Reddi-Wip was acquired), and by 1975 the food and service divisions of Norton-Simon, Inc. (primarily Hunt-Wesson) had sales and profit before taxes of approximately $848 million and $55 million respectively (see Exhibit 1).

THE DISTRIBUTION SYSTEM IN 1970

In 1970, Hunt-Wesson Foods, Inc. manufactured foods at 12 locations (Exhibit 2) consisting of Wesson refineries and Hunt canneries. National distribution from factories to customers was accomplished through 10 distribution centers (Exhibit 2) by rail and by common and contract truck carriers. For large customers, it was possible to eliminate the distribution center and transport directly by making use of a storage-in-transit privilege accorded by the rail carriers. The company's policy dictated that each

EXHIBIT 1 Food and Food Service Divisions Sales and Profit before Tax for the Years 1971–1975* ($ in 000's)

	1971	1972	1973	1974	1975
Sales	481,414	510,965	551,909	683,041	847,962
Profit before tax	32,268	32,772	32,633	28,152	55,362

* 1975 annual report of Norton Simon, Inc.

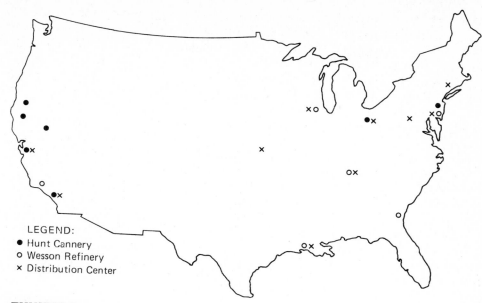

EXHIBIT 2

customer be serviced by a single distribution center. In addition to simplifying accounting and marketing functions and making customer inquiries easier to process, this policy offered several opportunities to take advantage of economies of scale through lower bulk shipping rates.

The firm's continued rapid growth had made it imperative that several distribution centers (DC's) be expanded or relocated and, in addition, the rail carriers' recent pricing policies permitted rate reductions (savings of approximately $.50 per hundred weight) whenever one million pounds or more were shipped via eight or more boxcars on the same train. In view of these developments, Hunt-Wesson's management sought a means of coordinating future expansions of the distribution system and of finding the least cost strategy for expansion. Initially, a "National Distribution Taskforce" was established, consisting of representatives of the Operations Planning, Traffic, Marketing and Distribution Departments. This taskforce recognized that the current method of doing a number of case studies of individual distribution centers was clearly sub-optimal and began searching for techniques to allow them to construct a medium-range (1–3 years) planning model which would interweave the complexities of the distribution process nationally.

Several experts in distribution systems were consulted. An early suggestion by one of these experts was a "planning board." This analog device was a large wooden board with holes drilled at each customer location. Strings between holes represented the varying distances (approximating transportation charges), and weights hung on pulleys at each "customer" represented demand. The board would then be shaken, the weights would fall, and a central knot would appear—the optimal location for the DC to service that set of customer demands. Unfortunately, however, this method posed a serious drawback—it required that the U.S. be divided into sections; the planning board would then find the optimal DC for each section, one at a time. Since this sectioning operation could be done in any number of ways, there was no assurance that the DC locations proposed by the planning board were optimal when taken in total.

An effort was then made to formulate the problem as a linear program, but this methodology also had serious limitations due to considerations such as mandatory service area constraints (i.e., no customer can deal with more than one DC), and the multicommodity aspect of the problem. At the same time, Hunt-Wesson's Director of Distribution recalled that Professor Arthur Geoffrion of UCLA's Graduate School of Management had been doing research on optimal distribution systems. He contacted Geoffrion and found that Hunt-Wesson's problem meshed quite well with Geoffrion's research, but that the problem was initially too large for Dr. Geoffrion to solve. At this point in time, early 1970, a new group was formed within Hunt-Wesson's Corporate Facilities Planning Department, the Operations Research Department. The OR group's first task was to work with Professor Geoffrion and determine whether a mathematical programming approach might be expected to yield a systematic and cost-effective solution to the problem of DC location and distribution. The verdict was affirmative.

DEVELOPMENT OF THE MODEL

In early 1971, a team was formed to develop a distribution model along the guidelines proposed by Professor Geoffrion. This team consisted of staff members from various corporate groups: Information Systems and Services (ISS); Distribution and Logistics Accounting; Distribution; Traffic; and Corporate Facilities Planning. The specific questions that management wanted the model to address were:

How many distribution centers should there be?

In which cities would they be located?

What size should each distribution center be?

How should each plant's output of each product be allocated among distribution centers or customers?

What should the annual transportation flows throughout the system be?

For a given level of customer service, how do the costs of the distribution system compare with a projection of the current system to the target period?

A summary of the model's constraints, assumptions, and simplifications is given in Exhibit 3.

EXHIBIT 3 Summary of the Model's Facts and Assumptions

1. The many hundreds of Hunt-Wesson's different products are aggregated into 17 product groups. Nearly all products in a given group are similar with respect to the plants which can make them, the production technology by which they are made, and their gross-to-net shipping weight ratios. All quantities are measured in gross shipping hundredweight (cwt.). Examples of the product groups are: bottled cooking oil, packaged shortenings, ketchup, tomato sauces, puddings, and matches.

2. The production capacity (cwt./yr.) of each of the company's 14 plants is given for each product group. Not every plant could make every group—in fact, only about 50 plant-product group combinations were possible.

3. Distribution center locations to be evaluated by the model are limited to a list of 45 cities composed of current locations, major metropolitan demand concentrations, the locations of major competitors' distribution centers, and other gateway cities.

4. The size of each distribution center chosen by the model must be between stipulated lower and upper limits expressed in terms of total annual throughput volume. The lower limit was due to the need to accommodate rail shipments of about eight boxcars, which permits important economies of scale.

5. The many thousands of individual customers are aggregated into 121 customer zones defined in terms of zip codes. The zones consist of a key city with a significant demand plus (usually) adjacent areas with relatively small associated demand. Each zone is efficiently small in geographical area so that the best distribution center for the key city is also the best one for the other customers in the zone.

6. The annual demand forecasted for each product group in each customer zone must be met. The demand forecasts were based on historical summaries prepared by computer from magnetic tape archives of shipment invoices. These tapes also included most of the information required to develop a realistic transportation cost structure.

7. Each customer must continue to be serviced from a single full-line distribution center for all products.

8. No distribution center location is allowed to service a customer zone unless it is sufficiently close to the zone that normal delivery time would be less than a specified maximum number of days. This maximum is the model's primary control over the level of customer service.

9. Differential production costs ($/cwt.) are given when there is a significant difference between unit costs at different plants for a given product group. Not to be overlooked among the reasons for differential production costs is the influence of plant location when it is significant in determining delivered raw material costs (as it was here in the case of refinery products).

EXHIBIT 3 *(Continued)*

10. The costs of each distribution center are expressed as a "fixed" charge if a location is selected for use by the model plus a "variable" cost ($/cwt.) applied to the total annual throughput volume over all product groups. These costs included all handling, storage, and other operating expenses, inventory carrying charges, and amortized capital costs associated with expanding an existing distribution center or acquiring a new one. A standard throughput cost curve like the hypothetical one shown in the figure was developed based on historical analysis of the current distribution centers' costs. This curve was then modified for each of the 45 locations to reflect geographical differences. A straight-line approximation proved adequate, although a more accurate broken-line approximation would have been used if necessary to portray economies and diseconomies of scale over the range of interest.

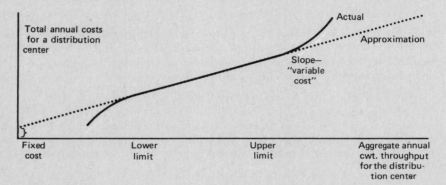

11. For each product group and possible plant-to-distribution center transportation link, a unit freight rate ($/cwt.) is specified. A judgment was made in each case whether truckload or rail carload lots were the most appropriate mode of supply.

12. For each product group and possible distribution center-to-customer zone link, a total annual freight cost ($) is specified. It made sense to specify an annual cost for a link, since each customer had to receive all of a product group from a given distribution center if he received any at all. Most of the delivery costs were generated by computer from specially constructed approximation tables, taking into account the proportions of mode (LTL, TL, CL) and shipment size likely to prevail in each case.

13. Transit rail rates are used whenever they are advantageous. The storage-in-transit rate applicable to some product groups is figured as though the shipment moves directly from plant to customer with a small charge for stopping over at the intermediate distribution center (so long as this stop is not too far off the direct line), instead of as the sum of the regular plant-to-distribution center and distribution center-to-customer rates.

Source: Reproduced with permission from Geoffrion, A. M., "Better Distribution Planning with Computer Models," *HBR*, July/August, 1976. p. 97.

Because it was impractical to expect the model to distribute each of the many hundred Hunt-Wesson products to the many thousand individual customers, some careful *aggregation* and *preselection* were required. The products were aggregated into 17 product groups; individual customers were aggregated into 121 zones based on the total demand associated with each zip code zone, its proximity to DC sites, and its proximity to demand concentrations. Since only a few plants would normally manufacture any one of the product groups, 49 plant-product group combinations were preselected from the 238 (14 plants × 17 product groups) theoretically possible. Possible DC's were limited to 45 preselected locations, including a "dummy" location to permit certain customers to receive commodities directly from the plant, making use of the applicable storage-in-transit rates. Lastly, from the possible 5445 (45 DC sites × 121 customer zones), 682 were preselected to be those in which the customer zone can be served by the DC with a certain maximum prescribed delay by rail or truck. These modeling specifications are described in Exhibit 3. Despite the simplifying effect of this aggregation and preselection, over 24,000 plant-product group-DC customer combinations were permissible, and from this group the model was to choose the optimal set.

THE MATHEMATICAL FORMULATION

A mixed integer program was formulated to minimize total distribution costs subject to the restrictions of Exhibit 3. The program determines which DC sites should be utilized, the optimal size of each DC, which customer zones should be served by each DC, and what the pattern of transportation flows should be for all commodities. The mathematical formulation follows.

DECISION VARIABLES

$x_{ijk\ell}$ — The amount of commodity i shipped from plant j through DC k to customer zone ℓ.

$y_{k\ell}$ — A 0–1 variable that will be 1 if DC k serves customer zone ℓ, and 0 otherwise.

z_k — A 0–1 variable that will be 1 if a DC is acquired at site k, and 0 otherwise.

THE OBJECTIVE FUNCTION

$$\text{Minimize} \sum_{ijk\ell} c_{ijk\ell} x_{ijk\ell} + \sum_{k} \left[f_k z_k + v_k \sum_{i\ell} D_{i\ell} y_{k\ell} \right]$$

for $x \geqq 0$; $y, z = 0, 1$;

where

c$_{ijk\ell}$ is the average unit cost of producing and shipping commodity i from plant j through DC k to customer zone ℓ,

f$_k$ is the fixed portion of the annual possession and operating costs for a DC at site k,

v$_k$ is the variable unit throughput cost for a DC at site k,

D$_{i\ell}$ is the demand for commodity i in customer zone ℓ.

THE CONSTRAINTS

1. $\sum_{k\ell} x_{ijk\ell} \leq S_{ij}$ for all i, j

where S$_{ij}$ is the production capacity for commodity i at j.

2. $\sum_{j} x_{ijk\ell} = D_{i\ell} y_{k\ell}$ for all i, k, ℓ.

3. $\sum_{k} y_{k\ell} = 1$ for all ℓ.

4. $\underline{V}_k z_k \leq \sum_{i\ell} D_{i\ell} y_{k\ell} \leq \overline{V}_k z_k$ for all k,

where $\underline{V}_k$ and $\overline{V}_k$ are, respectively, the minimum and maximum total annual throughput for a DC at site k.

5. Also, linear configuration constraints on y and/or z, e.g., to ensure that at most *one* DC is opened at each site; upper and/or lower bounds on the total number of DCs allowed, etc.

DATA COLLECTION

The collection and development of the data required by the model was (and remains) a considerable task, requiring the efforts of much of the OR group over a three- to four-month period.

The 49 capacity figures (S$_{ij}$) were developed individually based on existing capacities and anticipated changes. To collect the demand data, the firm, fortunately, had the previous year's shipment invoices stored on magnetic tape. The historical demands were calculated using the customer zones' zip codes, the individual commodity codes, and gross shipping weight. The demands (D$_{i\ell}$) could then be obtained by projecting the historical demands forward in time according to the company's market forecast. The upper and lower bounds ($\overline{V}_k$ and $\underline{V}_k$) on warehouse size were based on management's experience with the present distribution system. The corresponding fixed and variable cost coefficients (f$_k$ and v$_k$) were determined by developing a function W$_k$(w) (as pictured in Exhibit 3) defined as the total warehousing costs associated with leasing and operating a DC at site k with an annual throughput of w hundredweight per year. These $W_k(w)$s were estimated by fitting a linear approximation of the form

$$W_k(w) = f_k + v_k w$$

over the range $\underline{V_k}$ and $\overline{V_k}$ using linear regression.

Specifying the transportation costs ($c_{ijk\ell}$) was a complex task. As described above, the over 24,000 allowable $ijk\ell$ combinations had to be identified through a process of aggregation and preselection. Then, for each combination, it had to be determined by hand when the rail transit privilege applied. This privilege applies when the DC is not too far off the most direct rail route between plant and customer and permits substantial savings over simply adding the plant-DC and DC-customer rail rates. When the in-transit rate does *not* apply, $c_{ijk\ell}$ is the sum of a plant-DC rate and a DC-customer zone rate. For each plant-DC combination, everything moves either by rail or by truck. The DC-customer zone rates, however, involve both rail and truck shipping. The truck-load rate and rail rates were generated from tables and a weighted average of the sub-rates was then taken to obtain each DC-customer zone rate with the weights based on past experience of mode and shipment size for each demand center.

When the transit rate did apply, $c_{ijk\ell}$ was taken to be a weighted average of the appropriate transit rate (computed from tables) and the non-transit rate. There is always some non-transit truck shipping even when the transit privilege is applicable, since not all customers accept direct rail shipments.

Considerable effort was made to ensure that the required data was both correctly developed and correctly transferred to the data sets that would be accessed by the main computer program. The S_{ij}, $\underline{V_k}$, $\overline{V_k}$, f_k, and v_k coefficients were sufficiently few in number that they could be individually audited and entered manually into the program. The demand and shipping cost data, however, was of such a large volume that verification posed a problem. This data was transmitted on magnetic tapes, which then had to undergo considerable preprocessing in order to set up the properly indexed data sets required by the main program. Numerous editing and checking routines were among the programs which produced the demand and rate tapes, and further verification was done during the preprocessing. Selected and random samples were subjected to manual checking as well.

Final validation was done by carrying out a number of runs with many of the variables locked at particular values. The output was then scrutinized for anomalous or seemingly unreasonable results that might be indicative of inaccurate data or program malfunction.

RANCHO SHOPPING CENTER (A)

Anderson Associates of Burlingame, California, performs general construction work. In April 1980 the company had four jobs in progress: two twelve-family apartment houses, a gas station, and a four-store addition to the Rancho Shopping Center in Livermore.

The owner of the shopping center, Mr. Puckett, had recently returned from Akron, Ohio, where he had discussed with the executives of a large tire company the possibility of opening a tire sales and service shop in his shopping center. Mr. Puckett decided that a tire shop would be a profitable addition to his shopping center, and on the morning of April 2, 1980, he decided to proceed at once to arrange for the construction of a suitable building to house the tire shop in one corner of the shopping center parking lot. He then called Mr. Anderson, the president of Anderson Associates, to arrange a meeting to discuss plans for the building. During their meeting Mr. Puckett and Mr. Anderson agreed that a suitable building for the new tire shop would be a one-story frame structure somewhat similar in design to the gas station that Anderson Associates had under construction at that time.

Although the time was short, Mr. Puckett was anxious to have the tire shop building finished by the time the addition to the shopping center was completed. He felt that the grand opening of the tire shop should be tied in with the opening of the four stores in the new addition. The construction schedule for the addition, which was easily being met, indicated that the shopping center addition would be completed in 58 working days after April 2.

Following his meeting with the shopping center owner, Mr. Anderson spoke with Mr. Montero, Anderson Associates' planning specialist. Realizing time was short, Mr. Anderson asked Mr. Montero to plan the construction schedule for the tire shop building. Mr. Montero was instructed to use the plans and costs of the gas station under construction as guidelines for his preliminary planning of the tire shop.

In his initial analysis of the problem Mr. Montero noted the following relationships generally found in construction of this type:

1. A preliminary set of specifications would have to be completed before work could begin on the set of blueprints and before the foundation excavation could begin. After the excavation was completely finished the foundation could be poured. Installation of the automobile lifts could not begin until after the foundation was poured.

2. The preparation of the bill of materials would have to be deferred until the final set of blueprints was prepared. When the bill of materials was completed it would be used to prepare order invoices for lumber and other items. Construction of the frame could not begin until the lumber had arrived at the construction site and the foundation had been poured.

3. After the frame was completed, electrical work, erection of wallboard, plumbing, installation of millwork, and installation of siding could begin.

4. Painting of the interior could not start until the wallboard had been installed.

EXHIBIT 1

	Activity	Expected Completion Time under Normal Cost Conditions (Working Days)
A	Prepare preliminary specifications	10
B	Excavate foundation	5
C	Pour foundation	6
D	Electric work	5
E	Install wallboard	4
F	Plumbing	6
G	Install auto lifts	4
H	Paint interior walls	5
I	Millwork	8
J	Trim installation	5
K	Erect frame and roof	15
L	Final interior decoration	6
M	Installation of siding	7
N	Paint exterior	7
O	Blueprints finalized	5
P	Prepare bill of materials and order invoices	3
Q	Time required to receive lumber after order is sent	10
R	Window and exterior door installation	4

The wallboard installation could not be started until the plumbing and electrical work was completed.

5. The final interior decorating work could not begin until the interior walls were painted and the trim installed. Installation of the trim could not begin until the millwork was completely installed.

6. Painting of the building's exterior could not proceed until the windows and exterior doors were installed. Installation of the windows and doors, in turn, could not start until the siding was in place.

After studying the plans and construction schedule of the gas station under construction, Mr. Montero developed some estimates of the time required to complete each step of the building of the tire shop. These estimates appear in Exhibit 1 and in most cases were given to Mr. Montero by the foreman of the gas station job.

Mr. Montero desperately needed answers to the following questions:

1. Without reducing the time to do any activity, how long should the project take?
2. The activities involving electrical work, plumbing, millwork, and trim are subcontracted. At what date should he schedule the activities? What flexibility does Anderson have in scheduling the subcontractors? (This problem was becoming

acute because the subcontractors Anderson used were very busy, and it was imperative to set a date for them to arrive in order to avoid unnecessary delays.)

3. Mr. Anderson suggested that if the project took more than 58 days, the first activity time which could be reduced was pouring the foundation. The concrete supplier could send an additional truck if Anderson paid a premium of $300. This would reduce the time by two days. Would this be a good idea?

4. What activities are good candidates for reducing the project completion date?

5. If the subcontractor who installs the automobile lifts is not free for 30 days, will this delay the project?

RANCHO SHOPPING CENTER (B)

Mr. Montero, Anderson Associates' planning specialist, had just finished his initial analysis of the schedule for the tire shop building at Rancho Shopping Center. Before showing his results to Mr. Anderson, the president, he decided to check with the foreman of Anderson's gas station project.

He learned several new pieces of information:

1. The previous time estimate for installation of wallboard (four days) was incorrect. This task would take only two days.

2. The foreman was uncertain about the accuracy of the time estimates he had given Mr. Montero. He did feel that the estimate for each activity was the most likely time. However, he also believed that the actual time required would vary between a minimum value (an optimistic estimate, assuming that everything went well) and a maximum value (a pessimistic estimate, assuming that the work encountered problems). These times appear in Exhibit 2.

Given this new information, Mr. Montero needed answers to the following questions:

1. What is the probability of completing the project in 58 days?

2. If he wants a 90% probability of completing the project in 60 days or less, by how many days must he reduce the expected time for completion?

EXHIBIT 2

Job	Activity	Time Estimates in Days		
		Optimistic	Most Likely	Pessimistic
A	Prepare preliminary specifications	8	10	12
B	Excavate foundation	4	5	6
C	Pour foundation	5	6	7
D	Electric work	3	5	7
E	Install wallboard	2	2	2
F	Plumbing	6	6	6
G	Install auto lifts	3	4	5
H	Paint interior walls	3	5	7
I	Millwork	5	8	11
J	Trim installation	3	5	7
K	Erect frame and roof	12	15	18
L	Final interior decoration	6	6	6
M	Installation of siding	5	7	9
N	Paint exterior	5	7	9
O	Blueprints finalized	5	5	5
P	Prepare bill of materials and order invoices	3	3	3
Q	Time required to receive lumber after order is sent	4	10	16
R	Window and exterior door installation	1	4	7

RANCHO SHOPPING CENTER (C)

As he studied the latest estimates for the tire shop building at Rancho Shopping Center, Mr. Montero realized that some of the activities would have to be rushed in order to complete the job in 58 days. To provide more usable information on the effects of rushing some of the construction steps, Mr. Montero estimated the extra cost of reducing the normal time required for each step by one or more days (Exhibit 3). These costs would increase the cost of the tire shop over what might be called the cost under "optimal conditions" (i.e., the cost incurred if each step could be performed at normal pace without undue rushing, overtime, etc.). Realizing that any extra costs should be kept to an absolute minimum, Mr. Montero tried to develop a construction schedule that rushed only those activities where the extra cost was not too high. After several hours of work Mr. Montero devised the following tentative construction plan:

Step	Planned Duration (Days)	Step	Planned Duration (Days)	Step	Planned Duration (Days)
A	8	G	3	M	7
B	5	H	4	N	6
C	5	I	5	O	3
D	3	J	2	P	2
E	1	K	15	Q	8
F	4	L	4	R	4

Deciding the plan needed further work, Mr. Montero put all his notes on the tire shop job into his briefcase to do further work at home that evening.

EXHIBIT 3

	Step	Expected Time Required to Execute Step (Days under Optimal Cost Conditions)	Total Days Reduction	Total Cost
A	Prepare preliminary specifications	10	2	$ 50
			3	600
B	Excavate foundation	5	1	1,000
C	Pour foundation	6	1	900
D	Electric work	5	2	1,000
E	Install wallboard	2	1	100
F	Plumbing	6	2	400
G	Install auto lifts	4	1	200
			2	500
H	Paint interior walls	5	1	350
			2	750
I	Millwork	8	2	1,000
			3	1,750
J	Trim installation	5	2	450
			3	750
K	Erect frame and roof	15	2	5,000
			4	7,500
L	Final interior decoration	6	2	500
			4	4,000
M	Installation of siding	7	1	500
			3	3,000
N	Paint exterior	7	1	250
			2	750

EXHIBIT 3 (Continued)

Step		Expected Time Required to Execute Step (Days under Optimal Cost Conditions)	Total Days Reduction	Total Cost
O	Blueprints finalized	5	2	350
			3	600
P	Prepared bill of materials and order invoices	3	1	250
			2	850
Q	Time required to receive lumber after order is sent	10	2	500
			4	1,450
R	Window and exterior door installation	4	1	500

THE ONTARIO BREWING COMPANY

In January 1968 the Planning Committee of the Ontario Brewing Company met to consider proposals for the introduction of a new beer. The company hoped to strengthen its position in the younger, special occasion segment of the lager market by introducing a product that was discernibly different from the present line but was still close to the center of the taste preference curve (Exhibit 1). The marketing department had requested and received approval for $888,000 for a special campaign to promote either the existing lines or the introduction of a new product. The Marketing department was especially interested in producing a beer with a higher alcoholic content than was normally used. Thought had also been given to using an entirely new bottle design. The new beer proposal and investigation had been code-named "Quench" and had been classified confidential in order to protect the company's plans from its competitors. Alex Reid, the company President, hoped the January meeting would generate enough information to allow the best alternative available to be selected.

The Ontario Brewing Company was a wholly owned, semiautonomous subsidiary of Dominion Brewing Company Limited. Dominion and two other large breweries dominated the beer market throughout Canada. In Ontario the three companies accounted for 98% of the beer sold. Marketing was subject to the control and supervision of the Liquor Control Board of Ontario (L.C.B.O.). The board was responsible

Source: "The Ontario Brewing Company," A. A. Grindlay in *Management Science and the Manager: A Casebook,* E. F. Peter Newson (The University of Western Ontario), editor, © 1980, pp. 14–17. Reprinted by permission of Prentice-Hall, Inc., Englewood Cliffs, N.J.

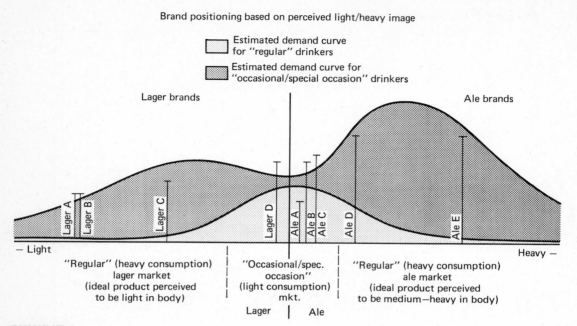

Brand positioning based on perceived light/heavy image

☐ Estimated demand curve for "regular" drinkers

▨ Estimated demand curve for "occasional/special occasion" drinkers

Lager brands   Ale brands

Lager A | Lager B | Lager C | Lager D | Ale A | Ale B | Ale C | Ale D | Ale E

— Light   Heavy —

"Regular" (heavy consumption) lager market (ideal product perceived to be light in body)

"Occasional/spec. occasion" (light consumption) mkt.

"Regular" (heavy consumption) ale market (ideal product perceived to be medium—heavy in body)

Lager | Ale

EXHIBIT 1

for controlling prices and approving any new innovations the breweries hoped to implement. Standard beers marketed in Ontario were sold through the Brewers Warehousing Company while imported beers were distributed through the Liquor Control Board of Ontario Retail Stores. A member of the board of directors of each brewery sat on the board of the Brewers Warehousing Company.

An eighteen month research program had been completed just prior to the January meeting. After analyzing the research results the marketing department was confident that a new product would be received favorably. Research results indicated that most consumers felt that very few new brands of beer had been introduced in Ontario recently, and that beer had not changed for many years. Austen Campbell, Vice-President of Marketing, and John Spears, Marketing Research Manager, attended the meeting to present their department's findings. Mr. Campbell led off by explaining the alternatives considered. "When we received the special promotion allocation we wanted to be sure the returns would exceed the $888,000 we would spend. Our initial step was to outline a campaign to promote our existing brands and to calculate the incremental returns after deducting all incremental costs. Although most of the effect will be felt in the first year we think there will be some carryover into the following years. Following the finance department's advice we used a 30% before tax discount rate in our calculations to express future cash flows at their present value. The campaign we outlined figured to return $1,900,000 in discounted incremental revenue after the incremental costs were subtracted. After deducting the $888,000, we would end up $1,012,000 ahead. Our next step was to compare the returns from promoting our present line to the returns for introducing and promoting a new product."

"Before we could estimate returns on a new product we had to establish what kind of beer we would sell," added Mr. Spears. "The marketing group has been anxious for some time to introduce something new and different. We think our research indicates a very strong market potential for a high alcohol beer. Unfortunately, a premium strength beer would have to be distributed through the liquor stores rather than the Brewers Retail due to the existing government regulations. A high alcohol product would be an innovation and would have to be approved by the L.C.B.O. We expect it would take about three months before a decision would be announced. We also considered introducing a new bottle. Again we would have to apply for permission. If we want both innovations we will have to hold off the bottle request until the high alcohol decision is made. We figure that our original application, whether it be high alcohol or new bottle, is about as likely to be passed as rejected."

"A new bottle application would have a better chance for approval if it followed a successful high alcohol application," interjected Mr. Campbell. "The L.C.B.O. would probably see more justification for a bottle change in this case since the product itself would be substantially different and since the beer would be marketed through the liquor stores. The chance for bottle approval would probably increase to about 60%."

"Let's get this straight," said Mr. Reid. "The Board will want to know what type of product the new bottle will be used with so we will have to clear up the high alcohol question before we apply for a new bottle. If we apply for both, the second decision will not be announced for about six months."

"Right," replied Mr. Campbell.

At this point, George Eckles, Vice-President of Production, entered the conversation. "It looks like our deadline is going to have a considerable influence on our decision. August 15th, 1969 was selected for the introductory date to take advantage of the heavy volume buying period preceding the Labour Day weekend. This period is important since it introduces our new beer when many of the light volume, occasional drinkers are stocking up. Since a full year is required to prepare and launch the marketing campaign, we will have to know which type of beer we will introduce by August of this year. All of the significant costs for developing a new bottle and a new beer are behind us, but it will take some time to outline and specify what the new product will be like. If we try for both innovations and are successful on the alcohol request we will have to do this final preparation while the bottle application is pending. If the bottle application is rejected after a successful high alcohol request we will not have time to switch the planning to another new product. We will simply have to spend the budget allocation promoting the existing brands."

"What can we do if our first application is rejected?" asked Mr. Reid. "Can we continue?"

"A rejection will force us to change our planning and will put us a week or two behind the original schedule," continued Mr. Eckles. "We will still have time to introduce a regular strength product in a standard bottle but there will not be time to make another application."

Mr. Reid asked Mr. Campbell what the dollar effect would be for each alternative.

"Although we expected a relatively fast increase in share volume during the introductory period followed by a falling off then leveling out period, we decided to make our decisions based on the average expected sales in the first five years. We didn't think the averaging would change the decision, especially since the sales trends would be the same for each alternative. A five year period was chosen arbitrarily since it is very difficult to project too far into the future. After five years our estimates would not be based on much more than a guess, and since the discount rate we are using is 30%, the following years would not have much weight anyway. For each alternative we tried to estimate a single average sales volume but we couldn't agree on any one figure. We found it easier to estimate a sales spread and to evaluate a probability for each level of the spread. By multiplying the sales volumes by their probabilities and taking the sum we produced an expected sales volume for each alternative. Realizing we were more interested in the amount generated to cover profit and existing overhead, we deducted all the incremental costs, except the amounts due to the high alcohol content and the new bottle, before we calculated present values. The results gave an estimated present value of $5,750,000 for a high alcohol product in a new bottle and $5,120,000 for high alcohol in a standard bottle. The present value of the contribution generated for a regular alcohol beer was $4,880,000 if a new bottle was used or $4,200,000 in a regular bottle. To figure our net gain we would, of course, have to deduct the $888,000 promotion cost.

"You expect the high alcohol contribution to be greater even though it has to be distributed through the liquor stores?" asked Mr. Reid.

"Yes, we do," replied Mr. Campbell. "We would use a higher selling price in the liquor stores than in the Brewers Retail resulting in a greater contribution per bottle. We think sales would have taken off if we had been able to distribute high alcohol through the Brewers Retail; however, we still believe we could achieve substantial sales distributing high alcohol through the liquor stores."

Mr. Eckles continued, "After Marketing gave us their expected sales volumes, we calculated the present value of the incremental costs over the five year period due to the higher alcohol content and the new bottle. The extra alcohol would cut present value contribution by $234,000 for the regular bottle volume forecast and $262,000 for the new bottle forecast. The new bottle would reduce present value contribution by about $755,000 due to extra production and handling expenses."

"Have you adjusted the volume forecasts to account for the reactions our competitors take?" Mr. Reid asked. "Also, have you estimated what portion of the new product sales will be drawn from our other beers? If most of our new product sales are at the expense of our other brands we won't be gaining much."

"We spent a lot of time estimating the effects of competitive reaction and cannibalization," replied Mr. Spears. "These are both highly uncertain events and are very difficult to put a figure on. We lumped them together and tried to estimate how much they would reduce the contribution figures that Austen mentioned. Since competitive reaction was rather intangible and hard to judge, we tended to discount it quite a bit. We classified the effects as either large or small. The large amount would reduce the present value of the contribution figures by about $1,600,000 while the small amount would be about $800,000. To establish the probability of the large and small effects we considered the original volume forecast, the distribution system, the buying characteristics of the new customer and the expected competitive reaction. If either of the innovations was used by itself there would be a 50% chance that cannibalization and competitive reaction would have a large effect. Using both innovations would increase the chance for a high effect to 70% primarily because of the greater volume forecast. A new product with the conventional alcohol content and the standard bottle would have a 40% chance that the combined effect would be large. We would not expect any effect at all if we used the entire budget to promote the existing brands."

The committee continued to discuss the decisions facing the company but after a few minutes Mr. Reid closed the meeting saying:

"I think we have outlined the alternatives, and the costs and revenues for each, but we have to organize these estimates. Austen, I would like you to go over what we have discussed and to outline on paper the alternatives and their consequences. When you have cleared things up and have come up with some sound recommendations, we will meet again to select the best strategy."

NOVON CEMENT COMPANY

The Novon Cement Company was founded in 1922 in Falstaff, a small town in southern California. In early 1961, Novon was engaged in the manufacture and distribution of cement, as well as the mining of raw materials required in cement manufacture.

Novon's Falstaff operations included a large cement-producing plant which has an annual capacity of 3,500,000 barrels of cement. Initial construction of this plant had begun in 1922. Since that time, the plant has been expanded on several occasions. This plant is located on a 2,000-acre tract which contained valuable raw material resources. Novon also operated a second and larger plant at Plata, California, 125 miles southeast of Falstaff. The 5,000 acres of land on which this plant was located were acquired in 1927 for the raw material deposits which the property contained. The plant itself, with an annual capacity of 5,500,000 barrels of cement, was constructed in 1954–1955. This plant was one of the most up-to-date facilities in the cement industry.

Each of Novon's plants was an independent, completely integrated operating unit. Each had, in addition to its own raw material deposits, complete crushing, grinding, clinker burning, cement grinding, and shipping facilities, as well as storage

Source: Copyright © 1971 by the President and Fellows of Harvard College. This case was prepared by Sherwood C. Frey, Jr. as a basis for class discussion rather than to illustrate effective or ineffective handling of an administrative situation. Reprinted by permission of the Harvard Business School.

facilities and complete maintenance shops. Novon also operated modern powerhouse facilities at each plant which were sufficient to provide most of the plant's power requirements.

The primary raw materials used by Novon came from the limestone deposits adjacent to its plants. The company estimated that its raw materials resources at each plant would be sufficient to sustain operations for more than 100 years. Besides the plants and property at Falstaff and Plata, Novon owned other raw material deposits in California, Utah, Wyoming, Arizona and Texas.

Novon marketed various types of cement under the "Novon" and "White Dot" brand names. These products were sold exclusively in southern California. The company's customers included ready-mix concrete dealers, building material dealers, concrete products manufacturers, heavy engineering construction contractors who worked under government contracts, and federal, state, and local governments. Within its southern California trading area, Novon experienced competition from five other cement plants that were operated by four companies.

Novon's balance sheets as of April 30, 1960 and December 31, 1960, and its statement of earnings for the fiscal years, 1958, 1959, 1960, and for the first eight months of fiscal 1961, are shown as Exhibits 1 and 2, respectively. The company had recently adopted a 17% after-tax hurdle rate for use in evaluating proposed expenditures.

INVESTIGATION OF NEW MARKETS

In early 1960, Novon's top executives had begun to think about what plans the company ought to adopt so that it could continue to achieve sales increases. At that time, there was extra capacity at both the Falstaff and Plata plants, but the southern California market was steadily growing and Novon's management believed that in the next several years Novon would be operating at capacity. The Executive Committee (composed of the President, Tom Denner, the Vice President–Production, George Ivers, the Vice President–Sales, Joe Merlis, and the Treasurer, Ralph Coleman) believed that in addition to considering further expansion in southern California, Novon should seriously consider entering new markets. Because of the desire to have a source of raw materials, at a plant site, primary attention was focused on locations where Novon already owned raw material deposits.

UPPER FEATHER RIVER PROJECT

In June 1960, the State of California approved a bond program in the amount of $1,750 million to be expended for water resource development. A major phase of the state supported, water development program was the Upper Feather River Project in northeastern California. This project had been advocated for many years, but up until June 1960 conservation groups, principally the Sierra Club, had successfully argued

EXHIBIT 1 Balance Sheets

	April 30, 1960	December 31, 1960 (unaudited)
Current Assets		
Cash	$ 3,900,095	$ 4,381,086
U.S. government and other securities (at cost)	1,210,000	2,725,939
Accounts receivable (net of allowance for doubtful accounts)	1,799,647	2,564,593
Inventories:		
Cement and process stock (at cost below market)	2,119,031	2,329,311
Packages and fuel (at cost)	440,646	632,870
General supplies (at cost)	1,544,328	1,676,674
Total current assets	$11,013,747	$14,310,493
Sundry assets	138,986	143,496
Long-Term Assets		
Land and quarries	$ 2,893,440	$ 3,079,000
Building, machinery and equipment	26,817,119	30,125,418
	$29,710,559	$33,204,418
Less depreciation:		
Amortization, depletion	12,060,570	13,618,177
	$17,649,989	$19,586,241
Deferred charges	194,916	248,140
Total assets	$28,997,638	$34,288,370
Current Liabilities		
Accounts payable	$ 1,150,655	$ 888,786
Accrued expenses	398,723	941,114
Dividend payable	528,000	148,500
Federal income tax (estimated)		759,220
Total current liabilities	$ 2,077,378	$ 2,737,620
Stockholders' Equity		
Preferred stock	6,600,000	6,600,000
Common stock	379,500	11,385,000*
Retained earnings	19,940,760	13,565,750
Total liabilities	$28,997,638	$34,288,370

* In August 1960 the company increased the par value of the common stock and declared a stock split in the form of a stock dividend.

EXHIBIT 2 Operating Statements

	Year Ended April 30			Eight Months Ended December 31, 1960 (unaudited)
	1958	**1959**	**1960**	
Sales	$26,317,229	$26,413,146	$30,959,062	$18,165,551
Cost of goods sold:				
Direct costs	15,531,755	14,305,431	17,377,504	10,598,456
Depreciation and depletion	1,425,703	2,129,969	2,464,134	1,605,541
Selling and administrative expenses	2,169,412	2,059,528	2,554,287	1,644,933
	$19,126,870	$18,494,928	$22,395,925	$13,848,931
Operating profit	7,190,359	7,918,218	8,563,137	4,316,620
Other income (expense)	(141,108)	84,633	(75,787)	(71,130)
Earnings before income taxes	7,049,251	8,002,851	8,487,350	4,245,490
Income taxes	3,084,178	3,584,841	3,528,602	1,771,000
Net profit	3,965,093	4,418,010	4,978,748	2,474,490

against it. The primary component of the Upper Feather River Project was the construction of the Glenn Butte Dam which would help control the frequent flooding by the Feather River. In addition to flood control, the reservoir would also provide water for irrigation, municipal and industrial needs, and power resource development. When full, the reservoir formed by this dam would have a volume of 3.5 million acre-feet. Five smaller earthen reservoirs, upstream from the Glenn Butte Dam, were included in the project. They would provide flood control and recreational facilities for northern California.

After approval of the bond, the State of California moved quickly to begin construction. The water requirement projections for the southern portions of the state were pressing; particularly, in light of the pending *Arizona-California* lawsuit over the Colorado River water rights.

In August 1960, Novon was asked by the State of California whether it "intended to bid on the Glenn Butte Dam and whether it was planning to build any new plants within economic shipping distances of the proposed structure." Novon replied that it was "interested in an opportunity to furnish the cement." In September 1960, Novon was informed by the State of California that invitations to bid on the three-million-barrel cement contract would not be called before November 1960 due to several minor changes required in the specifications for the cement. In late November, the State set 5:00 P.M., January 20, 1961, as the deadline for bids for the cement for the dam. The bids would be opened on February 6, 1961, and the contract would be awarded within a week of that date. The successful bidder would probably have to start supplying cement to the dam site in the summer of 1962. The company which was awarded the contract would be notified 15 days prior to the date on which the initial delivery would be required. In no case would cement be required after June 30, 1967. The anticipated delivery schedule was as follows:

Year	Barrels of Cement
1962	400,000
1963	900,000
1964	800,000
1965	700,000
1966	200,000

NOVON SPECIAL PROJECTS

As soon as the 1960 water resource bond was approved, Novon began an intensive study of the feasibility of construction of a new plant on their property in Lowe, eighty miles from the dam site. Their investigation was conducted on two fronts—the costs of a new plant and the basic market demand of northern California.

The estimated cost for a plant with an annual capacity of 1,500,000 barrels of cement was $4 million with construction time being slightly less than a year. The bulk of the construction expense would be incurred in the last phases of construction, that is, in late 1961–early 1962. Mr. Ivers had estimated that the variable manufacturing cost would be approximately $1.50 per barrel. The variable manufacturing cost did not include an allowance for administrative expenses (salaries for accounting, purchasing, sales, executive personnel and other related costs), depreciation, or depletion. The selling and administrative expenses were estimated to be $400,000 per year. For depreciation purposes, Mr. Ivers knew that Novon would use a straight line method with a ten-year life. Mr. Ivers also estimated a percentage depletion deduction for federal income tax purposes that would result in a reduction in taxable income of approximately 20 cents per barrel of cement sold. With respect to delivery of the cement, the dam contract was unusual. Industry practice usually required that all transportation costs be borne by the purchaser; however, when large contracts were "let" by the state, delivery to the construction site was to be included in the bid. Since the dam site was so close to the Lowe property, Novon felt that it would be able to use its own trucks, instead of contract trucks to transport the cement, and in so doing incur a cost of approximately $.10 per barrel rather than $.16 per barrel.

The analysis of the basic market demand for northern California was conducted by a well-known market research firm. Their results are given in Exhibit 3. These numbers confirmed the Executive Committee's suspicions that a plant capacity of

EXHIBIT 3 Estimates of Basic Cement Demand, Proposed Lowe Plant*

Calendar Year	Basic Demand** (000 Barrels)
1962	800
1963	800
1964	900
1965	1050
1966	1200
1967	1250
1968	1350
1969	1400
1970	1600
1971	1700
1972	1900

* Estimates assume (a) price $2.70 or 180% of variable manufacturing costs, (b) Novon is the only cement manufacturer in the region, (c) Lowe facility complete in first quarter 1962.

** Basic demand does *not* include the cement required for the dam.

1,500,000 barrels of cement would be adequate for at least the first eight years of the plant's life. Also it was clear to the Executive Committee that, if Novon were to lose the Glenn Butte contract, plans for the Lowe facility would have to be abandoned. The basic market demand simply was not adequate to support a large plant in its early years and a smaller plant would be far too inefficient. In addition, they would have to compete directly with the winner of the dam contract for that demand. Consequently, it would be foolish for Novon, or probably any firm, to build a plant in the area without having won the dam contract.

While the final conclusions of the report supported their intuition, the Executive Committee was very excited about some of the supporting information. As part of the analysis of Novon's entrance in the northern California market, a careful study of the competition was conducted. This included estimates of the production costs of the three primary competitors. Presently none had plants in the vicinity of the dam site and consequently the estimates were based on each firm's raw material sources, transportation costs, and the production technology. The estimates of the competitor's costs initiated a debate over the chances that Novon had of winning the dam contract at various bid prices. Ivers and Merlis maintained that Novon's bid had to be low enough to guarantee winning the contract and thereby insuring the success of a plant at Lowe. Denner and Coleman believed that Novon's bid price should be based on a fair estimate of costs plus a reasonable profit; they did not advocate setting "an unbeatable price." However, Ivers and Merlis thought that the contract was an opportune way of "getting the new plant rolling" and thereby ensuring production close to capacity while Novon was building a commercial market in the area. Denner and Coleman argued that if Novon submitted a very low bid and was awarded the contract, the amount of its winning bid would be published in many newspapers and trade journals. Because the low bid would be publicized, they thought that Novon would be receiving demands from its commercial customers for prices lower than what they were being charged, prices more in line with Novon's "unbeatable" price to the state.

At this point, Denner took control and insisted on estimating, based on the competitor's cost structure, Novon's chances of winning the Glenn Butte contract at various bid prices. Novon usually set its prices at 180% of variable manufacturing costs. Since the cement was to be delivered to the dam site, transportation costs would be added to the variable manufacturing costs. This implied a price of approximately $2.90 per barrel. The state contract was of such a magnitude that the full 180% pricing was probably inappropriate; but even so, a $2.90 bid would be discussed "just to see what it implied." Ivers and Merlis agreed that a factor of 130% was the lowest that Novon could economically go and thus wanted a bid of $2.10 per barrel included. Denner thought that a bid of $2.50 per barrel (160%) represented a reasonable profit and that there was probably a 50-50 chance of winning at that price. Others felt differently, but no more than 10% one way or the other. Ivers contended the low bid was so low that the competition could not economically beat it since Novon's production technology and plant site were at least as good as any of the competitors'. Of course, there might be some factors, although he couldn't imagine what, that would motivate the competition to bid very low. So he argued that there was at least a 90% chance of winning. The high bid was much more difficult. Eventually, they agreed that if they made the high bid of $2.90 per barrel, there would be only a one in ten chance of winning.

NELSON SPORTING GOODS, INC.

In late February of 1981, Arch Smith was preparing to schedule the production of the Summer Recreation Guide. The guide was a comprehensive directory of outdoor recreation facilities for camping, hiking, and fishing enthusiasts around the country. Each year its editorial staff carefully updated its information on prices and put together a new set of ratings based on survey data. The guide was sold to wholesalers in the sporting goods industry as well as to certain national bookstore chains. Demand for the guide had been growing, and Mr. Smith was not sure how large a printing to schedule for the coming year.

Nelson Sporting Goods was a manufacturer of a broad line of sportswear and sports equipment. Over the years, the firm had developed a number of catalogs and booklets, eventually deciding in 1970 to create an in-house department for all of its printing. Mr. Smith had become its manager in 1975 and had been successful at increasing the visibility of publications such as the guide.

Forecasts of annual demand for the guide were made by the Marketing Analysis Department. Meanwhile, the Sales Department processed all of the information on requests for the guide and compiled annual demand figures. Their records suggested how accurate the forecasts had been.

The Marketing Analysis Department had recently called Mr. Smith to discuss demand prospects for 1981. Working with contacts in the trade and factoring in economic conditions, the department had concluded that the guide would continue to grow in popularity. Their forecast was for 125,000 copies in 1981.

Mr. Smith knew the forecast had been optimistic by several thousand copies the previous year and wasn't confident that he should schedule a production run of 125,000. In addition, he didn't like the way it looked when he had thousands of copies left over at the end of the year. Although the guides brought in $12 each in sales, they cost $3 each to produce. An extra 6000 copies at the end of the year would show up as a cost of $18,000 in his departmental expense summary.

Hoping to find a way to improve the reliability of the forecast, Mr. Smith called the Sales Department. His idea was that by arranging for field rep's to visit the guide's large customers and by placing a number of telephone calls around the country, the Sales Department could probably get a near-perfect demand estimate. The Sales Department agreed, but said the company would end up spending about $50,000 on such an effort. They figured the expense would not be warranted.

TABLE 1

Year	Forecast	Demand	Demand-to-Forecast Ratio
1980	112,000	106,200	0.95
1979	100,000	99,800	1.00
1978	98,000	85,500	0.90
1977	86,000	86,100	1.00
1976	77,000	80,800	1.05
1975	74,000	74,300	1.00
1974	68,000	71,700	1.05
1973	62,000	62,200	1.10
1972	60,000	60,000	1.00
1971	60,000	57,100	0.95

HANOVER CONSUMER CO-OP

Arthur Gerstenberger, general manager of the Hanover Consumer Co-operative, was puzzled by the report given him by Rod Pierce, the Co-op's treasurer. After calling Rod on the telephone, Arthur said, "What do you mean saying that we can predict the Co-op's sales by using a mathematical formula? I started as a stock boy over 30 years ago and anybody connected with the retail food industry knows you can't tell what people will buy. OK, sales are affected by the economic climate, the buying power of the population served by the store, the weather, the existence of competition and many other factors, but it is hard to tell how much of an effect these factors have."

Rod replied, "I agree with you that there are problems in trying to come up with a method to forecast the Co-op's sales. But this kind of information would be so helpful to us in trying to budget that it seems worthwhile to experiment with a forecasting model."

"I have gathered some data describing the Co-op's sales in five areas (Groceries, Meat, Produce, Food Bin, and Total) for the last five years. (See Table 1.) After analyzing this data, and finding both a trend and significant monthly seasonal factors, I became convinced that some kind of forecasting technique would help us in preparing forecasts of sales. Although this technique is by no means a 'crystal ball,' its use would provide forecasts to serve as a guide in budgeting."

TABLE 1 Co-op Dollar Sales by Area

Period	Grocery	Meat	Produce	Food Bin	Total
1	200003	63867	23278	24776	311925
2	181301	58050	22648	21300	283301
3	202142	66327	28704	22706	319880
4	208338	72586	29127	23498	333549
5	193726	69516	29000	23645	315888
6	203598	67748	25876	25379	322602
7	207688	72225	25417	25179	330511
8	214414	70957	24767	27019	337159
9	209469	76957	25746	26309	338481
10	245382	84981	27045	37480	394890
11	222430	73725	27339	24805	348301
12	195483	64727	23509	23734	307455
13	219403	72776	27203	27091	346475
14	199133	64881	27352	24143	315510
15	220923	77367	34666	25517	358475
16	231746	79384	34106	27346	372583
17	213556	71338	32102	26015	343011
18	227201	77274	28367	30514	363358
19	213878	70580	26636	27552	338648
20	237986	73426	26535	30915	368863
21	226838	75908	30000	30685	363432
22	243539	82372	38980	43075	407968
23	235740	72213	27645	29853	365453
24	214119	69108	25068	28190	336487
25	213951	69082	25942	27846	336823
26	209711	71935	29489	29720	340857
27	233093	78542	39144	29024	379804
28	223162	71753	32557	30672	358146
29	231105	79208	32687	32219	375220
30	233172	82302	28952	32533	376961
31	225371	74313	27649	29609	356943
32	258344	82538	29753	34960	405596
33	225802	78533	29727	31577	364641
34	272185	91841	46736	47336	458099
35	252815	80731	31592	30427	395566
36	212529	68922	27450	28377	337279

TABLE 1 *(Continued)*

Period	Grocery	Meat	Produce	Food Bin	Total
37	222517	71759	30002	30066	354345
38	224614	75821	32621	31925	364982
39	235111	78143	40669	29084	383008
40	234980	81589	36007	30618	383196
41	248253	89857	38899	34537	411548
42	239137	81721	30589	34492	385941
43	247458	83397	30335	35669	396861
44	287704	91575	34278	40132	453691
45	250045	82962	33021	38476	404506
46	314146	100363	36684	55495	506690
47	267367	81143	35203	35642	419356
48	235424	73093	31886	34666	375071
49	248446	80895	36351	36167	401861
50	255890	83187	36581	36829	412488
51	268768	87009	37860	33553	427190
52	237302	81533	35324	34336	388495
53	298234	105975	48016	42325	494550
54	255448	89838	34818	39871	419974
55	265619	95346	32100	39561	432626
56	287233	100913	34083	43778	466006
57	272827	93172	36442	42112	444552
58	326236	112313	38024	61207	537779
59	269666	88938	36492	36138	431235
60	247145	81206	34708	38639	401698

JOHNSON PRODUCTS COMPANY

Fred Webster, general manager of Johnson Products Company (JPC), was contemplating several recent developments in the compressor market. Mr. Webster was concerned because in its production of industrial air conditioners, JPC used eight compressors each working day of the month. (JPC operated on a 20-day/month schedule). For several years the compressors had been produced in only two locations in the United States, one in New England and the other in Florida. Luckily for JPC, the New England producer was located several miles away and offered free delivery to JPC within hours.

Several months earlier Mr. Webster had compiled the following information about the compressors:

Information		Source of Information
Total annual usage	2000 units	Purchasing
Orders per year	50 times (weekly)	Purchasing
Units per order	40	Purchasing
Inventory carrying cost	30%/year	Controller
Weight per unit	500 pounds	Shipping and Receiving
Warehouse unloading cost	$3/hundredweight (100 pounds)	Warehouse Manager
Clerical cost	$10/requisition	Purchasing
Expediting cost	$22/requisition	Shipping and Receiving
Warehouse capacity	250 units	Warehouse Manager
Outside warehouse costs	$25/unit/year	Warehouse Manager

There is existing space in the warehouse for 250 units. Additional space must be leased by the year. As a result, if an order of more than 250 units arrives, part of the order must be stored in leased space.

Several months after compiling this information, Mr. Webster was informed by his purchasing agent that JPC's local supplier had followed his Southern competitor in announcing a new price structure:

Units per Order	Unit Price
First 100	$250
Next 100	$240
All over 200	$226

Just recently, JPC's local supplier announced that it was discontinuing production of compressors, forcing JPC to deal with the Southern supplier whose prices had been the same as the local supplier except that they were f.o.b. the Florida plant. The traffic department informed Mr. Webster that the transportation cost per hundredweight was $12 for carload lots of 50,000 pounds. The LCL (less than carload) rate was $20 per hundredweight. The replenishment cycle was expected to take 1 week.

Mr. Webster was wondering what effects these new developments would have on his cost structure.

GENOA ELECTRONICS

Wally Adams, manager of one of Genoa's seven distribution centers, reread the interoffice memo he had before him with incredulity. The memo was from Adams' supervisor, and it stated that in the next 2 months staff financial people would be visiting each of the distribution centers to assist them in developing a "should have" inventory analysis. The memo went on to state that this was a new concept in inventory control being pioneered by firms such as Raytheon and Western Electric. It involved calculating the theoretical dollar value of the inventory that each distribution center "should have" given the level of sales, forecast error, service level, and cost structure peculiar to it. This calculation would then serve as a standard against which the actual inventory investment could be compared.

The new concept was rather frightening to Wally Adams. He had never really been measured in his ability to control inventories. The traditional measures in his division had been the ratios of direct and indirect labor costs to sales, and service to the distribution center's customers.

THE DISTRIBUTION CENTER

The distribution center Wally Adams managed had the responsibility for serving over 300 wholesale and large chain customers in the western United States. The operation distributed radios, television sets, and other electronic appliances to these customers, as well as spare parts for repair purposes. All in all, the distribution center had an inventory of over 60,000 products and parts, worth a total of $13.5 million. This equated to about a 2 months' supply on a dollar basis. Most of Adams' customers also maintained small inventories of their own. A recent survey had indicated that the wholesalers and large chains that Genoa served maintained an average of 15 days' sales in inventory.

The system Genoa used to control its own inventories was a modification of the Reorder Point, Economic Order Quantity system. Order quantities were calculated using the Economic Order Quantity method. Then, because demand for many items had definite trend patterns, the Economic Order Quantity was converted to a "weeks' supply" basis by dividing it by the annual demand forecast and multiplying by 50 weeks. Then, as demand forecasts changed, the weeks' supply figure would remain constant, but the quantity ordered could change accordingly. In calculating the order quantity, Genoa used 25% of the item cost as the annual cost of holding inventories, and $10 as the cost of placing and receiving an order with either the company's main warehouse or the factory.[1] The reorder point was the level of inventory for a particular item at the time when an order was placed. Technically, it was calculated by multiplying the forecast demand for the item in weeks by the number of weeks it took to receive that order (usually 2 weeks from the main warehouse). In practice, however, inventory controllers used this figure as a baseline, often ordering before the reorder point was reached. Jerry Etchison, an inventory controller, explained it this way: "If I have a little too much inventory, I get a little reprimand, but if I can't fill a

---

[1] The $10 ordering cost was derived by summing the total personnel costs of the inventory control and receiving departments and dividing by the number of purchase orders processed in the previous year. This calculation resulted in $9, excluding the salaries of the inventory control and receiving department supervisors. To this figure was added $1, which was the estimated cost of paper, postal and telephone charges for processing an order.

customer's order, I really get chewed out. So, to protect myself, I raise the reorder point just to account for mistakes at the main warehouse and in case of forecast errors."

WALLY ADAMS' APPROACH

Wally Adams thought that it might be wise for him to run through some sample calculations to see how his "should have" inventory compared with the actual before the financial people arrived. He wanted to be prepared for their findings, and have some ideas for improvement before he came directly under the gun.

At first, he pulled out the results of a survey of 2% (a random sample) of all the items in his warehouse. (See Exhibit 1.) He quickly realized, however, that this was of little use since there were too many items in it to practically test out the "should have" concept without a computer. As an alternative then, he gathered some data on one of the distribution center's parts, #4915082, a resistor. He saw that the annual demand for this part was about 60,000 units, and that it cost $0.12. The average size of a customer order for this part was 500 units. He also noted that the forecast for the demand during the procurement lead time for this item was often in error. About 50% of the time, the forecast was for less than the actual demand for the part. Of the times that this occurred, the error was about 500 units 50% of the time, 750 units 25% of the time, 1000 units 15% of the time, and 1200 units 10% of the time. Jerry Etchison could never remember a forecast error being larger than 1250 units. Over the last year, the average inventory level for this part had been 6515.

Wally also saw that the resistor was a standard item stocked by his competitors. For such items he knew that Genoa's gross margin averaged about 40%.

EXHIBIT 1 Usage and Cost Distribution of the Sample Items

Annual Usage Range	Number of Different Items in Each Range	Cumulative Percent of Total Number of Items	Average Unit Cost for Each Item in the Range	Average Annual Usage for Each Item in the Range	Annual Cost of Sales for all Items in Each Range	Cumulative Annual Cost of Sales for Each Range	Cumulative Percent of Total Annual Cost of Sales
0–6	318	25.8	$13.22	1	$ 3,573	$ 3,573	0.26
7–24	96	33.6	5.72	13	7,610	11,184	0.82
25–48	74	39.6	3.54	34	8,945	20,130	1.47
49–100	122	49.5	3.49	73	31,392	51,522	3.77
101–200	103	57.8	2.46	147	37,373	88,896	6.51
201–300	54	62.2	1.56	248	20,974	109,870	8.05
301–400	35	65.0	2.06	340	24,532	134,403	9.84
401–500	26	67.1	0.84	447	9,770	144,173	10.56
501–750	48	71.0	1.07	601	30,904	175,078	12.82
751–1000	32	73.6	1.10	852	30,002	205,080	15.02
1001–2000	94	81.2	0.52	1,465	71,617	276,697	20.27
2001–3000	60	86.1	1.55	2,404	223,625	500,323	36.65
3001–4000	30	88.5	0.80	3,312	79,505	579,829	42.47
4001–5000	23	90.4	1.13	4,560	118,528	698,358	51.15
5001–10,000	60	95.2	0.43	6,625	170,946	869,304	63.67
10,001–50,000	41	98.5	0.22	20,753	187,197	1,056,502	77.38
50,001 or more	17	100.0	0.08	227,074	308,820	1,365,322	100.0
Total	1233	—	—	—	$1,365,322	—	—

XEROX CORPORATION: MANAGEMENT SCIENCE'S IMPACT ON SERVICE STRATEGY*

The practice of Management Science has made a significant impact on the performance of the Xerox service organization. The National Service department has implemented a new service strategy for the 9200 duplicator which provides better service to the customers to less cost at Xerox. The basic Management Science concept behind this service strategy is the utilization of queueing theory to reduce the service force idle time and simultaneously reduce the response time to a customer initiated call for service. The results of the queueing analysis indicated that a major productivity improvement could be achieved with mini-teams. It was decided that a three man mini-team was the best compromise (in terms of manageability) between a one-man territory and team territories which had four or more service men. Implementation of this service strategy has yielded the following results:

1. Specification to Xerox customers of response times for customer initiated service calls, and
2. An average increase in productivity of the service work force for the 9200 in excess of 50%.

HISTORICAL BACKGROUND

Xerox plays a dominant role in the office copier and duplicator market place. One reason for this dominance has been attributed to the service which Xerox provides its customers. Xerox has enjoyed a reputation of excellent service and intends to maintain that reputation.

Xerox service has, historically, attributed its success to the service technical representative, more commonly known as the "Tech Rep." The Tech Rep has been the face of the service organization in the eye of the customer. The general guidelines for the Xerox Tech Rep were, broadly stated, that he would be given a specified territory

Source: This article was written by W. H. Bleuel, currently Director of Marketing for the Environmental Controls Division of Barber-Colman Company, and appeared in *Interfaces*, Volume 6, No. 1, Part 2 (November 1975). Copyright © 1975, The Institute of Management Sciences.

* *Author's Acknowledgments.* This project could not have been completed alone. My thanks for cooperation and assistance is directed throughout the National Service Organization. I would like to extend particular gratitude to Dr. Rodda Reddy for his direct assistance and to Mr. Richard Pixley for his development of the simulation model. Mr. Casey Lopata in the Service Strategy and Planning Organization spent many hours in model validation. Mr. David Kachmaryk was particularly helpful in programming the analytical model and providing the graphical output. Finally, I would like to thank Mr. Thomas McCobb, former Vice President of National Service and now Senior Vice President of Operations, Latin America for his support and encouragement.

(number of machines) which became his responsibility to maintain. His territory was typically bounded geographically and thus his number of machines would increase as salesmen placed additional units within his geographical boundary and would decrease when machines were upgraded to machines that he was not trained to service or when machines were replaced by competitive units. The Tech Rep had the additional responsibility of installation of the new machines and, in most cases, the preparation for shipment of units to be removed. The on-going maintenance provided by the Tech Rep is broadly classified into three categories; namely, emergency maintenance, preventive maintenance and machine up-grading or retrofit.

It can be readily seen that a Tech Rep has become a valuable asset to Xerox since he performs as many as five functions. These functions are:

   (i) service man;

  (ii) public relations man—major customer interface after salesman places machine;

 (iii) supplies salesman—generally indicates when supplies are low;

 (iv) trainer—when machine malfunctions indicate misuse, the Tech Rep instructs operator(s) on proper procedures. He may also perform initial training during the installation;

  (v) territory manager—the Tech Rep has the responsibility of assigning priorities to the requests for service that occur in his territory.

Thus, the Xerox Tech Rep has become a one-man territory manager and when grouped as a national service organization for an expanding machine population, becomes a labor driven service expense as well as a limited resource.

BUSINESS BACKGROUND

The office copier and duplicator which represents the backbone of Xerox as well as an essential ingredient in the modern business office has been a "convenience" machine. Although the machine may be essential to office operations, the machine generally did not directly affect the revenue generation of the office. Hence, when a machine required service, it was important to respond in a timely manner in order to keep the customer happy and minimize his inconvenience.

The situation changed when Xerox announced the Model 9200 Duplicating System. The Model 9200 was directed toward the offset printing market and thus became a system designed primarily as a revenue generator for the offset printing industry. This product imposed a new service situation for Xerox since the impact of an inoperable machine at a customer site changed from inconvenience of the customer to loss of revenue for the customer.

The outcome of this product introduction was a service responsibility to the customer in terms of response to customer requests for service. The marketing organization developed a set of response time requirements for the service organization. It became obvious to members of the headquarters staff of the service organization that the historical service strategy would not be economically feasible if it were applied to the Model 9200. Once the service costs were presented to Headquarters Service Management, alternative service strategies became the only near term solution to meet the response time specifications within the service cost constraints of the product. Long term solutions could include alternatives not directly related to the service organization.

SERVICE STRATEGIES

The Xerox branch service organization is the field entity which provides administration to the Tech Reps. The Tech Reps are grouped under Field Service Managers with the number reporting to each manager varying from a low of about 6 to a high in the range of 20. It was generally concluded that the Tech Reps who service the Model 9200 should be included in this general organizational form rather than develop a separate or unique service organization.

One of the major objectives for the 9200 service strategy was full service management control of the response time to customer requests for service. This objective was in conflict with the territory management to which the Tech Rep had become accustomed. The first service strategy decision was to ignore, for the purpose of the analysis, the implication of elimination of territory management on Tech Rep morale. The service strategies then fell into three groups:

  (i) one-man territories
 (ii) mini-team territories
(iii) full-team territories (all Tech Reps reporting to the same Field Service Manager would be defined as a single team with a combined territory).

The first strategy, one-man territories, was uneconomical and was discarded. The second strategy, mini-team territories, had appeal since mini-teams had been attempted with limited success on other products and thus was considered a viable strategy. The third strategy, full-team territories, had appeal since full-team territories were commonly used by the Rank Xerox organization. Thus, it became a matter of deciding between the use of mini-teams and full-teams for the 9200 service.

SERVICE CONSTRAINTS

As with any applied problem, the constraints usually become the most influential force in the decision process. Each of the new service strategies had constraints associated with it. The list of constraints is grouped into the following categories in order to conserve space and omit nonessential details:

Old-Time Beliefs Any new service strategy must salve the many old-time beliefs held by many Xerox people as well as many customers. The most popular belief is that the customer likes to know the Tech Rep and prefers to see the same one on each service call. This old-time belief strongly supports the image of "personalized" service. Old-time beliefs held sacrosanct without supporting evidence became one of the major constraints for the full-team strategy. In this constraint the mini-team posed fewer faces to the customer and was thus preferred.

Unionization The Xerox service force has on several occasions attempted unionization. Each time the attempt has been made, the Tech Rep majority has opposed the action. Xerox Management believes that one of the major reasons behind the failure to unionize is the Tech Rep self image of territory manager. The Tech Rep is trained to act as a businessman to protect his territory and assume the service responsibility for "his" machines. Thus, any service strategy which alters the one-man, one-territory strategy provides a potential impetus toward unionization of the Tech Reps. Both of the proposed service strategies for the 9200 were considered as potentially dangerous in terms of unionization. A mini-team was preferred for this constraint since customer responsibility would be at the minimum with a full-team.

Job Requirements Since both proposed service strategies allowed more than one Tech Rep to service the same machines, individual Tech Rep skills became an important constraint. The concerns of service management both at headquarters and the field were that it would become more difficult to protect sensitive accounts from marginally performing Tech Reps and that Tech Rep morale might suffer on a service team if one or more of the Tech Reps did not "pull his weight." The one problem that had been noted in previous mini-team and full-team experiments was that a marginally poor performer could affect the team performance. Several reasons were cited for this reaction but were never proven satisfactorily with a controlled experiment. The mini-team was preferred in this instance since the team would have more interpersonal relations than a full-team and problems would be more easily detected and corrected.

Organization The procedure used to dispatch Tech Reps was considered a constraint to both of the proposed strategies. Long-range organizational changes concerning the dispatch of Tech Reps are still being analyzed. No preference appeared for this constraint.

These constraints, in general, opposed both of the proposed service strategies and supported the status quo. Since it has already been concluded that the status quo was not economically feasible, the decision was to select the strategy which posed to be the "lesser of the two evils." In each constraint the mini-team appeared to be the "lesser evil" and thus it was concluded that a mini-team would be used to service the Xerox Model 9200.

THE MANAGEMENT SCIENCE CONTRIBUTION

Although the Management Science effort was prominent in all phases of the service strategy development and implementation, the final decision of the size of the mini-team was based predominantly on the Management Science analysis. The analysis was performed at two levels. The first level was an analytical model developed using queueing theory. Once the analytical model had indicated the mini-team size, a simulation model was developed. The primary reasons for this two-level approach were economics and schedule. A queueing model had the advantages of timeliness as well as being parametrically sensitive. The simulation model provided the fine details required to evaluate implications not easily included in the analytical model.

The Analytical Models   The analytical model was based on four parameters:

  (i) the number of machines assigned to a territory,
  (ii) the number of Tech Reps assigned to a territory,
  (iii) the average rate at which the machines need service, and
  (iv) the average rate at which machines can be serviced by an average Tech Rep.

The following assumptions were made:

  (i) the machine population mix per territory is not significantly different from the national population mix,
  (ii) machine usage is variable to the point that PM calls within the territory are essentially random with respect to time,
  (iii) emergency maintenance calls and preventive maintenance calls are serviced according to a negative exponential distribution,
  (iv) calls carried over to the next day would not include time from stop of work until the next day in response time calculation,
  (v) travel time between calls was included as a fixed rather than variable time,
  (vi) vacation time, sick leave, training and business meetings were excluded.

Since this model was developed prior to market introduction, data were not available to support these assumptions. However, data on service call duration for an older product with high copy volume (but less than the expected copy volume of the Model 9200) indicates in Figure 1 that a negative exponential distribution of service times is not unreasonable. The Model 9200 is projected for several markets; however, the analytical model was derived for exactly two markets and only the average copy volumes were used for these markets. Thus, the analytical model was representative of an average team servicing average machines in an average market.

The analytical model was used successfully to derive the following relationships:

  (i) average response time,
  (ii) average queue length,
  (iii) percent active time per Tech Rep.

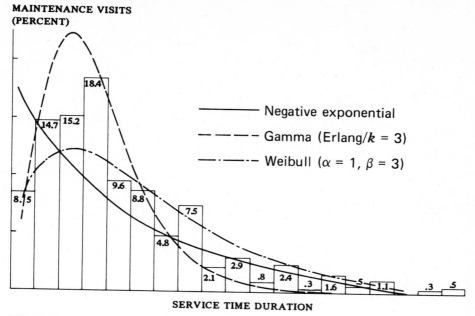

FIGURE 1

These relationships are indicated in Figures 2 through 7 for the case of mini-teams of 2 and 3 Tech Reps respectively.

The Management Science evaluation of feasible mini-team sizes ranged from 2 through 5. The parametric relationships for response time and Tech Rep active time indicated immediately that a 5 man mini-team did not present a sufficient improvement over a 4 man mini-team to warrant further consideration. Thus, the feasible sizes were reduced to 2, 3 and 4 men.

The parametric relationships of response time versus territory size for mini-teams of 2 man and 3 man teams were compared. For this situation it was apparent (see Figures 2 and 5) that for a one hour average response time, the 3 man mini-team could maintain 18% more machines per Tech Rep than the 2 man mini-team. Thus, the 2 man mini-team was rejected from further consideration and only mini-teams of 3 men or 4 men remained as feasible alternatives.

At this point, there was insufficient evidence to conclude which alternative was preferable, 3 men or 4 men. The final decision was that a 3 man mini-team would be selected in preference to a 4 man mini-team following the logic that a 3 man mini-team would require less leading by the team leader, would have less chance of personality conflict, would be more closely knit and thus avoid the marginal performer morale problem and would probably gain greater acceptance by the Tech Reps.

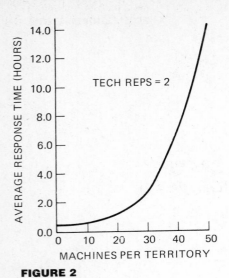

FIGURE 2

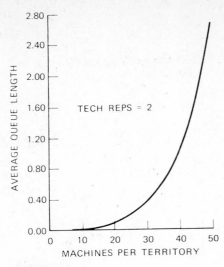

FIGURE 3

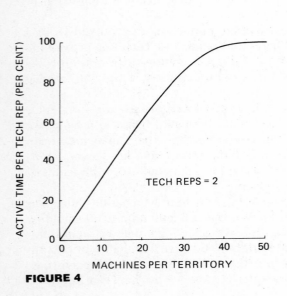

FIGURE 4

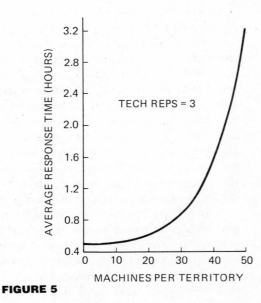

FIGURE 5

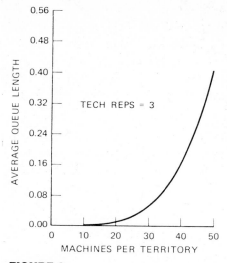

FIGURE 6

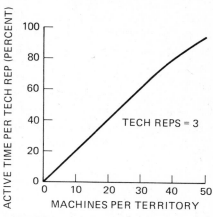

FIGURE 7

The Simulation Model The simulation model was designed to provide the necessary modeling detail to apply the 3 mini-team to specific territories. It was decided that the simulation model would require 5 parameters in addition to the parameters used in the analytical model. These additional parameters were:

   (i) geography,
   (ii) queue discipline,
   (iii) product copy-volume class (low, medium, high),
   (iv) time dependent usage of equipment, and
   (v) the Tech Rep work schedules.

This simulation model was developed to operate in a conversational mode at an interactive terminal so that headquarters planners could utilize the methodology on an as-needed basis. The output of this model included the Tech Rep utilization, overtime, travel time, and response time distribution.

Validation The data used in the models were collected from the Field Technical Information System (FTIS). Since the model had the flexibility to simulate the current one-man territory, validation was performed with field data from FTIS. The completion of the validation by headquarters service budgeting personnel was accepted as sufficient by headquarters service management. This decision allowed the simulation model to be released for full time support of the service planning efforts for the Model 9200.

ORGANIZATIONAL IMPACT AND SUMMARY

The 3 man mini-team for service support to the Model 9200 has been implemented at Xerox. The mini-teams have been accepted by the Tech Reps. The branch service organization is responsible for implementation of the mini-teams in the branches where the Model 9200 is being marketed. As a result of this service strategy Xerox can now include response time specifications to the prospective customer as an additional feature.

The computed program life savings for the new service strategy does not include savings to be realized from reduced training requirements which result from a smaller 9200 service force. For one of the copy volume markets, the savings over the program life in labor dollars per one thousand copies is 90% and the savings over the program life in total service cost is 46%.

CALIFORNIA MINING COMPANY

Jim Levison, the operations manager at California Mining Company, put down the consultant's report after reading it for a third time. He remembered how important it had seemed to get a consultant's view of the equipment needs at the company's open pit mine. The consultant's recommendation was different from what Mr. Levison had intuitively anticipated, but what concerned him even more was the fact that he simply was not convinced by the queueing theory on which the recommendation was based.

BACKGROUND

The California Mining Company operated a number of mines in Arizona, Nevada, and New Mexico, in addition to its original mining site in Southern California. The California site was actually its least productive, but when demand began to rise sharply the company's management decided to raise the output goal at the mine to 35,000 tons per week. At the same time, the decision was made to determine whether the equipment at the site was adequate to the new output goal.

The firm operated one crusher, three 3-yard shovels, and ten 20-ton trucks at the site. It was generally recognized that this equipment had been underutilized in the past, but no study had ever been made of the equipment's capacity. Moreover, the trucks frequently needed servicing or repairs, and it was considered good practice to have more trucks than were theoretically needed, just for the sake of back-up capability.

Source: This case was prepared as a basis for class discussion rather than to illustrate effective or ineffective handling of an administrative situation. Portions have been reprinted from "Simple Queueing Theory Saves Unnecessary Equipment," *Industrial Engineering*, February 1971.

When the 35,000-ton goal was set, Mr. Levison felt that it was an appropriate time to have a capacity study done. Since there was no in-house expertise, he investigated a number of engineering consultants before hiring the Victor Company to do the job.

THE CONSULTANT'S STUDY

The consulting team first carried out an extensive time study to determine how much time it took to perform various phases of the process. They mainly employed the "snapback" method of time study, under which each element of the procedure (loading, transporting, dumping, etc.) was studied separately to determine time standards.

Having collected the data, the consultants proceeded to use queueing models to analyze alternative designs for the use of the equipment. The three shovels operated in different locations at different levels in the mine. The trucks were assigned to individual shovels and were not switched even when a waiting line occurred at one of the shovels. No set pattern of scheduling existed, although the most common configuration involved eight trucks (three trucks in Areas 2 and 3, and two trucks in Area 1).

The consultants recommended that there should be only two trucks per shovel on the first shift. They also suggested that a second shift be instituted to provide insurance for excessive downtime on the regular shift. This second shift would involve only one of the shovels, and it would also operate with just two trucks. The consultant's report justified this configuration using queueing analysis (Exhibit 1), claiming that costs would be minimized by assigning two trucks to each area.

Mr. Levison was mildly surprised to read the recommendation to use only two trucks per shovel in each of the areas, given that output levels were about to rise. In addition, he found the queueing analysis difficult to understand. He had, in fact, seen queueing theory briefly in a management development program some months previously, but he had not kept his class notes. Now, after reading the report three times without being able to follow the analysis, he wondered whether he should ask for an explanation or simply accept the report and work on implementing its recommendation.

EXHIBIT 1 Excerpt from the Victor Company Report

The primary crusher handles approximately 480 truckloads per shift (9600 tons). This capacity is based on the individual truck dump-time, which is 0.94 minutes. The weekly 5-day requirements for the mine's refinery are 35,000 tons of ore. Therefore, the mine has to produce an average of 7000 tons of ore per day.

To find the cycle times for the truck-shovel system, the entire system was first time-studied by the continuous method. However, truck travel times were sometimes interrupted by unnecessary delays, such as truck drivers pulling over to the side of the roadbed to talk, waiting for other trucks to pass or cross intersections, and waiting for or following a roadgrader or water truck. These delays had to be identified and

EXHIBIT 1 *(Continued)*

segregated to set correct standards for the complete system, so truck travel times were recorded using the snapback method of time study.

By positioning one engineer with a radio on the rim of the open pit and establishing reference points along the roadbed, we were able to record the actual time for the trucks to travel from one reference point to another. A second engineer with a radio monitored the truck routes in a station-wagon. He was dispatched by the engineer on the rim of the pit to a stopped truck to determine the reason for the delay. Load, dump and position times were developed from the continuous time studies. Elemental times were picked up by both methods (Table 1). With this basic information, the queueing model was developed.

It was necessary to define the queueing model in terms of customer population, number of channels, queue discipline and service distribution.

Customer population refers to someone or some item needing service. We had to determine whether the trucks, the shovel, or the primary crusher was the customer—in other words, which required service and which provided it. We determined that the trucks required service. We then had to identify our customer population as finite or infinite. The finite model was appropriate since the number of trucks was small (10). They were the customers waiting to be loaded or unloaded at either the shovel or primary crusher.

Next, the number of service channels had to be recognized. The system was closed-loop since each truck was serviced from only one shovel or the primary crusher. Therefore, the single-channel model was selected. Queue discipline is the order in which the trucks are serviced. In this case the first-come, first-served discipline was appropriate.

The arrival distribution is the manner in which the trucks arrive and become a part of the queue. During the fact-gathering phase, trucks were observed arriving at random intervals, so the exponential arrival pattern distribution was selected. The same distribution was used for the service distribution model. The service time varied at random around a mean of 2.06 minutes. With the model developed, the next step was to determine the study's parameters (Table 2).

Table 3 is a matrix showing the average number of trucks arriving at a shovel per hour, and the average number of trucks loaded per hour for one, two, three, and four trucks since the traffic intensity exceeds one when four trucks are in the system.

TABLE 1 Cycle Times of Ore Trucks

Shovel Area	Time (minutes)					
	Load	To Crusher	Dump	From Crusher	Position at Shovel	Total Time (minutes)
#1	2.06	1.93	0.94	1.01	0.51	6.54
#2	2.06	3.13	0.94	1.48	0.51	8.12
#3	2.06	2.26	0.94	1.80	0.51	7.57

EXHIBIT 1 (*Continued*)

TABLE 2 Parameters

N = Number of units in the waiting line at time T
A = Mean arrival rate (trucks/hour)
B = Mean service rate (trucks/hour)
I = Traffic intensity = A/B
PN = The probability of a waiting line of length N
$PN = (1 - I)I^N$
Costs:

Shovel	Fixed cost	$14.51/hour
	Shovel operator	
	($3.885 × 134%)	5.21/hour
	Total cost	$19.72/hour
Pit truck	Fixed cost	$ 3.03/hour
	Truck driver	
	($3.435 × 134%)	4.60/hour
	Total cost	$ 7.63/hour

TABLE 3 Traffic Intensity with Various Numbers of Trucks in the System

	Number of Trucks			
	1	2	3	4
Arrival rate	9.71	18.35	27.52	36.59
Service rate	29.13	29.13	29.13	29.13
Traffic intensity	0.315	0.630	0.945	1.26

Using the probability equation in Table 2, it can be calculated that, in a one-truck system, the probability of zero trucks waiting or being serviced is 0.685. Now since the sum of the probabilities of all possible situations must be equal to one, the probability that one truck is waiting or being serviced can be calculated as

$$1.00 - 0.685 = 0.315$$

(Note that if the equation were used to find the probability of one truck waiting or being serviced, a different probability would be obtained.) This figure is discarded since it applies to an infinite-truck system.

In a two-truck system the probabilities of zero and one trucks waiting or being serviced are 0.370 and 0.233 respectively. Again, since total probability must be equal to one, the probability that two trucks are waiting or being serviced is given by:

EXHIBIT 1 *(Continued)*

$$1.00 - (0.370 + 0.233) = 0.397$$

The probabilities of zero, one, two and three trucks waiting or being serviced in a three-truck system are calculated in a similar manner as 0.055, 0.052, and 0.049, and 0.844.

Hourly costs for the different systems can now be calculated as shown in Table 4.

TABLE 4 Comparison of Costs for One-, Two-, and Three-Truck Systems

Comparison of costs for a one-truck system:
Cost of shovel idle = $19.72/hour × 0.685 = $13.508/hour
Cost of one truck waiting or being serviced
  = $7.63/hour × 0.315 = $ 2.403/hour
                Total truck cost $13.508/hour
$13.508/hour − $2.403/hour = $11.105/hour

Comparison of costs for a two-truck system:
Cost of shovel idle = $19.72/hour × 0.370 = $ 7.296/hour
Cost of one truck waiting or being serviced
  = $7.63/hour × 0.233 = $ 1.778/hour
Cost of two trucks waiting or being serviced
  = 2(7.63/hour) × 0.397 =   6.058/hour
                Total truck cost $ 7.836/hour
$7.836/hour − $7.296/hour = $0.54/hour

Comparison of costs for a three-truck system:
Cost of shovel idle = $19.72/hour × 0.055 = $ 1.085/hour
Cost of one truck waiting or being serviced
  = $7.63/hour × 0.052 = $ 0.397/hour
Cost of two trucks waiting or being serviced
  = 2(7.63/hour) × 0.049 =   0.748/hour
Cost of three trucks waiting or being
  serviced = 3(7.63/hour) × 0.844 =   19.319/hour
                Total truck cost $20.464/hour
$20.464/hour − $1.085/hour = $19.379/hour

Table 4 shows that the most economical method of meeting the ore requirements is to use two trucks per shovel in all three areas and operate all three shovels during the same shift. When the operation of three shovels during the same shift is not feasible, due to downtime or shovel location, then two shovels should be used during the day-shift with two trucks per shovel; one shovel and two trucks should be used for the second shift.

GENERAL APPLIANCES, INC.

General Appliances, Incorporated, is a major producer of home appliances faced with the 12-month forecast shown in Table 1. The company is interested in developing a minimum-cost production plan for the year, taking into consideration the several trade-offs that apply. The relevant costs are considered to be: the cost of holding inventory ($1 per appliance per month); the cost of hiring a new worker ($600 per worker for training expenses); the cost of laying off a new worker ($400 per worker for severance pay); the regular-time salary cost ($800 per month based on a 40-hour week); and the cost of using overtime (125% of the regular time salary cost). Furthermore, a company policy dictates that all demand should be met on time.

The company considers its output capacity to be 50 appliances per month per worker. The regular time production rate can be controlled by varying the number of workers and rebalancing the assembly lines accordingly. Physical space, however, limits the production rate to at most 20,000 appliances per month. Overtime can be scheduled in any month up to 40% of the regular time output level.

At the beginning of January the work force is expected to be 150 employees, and 500 appliances will be in stock.

TABLE 1 Monthly Demand Forecasts

January	7,000	July	8,000
February	8,500	August	8,000
March	10,000	September	7,000
April	16,000	October	6,000
May	18,000	November	5,000
June	16,000	December	5,000

POTLATCH FORESTS, INC.

The controller at Potlatch Forests, Incorporated (PFI) is preparing the annual financial plans for presentation to the management executive committee. Planning for the company's plywood division is particularly difficult since there are major uncertainties. Recent increases in the mortgage interest rate could have a substantial effect on home construction, and hence on the demand and price of plywood. Cost increases in raw materials and supplies could also affect profits substantially. Finally, negotiations with the union are underway, and the wage agreement reached may have a big effect on costs.

Source: Adapted from "Puyallup Forest Products," in Charles P. Bonini, *Computer Models for Decision Analysis*, Scientific Press, Palo Alto (1980).

Several months ago the controller asked his planning staff to develop a model to study the effects of these uncertainties and others upon plywood mill operations and profitability. The planning staff has developed a computer financial model for the company's plywood mill. The model displays a pro-forma income statement for the mill by quarters for the next year, and allows the user to make changes in the estimates and assumptions upon which the model is based. The model is called POTFOR and is based on the description of plywood operations contained in Appendix A. The use of the model itself is described in Appendix B.

Demand for plywood had been expected to be strong next year, and forecasts have been based upon that assumption. In reviewing the base case results (see example output) it is apparent that the company is somewhat short of capacity for veneer production (that is, peeling and drying capacity) and to a lesser degree short of pressing capacity, except in quarter 3. This has led to considerable discussion about what expansion of the mill, if any, should be recommended to the company's executive committee. A financial analyst prefers expanding the veneer capacity since this is "where the company had the biggest gap." The plywood marketing manager is in favor of increasing pressing capacity to avoid lost plywood sales. She noted that the lack of veneer capacity did not really hurt the company since veneer could be purchased on the outside. The mill operating manager, naturally enough, wants to expand both capacities. The controller is worried whether any expansion is financially sound.

The Economic Analysis Department has expressed some doubt about the forecast for plywood demand and price. The interest rate for home mortgages has been rising sharply and this might reduce home building and hence plywood sales and prices. Such a possibility causes doubts about the plywood mill's profitability as well as any expansion plans.

In addition, negotiations are underway with the company's union. In building the planning model, a labor cost estimate of $10 per hour was used, based on the anticipated outcome of the negotiations. The executive committee is interested in the effect of different settlement amounts, and at what point the mill would become unprofitable.

Finally the controller is interested in which assumptions are most critical in determining the mill's profitability.

APPENDIX A: PLYWOOD MILL OPERATIONS

The operation of a plywood mill is moderately complex. The process starts when logs are peeled into thin strips of veneer which are then passed through an oven and dried. Different species of trees are used, different thicknesses of veneer are required, and veneer of differing quality results from the various log species and types. The veneer is cut, sorted, and upgraded by patching. Finally, a mix of different thicknesses and types of plywood is produced by gluing together veneer of specified grade and thickness. A glue press is used in this stage of production. Finally, the plywood is trimmed, sanded, and shipped to market. (See Figure 1.)

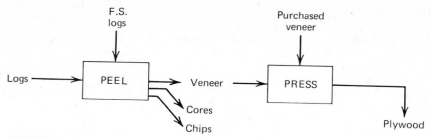

FIGURE 1. Sketch of plywood mill flows.

Certain byproducts result from the plywood manufacturing process. Wood that is unsatisfactory for veneer is converted into wood chips and sold to the company's paper making division. A log can only be peeled down to a certain diameter. The center part, or core, is shipped to a beam mill and cut up into 2 × 4's and other lumber products.

In addition, veneer can be purchased from outside vendors and used to make plywood.

A major decision problem is to match the plywood products manufactured with the market demand, on the one hand, and with the mix of logs and purchased veneer, on the other hand.

SIMPLIFIED DESCRIPTION

For planning purposes, the operation of the mill can be somewhat simplified. Logs to be peeled come from either the company's own timber lands or are purchased from outside sources (usually from cutting rights on U.S. Forest Service land). In the simplified case, logs are considered in aggregate, and are not classified by species or quality. The purchase cost for outside logs and the transfer price for the company's own logs are important variables in financial planning. In addition, the mix of own versus outside (U.S. Forest Service) logs is an important decision variable. At present, the company is anticipating a transfer price (cost) of $45 per MBF (thousand board feet) for its own logs and $55 per MBF purchased cost for outside logs. Currently the company expects to supply half of the logs it will need from its own supply and the other half from the Forest Service.

VENEER PRODUCTION

The logs are peeled into veneer and dried. On average each board foot of log results in 7.52 square feet of usable veneer. A major limitation is the peeling and drying capacity available. Currently the company has capacity to produce 720 million square feet (MMSF) of veneer per quarter. Veneer capacity can be increased by purchase of new equipment for peeling and drying.

VENEER PURCHASE

If PFI does not have enough peeling capacity to meet requirements, veneer can be purchased on the outside market. The estimated purchase price per thousand square feet (MSF) is

Quarter	Purchase Price for Veneer
1	$29
2	30
3	30
4	32

PLYWOOD PRODUCTION

Veneer, both internally produced or purchased, is glued into plywood sheets on the gluepress. On average it takes $3\frac{1}{3}$ square feet of veneer to make one square foot of plywood sheet (at standard $\frac{3}{8}$-inch width). The company currently has pressing capacity of 288 MMSF of plywood per quarter but has the possibility of increasing this capacity by purchase of additional equipment.

PLYWOOD DEMAND

The Marketing Department estimates the company can sell a maximum of 1176 MMSF of plywood during the next year, assuming it has the capacity to produce this much. Demand is not uniform but has a seasonal pattern, which is shown in the table below along with the average sale price per MSF that the marketing department expects to receive.

Quarter	Plywood Demand Potential	Average Plywood Price
1	300	$125
2	306	125
3	260	128
4	310	128
	1176 MMSF	

It is industry practice not to inventory plywood at the mill. Thus, in any quarter, the mill produces either at the demand level for that quarter, if capacity permits, or else at maximal capacity.

BYPRODUCT SHIPMENTS

As indicated earlier, lumber cores are left from logs after peeling. These are shipped to the company's beam mill for conversion into lumber. On average 0.02 MBF of lumber cores results from every MSF of veneer peeled.

Similarly, chips are also produced as a byproduct of the peeling operation. This results in 0.12 unit of chips for every MSF of veneer. The chips are shipped to the company's paper mill for conversion into paper products.

The transfer price received by the plywood mill for these byproducts is based upon the outside market price for comparable products. For the next year, these prices are expected to be

Quarter	Transfer Price per Unit Chips	Transfer Price per MBF Lumber
1	$18	$60
2	18	62
3	19	62
4	19	64

FINANCIAL FACTORS—SALES

Sales revenue is simply the amount of plywood, chips, and cores sold, multiplied by the sales or transfer price. The company allows a discount of 2% on plywood sales for payment within 10 days, and virtually all customers take advantage of this discount. In addition the company pays its brokers a 6% commission on plywood sales. There are no discounts or commissions on sales of chips or cores. Plywood is shipped by rail and the company bears this cost. Freight costs are expected to average $0.84 per MSF of plywood sold. Other fixed selling expenses are expected to be $750 thousand each quarter.

FINANCIAL FACTORS—OPERATING COSTS

For each MSF of veneer produced, the cost for operating materials and supplies is expected to be $3.61. For plywood, the cost for materials and supplies is estimated at $0.90/MSF.

Labor hours are also required for veneer and plywood at rates of 1.20 hours/MSF for veneer peeled and 0.50/MSF for plywood. The labor cost per hour is currently being negotiated with the union and an average cost of $10 per hour is expected under the new contract.

The fixed costs associated with operating the mill are expected to be $1.25 million per quarter. General and administrative expenses allocated to the mill are estimated at $750,000 per quarter, and other miscellaneous expenses are estimated to be $125,000 per quarter.

FINANCIAL FACTORS—INFLATION

With substantial inflation, the costs (and prices) are expected to change over the course of the next year. For certain of these factors, PFI has made detailed estimates. For example, the prices for plywood, veneer, chips, and lumber discussed earlier have been estimated, taking into account the effect of inflation. In addition, as mentioned earlier, the expected labor rate was under negotiation. However, the labor contract would have a cost-of-living clause that would increase the rate over the year.

In addition, the operating supplies cost for veneer and plywood production were expected to increase with inflation. Finally, the raw material cost for logs (both own logs and Forest Service logs) would also increase.

The annual percentage increases for these are expected to be

Labor cost growth rate	4% per year
Operating supplies cost growth rate	6% per year
Raw material cost growth rate	8% per year

APPENDIX B: USING PROGRAM POTFOR

Program POTFOR is largely interactive. That is, the user merely loads the program and then runs it. An income statement for the next year is printed, together with some supplemental information. The program then allows the user to interactively change any of the following eight factors:

1. Plywood sales potential (i.e., demand)
2. Plywood prices
3. Inflation rates for labor, supplies, and raw materials
4. Log purchase costs
5. Labor rate
6. Pressing capacity
7. Veneer capacity
8. Veneer purchase price

Caution: Changes made in any of the factors are cumulative. They do *not* revert back to the base case after each run. For example, if the user changes the labor rate to $12 per hour, it will remain at this level in subsequent runs unless specifically changed back to $10 per hour or some other level.

After the first run, the program has the option of a shorter version of output, showing only the sales, cost of sales, and net profit.

The following are explanations of calculated ratios and other factors:

GP/NS—Gross Profit/Net Sales
TIE/NS—Total Indirect Expenses/Net Sales
NP/NS—Net Profit/Net Sales
PCT VEN CAP ND—Percent (fraction) of Veneer Capacity Needed
PCT PRES CAP ND—Percent (fraction) of Pressing Capacity Needed
LABOR M M-HOURS—Labor hours used in thousands

If a change in capacity is indicated, the program will ask for any changes in Fixed Costs that may be needed.

An example run is attached. This is the base case with assumptions as described in Appendix A.

POTLATCH FOREST PRODUCTS

PROFIT AND LOSS STATEMENT -- (THOUS. OF DOLLARS)

LINE ITEMS	QR1	QR2	QR3	QR4	YRT
SALES PLY	36000	36000	33280	36864	142144
SALES CHIPS	1555	1555	1642	1642	6394
SALES LUMBER	864	893	893	922	3571
SALES ELIM	0	0	0	0	0
TOTAL SALES	38419	38448	35814	39427	152109
D&A PLYWOOD	720	720	666	737	2843
COM PLYWOOD	2160	2160	1997	2212	8529
FREIGHT PLY	242	242	218	242	944
TOT ALLOW	3122	3122	2881	3191	12316
NET SALES	35297	35326	32934	36236	139793
RAW MATERIAL	4787	4883	4979	5074	19723
VENEER PURCH	6960	7200	4400	7680	26240
OP SUPPLIES	2858	2901	2918	2987	11665
LABOR	10080	10181	10139	10382	40782
COST ELIM	0	0	0	0	0
COST OF SALE	24686	25165	22436	26124	98410
GROSS PROFIT	10612	10161	10498	10112	41383
FIXED COSTS	1250	1250	1250	1250	5000
SELLING EXP	750	750	750	750	3000
G&A EXP	750	750	750	750	3000
OTHER EXP	125	125	125	125	500
TOT IND EXP	2875	2875	2875	2875	11500
NET PROFIT	7737	7286	7623	7237	29883
RATIOS					
GP/NS	0.30	0.29	0.32	0.28	0.30
TIE/NS	0.08	0.08	0.09	0.08	0.08
NP/NS	0.22	0.21	0.23	0.20	0.21
PLY PROD MMSF	288	288	260	288	1124
VEN PROD MMSF	720	720	720	720	2880
LUM PROD MMBF	14	14	14	14	58
CHIP PROD UN	86	86	86	86	346
PCT VEN CAP ND	0.33	0.33	0.20	0.33	0.00
PCT PRES CAP ND	0.04	0.06	-0.10	0.08	0.00
LABOR M M-HR	1008	1008	994	1008	4018

```
        THE CURRENT ASSUMPTIONS FOR ALL FACTORS ARE:
FACTOR 1:   PLYWOOD SALES POTENTIAL (MILL SF) EACH QUARTER
      300         306         260         310
FACTOR 2:   PLYWOOD PRICES (DOLLARS PER MSF) EACH QUARTER
      125         125         128         128
FACTOR 3:   INFLATION FACTORS (PERCENT PER YEAR) FOR:
    LABOR COST INCREASES                  4.
    OPERATING SUPPLIES INCREASES          6.
    RAW MATERIALS COST INCREASES          8.
FACTOR 4:   PRICES PAID FOR LOGS (DOLLARS PER MBF):
    TRANSFER PRICE FOR INTERNAL LOGS            45
    PURCHASE PRICE FOR OUTSIDE LOGS             55
FACTOR 5:   BASE LABOR RATE 10 DOLLARS PER HOUR
FACTOR 6:   PRESSING CAPACITY:
    THE INITIAL CAPACITY IS 288 MILLION SF, AND THIS IS
    TO BE INCREASED 0 PERCENT IN QUARTER 1
FACTOR 7:   VENEER CAPACITY:
    THE INITIAL CAPACITY IS 720 MILLION SF, AND THIS IS
    TO BE INCREASED 0 PERCENT IN QUARTER 1
FACTOR 8:   VENEER PURCHASE PRICE (DOLLARS PER MSF)
      29          30          30          32


YOU MAY NOW MAKE CHANGES IN ANY OF THE 8 FACTORS GIVEN ABOVE.
TYPE THE NUMBER OF THE FACTOR (1-8), OR TYPE <0> TO STOP.? 5

THE BASE LABOR RATE CURRENTLY IN THE PROGRAM
IS $ 10 PER HOUR,  ENTER A NEW VALUE? 12.00


DO YOU WANT TO MAKE ADDITIONAL CHANGES? N
TYPE <S> FOR SHORT VERSION OF OUTPUT OR <E> FOR EXTENDED
VERSION.? S

NET SALES       35297       35326       32934       36236      139793
COST OF SALE    26702       27201       24463       28200      106567
NET PROFIT       5721        5250        5595        5161       21727

DO YOU WANT A LIST OF ASSUMPTIONS FOR THIS RUN? N

YOU MAY NOW MAKE CHANGES IN ANY OF THE 8 FACTORS GIVEN ABOVE.
TYPE THE NUMBER OF THE FACTOR (1-8), OR TYPE <0> TO STOP.? 0
```

The parameters and estimates are all included as DATA statements in the program. Thus they can be easily changed if desired. The parameters are described below, line by line, together with the base case values. These can be changed simply by retyping the line before running the program.

Line 1070: inflation rate labor; inflation rate operating supplies; inflation rate raw materials; initial pressing capacity; quarter in which capacity is to change; fractional change in capacity; initial veneer capacity; quarter of change; fraction change

```
1070 DATA  .04, .06, .08, 288, 1, 0, 720, 1, 0
```

Line 1100: price of own logs; price of FS logs; fraction of logs from own supply; fraction discount on plywood sale; fraction commission on plywood sales; freight rate for plywood; yield MSF veneer per log MBF; yield MSF plywood per MSF veneer; MSF veneer/MBF lumber; MSF veneer/units chips.

```
1100 DATA  45, 55, .5, .02, .06, .84, 7.52, .3, 50,
8.333
```

Line 1130: operating supplies—dollars/MSF veneer; operating supplies—dollars/MSF plywood; labor hours—hours/MSF veneer; labor hours—hours/MSF plywood; labor cost—dollars/hour.

```
1130 DATA  3.61, 0.90, 1.20, 0.50, 10
```

Line 1160: plywood demand (MMSF/quarter)

```
1160 DATA  300, 306, 260, 310
```

Line 1170: plywood price (dollars/MSF)

```
1170 DATA  125, 125, 128, 128
```

Line 1180: lumber cores transfer price (dollars/MBF)

```
1180 DATA  60, 62, 62, 64
```

Line 1190: chips transfer price (dollars/units of chips)

```
1190 DATA  18, 18, 19, 19
```

Line 1200: veneer purchase price (dollars/MSF)

```
1200 DATA  29, 30, 30, 32
```

Line 1210: Fixed costs (thousands of dollars)

```
1210 DATA   1250, 1250, 1250, 1250
```

Line 1220: selling expenses (thousands of dollars)

```
1220 DATA   750, 750, 750, 750
```

Line 1230: G&A expenses (thousands of dollars)

```
1230 DATA   750, 750, 750, 750
```

Line 1240: other expenses (thousands of dollars)

```
1240 DATA   125, 125, 125, 125
```

BRUNSWICK CORPORATION
The "Snurfer"

In mid-April 1967, Gerry O'Keefe, vice president for marketing of Brunswick Products, was trying to decide how many Snurfers he should request the manufacturing plant to produce for the 1967–1968 winter season.

The Snurfer was a new item, first introduced to the consumer market by Brunswick during July and August 1966, but because of the difficulty of predicting the actual sales requirements the factory had produced more Snurfers than were eventually sold. Mr. O'Keefe was anxious to avoid the same situation occurring in the 1967–1968 selling season.

THE SNURFER

The Snurfer was a surfboard-like device designed for use on snow. It consisted of a molded wooden plank 48 inches long by 7 inches wide upon which the rider stood and skied/surfed down snow-covered slopes. The company in its specification brochure described the Snurfer as follows:

> Snurfing is the all-new and exciting winter fun sport. Children, teens and young adults can now combine the many thrills and skills of surfing and skiing on the new Brunswick Snurfer. It's really maneuverable, fun-filled, and easy to learn. Goes on a minimum of snow—where saucers and sleds won't go. The Snurfer is just the thing for action-packed snow outings! Also fun for sand surfing![1]

The Snurfer was produced in two types, the regular and the super. Exhibit 1 shows pictures of both versions. The regular model consisted of a molded laminated wood shell, painted yellow with black stripes, which used metal staples as foot grips. The super Snurfer was the same basic shape as the regular but incorporated a metal keel for greater maneuverability. In place of the painted finish the super had a genuine natural wood surface, included deluxe metal traction button-type Snurf-treads (foot grips), was decorated with an official red racing stripe and was sold complete with Snurf-Wax. The wax allowed the bottom surface to be polished for even greater speeds. Exhibit 2 shows a sample of advertising material which describes the advantages of the Snurfer over other snow products such as sleds.

THE DEVELOPMENT OF THE SNURFER, JANUARY 1966—MARCH 1967

The idea for the Snurfer had originated in Muskegon, Michigan in early 1966. A plumbing supply salesman had converted a water ski for his children to use in the snow. The idea interested him and he experimented with different sizes and shapes and coined the name Snurfer.

During February the product came to the notice of a Brunswick employee who felt that the item might be of interest to the corporation. On April 1, 1966, after some negotiation, Brunswick bought both the rights to the design and the registered name from the Muskegon salesman. The contract involved a lump-sum payment and a royalty that was based on Brunswick's gross sales of the product. The royalty was not to become effective, however, until a set number of Snurfers had been sold.

Following the signing of the contract the Brunswick engineers commenced a careful study aimed at optimizing the shape of the Snurfer. Many samples were made and field tests conducted on the rapidly disappearing snow fields. By the end of April the design had been finalized and the engineers were ready to turn the project over to the production personnel.

While the engineers had been working on the design Noel Biery, a product manager, and Mr. O'Keefe, the marketing vice president, had been attempting to determine the size of the potential market and to settle upon channels of distribution. Because the product had been proved to be more readily usable by children than

---

[1] 1967 sales brochure.

EXHIBIT 1

Regular Snurfer

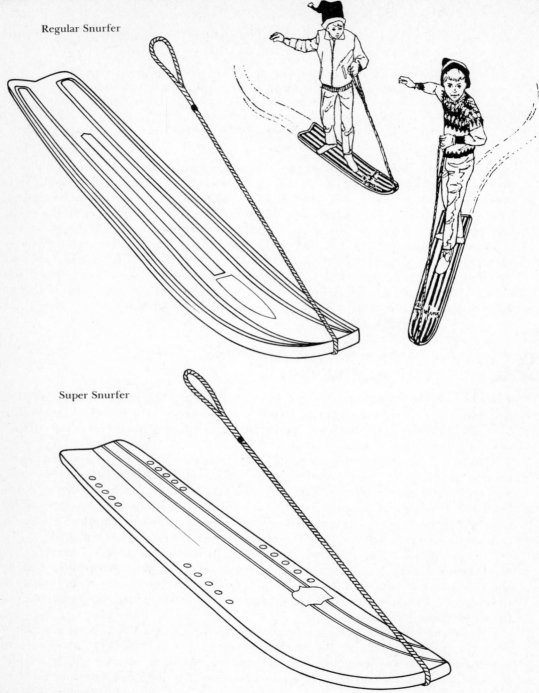

Super Snurfer

Source: Company sales brochure.

EXHIBIT 2 Advertising Copy

Source: Company sales brochure.

adults, Brunswick had decided to distribute the product through toy channels. After making rather slow progress with the local toy stores and jobbers, the decision was made to show the Snurfer at the New York Toy Show in late March. Only one prototype Snurfer was available at that time, yet the response at the show was encouraging. During the show, manufacturers' representatives covering 38 states were appointed. The product at this time which consisted of only a single model (which later became the regular) was sold at a factory price of $3.60 with a suggested retail price of $5.95. During the second week in April engineering prototypes together with specification sheets were sent to all representatives and Brunswick asked them to sound out the market and push for orders during the remainder of April.

By the end of April, Mr. O'Keefe had to make the decision whether or not to continue with Snurfer and, if so, to decide how many units he would order from the factory. The Brunswick production people were insistent that if the units were to be produced in time for the winter selling season, they must have the firm annual production requirements for the Snurfer by the end of April. With only one firm order for 3,000 units, Mr. O'Keefe decided to go ahead with the project and ordered 60,000 units from the factory for delivery during the 1966–1967 winter season. Fifty thousand units were to be the regular Snurfer and 10,000 units the super.

The tooling, capable of producing up to 150,000 units, was ordered at a cost of $50,000, and production scheduled to commence in early September.

By June no further orders of note had been received and both Mr. Biery and Mr. O'Keefe became concerned as to what action should be taken. Brunswick's own full-time representative in New York was asked to investigate the reasons why the Snurfer was not being sold. With this assignment, and a Snurfer in hand, he visited several sporting goods stores, as distinct from toy shops, and found the reaction to be very good. By July, Mr. Biery realized that the original decision to sell through toy jobbers and manufacturers' representatives had probably been a mistake; consequently the original distribution channels were closed down and Brunswick made an all-out effort to generate interest through their own dealer salesmen. However, by this time most sporting goods stores had completed their winter buying and although a good reaction was forthcoming, many stores were unwilling to order in quantity for the current season because of the late date. During August the decision was made to retrench, and the factory managed to cut back production from 60,000 to just over 50,000 units. In addition they agreed to change the product mix between regulars and supers.

The total number of Snurfers sold during the 1966–1967 season reached only 35,000 units, with the ratio between supers and regulars being approximately 60 : 40. By mid-March 1967 there were nearly 17,000 Snurfers in inventory, consisting of 12,000 regulars and 5,000 supers.

THE PRODUCTION DECISION—APRIL 1967

Because of the difficulties and setbacks that they had experienced during 1966, Mr. O'Keefe and Mr. Biery were anxious to ensure that the plans for 1967 were firmly based on what they had already learned.

In reviewing the situation they had reason to believe that most of the early problems had arisen from their decision to class the Snurfer as a toy. Experience had shown that a considerable degree of skill could be developed by Snurfer enthusiasts and that speeds in excess of 30 miles per hour were attainable. This fact coupled with the good, although somewhat late, response received from the sporting good shops suggested that by careful distribution and promotion 1967 sales were potentially well in excess of the 1966 predictions. Although both Mr. Biery and Mr. O'Keefe were convinced that the immediate prospects for the Snurfer were excellent, they were uncertain as to the actual market demand for the coming year and as to the share of this market that would be taken by the super Snurfer. They were certain, however, that in order to maximize the over-all profitability of the product they would have to estimate the size of the production order in a careful and systematic manner. The factory order for 1967–1968 production run had to be in the hands of the production people by the end of April.

As a first step in determining this quantity Mr. Biery decided to review the new cost estimates for the two Snurfer models. The production department advised him that the existing tooling, which had been purchased at a cost of $50,000, was in good shape and would be capable of producing a total of 150,000 units/year in any mix of models. To produce anywhere between 150,000 and 200,000 units would require an additional $15,000 of tooling. To increase the production above 200,000 units/year would require yet another $55,000 in addition to the extra $15,000 already mentioned. This latter step-up in tooling would allow the factory to produce up to 500,000 Snurfers a year. In calculating costs Mr. Biery planned to amortize tooling completely during the year in which it was ordered.

After consultation with the salesman it had been decided to sell the Snurfers in 1967 at an average price from the factory (quantity discounts were involved) of $4.30 for the regular and $5.50 for the super. Brunswick's direct costs for these items were $2.50 and $3.20 respectively. In addition to direct costs Mr. Biery estimated that 9% of the gross margin for both models would be required for selling expenses, royalties and discounts, while a further 3% would be allocated to advertising and promotion. In addition there would be a penalty for overproduction in the form of an inventory carrying cost that was charged at the rate of 2% per month based on Brunswick's direct costs. Mr. Biery estimated that any excess inventory could be considered as being carried for an average of six months.

Having outlined the costs involved Mr. Biery turned his attention to the question of demand. Although he was uncertain as to what figure he should choose, he believed that it was unlikely there would be any major intrusion into the 1967 market from competitive manufacturers. In addition he realized that the Snurfer was something of a novelty item, and, as such, might follow the trend of the skate board or hoola-hoop with sales rising extremely rapidly for one or two years and then tailing off just as quickly. Because of the extreme uncertainty arising from these factors he determined to concentrate solely on the demand for the 1967–1968 season.

To help in ascertaining the demand he called on Mr. O'Keefe, and together they considered the possible sales figures for Brunswick's Snurfers. They finally decided that the median demand was 150,000 units. They were certain that the demand would not be below 50,000 or above 300,000 units, and they believed that there was one chance in four that demand would be at least 190,000 units, and three chances in four that the demand would be at least 125,000 units.

In order to decide on what quantity of units to order from the factory Mr. O'Keefe felt that they should estimate how this demand would be broken down between the super and regular model Snurfers. This was necessary because the factory had to order raw materials well in advance and he didn't want to be left carrying regular Snurfers in inventory while the market was demanding supers, or vice-versa. Both Mr. Biery and Mr. O'Keefe believed that this breakdown of demand between models was independent of the over-all level of demand. They reasoned that the consumer would purchase either the regular or the super entirely on each one's distinctive selling features and this decision as to which to purchase would in no way be influenced by the total number of Snurfers being sold.

Mr. O'Keefe and Mr. Biery agreed that in their judgment there was a 50% probability that the super model would account for at least a 40% slice of the total demand. They felt almost positive that the fraction preferring the super model would not be below 30% or above 60%. They further concluded there was one chance in four that the fraction preferring the super model would be below 36% and one chance in four that it would be above 45% of the total demand for Snurfers.

APPENDIX

TABLE A Standard Normal Probability Density Function

z	0.00	0.01	0.02	0.03	0.04	0.05	0.06	0.07	0.08	0.09
0.0	0.3989	0.3989	0.3989	0.3988	0.3986	0.3984	0.3982	0.3980	0.3977	0.3973
0.1	0.3970	0.3965	0.3961	0.3956	0.3951	0.3945	0.3939	0.3932	0.3925	0.3918
0.2	0.3910	0.3902	0.3894	0.3885	0.3876	0.3867	0.3857	0.3847	0.3836	0.3825
0.3	0.3814	0.3802	0.3790	0.3778	0.3765	0.3752	0.3739	0.3725	0.3712	0.3697
0.4	0.3683	0.3668	0.3653	0.3637	0.3621	0.3605	0.3589	0.3572	0.3555	0.3538
0.5	0.3521	0.3503	0.3485	0.3467	0.3448	0.3429	0.3410	0.3391	0.3372	0.3352
0.6	0.3332	0.3312	0.3292	0.3271	0.3251	0.3230	0.3209	0.3187	0.3166	0.3144
0.7	0.3123	0.3101	0.3079	0.3056	0.3034	0.3011	0.2989	0.2966	0.2943	0.2920
0.8	0.2897	0.2874	0.2850	0.2827	0.2803	0.2780	0.2756	0.2732	0.2709	0.2685
0.9	0.2661	0.2637	0.2613	0.2589	0.2565	0.2541	0.2516	0.2492	0.2468	0.2444
1.0	0.2420	0.2396	0.2371	0.2347	0.2323	0.2299	0.2275	0.2251	0.2227	0.2203
1.1	0.2179	0.2155	0.2131	0.2107	0.2083	0.2059	0.2036	0.2012	0.1989	0.1965
1.2	0.1942	0.1919	0.1895	0.1872	0.1849	0.1826	0.1804	0.1781	0.1758	0.1736
1.3	0.1714	0.1691	0.1669	0.1647	0.1626	0.1604	0.1582	0.1561	0.1539	0.1518
1.4	0.1497	0.1476	0.1456	0.1435	0.1415	0.1394	0.1374	0.1354	0.1334	0.1315
1.5	0.1295	0.1276	0.1257	0.1238	0.1219	0.1200	0.1182	0.1163	0.1145	0.1127
1.6	0.1109	0.1092	0.1074	0.1057	0.1040	0.1023	0.1006	0.0989	0.0973	0.0957
1.7	0.0940	0.0925	0.0909	0.0893	0.0878	0.0863	0.0848	0.0833	0.0818	0.0804
1.8	0.0790	0.0775	0.0761	0.0748	0.0734	0.0721	0.0707	0.0694	0.0681	0.0669
1.9	0.0656	0.0644	0.0632	0.0620	0.0608	0.0596	0.0584	0.0573	0.0562	0.0551
2.0	0.0540	0.0529	0.0519	0.0508	0.0498	0.0488	0.0478	0.0468	0.0459	0.0449
2.1	0.0440	0.0431	0.0422	0.0413	0.0404	0.0396	0.0387	0.0379	0.0371	0.0363
2.2	0.0355	0.0347	0.0339	0.0332	0.0325	0.0317	0.0310	0.0303	0.0297	0.0290
2.3	0.0283	0.0277	0.0270	0.0264	0.0258	0.0252	0.0246	0.0241	0.0235	0.0229
2.4	0.0224	0.0219	0.0213	0.0208	0.0203	0.0198	0.0194	0.0189	0.0184	0.0180
2.5	0.0175	0.0171	0.0167	0.0163	0.0158	0.0154	0.0151	0.0147	0.0143	0.0139
2.6	0.0136	0.0132	0.0129	0.0126	0.0122	0.0119	0.0116	0.0113	0.0110	0.0107
2.7	0.0104	0.0101	0.0099	0.0096	0.0093	0.0091	0.0088	0.0086	0.0084	0.0081
2.8	0.0079	0.0077	0.0075	0.0073	0.0071	0.0069	0.0067	0.0065	0.0063	0.0061
2.9	0.0060	0.0058	0.0056	0.0055	0.0053	0.0051	0.0050	0.0048	0.0047	0.0046
3.0	0.0044	0.0043	0.0042	0.0040	0.0039	0.0038	0.0037	0.0036	0.0035	0.0034
3.1	0.0033	0.0032	0.0031	0.0030	0.0029	0.0028	0.0027	0.0026	0.0025	0.0025
3.2	0.0024	0.0023	0.0022	0.0022	0.0021	0.0020	0.0020	0.0019	0.0018	0.0018
3.3	0.0017	0.0017	0.0016	0.0016	0.0015	0.0015	0.0014	0.0014	0.0013	0.0013
3.4	0.0012	0.0012	0.0012	0.0011	0.0011	0.0010	0.0010	0.0010	0.0009	0.0009
3.5	0.0009	0.0008	0.0008	0.0008	0.0008	0.0007	0.0007	0.0007	0.0007	0.0006

Source: R. Peterson and E. A. Silver, *Decision Systems for Inventory Management and Production Planning*, John Wiley & Sons (1985), 2nd ed., pp. 699–708.

TABLE B Standard Normal Cumulative Distribution Function

z	0.00	0.01	0.02	0.03	0.04	0.05	0.06	0.07	0.08	0.09
0.0	0.5000	0.4960	0.4920	0.4880	0.4840	0.4801	0.4761	0.4721	0.4681	0.4641
−0.1	0.4602	0.4562	0.4522	0.4483	0.4443	0.4404	0.4364	0.4325	0.4286	0.4247
−0.2	0.4207	0.4168	0.4129	0.4090	0.4052	0.4013	0.3974	0.3936	0.3897	0.3859
−0.3	0.3821	0.3783	0.3745	0.3707	0.3669	0.3632	0.3594	0.3557	0.3520	0.3483
−0.4	0.3446	0.3409	0.3372	0.3336	0.3300	0.3264	0.3228	0.3192	0.3156	0.3121
−0.5	0.3085	0.3050	0.3015	0.2981	0.2946	0.2912	0.2877	0.2843	0.2810	0.2776
−0.6	0.2743	0.2709	0.2676	0.2643	0.2611	0.2578	0.2546	0.2514	0.2483	0.2451
−0.7	0.2420	0.2389	0.2358	0.2327	0.2297	0.2266	0.2236	0.2206	0.2177	0.2148
−0.8	0.2119	0.2090	0.2061	0.2033	0.2005	0.1977	0.1949	0.1922	0.1894	0.1867
−0.9	0.1841	0.1814	0.1788	0.1762	0.1736	0.1711	0.1685	0.1660	0.1635	0.1611
−1.0	0.1587	0.1562	0.1539	0.1515	0.1492	0.1469	0.1446	0.1423	0.1401	0.1379
−1.1	0.1357	0.1335	0.1314	0.1292	0.1271	0.1251	0.1230	0.1210	0.1190	0.1170
−1.2	0.1151	0.1131	0.1112	0.1093	0.1075	0.1056	0.1038	0.1020	0.1003	0.09853
−1.3	0.09680	0.09510	0.09342	0.09176	0.09012	0.08851	0.08692	0.08534	0.08379	0.08226
−1.4	0.08076	0.07927	0.07780	0.07636	0.07493	0.07353	0.07215	0.07078	0.06944	0.06811
−1.5	0.06681	0.06552	0.06426	0.06301	0.06178	0.06057	0.05938	0.05821	0.05705	0.05592
−1.6	0.05480	0.05370	0.05262	0.05155	0.05050	0.04947	0.04846	0.04746	0.04648	0.04551
−1.7	0.04457	0.04363	0.04272	0.04182	0.04093	0.04006	0.03920	0.03836	0.03754	0.03673
−1.8	0.03593	0.03515	0.03438	0.03362	0.03288	0.03216	0.03144	0.03074	0.03005	0.02938
−1.9	0.02872	0.02807	0.02743	0.02680	0.02619	0.02559	0.02500	0.02442	0.02385	0.02330
−2.0	0.02275	0.02222	0.02169	0.02118	0.02068	0.02018	0.01970	0.01923	0.01876	0.01831
−2.1	0.01786	0.01743	0.01700	0.01659	0.01618	0.01578	0.01539	0.01500	0.01463	0.01426
−2.2	0.01390	0.01355	0.01321	0.01287	0.01255	0.01222	0.01191	0.01160	0.01130	0.01101
−2.3	0.01072	0.01044	0.01017	0.009903	0.009642	0.009387	0.009137	0.008894	0.008656	0.008424
−2.4	0.008198	0.007976	0.007760	0.007549	0.007344	0.007143	0.006947	0.006756	0.006569	0.006387
−2.5	0.006210	0.006037	0.005868	0.005703	0.005543	0.005386	0.005234	0.005085	0.004940	0.004799
−2.6	0.004661	0.004527	0.004396	0.004269	0.004145	0.004025	0.003907	0.003793	0.003681	0.003573
−2.7	0.003467	0.003364	0.003264	0.003167	0.003072	0.002980	0.002890	0.002803	0.002718	0.002635
−2.8	0.002555	0.002477	0.002401	0.002327	0.002256	0.002186	0.002118	0.002052	0.001988	0.001926
−2.9	0.001866	0.001807	0.001750	0.001695	0.001641	0.001589	0.001538	0.001489	0.001441	0.001395
−3.0	0.001350	0.001306	0.001264	0.001223	0.001183	0.001144	0.001107	0.001070	0.001035	0.001001
−3.1	0.000968	0.000935	0.000904	0.000874	0.000845	0.000816	0.000789	0.000762	0.000736	0.000711
−3.2	0.000687	0.000664	0.000641	0.000619	0.000598	0.000577	0.000557	0.000538	0.000519	0.000501
−3.3	0.000483	0.000467	0.000450	0.000434	0.000419	0.000404	0.000390	0.000376	0.000362	0.000350
−3.4	0.000337	0.000325	0.000313	0.000302	0.000291	0.000280	0.000270	0.000260	0.000251	0.000242
−3.5	0.000233	0.000224	0.000216	0.000208	0.000200	0.000193	0.000185	0.000179	0.000172	0.000165

z	0.00	0.01	0.02	0.03	0.04	0.05	0.06	0.07	0.08	0.09
0.0	0.5000	0.5040	0.5080	0.5120	0.5160	0.5199	0.5239	0.5279	0.5319	0.5359
0.1	0.5398	0.5438	0.5478	0.5517	0.5557	0.5596	0.5636	0.5675	0.5714	0.5753
0.2	0.5793	0.5832	0.5871	0.5910	0.5948	0.5987	0.6026	0.6064	0.6103	0.6141
0.3	0.6179	0.6217	0.6255	0.6293	0.6331	0.6368	0.6406	0.6443	0.6480	0.6517
0.4	0.6554	0.6591	0.6628	0.6664	0.6700	0.6736	0.6772	0.6808	0.6844	0.6879
0.5	0.6915	0.6950	0.6985	0.7019	0.7054	0.7088	0.7123	0.7157	0.7190	0.7224
0.6	0.7257	0.7291	0.7324	0.7357	0.7389	0.7422	0.7454	0.7486	0.7517	0.7549
0.7	0.7580	0.7611	0.7642	0.7673	0.7704	0.7734	0.7764	0.7794	0.7823	0.7852
0.8	0.7881	0.7910	0.7939	0.7967	0.7995	0.8023	0.8051	0.8079	0.8106	0.8133
0.9	0.8159	0.8186	0.8212	0.8238	0.8264	0.8289	0.8315	0.8340	0.8365	0.8389
1.0	0.8413	0.8438	0.8461	0.8485	0.8508	0.8531	0.8554	0.8577	0.8599	0.8621
1.1	0.8643	0.8665	0.8686	0.8708	0.8729	0.8749	0.8770	0.8790	0.8810	0.8830
1.2	0.8849	0.8869	0.8888	0.8907	0.8925	0.8944	0.8962	0.8980	0.8997	0.9015
1.3	0.9032	0.9049	0.9066	0.9082	0.9099	0.9115	0.9131	0.9147	0.9162	0.9177
1.4	0.9192	0.9207	0.9222	0.9236	0.9251	0.9265	0.9279	0.9292	0.9306	0.9319
1.5	0.9332	0.9345	0.9357	0.9370	0.9382	0.9394	0.9406	0.9418	0.9429	0.9441
1.6	0.9452	0.9463	0.9474	0.9484	0.9495	0.9505	0.9515	0.9525	0.9535	0.9545
1.7	0.9554	0.9564	0.9573	0.9582	0.9591	0.9599	0.9608	0.9616	0.9625	0.9633
1.8	0.9641	0.9649	0.9656	0.9664	0.9671	0.9678	0.9686	0.9693	0.9699	0.9706
1.9	0.9713	0.9719	0.9726	0.9732	0.9738	0.9744	0.9750	0.9756	0.9761	0.9767
2.0	0.9773	0.9778	0.9783	0.9788	0.9793	0.9798	0.9803	0.9808	0.9812	0.9817
2.1	0.9821	0.9826	0.9830	0.9834	0.9838	0.9842	0.9846	0.9850	0.9854	0.9857
2.2	0.9861	0.9864	0.9868	0.9871	0.9875	0.9878	0.9881	0.9884	0.9887	0.9890
2.3	0.9893	0.9896	0.9898	0.9901	0.9904	0.9906	0.9909	0.9911	0.9913	0.9916
2.4	0.9918	0.9920	0.9922	0.9925	0.9927	0.9929	0.9931	0.9932	0.9934	0.9936
2.5	0.9938	0.9940	0.9941	0.9943	0.9945	0.9946	0.9948	0.9949	0.9951	0.9952
2.6	0.9953	0.9955	0.9956	0.9957	0.9959	0.9960	0.9961	0.9962	0.9963	0.9964
2.7	0.9965	0.9966	0.9967	0.9968	0.9969	0.9970	0.9971	0.9972	0.9973	0.9974
2.8	0.9974	0.9975	0.9976	0.9977	0.9977	0.9978	0.9979	0.9979	0.9980	0.9981
2.9	0.9981	0.9982	0.9983	0.9983	0.9984	0.9984	0.9985	0.9985	0.9986	0.9986
3.0	0.99865	0.99869	0.99874	0.99878	0.99882	0.99886	0.99889	0.99893	0.99896	0.99900
3.1	0.99903	0.99906	0.99910	0.99913	0.99915	0.99918	0.99921	0.99924	0.99926	0.99929
3.2	0.99931	0.99934	0.99936	0.99938	0.99940	0.99942	0.99944	0.99946	0.99948	0.99950
3.3	0.99952	0.99953	0.99955	0.99957	0.99958	0.99960	0.99961	0.99962	0.99964	0.99965
3.4	0.99966	0.99967	0.99969	0.99970	0.99971	0.99972	0.99973	0.99974	0.99975	0.99976
3.5	0.99977	0.99978	0.99978	0.99979	0.99980	0.99981	0.99981	0.99982	0.99983	0.99983

Source: R. Peterson and E. A. Silver, *Decision Systems for Inventory Management and Production Planning*, John Wiley & Sons (1985), 2nd ed., pp. 699–708.

TABLE C Unit Normal Loss Table

z	0.00	0.01	0.02	0.03	0.04	0.05	0.06	0.07	0.08	0.09
0.0	0.3989	0.3940	0.3890	0.3841	0.3793	0.3744	0.3697	0.3649	0.3602	0.3556
0.1	0.3509	0.3464	0.3418	0.3373	0.3328	0.3284	0.3240	0.3197	0.3154	0.3111
0.2	0.3069	0.3027	0.2986	0.2944	0.2904	0.2863	0.2824	0.2784	0.2745	0.2706
0.3	0.2668	0.2630	0.2592	0.2555	0.2518	0.2481	0.2445	0.2409	0.2374	0.2339
0.4	0.2304	0.2270	0.2236	0.2203	0.2169	0.2137	0.2104	0.2072	0.2040	0.2009
0.5	0.1978	0.1947	0.1917	0.1887	0.1857	0.1828	0.1799	0.1771	0.1742	0.1714
0.6	0.1687	0.1659	0.1633	0.1606	0.1580	0.1554	0.1528	0.1503	0.1478	0.1453
0.7	0.1429	0.1405	0.1381	0.1358	0.1334	0.1312	0.1289	0.1267	0.1245	0.1223
0.8	0.1202	0.1181	0.1160	0.1140	0.1120	0.1100	0.1080	0.1061	0.1042	0.1023
0.9	0.1004	0.09860	0.09680	0.09503	0.09328	0.09156	0.08986	0.08819	0.08654	0.08491
1.0	0.08332	0.08174	0.08019	0.07866	0.07716	0.07568	0.07422	0.07279	0.07138	0.06999
1.1	0.06862	0.06727	0.06595	0.06465	0.06336	0.06210	0.06086	0.05964	0.05844	0.05726
1.2	0.05610	0.05496	0.05384	0.05274	0.05165	0.05059	0.04954	0.04851	0.04750	0.04650
1.3	0.04553	0.04457	0.04363	0.04270	0.04179	0.04090	0.04002	0.03916	0.03831	0.03748
1.4	0.03667	0.03587	0.03508	0.03431	0.03356	0.03281	0.03208	0.03137	0.03067	0.02998
1.5	0.02931	0.02865	0.02800	0.02736	0.02674	0.02612	0.02552	0.02494	0.02436	0.02380
1.6	0.02324	0.02270	0.02217	0.02165	0.02114	0.02064	0.02015	0.01967	0.01920	0.01874
1.7	0.01829	0.01785	0.01742	0.01699	0.01658	0.01617	0.01578	0.01539	0.01501	0.01464
1.8	0.01428	0.01392	0.01357	0.01323	0.01290	0.01257	0.01226	0.01195	0.01164	0.01134
1.9	0.01105	0.01077	0.01049	0.01022	0.009957	0.009698	0.009445	0.009198	0.008957	0.008721
2.0	0.008491	0.008266	0.008046	0.007832	0.007623	0.007418	0.007219	0.007024	0.006835	0.006649
2.1	0.006468	0.006292	0.006120	0.005952	0.005788	0.005628	0.005472	0.005320	0.005172	0.005028
2.2	0.004887	0.004750	0.004616	0.004486	0.004358	0.004235	0.004114	0.003996	0.003882	0.003770
2.3	0.003662	0.003556	0.003453	0.003352	0.003255	0.003159	0.003067	0.002977	0.002889	0.002804
2.4	0.002720	0.002640	0.002561	0.002484	0.002410	0.002337	0.002267	0.002199	0.002132	0.002067
2.5	0.002004	0.001943	0.001883	0.001826	0.001769	0.001715	0.001662	0.001610	0.001560	0.001511
2.6	0.001464	0.001418	0.001373	0.001330	0.001288	0.001247	0.001207	0.001169	0.001132	0.001095
2.7	0.001060	0.001026	0.000993	0.000961	0.000930	0.000899	0.000870	0.000841	0.000814	0.000787
2.8	0.000761	0.000736	0.000712	0.000688	0.000665	0.000643	0.000621	0.000600	0.000580	0.000561
2.9	0.000542	0.000523	0.000506	0.000488	0.000472	0.000456	0.000440	0.000425	0.000410	0.000396
3.0	0.000382	0.000369	0.000356	0.000344	0.000332	0.000320	0.000309	0.000298	0.000287	0.000277
3.1	0.000267	0.000258	0.000249	0.000240	0.000231	0.000223	0.000215	0.000207	0.000200	0.000192
3.2	0.000185	0.000179	0.000172	0.000166	0.000160	0.000154	0.000148	0.000143	0.000137	0.000132
3.3	0.000127	0.000123	0.000118	0.000114	0.000109	0.000105	0.000101	0.000097	0.000094	0.000090
3.4	0.000087	0.000083	0.000080	0.000077	0.000074	0.000071	0.000069	0.000066	0.000063	0.000061
3.5	0.000058	0.000056	0.000054	0.000052	0.000050	0.000048	0.000046	0.000044	0.000042	0.000041

Source: R. Peterson and E. A. Silver, *Decision Systems for Inventory Management and Production Planning*, John Wiley & Sons (1985), pp. 699–708.

TABLE D Poisson Cumulative Distribution Function for Various Means

x/Mean	1	2	3	4	5	6	7	8	9	10	12	14	16	18	20
0	0.3679	0.1353	0.0498	0.0183	0.0067	0.0025	0.0009	0.0003	0.0001	0.0000	0.0000	0.0000	0.0000	0.0000	0.0000
1	0.7358	0.4060	0.1991	0.0916	0.0404	0.0174	0.0073	0.0030	0.0012	0.0005	0.0001	0.0000	0.0000	0.0000	0.0000
2	0.9197	0.6767	0.4232	0.2381	0.1247	0.0620	0.0296	0.0138	0.0062	0.0028	0.0005	0.0001	0.0000	0.0000	0.0000
3	0.9810	0.8571	0.6472	0.4335	0.2650	0.1512	0.0818	0.0424	0.0212	0.0103	0.0023	0.0005	0.0001	0.0000	0.0000
4	0.9963	0.9473	0.8153	0.6288	0.4405	0.2851	0.1730	0.0996	0.0550	0.0293	0.0076	0.0018	0.0004	0.0001	0.0000
5	0.9994	0.9834	0.9161	0.7851	0.6160	0.4457	0.3007	0.1912	0.1157	0.0671	0.0203	0.0055	0.0014	0.0003	0.0001
6	0.9999	0.9955	0.9665	0.8893	0.7622	0.6063	0.4497	0.3134	0.2068	0.1301	0.0458	0.0142	0.0040	0.0010	0.0003
7	1.0000	0.9989	0.9881	0.9489	0.8666	0.7440	0.5987	0.4530	0.3239	0.2202	0.0895	0.0316	0.0100	0.0029	0.0008
8		0.9998	0.9962	0.9786	0.9319	0.8472	0.7291	0.5925	0.4557	0.3328	0.1550	0.0621	0.0220	0.0071	0.0021
9		1.0000	0.9989	0.9919	0.9682	0.9161	0.8305	0.7166	0.5874	0.4579	0.2424	0.1094	0.0433	0.0154	0.0050
10			0.9997	0.9972	0.9863	0.9574	0.9015	0.8159	0.7060	0.5830	0.3472	0.1757	0.0774	0.0304	0.0108
11			0.9999	0.9991	0.9945	0.9799	0.9467	0.8881	0.8030	0.6968	0.4616	0.2600	0.1270	0.0549	0.0214
12			1.0000	0.9997	0.9980	0.9912	0.9730	0.9362	0.8758	0.7916	0.5760	0.3585	0.1931	0.0917	0.0390
13				0.9999	0.9993	0.9964	0.9872	0.9658	0.9261	0.8645	0.6815	0.4644	0.2745	0.1426	0.0661
14				1.0000	0.9998	0.9986	0.9943	0.9827	0.9585	0.9165	0.7720	0.5704	0.3675	0.2081	0.1049
15					0.9999	0.9995	0.9976	0.9918	0.9780	0.9513	0.8444	0.6694	0.4667	0.2867	0.1565
16					1.0000	0.9998	0.9990	0.9963	0.9889	0.9730	0.8987	0.7559	0.5660	0.3751	0.2211
17						0.9999	0.9996	0.9984	0.9947	0.9857	0.9370	0.8272	0.6593	0.4686	0.2970
18						1.0000	0.9999	0.9993	0.9976	0.9928	0.9626	0.8826	0.7423	0.5622	0.3814
19							1.0000	0.9997	0.9989	0.9965	0.9787	0.9235	0.8122	0.6509	0.4703
20								0.9999	0.9996	0.9984	0.9884	0.9521	0.8682	0.7307	0.5591
21								1.0000	0.9998	0.9993	0.9939	0.9712	0.9108	0.7991	0.6437
22									0.9999	0.9997	0.9970	0.9833	0.9418	0.8551	0.7206
23									1.0000	0.9999	0.9985	0.9907	0.9633	0.8989	0.7875
24										0.9993	0.9950	0.9777	0.9317	0.8432
25										0.9997	0.9974	0.9869	0.9554	0.8878
26										0.9999	0.9987	0.9925	0.9718	0.9221
27										0.9999	0.9994	0.9959	0.9827	0.9475
28										1.0000	0.9997	0.9978	0.9897	0.9657
29											0.9999	0.9989	0.9941	0.9782
30											0.9999	0.9994	0.9967	0.9865
31											1.0000	0.9997	0.9982	0.9919
32												0.9999	0.9990	0.9953
33												0.9999	0.9995	0.9973
34												1.0000	0.9998	0.9985
35													0.9999	0.9992
36													0.9999	0.9996
37													1.0000	0.9998
38														0.9999
39														0.9999
														1.0000

TABLE E Random Numbers from 00 to 99

43	75	29	72	11	04	50	75	98	41	14	08	24	25	61	24	54	36	02	27	35	92	14	59	32
05	41	99	19	09	49	52	87	48	78	34	02	88	69	37	27	21	46	76	29	70	09	02	50	01
61	44	16	54	82	69	31	13	29	68	00	61	30	60	83	78	69	25	61	39	64	90	15	82	80
24	83	67	09	91	39	24	38	65	25	12	35	69	83	52	97	84	24	76	41	70	56	40	08	91
81	33	14	15	73	27	43	21	56	34	43	50	96	97	69	76	26	72	14	99	15	02	40	58	30
93	42	93	94	45	72	73	99	77	59	13	05	78	35	34	82	27	68	44	44	02	95	49	33	65
96	34	17	47	79	08	77	81	74	34	35	72	53	02	20	54	97	86	06	87	04	78	76	10	39
03	09	70	97	53	31	91	52	74	71	18	97	36	81	75	08	14	75	15	08	71	66	04	38	69
99	39	14	43	89	65	25	71	73	56	66	01	12	23	19	30	35	56	60	64	25	50	89	40	45
44	74	87	57	08	07	67	73	46	54	28	76	44	58	46	83	88	24	04	82	62	91	62	14	32
82	14	39	65	52	77	99	23	34	08	29	91	64	85	26	02	74	49	81	68	53	28	26	30	66
08	72	24	73	74	28	82	29	06	97	33	87	81	81	99	95	70	74	03	97	41	70	59	33	60
56	80	39	85	16	74	48	74	31	45	88	78	76	93	83	45	25	15	52	19	44	02	12	41	98
43	76	46	48	21	50	67	49	17	40	32	53	07	45	65	08	63	62	86	59	52	82	11	46	40
94	52	04	87	82	17	66	47	25	11	60	74	01	33	10	15	80	80	35	15	31	43	53	13	19
10	75	46	02	67	09	46	38	92	60	40	78	61	26	54	70	48	05	06	59	19	88	12	84	40
64	86	81	69	16	35	83	63	24	62	17	74	65	69	07	50	11	50	75	35	29	99	34	69	83
03	98	88	34	45	75	24	38	07	68	05	46	63	78	56	06	87	01	95	63	46	27	39	57	03
47	00	23	20	42	86	93	52	95	01	96	50	79	45	56	64	69	14	92	36	30	00	20	08	28
91	52	14	22	70	97	87	69	19	58	54	19	12	35	40	22	21	25	65	21	15	18	45	56	58
04	91	63	09	65	11	73	25	82	10	16	56	31	87	15	53	84	38	89	57	08	55	54	09	68
27	24	46	24	36	04	98	31	63	00	94	41	84	11	58	02	71	34	09	59	91	59	64	50	08
76	34	12	83	67	28	77	71	12	48	73	24	89	96	23	91	67	67	47	14	17	52	62	33	00
40	79	86	77	15	05	02	04	55	46	11	33	38	00	36	12	36	64	97	84	15	29	10	89	39
83	87	63	70	10	35	38	61	91	58	42	66	00	57	99	32	09	27	28	03	87	59	46	19	97
42	63	15	99	59	88	24	48	91	26	73	98	13	74	85	94	96	30	82	82	09	85	77	01	16
27	85	87	76	39	11	71	44	02	60	82	74	91	32	42	12	78	23	73	03	31	23	89	86	14
22	03	96	86	02	22	66	03	44	50	24	16	23	86	92	75	12	27	92	21	77	65	38	96	82
86	43	35	88	75	14	69	49	11	54	26	19	70	65	31	44	25	40	02	68	42	73	56	31	85
50	03	68	14	56	53	12	85	70	08	90	50	68	69	26	56	21	31	39	46	98	85	46	62	62
20	57	37	72	19	80	04	85	62	20	91	52	24	76	22	20	77	43	15	34	89	14	87	33	24
75	49	53	41	11	09	25	96	02	71	78	40	22	35	34	21	44	95	13	83	35	44	31	65	58
69	01	04	75	54	28	30	39	78	17	72	03	18	68	53	15	44	76	92	17	25	33	05	51	24
27	05	50	01	40	98	47	11	53	87	70	06	42	74	42	33	77	53	83	36	27	16	08	55	55
50	29	26	21	39	53	79	80	64	85	43	84	98	23	41	80	14	63	92	12	80	97	13	20	58
13	14	39	10	93	04	01	89	18	86	33	48	63	59	59	34	00	19	98	91	96	58	67	59	15
63	76	72	16	17	33	63	55	01	41	58	83	90	01	83	48	55	07	55	93	63	52	91	59	79
22	02	80	62	01	95	87	67	69	75	10	46	02	40	70	47	70	87	88	12	42	06	79	82	80
85	54	91	44	08	22	72	91	54	85	52	70	98	43	54	30	13	91	99	15	65	22	00	63	19
21	70	10	33	74	17	88	63	59	43	24	60	52	48	42	72	24	28	60	43	43	74	95	11	72

TABLE F P_0 Values for Parallel Server Queues

λ/μ	$s = 1$	2	3	4	5	6	7	8	9	10
0.05	0.9500	0.9512	0.9512	0.9512	0.9512	0.9512	0.9512	0.9512	0.9512	0.9512
0.10	0.9000	0.9048	0.9048	0.9048	0.9048	0.9048	0.9048	0.9048	0.9048	0.9048
0.15	0.8500	0.8605	0.8607	0.8607	0.8607	0.8607	0.8607	0.8607	0.8607	0.8607
0.20	0.8000	0.8182	0.8187	0.8187	0.8187	0.8187	0.8187	0.8187	0.8187	0.8187
0.25	0.7500	0.7778	0.7788	0.7788	0.7788	0.7788	0.7788	0.7788	0.7788	0.7788
0.30	0.7000	0.7391	0.7407	0.7408	0.7408	0.7408	0.7408	0.7408	0.7408	0.7408
0.35	0.6500	0.7021	0.7046	0.7047	0.7047	0.7047	0.7047	0.7047	0.7047	0.7047
0.40	0.6000	0.6667	0.6701	0.6703	0.6703	0.6703	0.6703	0.6703	0.6703	0.6703
0.45	0.5500	0.6327	0.6373	0.6376	0.6376	0.6376	0.6376	0.6376	0.6376	0.6376
0.50	0.5000	0.6000	0.6061	0.6065	0.6065	0.6065	0.6065	0.6065	0.6065	0.6065
0.55	0.4500	0.5686	0.5763	0.5769	0.5769	0.5769	0.5769	0.5769	0.5769	0.5769
0.60	0.4000	0.5385	0.5479	0.5487	0.5488	0.5488	0.5488	0.5488	0.5488	0.5488
0.65	0.3500	0.5094	0.5209	0.5219	0.5220	0.5220	0.5220	0.5220	0.5220	0.5220
0.70	0.3000	0.4815	0.4952	0.4965	0.4966	0.4966	0.4966	0.4966	0.4966	0.4966
0.75	0.2500	0.4545	0.4706	0.4722	0.4724	0.4724	0.4724	0.4724	0.4724	0.4724
0.80	0.2000	0.4286	0.4472	0.4491	0.4493	0.4493	0.4493	0.4493	0.4493	0.4493
0.85	0.1500	0.4035	0.4248	0.4271	0.4274	0.4274	0.4274	0.4274	0.4274	0.4274
0.90	0.1000	0.3793	0.4035	0.4062	0.4065	0.4066	0.4066	0.4066	0.4066	0.4066
0.95	0.0500	0.3559	0.3831	0.3863	0.3867	0.3867	0.3867	0.3867	0.3867	0.3867
1.00		0.3333	0.3636	0.3673	0.3678	0.3679	0.3679	0.3679	0.3679	0.3679
1.05		0.3115	0.3451	0.3493	0.3499	0.3499	0.3499	0.3499	0.3499	0.3499
1.10		0.2903	0.3273	0.3321	0.3328	0.3329	0.3329	0.3329	0.3329	0.3329
1.15		0.2698	0.3103	0.3158	0.3165	0.3166	0.3166	0.3166	0.3166	0.3166
1.20		0.2500	0.2941	0.3002	0.3011	0.3012	0.3012	0.3012	0.3012	0.3012
1.25		0.2308	0.2786	0.2853	0.2863	0.2865	0.2865	0.2865	0.2865	0.2865
1.30		0.2121	0.2638	0.2712	0.2723	0.2725	0.2725	0.2725	0.2725	0.2725
1.35		0.1940	0.2496	0.2577	0.2590	0.2592	0.2592	0.2592	0.2592	0.2592
1.40		0.1765	0.2360	0.2449	0.2463	0.2466	0.2466	0.2466	0.2466	0.2466
1.45		0.1594	0.2230	0.2327	0.2343	0.2345	0.2346	0.2346	0.2346	0.2346
1.50		0.1429	0.2105	0.2210	0.2228	0.2231	0.2231	0.2231	0.2231	0.2231
1.55		0.1268	0.1986	0.2099	0.2118	0.2122	0.2122	0.2122	0.2122	0.2122
1.60		0.1111	0.1872	0.1993	0.2014	0.2018	0.2019	0.2019	0.2019	0.2019
1.65		0.0959	0.1762	0.1892	0.1915	0.1920	0.1920	0.1920	0.1920	0.1920
1.70		0.0811	0.1657	0.1796	0.1821	0.1826	0.1827	0.1827	0.1827	0.1827
1.75		0.0667	0.1556	0.1704	0.1731	0.1737	0.1738	0.1738	0.1738	0.1738
1.80		0.0526	0.1460	0.1616	0.1646	0.1652	0.1653	0.1653	0.1653	0.1653
1.85		0.0390	0.1367	0.1533	0.1565	0.1571	0.1572	0.1572	0.1572	0.1572
1.90		0.0256	0.1278	0.1453	0.1487	0.1494	0.1495	0.1496	0.1496	0.1496

TABLE F *(Continued)*

λ/μ	$s = 1$	2	3	4	5	6	7	8	9	10
1.95		0.0127	0.1193	0.1377	0.1413	0.1421	0.1422	0.1423	0.1423	0.1423
2.00			0.1111	0.1304	0.1343	0.1351	0.1353	0.1353	0.1353	0.1353
2.05			0.1032	0.1235	0.1276	0.1285	0.1287	0.1287	0.1287	0.1287
2.10			0.0957	0.1169	0.1213	0.1222	0.1224	0.1224	0.1225	0.1225
2.15			0.0884	0.1106	0.1152	0.1162	0.1164	0.1165	0.1165	0.1165
2.20			0.0815	0.1046	0.1094	0.1105	0.1107	0.1108	0.1108	0.1108
2.25			0.0748	0.0988	0.1039	0.1051	0.1053	0.1054	0.1054	0.1054
2.30			0.0683	0.0933	0.0987	0.0999	0.1002	0.1002	0.1003	0.1003
2.35			0.0621	0.0881	0.0937	0.0950	0.0953	0.0954	0.0954	0.0954
2.40			0.0562	0.0831	0.0889	0.0903	0.0906	0.0907	0.0907	0.0907
2.45			0.0505	0.0783	0.0844	0.0859	0.0862	0.0863	0.0863	0.0863
2.50			0.0449	0.0737	0.0801	0.0816	0.0820	0.0821	0.0821	0.0821
2.55			0.0396	0.0693	0.0760	0.0776	0.0780	0.0781	0.0781	0.0781
2.60			0.0345	0.0651	0.0721	0.0737	0.0742	0.0742	0.0743	0.0743
2.65			0.0296	0.0612	0.0683	0.0701	0.0705	0.0706	0.0706	0.0706
2.70			0.0249	0.0573	0.0648	0.0666	0.0671	0.0672	0.0672	0.0672
2.75			0.0204	0.0537	0.0614	0.0633	0.0638	0.0639	0.0639	0.0639
2.80			0.0160	0.0502	0.0581	0.0601	0.0606	0.0608	0.0608	0.0608
2.85			0.0118	0.0469	0.0551	0.0571	0.0577	0.0578	0.0578	0.0578
2.90			0.0077	0.0437	0.0521	0.0543	0.0548	0.0550	0.0550	0.0550
2.95			0.0038	0.0406	0.0493	0.0516	0.0521	0.0523	0.0523	0.0523
3.00				0.0377	0.0466	0.0490	0.0496	0.0497	0.0498	0.0498

Bibliography

Models and Modeling

Ackoff, Russell L. and Patrick Rivett, *A Manager's Guide to Operations Research*, Wiley, New York, 1963.

Schultz, Randall L. and Dennis P. Slevin, *Implementing Operations Research/Management Science*, American Elsevier, New York, 1975.

The Transportation Model

Gaver, Donald P., and Gerald L. Thompson, *Programming and Probability Models in Operations Research*, Brooks/Cole, Monterey, Calif., 1973. Chap. 1.

Lapin, Lawrence L., *Quantitative Methods for Business Decisions*, Harcourt, Brace, Jovanovich, New York, 1980, 2nd Ed., Chap. 15.

Linear Programming

Driebeck, Norman J., *Applied Linear Programming*, Addison-Wesley, Reading, Mass., 1969.

Schrage, Linus E., *Linear, Integer, and Quadratic Programming with LINDO*, Scientific Press, Palo Alto, Calif., 1984.

The Simplex Method

Bradley, Stephen P., Arnoldo C. Hax, and Thomas L. Magnanti, *Applied Mathematical Programming*, Addison-Wesley, Reading, Mass., 1977.

Gass, Saul I., *Linear Programming Methods and Applications*, McGraw-Hill, New York, 1975. 4th Ed.

Murty, Katta G., *Linear and Combinatorial Programming*, Wiley, New York, 1976.

Integer Programming

Garfinkel, Robert S., and George L. Nemhauser, *Integer Programming*, Wiley, New York, 1972.

Salkin, Harvey M., *Integer Programming*, Addison-Wesley, Reading, Mass., 1975.

Taha, Hamdy A., *Integer Programming: Theory, Applications and Computations*, Academic Press, New York, 1975.

Network Models for Project Scheduling

Elmaghraby, S. E., *Activity Networks: Project Planning and Control by Network Methods*, Wiley, New York, 1977.

Moder, Joseph J., Cecil R. Phillips, and Edward W. Davis, *Project Management with CPM, PERT and Precedence Diagramming*, Van Nostrand Reinhold, New York, 1983.

Wiest, Jerome D., and Ferdinand K. Levy, *A Management Guide to PERT/CPM*, Prentice-Hall, Englewood Cliffs, N.J., 1977. 2nd Ed.

Decision Analysis

Holloway, Charles A., *Decision Making Under Uncertainty*, Prentice-Hall, Englewood Cliffs, N.J., 1979.

Winkler, Robert L., *Introduction to Bayesian Inference and Decision*, Holt, Rinehart and Winston, New York, 1972.

Trade-Off Models for Surplus and Shortage

Baird, Bruce F., *Introduction to Decision Analysis*, Duxbury Press, North Scituate, Mass., 1978. Ch. 6.

Wagner, Harvey M. *Principles of Operations Research*, Prentice-Hall, Englewood Cliffs, N.J., 1975, 2nd Ed., Chap. 19.

Forecasting Models

Makridakis, Spiros G., Steven C. Wheelwright, and Victor E. McGee, *Forecasting, Methods and Applications*, Wiley, New York, 1983. 2nd Ed.

Montgomery, Douglas A. and Lynwood A. Johnson, *Forecasting and Time Series Analysis*, McGraw-Hill, New York, 1976.

Inventory Models

Brown, Robert G., *Decision Rules for Inventory Management*, Holt, Rinehart and Winston, New York, 1967.

Hadley, G., and T. M. Whitin, *Analysis of Inventory Systems*, Prentice-Hall, Englewood Cliffs, N.J., 1963.

Peterson, Rein, and Edward A. Silver, *Decision Systems for Inventory Management and Production Planning*, Wiley, New York, 1985. 2nd Ed.

Tersine, Richard J., *Principles of Inventory and Materials Management*, North Holland, New York, 1982. 2nd Ed.

Queueing Models

Cooper, Robert B., *Introduction to Queueing Theory*, Macmillan, New York, 1972.

Giffin, Walter C., *Queueing*, Grid, Inc., Columbus, Ohio, 1978.

Kleinrock, Leonard, *Queueing Systems*, Volume I, *Theory*, Wiley, New York, 1975.

White, J. A., J. W. Schmidt, and G. K. Bennett, *Analysis of Queueing Systems*, Academic Press, New York, 1975.

Simulation

Fishman, George S., *Principles of Discrete Event Simulation*, Wiley, New York, 1978.

Law, Averill M. and W. David Kelton, *Simulation Modeling and Analysis*, McGraw-Hill, New York, 1982.

Shannon, Robert E., *Systems Simulation*, Prentice-Hall, Englewood Cliffs, N.J., 1975.

Watson, Hugh J., *Computer Simulation in Business*, Wiley, New York, 1981.

Index